Lonely Planet Publications
Melbourne | Oakland | London

Mara Vorhees &
John Spelman

Boston

Introducing Boston

The Cradle of Liberty. The Hub of the Universe. The Athens of America. These are big words for a mid-sized city. But Boston lives up to them. With its rich history, grand architecture and world-renowned academic and cultural institutions, the city retains and radiates the glory it has garnered over the last four centuries.

It was the Puritans who set out in search of religious freedom and founded Boston as their 'shining city on a hill.' In the following century, the Sons of Freedom were born in Boston, where they caroused and rabble-roused until the colonies found themselves in the midst of a War for Independence. A hundred years later, it was Boston's poets and philosophers who were leading a cultural revolution – pushing progressive causes like abolitionism, feminism and transcendentalism.

That's the stuff of history, but today's Boston fulfils these promises. Boston is among the country's forward-thinking and barrier-breaking cities. This is most evident politically, where Boston is at the forefront of controversial issues like same-sex marriage and universal healthcare. It's also visible in the changing landscape of the city, as Boston and environs are now home to some of the country's most cutting-edge architecture and innovative urban planning projects.

Culturally, Boston is shedding its staid and stodgy reputation, as artists, literati, thespians and filmmakers rediscover the city's rich resources and create new ones. With the recent explosion of avant-garde studios and the opening of the Institute for Contemporary Arts, Boston is poised to play a role in visual arts more prominent than ever before.

No single element has influenced the city so profoundly as its educational institutions. Over the years, Boston's colleges and universities have attracted scholars, scientists, philosophers and writers who have thrived off and contributed to the city's evolving culture. Contemporary Boston is no exception, especially as it draws students from around the world. From September through May, the city overflows with their exuberance. This renewable source of cultural energy supports sporting events, film festivals, music scenes, art galleries, coffee shops, hip clubs and Irish pubs.

The city is magnificent in late spring (May and June) or early fall (September and October), when parks are filled with flowering trees or colorful leaves. In summer, the city goes all out for Independence Day, with a week's worth of celebrations during Harborfest. Any time of year, the cultural calendar is packed.

1 *Town houses, Beacon Hill (p74)* **2** *Reveling in the Public Garden (p76)* **3** *Café terraces line lively Newbury St (p97)* **previous pages** *Hood milk bottle (p94) at the Children's Museum, Fort Point Channel; Sailing off the Esplanade on the Charles River (p198)*

1 *USS Constitution (p85)*
2 *Inside the House of Representatives, State House (p76)* **3** *Paul Revere's tombstone, Granary Burying Ground (p75)*

1 *Mike's City Diner (p149)*
2 *Making pizza at Figs (p137)*
3 *Boston Beer Works (p162)*

1 *Performers, Club Passim (p180)* 2 *Koch Gallery in the Museum of Fine Arts (p103)* 3 *Chinatown (p94)*

following page *St Patrick's Day (p13) crowds*

Contents

Published by Lonely Planet Publications Pty Ltd
ABN 36 005 607 983

Australia Head Office, Locked Bag 1, Footscray,
Victoria 3011, ☎ 03 8379 8000, fax 03 8379 8111,
talk2us@lonelyplanet.com.au

USA 150 Linden St, Oakland, CA 94607,
☎ 510 893 8555, toll free 800 275 8555,
fax 510 893 8572, info@lonelyplanet.com

UK 72–82 Rosebery Ave, Clerkenwell, London,
EC1R 4RW, ☎ 020 7841 9000, fax 020 7841 9001,
go@lonelyplanet.co.uk

The Authors

Mara Vorhees

Born and raised in St Clair Shores, Michigan, Mara traveled the world (if not the universe) before finally settling in the Hub. She now lives in Somerville, Boston, with her husband and her cat. Mara spent several years pushing papers and tapping keys at Harvard University, but she has since embraced the life of a full-time travel writer. She is often spotted sipping Sam Adams seasonals in Union Sq and pedaling her road bike along the Charles River.

Mara is a frequent contributor to the *Boston Globe* Travel. She has also worked on Lonely Planet's guides to *Cape Cod & the Islands* and *New England*.

MARA'S BEST DAY IN BOSTON

It's a sunny morning in early autumn, and I wake up in Somerville. I hop on my bicycle and pedal over to Harvard Sq for my daily fix from Darwin's (p156). After fueling up, I follow my favorite riding route along the banks of the Charles (p126), stopping to catch a few morning rays on the Esplanade. I drop off my bike and head back into the city for some reading and eating at Trident Booksellers & Cafe (p151), where I lose a couple of hours to the huge selection of magazines.

After lunch, it's time for a little 'kultchah,' so I head to the Museum of Fine Arts (p103) to check out the Paul Gauguin exhibit, especially his provocative *Where did we come from? What are we? Where are we going?* I contemplate those questions as I stroll through the Back Bay Fens (p197) to Kenmore Sq.

I meet up with friends for a pre-game drink on the outdoor patio at Eastern Standard (p153). Then we follow the crowds to Fenway Park (p101) to watch the Sox spank the Yankees and clinch their spot in the playoffs (we can dream, can't we?).

After the game, we head back to the other side of the river to devour a savory pizza at Cambridge, 1 (p157). I have saved room for dessert so I can stop at Christina's (p52) for her irresistible pumpkin ice cream on my way home.

John Spelman

John Spelman grew up in a boring town outside Boston. His early years featured many trips to the city, where he was admonished to not touch subway station walls (people pee on them) and passed productive days at the children's museum, aquarium and Quincy Market. He later enjoyed the fate of many area teenagers who think that they are artists, and began wearing awkward clothes as a pseudo-punk regularly hanging out in Harvard Sq and on Newbury St. As an adult living in Cambridge, he developed slightly better fashion sensibilities and became very sentimental about the Boston/Providence rock scene.

More recently, John earned a Masters in Design Studies from Harvard's Graduate School of Design and is now a PhD student studying architectural and urban history at the University of Virginia, where he is working on a dissertation about Boston. He has written for multiple Lonely Planet titles, including *New England*.

City Life

City Life

BOSTON TODAY

Bostonians are going to be talking about the Big Dig for a long time. Considering that their city was a gigantic construction site for more than 15 years, running up bills in excess of $15 billion, they have a lot to talk about. Even upon completion, the famous Central Artery/Tunnel Project provides fodder for newspaper scoops and general outrage, as the tunnels continue to spring leaks and require repairs. Opinion about the project reached an all-time low in 2006, when a ceiling panel crashed on a car and killed a motorist.

At the same time, the city is finally reaping the benefits of this controversial construction project. Traffic has never flowed more freely (with the notable exception of the Ted Williams Tunnel, still closed for repairs at the time of research). The beautiful Zakim Bunker Hill Bridge spans the Charles in an impressive display of engineering and elegance. Neighborhoods like the North End, West End and Waterfront are being rediscovered and reconnected to the rest of the city by a network of green parks and inviting plazas. One can only hope that these positives will eventually outweigh the negatives of this much-maligned endeavor.

The Big Dig is only one of the many changes sweeping the city streets. The South End has become Boston's trendiest destination for creative cuisine and avant-garde art, while the West End is also reaching out beyond its traditional sports-fan clientele. The Leather District is now an up-and-coming area with cool, contemporary clubs and loft condominiums. And the Seaport District – once an industrial warehouse zone abandoned to the artists – is now the city's hottest real-estate market. Even out-of-the-way Allston, site of Boston's 'student ghetto,' is slated for a complete overhaul at the expense of its wealthy neighbor across the river, Harvard University. From Downtown to Chinatown, Boston's neighborhoods are enjoying the fruits of revitalization efforts that celebrate their distinct characters.

Revitalization means hip restaurants and clubs and valuable community services. It means renovation of buildings and an influx of new residents. It also means increasing property values and rising rents. And inevitably, it means forcing out less affluent longtime residents who can no longer afford to stay.

In Boston, this conflict is invariably perceived as one of class and ethnicity: yuppies are scooping up properties in formerly tight-knit ethnic enclaves like Southie and Somerville, while middle-class Irish families split for the suburbs; and developers are building high-rise hotels and luxury condos all around Chinatown, forcing many Asian immigrants to flee to the South End and Dorchester.

Meanwhile, immigrants continue to pour into Boston and surrounding cities, especially from Brazil, Haiti and Vietnam. Immigrants from this new wave are setting up their own ethnic enclaves in Somerville, Jamaica Plain and Dorchester. And the cycle begins again and the stew in the melting pot thickens.

CITY CALENDAR

JANUARY & FEBRUARY

The deepest, darkest part of winter. Expect snow and cold temperatures – great weather for sledding and skating. Public holidays include Martin Luther King Jr's birthday, celebrated on the third Monday of January, and Presidents' Day, celebrated on the third Monday of February.

DANCE ACROSS THE CITY

☎ 617-532-1263; www.danceacrossthecity.org
The Wang Center sponsors one day of free classes and performances in every type of dance. Held at venues around the Theater District on the first Saturday in January.

CHINESE NEW YEAR

In late January or early February, Chinatown lights up with a colorful parade, firecrackers, fireworks and lots of food.

MARCH

Boston is officially sick of winter. March 17 is Evacuation Day, the day the British pulled out of Boston Harbor in 1775.

ST PATRICK'S DAY

☎ 617-268-7955; www.saintpatricksdayparade.com
On March 17, Ireland's patron saint is honored by all those who feel the Irish in their blood and by those who want to feel Irish beer in their blood. Everyone wears green (or you might get pinched). The large and vocal South Boston Irish community hosts a parade on West Broadway St, but since the mid-1990s, it's been marred by the decision to exclude gay and lesbian Irish groups from marching.

APRIL

Spring arrives, signaled by the emerging of crocuses and the blooming of forsythia. Baseball fans await Opening Day at Fenway Park. Temperatures range from 40°F to 55°F, although the occasional snowstorm also occurs.

PATRIOTS' DAY

www.battleroad.org
On the third Monday in April, history buffs commemorate the start of the American Revolution. Stoic riders follow the route of Paul Revere and William Dawes' historic rides and the Lexington Minutemen re-enact the battle on Lexington Green (11 miles west of Boston) at 5:30am. Concord (17 miles west of Boston) hosts a commemoration ceremony at 8:30am at the North Bridge. Parades and parties occur throughout the weekend.

BOSTON MARATHON

☎ 617-236-1652; www.bostonmarathon.org
Later in the morning on Patriot's Day, thousands of runners compete in this 26.2-mile run – the longest-running marathon in the world. The race starts at 10am in Hopkinton and finishes on Boylston St in front of the Boston Public Library. See the boxed text, p197 for more info.

INDEPENDENT FILM FESTIVAL OF BOSTON

www.iffboston.org
During the last week in April, venues around the city host independent films, including shorts, documentaries and drama produced locally and nationally.

MAY

May is one of Boston's most beautiful months, as the sun comes out on a semipermanent basis and the magnolia trees bloom all along Newbury St and Commonwealth Ave. Memorial Day, the last Monday in May, officially kicks off the summer season.

MAYFAIR

www.harvardsquare.com
When the sun comes out, so do the good folks in Harvard Sq. On the first or second Sunday in May, artists, merchants, and restaurants set up booths on the streets, while children's events and live entertainment take place on stages around the square.

LILAC SUNDAY

www.arboretum.harvard.edu
On the third Sunday in May, Arnold Arboretum celebrates the arrival of spring, when more than 400 varieties of fragrant lilac are in bloom. It is the only day of the year that visitors can picnic on the grass.

JUNE

Temperatures range from 55° to 70°F, with lots of rain. Student calendars are packed with end-of-academic-year events and graduation ceremonies. Then they depart the city, causing a noticeable decline in traffic and noise.

BOSTON PRIDE FESTIVAL

☎ 617-262-9405; www.bostonpride.org
During the first week in June, Boston does its part for this now-national celebration, kicking off with a rainbow-flag-raising on City Hall Plaza. Events occur throughout the week. The highlight is the Pride Parade & Festival on the second Sunday in June, attracting tens of thousands of participants, decked out in outrageous costumes and showing off their gay pride, culminating in a huge party on the Boston Common.

BUNKER HILL DAY

On June 17, Charlestown reenacts the crucial Battle of Bunker Hill and celebrates with a parade.

JULY

The city empties out, as students vacate for the summer and Bostonians head to their summerhouses. July is Boston's hottest month. Temperatures range from 70°F to 85°F, but there's always a week or two when the mercury shoots to the high 90s.

HARBORFEST

☎ 617-227-1528; www.bostonharborfest.org
The week-long Independence Day festival starts on the last weekend in June. One

day is Children's Day, with face painting, balloons and children's entertainment at venues around the city. The tastiest part of the festival is Chowderfest, where you sample dozens of fish and clam chowders prepared by Boston's top chefs.

INDEPENDENCE DAY

☎ 888-484-7677; www.july4th.org
On July 4, Boston hosts a line-up of free performances that culminates with the Boston Pops playing Tchaikovsky's *1812 Overture*, complete with brass cannon and synchronized fireworks. Half a million people descend on Boston to watch it live. The event traditionally takes place on the Esplanade.

SOMERVILLE ARTBEAT

☎ 617-625-6600; www.somervilleartscouncil.org
Davis Sq goes bohemian on the third weekend in July. Three stages host live performances, while artists and food vendors set up shop on the streets.

AUGUST

Summer in the city continues. Only at the end of August do we begin to feel fall coming back on.

AUGUST MOON FESTIVAL

The Chinese harvest celebration takes place in mid-August in Chinatown. It also commemorates the overthrow of the Mongolian Yuan dynasty in the 14th century, when rebels apparently communicated with each other by smuggling messages inside small cakes. So people celebrate by eating mooncakes, made from ground lotus and sesame seeds and containing secret messages.

BOSTON CARIBBEAN CARNIVAL

☎ 617-296-7083; www.bostoncarnival.org
Spanning two weekends in August, Boston's Caribbean community re-creates Carnival, a celebration of Caribbean culture complete with spectacular costumes, sultry music and spicy cooking. The third weekend in August is usually the Kiddies Carnival Celebration, while the last weekend in August is reserved for the annual ing & Queen Show and the all-out, over-the-top 'Trini-style' Carnival parade.

ITALIAN FESTIVALS

www.northendboston.com/news-religious.htm
Throughout July and August, the North End's religious societies sponsor feasts and processions honoring their patron saints (see the boxed text, p82). Major celebrations include the Fishermen's Feast (http://fishermansfeast.com) on the third weekend in August and St Anthony's Feast (http://stanthonysfeast.com) on the last weekend in August.

RESTAURANT WEEK

www.restaurantweekboston.com
This week is two weeks, really. At the end of August, participating restaurants around the city offer prix-fixe menus: $20 for lunch, $30 for dinner. The menus are usually excellent value – an awesome opportunity to sample some restaurants that are otherwise out of your price range.

SEPTEMBER

The humidity disappears, leaving slightly cooler temperatures and a crispness in the air. The students return and the streets are filled with U-Hauls during the first week. The first Monday in September is Labor Day, the official end of the summer season.

BOSTON FILM FESTIVAL

☎ 617-523-8388; www.bostonfilmfestival.org
For 10 days in mid-September, all Bostonians become film critics, as they are invited to attend screenings of some 50 different films at theaters around the city.

BLUES TRUST

www.bluestrust.com
Feeling blue? Don't miss the last weekend of September, when Blues Trust sponsors two days of (free) live jazz music at the Hatch Shell. Performers are veteran musicians and local bands. Blues Trust is the culmination of Boston Blues Week, which features live acts at clubs around the city.

BEANTOWN JAZZ FESTIVAL

☎ 617-747-2261; www.beantownjazz.org; Columbus Ave btwn Burke St & Massachusetts Ave
The Berklee College of Music sponsors this free two-day festival in the South End. Three stages show performances by jazz greats as well as local artists and Berklee students. Panel discussions, food vendors, kids' activities and all that jazz.

NEMO MUSIC FESTIVAL

www.nemoboston.com
Also on the last weekend in September, NEMO is dedicated to showcasing up-and-coming indie and alt-rock artists. Hundreds of musicians perform at venues around the city; buy one badge and hear them all.

OCTOBER

Boston's best month. The academic year is rolling; the weather is crisp and cool; and the trees take on shades of red, gold

Head of the Charles Regatta (p16)

and amber. Columbus Day falls on the second Monday in October, and Halloween is October 31.

LOWELL CELEBRATES KEROUAC
LCK; ☎ 877-537-6822; lckorg.tripod.com
During the first weekend in October, Lowell (34 miles northwest of Boston) hosts a weekend of events dedicated to Beat writer Jack Kerouac, featuring tours of many places in his novels, as well as panel discussions, readings, music and poetry. Literature buffs travel from around the world for this unique event.

OKTOBERFEST
www.harvardsquare.com/oktoberfest
On the first or second Sunday in October, Harvard Sq artisans and entertainers take to the streets. This annual street fair is great for kids, with puppet shows, face painting, fair rides and dance troupes.

HEAD OF THE CHARLES REGATTA
☎ 617-868-6200; www.hocr.org
During the third weekend in October, the Charles River hosts the world's largest rowing event, drawing more than 3000 collegiate, club and independent rowers. Fans line the banks of the river, lounging on blankets and cheering the boats.

PUMPKIN FESTIVAL
www.lifeisgood.com
The third Saturday in October is also the Saturday before Halloween. Local company Life is Good (p216) invites everyone to bring a pumpkin to the Boston Common and carve it for a cause. Well, two causes: first, to raise money for Camp Sunshine; also, to try to beat the record for the most lit jack-o'-lanterns (30,128 and counting).

HAUNTED HAPPENINGS
☎ 877-725-3662; www.hauntedhappenings.org
Salem (16 miles north of Boston) takes Halloween seriously – that's everyone, not just the witches. The city celebrates for much of the month of October, when there are special exhibits, parades, concerts, pumpkin carvings, costume parties and trick-or-treating. It all culminates on October 31, with the crowning of the King and Queen of Halloween. Oooh, that's scary.

NOVEMBER & DECEMBER
Winter is coming, and you can feel it in the air. You may see snow flurries in November, and there is usually one good snowstorm in December. Thanksgiving Day – the third Thursday in November – kicks off the holiday season. In early December, the huge Christmas trees at the Prudential Center and the Boston Common are lit, lending the city a festive air that remains throughout the month.

BOSTON TEA PARTY REENACTMENT
www.oldsouthmeetinghouse.org
On the Sunday prior to December 16, costumed actors march from Old South Meeting House to the waterfront and toss crates of tea into the harbor. For more information see p88.

FIRST NIGHT
www.firstnight.org; admission $15
New Year celebrations begin early on December 31 and continue past midnight, culminating in fireworks over the harbor. Purchase a special button that permits entrance into events citywide.

CULTURE
IDENTITY
At the end of WWII, nearly 800,000 people lived in Boston, the majority of whom were Irish. Urban renewal and suburban flight reduced those numbers, but the core of the city was never abandoned. Today, Boston is home to about 590,000, making it the 20th-largest US city. More than 3 million people inhabit Greater Boston.

As of the 2000 census, the breakdown goes like this: 54% Caucasian (or white), 25% African American, 14% Latino, 7% Asian, and less than 1% trace their ancestry to Native American peoples.

The largest ethnic group is still the Irish, who constitute about 16% of the population. Boston's Irish identity is felt strongly in Jamaica Plain (p113), Somerville (p119) and most noticeably South Boston (p120). Italians – most visible in the North End (p81) – account for about 8% of the population. These ethnic enclaves remain from the earliest waves of immigration, when newcomers established insular communities as a defense mechanism against the discrimination they were enduring.

In the 21st century, Boston continues to attract immigrants – now mostly from Brazil, Haiti, Vietnam and China. The Brazilians are settling in Somerville, while Haitian and Asian communities are growing in the South End, Dorchester and Jamaica Plain. Chinatown (p94) continues to be a focal point for the Asian community. These new immigrants have established their own shops selling specialty food items and foreign-language videos; they have opened their own clubs playing Brazilian samba and restaurants serving Creole cooking.

Racial tension has diminished significantly since the 1970s, when forced desegregation of Boston public schools incited violent reactions from all sides. However, the city is still noticeably segregated, which is one reason why these diverse groups are able to coexist more or less peacefully.

Many old Boston families cling to their identity as Boston Yankees – the descendents of the Massachusetts Bay Colony, the blue-blooded Brahmins who built the city. Well educated and well funded, these would-be aristocrats have blended into Boston's professional class. They may recognize each other's names, but nobody else does.

Boston's student population also represents a distinct identity group, overlapping with the others. Students may think they are poor, but they often have outside sources of financial support (read: parents). By definition, they are educated, which means they have job prospects and will soon join the ranks of the professional class.

Which brings us to the 'yuppies.' Boston has more than its fair share of young urban professionals, thanks to the strong economy and the endless supply from area universities. An estimated one-third of private-school students and two-thirds of public-school students remain in Boston after graduation. Yuppies are often blamed for driving up real-estate prices and diluting communities, especially as they move into formerly closed neighborhoods like the North End, Jamaica Plain, Somerville and South Boston.

Many people in these old enclaves welcome newcomers, recognizing the advantages of diversity and development. But others resent being invaded by outsiders, whether immigrants or yuppies; and who needs development if it means they can't pay the rent?

LIFESTYLE

Bostonians are culture vultures. Whether it's Stravinsky's *Symphony of Psalms* performed by the Boston Symphony Orchestra or *I Will Survive* performed by a drag-queen Gloria Gaynor, Boston is into creating and consuming art of every variety (see p28).

Bostonians are also sports fans. Sure, almost everybody loves to watch the Sox; but Bostonians also recognize that life is not a spectator sport. They are just as likely to be playing on the company softball team as watching the boys on TV. Pick a sport and Boston has an intramural league; find an open space and you'll see someone throwing a Frisbee. Bike paths, basketball courts, boathouses and beaches are always in use by Boston's young, energetic population (p194).

Bostonians are liberal thinkers. At least that's what the numbers say, as the city votes Democratic in elections on almost every level. While the reality is always more complex than the numbers, Boston has emerged ahead of the pack on issues from gay marriage to universal healthcare (p23).

Bostonians are education addicts. Perhaps there is something in the water – and perhaps the local universities and colleges put it there – but residents of Boston have an unquenchable thirst for learning at all ages. The Cambridge Center for Adult Education is the country's oldest community education program, but Boston and Brookline also have similar line-ups (see p272 for courses). Many local institutions – including Harvard, BU and Northeastern – have 'continuing education' programs for non-degree students. Whether it's belly dancing, poetry or astronomy, classes cater to curious folks who seek to develop new skills and interests.

FASHION

Fashion has never been Boston's top priority. Maybe the high-minded population has been too busy writing books, solving equations and getting PhDs to consider such trivialities as how they look while they are doing it.

This general trend is showing signs of change, however. It is thanks, in part, to Boston's increasingly international population, many of whom arrive with a Euro-chic style sensibility. Boston's own beautiful people also play a role, as they try to keep up with their more modish counterparts in NYC.

In recent years, Newbury St has become designer row: you'll have no problem procuring Diesel jeans, Mark Jacobs boots, La Perla lingerie, a Fendi bag or an Armani suit. Even the *Boston Globe* has become more fashionable, with a new weekly 'Style & Arts' section targeting vogue-conscious Bostonians.

This newfound awareness of style is not so noticeable across the river in Cambridge, where residents are perhaps still busy getting PhDs. Cantabrigians do not experiment too much beyond the ever-popular jeans-and-fleece look and the long-standing tweed-jacket-no-tie look.

Fashionistas continue to take their cues from New York, but a few local designers are trying to put Boston on the map à la mode. Recognizing Boston's conservative tastes in clothes, the styles tend to be relatively down-to-earth and decidedly wearable compared to what you might see in *Vogue* magazine.

Cibeline Sariano identifies herself as a New York designer because she hails from the city. But she works right here in Somerville, where she puts innovative twists on classic clothing designs. Abigail LeBay is a swimwear designer (based in Maine) who aims to create sexy styles without sacrificing comfort or quality. Turkish-born Nirva Derbekyan trained at the Massachusetts College of Art before launching her fashion house, which specializes in playful skirts made from natural cottons, wools and silks. Based in Cambridge, Gypsy Moon features graceful, internationally inspired styles that appeal to the romantic in practical Boston. But the brand also emphasizes that the clothing is designed 'to fit and flatter the bodies of real women.'

SPORTS

There might as well be signs on I-90 and I-93 reading 'Now Entering Red Sox Nation.' The intensity of baseball fans has only grown since the Boston Red Sox broke their agonizing 86-year losing streak and won the 2004 World Series. For many folks around the country, this band of scruffy players came to symbolize triumph over adversity. In successive years, the Sox have not fared quite so well, and fans curse them for it. Nevertheless, Fenway Park, the home of the Red Sox, continues to sell out every game. They'll wait another 86 years if they have to.

Sports fanaticism is not limited to baseball. This is evident from the face painters and beer bellies that brave subzero temperatures to watch the Patriots play football. Super Bowl champions in 2002, 2004 and 2005 – that's a 'three-peat' for football fans – this team put individualism aside and pulled together to beat others who looked better on paper. They also took one game at a time, season after season.

Sports fandom in Boston crosses lines of class, education and ethnicity. Again, it comes back to baseball. It was the renowned evolutionary biologist and paleontologist Stephen J Gould who argued that baseball is an intellectual's sport – a game of strategy, not just strength; brains more than brawn. Gould supported the NY Yankees, forgive him, but his sentiments strike a chord with Boston fans, who count among their ranks members of the literati like John Updike and Stephen King. John Cheever went so far as to declare that 'all literary men are Red Sox fans.'

Since the 1990s, the ball club has overcome the legacy of racism that plagued it for many years (see the boxed text, p195). Not too many black American players have played for Boston. But many of the team's biggest stars have been Latino players, especially from the Dominican Republic. And as many colors (and countries) are represented on the bench, are represented in Red Sox Nation.

WE DON'T NEED ANOTHER HERO, JUST ANOTHER WORLD SERIES

Boston loves its sports teams. The local sports culture has been described as passionate and well informed by some; psychotic and boneheaded by others. It is probably all true. Suggesting a list of Boston's all-time sports heroes might seem like an innocent enough exercise, but if you do it in a local bar, get ready to fight or run.

- David 'Big Papi' Ortiz – Boston baseball has been very good to the Big O, and the Big O has been very good to Boston baseball. The indomitable DH from the DR, with the big smile and big bat, is the most feared Red Sox hitter since Ted Williams. His incredible knack for game-winning home runs is already the stuff of baseball lore.
- Tom 'Terrific' Brady – the coy quarterback with the California cool has led the Patriots to three Super Bowl victories and garnered two big-game MVPs for himself. Since the GQ cover boy took the helm, the longsuffering Pats are patsies no more, but now reign among football's elite.
- Larry 'Legend' Bird – the Hick from French Lick took the already starry and storied Boston Celtics to new basketball heights in the 1980s. The Celts simply owned the town. With deft passing and deadeye shooting, Bird led the team to three championships and earned three MVPs.
- Robert Gordon 'Bobby' Orr – forever etched in the minds of Bruins fans is the image of Number Four, soaring through mid-air in celebration after scoring 'the goal' that brought Boston its first Stanley Cup in twenty years. The Pride of Parry Sound revolutionized hockey with his incredible speed, strength and skill. Voted league MVP three times and best defenseman eight times. Seeing was believing.

Unfortunately, Sox ownership does not reach out to this diverse community in basic ways. Games are not shown on network TV, but on the local cable sports station. And tickets – when available – are prohibitively expensive. So the hometown team is actually less accessible, even as its appeal extends to new audiences.

MEDIA

America's first newspaper, the unauthorized *Publick Occurrences, Both Foreign and Domestick*, was published in Boston in 1690, then immediately suppressed. The *Boston News-Letter* was the first regularly published periodical, starting in 1704. The *New England Courant*, published by Benjamin Franklin's older brother James, added an outlet for news and fiction in 1720.

Three hundred years later, there are still two major newspapers in Boston. The most prominent daily is the *Boston Globe*. Widely read and widely respected, the Globe is Boston's top media organization. In the early 2000s, Globe reporters were instrumental in uncovering the Catholic Church abuse scandal, for which they were awarded a Pulitzer Prize. Like all respectable newspapers, the Globe is sometimes accused of having a liberal bias. Its competitor, the tabloid *Boston Herald*, has a smaller circulation, perhaps due to its conservative editorial stance.

Boston's independent media offer a refreshing alternative to these two mainstream papers. *The Boston Phoenix* (www.bostonphoenix.com) is a sassy weekly with a fresh perspective on local politics and trends. The Independent Media Corporation (www.boston.indymedia.org) also addresses events and issues that are often overlooked.

LANGUAGE

You won't be long in this town before you hear the broad vowels of the famous Boston accent. 'Pahk the cah in Hahvahd Yahd' is the overused example (translation: Park the car in Harvard Yard). Locals scoff at this attempt to imitate their speech patterns, as everyone knows that cars are prohibited in Harvard Yard.

But this distinct dialect rings out loud and clear on Boston streets, particularly among working-class and middle-class Irish, Italian and Portuguese residents. The letter R frequently disappears at the end of words ('chowdah' instead of chowder); then mysteriously reappears on the end of other words ('ideer' instead of idea). You are most likely to hear it when you ask directions from your bus driver or the local policeman.

If you really want to demonstrate that you are down with the Boston dialect, use the more appropriate (and accurate) sentence: 'The weathah heah is wikkid bizah.'

RELIGION

The colonists who founded the Massachusetts Bay Colony were Puritans, adherents to a strict form of Calvinism that sought to 'purify' the church of the excesses of ceremony acquired over the centuries. They believed the Bible was not to be subjected to elaborate theological interpretations.

Few traces of these fundamentalist beliefs are found in Boston today. More visible are the spiritual descendants of Boston's 18th- and 19th-century philosophers. Believers who questioned the concept of the trinity split off to found the first Unitarian Church at King's Chapel in 1782; the Unitarians were strongly influenced by transcendentalism, which flourished in Boston and Concord from 1836 to 1860. The belief that God 'transcended' all people and things attracted the era's greatest philosophers, including Emerson, Thoreau, Hawthorne and Melville. Its modern incarnation is Unitarian-Universalism. In 1866, Mary Baker Eddy founded the Christian Science Church, which professes personal healing through prayer. The 'mother church' is in Boston, but it has some 2000 churches internationally.

The immigrants that arrived in droves throughout the 19th century changed Boston's religious makeup. They were mostly Irish, Italian and Portuguese – all strongly Catholic. Nowadays, almost 70% of city residents who claim a religious identity claim Catholicism. Conservative Catholics have sometimes come into conflict with more liberal-thinking elements in society; for example, the annual St Patrick's Day Parade in overwhelmingly Irish South Boston still does not allow gays to march, even though the Commonwealth of Massachusetts allows them to marry.

But recently, the more prominent controversies are *within* the Catholic Church in Boston. In recent years, the horror at the reports of child molestation by local parish priests was outdone only by the outrage at the cover-up by the archdiocese. Following that scandal, the archdiocese has been forced to close many community churches, causing further heartbreak within the parishes (see the boxed text, p97).

Although relatively few in numbers, Eastern European Jews have also made their mark on Boston neighborhoods. Their descendants have created a notable Jewish cultural enclave in Brookline (see p103) and an internationally recognized education facility, Brandeis University, just outside of Boston in Waltham, Massachusetts.

EDUCATION

With 35 institutions of higher education and the country's highest number of students per capita, Boston is what you might call a 'college town.' Kenmore Sq and Fenway are home to the Boston University behemoth, as well as myriad smaller colleges and professional schools. In the western reaches of the city, sections of Allston and Brighton have been

BOSTON: COLLEGE TOWN

The greater Boston area has many, many college campuses – too many to mention here. The vibrancy of the student population is one of the defining characteristics of this youthful city. Cultural and sporting events are often open to the public (see p194).

Berklee College of Music (Map pp308–9; ☎ 617-747-2222; www.berklee.edu; 1140 Boylston St; 🚇 Hynes) One of the country's finest music schools.

Boston University (BU; Map pp308–9; ☎ 617-353-2000, 617-353-2169; www.bu.edu; 881 Commonwealth Ave; 🚇 BU Central) West of Kenmore Sq, enrolls about 30,000 graduate and undergraduate students, and has a huge campus and popular sports teams.

Harvard University (see p117)

Massachusetts College of Art (Massart; see p103)

Massachusetts Institute of Technology (see p118)

Northeastern University (Map pp306–7; ☎ 617-373-2000; www.northeastern.edu; 360 Huntington Ave; 🚇 Ruggles or Northeastern) Boasts one of the country's largest work-study cooperative programs.

University of Massachusetts, Boston (UMass; ☎ 617-287-5000; www.umb.edu; 100 Morrissey Blvd; 🚇 UMass/JFK) Host to the John F Kennedy Library & Museum (see p121).

Other well-established colleges and universities on the city's fringe:

Boston College (BC; Map pp298–9; ☎ 617-552-8000; www.bc.edu; 140 Commonwealth Ave/MA 30, Chestnut Hill; 🚇 Boston College or Cleveland Circle) The nation's largest Jesuit community. The large green campus has Gothic towers, stained glass, a good art museum and excellent Irish and Catholic ephemera collections in the library. Its basketball and football teams are usually high in national rankings. Take the green B-line to Boston College or the C-line to Cleveland Circle.

Brandeis University (Map pp298–9; ☎ 781-736-2000; www.brandeis.edu; South St, Waltham) A small campus that includes the Rose Art Museum, specializing in New England art. Take the MBTA commuter rail from North Station to the Brandeis/Roberts stop.

Tufts University (Map pp298–9; ☎ 617-628-5000; www.tufts.edu; College Ave, Medford) Home to the acclaimed Fletcher School of International Affairs. Take the Red Line to Davis Sq, then a free Tufts shuttle across from the station takes you directly to the campus.

Wellesley College (Map pp298–9; ☎ 781-283-1000; www.wellesley.edu; 106 Central St, Wellesley) A Seven Sisters women's college that has a hilly, wooded campus and the excellent Davis Museum & Cultural Center. Walk from the MBTA commuter rail or drive MA 16 to MA 135.

Harvard Yard, Harvard University (p117)

dubbed the 'student ghetto' for their low-rent apartments that attract students from BC and BU. And across the river, Cambridge is home to scholarly superstars Harvard and MIT, as well as a handful of smaller schools.

This abundance of colleges and universities guarantees a constant youthful presence in Boston; residents age 19 to 24 represent 16% of the population. Many students remain in Boston after graduation, bolstering the highly educated workforce. The young, educated population ensures a vibrant music scene (p33), an innovative art scene (p31) and a hot singles scene (37% of households are 'individuals': read 'available').

ECONOMY & COSTS

The greater Boston area is the seventh-largest regional economy in the United States, with a gross regional product of $255 million in 2005. The Boston economy is fueled by its educational institutions, which are major employers in their own right. They also provide a permanent source of employees for thriving private-sector industries.

The technology and biotechnology industries have spawned from university research labs (quite literally, as MIT researchers developed the first computer in 1928). Wang Computers, Digital Computers, Prime and Data General all began in the Boston area. Cambridge, especially Central Sq and Kendall Sq, is a center for the pharmaceutical industry, hosting companies like Millennium and Biogen.

Boston is home to at least six major hospitals. Again, the hospitals form collaborative relationships with universities for teaching and research. The world-class facilities at the Longwood Medical Area and Massachusetts General Hospital are affiliated with the Harvard Medical School, while the New England Medical Center maintains a relationship with Tufts University. Boston institutions receive more funding than those in any other urban area from the National Institute for Health.

HOW MUCH?
Bike rental (24 hours) $25
'Boston: Wicked Pissah' T-shirt $20
Bowl of clam chowder $3.75
Cappuccino $3.50
Cover charge Abbey Lounge $8-12
Gallon of gas $2.80
Liter of water $2.50
Pint of Sam Adams $5
T-ride $1.70
Red Sox ticket bleacher seat (face value) $23

Finally, Boston is a major center for financial services. Mutual funds originated in Massachusetts and became an enormously popular investment tool for individual retirement plans, due in part to promotion by Boston-based Fidelity Investments. Insurance and venture capital are also significant.

Much of this white-collar industry developed in the 1980s and 1990s – breathing new life into a city that was suffering from the decline of its manufacturing sector. This economic turnaround is sometimes called the 'Massachusetts Miracle.'

The result today is a robust economy that continues to grow. The downside of the city's prosperity, of course, is its high cost of living. Some reports estimate that Boston is the most expensive metropolitan area in the country. Housing prices are prohibitively high, having increased more than 80% in the first five years of the new millennium. This concerns companies and schools who want to attract talent from elsewhere. Recruiters lament the low- to moderate-income family being frozen out of the housing market, as do the low- to moderate-income families.

Boston is also an expensive place to visit. Once in town, the bulk of your expenses will be for accommodation. Fancy hotels in Boston can cost as much as you are willing to pay, but it is possible – taking advantage of discounted web rates – to stay in a respectable, central hotel for $125 to $175 (per night, per double room). Guesthouses and budget hotels run to $100 to $125, while hostels cost $25 to $40 for a bed. See p226 for more details.

Eating is also not cheap. Three sit-down meals a day, including one at an upscale restaurant, will easily cost $60 per person. Forgoing drinks or grabbing a meal at a less expensive venue trims that estimate to $40. At best, self-catering and cheap eats make it possible to eat for about $20 per day. See p134 for some suggestions on how to eat and save.

Keep in mind that Boston offers many opportunities to save money. See the boxed text on p98 for some suggestions.

GOVERNMENT & POLITICS

The late Thomas P 'Tip' O'Neill, Boston native and respected Speaker of the House, coined the phrase 'All politics is local.' So for example, if the mayor can keep control of the day-to-day practicalities of the functioning of the city, he's 'in like Flynn' (the long-serving Irish-Catholic mayor Ray Flynn, that is).

Boston's current chief is Thomas Menino, the city's first Italian-American mayor (and first non-Irish mayor since 1884). Fondly called 'Mumbles Menino' for his poor diction, Menino is nonetheless well liked. By the time he completes his current, fourth term in office, he will be the longest-serving mayor in Boston history. His popularity is due to his hands-on approach to managing the city. Trash pick-up and snow removal are reliable, somehow a sign that all is right with the world; the city's parks are green and well maintained, and if they're not, the parks department has a hotline where you can call to complain.

Despite Menino's positive standing, the city administration faces criticism on several fronts. The lack of affordable housing is a huge issue, as neighborhood gentrification continues to drive up real-estate prices. Also on the rise is violent crime, on par with a nationwide trend in urban areas.

Even if Tip O'Neill was right, Boston continues to play an important role in national politics. On that front, Boston is often considered the epitome of the 'liberal East Coast.' And it's true that the city strongly supports Democratic candidates. Massachusetts has been at the forefront of countless 'liberal' issues, including anti-smoking legislation (Massachusetts banned smoking in the workplace in 2003), same-sex marriage (legalized in Massachusetts in 2004), and healthcare (as of 2007, health insurance is required for all state residents and subsidized for low-income residents).

Conservatives argue that these progressive values are out of touch with mainstream America. Indeed, when Massachusetts Senator John Kerry ran for president in 2004, his opponents portrayed him as a member of the 'East-Coast elite', which likely contributed to his defeat. Bostonians, for their part, have come to accept that perhaps they are out of touch with mainstream America; but considering what's going on in mainstream America, they're okay with that.

There is much speculation that Massachusetts politicians will also be involved in the 2008 presidential election. At the time of research, Governor Mitt Romney had not declared his intentions to run, but he had spent plenty of time giving speeches and shaking hands in crucial primary states. Of course Romney also belongs to the East-Coast elite; whether or not that will be held against him remains to be seen.

ENVIRONMENT

CLIMATE

Here's a promise: at least once during your visit to Boston, somebody will say 'If you don't like the weather, wait a minute!' With the ocean to the east and mountains to the north and west, Boston's weather is subject to extremes.

Besides the day-to-day (or minute-to-minute) fluctuations, Boston enjoys wonderful seasonal variations. Spring brings temperate weather and blooming trees, usually in April. This mild weather often lasts until mid-June, but it is also accompanied by plenty of rain. July and August are hot and humid.

Autumn is Boston's most glorious season. Weather usually remains warm throughout September, while cooler temperatures in October bring out the colorful foliage. Winter lasts too long for most people's tastes, stretching from December to April. During this period, visitors can expect temperatures below freezing and plenty of snow.

THE LAND

The city of Boston was founded on Shawmut, a peninsula that protruded into the natural harbor of the Massachusetts Bay. On the western side of the peninsula, the wide back bay eventually gave way to the Charles River, which wound its way west. When European settlers arrived in the 17th century, they congregated on the peninsula itself (now the North End, West End, Beacon Hill and Downtown) and all along the north shore of the Back Bay and Charles River (now Cambridge and Charlestown).

In those early days, the peninsula's topography was defined by three hills (which explains the origins of street names like 'Tremont'). Beacon Hill, the smallest of the three, is the only hill that remains today – though it too used to be much higher.

In the 19th century when Boston was experiencing a population boom, the city undertook a massive expansion project, filling in much of the swampy, marshy bay on the back side of the peninsula; Shawmut's three hills became the source of landfill. So Boston built the south shore of the Charles River. What once was marshland became the neighborhoods known as the Back Bay, Kenmore Sq and Fenway.

The city continued to expand west and south, so that Boston today occupies 48.4 square miles.

GREEN BOSTON

Bostonians have the great fortune to witness the greening of their city, quite literally. The Central Artery is underground, out of sight, soon to be replaced by the Rose Kennedy Greenway (boxed text, opposite). The new park will provide a pleasant counterpart to the Charles River Esplanade (p198), on the south shore of the river, and the Emerald Necklace (boxed text, p104), stretching from the Boston Common to Franklin Park. And certainly after 15 years of construction, the greenway is a welcome addition to an otherwise concrete landscape.

Bridge over the lake on the Boston Common (p77)

BEYOND THE BIG DIG

All federal highway projects are local. And few road-improvement schemes have been so infamously linked with a locality as the Central Artery/Tunnel project is with the city of Boston. The Big Dig, as it is better known, is now well into its second decade of construction and well past its 15th billion dollar in cost. The project, which is finally nearing completion, has won acclaim and been defamed. Boston motorists have gone from infuriated, to confounded, to fearful (see p58).

The project involved the dismantling of the Central Artery, the perpetually congested raised highway that cut through the downtown. In its place, the Big Dig built more than 40 miles of subterranean superhighway. To undertake a massive public-works project in the heart of the city, according to the former project director, was like 'performing by-pass surgery on a patient while he continues to work and play tennis.'

The Big Dig is more than just a long and winding underground road; it also dramatically changed the face of the city and improved the quality of life. Just north of this high-tech cavern, the highway meets the Charles River. The graceful Leonard Zakim Bridge, named for a local civil-rights activist, spans the water. Against the historic backdrop of Bunker Hill, it is the widest cable-stayed bridge in the world. To the south, the Big Dig includes a new harbor tunnel, connecting Interstate-90 with the airport and north shore. The Ted Williams Tunnel, named for a local leftfielder, was considered an engineering feat (at least until its roof collapsed).

Finally, the project will reclaim about 27 acres of industrial wasteland for parks and civic plazas. Where the hulking Central Artery once created barriers and shadows, Bostonians will soon enjoy a tree-lined open space, the Rose Kennedy Greenway, named for a local matriarch.

When everything is functioning properly, the new network of subterranean highways dramatically reduces commuting times and facilitates airport traffic. That the various tunnels require periodic closing for repairs is a source of frustration and scorn. Above ground, the Rose Kennedy Greenway is still in the conceptual stages. Environmental regulations require that 75% of the reclaimed land must be devoted to parks or open space, while other segments will be developed for visitor facilities and other buildings.

One stretch near the Fort Point Channel has been designated for the Massachusetts Horticultural Society, which proposed building a conservatory and a botanical garden. Further south, between Chinatown and the Leather District, the new space will constitute an Asian-accented park to complement Chinatown Gate. Other parcels call for civic plazas with fountains and lawns, sculpture gardens, cafés and cultural facilities.

It sounds lovely, and Bostonians look forward to the day when they can walk along a ribbon of green from North Station to South Station. That said, if they've learned anything from the Big Dig, they have learned not to hold their breath.

Other ongoing environmental initiatives are also coming to fruition. For hundreds of years, the Boston Harbor was a dumping site for sewage, earning its reputation as the most polluted waterfront in the country. In the mid-1980s, the city was ordered by the EPA to clean up its act.

The 11-year effort is finally reaping benefits. For the first time in over a century, water quality in the harbor is safe for swimming; beaches are clean and enjoyable places to play; and thanks to the HarborWalk (p198), the Waterfront has become a wonderful area for strolling.

A similar effort is underway in the Charles River, inspiration for the Standell's song *Dirty Water*. Improvements have been significant. In 2006 – for the second year in a row – the Charles River Initiative received a B+ on its report card from the EPA, a vast improvement from the D it received a decade ago. A local advocacy group saw fit to celebrate the good report card by organizing the first-ever Charles River Swim, a tradition that will hopefully continue as water quality continues to improve.

Another green goal in Boston is reducing the number of cars on the roads, thus diminishing greenhouse gas emissions. Boston-based Zipcar – the country's largest car-sharing company – encourages urbanites to shed cars, drive less and use other forms of transportation. This trend complements the city's long-term transportation plans to extend the subway and build more bike paths ('long-term' being the operative word). Whether or not they realize it, T-riders, bike riders and Zipcar drivers are all contributing to the greening of Boston.

ON THE HORIZON

What's that on the horizon, a crane? Here are a few more major development projects that are underway:

- Allston initiative – Harvard University intends to radically alter Allston's landscape, creating a new urban campus and community environment.
- Green-line extension – one condition for receipt of the Federal funding for the Big Dig is extending the green line from Lechmere out to Medford via Union Sq.
- Northpoint Cambridge – city residents and urban planners hope this real estate development and green space will revive East Cambridge.

URBAN PLANNING & DEVELOPMENT

Downtown Boston has long felt like one giant construction project. With the completion of the Big Dig (see p25), residents and visitors can finally breathe a sigh of relief and enjoy some quiet. But not for long, as the next major development project is already underway.

In recent years, the Seaport District has been transformed with the construction of the convention center, the Moakley Federal Courthouse and the new ICA on the waterfront. But that's only the beginning. To cater to the business people attending conventions, luxury hotels are sprouting up all over this area. Two prominent pieces of property along Northern Ave are slated for development for housing, condos, offices, shops and restaurants.

Arts

Arts

From high culture to low-down blues, the Boston arts scene has something for everyone. Indeed, the arts are what made this city the 'Athens of America.'

Although much of Boston's culture goes back to its Puritan roots, the arts are an exception. The early settlers were a spiritual people, uninterested in such small-minded pursuits as art or music. The colonial period is notable for its political – not artistic – contributions.

It was not until the 19th century that Boston developed as an artistic center. Almost all of Boston's illustrious cultural institutions date to this Golden Age, including the Boston Public Library, the Boston Symphony Orchestra and the Museum of Fine Arts.

It's worth noting, however, that Boston can thank the Puritans for at least one contribution – one so crucial that it would influence every aspect of the city's artistic development. For the Puritans founded Harvard College, establishing the Boston area as a center for learning. Attracted by the intellectual atmosphere, other institutions followed suit; not only traditional universities but also art schools, music colleges, conservatories and more. To this day, the vibrant university culture enhances the breadth and depth of cultural offerings on both sides of the river.

For reviews of specific venues, see Entertainment, p176.

LITERATURE

The city's reverence for the written word was brought by the Puritans and nurtured over the centuries by the area's great universities and literary societies. This literary tradition thrives today, as writers and scholars continue to congregate in university classrooms and crowded cafés.

Grub Street (p272) is an active nonprofit that offers writing workshops and seminars, as well as book clubs, networking events, open-mike readings and Saturday-morning discussions. It is an invigorating forum for writers and literature-lovers alike.

Another notable event in Boston's literary life is Lowell Celebrates Kerouac (LCK; see the boxed text, p30).

COLONIAL LITERATURE

Boston's literary tradition dates to the days of Puritan settlement. As early as 1631, Anne Bradstreet was writing poetry and meditations. Shortly thereafter, Harvard College was founded (1636) and the first printing press was set up (1638), thus establishing Boston (and Cambridge) as an important literary center that would attract writers and scholars for generations to come.

Early colonial writings were either spiritual or historical in nature. Governor John Winthrop chronicled the foundation of Boston in his journals. Governor William Bradford, the second governor of Plymouth Colony, was the author of the primary historical reference about the Pilgrims, *Of Plimouth Plantation*. The most prolific writer was Reverend Cotton Mather (1663–1728), who wrote more than 400 books on issues of spirituality – most notably the Salem witch trials.

THE GOLDEN AGE

It was during the 19th century that Boston developed its reputation as the 'Athens of America.' The universities had become a magnet for writers, poets and philosophers, as well as publishers and bookstores. The local literati were expounding on social issues such as slavery, women's rights and religious reawakening. Boston, Cambridge and Concord were fertile breeding grounds for ideas, nurturing the seeds of America's literary and

BOSTON IN LITERATURE

- Nathaniel Hawthorne wrote *The Scarlet Letter* (1850) about a woman in Puritan New England who is vilified when she becomes pregnant with her minister's child. Hawthorne was apparently inspired by the gravestone of Elizabeth Pain, in King's Chapel Burial Ground, for his protagonist Hester Prynne.
- Henry James wrote several novels set in Boston, including the aptly named *The Bostonians* (1886). A Boston feminist takes her conservative male cousin to hear a speech by a rising star of the women's movement. They both fall in love with her, resulting in a tragicomic love triangle.
- *The Last Puritan* (1935), by George Santayana, explores what it might be like for someone with 17th-century Puritan ideals to attend Harvard in the 20th century.
- Robert McCloskey's *Make Way for Ducklings* (1941), a classic children's book, describes the story of a mother duck and her ducklings lost in Back Bay.
- The children's novel *Johnny Tremain* (1943), by Esther Forbes, describes the Revolutionary War from the point of view of a fictional boy.
- Edwin O'Connor's *The Last Hurrah* (1955), a fictional work based on Mayor Curley's antics, is as much fun as Jack Beatty's *The Rascal King* (1992), a biographical account of Curley's flamboyance.
- *The Friends of Eddie Coyle* (1972), by George Higgins, is a crime novel that is praised for its realistic dialogue, thus providing a crash course in the Boston dialect.
- David Foster Wallace's *Infinite Jest* (1996) includes intricate descriptions of Commonwealth Ave, Back Bay and the Boston Common. The 1000-page tome is at once philosophical and satirical.
- The former governor William Weld penned a sometimes-witty political mystery, *Mackerel by Moonlight* (1998).
- Dennis Lehane's novel *Mystic River* (2001) recounts the dark story of three childhood friends who are thrown together in adulthood when one of their daughters is murdered.

philosophical flowering. This was the Golden Age of American literature, and Boston was its nucleus.

Ralph Waldo Emerson (1803–82) promulgated his teachings from his home in Concord (p247). He and Henry David Thoreau (1817–62) wrote compelling essays about their beliefs and their attempts to live in accordance with the mystical unity of all creation (transcendentalism; see p64). Thoreau's notable writings included *Walden, or Life in the Woods* (1854), which advocated a life of simplicity and living in harmony with nature, and *Civil Disobedience* (1849), a treatise well before its time.

Nathaniel Hawthorne (1804–64) traveled in this Concordian literary circle. America's first great short-story writer, Hawthorne was the author of *The Scarlet Letter* (1850) and *The House of the Seven Gables* (1851), both offering insightful commentary on colonial culture. Louisa May Alcott (1832–88) grew up at Orchard House (p248), also in Concord, where she wrote her largely autobiographical novel *Little Women* (1868). This classic is beloved by generations of young women. After this success, Alcott moved to Beacon Hill, where her home is still a landmark on Louisburg Sq.

Around this time, poet Henry Wadsworth Longfellow (1807–82) was the most illustrious resident of Cambridge, where he taught at Harvard. Longfellow often hosted his contemporaries from Concord for philosophical discussions at his home on Brattle St. Here he wrote poems such as 'Song of Hiawatha' and 'Paul Revere's Ride', both cherished accounts of American lore.

Meanwhile these luminaries would travel one Saturday a month to Boston to congregate with their contemporaries at the old Parker House (see p230). Presided over by Oliver Wendell Holmes, the Saturday Club was known for its jovial atmosphere and stimulating discourse, attracting such renowned visitors as Charles Dickens. Out of these meetings was born the *Atlantic Monthly*, a literary institution that continues to showcase innovative authors and ideas.

Down the street, the Old Corner Bookstore was the site of Ticknor & Fields, the first publishing house to offer author royalties. Apparently Mr Fields had a special talent for discovering new local talent; by all accounts, his bookstore was a lively meeting place for writers and readers.

LOWELL: THE TOWN & THE CITY

'Follow along to the center of town, the Square, where at noon everybody knows everybody else.' So Beat Generation author Jack Kerouac described his hometown of Lowell, Massachusetts in his novel *The Town & The City*.

One of the most influential American authors of the 20th century, Jack Kerouac (1922–69) was born in Lowell, 34 miles north of Boston, at the mill town's industrial peak. He inhabited Lowell's neighborhoods and he graduated from Lowell High School. It is not surprising, then, that the author used Lowell as the setting for five of his novels that draw on his youth in the 1920s, '30s and '40s.

Kerouac is remembered annually during the Lowell Celebrates Kerouac (LCK) festival (see p16). LCK – in conjunction with the Jack Kerouac Subterranean Information Society – has also compiled a fantastically detailed walking tour (http://ecommunity.uml.edu/jklowell) of Lowell, based on places that Kerouac wrote about and experienced.

Of course Kerouac is most famous for his classic novel *On the Road*. With it, he became a symbol of the spirit of the open road. He eventually went to New York, where he and Allen Ginsberg and William Burroughs formed the core of the Beat Generation of writers. Nonetheless, Kerouac always maintained ties to Lowell, and he is buried in Edson Cemetery (on the corner of Gorham and Saratoga Sts), a pilgrimage site for devotees who were inspired by his free spirit.

Across the Common on Beacon Hill, William Lloyd Garrison, Julia Ward Howe and Harriet Beecher Stowe fueled the abolitionist movement with fiery writings. Indeed, social activist Lydia Maria Child had her privileges at the Boston Athenaeum (p75) revoked for her provocative antislavery pamphlets.

In 1895, WEB DuBois (1868–1963) became the first black man to receive a PhD from Harvard University. A few years later, he wrote his seminal tract *The Souls of Black Folk*, in which he sought to influence the way blacks dealt with segregation, urging pride in African heritage.

BANNED IN BOSTON

In the 20th century, Boston continued to attract authors, poets and playwrights, but the Golden Age was over. This city was no longer the center of progressive thought and social activism that had so inspired American literature.

This shift in cultural geography was due in part to a shift in moral consciousness in the late 19th century. Moral crusaders and city officials promoted stringent censorship of books, films and plays that they deemed offensive or obscene. Many writers were 'banned in Boston' – a trend that contributed to the city's image as provincial outpost instead of cultural capital. Eugene O'Neill (1888–1953) is the most celebrated example. O'Neill attended Harvard, he founded the Provincetown Players on Cape Cod and he spent the last two years of his life in Back Bay; but his experimental play *Strange Interlude* was prohibited from showing on Boston stages.

Henry James (1843–1916) grew up in Cambridge. Although he was undoubtedly influenced by his Bostonian upbringing, he eventually immigrated to England. A prolific writer, he often commented on American society in his novels, which included *Daisy Miller* and *The Bostonians*.

The revolutionary poet ee cummings (1894–1962) was also born in Cambridge, although it was his experiences in Europe that inspired his most famous novel, *The Enormous Room*. Descended from an old New England family, TS Eliot (1888–1965) taught at Harvard for a spell, but he wrote his best work in England.

Robert Lowell (1917–77) was another Boston native who was restless in his hometown. He spent many years living in Back Bay and teaching at Boston University, where he wrote *Life Studies* and *For the Union Dead*. Encouraged by his interactions with Beat-Generation poet Alan Ginsberg, Lowell became the seminal 'Confessional poet.' At BU, he counted Sylvia Plath (1932–63) and Anne Sexton (1928–74) among the students he inspired before he finally moved to Manhattan.

One of the Beat Generation's defining authors, Jack Kerouac was born in Lowell, Massachusetts. His hometown features prominently in many of his novels (see the boxed text, above), but he too eventually decamped to the new cultural capital to the south.

CONTEMPORARY LITERATURE

Boston never regained its status as the hub of the literary solar system. But its rich legacy and ever-influential universities ensure that the city continues to contribute to American literature. Many of Boston's most prominent writers are transplants from other cities or countries, drawn to its academic and creative institutions. John Updike (1932–), author of the Pulitzer Prize–winning Rabbit series, moved to Boston to attend Harvard (where he was president of *Harvard Lampoon*), before settling in Ipswich, Massachusetts.

Recipient of the National Book Award and PEN/Faulkner Award, Ha Jin (1956–) is a Chinese-American writer who teaches at Boston University. His poems and stories have been lauded for their insightful commentary about contemporary China.

Jhumpa Lahiri (1967–) is a Bengali Indian-American writer who studied creative writing at Boston University. Both of her books, which address the challenges and triumphs in the lives of her Indian-American characters, are set in Boston and surrounding neighborhoods.

Born in Ithaca, New York, David Foster Wallace (1962–) studied philosophy at Harvard. Although he abandoned this course and moved out of the city, his Boston-based novel, *Infinite Jest,* earned him a MacArthur Genius Award.

Of course, Boston has also fostered some homegrown talent. John Cheever (1912–82) was born in Quincy and lived in Boston. His novel, the *Wapshot Chronicle*, takes place in a Massachusetts fishing village, although his most famous stories come from the Pulitzer Prize winner, *The Stories of John Cheever.* Born and raised in Dorchester, Dennis Lehane (1966–) wrote *Mystic River*, a compelling tale set in a working-class Boston 'hood, which was made into an Oscar-winning film.

PAINTING & VISUAL ARTS

For all its wealth, early 19th-century Boston could not fully nurture its artists, most of whom sought fulfillment abroad. This included James Abbot McNeill Whistler (1834–1903), who challenged the tradition of representational painting by blurring lines and emphasizing the play of light in his work. John Singleton Copley (1738–1815) is considered the first great American portrait painter, but he completed many of his best-known works after relocating to London (though you can see both artists today at the Museum of Fine Arts, p103).

Later in the century, Boston was capable of supporting world-class artists, due in part to the new public buildings being constructed in Back Bay. Boston's most celebrated artist is John Singer Sargent (1856–1925), who painted telling portraits of Boston's upper class. Sargent's murals adorn the central staircase at the Museum of Fine Arts and the walls of the Boston Public Library (p98).

Austere statue of John Harvard in Harvard Yard (p117)

Winslow Homer (1836–1910) pursued a career as an illustrator for the popular press, but later dedicated his talents to painting. Homer is famous for his scenes of the New England coast. Childe Hassam (1859–1935) used the Boston Common and other local cityscapes as subjects for his impressionist works.

Daniel Chester French (1850–1931) is the creator of the Minuteman statue in Concord (p247) and the John Harvard statue in Harvard Yard (p117), not to mention better-known works in Washington, DC. Augustus St Gaudens (1848–1907) is famous for the Robert Gould Shaw Memorial on the Boston Common (p78), but he was also a key figure in the design of the Boston Public Library, where his work is also on display.

Critics claim that Boston lost pace with the artistic world in the second half of the 20th century. But the visual arts are returning to the forefront of contemporary cultural life in the new millennium. Recent exhibits at the Museum of Fine Arts have brought attention to the museum's impressive existing holdings. This preeminent institution is undergoing a major expansion, allowing for more interactive exhibits and enhanced space for the museum's most visited artwork. Meanwhile, the 2006 opening of the new ICA (see the boxed text, below) has shone the spotlight onto Boston's contemporary art scene, which had long been overshadowed.

Art-lovers can nurture their own creative spirit at the Museum of Fine Arts and at De-Cordova Museum & Sculpture Park in Concord (see p248). Both museums offer packed schedules of classes, workshops and lecture series, including many programs for kids.

ART GALLERIES

Newbury St in Back Bay and Charles St on Beacon Hill are Boston's traditional venues for gallery-hopping. Art connoisseurs, however, may find them rather staid. To experience the cutting edge of Boston's burgeoning art scene, look for open-studio events in the Seaport District, the South End, Jamaica Plain and Somerville.

The old brick warehouses on the southeast side of Fort Point Channel were the center of the nation's wool trade until the 1960s, when they were converted to art studios. As the Seaport District gets developed, the artists who initiated the revitalization are being squeezed out. The **Fort Point Arts Community** (www.fortpointarts.org) continues to be an active, energetic group of artists that includes painters, designers, photographers and mixed-media artists. The community has a gallery (see p183); or you can visit during the seasonal two-day Open Studios event.

In Jamaica Plain, a local community group sponsors **First Thursdays** (www.jpcentresouth .org), when shops and restaurants along the main drag are transformed into galleries where local artists can exhibit their works. Each business hosts a reception so visitors can meet the artists and partake of refreshment. The festive atmosphere is enhanced by live music and poetry readings.

Across the river, the **Somerville Arts Council** (www.somervilleartscouncil.org) organizes many ways for artists and art-lovers to interact, including Artbeat (see p14) and **Somerville Open**

CONTEMPORARY ART IN TRADITIONAL BOSTON

Boston may appear radical in its politics, but in affairs of the art, the city shows more conservative tastes. The Museum of Fine Arts and the Isabella Stewart Gardner Museum are first-rate cultural institutions, but their strength is art of the past. The 2006 unveiling of a gleaming new Institute of Contemporary Art on the waterfront established the city as a hub for the art of the present and the future as well.

ICA Boston was established in 1936 as a little sister to New York's MOMA, but long struggled to establish its place on the local art scene. Boston was not inactive in post-modern movements: it was the home of art minimalist pioneers Frank Stella and Carl Andre, and it was one of the first institutes to showcase the works of Andy Warhol and Robert Rauschenberg. For years, however, the ICA lacked adequate facilities, making do since the 1970s in a converted police station.

A growing appreciation for art after Arles led to the construction of the city's first major art building in over 100 years. Like most contemporary art museums, the new ICA is as much about the space as it is about the art. The four-storey cantilevered gallery on Fan Pier appears to hover over the harbor. Its tall glass walls seem to eliminate the boundary between inside and outside. Tight rooms and walls are replaced by wide open, sunlit exhibit halls. The site also includes a theater, media center, learning lab and waterfront café.

Contemporary art attempts to be about real social issues and uses real materials from everyday life as a means of expression; in this way, the design holds promise to fulfill the mission of the ICA, 'to become both a dynamic space for public activity and a contemplative space for experiencing the art of our time.' See p94 for more information.

Studios (www.somervilleopenstudios.org). As well, a large community of artists lives and works at **Brickbottom** (www.brickbottomartists .com), a former A&P canning facility and bakery near Union Sq that was converted into cooperative studio and living space. Brickbottom also hosts a semi-annual open-studios weekend and ongoing exhibits in its gallery space.

UNIVERSITY COLLECTIONS

Just as universities have fostered Boston's literary and scientific development, so too do these institutions contribute to its artistic tradition. Harvard University maintains an art collection that rivals most public museums. Housed in three buildings, the Harvard Art Museums (p117) include a

SOWA

In the South End, the area south of Washington St has been dubbed SoWa. In the 19th century it was a mill building district, producing pianos, canned goods, shoes and other merchandise. Out of the former ware-houses and factories, artists have carved out studios and gallery space. Many of these artists exhibit on a weekly basis at the South End Open Market (p215) an open-air arts and crafts market.

The market's seasonal opening in May coincides with the annual **SoWa Art Walk** (www.sowaartwalk .com) and **Film Festival** (www.sowafilmfestival.com). During this two-day event, artists invite the community into their studios and show off the painting, sculpture, film and multimedia work that was produced here.

world-class collection of western art, spanning history from the medieval era to the present, as well as one of the country's most impressive collections of Asian and Islamic art. At MIT, the List Visual Arts Center (p118) mounts sophisticated shows that stretch creative limits, although MIT's artistic highlight is its assortment of outdoor and public art (see below).

The **Rose Art Museum at Brandeis University** (☎ 781-736-3434; www.brandeis.edu/rose; 415 South St, Waltham; $3; ⊗ 9am-5pm Tue-Sun) is a museum of modern and contemporary art. It has a collection of more than 8000 pieces, which is particularly strong in American art from the 1960s and 1970s, including works by Jasper Johns, Roy Lichtenstein and Andy Warhol.

At Boston College, the **McMullen Museum of Art** (☎ 617-552-8587; www.bc.edu; 140 Commonwealth Ave, Chestnut Hill; admission free; ⊗ 11am-4pm Mon-Fri, noon-5pm Sat & Sun) showcases a wide-ranging collection. Highlights include Italian paintings, mostly religious paintings and portraits from the 16th to 18th centuries; ornate Flemish tapestries dating to the 16th century; and American landscapes and portraits from the 19th and 20th centuries.

PUBLIC ART

Art is everywhere in Boston, from the avant-garde Arthur Fiedler bust on the Charles River Esplanade (p198) to the whimsical 'Tortoise & Hare' on Copley Sq (p99). The most adored sculpture in Boston is Nancy Schon's 'Mrs Mallard & Her Ducklings' in the Public Garden (boxed text, p76).

No place in Boston packs so much public art into a relatively small space as the MIT campus. The university's progressive Percent for Art program requires that all new construction project budgets include a line item for art for public consumption. The result is a campus dotted with sculpture, walls painted with murals and lobbies hung with mobiles. Highlights include sculptures by Alexander Calder, Pablo Picasso and Henry Moore. Pick up a map at the List Visual Center (p118).

MUSIC

'From Boston, Massachusetts, we are Morphine at your service.' So legendary local rocker Mark Sandman used to introduce his band when playing gigs around the country. From the 1980s supergroup Boston to the ska-core Mighty Mighty Bosstones, Boston bands like to be associated with their hometown. That's because this city has a tradition of grooving to great music.

Classic rockers will agree, for they associate the city with the Boston Beat, exemplified by rock'n'roll and New Wave stars like Aerosmith, the Cars and the J Geils Band.

BOSTON PLAYLIST

- The Cars, 'Let the Good Times Roll'
- James Montgomery, 'Sweet Sixteen '
- Aerosmith, 'Last Child'
- J Geils Band, 'Start All Over'
- Tracy Bonham, 'Behind Every Good Woman'
- Barry and the Remains, 'Why Do I Cry'
- Willie Alexander, 'Mass Ave'
- The Pixies, 'Bone Machine'
- Human Sexual Response, 'Jackie Onassis'
- James Taylor, 'Sweet Baby James'
- The Real Kids, 'Do the Boob'
- Mighty Mighty Bosstones, 'Rascal King'
- Kingston Trio, 'Charlie on the MTA'
- The Neighborhoods, 'No Place Like Home'
- Mission of Burma, 'Einstein's Day'
- 'Til Tuesday, 'Voices Carry'
- Morphine, 'Cure for Pain'
- Donna Summer, 'I Feel Love'
- Dropkick Murphys, 'Tessie'
- The Standells, 'Dirty Water'

(Peter Wolf, lead singer of the J Geils Band, has been frequently sighted at celebrity events around Boston, even before the band's surprise reunion in 2006.)

Although Aerosmith established itself as 'America's Greatest Rock'n'Roll Band' in the 1970s, the band enjoyed its biggest successes during its comeback in the late 1980s and early 1990s. Even in the new millennium, Aerosmith participated in the star-studded Super Bowl halftime show in 2001, and was inducted into the Rock 'n' Roll Hall of Fame shortly thereafter. The group continues to tour with old-time favorites like Cheap Trick and Lenny Kravitz, selling out arenas along the way.

The influence of punk on the Boston music scene cannot be underestimated. The Mighty Mighty Bosstones combined elements of Caribbean-influenced ska with hardcore punk, creating a unique genre dubbed 'ska-core'. The Bosstones were the city's preeminent band throughout the 1990s. Similarly, the Pixies fused alt-rock with elements of punk and surf music, somehow achieving a balance between harmonious and abrasive. The overextended quartet disbanded in 1993 – long before Boston fans had had enough. Their absence only made the musical heart grow fonder, and the band attained a superhuman status in Boston. When the Pixies did their reunion tour in 2004, the concert at Avalon (p179) sold out in less than 60 seconds.

Both of these influential bands recorded at Fort Apache Studios, an internationally known recording studio that was based in Boston and Cambridge. Fort Apache deserves at least partial credit for the slew of alternative rock bands that arose in Boston throughout the 1990s, many of which exhibited the same punky elements embraced by the Bosstones and the Pixies. Now under new ownership, the music studio has relocated to Vermont.

Aimee Mann dropped out of the Berklee School of Music to form the punk band Young Snakes, which later gave way to the more melodious 'Til Tuesday. Mann continues to put out unremarkable solo albums, though she did front the Boston Pops in 2006. Letters to Cleo followed in the footsteps of the Bosstones, playing ska and growing increasingly punk throughout the 1990s. After the band's break-up in 2000, lead singer Kay Hanley launched her solo career, while Stacy Jones went on to form the band American Hi-Fi.

The Lemonheads were a popular alt-rock group that demonstrated tendencies toward punk, country and metal, before they disbanded in 1998. Following the lead of the Pixies, the Lemonheads quietly regrouped in 2005 and were working on a new self-titled CD. Other great examples from Boston's alt-rock heyday in the 1990s include Morphine, Buffalo Tom, The Neighborhoods and Tracy Bonham.

Meanwhile, no band makes more real, honest hardcore punk than the wildly popular Dropkick Murphys. A bunch of blue-collar Irish boys, the Dropkicks started playing in the basement of a barbershop in Quincy. They got together for a lark in 1996; and ten years later, the hard-working, hard-playing Dropkick Murphys are the quintessential Boston band.

While these bright lights from the 1990s continue to shine (or at least glimmer), there are many rising stars on the horizon, and they are still playing punk. Combining incongruous elements from punk and vaudeville, the Dresden Dolls' dark cabaret style carries on Boston's punk tradition. The Dolls were in the news in 2005 when a free concert at the Paradise Lounge (p178) inspired a spontaneous street festival. Other punked-out contemporary Boston bands include The Explosion and the 'post-hardcore' TREOS (The Receiving End of Sirens).

The hip-hop craze has not completely bypassed Boston. Local rappers 7L + Esoteric gained notoriety in the late 1990s when they sampled sounds from the cartoon *Transformers* ('More than Meets the Eye') on their song 'Be Alert.' Twelve years later, they have followed up with three full-length CDs that keep them on the local charts.

In the town that gave birth to the New Kids on the Block, we can't overlook the pop rockers. Not when American Idol finalist Ayla Brown is a student and basketball star at Boston College.

Boston is also home to a thriving folk tradition. The venerable non-profit Club Passim (p180) is known nationally for supporting the early careers of singer-songwriters Jackson Browne, Tracy Chapman, Nanci Griffith and Patty Larkin. These days, one of Boston's most popular artists is Ben Taylor, whose mellow acoustics follow in the tradition of his parents, James Taylor and Carly Simon.

A few venues sustain a lively jazz and blues scene – most notably the performance center at the Berklee College of Music. (This is where you'll hear some of the city's most innovative music; see p180). Inveterate blues rocker James Montgomery – father of the Boston Beat, which was so influential on all those great 1970s rock'n'roll bands – continues to play at clubs around town. Wally's Café (p179) is the city's best venue for down-home, local blues.

There are three primary ways to get to know Boston's flourishing music scene. First, hang out at Newbury Comics (see p217). This Boston chain of record shops carries a great selection of CDs by local bands, keeping track of rising stars with its running list of top-sellers. While you're there, also take a look at the 'Wicked Good Boston Bands' CD produced in-house.

Second, check out the local music festivals, including NEMO Music Festival, Blues Trust and Beantown Jazz Festival (p15). Finally, festival or not, visit the music clubs around the city to hear Boston bands in their element. See p177 for details.

PERFORMING ARTS

CLASSICAL MUSIC

Possibly Boston's most venerated cultural institution, the **Boston Symphony Orchestra** (www.bso .org) was founded in 1881 and is rated among the world's best orchestras, thanks to the leadership of several talented conductors. It was under Serge Koussevitsky's reign that the BSO gained its world-renowned reputation, due to its radio broadcasts and its noteworthy world premiers. Koussevitsky commissioned Stravinsky's celebrated Symphony of Psalms. The BSO's longest-tenured maestro (1973–2002), Seiji Ozawa was beloved in Boston for his passionate style.

Ozawa was succeeded by James Levine, who also heads the Metropolitan Opera. Levine is known for challenging Boston audiences with a less traditional repertoire.

Many BSO performers are graduates of the New England Conservatory, located down the street from Symphony Hall. In summer, the BSO heads for its season at the Tanglewood estate in Lenox, Massachusetts, where it performs along with guest and student artists and ensembles.

The **Boston Pops Orchestra** was founded four years after the BSO in an effort to offer audiences lighter fare, such as popular classics, marches and show tunes. The Pops are basically the BSO without its elite 'first-chair' musicians.

Arthur Fiedler, who took the helm of the Pops in 1930, was responsible for realizing its goal of attracting more diverse audiences. Fiedler initiated a series of free concerts at the Hatch Shell Memorial on the Charles River Esplanade, making it a fitting locale for his oversized bronze bust. He instigated the annual July 4 concert – accompanied by fireworks – which is still one of the country's most widely viewed celebrations (see p14).

The Pops' current conductor is the young, charismatic Keith Lockhart, who has reached out to audiences in new ways – namely bringing in pop and rock singers to perform with the orchestra. In the first season of the 'Pops on the Edge' series, the orchestra backed alt-rockers Aimee Mann and My Morning Jacket.

OPERA

There was a time when Boston was lauded for its opera – specifically, when the esteemed Sarah Caldwell was director of the Boston Opera Company. Caldwell founded the opera company in 1958 with $5000. She staged the first production on the Boston Common; the following year she upgraded to a converted movie theater. The company gained worldwide renown, staging premiers and hosting divas, with Caldwell's flamboyant persona leading the way. Caldwell was a better stage director than she was a financial manager, and sadly, the Boston Opera Company was forced to lower its curtain in 1990.

Boston opera has never recovered from this loss, although the city does boast two respected opera companies. **Opera Boston** (www.operaboston.org) is the more adventurous, specializing in little-known works. The company does three shows each year at the Cutler Majestic Theater (p186).

Founded in 1976, **Boston Lyric Opera** (www.blo.org) each year puts on four productions of masterpieces by Puccini and Mozart and others. Performances take place at the Shubert Theater (p185). Musical Director Stephen Lord has been cited as one of the country's most significant figures in American Opera; unfortunately he had recently announced his pending departure at the time of research.

In 2002, BLO staged two free productions of *Carmen* on the Boston Common, attracting over 100,000 spectators. But the enthusiastic turnout did not convince the opera company to make it an annual event.

DANCE

Boston's]preeminent dance company is the **Boston Ballet** (www.bostonballet.com), founded by E Virginia Williams in 1965. That December, Arthur Fiedler conducted the first two performances of *The Nutcracker*, a Boston tradition that would grow to 50 performances.

The Boston Ballet's current director is Mikko Nissenen, veteran of the Kirov Ballet in St Petersburg, Russia and the Finnish National Ballet. The season usually includes timeless pieces by choreographers like Rudolph Nureyev and George Balanchine, as well as more daring work by choreographers-in-residence. And it always includes the classic performance of *The Nutcracker* at the Opera House (p185) at Christmas. Otherwise, the Boston Ballet performs at the Wang Theatre (p185).

Some smaller dance companies focus on more modern and innovative dance. The largest and longest standing is the 31-year-old **Boston Dance Collective** (www.dancecollective.org), which focuses on mentoring and outreach. The **Snappy Dance Theater** (www.snappydance.com) is one of the more accessible dance companies, incorporating acrobatics and gymnastics into performances.

Bennett Dance Company (www.bennettdancecompany.org) blends modern dance with sculpture, photography, martial arts and original music. **Lostwax** (www.lostwax.org) uses multimedia to explore the relationship between live and digital performances. **Zoé dance** (www.zoedance.org) seeks to convey honesty and emotion through simple, pure dance movements.

So you think you can dance? **Swing** (www.totalswing.com or www.havetodance.com), **salsa** (www.salsaboston.com) and **ballroom dancing** (www.danceinboston.com) all attract a lively following. Every year the Wang Center sponsors **Dance Across the City** (see p13), a full day of free classes and performances. **The Boston Dance Alliance** (www.bostondancealliance.org) is another excellent resource.

THEATER

Boston's strong Puritan roots have always exercised a stranglehold over her desire to become a world-class city, and this clash is most apparent in the city's stunted theater tradition. Churchgoing Bostonians were markedly suspicious of plays and show folk, but reports of London theater sparked their curiosity.

In 1750, professional actors from England staged Tomas Otway's tragedy *The Orphan* at a coffee house on State St; it was such a curiosity that the coffee house was mobbed and a near riot broke out. The ensuing scandal caused the General Court to enforce a law making it a crime to act or be a spectator of theater.

The puritanical order broke down in the 19th century, however, despite various societies clamoring for decorum. During this period, a theater district grew up around Scollay Sq, the grand Old Howard opened as a vaudeville theater, to rave reviews, and other venues eventually followed suit.

Boston's high-handed morality made it the butt of many jokes, as savvy marketing moguls designated their productions 'banned in Boston' and were therefore guaranteed a full house elsewhere. In 1929 Eugene O'Neill's *Strange Interlude* was banned and moved to nearby Quincy, where it was enthusiastically received.

Boston loosened up in the 1940s and '50s and became a tryout venue for Broadway-bound shows like Tennessee Williams' *A Streetcar Named Desire*, and the musical extravaganza *Oklahoma!*

In 1965 the American Civil Liberties Union (ACLU), stalwart guardian of free expression, took the city to court, finally exposing the tacit censorship agreement that existed between City Hall and theater managers. Still, the Puritans' posthumous hold was not entirely severed. The musical *Hair* was closed prematurely in 1970, allegedly because it depicted the desecration of the American flag.

Censorship is no longer a problem in Boston, but its legacy casts a long shadow. Only in recent years has the city developed as a destination for interesting alternative or cutting-edge theatrical productions.

Theater Companies

Several excellent independent and university groups stage adventurous shows, mostly outside the Theater District.

Boston's leading production company is the long-running, Tony-award-winning **Huntington Theatre Company** (☎ 617-266-0800; www.huntingtontheatre.org), which stages plays at the Boston University Theater and at the Calderwood Pavilion at the Boston Center for the Arts. Affiliated with BU School of Theater, Huntington is known for introducing new plays for American theater and for reinvigorating old classics. Most recently, the company has staged a series of plays by Pulitzer Prize–winning playwright, August Wilson, shown in Boston before their debut on Broadway.

Across the river, the **American Repertory Theater** (ART; ☎ 617-547-8300; www.amrep.org), affiliated with Harvard University, is renowned for its experimental interpretations of classics, although it also stages new shows. The ART has a cooperative relationship with the Moscow Art Theater, so it often features interesting takes on Russian playwrights like Chekhov and Bulgakov.

The city's newest venue is the Boston Center for the Arts (see p185), which is home to four independent resident theater companies. This is theater at its most inventive. For an overview of what's happening on all of BCA's stages, see www.bostontheaterscene.com.

The 14-year-old **Speakeasy Stage Company** (www.speakeasystage.com) has established a reputation for Boston and New England premieres, especially offbeat, unknown musicals. **Pilgrim Theatre** (www.pilgrimtheatre.com) is a 'research and performance collaborative' that offers sliding-scale ticket prices, special services for blind and deaf audiences, open rehearsals and discussions with the directors, and other educational programs. **Company One** (www .companyone.org) strives for radical work, in attempt to reach less traditional, younger, ethnically diverse audiences.

The Theater Offensive (www.thetheateroffensive.org) uses its stage to examine varied aspects of gay and lesbian life. In addition to its seasonal line-up, the Theater Offensive hosts the annual Out on the Edge Festival of Queer Theater.

The opening of the BCA, as well as the ART's new space at Zero Arrow St, has sparked a proliferation of small, professional companies that stage engaging and unconventional shows. For an overview and links to individual companies, see Larry Stark's **Theater Mirror** (www.theatermirror.com). For the inside lowdown on Boston's theater scene, see **New England Theater 411** (www.netheater411.com).

Boston stages continue to play the role of testing ground for major musicals, which are often shown here before heading to Broadway in New York. Several of the gilded venues in the Theater District – including the Opera House and the Colonial Theater – participate in **Broadway Across America** (☎ 617-931-2787; www.broadwayacrossamerica.com), which allows spectators across the country to see the best of New York theater. Tickets are available online or at the venue's box office.

CINEMA

As with theater and visual arts, Boston's demand for and production of independent film has blossomed in recent years. Suddenly, independent production companies are sprouting up around town, especially in the South End, Jamaica Plain and other artistic communities. Film festivals are all the rage, with local interest groups organizing events to showcase films catering to their people, be they bikers or bisexuals.

The **Chlotrudis Society for Independent Film** (www.chlotrudis.org) is a local nonprofit that aims to encourage active and thoughtful viewing of films. The idea is to promote film as an active and interactive art form, to encourage critique, discussion and feedback. The society sponsors a short film festival, reviews movies and offers a host of resources on its website.

The premier resource for local independent filmmakers is **NE Film** (www.newenglandfilm .com), though it's not exclusive to Boston. Midnight Chimes Productions hosts the **Boston Film Site** (www.midnightchimesproductions.com), a website designed to promote and unite the city's independent film community.

Boston and environs is home to several fine independent cinemas, including the Coolidge Corner Theater (p188), Landmark Kendall Square Theater (p187) and Somerville Theater (p189), all of which show a good selection of international and independent films. The Harvard Film Archive (p189) is also a rich resource, with its vast collection of offbeat pictures and cinema classics.

BOSTON ON FILM

- The original *Thomas Crown Affair* (1968), starring Steve McQueen and Faye Dunaway, depicts the city as the perfect place to stage the perfect crime. Speaking of which, director William Friedkin of *The Brink's Job* (1978) insisted on authentic North End locations and hired local ex-cons to play toughs.
- *Love Story* (1970), with Ryan O'Neal and Ali MacGraw as Harvard and Radcliffe undergraduates, told us that 'love means never having to say you're sorry.' *The Paper Chase* (1973) stars John Houseman as the classically stern, Socratic Harvard law professor.
- Set on Martha's Vineyard, *Jaws* (1975) is an improbable but still terrifying story of a great white shark attacking swimmers on New England beaches.
- In *The Verdict* (1982), Paul Newman plays a Boston lawyer who – against his better judgement – takes on a medical malpractice case.
- *The Bostonians* (1984) stars Vanessa Redgrave and Christopher Reeve in a period piece based on the Henry James novel of Boston politics and manners circa 1876.
- *Glory* (1989), starring Denzel Washington and Matthew Broderick, tells the true story of the first Civil War black volunteer infantry unit.
- *Little Women* (1994) is based on Louisa May Alcott's wonderful book about girls growing up in 19th-century Concord. Stars Susan Sarandon as Marmie and Winona Ryder as Jo.
- *The Crucible* (1996), with Daniel Day-Lewis and Winona Ryder, is a film adaptation of Arthur Miller's play about the Salem witch trials.
- *Amistad* (1997), with an all-star cast directed by Stephen Spielberg, tells the true story of an 1839 mutiny aboard a slave ship and the ensuing legal battle to vindicate and free the mutineers.
- *Good Will Hunting* (1997) put Southie on the Hollywood map and started the careers of Cambridge boys Matt Damon and Ben Affleck (who wrote the screenplay and starred along with Robin Williams).
- The art-house hit *Next Stop Wonderland* (1997), a heartwarming independent film about a young woman's dating travails, refers to the final outbound stop on the T Blue Line.

No Boston movie house is more beloved than the historic Brattle Theater (p188). On the occasion of its 100th anniversary in 1990, one local journalist wrote that 'the Brattle Theater… inspires a kind of nostalgia verging on worship.' In recent years, this longstanding cultural landmark has threatened to close for lack of funding, but local film buffs rallied to raise the cash needed to sustain it. Since opening as a cinema in the 1950s, the Brattle has been Boston's primary source of international, artsy and otherwise offbeat films.

The **Museum of Fine Arts** (www.mfa.org) also has a rich film program, which includes a full roster of foreign, indie and classic films. The MFA's annual film festivals includes the African Film Festival, Boston Festival of Films from Iran, Boston Gay & Lesbian Film Festival, Boston Jewish Film Festival, French Film Festival and Human Rights Watch International Film Festival.

Other Boston film festivals include:

48 Hour Film Project (www.48hourfilm.com) Filmmakers have 48 hours to make a four-minute movie, yielding results ranging from bad to brilliant. The films are screened in April.

Boston Bike Film Festival (www.bostonbikefilmfest.org) Films shot on or about bikes. Two nights in October at the Somerville Theater.

Boston Film Festival (www.bostonfilmfestival.org) The longest-running (22 years and counting) and the most mainstream. Over the years, BFF has premiered such hits as *Kiss Kiss Bang Bang*, *American Beauty* and *The Piano*. See p15 for details.

Boston Independent Film Festival (www.iffboston.org) Aims to showcase the best indie films from around the world. In its fifth year and growing fast. See p13 for details.

Boston Jewish Film Festival (www.bjff.org) The MFA showcases Jewish filmmakers and Jewish-themed films for the first two weeks in November.

Boston Latin International Film Festival (www.bliff.org) Features local, national and international Latino filmmakers. Held two weekends in October at the Harvard Film Archive and the MIT Strata Center; all films are subtitled in English.

Boston Turkish Film Festival (www.bostonturkishfilmfestival.org) Also at the MFA, a week of Turkish film, as well as a music series featuring contemporary and traditional Turkish live music.

Boston Underground Film Festival (www.bostonundergroundfilmfestival.com) Three days in March that celebrate the bizarre, demonic and insane.

Magners Irish Film Festival (www.irishfilmfestival.com) Showcases contemporary Irish film; one weekend in November.

Somewhat North of Boston (SNOB; www.snobfilmfestival.org) Five-day festival in Concord, Massachusetts, held in November.

Architecture ▪

Architecture

To best understand Boston's built landscape, ditch the limited concept of architecture as extraordinary buildings made by celebrated designers. While Boston has fathered some seminal figures such as Henry Hobson Richardson (many claim he is the greatest 19th century American architect) and Charles Bulfinch (arguably America's first home-grown professional architect), their exceptional works are merely an important layer among many. The layers of Boston's parks, towers, markets and homes can be used not only to understand the city of today, but also to look back at important moments since it took shape in the 17th century.

In part because Boston's period of brash 19th-century capitalism wasn't as fertile as in other American metropolises, the city's monumental architecture staggered into and through the modernist period with few pioneering projects between the death of Richardson in 1886 and the major building campaigns that transformed the city following WWII (the most prominent of these being the brutalist Government Center). In the lengthy intervening period, truly innovative works were scant compared to places like Chicago and New York, evidenced by Boston's competent, but not extraordinary, train stations and absence of inventive skyscrapers. In fact, many of Boston's 20th-century trendsetting achievements involve the city retaining and reusing historic bits of its old core to recast itself as a tourist destination without actually falling into the trap of becoming a fossilized 'museum city.'

INSTITUTIONAL BOSTON

The various universities, government agencies and public bodies that operate within Boston have had a tremendous impact on the city's cultural and material landscapes. Walk through Harvard's campus and you'll be confronted with a collection of some of the United States' most prestigious architecture. Harvard's oldest surviving building, the plain brick **Massachusetts Hall** (1718; Map p310) provides a glimpse into the character of the early grounds. Richardson's nearby **Sever Hall** (1878; Map p310) is a tour de force, with incredible brickwork, subtle moldings, rich materials and rhythmically spaced windows. Walk around it. Look hard. No matter where you stand, no matter how foreshortened the building in relation to your body, no element ever looks out of balance. It faces the **Carpenter Center** (1961–63; Map p310), the only building in the US designed by Le Corbusier. It contains Harvard's visual arts department, and has a giant ramp that rises to slice through the building's center and curves to descend to

GROUNDBREAKING ARCHITECTURAL SPACES

- Mt Auburn Cemetery (p116) – the park-like grounds of this pastorally landscaped graveyard impacted the national garden movement and informed the design of early American urban parks.
- Brookline Village (p103) – one of the United States' first commuter suburbs, Brookline has an affluent collection of residential buildings that presaged (but with elegance, not later-day tackiness) a trend that would become the defining feature of the American Landscape.
- Quincy Market restoration (p89) – the transformation of the granite beauty from derelict market to fast-food court is an early and successful example of the American approach to the preservation of historically and architecturally significant sites.
- Trinity Church (p100) – Henry Hobson Richardson's first benchmark building, the high-profile church popularized his heavy Romanesque design sensibility and his approach to overwhelming decorative interiors. It also made him America's first true celebrity architect.
- Central Artery & Big Dig (p58) – anyone driving on the old elevated freeway should have noted the graceful manner in which their gaze was directed in god-like fashion over the city core. Cruel below, it was masterful above. The Big Dig replacement might be a pile of shoddy engineering, but the thing reeks of ambition and points to a new direction in privileging civic space over cars.

a road beyond. Along the route, passers-by peer into classroom and galley spaces, and there's a café where you can sit on a rooftop deck to admire this building-cum-sculpture.

Harvard's significance for modern American architecture cannot be overstated. In 1937, Walter Gropius (of Bauhaus fame) arrived with fanfare at the Graduate School of Design (GSD). Under his tenure, the school assembled a cast of internationally regarded modernists who would educate a generation of architects. Their students would then disperse across the United States, carrying the GSD's imprint with them. The celebrity status of Harvard's design faculty would cause it to attract more rock-star architects (Sert, Koolhaas) whose work is often visible either as a building on Harvard's campus (Gropius's **North Yard**, Sert's **Science Center**; both on Map p310) or in the hallway/gallery of **Gund Hall** (Map p310), which houses the GSD.

MIT imposes its own design might on Cambridge's fabric and lately seems to be dueling with Harvard to produce increasingly innovating works. With the completion of Frank Gehry's **Stata Center** (Map p311; at night a luminous crunch of boxes slammed together) and Steven Holl's **Simmons Hall** (a shimmering rectangle punctuated with dramatic cuts, and swatches of orange, yellow and blue), MIT has landed the latest blows. Also see Eero Saarinen's **Kresge Auditorium** (1955; Map p311) and Alvar Aalto's **Baker House** (1949) as earlier examples of MIT's design prowess. Both campuses exemplify the ways that an assemblage of architecture can create an atmosphere of scholarly meditation. Harvard's Old Yard, cloistered by a ring of gates and barrier dormitories, models itself on a medieval monastic tradition. MIT's vibe is harder to quantify, but stroll through its campus and you'll find buildings that drip with metaphors for scientific vitality (even if some are straightforward no-frills concrete boxes).

On the peninsula, the **Old State House** (1712–13; p88) originally functioned as headquarters for royal power when it controlled the colony, this role made obvious by freestanding figures of a lion and unicorn, official symbols of the Crown. Walk around Charles Bulfinch's later **Massachusetts State House** (p76) with its gold dome, and you'll see how quickly the scale of government changed with the rapid growth of Massachusetts and its capital. That Bulfinch designed a building as politically significant as the State House points to his renown as a Boston architect. His institutional works can be viewed in **Massachusetts General Hospital** (1818-23; Map pp300–1), the street network of the Bulfinch Triangle, multiple wharf buildings, and several land reclamation schemes. Given the scope and stylistically unifying nature of his projects, Bulfinch is sometimes argued to be Boston's first urban designer.

Exceptional institutional architecture can also be enjoyed in Copley Sq, a monumental space surrounded by some of Boston's finest structures. Henry Hobson Richardson's **Trinity Church** (p100), with its heavy massing, subdued towers and opalescent stained-glass interior, directly fronts McKim Mead and White's **Boston Public Library** (1887–95; p98), a Renaissance Revival masterpiece modeled after an Italian Renaissance palazzo. Like Trinity Church, the library has a stunningly lavish interior, with huge coffered vaults covering its reading rooms and a grand entry hall festooned with polychromatic marble. Scholars of McKim Mead and White claim that it set the standard for American libraries for the next 50 years. Since there is no admission fee, you should probably go inside.

Boston's most contentious space is another major public square – **Government Center**, dominated by **City Hall Plaza** (1961–68; p80). Vast, windswept and often devoid of life (scurrying business types or tourists shielding their eyes from a blazing sun pounding the shade-free expanse). The buildings that make up Government Center remain architecturally intriguing in the ways that they use massing, position and a common material palette to communicate with one another. They're emblematic of the brutalist style (so-called because of the rugged use of concrete), and many feel the term applies to the way in which the space was built – by demolishing 64 acres of the old city fabric, including beloved (and seedy) Scollay Sq.

WORKING BOSTON

As in many cities, more of the working population labors outside of the center than in it. In this regard, the transportation systems used to shuttle Bostonians about are a huge part of the working landscape. Some of the most charmingly grimy architectural spaces can be found in the colored lines of the subway system, the oldest in the United States. Some stations, notably **Park Street**, wear this age like a badge of honor, with modern cars squealing around

TOP FIVE ARCHITECTURAL SPACES

- City Hall Plaza (p80) – love it or hate it, Boston's Tiananmen Sq dominates the city center with stark windswept plazas, angular lines and corduroy concrete. The site is so prominent that nearly everyone is forced to walk through it.
- Carpenter Center (p42) – when modernism's most cherished architect builds his only American building in Cambridge, you kind of have to list it. The place is predictably awesome, even if the ceiling leaks.
- Boston Public Library (p98) – pass through McKim Mead and White's classically proportioned and calmly ordered exterior to find tranquil courts and ennobling reading rooms lit by huge arched windows.
- The Emerald Necklace (boxed text, p104) – Olmstead's park system is the bar to which other American cities can only aspire to.
- Trinity Church (p100) – Boston's own Henry Hobson Richardson reached the maturation of the Romanesque style he popularized with this building.

tracks that curve too tightly, a garish slathering of red and green tiling and old signage that looks homemade. Other stations, such as **Back Bay** (1987), have a stark utilitarian concrete palette mitigated by a few sculptural efforts and welcoming archways.

Another major element of the transit system are the freeway ring roads that surround the metropolitan area. A prime example is route 128, the so-called **Space Highway**, whose sci-fi nickname was applied in the 1950s when electronic, industrial and technological firms moved to wooded grounds along this commuters' boulevard. Now dated and shoddy, the Space Highway helps to contextualize the rather gleaming transformation of East Cambridge. This repurposing speaks to the braininess of MIT, which is continually expanding its land holdings in this area, and to the arrival of multiple biotech and biomedical firms. The buildings produced by these twin powers have given the area a postmodern panache, forming a horizontal non-skyline of fortified technology campuses of contemporary design.

Closer to downtown, Boston's legacy as a mercantile city is plain in the megalithic granite warehouses (**Mercantile Wharf** and **Commercial Wharf**, both 1856) that surround the waterfront. Their positions on the ground can help tell you where the water's edge once was. Legend suggests that HH Richardson's heavy designs were influenced by these warehouses.

Near the 19th-century waterfront and prominently positioned on State St, the **Custom House** (p86) was a nucleus of exchange in Boston's mercantile days. The original building (1837), a stout granite block with a temple front on each side, was later topped with Boston's first skyscraper, Peabody and Stearns Classical Revival tower (1913). The later tall buildings and banks that now form the financial district tie their roots to the area's mercantile trading, and their typically low forms express Boston's apathetic approach to height. In fact, Boston's signature tall building, IM Pei's **John Hancock Tower** (p99), would not be built until 1975. Depending on the angle of view and the quality of daylight, its sheer glass walls have been variously described as attempting to build a necessary mass of office space, to vanish into the sky, and to behave as a mirror on the edge of Copley Sq, respectfully reflecting the form of Trinity Church and by this process avoiding visual competition with its venerable buildings. Thus even this prominent modern tower takes its design cues from Boston's past, a recurring trope in the city.

SHOPPING BOSTON

Architecture has well served Boston's shoppers since the city's foundation. You can get a good idea about the practices of yore by visiting the **Faneuil Hall complex** (p213), which for a time stood as Boston's principal market. While the original hall was built in 1740, the version you see today is an enlargement of Bulfinch's design (1805), which doubled the market's size. The exterior brick walls, with their symmetrical layering of pilasters and cupola top, recall both the character of the original market as well as English design sensibilities which informed the appearance of every building in early Boston.

Boston quickly outgrew Faneuil Hall, which led to the creation of **Quincy Market** (p89). Noble, severe and emblematic of the Greek Revival style, the two-story affair was over 500ft long and built with heavy granite blocks, interrupted in the middle by a dramatic rotunda. Back in the day, it lent a bit of awe (and light) to those toting around dead beef carcasses in the market below. Today, this same awe is directed towards those occupying communal counters in New England's most famous food court.

In Boston's youth, pushcarts would pile around the base of Faneuil Hall and Quincy Market and up to adjacent streets to define a large open-air food market. An amazing survivor of this ritual is the nearby **Haymarket** (Map pp300–1), a temporary marketing event that assembles and reassembles itself every weekend on Blackstone St. In a sense, the Haymarket, despite being made from modern materials (plastic tarps, collapsible metal tables), more authentically reflects the condition of Old Boston than its well-preserved and celebrated neighbors. Embedded in its filth is a beautiful vibrancy tied to old patterns of ritual and behavior. It's a direct survivor of the old mode of shopping that characterized the economy of the district long before one could make a living selling T-shirts.

Citgo sign (p101), towering over Kenmore Sq

Washington St marks a great center of retail that characterizes several periods. **Filene's Basement** (1912; Map pp302–3), the flagship of the defunct chain, displays the sumptuousness of early department store design. It was built by Daniel Burnham, America's premier department store architect, responsible for the renowned Marshall Fields Building in Chicago. The thing is awash with terracotta tiles and the sculptural program on the exterior rivals some Greek temples in its complexity. Buy a hot dog, stand on the street and admire.

If grand department stores speak to the design principles of the past, the pedestrianization of Washington St reveals modern impulses and urban circumstances. By forcing cars away from this central strip, a greater density of shoppers can more easily access the department and clothing stores that dominate the district. The privileging of swelling numbers of pedestrian shoppers in turn lends a kind of ceremonial aspect to the shopping experience.

LIVING BOSTON

While little of Boston's 17th-century past remains visible in the city fabric, the **Paul Revere House** (begun 1680; p83) still stands to remind us of older modes of living. The diamond-paned windows, timber construction and overhanging second floor are unlike anything else in the city, and the building contrasts startlingly with the 19th-century brick row houses that surround it. The wooden house is a rarity in central Boston and points to a recurring worry

ICONIC BOSTON

- Pink & Orange – if you aren't yet mesmerized by those Dunkin' Donuts signs, you will be within 15 minutes after your plane touches down.
- Fenway Park (p101) – while your seat will be truly uncomfortable, wandering around the ancient stadium virtually guarantees that you will stir up romantic ghosts, even if you don't like baseball.
- The Steaming Tea Kettle (boxed text, p80) – the 227-gallon kettle at 65 Court St is fed from the building's boiler. Cast in 1883, the sign is a remnant of Scollay Sq before Government Center destroyed it. It has nothing to do with the Starbucks that currently lives below.
- Vinyl & Aluminum Siding – head into any neighborhood outside of Back Bay, and you'll find it blanketing everything from 18th-century homes to triple-deckers. It's amazing they haven't put the stuff on the State House.
- Citgo Sign (boxed text, p101) – Boston's favorite enormous sign blazes its giant pink triangle over the alpha males rounding the bases at Fenway Park.
- Filene's Basement (p212) – The low-budget retail basement remains legendary in the city, and its commonness, exhibited by poor signs, congested aisles and dated display racks, provides a distinctive spatial experience.
- Dorchester Gas Tanks – those approaching Boston from the south (Interstate-93) can't miss Corita Kent's giant rainbow design (1971) slathered over an enormous gas tank. Look close and you might see the face of Ho Chi Minh.

THREE NEW ADDITIONS

Only after the passing of much time will we be able to judge if these buildings are actually significant or merely hyped-up pretenders, but for now they are what people talk about when they think of Boston's contemporary productions. (That is, these are the buildings that come up when conversation turns away from the Big Dig, the new addition that reigns over all.)

- Stata Center, Frank Gehry's building No 32, is already famous and is emblematic of MIT's highly visual impact on the form of the Charles River waterfront.
- Zakim Bridge – for architecture that seems to be influenced by the design of toys, drive over the work of engineer Theodore Zoli. The bridge's towers supposedly evoke the shape of the Bunker Hill memorial, which is a generic obelisk.
- Large, cantilevered and playful with its transparency, Diller Scofidio + Renfro's new museum, ICA, was being completed at time of research.

never far from the minds of the city fathers – large-scale urban conflagrations. The brick material palate that continues to comprise much of the housing stock of the oldest neighborhoods (Beacon Hill) points to the restrictions on construction early imposed on the city.

Some of Boston's finest old homes can be found in Beacon Hill, where the narrow streets and congested fabric of three- and four-story brick row houses viscerally evoke another era. Many of these residences date to the first half of the 19th century and are variously emblematic of the Federal, Georgian and Greek Revival periods, pointing to the strong influence of English fashion on the young city. Embedded in this context are Bulfinch's three **Harrison Gray Otis houses** (from 1795, 1800 and 1805, respectively; Map pp302–3), designed for a gluttonous mayor and senator. All are supremely grand, and all reveal a Federal aesthetic. At first glance they seem alike, but look closely and in chronological sequence and you'll find that they reveal Bulfinch's increasingly sophisticated sense of composition and massing. House three is a triumph in its simplicity; a planar brick volume forcefully punctured by crisp rectangular windows whose subtly different sizes and spacing create a gentle rhythm across the façade. In the heart of the hill you'll find **Louisburg Sq** (planned 1826; Map pp302–3), one of the country's most exclusive addresses. The cobbled pavement contains a private garden surrounded by an iron fence. Flanking it on either side is a collection of houses with the bow fronts that characterize many of the residences built in Boston throughout the 19th century.

In 1857, one of Boston's most noteworthy land reclamation schemes was developed with the **Back Bay infill**. Walk along it from the Public Garden towards Fenway Park and you'll follow the growth of the neighborhood, its buildings growing gradually taller and shifting in style. Many take a mansard roof and Second Empire ornamentation, revealing a move in Boston fashion towards French taste. Back Bay buildings further underscore the French influence when one considers their plans – divided into apartments based on Parisian models.

As picturesque as many parts of the city were, the experience of industrial-age Boston was for most a daily navigation through filth, noise and disease. With the development of the streetcar and public transit in general, early pre-automobile suburbs were established at Brookline and Cambridge, often with shockingly fine buildings, reflecting the social status of those who could afford to leave the center. These also conflict with latter-day notions of suburbs as placeless sprawl. In Cambridge, head west along Battle St and you'll find Richardson's **Stoughton House** (1882; Map p310) and will begin to see some of the protosuburban landscape.

Despite the prominence of residential Back Bay and Beacon Hill in the minds of Bostonians and despite the remarkable quality of many buildings lying within tracks of the streetcar suburbs, if one were to chose a single form to characterize Boston's housing stock, it would have to be the triple-decker. From Somerville to Cambridge to Allston to Brookline to Jamaica Plain, this ubiquitous type became the choice de jour as dense suburban areas grew around the city. Often ordinary in appearance and home to a huge middle-class population, these buildings are typically flat-roofed and three stories tall. On each level is a flat with two to four bedrooms, and triple stacked porches often adorn their front or rear.

Food

Food

Advances in culinary culture have changed the landscapes of cities nationwide, and Boston is no exception. In the last decade, Boston has developed a multifaceted local cuisine, drawing on its unique regional traditions and the richness and variety of its international influences.

New England is the home of the first Thanksgiving and of bountiful autumnal harvests. It is America's seafood capital, home to clam chowder and boiled lobster. This regional cuisine has deep cultural roots; and like all things cultural, it is dynamic and developing.

HISTORY OF BOSTON CUISINE

Old-fashioned Boston cuisine is a blend of Anglo American, European and Native American food traditions. It combined established English recipes with local offerings from the earth. Thus evolving from its environment, Boston cuisine featured plenty of seafood, especially the 'sacred cod,' halibut and various shellfish. Back in the day, the seemingly endless supply of lobster was the food of the poorest classes, sometimes fed only to prisoners.

The local bounty included corn, potatoes, squash, peppers and tomatoes – all vegetables that were unknown in Europe prior to the discovery of the Americas. Culinary historians believe that Native Americans cooked beans with bear fat and molasses in an earthenware pot. Early settlers likely adapted this recipe, substituting pork for bear meat, resulting in the famed Boston baked beans (and thus earning the city its nickname of Beantown).

Molasses, honey and maple syrup were staple sweeteners. Early Bostonians went easy on the herbs and spices – no need to excite the sensitive palates of those Puritans! For a taste of ye olde New England, head to ye olde Union Oyster House (p144) or Durgin Park (p143).

The influx of immigrants in the 19th century had profound impacts on local cuisine. Seafood was still prominently featured, but now it was served under Italian tomato sauces and in spicy Portuguese stews. The southern Europeans – who had inherited the tomato from the Americas – now brought it back to the New World in unrecognizable but undeniably delicious forms.

A tight-knit immigrant enclave, the North End (p139) became an upholder of old-fashioned Italian American cooking, with tomato sauces simmering and pasta boiling on every stove. But it did not take long for this strange foreign fare to become mainstream, as Americans recognized its versatility and simplicity.

Irish influences on cooking were not as drastically felt, since the cuisine of Ireland focused on seafood and potatoes – already New England staples. But the Irish can claim responsibility for the famous New England boiled dinner – boiled beef with cabbage, carrots and potatoes. Perhaps Ireland's most important contribution to Boston dining is the city's love of beer – sample it at any one of many Irish pubs (p162).

EAT YOUR WORDS

When it comes to food and drink, sometimes Bostonians have a funny way of expressing themselves:

Bubbler Water fountain

Frappe Milkshake

Grinder A heated submarine sandwich

Jimmies Chocolate sprinkles (on ice cream)

Order Groceries

Packie Liquor store

Scrod White-fish catch of the day

Steamers Steamed clams

Tonic Carbonated soft drink; soda

For tips on ordering coffee, see p138.

CULINARY CULTURE

Since the end of the 20th century, Boston's food culture has undergone a significant shift, fueled by the breakup of the old ethnic enclaves; a new influx of immigrants, this time from Asia and South America; and increasing awareness of health and environmental issues.

The international influence on Boston cuisine cannot be underestimated. Italian, Irish and Portuguese is already old hat. Now Bostonians are sampling Brazilian, Chinese, Indian, Thai and Vietnamese (see p146). Immigrants open restaurants to cater to their own community, but these exotic eats are also attracting the attention of well-traveled Bostonians who are curious about global cultures.

Preparing oysters at the Union Oyster House (p144)

In this era of creative culinary discovery, more and more Bostonians are reclaiming their roots in one crucial way: their appreciation of fresh, seasonal and organic products. Frozen foods and canned goods – once liberating – are now anathema, as food-lovers are reminded how much better ingredients taste when they are fresh (and even more so when they are pulled straight from the ground, without chemical fertilization or genetic modification).

How Locals Eat

Eating habits vary widely between communities, families and individuals. Breakfast is popularly considered 'the most important meal of the day,' but is nonetheless sometimes skipped, as busy professionals run off to work. Otherwise, it often features toast and cereal, egg dishes or stacks of pancakes, possibly drenched in blueberries and the New England specialty – maple syrup. The quintessential Boston breakfast is coffee and a doughnut from Dunkin' Donuts (see p138).

FLUFFY STUFF

As any native New Englander knows, it takes 'fluff, fluff, fluff to make a Fuffernutter, Marshmallow Fluff and lots of peanut butter.' Surely, very few kids made it through elementary school without enjoying a marshmallow creme and peanut butter sandwich for lunch now and then. Hard to believe that a Massachusetts senator sought to have the sticky staple expelled.

In 2006, Senator Jarrett Barrios proposed a state ban on Marshmallow Fluff, as part of a campaign against junk food in public schools. Maybe it is mostly air-whipped sugar and not real marshmallow (a plant that actually grows in marshes), but the squat white-and-blue jar of Fluff has been present in cupboards across the region for more than three-quarters of a century.

In 1917, Archibald Query went door-to-door to sell the gooey treat made in his Somerville kitchen. A few years later, two enterprising WWI veterans bought the secret recipe for $500, and moved the operation to Lynn. Good management and even better marketing made the Fluff business a sweet success.

Marshmallow Fluff is more than just a creamy confectionary that sneaked onto the lunch menu, it is part of the popular culture, a link to a past when Boston was a candy capital. Not surprisingly, the senator's proposal provoked a swift and angry reaction. The 80-year-old son of the company's founder swears by the good health effects of marshmallow. An outraged state representative put forth a counter-proposal to have the Fluffernutter declared the official state sandwich. The fluffy flap ended when both proposals were withdrawn. Meanwhile, sales quadrupled, as the dentist lobby remained noticeably quiet.

In 2006, the city of Somerville celebrated this sweet history at the first annual Fluff Festival, which featured cooking contests, science experiments, performances by the 'Flufferettes' and – of course – Fluffernutters for sale.

Weekend brunch is an increasingly popular tradition. Following a country-wide urban trend, Bostonians enjoy a leisurely morning on Saturday or Sunday and indulge in a large midday meal, often featuring traditional breakfast foods. For recommendations for brunch, see the boxed text on p150.

Otherwise, lunch centers on that all-American omnipresent invention, the sandwich. Traditionally, sandwiches are simple affairs like a PB&J (peanut butter and jelly) or BLT (bacon, lettuce and tomato). In the new foodie culture, sandwiches have reached new heights, with homemade, multigrain breads, fancy chutneys and aioli spreads, smoked or salted meats and artisinal cheeses. To sample some of Boston's best, visit the All-American Sandwich Bar (p158), Darwin's (p156), Chacarero (p142), Sam La Grassa's (p142) or Pressed (p142).

Unlike many European countries, alcohol is not often drunk at lunchtime (another holdover from the Puritans).

Dinner is the biggest meal of the day, whether eaten at home or in a restaurant. In recent years, dining out has become a form of entertainment and the most common venue for socializing. According to standard etiquette, each person orders an individual meal, but it's common to share appetizers and desserts.

If you are dining in a private home with an American family, it is polite to bring a bottle of wine or something to share.

STAPLES & SPECIALTIES

Most of Boston's staples and specialties derive from the region's earliest cuisine, which was heavily influenced by environmental factors. As the international elements become mainstream, they often take on the status of 'staple.'

Seafood & Shellfish

First things first: ask ten locals about Boston's best chowder and you're likely to get ten different answers. The thick, cream-based soup is chock-full of clams or fish, though clam chowder is more prevalent. Usually, the meaty insides of giant surf clams are used to make the famous New England concoction (see opposite).

Other varieties of clam include soft-shelled clams, or 'steamers' (so-called because they are steamed to eat). Many seafood restaurants showcase their shellfish at a 'raw

---

HOW TO EAT A LOBSTER

Eating a lobster is a messy affair (as you may have guessed when you were provided a bib).

At lobster pounds, live lobsters are cooked to order. They range in size from 1lb (chicken lobsters, or 'chicks') and 1¼lb to 1½lb (selects) to large lobsters weighing from 2lb to 20lb. Culls – lobsters missing a claw – are sold at a discount, as the claw meat is considered choice. Anything smaller than a chick is a 'short' and does not meet the legal minimum size for harvesting.

Besides the bib, a lobster comes with a cracker for breaking the claws, a small fork or pick for excavating, a container of drawn butter and a slice of lemon.

Start by twisting off the skinny legs and sucking out the slender bits of meat inside. Then move on to the claws: twist the claws and knuckles off the body, break them with the cracker and dip the tender meat in butter before eating.

Pick up the lobster body in one hand and the tail in the other. Twist the tail back and forth to break it. Tear off each flipper at the end of the tail and suck out the meat. Then use your finger or an implement to push the bigger pieces of meat out of the tail.

There is delicious meat in the body as well, but it takes extra work (and many people just discard it). Tear off the carapace (back shell), then split the body in two lengthwise. Use a pick to dig out the meat from behind the spot where the skinny legs were attached.

Now it's finally safe to remove your bib; and here's where you'll need that towelette to wipe your hands.

CLAM CHOWDER

4 lb chopped clams	½ cup chopped onion
40 oz clam juice	2 bay leaves
salt and pepper	¼ cup chopped parsley
1 tbsp olive oil	1 lb butter
5 potatoes	1 lb flour
1 cup chopped celery	1 quart half-and-half

Place oil in large stockpot with onion and celery and cook over medium heat until softened. Add the clams and clam juice to the pot, along with salt, pepper and bay leaves. Peel and dice potatoes and add to stockpot. Bring to a boil, then lower heat, cover and simmer until thickened. In a saucepan, melt the butter, then add the flour to make a roux. Whisk the roux into the clam broth. Add the half-and-half, then simmer for 30 minutes. Garnish with parsley. Makes 4 to 6 servings.

bar,' where a dedicated bartender works to shuck raw oysters and clams to be served on the half-shell. Any self-respecting raw bar will have a selection of hard-shelled clams or 'quahogs,' often including littlenecks and cherrystones. Other raw bar specialties include oysters, the best being Wellfleet oysters from Cape Cod. Littlenecks, cherrystones and oysters are usually eaten raw with a good dollop of cocktail sauce and a few drops of lemon. For your own raw bar experience, try B&G Oysters, Ltd (p150) or Jasper White's Summer Shack (p151).

New England is a mecca for seafood lovers who come to get their fix of fresh lobster. Boston has no shortage of excellent restaurants who serve it up in the traditional style. Jasper White's Summer Shack is one possibility; or head to J Hook & Sons, a lobster retailer in the Seaport District (p93). The lobster gets steamed or boiled, then the fun begins; see the boxed text on opposite for tips on how to eat a lobster.

Scrod (which might be any white-fleshed fish) is often broiled or fried and served with french fries, creating the classic fish and chips combo. The venerable Omni Parker House (p230) claims responsibility for coining the term 'scrod.' Apparently, sailing captains would pick out the best of the day's catch and store it in a container marked 'Select Catch Remains On Deck,' or SCROD. Other fresh fish making regular appearances on Boston menus include bluefish and mackerel, as well as swordfish, tuna steaks and striped bass.

Fruit & Vegetables

Fruit grows in abundance throughout New England, including farms and orchards on the outskirts of Boston. Apples, peaches and berries are available at roadside stands, farmers markets (see p134) and pick-your-own farms. In the fall, bogs on Cape Cod yield crimson cranberry crops, spectacular to look at and tart to taste. With a healthy dose of sugar, cranberries make delicious juices, muffins and pies. Thanksgiving dinner (see p53) is not complete without cranberry sauce.

Corn, beans and squash – dubbed the 'life-giving sisters' – are staple foods in New England. They are the ingredients of another traditional Thanksgiving dish, succotash (see p53). The single food item most-associated with Boston is certainly baked beans, thanks to the city's nickname Beantown. Boston baked beans are white or navy beans, molasses, salt pork and onions slow-cooked in a crock-pot. Baked beans were a traditional Sunday meal, since they could be made in advance and the Puritans did not cook on Sundays.

Cheese & Dairy

New England's largest dairy is Hood, known even to non-milk-drinking Bostonians, thanks to the iconic Hood milk bottle near the Boston Children's Museum (see p94).

Bostonians are benefiting from a regional interest in returning to organic, hormone-free dairy products. Massachusetts' neighbor to the north, Vermont, is leading this movement.

I SCREAM, YOU SCREAM

We all scream for ice cream:

- **Steve's** (Map pp302–3; ☎ 617-367-0569; Quincy Market, Faneuil Hall Marketplace; 🚇 Haymarket) Won fame for 'smush ins,' chunks of candy or nuts mixed into the flavor of your choice.
- **Emack & Bolio's** (Map pp306–7; ☎ 617-247-8772; 290 Newbury St; 🚇 Copley) An old-timer on the local gourmet scene, makes the definitive Oreo cookie ice cream (and good nonfat yogurt creations). Another outlet is in Jamaica Plain.
- **JP Licks** (Map pp306–7 ☎ 617-236-1666; 352 Newbury St; 🚇 Hynes/ICA; Map pp308–9; ☎ 617-738-8252; 311 Harvard St, Brookline; 🚇 Coolidge Corner) It's a toss-up between white coffee and caramel apple. The original outlet is in namesake Jamaica Plain (JP).
- **Herrell's** (Map p310; ☎ 617-497-2179; 15 Dunster St, Cambridge; 🚇 Harvard; Map pp306–7; ☎ 617-236-0857; 224 Newbury St; 🚇 Hynes/ICA) Will it be malted vanilla or chocolate pudding?
- **Toscanini's** (Map p311; ☎ 617-491-5877; 899 Main St, Cambridge; 🚇 Central; Map p310; ☎ 617-354-9350; 1310 Massachusetts Ave, Cambridge; 🚇 Central) Try the gingersnap molasses or Vienna finger cookie.
- **Christina's** (Map p311; ☎ 617-492-7021; 1255 Cambridge St, Cambridge; 🚇 Central) Eclectic flavors such as burnt sugar and fresh mint; located in Inman Sq.

Dozens of family farms and small producers are making artisinal cheeses from goat, sheep and cow milk. The great variety and high quality of New England cheeses (www .newenglandcheese.com) will thrill the most discriminating gourmet. But the old stand-by Vermont cheddar is still the most popular. Sample the goods at Harvest Food Co-op (p223), Cardullo's (p220) or South End Formaggio (p215).

Desserts

Old-fashioned New England meals are sometime followed by bread pudding or Indian pudding, which is a soupy gingerbread. In fall, menus feature seasonal pies like pumpkin, apple and squash (often considered the most important part of Thanksgiving dinner, see opposite). Apple crisp and apple cobbler are delicious variations on the theme, especially when topped with homemade ice cream. In June and July, strawberries and rhubarb are in season, making it prime time for strawberry-rhubarb pie. Boston has a countrywide reputation for excellent ice cream (see above).

Beer

Bostonians take beer seriously and the city is home to many microbreweries. Although the regional breweries don't often distribute beyond their local communities, Sam Adams has achieved national and international recognition. For local breweries offering tours and tastings see the boxed text on p169.

CELEBRATING WITH FOOD

If you want to pack in sampling a lot of food in a short amount of time, check out one of these local food festivals:

Boston Vegetarian Food Festival (www.bostonveg.org) Veggie products, recipes and speakers, including lots of free samples. One Saturday in October.

Boston Wine Expo (www.wine-expos.com) A classy two-day affair with wine tastings and appearances by celebrity chefs. This event is ticketed.

Cambridge Food & Drink Festival (www.camfoodfest.org) This new week-long festival celebrates local food and good eating. Held in spring, with other events occurring throughout the year.

Phantom Gourmet Food Festival (www.phantomgourmetfoodfestival.com) A one-day event in September. The admission price ($30) to this street fair covers samples from dozens of participating restaurants and live music.

Taste of Boston (www.tasteofboston.com) Dozens of restaurants take to the streets for this weekend event.

Special Events

Almost all American holidays are associated with specific foods, which are incorporated into celebration rituals. Lovers celebrate Valentine's Day with champagne and chocolates. St Patrick's Day is an important beer-drinking holiday. Easter is associated with the symbolic Easter egg, but a traditional Easter dinner involves rack of lamb or honey-baked ham.

The summer holidays – Memorial Day, Independence Day and Labor Day – are traditionally dedicated to that all-American summertime activity, the cookout. It usually means burgers and hot dogs cooked on the grill, pickles, potato salad and jello molds. In recent years, grilling has become a celebration in and of itself, and gourmands use their outdoor oven to grill steaks, vegetables and fish.

Trick or Treat! The primary Halloween food is candy – the promised 'treat' that costumed kids collect, else they seek revenge with a 'trick.' Patient pumpkin-carvers also roast and salt pumpkin seeds, another addictive treat.

November is the holiday most closely associated with food (see below), but Christmas dinner is also an important celebration. You may read about the traditional Christmas goose, but these days families are more likely to eat a turkey or a ham, with all the accompaniments. Seasonal drinks include mulled wine (heated red wine, mixed with cinnamon and cloves) and eggnog (a thick, rich drink of milk, eggs and sugar, often with rum). Those with a sweet tooth look forward to gingerbread and Christmas cookies, as well as the orange that always appears in the bottom of the stocking.

New England Thanksgiving

Every year on the third Thursday of November, Americans give thanks for a bountiful harvest (metaphorically speaking, in most cases). American folklore dictates the menu. It is modeled after the meal the Pilgrims shared with the Wampanoag (see below), which

The First Thanksgiving

Plymouth is known for one thing most of all – Pilgrims. And, as all schoolchildren are taught, Pilgrims are known for one thing most of all – Thanksgiving. Maybe two things – Thanksgiving and big buckled shoes. While footwear styles come and go, Thanksgiving remains a time-honored tradition of feasting and football for American families. But to what extent is our celebration of Thanksgiving consistent with our Pilgrim forbearers?

The first Thanksgiving was held in the early fall of 1621 and lasted for three days. The Pilgrims were thankful, but not for a bountiful harvest. In fact, virtually everything they planted that year failed to come up, except for some native corn. The Pilgrims were thankful simply to be alive. Of the 100 passengers aboard the *Mayflower*, only half survived the first year in the wilderness. There may have been a wild turkey on the table, but the plates more likely featured venison, lobster and squirrel…mmm. There was no pumpkin pie, alas, the Pilgrims did not have any ovens.

True to legend, the Indians were on hand for the first feast. Chief Massasoit of the Wampanoag had no problems with the pathetic Pilgrims, since he had set them up on the land of a rival tribe, the Patuxet. The Patuxet certainly would have objected, but they were wiped out by smallpox a year earlier. The Wampanoag, in fact, provided most of the food. The Pilgrims really were not very good hosts.

There were no Lions or Cowboys, but there were games played that weekend. The Pilgrim menfolk competed against the natives in shooting, archery and a crude colonial version of croquet.

Thanksgiving with the Pilgrims pretty much ended there. The fall festival was not repeated in subsequent years. The Pilgrims were pious, not partiers. The Wampanoag soon came to reconsider their position on the newcomers. Over the years, an annual harvest feast was common in some colonies, especially in New England. In 1789, George Washington called for a national day of Thanksgiving to honor the new constitution, but again this did not become a widespread annual event.

The Thanksgiving that we celebrate today has more to do with 19th-century nationalism, than with 17th-century settlers. It is an invented tradition. In 1863, in the midst of civil war, Abraham Lincoln proclaimed the last Thursday in November as a national Thanksgiving holiday. The popular depiction of the Pilgrims in peace and harmony with natives and nature was meant to emphasize the common heritage of a people at war with itself. The Thanksgiving tradition is the celebration of a myth, but a myth that unifies the nation.

Oh, and by the way, the Pilgrims did not really wear big buckled shoes either.

undoubtedly derived from the bounty of the earth. So once again, seafood and seasonal produce play a role.

Warm up with a thick, rich soup, either traditional clam chowder or a bisque made from seasonal vegetables like butternut squash. Follow that with a palette-cleansing salad of mixed greens, tossed with apples, walnuts and dried cranberries.

Onto the main course. The centerpiece, of course, is roast turkey. The cooking of the turkey has long filled cooks with fear and delight. Young married couples phone home, begging breathlessly for better basting techniques; parents run around in frilly aprons; grandmothers serve as quality control. Ben Franklin so loved his turkey that he nominated it to be the national bird. In a long-standing tradition, the US president always pardons one turkey before the mass slaughter. We don't actually know if the Pilgrims even ate turkey on the first Thanksgiving, but nobody in America is willing to give it up.

The bird is always stuffed with celery, onions and bread, which absorbs the flavorful juices; but New England birds are stuffed with oysters along with the traditional ingredients.

The list of Thanksgiving side dishes is long. Succotash, originating from a Native American recipe, is a casserole of lima beans, corn and tomatoes. The natives apparently used salt pork for flavor, but modern recipes usually call for bacon. Our forbearers used molasses to sweeten root vegetables like carrots, parsnips and turnips, which is the basis for the candied yams we eat today. Cranberry sauce complements the turkey. And don't forget the mashed potatoes and gravy.

You didn't save room for dessert, but somehow you'll find a way. The most typical Thanksgiving dessert is a pie showing off the fruits of the season – especially pumpkin, apple or pecan (or all of the above).

WHERE TO EAT & DRINK

Wherever you are in Boston, you are never far from a food source. The most touristy restaurant area is Faneuil Hall and Quincy Market (p143), which offers plenty of low-cost alternatives; while the neighborhoods with the widest selection of excellent eating establishments include the South End (p148) and Back Bay (p150). Charles St on Beacon Hill (p136)

Café window in Boston's North End

TALKING WITH YOUR MOUTH FULL

An Interview with Gordon Hamersley

Gordon Hamersley is the chef and proprietor at Hamersley's Bistro (p150), in the South End. Gordon began cooking as a student at Boston University in the early 1970s. After receiving formal training in Los Angeles and in France, he moved back to Boston with his wife Fiona and opened Hamersley's in 1987.

I understand that your career-defining training came under Wolfgang Puck in Los Angeles. What was it about Boston that made you decide to move back and open your restaurant here?
Honestly, Fiona and I almost moved back to California from France, but a conversation with Julia Child convinced me that coming back to Boston was a great idea. She mentioned Jasper White, Lydia Shire, Moncef Meddeb and others who were doing good food here and a young restaurant scene with potential. I also hated rooting for the Red Sox from the West Coast. That was it really. We decided to move back here – the place I began cooking and where I went to school.

What is unique about Boston cuisine or dining?
The natural products from New England set us apart from other states. Our great shellfish and ground fish, small farms raising high quality animals like ducks, lambs, rabbits, goats and pigs, and a vibrant vegetable farm scene very close to the city really make Boston a unique place to cook.

What would you recommend off the menu at Hamersley's Bistro for a visitor to our city?
I guess items in that season that represent New England and my particular style of cooking. For example, tonight we're doing a halibut and clam roast with black trumpet mushrooms and bacon. It typifies the New England products and is cooked in a way which shows off my style.

How has Boston's restaurant 'scene' changed over the past decade?
The scene in Boston has gone from a very formal dining scene with fancy rooms, high prices and stuffy service to one where we are more casual now. What seems to be important for diners is the quality of the food and wine lists and a relaxed (not necessarily less expensive) atmosphere.

But the food here is really quite diverse now too. As a diner you can find a vast array of food styles that are really top-notch. French, Italian, Thai, Japanese, Chinese, Spanish and American cooking really shine now more than ever, and are cooked by well trained and dedicated chefs.

What trends and changes can diners look forward to in the future?
I think the trend of the small, privately-owned high-quality places is going to continue to grow here. I'm really pleased that new young chefs are emerging and that the chain types are being successfully kept at bay. The trend toward more organic food is here to stay I think and you'll find it making inroads into less expensive places as the price of organic produce comes down.

and Cambridge St in Inman Sq (p158) also offer a huge variety and top-notch quality. The North End (p139) is the obvious top choice for Italian cuisine.

Boston's little-known but best-value eat-street is Peterborough St in Fenway (p152). Another option for cheap eating is Chinatown (p145). Chinatown and the Theater District are the places to come for late-night dining. At lunchtime, Downtown (p142) has many sandwich shops and street vendors.

VEGETARIANS & VEGANS

Any Boston-area restaurateur who has done an ounce of market research is going to offer at least a few options for the non-meat-eating clientele. Gone are the days when most meals center around a meat dish.

Boston ethnic cuisines are particularly veggie friendly, especially Indian (see Tanjore on p157 or Punjabi Dhaba on p158), Italian (see p139), Chinese and Thai (p145). Buddha's

Delight (p146) is an exclusively vegetarian option that serves all the major food groups made out of soy.

EATING WITH KIDS

Everyone gets cranky when they are hungry, especially children. To keep your kids happy on the road, try not to disrupt their eating schedule; don't force unfamiliar foods on them; and try to give them some room to move. See p143 for some suggestions for kid-friendly restaurants. You might also plan to picnic outdoors so the little ones don't have to sit still. Consider staying at a hotel with a kitchenette, especially if you have spawned picky eaters.

COOKING COURSES

Patron food saint Julia Child, long-time Cambridge resident and star of many cooking shows, spent four decades teaching people to cook before she died in 2004. She was active in the Cambridge and Boston community and supported a scholarship program for aspiring culinary arts students. If you want to embody Julia's bon vivant, bon appétit spirit, take a class at the Cambridge School of Culinary Arts (p272).

History

History

THE RECENT PAST

For all its ties to history, Boston has steadily looked forward. At the turn of the 21st century, the city is in good form, its duck boats all in a row.

Boston would not be Boston without a major redevelopment project underway. In this regard, the Big Dig is an unmatched marvel of civil engineering, urban planning and pork-barrel politics. The project employed the most advanced techniques of urban engineering and environmental science. Within a slurry-lined swath of city, construction workers excavated around building foundations and subway tunnels, through hazardous landfill and solid bedrock, and under the sludgy harbor floor. At its peak in the 1990s, the project employed over 5000 full-time laborers plus 10,000 support staff. The project fell way behind schedule and costs ran way over budget, eventually topping $15 billion. When it finally opened in 2004, the walls leaked; two years later a fallen ceiling panel killed a motorist. The investigations and litigations over mismanagement, misappropriation and malfeasance are likely to last longer than the construction time (see the boxed text, p25).

The local economy is sustained by medicine, finance, higher education and tourism, with a big boost now from information and biotechnologies (see p22). Entrepreneurial spirit and technological imagination combined to make the 'Massachusetts Miracle' in the 1980s; even with market corrections and burst bubbles, the high-tech revolution continues to invigorate the city. The globalization-induced wave of corporate takeovers, however, means that some of the city's best-known companies, like Gillette Razor and First Boston Bank, are no longer masters of their domain.

Economic change affects social trends, in this case with a real-estate boom. After several generations of retreat, people are moving back into the city. The downtown is being revitalized as abandoned warehouses are converted into living space and retail. Rising property values hastened the break-up of the old working-class ethnic neighborhoods. This trend causes some resentment, hence the city's culture clash between Dunkin' Donuts and Starbucks.

While living costs and harsh winters cause some residents to leave, Boston's population is regularly replenished by the annual influx of college students, some of whom remain after graduation, and new waves of immigrants, who now arrive from East Asia, the Caribbean and Brazil. See p16 for more information on Boston's changing identity.

In 1993 Mayor Thomas Menino (currently in his fourth term) became the city's first mayor of Italian descent, breaking the century-old Irish hold on the office. The politics of Boston, as well as the People's Republic of Cambridge, is left of center (see p23). Since colonial times, Boston has been out in front on issues of political equality, civil rights and social reform. In 2003 Boston again became a political battle site, this time for gay and lesbian rights. Massachusetts became the first, and only, state to give legal recognition to same-sex marriages.

Boston's Catholic Church was a strong opponent of gay marriage on moral grounds, but its influence was undermined by its own moral troubles. In a scandal beginning in 2002, the city's sizable Catholic community was rocked by revelations of sexual abuse involving children, and the sin was compounded by the willful cover-up by the hierarchy. The episode had major repercussions on what was one of the country's most prominent Catholic dioceses. Financially, the cost of legal settlements caused bankruptcy, forcing the selling of the bishop's estate and closing of numerous community churches (see the boxed text, p97). Politically, the scandal led to the disgraced resignation of the archbishop and a revolt among the laity, who organized the Voice of the Faithful, an activist group seeking to make church leaders more accountable to their followers.

1614	1630
English explorer Captain John Smith surveys the coast of New England	Puritans led by governor John Winthrop establish the Massachusetts Bay Colony

HISTORY SYLLABUS

Read on, students of history:

- Thomas H O'Connor, the dean of Boston historians, provides a nice overview of the city's political and social history in *The Hub: Boston Past and Present*.
- *The Puritan Idea: The Story of John Winthrop* is the story of the Puritans as told by the foremost specialist of early Boston, Edmund S Morgan.
- David Hackett Fischer gives a suspenseful account of Boston's patriots and the events that started a revolution in *Paul Revere's Ride*.
- Russell Duncan's *Where Death Meets Glory* is a personalized take on Robert Gould Shaw and the 54th Regiment of black soldiers and their heroically tragic campaign.
- In *Black Mass: The True Story of an Unholy Alliance between the FBI and the Irish Mob*, Dick Lehr and Gerard O'Neil give the dope on local hood Whitey Bulger and why he is on the lam, instead of in the slammer.

The news of late for the city's other major religion, baseball, is notably better. After more than eight decades of heartbreaking near misses, the Olde Towne Team, the Boston Red Sox, finally finished first in 2004 (see the boxed text, p195). After dispatching long-time nemesis, the New York Yankees, in dramatic fashion, the Red Sox made short work of the St Louis Cardinals to win the World Series. The party began immediately after the final out and continued through the New Year. The Red Sox shared the sports spotlight with local gridiron gladiators, the New England Patriots, who won an amazing three Super Bowls in four years from 2002 to 2005. Boston was truly a City of Champions.

FROM THE BEGINNING
THE SHAWMUT PENINSULA

In 1614, English explorer Captain John Smith, at the behest of the future King Charles I, set sail to assess the New World's commercial opportunities. Braving the frigid North Atlantic, the plucky explorer reached the rocky coast of present-day Maine and made his way southward to Cape Cod, making contact with the natives, mapping out the coastline and dubbing the region 'New England.' Smith noted a tricapped hilly peninsula with an excellent harbor fed by three rivers and connected to the mainland by a narrow neck across a shallow back bay. Valued for its freshwater spring, it was known to the natives as Shawmut.

Prior to the 17th century, there were as many as 100,000 native inhabitants in New England, mostly of the Algonquin nation. Organized into small regional tribes, they fished, hunted and gathered. In summer, women raised corn, squash and beans, using primitive slash-and-burn techniques. The tribes cooperated and quarrelled with one another. Their subsistence economy required seasonal migration, following food sources between the coast and the interior, making it seem to the property-conscious English that the land was abandoned.

Before England's religious outcasts showed up, local natives were already acquainted with Portuguese fishermen, French fur traders, Dutch merchants and Jesuit missionaries. The Europeans were welcomed as a source of valued goods, but they were also feared. In the Great Sadness of 1616–17, a smallpox epidemic devastated the native population by three-quarters. As a result, the Shawmut Peninsula was practically uninhabited when the Puritans arrived.

English colonial coastal encampments quickly spread, as seemingly unoccupied lands were claimed for King and commodity. According to John Winthrop, the first governor of the colony, 'God hath hereby cleared our title to this place.'

1635	1636
The first public school is founded	Harvard College is founded

In 1675 Chief Metacomet, son of the famed Massasoit who befriended the starving Pilgrims (see the boxed text, p53), organized a desperate last stand against the ever-encroaching English. He was known as King Philip to the settlers, and his war terrorized the frontier for more than a year before he was finally ambushed and killed. The chief's body was drawn and quartered and his heathen head perched on a pole, while his son was sold into slavery. In less than a hundred years, the indigenous population was reduced by 90% from disease, war and forced migration.

MISSION FROM GOD

Seventeenth-century England was torn by religious strife. Henry VIII's turn to Protestantism was not enough for some Englishmen, who wanted to purify the Anglican Church of all vestiges of pomp, pope and privilege. These Puritans were austere Calvinists, who believed in the predestination of souls beyond the influence of King or Canterbury. Annoyed by the nonconformists, James I threatened to 'harry them out of the country.'

As the fortunes of the faithful diminished, New England held out hope of renewal. The first trickle of Protestant immigrants came in 1620, when the Pilgrims established a small colony in Plymouth (see p254). Ten years later, the flagship *Arbella* led a flotilla of a thousand Puritans on the treacherous transatlantic crossing. In June 1630, their leader, country squire John Winthrop, gazed out on the Shawmut Peninsula and declared, 'we shall be as a City upon a Hill, with the eyes of all people upon us.'

Winthrop and his Puritan partners were gentlemen of middle social rank and wealth, and like-minded religious temperament. A year earlier, they agreed to pool their assets to become majority shareholders in a recently commissioned royal charter to establish a commercial enterprise in the New World. But their interest as investors was more spiritual than financial.

The Massachusetts Bay Colony reflected the ambitions of Puritan gentry, who sought to build 'a model of Christian clarity,' where modest personal virtue and industry replaced the smug class hierarchy and decadence of aristocratic England. Instead of tyranny, they would construct a community of devout hardworking freemen. If they should prosper in the endeavor, it signified the Almighty's approval.

They landed first near Salem and settled further south at present-day Charlestown. Across the river, the Shawmut Peninsula was at this time occupied by the Reverend William Blackstone, who survived an earlier failed settlement and now lived comfortably in his apple orchard on the western slope. He invited Winthrop and his scurvy-ridden company closer to fresh water. They named their new home Boston, after the town in Lincolnshire where many had lived.

The challenge of survival in God's country nearly ruined their plans. Low on food and supplies, their ranks were reduced by 200 deaths that first winter and another 200 departures back to England when spring arrived. Winthrop's son drowned, but the driven governor persevered, leading by example and constantly reminding the settlers of their divine mission.

PIETY, POWER & PROFITS

To ensure the colony's decent development, the new settlement was governed by a spiritual elite – a Puritan theocracy. As such, the Church dominated early colonial life. Local congregations were managed by members; church elders bestowed membership on those deemed worthy, as indicated by moral character, religious devotion and economic success. Theirs was a kind of legalistic Calvinism, enforced Old Testament style. Anyone missing church without good cause was apt to catch a whipping. There were no sects in this city: Catholics, Quakers and other heretics were made unwelcome by threat of flogging, banishing and hanging.

1700	1750
The population of Boston reaches 7000	The population of Boston reaches 15,000

Divine Law was above all, and the state was put in service to the Church. The General Court, a select assembly of Church members, became the principal mechanism for law-making, while the governor was endowed with extensive powers to enforce the laws. Local affairs were settled at regular meetings, open to the freemen of each town. (Women were allowed to attend if they did not talk.) The tradition of town meetings became a cornerstone of American democracy.

The Puritan theocracy did not go unchallenged. Anne Hutchinson started a women's Bible circle, promoting the idea of salvation through personal revelation. The popularity of this individualist-inspired view threatened the reigning patriarchy, who exiled her to an island. In Salem, Reverend Roger Williams chafed under the General Court's meddling in spiritual matters. He called for separation of church and state, and was soon sent packing south to Rhode Island.

The Puritans valued education. The General Court ordered communities of 50 or more households to hire and fund schoolteachers. To promote literacy, they established America's first public school (on the site of Old City Hall; see p87) and public library. In 1636, Harvard College was founded to supply the colony with homegrown enlightened ministers. America's first regularly published newspaper was the *Boston News-Letter*.

Meanwhile, Boston became a boomtown. The first inhabitants concentrated near the waterfront, behind the town dock. The back side of the hill served as 'common' lands. Newcomers fanned out along the rivers, looking for farmland and founding new settlements. Fortunes were made in the maritime trades – fishing, shipbuilding and commerce with the Old World. Well into the 18th century, Boston was the richest city in the American colonies.

But population and prosperity put pressure on Puritan principles. Modesty gave way to display. Red-brick mansions appeared on Beacon Hill, tables were set with fine china and silk linens, and women's shoulders were fashionably exposed.

Life in Colonial Boston increasingly felt tension between community and individual, piety and profit. The Church lost its monopoly on governing, when the royal charter was revised to make property-holding the basis for political rights. As the old order declined, Puritan preachers railed against vice and hunted for witches. The Puritan experiment fell victim to its own success, as the rise of commercial culture transformed the 'City upon a Hill.'

FROM EMPIRE TO INDEPENDENCE

Massachusetts Bay enjoyed virtual independence at first, as England was consumed by civil war. In 1660 Charles II was restored to the throne. Puritanism was defeated at home and detested abroad. The Stuart kings were no friends of New England's Protestants.

In 1686 King James II appointed his friend Sir Edmund Andros as new colonial governor to curb independence. Andros suspended the General Court, levied new taxes, forbade town meetings and Anglicized the church. When James was deposed in the Glorious Revolution, the colonists rose in rebellion, seizing the obnoxious Andros and shipping him back to England in chains.

The demands of empire kept England at war. Colonists were drawn into the fighting in the French and Indian War. Despite their victory, all the colonists got was a tax bill from the King. Covetous of New England's maritime wealth, the Crown pronounced a series of Navigation Acts, restricting colonial trade. Boston merchants conducted business as usual, except now it was on the sly.

The issue of taxation brought the clash between King and Colony to a head. In 1765, Parliament passed the Stamp Act. Royal stamps, obtained for a fee, were required to execute wills, purchase property, sell alcohol or just buy a newspaper. Sam Adams, a beer brewer turned political agitator, incited a mob to ransack the Royal Stamp Office. This act of defiance was defended by his more respectable lawyer cousin, John Adams, who cited the Magna Carta's principle of 'no taxation without representation.' When Bostonians joined in a boycott of British imports, the Stamp Act was repealed.

1760	1770
A devastating fire destroys 300 buildings in the young city	British troops kill five rowdy protesters in an event dubbed the Boston Massacre

CRADLE OF LIBERTY

King George III took the matter of colonial insubordination personally. He engaged the upstart Americans in a test of wills, and chose to make an example of Boston.

Royal revenue agents were sent from London to take control of the Boston customs house. They targeted one of the city's richest merchants, John Hancock, impounding his ship, *Liberty*, which was laden with undeclared cargo. This newfound royal resolve aroused a local riot, triggering the dispatch of two Redcoat regiments to restore order and protect the king's tax collectors. The local legislature was suspended and all political power transferred to Royal Governor Thomas Hutchinson

Under siege on the street, unrepentant Bostonians went underground. The Sons of Liberty was a clandestine network of patriots who stirred up public resistance to British policy and harassed the king's loyalists. They were led by some well-known townsmen, including esteemed surgeon Dr Joseph Warren, upper-class merchant John Hancock, skilled silversmith Paul Revere and bankrupt brewer Sam Adams. Branded as treasonous rebels by the king, the Sons of Liberty became more radical and popular as the imperial grip tightened.

The resented Redcoat presence did not extinguish but rather inflamed local passions. In March 1770 a motley street gang provoked British regulars with slurs and snowballs until the troops fired into the crowd, killing five and wounding six. John Adams successfully defended the British troops, who were found at trial to be acting in self-defense. The Sons of Liberty, however, scored a propaganda coup with their depictions of the Boston Massacre (see p86).

TEMPEST IN A TEAPOT

In 1773 Parliament passed the Tea Act, granting a trade monopoly to the politically influential but financially troubled East India Company. In December three tea-bearing vessels arrived in Boston Harbor, but colonial merchants refused the shipments. When they tried to depart, Governor Hutchinson demanded their cargo be unloaded. At a meeting in the Old South Church (see p88), the Sons of Liberty decided to take matters into their own hands. Disguised as Mohawk Indians, they descended on the waterfront, boarded the ships and dumped 90,000 pounds of taxable tea into the harbor.

The king's retribution was swift. Legislation was rushed through Parliament to punish Boston, 'the center of rebellious commotion in America, the ring leader in every riot.' The port was blockaded and the city placed under military rule. The Sons of Liberty spread the news of this latest outrage down the seaboard. The cause of Boston was becoming the cause of all the colonies – American Independence versus British Tyranny.

SHOT HEARD ROUND THE WORLD

Until now, all but the most pugnacious of patriots would have been satisfied with colonial economic autonomy and political representation. But the king's coercive tactics aroused indignity and acrimony. Boston had exposed the colonial inner conflict between loyalty and liberty.

Both sides were spoiling for a fight. British General Gage, a veteran of the French and Indian War, was sent over with 4000 troops and a fleet of warships. Local townsfolk and yeoman farmers organized themselves into Minutemen groups, citizen militias that could mobilize in a minute. They drilled on town commons and stockpiled weapons in secret stores (see p119).

In April 1775 Gage saw the chance to break colonial resistance. Acting on a tip from a local informant, Gage dispatched 700 troops on the road west to arrest fugitives Sam Adams and John Hancock and to seize a hidden stash of gunpowder. Bostonians had their own informants, including Gage's wife, who tipped off Joseph Warren on the troop movement.

1773	1775
British Parliament levies the Tea Act, inciting protesting colonists to dump crates of tea into Boston Harbor	The Minutemen confront the Redcoats in Lexington and Concord, commencing the War for Independence

Word was passed to the Old North Church sexton to hang two signal lanterns in the steeple. Paul Revere quietly slipped across the river into Charlestown, where he mounted Brown Beauty and galloped into the night to alert the Minutemen.

At daybreak, the confrontation finally occurred. 'Here once the embattled farmer stood,' Emerson later wrote, 'and fired the shot heard round the world.' Imperial troops skirmished with Minutemen on the Old North Bridge in Concord (p247) and the Lexington Green (p246). By mid-morning, more militia had arrived and chased the bloodied Redcoats back to Boston in ignominious defeat. The inevitable had arrived: war for independence.

Boston figured prominently in the early phase of the American Revolution. In June 1775 Bostonians inflicted a hurtful blow to British morale at the Battle of Bunker Hill (p84). The British took the hill after three tries, but their losses were greater than expected. Fighting on the frontline, Dr Warren was killed by a musket shot to the head in the final British charge. A few weeks later, George Washington assumed command of the ragged Continental Army on the Cambridge Common.

Britain's military occupation of the city continued until March 1776, when Washington mounted captured British cannons on Dorchester Heights (p121) and trained them on the British fleet in Boston Harbor. Rather than see the king's expensive warships sent to the bottom, the British evacuated the city, trashing and looting as they went. Boston was liberated.

The fighting moved to the mid-Atlantic colonies. In the meantime, merchant-turned-rebel John Hancock was appointed President of the Second Continental Congress in Philadelphia, which ordered the drafting of a Declaration of Independence. On July 18, 1776, Bostonians first heard the declaration read from the balcony of the Old State House (p88), and there was much rejoicing.

The British occupation ravaged the city. During winter, townspeople cut down the great elms on the Common and razed wooden buildings to stay warm. Desperate and hungry, the population fell from 20,000 to 6000.

ATHENS OF AMERICA

With victory came the post-revolution sorting out. The war exposed social divisions within the colony. On one side, the well-off Tories remained loyal to the Crown and opposed the rebellion; they included royally connected merchants, manufacturers and financiers. On the opposing side, the Patriots included independent merchants, artisans, yeoman farmers and working poor. Tories became the target of vengeful attacks. Set upon by mobs, they abandoned their posh digs and took flight to Canada.

Among the victors, political divisions arose. John Hancock and Sam Adams, in fact, did not get along. Hancock wanted to replace British rule with an American aristocracy, but Adams favored a Puritan-inspired democracy. The fears of Eastern merchants were roused by Shays' Rebellion, an angry protest movement by western farmers against the new government's tight fiscal policy. The insurrection was put down with cannons, as the new conservative order effectively tamed the revolutionary spirit. In a contentious vote, Massachusetts

Statue of Samuel Adams at Dock Sq, Faneuil Hall (p90)

1776	1776
The British evacuate Boston; the colonies declare independence from the British crown	The population falls to 6000

WHO CHANGED HISTORY?

One person really can make a difference. Here's the proof from Boston:

- John Adams – founding father who authored in 1780 the Massachusetts Constitution, which served as the model for the US Constitution in 1788
- Alexander Graham Bell – Boston teacher of the deaf who made good with a new-fangled invention
- Theo Epstein – boy genius baseball executive who ended 80-plus years of grief by bringing the World Series championship to Boston
- Angelina Grimké – suffragette and abolitionist who became the first woman to address the Massachusetts legislature
- Jim Koch – successful Boston brewer (unlike his beer's namesake, Sam Adams) who launched the microbrew revolution
- JCR Licklidder – MIT computer scientist who first conceived of a 'galactic network,' which would later spawn the internet

narrowly approved the new Federal Constitution after John Hancock left his sickbed to argue for its passage. The merchant class consolidated its power and status in independent Boston.

In the early 19th century, Boston emerged as a center of enlightenment in the young republic. The city's second mayor, Josiah Quincy, led an effort to remake the city's underclass into industrious and responsible citizens. He expanded public education and made the streets safer and cleaner. The 'Great Mayor' revitalized the decaying waterfront with a refurbished Faneuil Hall and the new Greek Revival marketplace, which bears his name (see p89).

Influenced by the idealistic legacy of Puritanism and revolution, Boston gave rise to the first uniquely American intellectual movement. Led by Unitarian minister Ralph Waldo Emerson, the transcendentalists shocked and challenged the Christian establishment with their belief in the inherent goodness of human nature and emphasis on individual self-reliance to achieve spiritual fulfillment. Transcendental influences are exemplified in the romantic literature of Nathaniel Hawthorne and the civil disobedience of Henry David Thoreau (see p28). Besides philosophy, the city became a vibrant cultural center for poetry, painting, architecture, science and scholarship, earning Boston the reputation as the Athens of America.

FROM SAIL TO STEAM

Boston thrived during the Age of Sail. In the 17th century the infamous 'triangular trade' route was developed, involving sugar, rum and slaves. Merchants who chose not to traffic in human cargo could still make large profits by illicitly undercutting European trade monopolies in the West Indies. In his East Boston shipyard, Donald McKay perfected the design of the clipper ship.

The advent of the steam engine in the second half of the 19th century marked the decline of Boston seafaring prominence. Early on, Boston industry was related to overseas trading: ship building, fishing and rum. Otherwise, the city had small-scale artisan shops. During the war, the disruption of commerce caused acute shortages of manufactured goods. In response, some merchants shifted their investments into industry, with revolutionary results.

By the middle of the 19th century, steam power and metal machines transformed the city. Boston became the railroad hub of New England. Leather works and shoe-making factories appeared on the edge of the city. Even Paul Revere abandoned his silversmith shop and set up a rolling copper mill and foundry.

Northwest of Boston, a group of wealthy merchants built one of the wonders of the industrial age: a planned city of five-story red-brick factories lining the Merrimack River. Named Lowell for the project's deceased visionary, Francis Cabot Lowell, the city counted

1800	1831
The population of Boston reaches 25,000	Abolitionist agitator William Lloyd Garrison first publishes the *Liberator*

over 40 mills and employed over 10,000 workers; machines hummed 12 hours a day, six days a week.

Industrial wealth transformed the city. The tops of hills were cropped and used for landfill to expand its size. Back Bay (p97) became a French-style neighborhood of elegant boulevards, and the South End (p96), an English-style quarter of intimate courtyards. The adjacent towns of Roxbury, Dorchester, Brighton and Charlestown were annexed. The Museum of Fine Arts (p103) and the Boston Symphony Orchestra (p36) were established. On Copley Sq (p99), HH Richardson's beautiful Romanesque Trinity Church (p100) and the Renaissance-inspired Boston Public Library (p98) were unveiled. Frederick Law Olmsted created the 'Emerald Necklace,' a string of ponds and parks stretching from the Public Garden to Franklin Park (see the boxed text, p104). Profits and patronage had its benefits.

BOSTON MELTING POT

For nearly two centuries, the city was ruled by a select group of leading families, the Boston Brahmins. The self-deprecating term was coined by Oliver Wendell Holmes Sr, but was readily adopted by the caste-conscious. Their elite status was claimed through lineage to the colonial founders or through wealth from the merchant heyday. They dominated city politics and business, and mimicked the style and manners of the European aristocracy. They created exclusive clubs for themselves and cultural institutions for the city.

The rapid rise of industry led to social change. The industrial workforce initially was drawn from the region's young farm women, who lived in dormitories under paternalistic supervision. The 'mill girls' were replaced by cheaper immigrant Irish labor in the 1820s. Although their numbers were still modest, the effect of immigration on local attitudes was great. The world of English-descended Whig Protestants was thrown into turmoil.

Disparaged by proper Bostonians, the Irish were considered an inferior race of moral delinquents, whose spoken brogue was not endearing, but rather suggested a shoe in one's mouth. They undercut workers in the job market. Worse yet, the Irish brought the dreaded religion of pomp and popery that the Puritans so detested. In the 1830s, rumors of licentiousness led a Protestant mob to torch the Catholic Ursuline Convent in present-day Somerville. In another incident, an Irish funeral procession met a volunteer fire company along Boston's Broad Street, and a melee ensued, leaving a row of Irish flats burned to the ground.

A potato famine back home spurred an upsurge in Irish immigration. Between 1846 and 1856 more than 1000 new immigrants stepped off the boat every month. It was a human floodtide that the city was not prepared to absorb. Anti-immigrant and anti-Catholic sentiments were shrill. The Know Nothing Party sprang up as a political expression of this rabid nativist reaction. Know Nothings swept into political office, promising to reverse the immigration tide, deny newcomers political rights, and mandate Protestant Bible readings in school.

Subsequent groups of Italian, Portuguese and East European Jewish immigrants suffered similar indignities. By the end of the 19th century, the urban landscape resembled a mosaic of clannish ethnic enclaves. Sticking together became an immigrant survival strategy for finding work, housing and like-minded companionship. Neighborhoods took on the feel of the old country with familiar language, cuisine and customs. The Boston melting pot was more stew than purée.

ALL POLITICS IS LOCAL

With social change, Brahmin dominance of Boston politics slipped away. By the end of the 19th century, ethnic-based political machines wrested control of local government from the old elite.

The fears of the Yankee old guard led to the formation of a new political party. In the mid-19th century, the Whigs, Know Nothings and anti-slavery movement cobbled together

1857–1900	1870
Swampy marshland is filled in to build neighborhoods in Back Bay, Kenmore and Fenway	The Museum of Fine Arts is established

Boston's Republican Party. It eventually became the political vehicle for promotion of the values of the old English-descended elite, envisioning a paternalistic and frugal government, preaching self-help and sobriety.

While the Democratic Party was initially associated with rural and radical interests, it became the political instrument of the working poor. Irish immigrant neighborhoods provided ready-made voting blocs, which empowered a new type of political boss. These flamboyant populists took an activist approach to government and traded in patronage and graft.

No other Boston boss outshone James Michael Curley. He was conniving, corrupt and beloved. The Rascal King had a seemingly endless supply of holiday turkeys and city jobs for constituents, who between 1914 and 1949 elected him mayor four times and governor and congressman once. He built hospitals, bridges, tunnels, bathhouses and parks. He also raised taxes and mired the city in debt.

In the early 20th century, the new political activists started preaching working-class solidarity and inciting the wrath of Yankee capitalists. Labor unrest in factories was blamed on new immigrants from Southern and Eastern Europe, feeding the twin fears of foreigners and socialism.

BOSTON ROGUES GALLERY

Boston folklore is replete with more than patriots, poets and preachers; the city has also produced its fair share of the muggers, buggers and thieves. Here is a sample of the most infamous.

John White Webster In 1849, this distinguished Harvard chemistry professor committed 'the murder of the century' when he bashed in his colleague's head in the college laboratory. Webster's attempt to conceal the crime by dismembering and burning the corpse was foiled by a school janitor. The trial attracted thousands of spectators seeking a glimpse of the fallen Brahmin. The professor was found guilty and hanged. His story and the evidence are reassembled in Simon Schama's mystery novel, *Dead Certainties*.

James Michael Curley Mayor Curley was the archetypal city boss, who once won an election while serving time for cheating on a civil service exam. 'I did it for a friend,' he explained to sympathetic voters. Corruption, graft and blackmail marked his time in the political spotlight. He completed his final term as mayor in 1846 in a jail cell, following a mail fraud conviction. Curley was the model for the protagonist in Frank Skeffington's novel *The Last Hurrah*; he was played by Spencer Tracy in the film.

Albert De Salvo You've heard about the Boston Strangler, whose serial murders terrorized the city in the early 1960s. De Salvo raped and killed 13 women, leaving their naked bodies in lewd poses with their stockings tied tightly in a bow under the chin. De Salvo finally gave himself away when in the middle of an attack he apologized to the intended victim and left. De Salvo was found to be a psychotic schizophrenic and given a life sentence. The Boston Strangler was defended by F Lee Bailey in court and portrayed by Tony Curtis on screen.

The Brinks Robbers In 1950, seven armed masked men entered the Brinks office in the North End and pulled off the richest heist in US history, taking over one million dollars in cash and even more in securities and checks. So well executed was this 'crime of the century' that police were stumped. Suspicion finally centered on a local gang of petty hoodlums led by Tony Pino. The FBI spent $30 million and six years trying to crack the case. Finally, 11 days before the statute of limitations ran out, a confession was extracted from a minor gang member, disgruntled over his share of the loot. Peter Falk depicted likable Tony Pino in the 1978 film *The Brinks Job*.

James 'Whitey' Bulger The volatile bad brother of the former head of the Massachusetts state senate, Whitey has appeared weekly atop the FBI's Most Wanted list since 2000. The bureau is offering a one million dollar reward for information leading to his capture. With Bulger it is personal, since he used his protected status as FBI informant to rise to the top of Boston's criminal underworld as head of the Winter Hill Gang in the 1980s. Wanted for racketeering, drug trafficking and 18 counts of murder, the 75-year-old has been on the lam for nearly a decade. The sordid details are compiled in Dick Lehr and Gerald O'Neil's book *Black Mass*. Whitey's photograph is now showing in a post office near you.

1881	1900
The Boston Symphony Orchestra is established	The population of Boston exceeds 560,000

After more than 125 years, Massachusetts once again took center stage in national politics with John Kennedy's election to the presidency in 1960. The youthful JFK was the pride of Boston's Irish Catholics for being the one who finally made it. A troupe of Boston politicians and Cambridge professors descended on the capital. Kennedy's brief Camelot inspired a new generation of Americans into public service and founded a political family dynasty that rivaled the Adamses. Kennedy's old congressional seat became the property of Thomas 'Tip' O'Neill, who climbed to the top of the legislative ladder as Speaker of the House while sticking to the adage that 'All Politics is Local.'

REFORM AND RACISM

The legacy of race relations in Boston is marred by contradictions. Abolitionists and segregationists, reformers and racists have all left their mark. Massachusetts was the first colony to recognize slavery as a legal institution in 1641, and the first to abolish slavery in 1783.

The first slaves, delivered to Massachusetts Bay Colony from the West Indies, became the personal property of wealthy Puritans. By 1700, Boston was home to roughly 400 slaves and a few free blacks. A number of black slaves earned their freedom by fighting with the colonists against the British in the revolution. Crispus Attucks, a runaway African-Indian slave, became a martyr by falling victim in the Boston Massacre. Salem Poor, an ex-slave who bought his freedom, was distinguished for heroism in the Battle of Bunker Hill.

By 1800, some 1100 black Bostonians comprised one of the country's largest free African-American communities, mostly on the northern slope of Beacon Hill. They worked as artisans and servants, catering to the wealthy Brahmins that were settling the southern slope. In 1806 they built the African Meeting House (see p76). Driven out of segregated white churches, the black populations used the building as the African Baptist Church, but it would also become the site of the first black school, a meeting place for abolitionists and a center for social activism.

Boston emerged as a nucleus of the abolition movement. Newspaper publisher William Lloyd Garrison, Unitarian minister Theodore Parker and aristocratic lawyer Wendell Phillips launched the Anti-Slavery Society to agitate public sentiment. The city provided safe houses for runaway slaves who took the Underground Railroad to freedom in Canada.

In the Civil War, Robert Gould Shaw led the famous 54th Regiment of black troops into battle in South Carolina. Colonel Shaw was killed in action and was buried by the Confederates in a common grave next to the fallen black soldiers as a mark of disrespect, which was said to please his abolitionist parents very much.

After the Civil War, many blacks rose to prominent positions in Boston society, including John S Rock, who became the first African-American to practice in the US Supreme Court; John J Smith, who was elected to the Massachusetts House of Representatives; Lewis Hayden, who was elected to the

View from the Museum of Afro-American History (p76)

1927	1950
Two Italian anarchists, Nicola Sacco and Bartolomeo Vanzetti, are executed on trumped-up murder charges	The population of Boston tops 800,000

Massachusetts General Court; and William DuBois, who was the first African-American to receive a PhD from Harvard.

In the early 20th century manufacturing jobs attracted southern blacks as part of the Great Migration. For newcomers, the north promised refuge from racism and poverty. More than 20,000 strong, Boston's expanding black community relocated to Roxbury and the South End, where a thriving jazz and dance scene enlivened city nights. At one point, both Martin Luther King, a Boston University divinity student, and Malcolm X, a pool-hall-hustling teenager, called the city home.

Boston did not have Jim Crow laws per se, but it did have its own informal patterns of racial segregation with African Americans as an underclass. As the city's economy declined, racial antagonisms increased. In the 1970s, a judge determined that separate was not equal in the public school system. His court order to desegregate the schools through forced busing violated the sanctity of the city's ethnic neighborhoods and exposed underlying racial tensions. The school year was marked by a series of violent incidents involving students and parents, most infamously in South Boston (p120). The experiment in racial integration was eventually abandoned, and the healing was slow.

MAKING BOSTON MODERN

Boston has experienced booms and busts. The good times of the early 20th century came to a crash in the Great Depression. The foundations of Boston's economy were crumbling: manufacturers moved out, seaport traffic dwindled, defense spending declined. The city languished and fell into disrepair, and the middle class sought suburban sanctuary.

In response, Yankee businessmen began to cooperate with their erstwhile antagonists, the Irish mayors, to bring about urban renewal. Meeting informally in a room next to the underground safe of a local bank, a select group of business leaders known as 'The Vault' fashioned a plan for the city. Mayors John Hynes and John Collins secured federal funding and local support for a modern Boston.

In the mid-20th century, the city underwent a remarkable physical transformation. Two of the city's oldest neighborhoods were targeted: Scollay Sq, which once bustled with theaters and music halls, but had since become a rundown red-light district; and the West End, where working poor immigrants eked out an existence amid a grubby labyrinth of row houses and alleyways (see the boxed text, p79). Urban redemption came in the form of the grim bulldozer, which sent both neighborhoods into oblivion. While only the sailors in the old Navy Yard wept for Scollay Sq, a popular outcry was caused by the demolition of homes and flight of refugees from the West End. Ethnic communities in the North End, Charlestown and Southie organized themselves to prevent 'renewal' of their neighborhoods.

Next came the cement mixers that filled the modernist moldings of a new Government Center for Boston's sizable civil-servant sector. The centerpiece was an inverted pyramid, the monumental and cavernous City Hall, which has since become prime evidence in the architectural case against 1960s modernism. The city's skyline reached upwards with luxury condominiums and office buildings. The old customs tower on the waterfront, long the tallest building in town, was overtaken by the proud Prudential Tower and Henry Cobb's elegant John Hancock Tower.

Boston was on the rebound. After the West End disaster, urban planners focused on revitalizing, rather than razing, neglected neighborhoods. Modern Boston came to embody the old and the new, a coexistence of red brick with steel and glass.

In 1976, the city organized a triumphant Bicentennial celebration, capped with spectacular fireworks and a spirited concert by the River Charles. A half-million people attended the patriotic party, including British monarch Queen Elizabeth II, who showed no hard feelings over past misunderstandings in her salute to independent Bostonians from the balcony of the Old State House.

1960	1991–2006
Boston native John F Kennedy is elected president, ushering in the era of Camelot	The Central Artery/Tunnel Project keeps all of Boston under construction

Sights ■

Sights

Boston's 18th-century historic spots stand side-by-side with 19th-century architectural gems, 20th-century museums and 21st-century innovations. It's an amazing amalgam of history, art and entertainment, packed into the country's oldest city streets.

As difficult it is to drive in Boston (very) is as wonderful as it is to walk. While the city is almost 50 square miles, most of the attractions are in one of 14 neighborhoods, all of which are accessible by subway (or 'T'), and navigable by foot. Even the outlying areas are easy enough to reach by public transportation. For the purposes of this book, Brookline, Cambridge and Somerville are treated as Boston neighborhoods, even though they are separate administrative entities.

Abutted by the Boston Common and topped with the gold-domed Massachusetts State House, Beacon Hill (p75) is the neighborhood most oft-featured on Boston postcards. Standing in stark contrast are Government Center and the West End (p79), both victims of reconstruction in the 1960s, but enjoying some revitalization with the completion of the Big Dig. Likewise, the North End (p81) is finally rejoining the rest of the city, but its narrow streets with Italian accents still feel like another world – the Old World. Across the bridge, Charlestown (p83) is the site of the Battle of Bunker Hill and the Charlestown Navy Yard.

The Freedom Trail blazes through bustling Downtown (p86), a business district crammed with colonial buildings and modern complexes. Including Faneuil Hall, the New England Aquarium and the HaborWalk, the Waterfront (p89) is a tourist epicenter. Across the Fort Point Channel, the Seaport District (p93) is fast developing as an another attractive waterside destination.

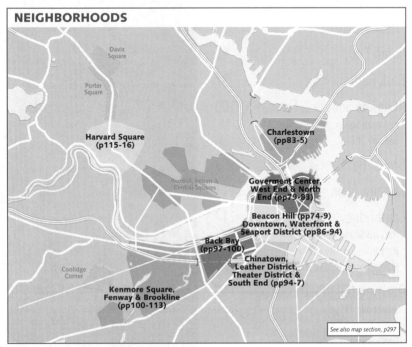

NEIGHBORHOODS

Davis Square

Porter Square

Harvard Square (p115-16)

Charlestown (pp83-5)

Kendall, Inman & Central Squares

Goverment Center, West End & North End (pp79-83)

Beacon Hill (pp74-9) Downtown, Waterfront & Seaport District (pp86-94)

Back Bay (pp97-100)

Chinatown, Leather District, Theater District & South End (pp94-7)

Coolidge Corner

Kenmore Square, Fenway & Brookline (pp100-113)

See also map section, p297

Harvard Sq (p115) in fall

Chinatown, Leather District and Theater District (p94) are overlapping areas, filled with glitzy theaters, Chinese restaurants and the remnants of Boston's shoe and leather industry (now converted lofts and trendy clubs). Nearby, the Victorian manses in the South End (p96) have been claimed by artists and gays, who are creating a vibrant restaurant and gallery scene in the formerly rough-and-tumble neighborhood.

Back Bay (p97) includes the city's most fashionable window-shopping, latte-drinking and people-watching on Newbury St, as well as its most elegant architecture around Copley Sq. Further west, Kenmore Sq & Fenway (p100) attract rowdy club-goers and Red Sox fans, as well as art-lovers and culture vultures.

With deeply rooted Jewish and Russian populations, Brookline (p103) is a separate city set in the midst of Boston proper. Follow the Emerald Necklace – Boston's chain of green parks – south to Jamaica Plain (p113), a progressive residential community with gracious Victorian architecture and a cutting-edge music scene. Further west are the lively student areas of Allston and Brighton, while South Boston (p120) and Dorchester (p121) lie to the south.

Across the Charles River, Cambridge is a distinct city that boasts two distinguished universities, a host of historic sites and no shortage of artistic, architectural and cultural attractions. North of Cambridge and Charlestown, Somerville (p119) is enjoying some spillover from the former.

ITINERARIES

Two Days

Spend one day reliving revolutionary history by following the **Freedom Trail** (p105). Take time to lounge on the **Boston Common** (p77), peek in the **Old State House** (p88) and visit the **Paul Revere House** (p83). At the end of the walking tour, stroll back into the **North End** (p139) for dinner at an atmospheric Italian restaurant. On your second day, pack a picnic, rent a bike and ride the **Charles River Bike Loop** (p126). Go as far as **Harvard Square** (p115) to cruise the campus and browse the bookstores. Spend the evening in Cambridge hanging out with students and hearing **live music** (p177).

Four Days

Follow the two-day itinerary and then on your third day head out to the **Harbor Islands** (p91). Visit **Fort Warren** (p91) and go berry picking on **Grape Island** (p91). Spend your last day discovering **Back Bay** (p97). Take a stroll across the **Public Garden** (p76), window shop and gallery hop on **Newbury St** (p215), go to the top of the **Prudential Center** (p100) and browse the **Boston Public Library** (p98).

One Week

If you have a week to spare, you can see all the sights listed in the two previous itineraries. Plus you have time to peruse the impressive American collection at the **Museum of Fine Arts** (p103), catch a **Red Sox game** (p194) or tour the **Massachusetts State House** (p76). If revolutionary history is your thing, head to **Lexington** and **Concord** (p246) to see where it all began. Otherwise, go north to **Salem** (p250) to investigate its maritime culture or south to **Cape Cod** (p256) for a day at the beach.

ORGANIZED TOURS

For a series of self-guided walking tours, see p124.

Bike Tours

BOSTON BIKE TOURS

☎ 617-308-5902; www.bostonbiketours.com; with/without bike rental$25/20; 11am Sat & Sun
Every weekend Boston Bike Tours follows a different route, whether it's Paul Revere's Ride, the Freedom Trail or the Emerald Necklace. On the third Saturday of the month, combine your favorite pastimes on the Bike, Beach and Brew Tour, which visits Castle Island, Carson Beach and the Harpoon Brewery.

URBAN ADVENTURS Map pp308-9

☎ 617-233-7595; www.urbanadventours.com; 842 Beacon St; tours $50-75; 10am, 2pm & 6pm; St Mary's
Founded by avid cyclists who believe the best views of Boston are from a bicycle. The City View Ride provides a great overview of how to get around by bike. Other more specialized tours are for photographers and art and architecture buffs. Prices include bikes and helmets; reservations required.

Boat Tours

BOSTON HARBOR CRUISES Map pp302–3

☎ 617-227-4320; www.bostonharborcruises .com; 1 Long Wharf; adult/senior & student/child $19/17/15; 11am, 1pm & 3pm daily Jun-Aug, Sat & Sun only in Sep; Aquarium
Narrated sightseeing trips around the harbor. Other boats go on sunset cruises ($20/18/16, 7pm daily in Jun and Aug, 6pm Thursday to Sunday in Sep), through the Charles River locks ($19/17/15, 10am and noon daily, plus 2pm Saturday and Sunday in Jul and Aug) and to Charlestown ($14/12/10, 10:30am to 4:30pm, mid-Apr to mid-Nov).

CHARLES RIVER BOAT CO

☎ 617-621-3001; www.charlesriverboat.com; Cambridgeside Galleria; adult/senior/child $12/10/6; 10am-7pm daily Jun-Aug, 10am-7pm Sat & Sun Apr, May & Sep; Lechmere
The 75-minute narrated trip travels the Charles River Basin between Harvard and the Boston Harbor locks. Cruises depart from Canal Park at the Cambridgeside Galleria.

DUCK TOURS Map pp306-7 and pp300-1

☎ 617-723-3825; www.bostonducktours.com; adult/senior & student/child $26/23/17; 9am-dusk Apr-Nov; Copley or Science Park
Land and water tours using amphibious vehicles from WWII depart from the Prudential Center and the Museum of Science. Rain or shine, the 90-minute narrated tour splashes around the Charles River, then takes to Boston city streets. Buy tickets in advance.

GONDOLA DI VENEZIA Map pp302-3

☎ 617-876-2800; www.bostongondolas.com; Community Boating, Charles River Esplanade; tours per couple $69-219; 2-10:30pm Wed-Sun Jun-Oct; Charles/MGH
Make no mistake about it – the Charles River is not the Grand Canal. However, the gondolier's technique and the craftsmanship of the boat make these private gondola rides a romantic treat. Tours range from 'traditional' (35 minutes) to 'bellissimo' (one hour), complete with chocolates, roses and a live accordion player. All boat rides are private so reservations are required.

LIBERTY CLIPPER Map pp302-3

☎ 617-742-0333; www.libertyfleet.com; 67 Long Wharf; adult/child $30/18; noon, 3pm & 6pm Jun-Sep; Aquarium
This 125-ft schooner takes a two-hour, 12-mile sail around the harbor several times a day. It is docked on Central Wharf, north of the Aquarium.

MASSACHUSETTS BAY LINES

Map pp302-3

☎ 617-542-8000; www.massbaylines.com; Rowes Wharf; adult/child $16/12; ⏰ 11am-6pm May-Sep; 🚇 Aquarium

The 'Birth of a Nation' tour retraces the events of the Boston Tea Party, Paul Revere's ride and Old Ironsides' legendary battles. Other tours include music cruises (over 21 only, $18 to $20, 8pm Friday and Saturday), dusk cruises (adult/child $19/16, 7pm Jun and Aug, 6pm Sep) and moonlight cruises ($19/16, 8:45pm Friday and Saturday in Jun and Aug, 8pm Friday and Saturday in Sep).

Trolley Tours

Overheard on a Duck Tour: 'Trolleys can go in the water too…Once.' Nonetheless, trolley tours offer great flexibility because you can hop off at sites along the route and hop on the next trolley that comes along. There is little to distinguish the various companies (besides the color of the trolley).

BEANTOWN TROLLEY

☎ 781-986-6100, 800-343-1328; www.brushhill tours.com; adult/senior/child $29/27/7; ⏰ 9:30am-4:30pm; 🚇 Boylston

The only trolley that offers service to the Museum of Fine Arts and the Seaport District. The price also includes a harbor cruise from the New England Aquarium. Trolley color: red.

DISCOVER BOSTON TOURS Map pp302-3

☎ 617-742-1440; www.discoverbostontours .com; 66 Long Wharf; adult/senior/child one day $28/25/15, two days $38/35/25; ⏰ 9am-5pm; 🚇 Aquarium

Audio tapes available in Spanish, French, German and Japanese for multilingual guests. Besides the standard city tour, Discover Boston Trolley has some specialty offerings, such as the Night Life Express, which travels between a bunch of bars. Trolley color: white.

GHOSTS & GRAVEYARDS Map pp302-3

☎ 617-269-3626; www.ghostsandgravestones.com; Long Wharf; adult/child $32/19; ⏰ 6pm, 7pm, 8pm & 9pm Fri-Sun May, daily Jun-Oct; 🚇 Aquarium

Hosted by a cursed gravedigger, this hair-raising tour tells tales of Boston's darker

side. Visit the city's two oldest graveyards and learn about its most haunted houses. Reservations are required

OLD TOWN TROLLEY TOURS

Map pp302-3

☎ 1800-868-7482; www.historictours.com; adult/senior/student/child one day $26/23/23/5, two days $40/37/37/9; ⏰ 9am-4pm Nov-Apr, to 5pm May-Oct; 🚇 Aquarium

Price includes a guided walking tour of Beacon Hill and half-price admission to the Old State House. Trolley color: orange.

Walking Tours

The granddaddy of walking tours is the Freedom Trail, a 2½-mile trail that traverses the city, from the Boston Common to Charlestown. For details see p106. Most walking tours depart from the Greater Boston Convention & Visitors Bureau information kiosk on the Boston Common.

BLACK HERITAGE TRAIL

☎ 617-742-5415; free; ⏰ tours 10am, noon & 2pm Mon-Sat Jul & Aug

A 1.6-mile walking tour that explores the history of the abolitionist movement and African American settlement on Beacon Hill. The National Park Service (NPS) conducts guided tours in summer, but maps and descriptions for self-guided tours are available at the Museum of Afro-American History (see p76).

BOSTON BY FOOT

☎ 617-367-3766; www.bostonbyfoot.com; adult/child $10/8

This fantastic nonprofit offers 90-minute walking tours of Boston's neighborhoods. Specialty tours include Literary Landmarks, Boston Underfoot (with highlights from the Big Dig and the T) and Boston for Little Feet – a kid-friendly version of the Freedom Trail. Check the website for tour info.

BOSTON MOVIE TOUR

☎ 866-668-4345; www.bostonmovietours.net; adult/senior & student/child $20/16/10; ⏰ 11am & 2pm Wed-Mon

It's not Hollywood, but Boston has hosted its share of famous movie scenes. Stroll along the Movie Mile, site of scenes from *Good*

Will Hunting, *A Civil Action* and *The Verdict*. Boston-based TV shows are covered too. Real movie mavens might consider Theater-on-Wheels, the bus version of the tour.

CHINATOWN WALKING TOUR COLLECTIVE

☎ 617-507-7927; www.chinatownheritage.org
A cooperative effort allows visitors to explore Chinatown markets, restaurants and historical sights. Gain insight from community members' personal stories.

HAHVAHD TOUR Map p310

☎ 203-305-9735; www.hahvahdtour.com; suggested donation adult/senior $10/5; ☺ 10am, noon & 2pm; ⓡ Harvard
This unofficial Harvard tour was founded by two dynamic students – 'a New England liberal and a conservative Texan' – who give the inside scoop on Harvard's history and student life at the university. Tours depart from the Cambridge Visitors' Information Kiosk outside the Harvard Sq T stop.

MICHELE TOPOR'S NORTH END MARKET TOURS

☎ 617-523-6032; www.northendmarkettours.com; per person $48; ☺ 10am & 2pm Wed & Sat, 10am & 3pm Fri
This 3½-hour tour around the North End includes shopping in a *salumeria* (deli), sampling pastries at the local *pasticceria* (pastry store) and touring an *enoteca* (wine bar). The sights and smells of the North End provide a great introduction to Italian cuisine and culture. Reservations required.

MY TOWN TOURS

☎ 617-536-8696; www.mytowninc.org; adults$15, less for students & youth
If you've had your fill of white men like Paul Revere and John Hancock, head to the South End to hear stories about immigrants, people of color and other working class heroes. Student-run tours highlight citizen activism and its effects on affordable housing, green space, civil rights and other contemporary issues. Tour times vary.

PHOTO WALKS

☎ 617-851-2273; www.photowalks.com; adult/youth $25/12; ☺ 10am & 1pm May-Sep, less often Oct-Apr

A walking tour combined with a photography lesson. Visit Boston's most scenic spots and get some picture-taking tips along the way. The price includes a copy of the booklet *Photo Walks Guide to Creative Photography*. Check the website for specifics on tours, points of departure and reservations.

SECRET TOUR Map pp300-1

☎ 617-720-2283; www.northendboston.com /secrettour; $30; ☺ 10am, 1pm & 4pm Fri & Sat; ⓡ Haymarket
This two-hour tour begins at North Sq – opposite Paul Revere's House – and explores the North End's hidden courtyards and passageways, thus uncovering the neighborhood's checkered past.

TALES OF OLDE CAMBRIDGE

☎ 617-354-3344; www.livelylore.com; per person $15
A husband-wife team – an actor and an educator – has developed an interactive, entertaining tour of historic Harvard Sq. Hear 'true tales of witches, patriots, heroes, heretics, revolutionaries, spies and (gasp) liberals.' Tours can be scheduled at your convenience.

BEACON HILL & BOSTON COMMON

Eating p136, Shopping p209, Sleeping p227

When the local news reports the day's events 'on Beacon Hill', it usually refers to goings-on in the Massachusetts State House (p76), the focal point of politics in the Commonwealth, the building famously dubbed 'the hub of the solar system.' The State House is an impressive jewel that crowns Beacon Hill; but that is not what makes this neighborhood the most prestigious in Boston.

Perhaps what makes Beacon Hill is its history. This enclave has been home to centuries of great thinkers, from writer Henry David Thoreau to statesman Daniel Webster to abolitionist Wendell Phillips. In the 19th century, Beacon Hill was the site of literary salons and publishing houses. As well, it was the center of the abolitionist movement. (See p124 for a walking tour of Beacon Hill's most historic spots.)

Sights

BEACON HILL & BOSTON COMMON

Or perhaps the appeal of Beacon Hill is the utter loveliness of the place: the narrow cobblestone streets lit with gas lanterns; the distinguished brick town houses decked with purple windowpanes and blooming flowerboxes. These enchanting residential streets are reminiscent of London, and streets such as stately Louisburg Sq indeed capture the grandeur that was intended.

Or perhaps it is the charm of Charles St, the commercial street that traverses the flat of the hill. This is Boston's most enchanting spot for browsing boutiques and haggling over antiques. A steaming cappuccino is all the more satisfying, a fine dinner all the more romantic, when it is enjoyed in such a delightful setting.

Truth be told, it matters not what makes Beacon Hill so bewitching, only that it is so. Visitors can pick their pleasure – explore the Boston Common, tour the State House, visit the historic homes and patronize the shops and restaurants – or explore all aspects of this quintessential Boston neighborhood.

Orientation

With the Boston Common as its southern border, Beacon Hill extends north to Cambridge St and west to the Charles River. The neighborhood's most distinctive landmark is the Massachusetts State House, whose gold dome towers over the elegant row houses and the Boston Common, while the granite blocks of Suffolk University dominate the rest of the eastern end. At the western end of the neighborhood – the flat end – Charles St is lined with antique shops and European-style cafés. While most of Beacon Hill is staunchly upper class, the back side of the hill (north of Myrtle St) is the home of those of relatively modest means.

TRANSPORTATION

Subway Three corners of Beacon Hill are punctuated by T stops. On the red line, Charles/MGH T station is convenient to Charles and Cambridge Sts, as well as the Charles River Esplanade. Also on the red line, Park St T station services the Boston Common and sights in the southeastern part of Beacon Hill. At the end of the blue line, Bowdoin T station is a lesser-used stop that is convenient to the eastern end of Cambridge St.

BEACON HILL

BOSTON ATHENAEUM Map pp302-3

☎ 617-227-0270; www.bostonathenaeum.org; 10½ Beacon St; admission free; ☻ 8:30am-8pm Mon, 8:30am-5:30pm Tue-Sat, closed Sat Jun-Aug; 🚇 Park St

Founded in 1807, the Boston Athenaeum is an old and distinguished private library, having hosted the likes of Ralph Waldo Emerson and Nathaniel Hawthorne, as well as less traditional members like Amy Lowell. While the writers and bibliophiles that are members today are perhaps less known, the place is no less esteemed. Its collection has over a half a million volumes, including an impressive selection of art which is showcased in the onsite gallery. Unfortunately, the library itself is open to members only, but tourists can visit the gallery.

GRANARY BURYING GROUND

Map pp302-3

☎ 617-635-4505; Tremont St; admission free; ☻ 9am-5pm; 🚇 Park St

Adjacent to Park St Church, this ancient cemetery dates to 1660. As the name implies, the location of the church was once the site of the town granary. As the burying ground pre-dates the church, it is named after the grain storage facility instead.

While it is sometimes called the *Old* Granary Burying Ground, it's not the oldest; King's Chapel (p87) and Copp's Hill (p82) date back even further. Nonetheless, this atmospheric atoll is crammed with historic headstones, many with evocative (if not creepy) carvings. It is the final resting place of all your favorite revolutionary heroes including Paul Revere, Samuel Adams, John Hancock and James Otis. Benjamin Franklin is missing, as he is buried in Philadelphia, but the Franklin family plot contains his parents. The five victims of the Boston Massacre share a common grave, though the only name you are likely to recognize is that of Crispus Attucks, the freed slave who is considered the first person to lose his life in the struggle for American independence. Other noteworthy permanent residents include Peter Faneuil, of Faneuil Hall fame, and Judge Sewall, the only magistrate to denounce the hanging of the so-called Salem witches.

Sights

BEACON HILL & BOSTON COMMON

MASSACHUSETTS STATE HOUSE

Map pp302-3

☎ tours 617-727-3676; www.sec.state.ma.us; cnr Beacon & Bowdoin Sts; admission free; ✆ open 9am-5pm, tours 10am-4pm Mon-Fri; 🚇 Park St

High atop Beacon Hill, Massachusetts leaders and legislators attempt to turn their ideas into concrete policies and practices within the State House. Charles Bulfinch designed the commanding state capitol, but it was Oliver Wendell Holmes who called it 'the hub of the solar system' (thus earning Boston the nickname 'the Hub').

For most of the 18th century, the seat of the Massachusetts government was the Old State House (see p88). After the revolution, when state leaders decided they needed an upgrade, they chose the city's highest peak – land that was previously part of John Hancock's cow pasture. Other Sons of Liberty also had their hands in building the new capitol, literally: Sam Adams and Paul Revere laid the cornerstones. Paul Revere's silversmith skills were later tapped when the leaking dome was covered with copper.

Today the State House is much bigger than Bulfinch's original design, thanks to later additions. Another evident difference is that the dome is no longer copper, but rather gilded with 23-carat gold leaf.

A free 40-minute tour of the State House covers its history, artwork, architecture and political personalities. It starts in the Doric Hall, the columned reception area directly below the dome. Once the main entryway for the State House, these front doors are now used only by a visiting US president or by a departing governor taking 'the long walk' on his last day in office.

Knowledgeable 'Doric Docents' provide details about the many statues, flags and murals that decorate the various halls. Tours also visit the legislative chambers: the House of Representatives, also house of the famous 'Sacred Cod'; and the Senate Chamber, where Angelina Grimke spoke out against slavery in 1838. These chambers are particularly intriguing when congress is in session, so you can see who's voting 'yea' or 'nay'.

On the front lawn, statues honor important Massachusetts figures, among them orator Daniel Webster, Civil War general Joseph Hooker, religious martyrs Anne Hutchinson and Mary Dyer, President John F Kennedy, and educator Horace Mann. Unfortunately, these lovely grounds are now closed to the public, so you'll have to peek through the iron fence to catch a glimpse.

MUSEUM OF AFRO-AMERICAN HISTORY Map pp302-3

☎ 617-725-0022; www.afroammuseum.org; 46 Joy St; donation $5; ✆ 10am-4pm Mon-Sat; 🚇 Park St

Beacon Hill was never the exclusive domain of blue-blood Brahmins. Waves of immi-

PUBLIC GARDEN

The Public Garden is a 24-acre botanical oasis of Victorian flowerbeds, verdant grass, and weeping willow trees shading a tranquil lagoon. Until it was filled in the early 19th century, it was (like the rest of Back Bay) a tidal salt marsh. Now, at any time of year, it is an island of loveliness, awash in seasonal blooms, gold-toned leaves or untrammeled snow. At the main entrance (from Arlington St), visitors are greeted by a **statue of George Washington**, looking stately atop his horse. But other pieces of public art are more whimsical.

The most endearing is **Make Way for Ducklings**, always a favorite with tiny tots who can climb and sit on the bronze ducks. The sculpture depicts Mrs Mallard and her eight ducklings, the main characters in the beloved book by Robert McKloskey. As the story goes, Mrs Mallard and her ducklings are stuck at a busy street until a friendly Boston policeman helps them across.

On the northeast side of the lagoon, the **Ether Monument** commemorates the first use of anesthesia for medical purposes, which took place in Boston (see the Ether Dome on p80).

If the slow-going **swan boats** (☎ 617-522-1966; www.swanboats.com; adult/senior/child $2.75/2/1.25; ✆ 10am-4pm mid-Apr–mid-Jun, 10am-5pm daily mid-Jun–Aug, 10am-4pm Sat & Sun, noon-4pm Mon-Fri Sep–mid-Oct) seem out of place in today's fast-paced city setting, they are. The story of the swan boats goes back to 1877, when Robert Paget developed a catamaran with a paddlewheel that was propelled by pedal. Inspired by the opera *Lohengrin*, in which a heroic knight rides across a river in a swan-drawn boat, Paget designed a graceful swan to hide the boat captain. While today's swan boats are larger than the 1877 original, they still utilize the same technology and they are still managed by Paget's descendents. A relic of Boston's bygone days, the swan boats present an image of serenity and contentment.

grants, and especially African Americans, freed from slavery, settled on the back side of the hill in the 19th century. The Museum of Afro-American History occupies two adjacent historic buildings: the African Meeting House, the country's oldest black church and meeting house; and Abiel Smith School, the country's first school for blacks.

Within these walls, William Lloyd Garrison began the New England Antislavery Society. Here, Maria Stewart became the first American woman – a black woman, no less – to speak before a mixed-gender audience. Frederick Douglass delivered stirring calls to action within this hall, and Robert Gould Shaw recruited black soldiers for the Civil War effort. Today, the Museum of Afro-American History offers exhibits about these historic events, as well as an extensive library and interactive computer kiosks.

The museum is also a source of information about and the final destination of the Black Heritage Trail (see p73).

NICHOLS HOUSE MUSEUM Map pp302-3

☎ 617-227-6993; www.nicholshousemuseum.org; 55 Mt Vernon St; adult/child $7/free; ⏱ noon-4pm Tue-Sat May-Oct, Thu-Sat Nov-Apr; 🚇 Park St
This 1804 town house might be your only opportunity to peek inside one of these classic Beacon Hill beauties. Attributed to Charles Bulfinch, it is unique in its merger of Federal and Greek Revival architectural styles. Equally impressive is the story told inside the museum – that of the day-to-day life of Miss Rose Standish Nichols, who lived here from 1885 to 1960. Miss Rose was an author, pacifist and suffragette. The museum has reconstructed her home, furnished with art and antiques from all over the world, as well as some impressive examples of her own needlepoint and woodwork.

PARK ST CHURCH Map pp302-3

☎ 617-523-3383; www.parkstreet.org; cnr Tremont & Park Sts; ⏱ 9:30am-3:30pm Tue-Sat mid-Jun–Aug; 🚇 Park St
Shortly after the construction of Park St Church, powder for the War of 1812 was stored in the basement, earning this location the moniker 'Brimstone Corner.' But that was hardly the most inflammatory event that took place here. Noted for its graceful, 217ft steeple, this Boston land-

BOSTON FOR SHUTTERBUGS

Photographers will delight in Boston's awesome architecture, gorgeous green spaces and seaside setting. If you think you might appreciate some picture-taking pointers, consider Photo Walks (p74). Otherwise, here are some photo-ops that are guaranteed to impress your friends at home.

Acorn St The city's narrowest street, on Beacon Hill.

Ben Franklin look-alike This guy usually hangs around Faneuil Hall (p90). He's happy to pose, but he may charge you a few dollars.

City skyline From the Longfellow Bridge – the panorama is especially attractive just before sunset.

Granary Burying Ground (p75) Get up close and personal with the gravestones.

Make Way for Ducklings Sculpture in the Public Garden (opposite). Particularly charming when the children are playing on the ducks.

Sculls on the Charles River The Weeks Footbridge offers a good vantage point.

mark has been hosting historic lectures and musical performances since its founding. In 1829, William Lloyd Garrison railed against slavery from the church's pulpit. And on Independence Day in 1831, Samuel Francis Smith's hymn 'America' (My Country 'Tis of Thee) was first sung. These days, Park St is a conservative congregational church.

BOSTON COMMON

The 50-acre Boston Common is the country's oldest public park. If you have any doubt, refer to the plaque emblazoned with the words of the treaty between Governor Winthrop and William Blaxton, who sold the land for £30 in 1634.

The Common has served many purposes over the years, including as a campground for British troops during the Revolutionary War and as green grass for cattle grazing until 1830. Although there is still a grazing ordinance on the books, the Common today serves picnickers, sunbathers and people-watchers. In winter, the Frog Pond attracts ice-skaters (p202); while summer draws theater lovers for Shakespeare on the Common (p190).

For a free tour of the Boston Common and the Public Garden, inquire at the visitors information kiosk (see p278).

BOSTON MASSACRE MONUMENT

Map pp302-3

This 25ft monument pays tribute to the five victims of the Boston Massacre, which took place down the street near the **Old State House** (see p88). It replicates Paul Revere's famous engraving of this tragic event. Revere's effective propaganda depicts the soldiers shooting down defenseless colonists in cold blood, when in reality they were reacting to the aggressive crowd in self defense.

CENTRAL BURYING GROUND

Map pp302-3

Boylston St; 🕑 9am-5pm; 🚇 Boylston
Dating to 1756, the Central Burying Ground is the least celebrated of the old cemeteries as it was the burial ground of the down-and-out (according to one account, used for 'Roman Catholics and strangers dying in the town'). Some reports indicate that it contains an unmarked mass grave for British soldiers who died in the Battle of Bunker Hill. The most recognized name here is the artist-in-residence, Gilbert Stuart. Sometimes called the 'Father of American Portraiture,' Stuart painted the portrait of George Washington that now graces the dollar bill.

GREAT ELM SITE Map pp302-3

The trees that occupy this site are probably descendents of the Old Elm that stood here for more than 200 years. History has it that Ann Hibbens was hanged on the branch of the elm tree for witchery in 1656, and Mary

Central Burying Ground (above)

Dyer for religious heresy in 1660. Boston's 'oldest inhabitant' was damaged in 1869 in a brutal storm that reportedly took down the spires of many churches, and destroyed for good by another storm in 1876.

ROBERT GOULD SHAW MEMORIAL

Map pp302-3

cnr Beacon & Park Sts; 🚇 Park St
The magnificent bas-relief opposite the State House was sculpted by Augustus St Gaudens over nearly 13 years of work. It honors the 54th Massachusetts Regiment of the Union Army, the nation's first all-black Civil War regiment, depicted in the 1989 film *Glory*. The soldiers, led by 26-year-old Shaw (the son of a wealthy Brahmin family), steadfastly refused their monthly stipend for two years, until Congress increased it to match the amount that white regiments received. Shaw and half his men were killed in a battle at Fort Wagner, South Carolina. The NPS tour of the Black Heritage Trail departs from here (see p73).

SOLDIERS & SAILORS MONUMENT

Map pp302-3

Dedicated in 1877, this massive monument atop Flagstaff Hill pays tribute to the namesake soldiers and sailors that died in the Civil War. The four bronze statues represent Peace, the female figure looking to the South; the Sailor, the seaman looking toward the ocean; History, the Greek figure looking to heaven; and the Soldier, an infantryman standing at ease. See if you can recognize the many historical figures in the elaborate bronze reliefs.

GOVERNMENT CENTER & WEST END

Eating p138, Shopping p210, Sleeping p228

Government Center is on the site of the notorious Scollay Sq of yesteryear (see below), while the West End is sometimes called the 'Old West End' because there's not much left of this formerly vibrant neighborhood. After a wave of redevelopment in the 1950s and 1960s, both areas are now dominated by mammoth, institutional buildings that leave little room for character.

The massive institutions that now dominate this neighborhood include City Hall and other government facilities, as well as the many annexes of Mass General Hospital. Of more interest to travelers is Banknorth Garden, home of the Boston Celtics and the Boston Bruins (p194), and site of Boston's biggest crowd-drawing concerts.

Tucked in between all these gargantuan buildings, there is a little grid of narrow streets and brick commercial buildings that gives some sense of what the Old West End was like. As part of the Big Dig, the elevated train was recently dismantled, allowing light to filter down onto Causeway St. It seems to have scared away the adult-only theaters and seedy bars that once dominated these streets. Now it is packed with pubs – a popular spot for sports fans (see p162) – as well as a few fine hotels (p228) and restaurants (p138). The neighborhood is repackaging itself as the Bulfinch Triangle – a destination to work, live and play.

Orientation

Government Center is the block that is bound by New Sudbury, Cambridge, Court and Congress Sts. It is dominated by City Hall Plaza and surrounded on all sides by nondescript office buildings. The West End stretches from Government Center west to the Charles River, occupying the area north of Cambridge St. More government buildings and the endless development around Massachusetts General Hospital fill this space. Of interest to

Sights

GOVERNMENT CENTER & WEST END

SCOLLAY SQUARE

Scollay Sq is gone, razed by developers and renamed by city planners in the 1960s. But Boston remains nostalgic for this bygone bastion of iniquity, as evidenced by the namesake restaurant that recently opened nearby on Beacon St (see p137).

Historically, Scollay Sq was home to many of Boston's most esteemed residents, including the Adams family (John and Abigail, that is), while the socialite Otis family lived just up the street. Alexander Graham Bell worked in a laboratory here; and Thomas Edison invented the stock ticker in the very same building. In 1880, a centerpiece statue of John Winthrop – a replica of the sculpture in the US Capitol – was dedicated in Scollay Sq, emblematic of its prominence in Boston geography.

With the influx of European immigrants in the 19th century, however, the character of this neighborhood began to change. Wealthy families retreated up Beacon Hill and to the Back Bay, as working class Irish took over the streets west of Scollay Sq. Poor black populations overflowed from the northern slope of Beacon Hill to the crowded streets below.

A thriving commercial center, Scollay Sq bustled with restaurants and nightclubs. Yet it became known not for its intellect and innovation, as in former years, but for its debauchery and depravity. It was Boston's center of burlesque, lined with theaters like the Old Howard and the Olympia. It was a popular destination for sailors, drunks and thieves who would frequent the bars and brothels. At the same time, the West End was a teeming maze of narrow streets, lined with clapboard houses with cold-water flats.

Both of these areas were razed in the mid-20th century. A group of motivated theater-lovers rallied to save the historic Howard Theater, but a mysterious fire destroyed the building before they could raise sufficient funds. Approximately 20,000 residents were displaced, moving primarily to the South End, South Boston, Dorchester and Roxbury.

With $40 million in federal funding, Scollay Sq was replaced with a collection of office buildings, representing a new, modern Boston – wider roads but no sidewalks, lots of concrete and few trees, high-rise housing but no soul. In retrospect, they are often held up as examples of urban planning: what not to do.

TRANSPORTATION

Subway Government Center is serviced by the T station of the same name, which is at the intersection of the green and blue lines. The West End has a T station in every corner. Use the red-line Charles/MGH for Mass General Hospital and the western end of Cambridge St, while blue-line Bowdoin is closer to the eastern end of Cambridge St. On the orange and green lines, North Station provides easy access to the Banknorth Garden and the Bulfinch Triangle.

travelers is North Station, a transit center for northbound commuter trains and the Banknorth Garden, home of the Celtics and the Bruins. These facilities share a building in the northern corner of this large swathe of land. Just south, a few places to stay, eat and drink are located in the Bulfinch Triangle, the blocks bounded by Merrimac, Haverhill and Causeway Sts.

CITY HALL PLAZA Map pp300-1

Erected in the 1960s, City Hall Plaza is a cold 56-acre concrete plaza surrounded by government office buildings. Designed by IM Pei (who also designed the Kennedy Library), it's home to the fortress-like Boston City Hall, a top-heavy mass of concrete, brick and glass, and the John F Kennedy Federal Building, which anchors the northern edge. The plaza sometimes hosts public gatherings and summertime performances.

The plaza's high points are the gracefully curved brick **Sears Crescent** (cnr Court & Tremont Sts), one of the few buildings that remains from the Scollay Sq days. The sweeping curve of the modern **Center Plaza** (Cambridge St) mirrors the Sears Crescent.

ETHER DOME Map pp300-1

☎ 617-726-2121; Mass General Hospital, 4th fl; admission free; ◷ 9am-8pm; ⓡ Charles/MGH
On October 16, 1846, Thomas WG Morton administered ether to the patient Gilbert Abbott, while Dr John Collins Warren cut a tumor from his neck. It was the first use of anesthesia in a surgical procedure and it happened in this domed operating room in Mass General Hospital. The dome looks like a typical, old-fashioned hall used for lectures and medical demonstrations, up to and including the skeleton hanging in the corner. The dome is still used today for

meetings and lectures, so it is sometimes closed to the public.

MUSEUM OF SCIENCE Map pp300-1

☎ 617-723-2500; www.mos.org; Science Park, Charles River Dam; adult/senior/child $16/14/13; ◷ 9am-5pm Sat-Thu Sep-Jun, to 7pm Jul & Aug, 9am-9pm Fri year-round; ⓡ Science Park
This educational playground has more than 600 interactive exhibits. Favorites include the world's largest lightning bolt generator, a full-scale space capsule, a world population meter and a virtual fish tank. The amazing array of exhibits explores computers, technology, complex systems, algae, maps, models, dinosaurs, birds and much more. Live science demonstrations involve animals and experiments taking place before your eyes, while the Discovery Center offers other hands-on fun that's cool for kids.

The museum also houses the **Hayden Planetarium and Mugar Omni Theater** (shows $9/8/7, show & museum $20/17.50/16). The planetarium boasts a state-of-the-art projection system that casts a heavenly star show, programs about black holes and other astronomical mysteries, and evening laser light shows with rock music. The Skyline Room Cafeteria offers good food and skyline views.

NEW ENGLAND SPORTS MUSEUM

Map pp300-1
☎ 617-624-1234; www.sportsmuseum.org; Banknorth Garden; adult/child $6/4; ◷ 11am-2pm game days, 11am-3pm non-game days; ⓡ North Station
Nobody can say that Bostonians are not passionate about their sports teams. The

LETTING OFF STEAM

The steaming kettle on the Sears Crescent has been a Boston landmark since 1873, when it was hung over the door of the Oriental Tea Co at 57 Court St. The teashop held a contest to determine how much tea the giant kettle might hold. The answer – awarded with a chest of premium tea – was 227 gallons, two quarts, one pint and three gills.

The tea kettle was relocated to its current location on the western tip of the Sears Crescent building in 1967, when 'urban renewal' swept this neighborhood. Tea drinkers are grateful that this icon of old Boston was saved; although they are miffed that it now marks the spot of a Starbucks.

New England Sports Museum is not the best place to witness this deep-rooted devotion (that would be Fenway Park), but sports fans might enjoy the tribute to the retired numbers of the Boston Celtics or the dramatic stories of Red Sox Century. Unfortunately, the exhibits are strong on photographs and jerseys and not much else, though they do cover all of the major professional sports. The highlight is the penalty box from the old Boston Garden.

This museum is actually in the concourse area of the Garden's box seats. The good news is that if you go on a game day, you may see the Celtics or the Bruins warming up. The bad news is that it often closes for special events at the Garden; and even when it is open, admission is only at designated times (call to confirm).

OTIS HOUSE MUSEUM Map pp300-1
☎ 617-227-3956; www.historicnewengland.org; 141 Cambridge St; adult/senior/child $8/7/4; ⏰ 11am-5pm Wed-Sun; 🚇 Charles/MGH
The stern, Federal brick building stands in stark contrast to the modern development all around it. It was the first of three houses designed by Charles Bulfinch for Mr Harrison Gray Otis at the end of the 18th century. A real estate developer, congressman and mayor of Boston, Otis and his wife Sally were renowned entertainers who hosted many lavish parties here. Since then, the house has had quite a history, serving as a women's bath and rooming house. These days, it is the headquarters of Historic New England, a preservation society that has recreated the interior of the Otis' day.

NORTH END

Eating p139, Shopping p210, Sleeping p229
Despite the ongoing process of physically reconnecting the North End to the rest of the city, this Old World enclave is still a continent and a century away. Italian immigrants and their descendents have held court in this warren of narrow, winding streets and alleys since the 1920s. Old-timers carry on passionate discussions in Italian and play bocce in the parks. Others complete their ritual shopping at specialty stores selling fresh flowers, handmade pasta, cannoli or *biscotti* and fresh baked bread. (For a food-lover's tour of the North End, see p130.)

BOSTON FOR CHILDREN

Boston is one giant history museum, the setting for many educational and lively field trips. Cobblestone streets and costume-clad tour guides can bring to life the events that kids read about in history books. Hands-on experimentation and interactive exhibits fuse education and entertainment. Here is the rundown of Boston's top spots for kids.

Boston Tea Party Ship & Museum (p93) What's more fun than dumping bales of tea overboard?

Children's Museum (p94) Hours of fun climbing, constructing and creating. Especially good for kids aged three to eight years.

Duck Tours (p72) Kids of all ages are invited to drive the duck on the raging waters of the Charles River. Bonus: quacking loudly is encouraged.

Franklin Park Zoo (p114) Visit the Serengeti Plain, the Australian Outback and the Amazonian Rain Forest all in one afternoon.

Freedom Trail (p106) Download a scavenger hunt or a reading list for your child before setting out. Also consider 'Boston by Little Feet,' a walking tour designed especially for children. For more information, see Boston by Foot on p73.

Massachusetts State House (p76) Check out the Kids' Zone on the website. It features word games, trivia quizzes and the priceless Ladybug Story, a story of how a group of kids used the legislative process to make the ladybug the official bug of Massachusetts.

Museum of Fine Arts (p103) Offers loads of programs for kids of all ages. For example, Family Place (⏰ Tue & Thu) teaches children over age four to use art, music and poetry to explore the gallery's collections. Different series of Saturday classes target kids and teens.

Museum of Science (opposite) More opportunities to combine fun and learning than anywhere in the city.

New England Aquarium (p91) Explore the most exotic of natural environments… under the sea.

Paul Revere House (p83) 'Just for Kids' allows children to learn about the Revere family kitchen (including a recipe for a colonial snack), play old-fashioned games, read age-specific articles and complete a crossword puzzle about the historic house.

Prudential Center Skywalk (p100) Assuming your kids are not afraid of heights. A special audio tour caters to little ones.

Stella Bella (p223) Boston's favorite toy store; playing is encouraged.

While it's always active, the North End really comes to life on weekends in the summer, when various saints' days are celebrated with dedicated festivals (see below).

The North End was not always Boston's Little Italy. Prior to the revolution, the North End was a fashionable Tory community. When the Loyalists decamped for Nova Scotia, free blacks settled around Copp's Hill, calling the area 'New Guinea.' They relocated to Beacon Hill in search of better employment opportunities, and successive waves of Irish, Eastern European Jews, Portuguese and Italians settled here and opened small businesses throughout the 19th and early 20th centuries.

These days, the North End's Italian flavor is the strongest, but the neighborhood's rich history is not forgotten. The events of the fateful night of April 18, 1775 – Paul Revere's famous ride – were kick ed off right here. Follow the Freedom Trail past his house to the storied Old North Church. Then follow up with a heaping plate of pasta or a cappuccino and a cannoli, and you'll have a pretty good sense of what the North End is all about.

Orientation

In the northeast corner of the city, the North End occupies a peninsula which juts out into Boston Harbor. The main drag is Hanover St, which starts at Congress St, crosses the highway (now underground) and traverses the entire length of the North End. Salem St runs parallel, just west of

---

TRANSPORTATION

Subway For easy access to the North End, get off at Haymarket T station, a stop on both the green and orange lines.

Hanover St, as far as the Old North Church. The area is encircled by Commercial St (also called Atlantic Ave) on the waterfront.

COPP'S HILL BURYING GROUND
Map pp300-1
Hull St; ⓣ **Haymarket**
The city's second-oldest cemetery – dating to 1660 – is named for William Copp, who originally owned this land. The oldest graves here belong to his children. An estimated 10,000 souls occupy this small plot of land, including more than 1000 free blacks, many of whom lived in the North End. Near the Charter St gate you'll find the graves of the Mather family – Increase, Cotton and Samuel – all of whom were politically powerful religious leaders in the black community.

Find the grave of Daniel Malcolm, whose headstone commemorates his rebel activism. British soldiers apparently took offense at this claim and used the headstone for target practice.

Across the street, 44 Hull St is Boston's narrowest house, measuring a whopping 9½ft wide. The c 1800 house was reportedly built out of spite to block light from the neighbor's house and to obliterate the view of the house behind it.

OLD NORTH CHURCH Map pp300-1
☎ 617-523-6676; www.oldnorth.com; 193 Salem St; ⏰ 9am-6pm Mon-Fri, 9am-5pm Sat & Sun, services 9am & 11am Sun; ⓣ Haymarket
On the night of April 18, 1775, the sexton hung two lanterns from this steeple as a signal that the British would march on Lexington and Concord via the sea route.

Also called Christ Church, this 1723 place of worship is Boston's oldest church. Many of the tall pew boxes bear the brass nameplates of early parishioners who had to purchase their pews. The brass chandeliers used today were first lit on Christmas in 1724. Note the candles – there is no electric lighting in the church. This remains an active church; the grand organ is played at the 11am Sunday service.

ITALIAN FESTIVALS

In July and August, the North End takes on a celebratory air, as old-timer Italians host festivals to honor their patron saints. The streets fill with local residents listening to music, playing games and – of course – eating. The highlight of every festival is the saint's parade, which features local marching bands and social clubs and the star participant, a statue of the patron saint. The lifesize likeness is hoisted onto a wooden platform and carried through the streets, while residents cheer and toss confetti. Banners stream behind the statue so that believers can pin on their dollar bills, thus earning the protection of the saint's watchful eye. While the saints' festivals occur throughout the summer, the biggest events are the Fisherman's Feast and St Anthony's Feast, both in late August (see p15).

The 175ft steeple houses the oldest bells (1744) still rung in the US. Today's steeple is a 1954 replica, since severe weather toppled two prior ones, but the 1740 weather vane is original. Behind the church, several hidden brick courtyards offer quiet respite for a moment of peaceful meditation.

In summer and autumn, Old North hosts a weekly show called Paul Revere Tonight (adult/child $12/8). A costumed actor portrays the midnight rider in this engaging reenactment.

PAUL REVERE HOUSE Map pp300-1
☎ 617-523-1676; www.paulreverehouse.org; 19 North Sq; adult/senior & student/child $3/2.50/1; ☼ 9am-5:15pm mid-Apr–Oct, 9:30am-4:15pm Nov–mid-Apr, closed Mon Jan-Mar; 🚇 Haymarket
When silversmith Paul Revere rode to warn patriots of the British march to Lexington and Concord, he set out from his home on North Sq. This small clapboard house was built in 1680, making it the oldest house in Boston. The structure actually violated building codes of the day, which – in the wake of the fire of 1676 – required brick construction. Nonetheless, the house survived and has now been restored to its 17th-century appearance.

A self-guided tour through the house and courtyard gives a glimpse of what life was like for the Revere family (which included 16 children!). Also on display are some examples of his silversmithing and engraving talents, as well as an impressive bell that was forged in his foundry. A joint ticket with entry to the Old State House and the Old South Meeting House is $11.

The adjacent **Pierce-Hichborn House**, built in 1710, is a fine example of an English Renaissance brick house. It is also maintained by the Paul Revere Memorial Association, but you can visit it by guided tour (appointment only).

NOT SO SLOW

For years Boston was a leader in the production and export of rum, made from West Indian sugar cane. Near water's edge in the North End stood a storage tank for the Purity Distilling Company. On a January morning in 1919, the large tank, filled to the brim with brown molasses, suddenly began shuddering and rumbling as its bindings came undone.

The pressure caused the tank to explode, spewing two million gallons of molasses into the city like a volcano. The sweet explosion leveled surrounding tenements, knocked buildings off their foundations and wiped out a loaded freight train. Panic-stricken, man and beast fled the deadly ooze. A molasses wave surged down the streets drowning all in its sticky path. The Great Molasses Flood killed a dozen horses, 21 people and injured more than 100. The clean up lasted nearly six months.

CHARLESTOWN
Eating p141, Sleeping p229
The Charlestown Navy Yard was a thriving ship-building center throughout the 19th century. Although the navy yard was closed in 1974, the surrounding neighborhood has been making a comeback ever since. The impressive granite buildings have been transformed into shops, condos and offices, which enjoy a panoramic view of Boston. The narrow streets immediately surrounding Monument Sq are lined with restored 19th-century Federal and colonial houses, and Main St has a handful of trendy restaurants. However, a short stroll away from this center – four or five blocks in any direction – reveals that Charlestown has not strayed too far from its grittier, working-class roots.

Charlestown was settled the year before Boston and, in 1630 acted as the seat of government. This area saw some of the most atrocious fighting of the revolution during the bloody Battle of Bunker Hill. Indeed, the town was completely destroyed by the British during the revolution. Townspeople rebuilt quickly, however, and today most houses date from the early 19th century. The c 1780 Warren Tavern was one of the first buildings constructed

Paul Revere House (above)

after the town was burned (see right). Two centuries later, it's still a fine place for a drink. Charlestown was incorporated into Boston in 1873, but has always retained its own character.

Orientation

While technically part of Boston, Charlestown remains apart, both geographically and atmospherically. On the north shore of the Charles River, it is connected to the North End by the old Charlestown Bridge. A few restaurants are clustered around City Sq, while the bulk of business establishments line Main St, which runs north from here. Constitution Rd runs along the waterfront to the Navy Yard, where the USS *Constitution* is docked.

TRANSPORTATION

Subway From the North End or the orange/green-line North Station, you can walk across the Charlestown Bridge in about 15 minutes. Alternatively, ferries and water taxis travel from the Navy Yard to Long Wharf and Lovejoy Wharf (see p266).

BUNKER HILL MONUMENT

Map p304

☎ 617-242-5641; www.nps.gov/bost; Monument Sq; admission free; ☽ 9am-4:30pm, to 5pm Jul & Aug; ☒ North Station

'Don't fire until you see the whites of their eyes!' came the order from Colonel Prescott to revolutionary troops on June 17, 1775. Considering the ill preparedness of the revolutionary soldiers, the bloody battle that followed resulted in a surprising number of British casualties. Ultimately, however, the Redcoats prevailed (an oft-overlooked fact).

The so-called Battle of Bunker Hill is ironically named, as most of the fighting took place on Breed's Hill, where the Bunker Hill Monument stands today. The 200ft granite obelisk rewards physically fit visitors with fine views at the top of its 294 steps. The adjacent museum contains historical dioramas depicting the battle, and NPS park rangers give summer talks and musket-firing demonstrations. A reenactment of the battle takes place every June on Monument Sq.

BUNKER HILL PAVILION

Map p304

☎ 617-241-7575; www.nps.gov/bost; Charleston Navy Yard Visitor's Center, Constitution Rd; admission free; ☽ 9am-5pm Apr-Nov, 9am-6pm Jun-Aug; ☒ North Station

The pavilion provides an introduction to both the Navy Yard and Bunker Hill Monument. The 18-minute multimedia presentation, *The Whites of Their Eyes*, is screened every 30 minutes from 9:30am to 4:30pm (adult/senior/child $4/3/2) and uses music, slides and mannequins (in costume) to reenact the battle. The name, of course, comes from Colonel Prescott's famous command (see left).

CHARLESTOWN LOCKS

Map p304

Immediately west of the Charlestown Bridge, the dam and locks control the water levels between the Charles River Basin and Inner Harbor. In summer, upwards of 1000 pleasure boats and an inestimable number of fish pass through daily. Here, the Charles River shoreline is hidden, severed from the rest of the city by industry. Part of the HarborWalk, the adjacent Paul Revere Park is a link in an ongoing plan for 7 miles of recreational pathways.

WARREN TAVERN

Eliphelet Newell was an ardent supporter of the revolutionary cause and a supposed participant in the Boston Tea Party. When the War for Independence was over, he opened a tavern and named it after his dear friend General Joseph Warren. Although Warren had died in the Battle of Bunker Hill, he had been an active member of the Sons of Liberty and a respected leader of the revolution. Indeed, the Prime Minister of Great Britain described him as 'the greatest incendiary in North America.'

So when the Warren Tavern was opened in 1780 it quickly became a popular meeting place, especially among admirers of General Warren. Over the years, Paul Revere was a regular visitor and even George Washington stopped by for a visit when he was in town. Nowadays, locals still love to gather here to drink a few pints and engage in debates (perhaps not the heady discussions of building a new nation, but important stuff nonetheless). See p141 for details.

OLD IRONSIDES

'Her sides are made of iron!' So cried a crewman as he watched a shot bounce off the thick oak hull of the USS *Constitution* during the War of 1812. This bit of irony earned the legendary ship her nickname. Indeed, she won no less than three battles during that war, and she never went down in a battle. For her last mission in 1853 she seized an American slave ship off the coast of Africa.

The **USS Constitution** (☎ 617-242-2543; www.ussconstitution.navy.mil; Charlestown Navy Yard; admission free; ☺ 10am-6pm Tue-Sun Apr-Oct, 10am-4pm Thu-Sun Nov-Mar; ☒ North Station) is still the oldest commissioned US Navy ship, dating to 1797, and she is taken out onto Boston Harbor every July 4th in order to maintain her commissioned status. She has been moored here since 1897, when Congressman John F 'Honey Fitz' Fitzgerald introduced a bill to make Massachusetts her permanent residence.

Navy personnel give 30-minute guided tours of the top deck, gun deck and cramped quarters (last tour 3:30pm). You can also wander around the top deck by yourself, but access is limited. Plus, you won't learn all the USS *Constitution* fun facts, like how the captain's son died on her maiden voyage (an inauspicious start).

CHARLESTOWN NAVY YARD
Map p304

☎ 617-242-5601; www.nps.gov/bost; admission free; ☒ North Station

Besides the historic ships docked here and the museum dedicated to them, the Charlestown Navy Yard is a living monument to its own history of shipbuilding and naval command. The only other building open to the public is the old Paint Shop, which houses a collection of artifacts. But you can wander around the dry docks and see how the ships were repaired while resting on wooden blocks. The oldest building in the yard is the imposing Federal-style Commandant's House, dating to 1805. Other interesting buildings on the grounds include the 1000ft-long Ropewalk, where all the Navy's rope was made for 135 years. Next door, in the forge shop, metal workers hammered out 'die-lock' chains which eventually put the ropemakers out of business.

GREAT HOUSE SITE Map p304

City Sq; ☺ dawn-dusk; ☒ North Station

A sweet oasis in the midst of Charlestown, City Sq is also an archaeological site. Recent Central Artery construction unearthed the foundation for a structure called the Great House, widely believed to be John Winthrop's house and the seat of government in 1630. Winthrop soon moved across the Charles to the Shawmut Peninsula, and the Great House became the Three Cranes Tavern, as documented in 1635. Informative dioramas demonstrate the remains of the kitchen, the main hall and the wine cellar.

The shady, brick plaza north of here is John Harvard Mall, which leads up Town Hill. Back in the days of the earliest settlements, a fort crowned Town Hill, as you can read on the bronze plaques along the mall. Before the local minister – one John Harvard – died of consumption, he donated half his £800 estate and all 300 of his books to a young Cambridge college, which saw fit to name its school after him.

USS CASSIN YOUNG Map p304

☎ 617-242-5601; Charlestown Navy Yard; ☺ 10am-4pm, tours 11am, 2pm & 3pm; ☒ North Station

This 376ft WWII destroyer is one of 14 Fletcher-class destroyers built at the Charlestown Navy Yard. These are the Navy's fastest, most versatile ships. *Cassin Young* participated in the 1944 Battle of Leyte Gulf, as well as the 1945 invasion of Okinawa. Here, the ship sustained two kamikaze hits, leaving 23 crew members dead and many more wounded. These days she has been completely refurbished, as you can see during a free, 45-minute tour, or if you choose to wander around the main deck on your own.

USS CONSTITUTION MUSEUM Map p304

☎ 617-426-1812; First Ave, Charlestown Navy Yard; admission free; ☺ 9am-6pm May–mid-Oct, 10am-5pm mid-Oct–Apr; ☒ North Station

For a play-by-play of the USS *Constitution's* various battles, as well as her current role as the flagship of the US Navy, head indoors to the museum. More interesting is the exhibit on the Barbary War, which explains the birth of the US Navy during this relatively unknown conflict – America's first war at sea. Upstairs, kids can experience what it was like to be a sailor on the USS *Constitution* in 1812.

DOWNTOWN

Eating p142, Shopping p212, Sleeping p230

It's hard to tell that this area was once the domain of cows. The well-trodden 17th-century paths eventually gave rise to the maze of streets occupied by today's high rises. But the remnants of colonial architecture are vivid reminders that this is where Boston grew up. Most prominently, the Old State House – now dwarfed by surrounding skyscrapers – stands at the head of State St (formerly King St). See the boxed text on opposite for more colonial relics.

Although such vestiges of 17th-century Boston are not uncommon in this part of town, the atmosphere of these streets is hardly historic. Downtown is a bustling commercial center, its streets lined with department stores and smaller shops. Since 1912, Downtown Crossing was anchored by the big department store Filene's. Sadly, the Boston-based Filene's closed this flagship store in 2006, leaving little trace except a plaque on its former edifice. While the building is unlikely to remain empty for long, sentimental types lament the end of an era with the passing of this Boston institution.

But shoppers keep shopping, now patronizing Macy's instead of Filene's, or any number of sports stores, music stores, bookstores, etc. The surrounding skyscrapers, especially in the Financial District, are occupied by Boston's insurance companies, investment funds and law firms – suit-and-tie types that keep the business world ticking. Luxury hotels cater mainly to business travelers. White-collar professionals take quick lunch breaks at speedy sandwich shops, but frequent the many fine dining establishments when expense accounts kick in.

The Freedom Trail cuts through Downtown, highlighting the historic spots from the 17th and 18th centuries. But this neighborhood is all about commerce in the 21st century; and you won't need to follow the red-brick road to find it.

Orientation

Downtown is bound by Boylston, Tremont and State Sts, with the Central Artery (soon to be the Rose Kennedy Greenway) forming the eastern frontier; it includes Downtown Crossing (sometimes called the Ladder District) and the Financial District.

TRANSPORTATION

Subway If you are headed Downtown, there is definitely a T stop near your destination. The most central is Downtown Crossing, on the red and orange lines. State T station is also convenient, on the orange and blue lines. Along Tremont St on the western edge of this district, you'll find Boston's oldest subway stops: Park St (red and green lines) and Boylston (green line).

Downtown Crossing, the pedestrian-only shopping district near the intersection of Washington, Summer and Winter Sts, bustles with pushcart vendors and street musicians. Just west of here is the focal point of the city, the Boston Common, and a host of historic sights heading north along Tremont St. The Financial District lies east of Congress St and stretches all the way to the waterfront. Bounded by State St to the north and Purchase St to the south, this is the land of the daily grind, with little to offer travelers, save some nice hotels and restaurants.

BOSTON MASSACRE SITE Map pp302-3

cnr State & Washington Sts; Ⓣ State

Encircled by cobblestones, the Boston Massacre site marks the spot where the first blood was shed for the American independence movement. On March 5, 1770, an angry mob of colonists swarmed the British soldiers guarding the State House. Sam Adams, John Hancock and about 40 other protesters hurled snowballs, rocks and insults. Thus provoked, the soldiers fired into the crowd and killed five townspeople, including Crispus Attucks, a former slave.

The incident sparked enormous anti-British sentiment. Paul Revere helped fan the flames by widely disseminating an engraving that depicted the scene as an unmitigated slaughter (an original print is on display inside the Old State House, p88). Interestingly, John Adams and Josiah Quincy – both of whom opposed the heavy-handed authoritarian British rule – defended the accused soldiers in court, and seven of the nine were acquitted.

CUSTOM HOUSE Map pp302-3

☎ 617-310-6300; www.marriott.com; 3 McKinley Sq; admission free; Ⓣ Aquarium

Begun in 1837, the lower portion of the Custom House resembles a Greek temple.

But the federal government decided something grander was in order; so in 1913 it exempted itself from local height restrictions and financed a 500ft tower. Thus Boston's first skyscraper was born. At first Bostonians were aghast, but they have since grown to love it. The 22ft illuminated clock makes this gem the most recognizable structure of the city skyline.

The old Custom House now contains a Marriott hotel (see p231). But that doesn't mean you have to dole out big bucks to stay here to appreciate the building's history and aesthetics. The 1st-floor rotunda is a work of art in itself; it also houses a small exhibit of maritime art and artifacts from the **Peabody Essex Museum** (see p251). Even better, the public is welcome to enjoy the spectacular views from the 26th-floor **observation deck** (admission free; 🕙 10am & 4pm).

KING'S CHAPEL & BURYING GROUND
Map pp302-3

☎ 617-227-2155; www.kings-chapel.org; 58 Tremont St; suggested donation $1, self-guided tour $1; 🕙 10am-4pm Mon-Sat, 1:30-4pm Sun Jun-Aug, 10am-4pm Sat Sep-May, services 11am & 12:15pm Sun year-round; 🚇 Park or State

Bostonians were not pleased when the original Anglican church was erected on this site in 1688. (Remember, it was the Anglicans – the Church of England – whom the Puritans were fleeing.) The granite chapel standing today was built in 1754. If the church seems to be missing something, it is: funds ran out before a spire could be added. The church houses the largest bell

ever made by Paul Revere, as well as a historic organ. Note the prestigious Governor's pew, once occupied by George Washington who came to hear a concert.

After the revolution, King's Chapel became the first Unitarian church in America, and today it is an independent Christian church. Besides the bi-weekly services, recitals are held here every week (Tuesday at 12:15pm, $3).

The adjacent burying ground is the oldest in the city. The church was built on a corner of the city cemetery because the Puritans refused to allow the Anglicans to use any other land. As a result, these are some of the city's oldest headstones, including one that dates to 1623. Famous graves include John Winthrop, the first governor of the fledgling Massachusetts Bay Colony; William Dawes, who rode with Paul Revere; Elizabeth Pain, the model for Hawthorne's Hester Prynne in *The Scarlet Letter*; and Mary Chilton, the first woman to set foot in Plymouth.

OLD CITY HALL Map pp302-3

☎ 617-523-8678; www.oldcityhall.com; 45 School St; 🚇 State

This monumental French Second Empire building is now office space with one fancy restaurant, but this site has seen its share of history. Out front, a plaque commemorates the site of the first public school, Boston Latin, founded in 1635 and still operational in Fenway. The hopscotch sidewalk mosaic, *City Carpet*, marks the spot where Benjamin Franklin, Ralph Waldo Emerson and Charles Bulfinch were educated.

COLONIAL RELICS

History is everywhere in Boston. If you don't believe it, here are a few colonial relics that you might otherwise miss.

1712 Ebenezer Clough House (Mapp300–1; 21 Unity St) Behind the Paul Revere Mall in the North End. Ebenezer Clough, a Sons of Liberty member who participated in the Boston Tea Party, was a mason who worked on the adjacent Old North Church.

Blackstone Block (see p89) Boston's oldest block. These brick buildings clustered around cobblestone streets date to the 18th century.

Great House Site (p85) Okay, it's more of a ruin than a relic, but that's what's left from the earliest seat of government.

Province House Steps (Mapp302–3; cnr Province & Bosworth Sts) An innocuous set of steps is all that remains from the 17th-century royal governor's mansion. From here, General Gage ordered the Redcoats to Concord.

Tory Row (Map310; Brattle St, Cambridge) West of Harvard Sq, this mansion-lined street was a bastion of British sympathizers in the 18th century.

Statues of Benjamin Franklin, founding father, and Josiah Quincy, second mayor of Boston, stand inside the courtyard. They are accompanied by a lifesize replica of a donkey, symbol of the Democratic Party. ('Why the donkey?' you wonder. Read the plaque to find out.) Two bronze footprints 'stand in opposition.'

OLD CORNER BOOKSTORE

Map pp302-3

cnr School & Washington Sts; 🚇 Downtown Crossing

Built in 1718, this little brick building was originally a pharmacy and residence. In the 19th century, the house was leased to a bookseller, Carter & Hendlee. This was the first of nine bookshops and publishing companies that would occupy this spot, making it a breeding ground for literary and philosophic ideas. The most illustrious was Ticknor & Fields, publisher of books by Thoreau, Emerson, Hawthorne, Longfellow and Harriet Beecher Stowe. Today, the storefront houses a jewelry shop, which seems somewhat less lofty.

OLD SOUTH MEETING HOUSE

Map pp302-3

☎ 617-482-6439; www.oldsouthmeetinghouse .org; 310 Washington St; adult/senior & student/ child $5/4/1; 🕒 9:30am-5pm Apr-Oct, 10am-4pm Nov-Mar; 🚇 Downtown Crossing or State

'No tax on tea!' That was the decision on December 16, 1773, when 5000 angry colonists gathered here to protest British taxes, leading to the Boston Tea Party (see p93). This brick meeting house, with its soaring steeple, was also used as a church house. In fact Ben Franklin was baptized here. Which is why he found it so abhorrent when – after the Tea Party – British soldiers used the building for a stable and riding practice.

The Old South congregation moved to a new building in Back Bay in 1875 (see p97), when Ralph Waldo Emerson and Julia Ward Howe gathered support to convert the church into a museum. The graceful meeting house is still a gathering place for discussion, although not as much rabble-rousing goes on here anymore. Instead, the meeting house hosts concert and lecture series, as well as reenactments and other historical programs. When you visit, you can listen to an audio of the historic pre-Tea Party meeting. The Freedom Trail ticket, including the Old State House and the Paul Revere House, is $11.

OLD STATE HOUSE

Map pp302-3

☎ 617-720-3290; www.bostonhistory.org; 206 Washington St; adult/senior & student/child $5/4/1; 🕒 9am-5pm, to 4pm Jan, to 6pm Jul & Aug; 🚇 State

Dating to 1713, the Old State House is Boston's oldest surviving public building. It's where the Massachusetts Assembly used to debate the issues of the day. It occupies a once prominent spot at the top of State St (then known as King St), which was Boston's main thoroughfare. The building is best known for its balcony, where the Declaration of Independence was first read to Bostonians in 1776. The rooftop is graced with lions and unicorns, which were symbols of the British crown. These are replicas, as the originals were torn down in a fit of patriotism after the reading of the Declaration.

Operated by the Bostonian Society, the museum depicts Boston's role in the Revolutionary War, including videos on the history of the Old State House and the Boston Massacre (see p86). Their Freedom Trail ticket, including the Old South Meeting House and the Paul Revere House, is also $11.

'WATSON, COME HERE! I NEED YOU!'

Dr Alexander Graham Bell muttered these famous words when he made his first successful telephone call in his attic office on Scollay Sq. When the building was demolished in the 1920s, the wood, windows and equipment from the laboratory were carefully preserved. Which explains how you can now see the **birthplace of the telephone** (185 Franklin St; admission free; 🕒 8am-6pm; 🚇 Downtown Crossing) in the lobby of the Verizon Building on Post Office Sq. The laboratory is apparently historically accurate, down to the view that Bell would have had from his window. Architects consulted old maps and building drawings, while historians referred to Bell's patent testimonies and Watson's memoirs. Other telephone memorabilia is also on display, including the first telephone switchboard and the first commercial telephone.

WATERFRONT

Eating p143, Shopping p213, Sleeping p231

Back in the day, Boston's Waterfront was the focal point of activity in this mercantile center, as ships sailed in from Europe, the Caribbean and the Far East, laden with coffee, tea, sugarcane and spices. Fishermen docked their boats here, after spending the day hauling in lobsters, mackerel and cod.

Many points around the Boston Harbor still employ a working waterfront, especially in East Boston and the Seaport District. Here in downtown Boston, however, the Waterfront caters to tourists. Now the wharves are the docking place for passenger ferries and water taxis; the old warehouses have been converted into hotels; and the only fish are swimming around the New England Aquarium (p91) or sitting on somebody's plate in Legal Seafood (p144).

In recent years, the Waterfront has been transformed by the completion of the Big Dig. The dismantling of the Central Artery means that the call of seagulls and the lapping of waves no longer competes with the roar of the cars. It also means that this previously inaccessible area has been reconnected to the city, making it easy for pedestrians to wander from Quincy Market to Long Wharf and on to the Seaport District. And now, a public path, officially designated the HarborWalk, runs along the outer edge of the wharves from Columbus Park to the new Moakley Federal Courthouse and beyond (see p198).

While the Waterfront is often packed with tourists, several spots offer a sweet retreat. In Columbus Park, just north of Long Wharf, a cobblestone walkway winds through a trellised archway draped with wisteria, creating a shady spot to watch the sailboats moored in the harbor. At the southern end of the Waterfront, Rowes Wharf has plenty of waterside seating – perfect for sipping cocktails and recovering from too much sightseeing. For the ultimate escape from the city, hop on a ferry and go out to sea – specifically to one of the Boston Harbor Islands for a day of berry picking, beachcombing or sunbathing.

Orientation

East of Atlantic Ave, the Waterfront becomes more accessible with each passing year. From Christopher Columbus Park in

TRANSPORTATION

Subway The most useful T station for the Waterfront is the blue-line Aquarium, though Haymarket (green/orange line) and Government Center (blue/green line) are also convenient to Faneuil Hall. From Long Wharf, water taxis run to the Charlestown Navy Yard, the Harbor Islands and other destinations around the city, while airport water taxis runs from both Long Wharf and Rowes Wharf.

the north to South Station in the south, Boston's Waterfront consists a series of wharves, home to seafood restaurants and sightseeing cruises, as well as the New England Aquarium (p91). Rowes Wharf and Long Wharf also house ferry docks, where you can catch the ferry out to the Boston Harbor Islands. For the purposes of this book, the Waterfront also includes the area immediately around Faneuil Hall and Quincy Market, at the northern end of this stretch, as well as the Harbor Islands.

FANEUIL HALL & QUINCY MARKET AREA

Historic Faneuil Hall, as well as the three long granite buildings that make up Quincy Market, served as the center of the city's produce and meat industry for almost 150 years. In the 1970s, the old buildings were redeveloped into today's touristy, festive shopping and eating center, so it still serves its original purpose, albeit with all the modern trappings.

BLACKSTONE BLOCK Map pp302-3

cnr Union & Hanover Sts; 🚇 Haymarket or Government Center

Stepping off the T at Government Center, you emerge from the underground onto a vast plaza of cement and concrete. Mammoth, modern buildings surround you on all sides. You dodge the traffic to cross Congress St. Suddenly you find yourself on a quaint, cobblestone street, lined with brick row houses with paned windows and flower boxes. The traffic noise fades and instead you hear the cry of farmers hawking their produce at the open air market (see p134).

This is Blackstone Block, bounded by Union, Hanover, Blackstone and North Sts and named after Boston's first settler.

New England Aquarium (opposite)

Sights

WATERFRONT

This tiny warren of streets dates back to the 17th and 18th centuries. Established in 1826, the **Union Oyster House** (p144) is Boston's oldest restaurant. Around the corner in Creek Sq, the c 1767 **Ebenezer Hancock House** (10 Marshall St) was the home of John Hancock's brother. At the base of the shop next door, the 1737 **Boston Stone** served as the terminus for measuring distances to and from 'the Hub.' (The State House dome now serves this purpose.)

FANEUIL HALL Map pp302-3

☎ 617-242-5642; www.faneuilhall.com; Congress & North Sts; admission free; ⏱ 9am-5pm; ⎘ Haymarket or Aquarium

Faneuil Hall – a brick colonial building topped with the beloved grasshopper weather vane – was constructed as a market and public meeting place in 1740, at the urging of Boston benefactor and merchant Peter Faneuil. In 1805, Charles Bulfinch enlarged the building and enclosed the 1st-floor market, designing the 2nd-floor meeting space that's here today.

Although the hall was supposed to be exclusively for local issues, the Sons of Liberty called many meetings here, informing public opinion about their objections to British taxation without representation, thus earning Faneuil Hall its nickname, the 'Cradle of Liberty.' In December of 1773, meetings concerning the controversial consignment of tea that had recently arrived in Boston Harbor were drawing so many townspeople that they had to move to the larger Old South Meeting House (p88).

Public meetings and ceremonies are still held on the 2nd floor. It's normally open to the public, who can hear about the building's history from NPS rangers. On the 3rd floor, the **Ancient & Honorable Artillery Co of Massachusetts** (☎ 617-227-1638; ⏱ 9am-3:30pm), which was chartered in 1638, maintains a peculiar collection of antique firearms, political mementos and curious artifacts.

NEW ENGLAND HOLOCAUST MEMORIAL Map pp302-3

☎ 617-457-0755; btwn Union & Congress Sts; ⎘ Haymarket

The six luminescent glass columns of the New England Holocaust Memorial were constructed in 1995. The towers are engraved with six million numbers, representing those killed in the Holocaust. Each tower – with smoldering coals sending plumes of steam up through the glass corridors – represents a different Nazi death camp. The memorial sits along the Freedom Trail, a sobering reminder of its larger meaning.

WATERFRONT

Long gone are the days when sailing ships brought exotic spices, tea and coffee into these docks. While some remnants of this maritime trade are still visible in the architecture (especially on Long Wharf), the Waterfront is now a center for a new industry: tourism. Tourists and residents stroll the HarborWalk (p198), ferries shuttle visitors between historic sights and alfresco diners enjoy the breeze off the harbor.

NEW ENGLAND AQUARIUM Map pp302-3

☎ 617-973-5200; www.neaq.org; Central Wharf;
adult/child $18/10; ☣ 9am-6pm Mon-Thu, 9am-
7pm Fri-Sun; ☒ Aquarium

Teeming with sea creatures of all sizes,
shapes and colors, this giant fishbowl was
the first step Boston took to reconnect the
city to the sea. Harbor seals and sea otters
frolic in a large observation tank at the
entrance, but the main attraction is a three-
story, cylindrical saltwater tank. It swirls with
more than 600 creatures great and small, including turtles, sharks and eels. At the base
of the tank, the penguin pool is home to
three species of fun-loving penguins. Countless side exhibits explore the lives and habi-
tats of other underwater oddities, including
exhibits on ethereal jellyfish and rare, exotic
sea dragons. Daily programs include tank
dives, penguin presentations, harbor seal
training exhibits and puppet shows.

The 3-D IMAX theater (adult/child $10/8;
☣ 10am-10pm) features films with aquatic
themes. The aquarium also organizes
whale-watching cruises (adult/child $32/26;
☣ 9:30am or 10am & 1:30 or 2pm May-
Oct). Combination tickets are also available.

HARBOR ISLANDS

Boston Harbor is sprinkled with 34 islands,
many of which are open for trail walking,
bird-watching, fishing and swimming. The
Boston Harbor Islands (☎ 617-223-8666; www
.bostonislands.org; admission free) offer
a range of ecosystems – sandy beaches,
rocky cliffs, fresh and saltwater marsh
and forested trails – only 45 minutes from
downtown Boston. Since the massive, mul-
timillion-dollar cleanup of Boston Harbor
in the mid-1990s, the islands are one of
the city's most magnificent natural assets.
For information on camping on the islands,
see p203.

TRANSPORTATION

Ferry To get to most of the islands, Harbor Express
(☎ 617-222-6999; 1 Long Wharf, off Atlantic Ave;
round-trip adult/senior/child Mon-Wed $10/7/7,
Thu-Sun $12/9/7; ☣ 9am-5pm mid-Apr–mid-Oct)
offers seasonal ferry service from Long Wharf. Purchase a round-trip ticket to Georges Island or Spectacle Island, where you catch a free water taxi to the
smaller islands.

BUMPKIN ISLAND

☣ 9am-dusk daily mid-Jun–early-Sep, Sat & Sun
only mid-Apr–mid-Jun & early-Sep–mid-Oct

This small island has served many purposes
over the years, first farming then fish dry-
ing and smelting. In 1900 it was the site of
a children's hospital, but it was taken over
for navy training during WWI. You can still
explore the remains of a stone farmhouse
and the hospital. The beaches are not the
best for swimming, as they are slate and
seashell. A network of trails leads through
fields overgrown with wildflowers. One of
three islands with camping facilities (p203).

GEORGES ISLAND

☣ 9am-dusk from mid-Apr–mid-Oct

Georges Island is the transportation hub for
the islands, as the inter-island shuttle leaves
from here. It is also the site of Fort Warren,
a 19th-century fort and Civil War prison.
While NPS rangers give guided tours of the
fort, it is largely abandoned, with many
dark tunnels, creepy corners and magnificent lookouts to discover. The extensive
picnic area attracts large groups of kids,
as do the family programs like children's
theater (Fri) and family fun days (Sat & Sun).
This is one of the only islands with facilities
like a snack bar and rest rooms (most other
islands have outhouses).

GRAPE ISLAND

☣ 9am-dawn daily mid-Jun–early-Sep, Sat & Sun
only mid-Apr–mid-Jun & early-Sep–mid-Oct

Grape Island is rich with fruity goodness –
not grapes, but raspberries, bayberries and
elderberries, all growing wild amid the
scrubby wooded trails. The wild fruit attracts abundant bird life. Park rangers lead
an interesting 'wild edibles' tour highlighting the fruits of the earth. Unlike many of
the Harbor Islands, Grape Island has no
remains of forts or military prisons; but during the Revolutionary War, it was the site of
a skirmish over hay, known as the Battle of
Grape Island.

LITTLE BREWSTER

☎ 617-223-8666; adult/senior/child $28/25/17;
☣ 10am Thu, 10am & 2pm Fri-Sun Jun-Oct

Little Brewster is the country's oldest light
station and site of the iconic Boston Light.
Although the first lighthouse was built on
this spot in 1715, it was demolished by the

British in the revolution; today's lighthouse dates to 1783. To visit Little Brewster, you must take an organized tour (reservations recommended). Learn about Boston's maritime history during a one-hour sail around the harbor, then spend two hours exploring the island. Adventurous travelers can climb the 76 steps to the top of the light for a close-up view of the rotating light and a far-off view of the city skyline. Tours depart from Fan Pier in the Seaport District.

LOVELLS ISLAND

⏰ 9am-dusk daily mid-Jun–early-Sep, Sat & Sun only mid-Apr–mid-Jun & early-Sep–mid-Oct
Two deadly shipwrecks may bode badly for seafarers, but that doesn't seem to stop recreational boaters, swimmers and sunbathers from lounging on Lovells' long rocky beach. Some of the former uses of Lovells are evident: European settlers used the island as a rabbit run, and descendent bunnies are still running this place; Fort Standish dates from WWI but has yet to be excavated. With facilities for camping and picnicking, Lovells is one of the most popular Harbor Island destinations.

PEDDOCKS ISLAND

⏰ 9am-dusk daily mid-Jun–early-Sep, Sat & Sun only mid-Apr–mid-Jun & early-Sep–mid-Oct
One of the largest Harbor Islands, Peddocks consists of four headlands connected by sandbars. Hiking trails wander through marsh, pond and coastal environs. But the dominant feature of Peddocks Island is the remains of Fort Andrews, a large facility with more than 20 buildings. Peddocks' proximity to the mainland ensured its use as a military stronghold, from the Revolutionary War right through WWII. New utilities on Peddocks were being constructed in 2006 so look for an upgrade.

SPECTACLE ISLAND

⏰ dawn-dusk mid-Jun–early-Sep
Recently revamped, Spectacle Island has a brand new marina ($15 to $25 per day), visitors center, snack bar and supervised beaches. Five miles of walking trails provide access to a 157ft peak overlooking the harbor. Special events include live jazz and Dixie music on Sunday afternoons and occasional kite-flying festivals. Spectacle Island is relatively close to the city and a ferry

runs here directly from **Long Wharf** (⏰ 9am-5pm daily, to 6pm Sat & Sun).

THOMPSON ISLAND

☎ 617-328-3900; www.thompsonisland.org;
⏰ noon-5pm Saturday Jun & Aug
Thompson Island was settled as early as 1626 by a Scotsman, David Thompson, who set up a trading post to do business with the Neponset Indians. Today, this island is privately owned and inhabited by Thompson Island Outward Bound, a nonprofit organization that develops fun and challenging physical adventures, especially for training and developing leadership skills. As such, the public can explore its 200-plus acres only on Saturday. A dedicated ferry leaves from EDIC Pier in the Seaport District.

WORLD'S END

☎ 617-780-6665; www.thetrustees.org; 250 Martin's Lane, Hingham; adult/child $4.50/free; ⏰ 8am-dusk year-round
Not exactly an island, this 251-acre peninsula was originally designed by Frederick Law Olmsted for residential development in 1889. Carriage paths were laid out and trees were planted, but the houses were

---

HARBOR ISLANDS IN A DAY

Hop on the first ferry at 9am to Georges Island, where you can spend about two hours exploring Fort Warren. After lunch, take the shuttle to Lovells Island to catch some rays on the otherwise empty beach and cool off in the refreshing Atlantic waters. Spend a few hours on Lovells' rocky shores, but don't miss the afternoon shuttle to Grape Island. Here, you can tag along on the ranger-led 'wild edibles' tour, or find your own stash of wild berries. Take the last shuttle (around 4:30pm) back to Georges Island to catch the ferry to the mainland.

A few tips:

- Only Georges and Spectacle Islands have food and water, so you may want to pack a picnic.
- The inter-island shuttle runs several times a day, but not every hour. Make sure you check the schedule in advance and plan your day accordingly.
- Don't try to visit more than two or three islands in one day: you'll end up spending all your time riding or waiting for boats.

never built. Instead, wide grassy meadows attract butterflies and grass-nesting birds. Over the years, the area escaped proposals for development as a UN headquarters and a nuclear power plant, and today it is managed by the Trustees of Reservations, which guarantees continued serenity and beauty. The four-plus miles of tree-lined carriage paths are perfect for walking, mountain biking or cross-country skiing – download a map from the Trustees website. It is accessible by car from Hingham.

SEAPORT DISTRICT

Eating p144, Sleeping p232

Separated from Boston proper by the jellyfish-laden Fort Point Channel, this area has always afforded spectacular views of downtown Boston. But until recently, it had been neglected by city officials and ignored by developers. Such prime waterside real estate can only go unexploited for so long, however. The Seaport District is now the target of an ambitious development project, as evidenced by the huge convention center, several luxury hotels catering to business traffic and – the centerpiece – the new Institute of Contemporary Arts (ICA) on the water's edge (see p94).

Following the HarborWalk (p198), it's a pleasant stroll across Northern Ave Bridge to the Seaport District. Here, old-school establishments like James Hook & Co Lobsters and the Barking Crab (see p145) are holding their own alongside new development like the Moakley Federal Courthouse.

Once across the Fort Point Channel, the HarborWalk diverges. Walk around the courthouse to enjoy the landscaped parks and fantastic views from Fan Pier, eventually ending up at the ICA. Or head south along the Fort Point Channel to the Children's Museum and the Boston Tea Party Ship. While there is still a disproportionate amount of unused space, this entire area is targeted for condos, parks and shopping malls. Indeed, construction may be underway by the time you are reading this.

The Seaport District is still a funny mix of old and new. Further east, the wharfs are dominated by fish processing plants and a giant marine industrial park. It's worth walking at least as far as the Fish Pier to have lunch at the No Name (p145) and to catch a whiff of what this area used to be.

Orientation

The self-contained Seaport District is bounded by Fort Point Channel in the west and Boston Harbor in the north. The Moakley Federal Courthouse sits on the prominent spot where these two bodies of water intersect, while the World Trade Center and the Fish Pier are other landmarks along the harbor. The Seaport District's southern boundary is approximately Summer St, marked by the massive new Boston Convention Center. Continuing southeast along the HarborWalk, you will traverse the Boston Marine Industrial Park and find yourself in the heart of South Boston (see p120).

TRANSPORTATION

Bus The Seaport District is serviced by the Silver Line, which sounds like the subway but is really the bus. Get on at South Station T station and take it to the Moakley Federal Courthouse, the World Trade Center or the Fish Pier. Incidentally, the Silver Line offers fast access to the airport from Silver Line Way, near the Fish Pier.

Subway Alternatively, you can walk from Aquarium or South Station T stations in about 20 minutes.

BOSTON TEA PARTY SHIP
& MUSEUM Map pp302-3

☎ 617-269-7150; www.bostonteapartyship.com; Congress St Bridge; ⓡ South Station

On the cold night of December 16, 1773, a group of fiery colonists disguised as Mohawk Indians burst from the Old South Meeting House (p88) and headed to Griffin's Wharf, where they clambered aboard the three ships harbored there.

Outraged by the taxes that the British imposed on tea and other imports, the colonists reacted violently. Armed with axes and hatchets, they destroyed 342 crates of British tea, defiantly dumping the precious cargo into the sea. Today, the Boston Tea Party Ship remembers this spirited rebellious act. Artifacts include the Robinson Tea Chest, which was retrieved from the harbor on the morning after the Tea Party.

At the time of research, the museum was closed for rebuilding after suffering extensive fire damage. The new museum, expected to open in summer 2007, will include full-size replicas of the historic tall ships, the *Dartmouth* and the *Eleanor*, in addition to the brig *Beaver*. And no doubt visitors will still be invited to drink their fill of tax-free tea.

CHILDREN'S MUSEUM Map pp302-3
☎ 617-426-8855; www.bostonchildrensmuseum
.org; 300 Congress St; adult/senior/child/infant
$9/7/7/1, Fri evenings $1; ⏰ 10am-5pm Sat-Thu,
10am-9pm Fri; 🚇 South Station

The interactive, educational exhibits at the delightful Children's Museum keep kids entertained for hours. Highlights include a bubble exhibit, a two-story climbing maze, a rock-climbing wall, a hands-on construction site and intercultural immersion experiences. In 2006, the museum underwent major expansion, with the addition of a new light-filled atrium featuring an amazing climbing structure, bridges and glass elevators. In nice weather, kids can enjoy outdoor eating and playing in the waterside park. Look for the iconic Hood milk bottle on Fort Point Channel.

ICA Map pp298-9
☎ 617-927-6613; www.icaboston.org;
100 Northern Ave; 🚇 South Station

The Institute of Contemporary Arts used to be a minor institution, showing rotating exhibits in an old police station in Back Bay. Not that the exhibits were not innovative and exciting – they were. In fact, the ICA hosted the first museum shows for artists such as Andy Warhol and Cornelia Parker. But the small space was limiting and they never attracted much attention.

GOT MILK?

Up there with the Citgo sign and the Steaming Kettle, the giant Hood milk bottle is emblematic of Boston. Towering 40ft over Fort Point Channel, it would hold 50,000 gallons of milk if it could hold a drop (that's 800,000 glasses of milk, if anybody's counting). This unlikely wooden milk bottle was built in 1934 to house an ice cream stand, which it did for 30-some years before it was abandoned. The milk bottle was finally purchased by Hood Milk, New England's largest and oldest dairy, and moved to its current location in 1977. When the Children's Museum was renovated in 2006, the iconic milk bottle underwent some repairs of its own, but it is expected to open for business (selling hot dogs and ice cream) in fall 2007.

Times have changed. Boston is poised to become a focal point for contemporary art, with the highly-touted opening of the new ICA in its dramatic new quarters. The building is a work of art in itself – a striking glass structure cantilevered over a waterside plaza. The spacious light-filled interior allows for multimedia presentations, educational programs and studio space. More importantly, it provides the venue for the development of the ICA's permanent collection of 21st-century art. At the time of publication, four inaugural exhibits were planned to showcase works from the permanent collection, including *Momentum*, an ongoing series devoted to developments in contemporary art.

CHINATOWN, LEATHER DISTRICT & THEATER DISTRICT
Eating p145, Shopping p213, Sleeping p232

These three side-by-side neighborhoods are home to Boston's lively theater scene, its most hip-hop-happening nightclubs and its best international dining. Ethnically and economically diverse, they border Boston's Downtown districts, but they are edgier and artsier.

This area was pretty bleak in the 1970s, when it was known as the Combat Zone (see opposite). But like many parts of Boston, it has experienced a rebirth in recent years, as developers renovate old theaters, young professionals move into loft apartments and city-dwellers flock here for pricey performances and cheap Chinese food. While such development is generally positive and productive, rising rents threaten the immigrant communities that make this neighborhood what it is.

Although tiny by New York standards, Boston's Theater District has long served as a pre-Broadway staging area. In the 1940s, Boston had over 50 theaters. European actors performed on stages so close together that underground tunnels were built between them, allowing patrons to go from one to another without braving inclement weather. Many landmark theaters have recently received facelifts, and their colorful marquees and posh patrons have revived the aura of 'bright lights, big city' (see p184).

Chinatown is overflowing with ethnic restaurants (see p145), live poultry and fresh produce markets, teahouses and textile shops. Newspaper boxes carry Mandarin and Cantonese publications, while phone booths are topped with pagodas. As well as the Chinese, who began arriving in the late 1870s, this tight-knit community also includes Cambodians, Vietnamese and Laotians.

East of Chinatown, the Leather District is a pocket of uniform brick buildings tucked in between South Station and the remains of the Central Artery. It's named for the shoe and leather industries that prospered here in the late 19th century. This area was built up after the great fire of 1872, so most of the buildings are low-rise red brick creations with flat roofs and hints of classical revival and Richardsonian frills. They shelter some fine art galleries (p183), a few funky clubs (p180) and increasingly pricey residential lofts.

Orientation

The northern border of this area is Boylston St, where it runs along the Public Garden and the Boston Common. The Theater District is tucked into the streets between Arlington and Tremont Sts. Chinatown stretches from Tremont St to the Central Artery (or what's left of it). The Leather District occupies the area between the Central Artery and Atlantic Ave, where you'll find South Station. The southern boundary is I-90, the highway that divides this area from the South End.

TRANSPORTATION

Subway Chinatown is best served by the orange-line Chinatown stop, while the Leather District is easiest to access from South Station, on the red line. Green-line Boylston services the Theater District. That said, all of these areas are very close to each other and it's a short walk to any destination from any of these T stations.

CHINATOWN GATE & PARK Map p305
cnr Beach St & Surface Rd; 🚇 Chinatown

The official entrance to Chinatown is the decorative gate, or *paifong*, a gift from the city of Taipei. It is symbolic – not only as an entryway for guests visiting Chinatown, but also as an entryway for immigrants who are still settling here, as they come to establish relationships and roots in their newly claimed home. In 2006, ground was broken for the new Chinatown Park, which will surround the gate and anchor the southern end of the Rose Kennedy Greenway. Incorporating elements of feng shui, the park design is inspired by the many generations of Asian immigrants who have passed through this gate.

COMBAT ZONE

With the demolition of Scollay Sq in the 1960s (see p79), the city's go-go dancers, strippers and prostitutes – as well as their clientele – made their way to the blocks wedged between the Theater District and Chinatown. The city administration supported this move, believing that it could concentrate the city's sleaze into a sort of red light district (although prostitution was technically illegal), and free the rest of the city of riff-raff.

Washington St – between Boylston and Kneeland Sts – became the center of all skankiness in Boston. Lined with clubs like the Teddy Bare Lounge and the Naked I, this was the place to come for adult bookstores and X-rated movie theaters. Prostitutes congregated along LaGrange St. Local reporters dubbed it the 'Combat Zone.'

Residents were generally poor immigrants. They had little voice in local government and were unable to change official policy. The Combat Zone flourished.

The heyday of the Combat Zone has passed (although there are still a few strip clubs in this area). Due to rising real estate values, this area attracted the attention of developers in the 1980s: the Four Seasons Hotel and the State Transportation Building were built on Park Sq; Emerson College moved its campus here; other development followed suit. City officials cracked down on street crime, forcing the Combat Zone clientele to stay home and surf the internet. Many of the old theaters – such as the Opera House and the Paramount– were revamped for Broadway shows and upscale nightclubs.

Chinatown residents also engaged in grassroots efforts to shut down the Combat Zone, and for the most part they succeeded. Unfortunately, even as the neighborhood is enjoying revitalization, this ethnic enclave continues to be jeopardized – not by peep shows and porn theaters but by skyrocketing rents.

SOUTH END

Eating p148, Shopping p214, Sleeping p233

What the Castro is to San Francisco, what Dupont Circle is to Washington, DC, so the South End is to Boston – a once rough neighborhood that's been claimed and cleaned up by the gay community, and now everyone wants to live there.

And why not? The South End boasts the country's largest concentration of Victorian row houses, many of which have been painstakingly restored by aforementioned gay residents. It offers Boston's most innovative and exciting options for dining out, especially along trendy **Tremont St** (see p148). And now, the area south of Washington St has earned the moniker SoWa for the artistic community that is converting the old warehouses into studio and gallery space. The South End is everything that an urban community should be, including diverse.

Historically, the South End has been the most ethnically, racially and economically varied neighborhood in Boston. Sammy Davis Jr and Louis Mayer both grew up here, as did Lebanese immigrant and poet Kahlil Gibran. Martin Luther King Jr and Coretta Scott King lived here while MLK was a Boston University (BU) theology student.

These days, despite skyrocketing property values, this progressive community is committed to maintaining the diversity that makes it so rich. The most famous incident demonstrating this commitment was in the 1980s, when community members staged a rally protesting the destruction of affordable housing. The result of that protest was Tent City, a mixed-income housing project, which now occupies the corner of Dartmouth St and Columbus Ave. Other examples abound. And the outcome – visible when you stroll the South End streets – is a vibrant community of many races, many nationalities and many income levels.

The beautiful green strip of **Southwest Corridor Park** (p199) is another result of community activism, as this stretch was slated to be a highway, which would have destroyed neighborhoods. Residents protested, and now it is a multifunctional park and pathway, where housing projects and halfway houses rub up against student dorms and converted condos.

That said, the most enticing corners of the South End are not those with public housing projects, but those with exquisite London-style row houses with steep stoops and tiny ornamental gardens. Several sweet streets run between Tremont St and Shawmut Ave, particularly the lovely elliptical Union Park and intimate Rutland Sq.

Orientation

Southwest Corridor Park forms the northwestern boundary between the South End and Back Bay; the Mass Turnpike (I-90) forms the northern boundary with Chinatown. The main drag is Tremont St, where lots of activity surrounds the Boston Center for the Arts. Now Washington St is also being targeted by artists and restaurateurs, with Blackstone Sq becoming a hub in the southwestern part of this district. In the east, the South End is bounded by the Central Artery (I-93), while the southwestern border is Massachusetts Ave. Avoid going too far southwest of Massachusetts Ave, especially at night, as this area can be dangerous.

BOSTON CENTER FOR THE ARTS

Map p305

☎ 617-426-5000; www.bcaonline.org; 539 Tremont St; ⏰ noon-5pm Wed-Thu & Sun, noon-10pm Fri & Sat; 🚇 Back Bay or South End

Besides several different performance spaces (see p185), the main venue for visual arts at the BCA is the Mills Gallery, which hosts rotating exhibits of cutting-edge art, as well as opportunities to interact with the artists (eg artist and curator talks). Exhibits feature established and emerging artists, from Boston and from around the country, who put on shows appropriate to this trendsetting neighborhood. Annual events include the Drawing Show, featuring works by dozens of artists but only one medium; and the Medicine Wheel, which uses art to reflect on the AIDS epidemic.

TRANSPORTATION

Bus Silver Line buses run down Washington St from the New England Medical Center to Dudley Sq.

Subway No T station is super convenient to the South End, but the closest is orange-line Back Bay/South End. If you're headed to the western end of this neighborhood, use the orange-line Massachusetts Ave T station instead.

SCANDAL IN THE CHURCH

On December 13, 2002, Pope John Paul II accepted the resignation of Cardinal Bernard Law, who said 'To all those who have suffered from my shortcomings and mistakes I...beg forgiveness.' He was apologizing to the victims of sexual abuse by priests around the archdiocese of Boston. Law was accused of playing a major role in the cover-up of the scandal, going so far as to move priests between parishes despite allegations of molestation of children and teenagers. His resignation was the culmination of a year of almost daily protests at the Cathedral of the Holy Cross, which was Law's parish.

The fallout of the scandal is far-reaching, as the archdiocese paid millions of dollars in reparations to abuse victims. The cash-strapped diocese has had to close more than 60 churches around the city. Some heartbroken parishioners dispersed quietly, while others were galvanized to stage vigils and other forms of protest to save their communities. Activist church-members formed the Council of Parishes to assist congregations in organizing church occupations to block closures. Several church occupations were still on-going at the time of research, almost two years after the contentious closings began.

CATHEDRAL OF THE HOLY CROSS

Map p305

☎ 617-542-5682; www.rcab.org/tourofcathedral; 1400 Washington St; ☒ service 9am Mon-Sat, 7:30am & 11:30am Sun; ☒ Union Park St

When this neo-Gothic cathedral was built in 1875, it was America's largest Catholic cathedral, as big as Westminster Abbey. It serves as the main cathedral for the archdiocese of Boston and the seat of the archbishop. The exquisite rose window features King David playing his harp, while the rest of the cross-shaped building is peppered with stained glass windows and traditional church art.

FIRST CORPS OF CADETS ARMORY

Map p305

☎ 617-423-1112; 101 Arlington St; ☒ 11:30am-3pm Mon-Fri, 5-10pm daily; ☒ Arlington

Out of place amid Boston's Colonial, Federal and Victorian architecture, this medieval castle sits on a prominent corner. Complete with castle towers, oriel turrets and parapet walls, the building was constructed in 1891 as an armory for a volunteer militia of wealthy merchants and professionals. Although the First Corps of Cadets was originally founded

to guard the governor of the Massachusetts Bay Colony, at the end of the 19th century the group was more concerned with immigrant revolts and lower-class riots (they especially feared the Irish Catholics). Which explains why they constructed this defensive fortress. The castle now houses a swanky steakhouse; the gunroom, social hall and museum floor now contain opulent dining rooms, still catering to the likes of the cadets.

BACK BAY

Eating p150, Shopping p215, Sleeping p234

During the 1850s, Back Bay was an uninhabitable tidal flat. Boston was experiencing a population and building boom, so urban planners embarked on an ambitious 40-year project: filling in the marsh, laying out an orderly grid of streets, erecting magnificent Victorian brownstones and designing high-minded civic plazas. So Back Bay was born.

The grandest of Back Bay's grand boulevards is Commonwealth Ave (more 'commonly', Comm Ave). Boston's Champs Élysées, the dual carriageway connects the Public Garden to the Back Bay Fens, a green link in Olmsted's Emerald Necklace (see p104). The grassy mall is dotted with public art and grand elms and lined with stately brownstones.

North of here is lovely Marlborough St, its brick sidewalks lit with gas lamps and shaded by blooming magnolias. South is swanky **Newbury St**, a popular destination for the serious shopper (p215) or gallery-hopper (p183).

Newbury St shops

Sights

BACK BAY

BOSTON FOR FREE

It only takes a bit of research to entertain yourself for free in Boston. Here are some options for culture vultures with empty pockets:

Arnold Arboretum (p114) Free walking tours, free greenery and fresh air.

Black Heritage Trail (p73) Free walking tour, free history lesson.

Boston Public Library (below) Free internet access, free guided tours, free books (you have to give them back).

Bunker Hill, Charlestown Navy Yard & USS Constitution (p83) All free, all the time.

Charles River Memorial Hatch Shell (p190) Free concerts.

Custom House (p86) Free view from the top, 10am and 4pm.

Harvard Art Museums (p117) Free art in the morning, 9am to noon Sat.

Harvard Museum of Natural History (p117) Free fossils, 9am to noon Sun.

Harvard Square buskers (p115) Free music; quality is not guaranteed.

Museum of Fine Arts (p103) Free art in the evening, 4pm to 9:45pm Wed.

Shakespeare on the Common (p190) Free outdoor theater, picnic not included.

Copley Sq represents the best of Back Bay architecture, as it gracefully blends disparate elements like the Renaissance Revival Boston Public Library, the Richardsonian Trinity Church and the modern John Hancock Tower. While many high-end hotels are clustered around Copley Sq and the Hynes Convention Center (p234), you'll find sidewalk cafés, trendy bars (p166) and chic restaurants (p150) on nearly every block.

Orientation

Back Bay is bounded by the Public Garden and Arlington St in the east and Mass Ave in the west. The Charles River forms the northern boundary, and it stretches all the way to Southwest Corridor Park in the south. The main boulevards are Beacon St, Marlborough St, Commonwealth Ave, Newbury St and Boylston St. Huntington Ave runs southwest from Copley Sq. Cross streets are laid out alphabetically from Arlington St to Hereford St.

TRANSPORTATION

Subway The main branch of the green line runs the length of Boylston St, with stops at Arlington near the Public Garden, Copley at Copley Sq and Hynes at Mass Ave. At Copley, the E-line branches southwest along Huntington Ave to Prudential and Symphony. The orange-line Back Bay/South End sits on the border between these two neighborhoods.

ARLINGTON ST CHURCH Map pp306-7

☎ 617-536-7050; www.ascboston.org; 351 Boylston St; ⊙ noon-6pm Wed-Sun May-Oct; ⊕ Arlington

This 1861 church was the first public building erected in Back Bay. The original congregation gathered in 1729 in a barn on Federal and Franklin Sts. Three meeting houses later, this graceful church features extraordinary Tiffany windows and 16 bells in its steeple, which was modeled after London's well-known church St Martin-in-the-Fields. The church's Unitarian Universalist ministry is purely progressive, as it has been since Rev William Ellery Channing preached in the early 19th century. (A statue in his honor is across the street in the Public Garden.)

BOSTON PUBLIC LIBRARY Map pp306-7

☎ 617-536-5400; www.bpl.org; 700 Boylston St; admission free; ⊙ 9am-9pm Mon-Thu, 9am-5pm Fri & Sat, 1-5pm Sun Oct-May only; ⊕ Copley

Dating from 1852, the esteemed BPL lends credence to Boston's reputation as the 'Athens of America.' The old McKim building is notable for its magnificent façade and exquisite interior art. Pick up a free brochure and take a self-guided tour; alternatively, free guided tours (times vary) depart from the entrance hall.

The original McKim building, inspired by Italian Renaissance *palazzi*, features Daniel Chester French's enormous bronze doorways, flanked by iron gates and lanterns.

From there a marble staircase leads past Pierre Puvis de Chavannes' inspirational murals depicting poetry, philosophy, history and science, which he considered 'the four great expressions of the human mind.'

The staircase terminates at the splendid Bates Hall Reading Room, where even the most mundane musings are elevated by the barrel-vaulted, 50ft coffered ceilings. Nearby, the Abbey Room is named for the author of the 1895 murals recounting Sir Galahad's quest for the Holy Grail. The 3rd floor features John Singer Sargent's unfinished Judaic and Christian murals, which were criticized for anti-Semitic messages.

Besides this amazing artistry, the library holds untold treasures in its special collections, including John Adams' personal library. Frequent exhibits showcase some of the highlights – check the BPL website for details. An inviting café, Novel, overlooks the enchanting Italianate courtyard, which is a peaceful place to read.

CHRISTIAN SCIENCE CHURCH

Map pp306-7

☎ 617-450-3790; www.tfccs.com; 175 Huntington Ave; admission free; ☾ open 10am-4pm Mon-Sat, tours 11:30am-3:30pm Mon-Sat; 🚇 Symphony
Known to adherents as the 'Mother Church', this is the international home base for the Church of Christ, Scientist (Christian Science), founded by Mary Baker Eddy in 1866 (see p100). Tour the grand classical revival basilica, which can seat 3000 worshippers, listen to the 14,000-pipe organ and linger on the expansive plaza with its 670ft-long reflecting pool.

COPLEY SQUARE Map pp306-7

cnr Boylston & Dartmouth Sts; 🚇 Copley
Copley Sq is graced on all sides with amazing architecture. With eyes constantly drifting upward, it's easy to miss the square's plebeian-sized, down-to-earth elements. The famous Boston Marathon, finishes here. Runners congregate in a staging area, where they are commemorated by the Boston Marathon Monument embedded in the sidewalk (on Boylston St near Dartmouth St). Paying tribute to the runners who subscribe to the 'slow and steady' strategy is Nancy Schon's sculpture Tortoise & Hare (Schon also cast Make Way for Ducklings in the Public Garden).

GIBSON HOUSE MUSEUM

Map pp306-7

☎ 617-267-6338; www.thegibsonhouse.org; 137 Beacon St; tours adult/senior & student $7/5; ☾ tours 1pm, 2pm & 3pm Wed-Sun; 🚇 Arlington
When Catherine Hammond Gibson moved to this Italian Renaissance row house in 1860, the Back Bay was barely filled in. This was one of the first houses built on Beacon St, and Ms Gibson was considered quite the pioneer (that she was a female homeowner in this 'New Land' was even more unusual). The Gibson House attempts to preserve a piece of Victorian-era Boston, showcasing antique furniture and art that was collected by the Gibson family, especially Catherine's grandson Charles. Four of six levels are open, allowing visitors to see the servants' quarters, the high-ceilinged library and music room, and Charles' bedroom and study.

JOHN HANCOCK TOWER Map pp306-7

200 Clarendon St; 🚇 Copley
Constructed with more than 10,000 panels of mirrored glass, the 62-storey John Hancock Tower offers an amazing perspective on Trinity Church, often reflected in its façade. Designed in 1976 by Henry Cobb, the tower suffered serious initial problems: when the wind whipped up, some panes popped out, falling hundreds of feet to the ground. Fortunately, the panes were replaced and the design problem fixed before anyone was hurt. The top-floor observatory was closed for security reasons in the aftermath of September 11.

Sights

BACK BAY

WEATHER OR NOT

Steady blue, clear view
Flashing blue, clouds are due
Steady red, rain ahead
Flashing red, snow instead

Since 1950, Bostonians have used this simple rhyme and the weather beacon atop the old Hancock tower (next to the new John Hancock Tower) to determine if they need to bring their umbrella when they leave the house. And yes, the beacon has been known to flash red in mid-summer. But that is not a warning of some extremely inclement New England weather, but rather an indication that the Red Sox game has been canceled for the night.

MARY BAKER EDDY LIBRARY & MAPPARIUM Map pp306-7

☎ 617-450-7000, 888-222-3711; .www.mary
bakereddylibrary.org; adult/senior/student & child
$6/4/4; ☺ 10am-4pm Tue-Sun; ◉ Symphony
The Mary Baker Eddy Library for the Bet-
terment of Humanity is an odd amalgam,
housing the offices of the internationally
regarded newspaper, the *Christian Science
Monitor*, as well as one of Boston's hidden
treasures, the intriguing Mapparium. The
Mapparium is a room-size, stained-glass
globe that visitors walk through on a glass
bridge. It was created in 1935, which is
reflected by the globe's geopolitical boundaries. The acoustics, which surprised even
the designer, allow everyone in the room
to hear even the tiniest whisper.

Second-floor galleries deal with the
'search for the meaning of life,' both on a
personal and global level. From here, you
can also peer into the newsroom of the
Monitor, which Eddy founded when she
was 87. Interactive exhibits delve into a no-
tion of journalism that explores questions
that matter. The heart of the library's collections, Eddy's papers and transcripts, are on
the top floors and accessible by permission.

NEW OLD SOUTH CHURCH Map pp306-7

☎ 617-536-1970; 645 Boylston St; ☺ 9am-7pm
daily mid-Jun–early-Sep, 9am-4:30pm Mon-Fri,
9am-2pm Sat & Sun early-Sep–mid-Jun; ◉ Copley
This magnificent Venetian Gothic church
on Copley Sq is called the 'new' Old South
because up until 1875, the congregation
worshiped in the Old South Church on Milk
St (now the Old South Meeting House, see
p88). The new church's exterior stonework
is pudding stone and the interior woodwork
is exquisite Italian cherry. The Congregational church has an impressive collection of
stained glass windows, all shipped from London, and an organ that was rescued from a
Minneapolis church just before demolition.

PRUDENTIAL CENTER SKYWALK

Map pp306-7
☎ 617-859-0648; www.prudentialcenter.com;
adult/senior/child $10.50/8.50/7; ☺ 10am-9:30pm
Mar-Oct, 10am-8pm Nov-Feb; ◉ Prudential
Technically called the Shops at Prudential
Center (see p217), this landmark Boston
building is not much more than a fancy
shopping mall. But it does provide a bird's-

eye view of Boston from its 50th-floor
Skywalk. Completely enclosed by glass, the
skywalk offers spectacular 360° views of
Boston and Cambridge, accompanied by an
entertaining audio tour.

TRINITY CHURCH Map pp306-7

☎ 617-536-0944; www.trinitychurchboston
.org; 206 Clarendon St; adult/senior & student/child
$5/4/free; ☺ 9am-5:30pm Tue-Sat, 1-5pm Sun;
◉ Copley
A masterpiece of American architecture,
Trinity Church is the country's ultimate
example of Richardsonian Romanesque. The
granite exterior, with a massive portico and
side cloister, uses sandstone in colorful patterns. The interior is an awe-inspiring array
of vibrant murals and stained glass, most by
artist John LaFarge, who cooperated closely
with architect Henry Hobson Richardson to
create an integrated composition of shapes,
colors and textures. The walls of the great
central tower are covered by two tiers of
murals, divided by a gilded band bearing
the names of the building's artists and architects. The decorative coffered ceiling and
the stained glass windows are exquisite. In
the west gallery, the jeweled window *Christ
in Majesty* is considered one of America's
finest examples of stained glass art.

KENMORE SQUARE & FENWAY

Eating p152, Shopping p218, Sleeping p236
West of Back Bay, Beacon St and Commonwealth Ave converge at Kenmore Sq, the
epicenter of student life in Boston. In addition to the Boston University behemoth,
which stretches along Commonwealth Ave,
there are more than a half-dozen colleges in
the area. Kenmore Sq has a disproportionate share of clubs (see p182), inexpensive
but nondescript eateries (see p152) and dormitories disguised as brownstones. You'll
know you're in Kenmore Sq when you spot
the landmark Citgo sign (opposite).

Fenway refers to an urban residential
neighborhood south of Kenmore Sq, attractive to students for its low-cost housing and
dining (see p153). Fenway is also the name
of a road that runs through here. Not the
least, Fenway Park is where the Boston Red
Sox play baseball. But when people refer
to 'Fenway,' they're generally talking about

SIGN OF THE TIMES

'London has Big Ben, Paris has the Eiffel Tower, and Boston has the Citgo sign.' It's an unlikely landmark in this high-minded city, but Bostonians love the bright-blinking 'trimark' that has towered over Kenmore Sq since 1965.

For some, the Citgo sign means baseball: every time the Red Sox hit a home run over the leftfield wall at Fenway Park, Citgo's colorful logo is seen by thousands of fans. For others, it is symbolic of the end of the Boston Marathon, as it falls at mile 25 in the race.

For whatever reason, Bostonians have claimed these neon lights as their own. The sign was turned off in 1979 to conserve energy, and after four years, Citgo decided to dismantle the deteriorating sign. But local residents rallied, arguing it is a prime example of urban neon art. They fought to bestow landmark status on the sign to preserve it. And the Citgo sign stayed.

The sign was renovated in 2005, replacing the neon lights with LEDs (which are more durable, more energy-efficient and easier to maintain). Indeed, the previous version of the sign required more than five miles of neon tubing to light its 60ft-by-60ft face. Featured in film, photographs and song, the Citgo sign continues to shine.

the Back Bay Fens, a tranquil and interconnected park system that's an integral link in the Emerald Necklace (see p104).

Huntington Ave cuts across the neighborhood, south of Fenway. Dubbed 'Ave of the Arts,' this road represents a concentrated area of major and minor artistic and cultural venues, including Horticulture Hall, Symphony Hall, two universities and two art museums. Kenmore Sq and Fenway are a bit of the beaten tourist track, but they are home to some celebrated cultural institutions – Boston Symphony Orchestra, the Museum of Fine Arts and the Boston Red Sox.

Orientation

This area stretches from the Charles River in the north to Huntington Ave in the south, from Mass Ave in the east to Carlton St in the west. BU occupies both sides of Commonwealth Ave, which runs parallel to the river in the northern part of the neighborhood. Kenmore Sq anchors the eastern end of the BU campus, while Fenway Park and nightlife-central Landsdowne St are just

south of here. For the purposes of this book, Fenway refers to the area south of Fenway Park. The Muddy River and the Back Bay Fens wind across the whole neighborhood in an S-shape from southwest to northeast.

KENMORE SQUARE

FENWAY PARK Map pp308-9

☎ 617-236-6666; www.redsox.com; Gate E, Landsdowne St; adult/senior/child $12/11/10; ☼ 9am-4pm Apr-Oct; ⓣ Kenmore

Boston's most cherished landmark? Site of Boston's greatest dramas and worst defeats? To many Bostonians, it's not Bunker Hill or the Tea Party ship, but tiny old Fenway Park, home of the Boston Red Sox.

Built in 1912, Fenway Park is one of the last survivors of the old-style baseball parks. Only Wrigley Field in Chicago rivals its legendary status.

Baseball at Fenway is special thanks to the unique shape of the park, the intimate playing field and famous leftfield wall. Fenway has the one and only Green Monster, the towering leftfield wall that compensates for the relatively short distance from home plate. The Green Monster consistently alters the regular course of play – what appears to be a lazy fly ball could actually drop over the Monster for a home run, and what appears to be a sharp double into the gap may be played off the wall to hold the runner to a single.

The best way to experience Fenway Park is to watch a game (see p194), but tickets are hard to come by, especially since the Red Sox 2004 World Series victory (see p18). If you can't see a game, you can at least take the tour, which normally allows you inside the press box and up on

Sights

KENMORE SQUARE & FENWAY

TRANSPORTATION

Subway West of the center, the green line forks into four branches, all of which run through this neighborhood. So you have to pay attention not only to the color of your train, but also its letter (B, C, D or E). To reach Kenmore Sq or Fenway Park, take any of the green-line trains *except* the E-line to Kenmore T station. West of here, sites along Commonwealth Ave are served by stops on the B-line (especially BU Central and BU West). Sites along Beacon St are more easily accessible from the C-line (St Mary's). And sites along Huntington Ave are accessible from the E-line (Museum).

Fenway Park (p101) sign

top of the Monster. And you might get a chance to peak *inside* the wall, where anybody who's anybody in baseball has left their autograph. Avoid afternoon tours on game days; crowds are huge and tours shortened.

MUGAR MEMORIAL LIBRARY
Map pp308-9

☎ 617-353-3696; www.bu.edu/archives; 771 Commonwealth Ave; admission free; ☽ 8am-11pm Mon-Thu, 8am-5pm Fri & Sat, 10am-11pm Sun; Ⓡ BU Central

The special collections of BU's Mugar Memorial Library are housed in the Howard Gotlieb Archival Research Center, an outstanding 20th-century archives that balances pop culture and scholarly appeal. Rotating exhibits throughout the library showcase the holdings, including papers from Arthur Fiedler's collection, the archives of Douglas Fairbanks, Jr or the correspondence of BU alumnus Dr Martin Luther King, Jr. Hours posted are for the library; exhibit hours may vary depending on their exact location in the building.

PHOTOGRAPHIC RESOURCE CENTER
Map pp308-9

☎ 617-975-0600; www.bu.edu/prc; 832 Commonwealth Ave; adult/senior & student/child $3/2/free, Thu free to all; ☽ 10am-6pm Tue, Wed & Fri, 10am-8pm Thu, noon-5pm Sat & Sun; Ⓡ BU West

The independent Photographic Resource Center is one of the few centers in the country devoted exclusively to this art form. The PRC's ever-changing exhibits lean toward the modern and experimental, often featuring work by amateur members. Other resources include educational

programs, online exhibits, a well-stocked library and unique special events.

FENWAY
ISABELLA STEWART GARDNER MUSEUM Map pp308-9

☎ 617-566-1401; www.gardnermuseum.org; 280 The Fenway; adult/senior/student/child $12/10/5/ free; ☽ 11am-5pm Tue-Sun; Ⓡ Museum

The magnificent Venetian-style *palazzo* that houses the Isabella Stewart Gardner Museum was also home to 'Mrs Jack'

ART HEIST OF THE CENTURY

On March 18, 1990, two thieves disguised as police officers broke into the Isabella Stewart Gardner Museum. They left with nearly $200 million worth of artwork. The most famous painting stolen was Vermeer's *The Concert*, but the loot also included three works by Rembrandt, and others by Manet and Degas, not to mention French and Chinese artifacts. The crime was never solved.

While recovering the paintings after so many years seems unlikely, authorities continue to pursue it. In 2005, local newspapers reported that FBI agents flew to Paris to meet with authorities about a suspect French media mogul. This latest theory suggests that Boston mafia-types pulled off the heist, then sold the works to illicit underground art dealers in Italy and France.

Mrs Jack's will stipulated that the collection remain exactly as it was at the time of her death. So the walls where these paintings hung remain bare, even today. Meanwhile, the Gardner Museum continues to offer a $5 million reward for information leading to the recovery of the artwork. So if you have any leads, please let us know.

Gardner herself until her death in 1924. A monument to one woman's exquisite taste for acquiring art, the Gardner is filled with almost 2000 priceless objects, including outstanding tapestries and Italian Renaissance and 17th-century Dutch paintings. The *palazzo* itself, with a four-story greenhouse courtyard, is a masterpiece, a tranquil oasis worth the price of admission.

MASSART

Map pp308-9

☎ 617-879-7333; www.massart.edu; 621 Huntington Ave; admission free; ☼ 10am-6pm Mon-Fri, 11am-5pm Sat; 🚇 Longwood Ave

More formally known as the Massachusetts College of Art, this is the country's first and only four-year independent public art college. In 1873, state leaders decided the new textile mills in Lowell and Lawrence needed a steady stream of designers, so they established MassArt to educate some. The South Building houses over 9000 sq ft of exhibit space in the Arnheim, Bakalar and Paine galleries, while the Tower also houses the President's Gallery. There's always some thought-provoking or sense-stimulating exhibits to see.

MUSEUM OF FINE ARTS

Map pp308-9

☎ 617-267-9300; www.mfa.org; 465 Huntington Ave; adult/senior & student/child $15/13/6.50; ☼ 10am-4:45pm Sat-Tue, 10am-9:45pm Wed-Fri, Thu & Fri evening West Wing only; 🚇 Museum

The collections at the Museum of Fine Arts are second in this country only to New York's Metropolitan Museum of Art. The museum's highlight is undoubtedly its American collection, including American painting and decorative arts. The museum also has an incredible collection of European paintings, including many by French impressionists. The recent acquisition of *Duchessa di Montejasi with Her Daughters* makes the MFA's Degas collection one of the richest in the world. The museum also boasts excellent exhibits of Japanese art, including Buddhist and Shinto treasures.

Children under the age of 17 are admitted free after 3pm on weekdays and all day on weekends – a fantastic family bargain. Wednesday evenings admission is free for everyone. See the boxed text 'The MFA in Half a Day' (right) for more details.

THE MFA IN HALF A DAY

It's easy to while away many hours, exploring the special exhibits and admiring the permanent collections at the Museum of Fine Arts. If you don't have the time (or the attention span), here are some highlights that you can do in half a day.

Your first stop should be the first floor, through the lower rotunda, to the extensive holdings of American art. The collection includes more than 60 portraits by John Singleton Copley and 50 by Gilbert Stuart (including the dollar-bill portrait). You'll see many paintings by Winslow Homer, John Singer Sargent and Mary Cassat. Edward Hopper and the Hudson River School are also highlights. American decorative arts, including furniture, are well-represented. Hunt for the American silver collection, which includes Paul Revere's Liberty Bowl.

In the southwestern corner of the first floor, you'll find the Asian art. The museum has one of the world's most comprehensive collections of Japanese art, from porcelain to woodblock prints to painted silk screens and samurai regalia. Don't miss the dimly lit templelike room displaying six massive and awesome Buddhas.

When the museum joined forces with Harvard for a 1905 archaeological expedition at the Great Pyramids at Giza, they hauled back a world-famous collection of mummies and related objects. The refurbished galleries next to the Huntington Ave entrance provide the royal treatment these treasures deserve. You'll also find one of the most significant collections of Nubian art outside the Sudan.

On the second floor, the collection of European paintings is outstanding. Check out the huge stash of French impressionist paintings, including 36 by Claude Monet. This is where you will find the famous collection of Degas. Look also for Paul Gauguin's thought-provoking mural *Where do we come from? What are we? Where are we going?*

When it's time to rest, head to Tenshin-En (Garden of the Heart of Heaven), a tranquil Japanese garden, or the early-20th-century European garden, Fraser Garden Court. The outdoor Calderwood Courtyard café serves light meals.

BROOKLINE

Eating p154, Shopping p218, Sleeping p238

Although it seems to be part of Boston proper, Brookline is a distinct entity with a separate city government. It is a 'streetcar suburb,' a historical term describing its development after electric trolleys were introduced in the late 1800s. Brookline was built as a modest, middle-income neighborhood, suitable for young families (which explains

EMERALD NECKLACE

The Emerald Necklace is an evocative name for a series of parks and green spaces that weave through Boston, some seven miles from the Boston Common to Franklin Park. Designed by Frederick Law Olmsted in the late 19th century, the Emerald Necklace treats city residents to a bit of fresh air, green grass and flowing water, right within the city limits. It's particularly well-suited for cycling, so hop on a bike (see p197) and go for the green:

Arnold Arboretum (p114) The 265-acre arboretum is a gem, planted with more than 14,000 botanical specimens, including exotic trees and flowering shrubs. Dog walking, Frisbee throwing, bicycling and general contemplation are encouraged, but picnicking is not.

Back Bay Fens (p197) The Fens features the beloved Community Gardens, the elegant Kelleher Rose Garden and open grassy areas where college students sunbathe.

Franklin Park At 500-plus acres, the park is an underutilized resource – partly because it borders a sketchy neighborhood, and partly because it is so huge. Still, on weekend afternoons the park is full of families from the nearby neighborhoods of Jamaica Plain, Dorchester and Roxbury. The Franklin Park Zoo (p114) is contained within the park. Take the Orange Line to Stony Brook, Green St or Forest Hills and head east until you reach the park's western edge. But the park is dangerous after dark, so don't linger longer than the sun.

Jamaica Pond The idyllic spring-fed pond, on the west side of the Jamaicaway, is more than 50ft deep and great for boating, fishing, jogging and picnicking.

Olmsted Park A paved path hugs the banks of Leverett Pond and Ward Pond in Jamaica Plain.

the draw to Joseph and Rose Kennedy, who moved here in 1914).

Around this time, Boston saw a significant migration of Jews – especially from Poland and Lithuania – many of whom settled in Brookline. Boston's first synagogue, Ohabei Shalom, moved from the South End to Beacon St in the 1920s. Successive waves of Jewish immigrants have followed, especially following the turmoil in the former Soviet Union. Today, synagogues and kosher delis reveal these roots.

Nowadays, Brookline is one of Boston's most desirable addresses, offering stately homes and spacious lawns, all within minutes of the city. The tranquil residential areas are interspersed with lively commercial zones, including Coolidge Corner and Brookline Village, both of which offer excellent eating (p154) and shopping (p218). And Russian has become Brookline's second language, oft overheard on the green line and always seen at Russian restaurants and specialty shops clustered in these squares.

TRANSPORTATION

Subway Two branches of the green line run through Brookline. Take the C-line to Coolidge Corner, or take the D-line to Brookline Village or other sites in the southern part of town.

Orientation

Brookline is a town spread out over seven square miles between Commonwealth Ave and Boylston St. The eastern boundary is marked by Carlton St and the Muddy River. The main highway cutting through Brookline is Beacon St, which heads west from Kenmore Sq to Coolidge Corner and beyond. Coolidge Corner is at the intersection of Beacon and Harvard Sts, and Brookline Village is less than a mile south along Harvard St. Most of the sights – being homesteads – are scattered about the residential parts of Brookline.

FREDERICK LAW OLMSTED NATIONAL HISTORIC SITE

☎ 617-566-1689; www.nps.gov/frla; 99 Warren St, Brookline; admission free; ⏱ 8:30am-5pm Mon-Fri; 🚇 Brookline Hills (D-line)

Widely considered the father of landscape design architecture, Frederick Law Olmsted made an indelible mark on Boston's urban landscape, linking green space from the Boston Common to Franklin Park, some seven miles long. His firm spent nearly 20 years on the project, known as the Emerald Necklace. In the midst of this project, Olmsted moved his own home to Brookline, where he established

(Continued on page 113)

FREEDOM TRAIL

Prescott statue and Bunker Hill Monument, Monument Sq (p109)

Statue of Paul Revere near the Old North Church (p82)

The best introduction to revolutionary Boston is the Freedom Trail. This red brick path winds its way past 16 sites that earned this town its status as the cradle of liberty. The 2.5-mile trail follows the course of the conflict, from the Old State House, where Redcoats killed five men, marking the Boston Massacre, to the Old North Church, where the sexton hung two lanterns to warn that British troops would come by sea.

But even though it's called the Freedom Trail, it covers much more than just revolutionary history. Here you'll find some of Boston's oldest landmarks, including three cemeteries dating to the 17th century, America's first public park and the site of its first

Quincy Market, Faneuil Hall (p109)

Massachusetts State House (p108)

public school. You'll also find the sites where Boston prospered in the postrevolutionary period – the Massachusetts State House, built for the new Commonwealth in 1798; Park St Church, where abolitionists rallied in 1829; the Old Corner Bookstore, where literary salons were held throughout the 19th century; and the Charlestown Navy Yard, active into the 20th century.

This well-trafficked walking tour is officially operated by the National Park Service (NPS). It starts on the Boston Common and visits sights on Beacon Hill, Downtown, near the Waterfront and in the North End, before crossing the bridge and ending in Charlestown. As such, it provides an introduction to some of Boston's distinct neighborhoods, as well as its rich history.

Visit the tourist information kiosk at the Boston Common (see p278) to pick up a free map or to hook up with a 90-minute guided tour led by the **Freedom Trail Foundation** (☎ 617-357-8300; www .thefreedomtrail.org; adult/senior/child $12/10/6; ☽ 11am, noon & 1pm).

top ten

SURPRISES FROM THE FREEDOM TRAIL

- Great Elm or gallows? The Freedom Trail kicks off on the Boston Common, a popular spot for hanging religious heretics during Puritan times (p78).
- A hooker in front of the State House? That would be the statue honoring 'Fighting Joe' Hooker, Civil War general and Massachusetts native (p76). Despite his reputation as a heavy drinker and ladies' man, it is unlikely that he is the source of the term 'hooker.'
- Don't overlook the other midnight riders. Pay your respects to Paul Revere at the Granary Burying Ground (p75). But the politically-savvy silversmith was not the only patriot who rode to Lexington and Concord – he was joined by young William Dawes, now buried in King's Chapel Burial Ground (p87), and Samuel Prescott, buried in Concord (p247).
- Get your pies for the big pie fight! Boston Cream Pie – official state pie of Massachusetts – was invented at the Omni Parker House (p230).
- Pub crawl, 17th-century style. Blackstone Block (p89) is home to Boston's oldest architecture and liveliest bar scene. Check out Bell in Hand (p164) or Green Dragon (p164).
- How low can you go? Haggle with the vendors at Haymarket (p134) – you can't beat these prices anywhere!
- From Highway to Greenway. Witness the ongoing transformation of downtown Boston (p25).
- Could it be that Paul Revere was Italian? Well, no… but you can still sate your appetite with Boston's best pizza or pasta in the North End (p139).
- Whose Hill? Turns out the Battle of Bunker Hill actually took place on Breed's Hill, which is where the monument stands today (p84).
- You'll shoot your eye out! Catch musket practice at the Bunker Hill Monument (p84).

Splashing about in the pond, Boston Common (below)

BOSTON COMMON Map pp302-3

☎ 617-426-3115 (visitor information kiosk); btwn Beacon, Park, Tremont & Charles Sts; 🚇 Park St or Boylston

The Freedom Trail kicks off at the Boston Common, America's oldest public park and the centerpiece of the city. The onsite information kiosk is a great source of information, maps and tour guides. Otherwise, wander freely about this 50-acre green, crisscrossed with walking paths and dotted with monuments. Bostonians hustle to and from the nearby T stations; others stroll leisurely, enjoying the fresh air or engage in any number of Common activities, from free concerts to political rallies to seasonal festivities. Don't miss the Robert Gould Shaw Memorial, sculpted by Augustus St Gaudens.

MASSACHUSETTS STATE HOUSE Map pp302-3

☎ 617-727-3676; www.sec.state.ma.us; Beacon & Bowdoin Sts; admission free; 🕘 open 9am-5pm, tours 10am-4pm Mon-Fri; 🚇 Park St

Overlooking the Boston Common from the northeast corner, the Massachusetts State House occupies a proud spot atop the city's last remaining hill. Since 1798, this is the seat of the government of the Commonwealth. Knowledgeable volunteer guides, known as Doric Docents, lead tours of the many ceremonial halls and the legislative chambers. Tours cover the history and architecture of the building, as well as highlights of the artwork and flags that adorn the halls. When the Senate or the House of Representatives are in session, you can view the proceedings from the observation balcony.

OLD STATE HOUSE Map pp302-3

☎ 617-720-3290; 206 Washington St; adult/senior & student/child $3/2/1; 🕘 9am-5pm; 🚇 State

Before the revolution, the seat of the Massachusetts government was the Old State House, a red brick colonial building that is now surrounded by modern structures and busy streets. Dodge the traffic to inspect the cobblestone circle which marks the site of the Boston Massacre, the revolution's first violent conflict in 1770. And gaze up at the balcony, where the Declaration of Independence was first read to Bostonians in 1776. Inside, the Old State House contains a small museum of revolutionary

Inside Faneuil Hall (below)

memorabilia, with videos and multimedia presentations about the Boston Massacre. You can also learn more about the preservation of the Old State House, which now contains a T station in its basement.

FANEUIL HALL Map pp302-3

☎ 617-242-5642; www.faneuilhall.com; Congress & North Sts; admission free; ⏰ 9am-5pm; 🚇 Haymarket or Aquarium

Nearly every visitor to Boston stops at Quincy Market to grab a beer or shop for souvenirs; but most bypass historic Faneuil Hall, the original market and public meeting place that was built in 1740. Pause to admire the bronze statue of Sam Adams, who sits

GETTING THERE

The Freedom Trail starts at the Boston Common, easily accessed from Park St, the T stop at the intersection of the red and green lines. It ends in Charlestown, where there is an orange-line T stop called Community College. It's just as easy (and a more pleasant walk) to return across the Charlestown bridge to the T stop at North Station, on the green and orange lines.

astride his horse in Dock Sq. Then ascend to the 2nd-floor hall, where Sam Adams was one of many orators who spoke out against the British rule. The hall is still used for public ceremonies today, though you're more likely to witness a talk by a NPS ranger about the history of the 'cradle of liberty.'

BUNKER HILL MONUMENT Map p304

☎ 617-242-5641; Monument Sq; admission free; ⏰ 9am-4:30pm, to 5pm late Jun-early Sep; 🚇 North Station or Community College

This 220ft granite obelisk is visible from across the harbor in the North End, from the expanse of the Zakim Bridge and from almost anywhere in Charlestown. But only a walk through the winding cobblestone streets up to the monument's hilltop perch allows visitors to experience and appreciate the authentic, historic charm of this 18th-century neighborhood. Check out the dioramas to better understand what transpired on that fateful day in June 1775, when the Battle of Bunker Hill took place. Then climb 295 steps to the top of the monument to enjoy the panorama of the city, the harbor and the North Shore.

Copp's Hill Burying Ground, North End (p82)

WALKING TOUR

Start at the **Boston Common** (1; p77), America's oldest public park. On the northern side of the park, you can't miss the gold-domed **State House** (2; p76) sitting atop Beacon Hill. **Park St Church** (3; p77) stands on the eastern side of the Common. Walk north on Tremont St, where you will pass the Egyptian revival gates of the **Granary Burying Ground** (4; p75), the final resting place of many notable patriots.

Continue north to School St, where the Georgian **King's Chapel** (5; p87) overlooks its adjacent burying ground. Turn east on School St, and take note of the bronze statue of Benjamin Franklin outside Old City Hall (p87). A plaque commemorates this spot as the **site of the first public school** (6), founded in 1635.

Continue down School St to Washington St, where the little brick building, known as the **Old Corner Bookstore** (7; p88), has been a literary and intellectual hotspot for 75 years. Kiddy-corner across Washington St, where the **Old South Meeting House** (8; p88) saw the beginnings of one of the American Revolution's most vociferous protests – the Boston Tea Party.

Further north on Washington St, the **Old State House** (9; p88) was the scene of more historic drama: the first reading of the Declaration of Independence. Outside, a ring of cobblestones marks the **site of the Boston Massacre** (10; p88). Cross the traffic-filled square and head north on Congress St. Historic **Faneuil Hall** (11; p89) has served as a public meeting place and marketplace for over 250 years. This is a choice spot to stop for lunch from the food court in Quincy Market or from one of the nearby eateries (see p143).

From Faneuil Hall, walk north on Union St (p89); turn right on Hanover St, weaving through the fruit and vegetable stalls of Haymarket (p134), into the heart of the North End. Turn east on Richmond St and you will find yourself in charming North Sq, also the site of the **Paul Revere House** (12; p83).

Back on Hanover St, walk two blocks north to Paul Revere Mall. Besides a dramatic statue of the patriot himself, this park also provides a lovely vantage point to view your next destination, the **Old North Church** (13; p82). From the church, head west on Hull St to Copp's

Park St Church (p77)

Hill Burying Ground (14; p82), with grand views across the river to Charlestown.

Continue west on Hull St to its end. Turn left on Commercial St and walk across the Charlestown Bridge. Turning right on Constitution Rd brings you to the Charlestown Navy Yard, home of the world's oldest commissioned warship, the **USS Constitution** (15; p85).

Now wind your way through the historic streets of Charlestown to your final destination, the **Bunker Hill Monument** (16; p84), site of the Revolutionary War battle. From here, you can grab a bite to eat and recuperate in one of Charlestown's trendy or traditional eating establishments (see p141).

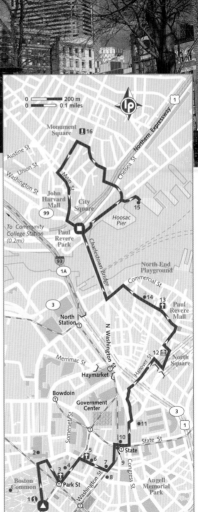

FREEDOM TRAIL FACTS

Start Boston Common
End Bunker Hill Monument, Charlestown
Distance 2.5 miles
Duration Anywhere from one hour to one day, if you stop at the museums and sights along the way
Fuel stops Quincy Market (p143), Giacomo's Ristorante (p140), Figs (p141)

The decorative tower of the Old State House (p108), against a backdrop of steel and glass

(Continued from page 104)

a full-scale landscape design office called 'Fairsted.'

Closed at the time of research, Fairsted will open for tours in fall 2007. You can visit Olmsted's office, which remains as it was a century ago, and peruse his designs for the country's most beloved green spaces: Central Park in New York City, Rock Creek Park in Washington, DC; national parks such as Acadia and the Great Smoky Mountains; and more. Olmsted was also influential in the creation of the National Park Service, which manages his homestead as a historic site.

JOHN F KENNEDY NATIONAL HISTORIC SITE Map pp308-9

☎ 617-566-7937; www.nps.gov/jofi; 83 Beals St, Brookline; adult/child $3/free; ✆ 10am-4:30pm Wed-Sun May-Oct; Ⓡ Coolidge Corner (C-line)
In 1914, newlyweds Joseph and Rose Kennedy moved into this modest three-story house in the shady streetcar suburb of Brookline. Four of their nine children would be born and raised here, including Jack, who was born in the master bedroom in 1917. Matriarch Rose Kennedy oversaw restoration and furnishing of the house in the late 1960s; today her narrative sheds light on the Kennedys' family life. Mandatory guided tours allow visitors to see furnishings, photographs and mementos that have been preserved from the time the family lived here. A self-guided walking tour of the surrounding neighborhood sets the scene for the Kennedy family's day-to-day life, including church, school and shopping.

LARZ ANDERSON AUTO MUSEUM

☎ 617-522-6547; www.mot.org; 15 Newton St, Brookline; adult/senior/student & child $5/3/3; ✆ 10am-5pm Tue-Sun; Ⓡ Reservoir (D-line)
Larz and Isabel Anderson, a high-society socialite couple, bought their first automobile in 1899: a Winton Runabout. It was the first of 32 autos that they would purchase over the next 50 years. When one car would become obsolete, it would retire to the carriage house, forming the foundation for 'America's oldest motorcar collection.' Fourteen of the 32 originals are a part of the current collection, which is still housed in the carriage house on the grounds of the

estate (now Larz Anderson Park). A walking tour of the park allows visitors to discover what these grounds were once like. Take bus 51 from the Forest Hill or Reservoir T station.

JAMAICA PLAIN

Eating p155, Sleeping p239

Jamaica Plain (or 'JP' as it is fondly known) centers on its namesake Jamaica Pond, a spring-fed pond that is pleasant for strolling or running. This lovely body of water, surrounded by park, is another link in the Emerald Necklace (see p104).

It was Jamaica Pond that attracted Boston's wealthy families to build summer homes near the water in the mid-19th century. Many of these beautiful Victorians still stand along the streets just east of the pond. Other parts of Jamaica Plain are not so patrician, however. Public housing projects and triple deckers are the norm here.

JP has strong Irish immigrant roots, but in recent years the population has diversified. The area has attracted Spanish-speaking populations from Cuba and Dominican Republic, Asian immigrants from China and Vietnam, and black families from neighboring Roxbury. In the 1990s, as real estate values soared around the city, JP became a destination for artists, political activists and lesbians, all of whom have fueled the ongoing transformation of the neighborhood. Now Centre St is lined with ethnic eateries, vegetarian restaurants and funky coffee shops (p155), as well as old-school Irish pubs (p170) and hip music clubs.

Orientation

In the southern part of the city, Jamaica Plain is nestled between Brookline and Roxbury, due south of Fenway. Its western border is formed by the Emerald Necklace – here Olmsted Park, Jamaica Pond and Arnold Arboretum – and the fast-moving Jamaicaway hugs its edge. JP's main drag is Centre St,

---

TRANSPORTATION

Subway The orange-line Green St T station provides the easiest access to Centre St and Jamaica Pond, though it's a good 20-minute walk. If you are headed to the other JP sights, use Forest Hills T station (also orange line).

running north to south, a few blocks east of Jamaica Pond. Centre St is home to JP's cool restaurants and clubs, while its loveliest architecture is in the Pondside neighborhood. Arnold Arboretum is south along Centre St, while Franklin Park is further east, on the border with Roxbury.

ARNOLD ARBORETUM

☎ 617-524-1718; www.arboretum.harvard.edu; 125 Arborway, Jamaica Plain; admission free; ☺ dawn-dusk; ⓡ Forest Hills

Under a public/private partnership with Harvard University, the 265-acre Arnold Arboretum is planted with over 13,000 exotic trees and flowering shrubs. This gem is pleasant year-round, but it's particularly beautiful in the bloom of spring. Dog walking, Frisbee throwing, bicycling, sledding and general contemplation are encouraged (but picnicking is not allowed). A visitor center (open from 9am to 4pm Monday to Friday, from 10am to 4pm Saturday, and from noon to 4pm Sunday) is located at the main gate, just south of the rotary at Rte 1 and Rte 203. Free one-hour walking tours are offered on alternate Wednesdays (12:15pm), Saturdays (10:30am) and Sundays (1pm) from April to November.

FRANKLIN PARK ZOO

☎ 617-541-5466; www.zoonewengland.com; 1 Franklin Park Rd; adult/senior/child $9.50/8/5.50; ☺ 10am-5pm Mon-Fri, 10am-6pm Sat & Sun Apr-Sep, 10am-4pm daily Oct-Mar; ⓡ Forest Hills

While the 70-acre Franklin Park Zoo is surrounded by one of the city's sketchier neighborhoods, the zoo itself is safe. It boasts a well-designed Tropical Forest pavilion, complete with lush vegetation, waterfalls, lowland gorillas, warthogs and over 30 species of free flight birds. The Serengeti Crossing features Grevy's zebras, Masai giraffes, wildebeests, ostrich and ibex, while the Australian Outback Trail allows visitors to walk among red kangaroos and wallabies. Don't miss the magical Butterfly Landing, where you can stroll among blooming perennials, gushing waterfalls, and 1000 fluttering butterflies in free flight.

The zoo's newest exhibit is Tiger Tales, which recounts the sad stories of Anal, a Bengal tiger, and Luther, a white tiger,

both of whom were 'purchased' by US Fish and Wildlife agents in an undercover sting operation. Other big cats include an African lion and an Amur leopard. Take bus 16 from Forest Hills.

CAMBRIDGE

Eating p156, Shopping p219, Sleeping p239

Boston's neighbor to the north was home to the country's first college and first printing press. Thus Cambridge established early on its reputation as fertile ground for intellectual and political thought – a reputation it has upheld over 350 years (and counting). This reputation is due primarily to its hosting of the two academic heavyweights Harvard University and Massachusetts Institute of Technology (MIT). No less than seven presidents of the United States and countless cabinet members have graduated from Harvard University; fifty-nine MIT faculty, staff and alums have won the Nobel Prize for chemistry, physics, economics, medicine and peace. Most importantly, Cambridge's thousands of student residents ensure the city's continued vibrancy and diversity.

Cambridge is fondly called the 'People's Republic' for its progressive politics. Cantabrigians, as residents are known, vehemently opposed the Vietnam War before others did; they embraced the environmental movement before recycling became profitable; and they were one of the first communities to ban smoking in public buildings.

In this vein, Cambridge has played a historic role in the gay and lesbian rights movement too. When Irish gays and lesbians were excluded from marching in South Boston's traditional St Patrick's Day parade in the mid-1990s, Cambridge immediately pledged to hold its own inclusive parade. More recently, Cambridge City Hall was the first to issue marriage licenses to gay and lesbian couples when same-sex marriages became legal in Massachusetts in 2004.

Life on the 'other side' is all about squares (pardon the pun). Harvard Sq is home to its namesake university, and Central Sq is the stomping ground of MIT students. Cambridge's lesser-known squares may not have a top-tier educational institute on the corner, but Kendall, Inman and Porter all have unique atmospheres, with plenty of

CAMBRIDGE IN A DAY

Even the best and brightest are forced to choose: Harvard or MIT. Take a tour of the historic Harvard campus (try the off-beat Hahvahd Tour for laughs, (p74), then visit one of the university's top-notch museums (p117). Alternatively, explore the MIT campus and discover its wealth of public art and innovative architecture (p118). While you are there, visit the MIT Museum to learn about robots, holograms and other fun technology.

Either way, have lunch in Harvard Sq at Mr Bartleby's Burger Cottage or Darwin's (p156). You can spend the afternoon browsing the bookshops and boutiques (p219), learning about literary Cambridge (p128) or sitting in a café doing the student thing.

When you get hungry, head to Inman Sq for dinner at the East Coast Grill or one of many excellent ethnic eateries (p158). Afterwards, check out the local bands at the Abby Lounge or the Middle East (p177).

restaurants (p156), bars (p170), shopping (p219) and entertainment (p177).

Orientation

When we say the 'other side' we mean the other side of the Charles River. Cambridge stretches along the north shore of the Charles, from the Museum of Science in the east to Mount Auburn Cemetery in the west. Just over the Longfellow Bridge from Beacon Hill, Kendall Sq centers on the intersection of Broadway, Hampshire and Main Sts. Follow Main St a few blocks west, and you'll find yourself in Central Sq at the intersection of Prospect St and Mass Ave. South and east of here, along the banks of the river, is the MIT campus; and north of here, at the intersection of Prospect, Inman and Hampshire Sts, is Inman Sq.

Continue west along Mass Ave and you'll come into the heart of Harvard Sq. The oldest part of the campus – Harvard Yard – is north of the commercial square. But the university stretches out in all directions like an imperialist nation. The business school and the athletic facilities are actually across the river in Allston (part of Boston), while future plans include more expansion south. Mass Ave swoops around Harvard Yard and continues north to Porter Sq.

TRANSPORTATION

Subway The red line is red because it goes to Harvard University, whose official color is crimson and whose nickname is 'The Crimson.' (Don't ask why it's not the crimson line. Clearly the MBTA officials are not Harvard grads.) The red line cuts across Cambridge, east to west, with aptly named stops at all the squares: Kendall, Central, Harvard and Porter. Inman Sq is a short walk up Prospect St from Central T station.

HARVARD SQUARE

Harvard Sq is overflowing with cafés, bookstores, restaurants and street musicians. Although many Cantabrigians rightly complain that the square has lost its edge – once independently-owned shops are continually gobbled up by national chains – Harvard Sq is still a vibrant, exciting place to hang out.

There's a lot to Harvard Sq besides the university: it's a hotbed of colonial and revolutionary history. Opposite the main entrance to Harvard Yard, **Cambridge Common** is the village green where General Washington took command of the Continental Army on July 3, 1775. The traffic island at the south end, known as Dawes Island, pays tribute to the 'other rider' William Dawes, who rode through here on April 18, 1775, to warn that the British were coming (look for bronze hoofprints embedded in the sidewalk). From here you can stroll over to Brattle St, the epitome of colonial posh. Lined with mansions that were once home to royal sympathizers, it earned the nickname Tory Row. But its proximity to the university also means that it is a well-known address for the country's intellectual elite (see also p128).

If you're more interested in today's Harvard Sq, then take a seat at the café in front of Holyoke Center (see p278). From here you have a front-row view of the congregations of students, the performances of buskers, the bustle of the shoppers, the pleas of the homeless, the challenges between chess players, and more.

CHRIST CHURCH Map p310
☎ 617-876-0200; 0 Garden St
Cambridge's oldest church was designed in 1761 by America's first formally trained architect, Peter Harrison (who also did King's Chapel in Boston). Washington's

Sights

CAMBRIDGE

115

SHTICK SHIFT

Here's a puzzler. How does a struggling auto repair shop owner parlay a brief spot on local public radio into national fame and fortune? Answer: he is one of the Magliozzi Brothers.

It helped, of course, to be invited back, which Tom Magliozzi was in 1977, when he first accepted the invitation of radio station WBUR in hopes of drumming up free publicity for his small Cambridge shop, the Good News Garage. It helped even more that Tom brought his wise-cracking younger brother Ray for his next radio gig.

The Magliozzi Brothers were not your typical auto repair guys, nor were they your typical public radio fare. The East Cambridge natives and MIT graduates were adept at leading listeners under the hood and unraveling the mysteries of internal gas combustion, while engaging in non-stop playful banter and sibling rivalry. They also offered insightful and unfiltered opinions of the auto repair profession, the auto industry as a whole and America's car culture.

The audience quickly grew beyond the do-it-yourselfer set as the Car Talk guys developed a local cult following. They were no longer the Magliozzi Brothers, humble garage technicians, they were now the Marx Brothers of auto repair, starring in their own weekly version of Grease Monkey Business.

In 1987, 'Click and Clack, the Tappett Brothers,' took their show on the road, via National Public Radio's nation-wide network of affiliates. Today, Car Talk is heard by more than 4 million listeners on over 500 radios stations each week. The brothers also have a syndicated automotive advice column that runs in 350 newspapers. Their production company, **Dewey, Cheetham & Howe** (cnr Brattle & JFK Sts) is located in Harvard Sq and their shop, the Good News Garage, still operates in Cambridge.

'Don't drive like my brother. Don't drive like my brother.'

troops used it as a barracks after its Tory congregation fled. Christ Church's favorite son is Teddy Roosevelt, who taught Sunday school here when he was a student at Harvard. The adjacent Old Burying Ground is a tranquil revolutionary-era cemetery, where Harvard's first eight presidents are buried.

HOOPER-LEE-NICHOLS HOUSE
Map pp298-9

☎ 617-547-4252; www.cambridgehistory.org; 159 Brattle St; adult/senior/student $5/3/3; ☺ tours 2pm & 3pm Tue & Thu; ☺ Harvard

This c 1685 Georgian mansion has been changed several times over the course of its 300-plus year history, first to modernize and hide its original appearance, and then to recover its historically accurate appearance. Now the headquarters of the Cambridge Historical Society, the house is open for occasional architectural tours. Highlights include the massive stone fireplace in the Chandler room and hand-painted wallpaper in the Bosphorous room.

LONGFELLOW NATIONAL HISTORIC SITE Map p310

☎ 617-876-4491; www.nps.gov/long; 105 Brattle St; adult/child $3/free; ☺ house 10am-4:30pm Wed-Sun May-Oct, grounds dawn to dusk year-round; ☺ Harvard

Brattle St's most famous resident was Henry Wadsworth Longfellow, whose stately

manor is now a National Historic Site. The poet lived and wrote here for 45 years, from 1837 to 1882, writing many of his most famous poems including *Evangeline* and *Hiawatha*. Now under the auspices of the NPS, the Georgian mansion contains many of Longfellow's belongings and lush period gardens. After a long period of restoration, the site now offers poetry readings and historical tours.

Incidentally, one reason Longfellow was so taken with this house was its historical significance. During the Revolutionary War, General Washington appropriated this beauty from its absent Loyalist owner and used it as his headquarters.

MT AUBURN CEMETERY Map pp298-9

☎ 617-547-7105; 580 Mt Auburn St; admission free, guided tour $5; ☺ 8am-5pm, daylight saving time to 6pm; ☺ Harvard

On a sunny day, this delightful spot at the end of Brattle St is worth the 30-minute walk west from Harvard Sq. Developed in 1831, it was the first 'garden cemetery' in the US. Maps pinpoint the rare botanical specimens and notable burial plots, including those for Mary Baker Eddy (founder of the Christian Science Church), Isabella Stewart Gardner (socialite and art collector), Winslow Homer (19th-century American painter), Oliver Wendell Holmes (US Supreme Court Justice) and Henry W Longfellow (19th-century writer). Take bus 71 or 73 from Harvard Sq.

HARVARD UNIVERSITY

Founded in 1636 to educate men for the ministry, Harvard is America's oldest college. (No other college came along until 1693.) The original Ivy League school has six graduates who went on to become US president, not to mention dozens of Nobel laureates and Pulitzer prize winners. It educates 6500 undergraduates and about 12,000 graduates yearly in 10 professional schools. Free campus tours (10am and 2pm Monday to Friday, 2pm Saturday and additional tours in summer) depart from Holyoke Center (see p278).

HARVARD ART MUSEUMS Map p310

☎ 617-495-9400; www.artmuseums.harvard .edu; 32 Quincy St; adult/senior & student/child $7.50/6/free; ☷ 10am-5pm Mon-Sat, 1-5pm Sun; 🚇 Harvard

Harvard's oldest museum is the **Fogg Art Museum** (☷ tours 11am Mon-Fri), which exhibits Western art from the Middle Ages to the present. Set around an Italian Renaissance courtyard, the Fogg has one of the country's finest collections of Impressionist and post-Impressionist works, as well as an excellent display of works by Picasso. The adjacent **Busch-Reisinger Museum** (☷ tours 1pm Mon-Fri) specializes in Central and Northern European art.

Across the street, the **Arthur M Sackler Museum** (☎ 617-495-9400; 485 Broadway; ☷ tours 2pm Wed) is devoted to Asian and Islamic art. It boasts the world's most impressive collection of Chinese jade as well as fine Japanese woodblock prints. One ticket allows entry to all three museums. Admission is free on Saturday mornings.

HARVARD MUSEUM OF NATURAL HISTORY Map p310

☎ 617-495-3045; www.hmnh.harvard.edu; 24 Oxford St; adult/senior & student/child $9/7/6, 9am-noon Sun free; ☷ 9am-5pm; 🚇 Harvard

This place is coming around to catering to the casual science buff, in addition to the botanists, zoologists and geologists that are its normal audience. The highlight is the famous botanical galleries, which feature more than 3000 lifelike pieces of handblown-glass flowers and plants. The zoological galleries house an unbelievable number of stuffed animals and reassembled skeletons, as well as an impressive fossil collection. (Look for the pheasant that was owned by George Washington.) And the mineralogical and geological galleries contain sparkling gemstones from all over the world, including some found right here in New England. The shining star is the 1642lb amethyst geode from Brazil. The price of admission includes entry into the Peabody Museum of Archaeology & Ethnology (see below).

HARVARD YARD Map p310

☎ 617-495-1573; www.harvard.edu; tours free; ☷ 10am & 2pm Mon-Fri & 2pm Sat Sep-May, 10am, 11:15am, 2pm & 3:15 Mon-Sat Jun & Aug; 🚇 Harvard

The geographic heart of Harvard University – where red-brick buildings and leaf-covered paths exude academia – is Harvard Yard (through Anderson Gates from Mass Ave). The focal point of the yard is the John Harvard statue, where every Harvard hopeful has a photo taken (and touches his shiny shoe for good luck). Daniel Chester French's sculpture, inscribed 'John Harvard, Founder of Harvard College, 1638,' is known as the statue of three lies: (1) it does not actually depict Harvard (since no image of him exists), but a student chosen at random; (2) John Harvard was not the founder of the college, but its first benefactor in 1638; (3) the college was actually founded two years earlier in 1636. The Harvard symbol hardly lives up to the university's motto, *Veritas*, or 'truth.'

Learn about this and many other fun facts on a campus tour, which departs several times a day from Holyoke Center (see p278).

PEABODY MUSEUM OF ARCHAEOLOGY & ETHNOLOGY Map p310

☎ 617-496-1027; www.peabody.harvard.edu; 11 Divinity Ave; adult/senior & student/child $9/7/6; ☷ 9am-5pm; 🚇 Harvard

Founded in 1866, the Peabody Museum is one of the world's oldest museums devoted to anthropology. Rotating exhibits showcase pieces from its impressive collection, which focuses on artifacts from Native Americans and other indigenous groups. The Hall of the North American Indian traces how native peoples responded to the arrival of Europeans from the 15th to

Sights

CAMBRIDGE

the 18th centuries. The price of admission includes entry to the Harvard Museum of Natural History.

WIDENER LIBRARY

Map p310

Behind this mass of Corinthian columns and steep stairs are more than 5 miles of books. Widener was built in memory of rare-book collector Harry Elkins Widener, who had the misfortune of returning from England aboard the *Titanic*. Apparently Harry gave up his seat in a lifeboat to retrieve his favorite book from his stateroom. The Widener family made two stipulations to their library grant: that the building's exterior mortar or bricks not be altered (Harvard circumvented this by connecting the library to another with a glass breezeway) and that a reading room like Harry's be built and fresh flowers placed in it daily. Legend states that the bequest also required that students pass a swimming test. The library, unfortunately, is not open to the public.

MASSACHUSETTS INSTITUTE OF TECHNOLOGY

The MIT campus – spread along Mass Ave east of Central Sq and along the Charles River – offers a completely novel perspective on Cambridge academia: proudly nerdy, but not quite as tweedy as Harvard. Notorious pranksters, MIT students have a long tradition of leaving large and very visible objects on the roof of the 'Great Dome.' And then there's the whole business about the official distance across the Harvard Bridge (see opposite).

MIT seems to pride itself on being offbeat. Wander into a courtyard and you might find it is graced with a sculpture by Henry Moore or Alexander Calder; or you might just as well find a Ping-Pong table or a trampoline. In the past few years, it seems the university has taken this irreverence to a new level, as a recent frenzy of building has resulted in some of the most architecturally unusual and intriguing structures you'll find on either side of the river.

It's worth a wander to see what they'll come up with next. Or join an excellent guided campus tour (10:45am and 2:45pm Monday to Friday) which departs from the information center (see p278).

LIST VISUAL ARTS CENTER

Map p311

☎ 617-253-4680; http://web.mit.edu/lvac; Weisner Bldg, 20 Ames St; suggested donation $5; ◷ noon-6pm Tue-Thu, Sat & Sun, noon-8pm Fri; ◖ Kendall

The stated goal of the List Center is to explore the boundaries of artistic inquiry – to use art to ask questions, not only about aesthetics, but also about culture, society and of course science. Rotating exhibits push the contemporary art envelope in painting, sculpture, photography, video and just about every other medium imaginable.

This is also where you can pick up a map of MIT's public art, proof enough that this university supports artistic as well as technological innovation. The university's progressive Percent-for-Art program requires that a certain percentage of every new building and renovation project be earmarked for art acquisitions.

MIT MUSEUM

Map p311

☎ 617-253-4444; http://web.mit.edu/museum; 265 Mass Ave; adult/senior & student $5/2; ◷ 10am-5pm Tue-Fri, noon-5pm Sat & Sun; ◖ Central

Leave it to the mischievous brainiacs at MIT to come up with the city's quirkiest museum. An exhibit called Robots and Beyond demonstrates MIT's ongoing work on artificial intelligence. You can meet humanoid robots like observant Cog and personable Kismet and decide for yourself if they are smarter than humans. Sculptor Arthur Ganson explores the fine line between art and engineering with his display of interactive sculpture. And the fantastic Light Fantastic is the world's largest exhibit of holograms – learn how they are made and how they are used in fields from art and architecture to medicine and engineering.

STATA CENTER

Map p311

☎ 617-253-5851; www.csail.mit.edu; 32 Vassar St; ◖ Kendall

Of all the funky buildings on the MIT campus, none has received more attention than this avant-garde edifice that was designed

A WALK ACROSS THE HARVARD BRIDGE

The Harvard Bridge – from Back Bay in Boston to MIT in Cambridge – is the longest bridge route across the Charles River. It is not too long to walk, but it is long enough to do some wondering while you walk. You might wonder, for example, why the bridge that leads into the heart of MIT is named the Harvard Bridge.

According to legend, the state offered to name the bridge after Cambridge's second university. But the brainiac engineers at MIT analyzed the plans for construction and found the bridge was structurally unsound. Not wanting the MIT moniker associated with a faulty feat of engineering, it was suggested that the bridge better be named for the neighboring university up the river. That the bridge was subsequently rebuilt validated the superior brainpower of MIT.

That is only a legend, however (one invented by an MIT student, no doubt). The fact is that the Harvard Bridge was first constructed in 1891, and MIT moved to its current location only in 1916. The bridge was rebuilt in the 1980s to modernize and expand it, but the original name has stuck, at least officially. Most Bostonians actually refer to this bridge as the 'Mass Ave bridge' because frankly it makes more sense.

By now, walking across the bridge, perhaps you have reached the halfway point: 'Halfway to Hell' reads the scrawled graffiti. What is this graffiti anyway? What is a 'smoot'?

A smoot is an obscure unit of measurement that was used to measure the distance of the Harvard Bridge, first in 1958 and every year since. One smoot is approximately five feet, seven inches, the height of Oliver R Smoot, who was a pledge of the MIT fraternity Lambda Chi Alpha in '58. He was the shortest pledge that year. And yes, his physical person was actually used for all the measurements.

And now that you have reached the other side of the river, surely you are wondering exactly how long this bridge is. We can't say about the Harvard students, but certainly every MIT student knows that the Harvard Bridge is 364.4 smoots plus one ear.

Sights

OUTLYING NEIGHBORHOODS

by architectural legend Frank Gehry. Like something out of Dr Seuss, the Stata Center for Computer Science & Artificial Intelligence Laboratory (CSAIL) is composed of whimsical, colorful shapes and tilting metallic towers. Pick up a map at the information desk for a self-guided tour of the public spaces. Or wander on your own to discover the hidden courtyards, multiple levels and light-filled spaces. If you are interested in the ongoing research taking place here, guided tours of the laboratories are available to the general public: submit your online request at least two weeks in advance.

OUTLYING NEIGHBORHOODS

SOMERVILLE

Wedged in between Cambridge and Charlestown, Somerville is an old-fashioned, working-class city that is experiencing an influx of immigrants – from Brazil, Korea, Haiti and – most noticeably – from Cambridge. As real estate prices continue to soar, all the artists and students that used to live in Cambridge are invading this neighbor to the north. This is where statues of the Virgin Mary rub shoulders with post-industrial garden artwork; where the local

arts council sponsors trolley tours of the brightest Christmas light displays; where young Harvard professors live next door to old-timer Harvard cafeteria ladies.

Somerville is changing, and nowhere is it more obvious than Davis Sq. This Cambridge-wannabe square has been transformed with trendy bars (p173), cappuccino counters, gourmet restaurants (p160) and public art. Gentrification is slower down the road in the Union Sq; but it is home to Boston's hottest lesbian club (p183), a sign that change is in the air. While Somerville is not big on tourist attractions, it is the site of some notable revolutionary history.

OLD POWDER HOUSE

cnr College Ave & Broadway; 🕙 dawn to dusk; 🚇 Davis

In the years leading up to the revolution, the Old Powder House contained the largest supply of gunpowder in the state.

TRANSPORTATION

Subway Davis Sq is directly above the red-line T stop of the same name.
Bus To get to Union Sq take a from Harvard Sq or the 87 from Davis Sq.

Which is why the patriots were alarmed when British troops raided the facility and confiscated the ammunition on September 1, 1774. It was part of a British attempt to keep the peace after levying the Intolerable Acts, but patriot sympathizers took the move to be threatening, and rumors spread wildly. Men came from all over the region, forming militia groups that were prepared to fight.

Known as the Powder Alarm, the tension was eventually diffused. But the incident caused the British to call for reinforcements from London; and it impressed upon the revolutionary movement the need for preparedness. During the War for Independence, this facility became the main munitions depot for the Continental Army. The powder house is not open but the park is a pleasant place to stroll. Walk north from Davis on College Ave.

PROSPECT HILL PARK
Munroe St; ☽ dawn to dusk
On January 1, 1776, George Washington ordered the Grand Union Flag be flown from a 76ft mast atop Prospect Hill. Bearing thirteen stripes representing the united colonies with the crosses of St Andrew in the corner, it is considered the first American flag and this is the first time it was so proudly waved. The flag flew over Prospect Hill until British troops were driven out of the city; and it served the purpose of the national flag until the new nation officially adopted the Stars and Stripes the following year.

The granite tower was built in 1903 to commemorate the site's historical significance. Today you can see why the patriots chose this spot to wave their flag, as the tall tower gives a spectacular panorama across Cambridge, Charlestown and Boston. The tower is open once a year – on New Year's Day – when the city of Somerville sponsors a reenactment of the flag-raising.

Prospect Hill overlooks Union Sq from the north. Walk up Stone St and climb the stairs to the top of the hill.

SOUTH BOSTON
This tight-knit, predominantly white, working-class, Irish-Catholic community is not the most alluring part of Boston.

It was caught in the national spotlight in the 1970s, when courts ordered the city to bus students between neighborhoods in order to integrate the schools. Violence broke out in South Boston, with protesters throwing stones, eggs and rotten tomatoes at buses filled with black students; other appalling incidents occurred throughout the school year, and as a result, several students were killed. Hardly Boston's finest hour.

More recent news has focused on Whitey Bulger – Boston's local mafia guy who made the FBI's 'Most Wanted' list – who hales from South Boston. 'Southie' is probably most famous because it was the stomping ground of Matt Damon's character in *Good Will Hunting*, the 1997 film about the genius from the wrong side of the tracks (or river, in this case).

Despite these less-than-flattering portrayals, South Boston has its own charm. The waterside community offers great harbor views, as well as Boston's best city beaches (p201). East and West Broadway, South Boston's main thoroughfare, are packed with Irish pubs. This neighborhood is getting a glimpse of the gentrification that has transformed other parts of the city; but Southie is still unapologetically old-school.

TRANSPORTATION
Subway Use the red-line Broadway to get to the center of South Boston. Or follow the HarborWalk southeast from the Seaport District.

CASTLE ISLAND & FORT INDEPENDENCE
☎ 617-727-5290; Marine Park; ☽ dawn to dusk May-Sep; 🚇 Broadway
Since 1634, eight different fortresses have occupied this strategic spot at the entrance to the Inner Harbor. Fort Independence – the five-point granite fort that stands here today – was built between 1834 and 1851. It sits on 22 acres of parkland called Castle Island (a misnomer, as it's connected to the mainland). A paved pathway follows the perimeter of the peninsula – good for strolling or biking – and there is a small swimming beach. Take bus 11 from Broadway T station.

DORCHESTER HEIGHTS MONUMENT

btwn G & Old Harbor Sts; 🕐 dawn to dusk;
🚇 Broadway

In the winter of 1776, rebel troops dragged 59 heavy cannons to Boston from Fort Ticonderoga in upstate New York. On the night of March 4, they perched them high atop Dorchester Heights, from where the British warships in the Harbor were at their mercy. The move caught the British completely by surprise, and ultimately convinced them to abandon Boston.

The Georgian revival tower that stands here today was erected in 1898. To reach the Dorchester Heights Monument, walk east along West Broadway from the T station, turn right onto Dorchester St and head up any of the little streets. (Or take bus 11 and get off near Dorchester St.)

DORCHESTER

Columbia Point juts into the harbor south of the city center in Dorchester, one of Boston's rougher neighborhoods. The location is unexpected, but it does offers dramatic views of the city and a pleasant place to stroll. The museums here – associated with University of Massachusetts, Boston – are a part of ongoing revitalization efforts. Unfortunately, the revitalization has not resulted in much activity outside the museums. There are, however, a few places to eat and sleep around here (see p242) and you can

TRANSPORTATION

Subway/Bus Take the red line to JFK/UMass and catch a free shuttle bus (departures every 20 minutes) to Columbia Point.

stroll or ride along the HarborWalk between Columbia Point and Castle Island (opposite) or the South Boston beaches (p201).

COMMONWEALTH MUSEUM

☎ 617-727-9268; 220 Morrissey Blvd, Columbia Point; admission free; 🕐 9am-5pm Mon-Fri, 9am-3pm Sat; 🚇 JFK/UMass

The Commonwealth Museum exhibits documents dating to the early days of colonization. Rotating exhibits showcase various aspects of state history, ranging from the archaeology of the Big Dig to the story of Italian anarchists Sacco and Vanzetti. Exhibits are drawn from the Massachusetts Archives (☎ 617-727-2816), a research facility housed on site.

JOHN F KENNEDY LIBRARY & MUSEUM

☎ 617-514-1600; www.jfklibrary.org; Columbia Point, Dorchester; adult/senior & student/child $10/8/7; 🕐 9am-5pm; 🚇 JFK/UMass

The legacy of JFK is ubiquitous in Boston, but the official memorial to the 35th president is the John F Kennedy Library

Sights

OUTLYING NEIGHBORHOODS

John F Kennedy Library & Museum (above)

& Museum. The striking, modern, marble building – designed by IM Pei – was dubbed 'the shining monument by the sea' when it opened in 1979. The architectural centerpiece is the glass pavilion, with soaring 115-foot ceilings and floor-to-ceiling windows overlooking Boston Harbor.

The museum is a fitting tribute to JFK's life and legacy. The effective use of video recreates history for visitors who may or may not remember the early 1960s. A highlight is the museum's treatment of the Cuban Missile Crisis: a short film explores the dilemmas and decisions that the president faced, while an archival exhibit displays actual documents and correspondence from these gripping thirteen days. Family photographs and private writings – of both John and Jacqueline – add a personal but not overly sentimental dimension to the exhibits.

Interestingly, the library has an archive of writer Ernest Hemingway's manuscripts and papers (though there is no exhibit space). Kennedy was key in helping Hemingway's widow get the manuscripts and papers out of Cuba during the most intense days of the embargo. She willed them to this library, because it offers more public access than most.

Walking & Biking Tours

Walking & Biking Tours

Boston's intimate neighborhoods are a tapestry of historical anecdotes, politics, personalities and architectural styles. The best way to discover this intriguing city is by feeling the uneven brick sidewalks beneath your feet (or wheels). The city's small size and compact layout make it easy to navigate by your own leg power.

The Freedom Trail is a walking tour of Boston's most talked-about sights (see p106). But this chapter provides some ideal and unusual ways to see the rest of Boston: contemporary cultural gems and historic 'hoods that may not be on every visitor's itinerary.

For an excellent overview, the Charles River Bike Loop is a bicycle ride along Boston's main waterway, traversing the green spaces of the Esplanade and Charlesbank Park on the Boston side, as well as the intellectual institutions on the Cambridge side.

History buffs have a few options. The Beacon Hill Hike takes you up and down one of Boston's oldest and most prestigious residential areas, recounting the interwoven histories of Boston Brahmins and black heritage. Literary Cambridge tours some of the sites where Boston-area writers and thinkers congregated, cogitated and composed.

Is all this talk about walking tours making you hungry? Or thirsty? Last but not least, foodies can explore Boston's Italian culinary heritage on the North End Nosh.

So lace up your sneakers and hit the road.

BEACON HILL HIKE

Wander the southern slope of Beacon Hill to admire the brick town houses with purple windowpanes and the cobblestone streets lit with gas lanterns, all of which somehow epitomize Boston's blue blood. Many famous families occupied these stately 19th-century homes – high-minded intellectuals, writers and philosophers, men and women with old money and new ideas. But the back side of Beacon Hill tells a different (if related) tale: in the early 19th century, the northern slope was the home of Boston's thriving community of free African Americans (in fact, the Black Heritage Trail roams around these parts; see p73). Between the liberal-thinking upper crust and the activist black Bostonians, Beacon Hill became the center of the abolitionist movement and a crucial stop on the Underground Railroad (the informal network of safe havens for runaway slaves).

This walking tour explores both sides of Beacon Hill's rich history. To begin, walk up Park St to the corner of Beacon St, where the **Robert Gould Shaw Memorial 1** (p78) honors the African American soldiers who fought in the Civil War and the Boston Brahmin captain who led them. Walk down Beacon St, in front of the Massachusetts State House, and head into Beacon Hill on Joy St.

Turn left on Mt Vernon St, one of the Hill's loveliest streets. The 1804 **Nichols House Museum 2** (p77), designed by Charles Bulfinch, was home to Miss Rose Standish Nichols, known for her skills in design and her leadership in the women's suffrage movement. It is one of the few Beacon Hill homes that is open to the public.

Continue down Mt Vernon St, which writer Henry James called the 'most respectable street in America.' You will pass the **Second Harrison Gray Otis House 3** at No 85. It is the second of three houses designed by Charles Bulfinch for Harrison Gray Otis, a real estate developer, US senator and Boston mayor at the turn of the 18th century. This one is not open to the public, but you can visit the Otis House Museum (see p81) in his third house on Cambridge St.

Turn south on Willow St and make your way to Boston's oft-photographed narrowest street, **Acorn St 4**. This cobblestone alleyway was once home to artisans and to the service people who worked for the adjacent mansion dwellers. The brick walls on the north side of the street enclose examples of Beacon Hill's hidden gardens.

Return to Mt Vernon St and turn up Louisburg Sq (pronounced Lewis-burg), a cluster of elegant brick row houses facing a private park. There is no more prestigious address in

Boston: after she gained literary success, **Louisa May Alcott's home 5** was at No 10; at the northern corner of the square is the **home of Senator John Kerry 6** and his wife Teresa Heinz.

Turn right up Pinckney St, particularly lovely in spring when the trees are blossoming. The house at **No 62 7** was owned by George and Susan Hillard. Though Mr Hillard was an ardent Webster Whig (who favored preserving the Union over freeing the slaves), he apparently did not interfere with his wife's activity aiding fugitive slaves. In the 1920s, renovations uncovered hidden attic space, leading historians to believe that this was a stopping point on the Underground Railroad. Across the street the **Phillips School 8**, formerly known as Boston English High School, was the first public grammar school in Boston to be racially – if not gender – integrated. (It's now condominiums.)

The small, clapboard home at No 5, the **Middleton-Glapion House 9**, was built in 1791 – perhaps the oldest house still standing on Beacon Hill. It was owned by George Middleton, an African American coachman who was a prominent member of the community. He had been commander of the Bucks of America (an all-black regiment in the Continental Army) during the Revolutionary War and he was the Grand Master of the African Lodge. The house was co-owned by one Louis Glapion, a mixed-race barber about whom little is known.

Pinckney St and parallel Myrtle St act as a dividing line between the stately south slope and the less conforming north slope. Not surprisingly, these streets also demarcated 19th-century white and black communities: whites lived on the south slope, blacks on the north. Head down Joy St to the **Museum of Afro-American History 10** (p76), incorporating the African Meeting House and the Abiel Smith School, which served local families in the 1830s.

At the end of Smith Court, pass through the narrow and winding **Holmes Alley 11**. This alley was well known to slaves but not to 'slavecatchers' (bounty hunters who

HIKE FACTS

Start/Finish Park St (Ⓣ Park St)
Distance 2 miles
Duration 2 hours
Fuel Stops Panificio (p136), Upper Crust (p136)

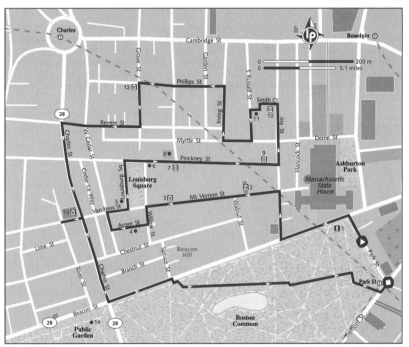

Charles St Meeting House (below), Beacon Hill

pursued runaway slaves across state borders and returned them to their owners). Since it appears to be a dead end, fleeing slaves could often 'disappear' by ducking down this alley. Often, the doors fronting the alley were left unlocked so slaves could hide inside, or they would try to blend into groups of free blacks congregating at the meeting house. Slave catchers were rarely successful in Boston, and a few were tarred and feathered for their efforts.

Turn left up South Russell St, right onto narrow Myrtle St and right onto Irving St. To the left is Phillips St, which was a hotbed of abolitionist activity in the 19th century, partly due to its proximity to the Charles River. At the corner of Phillips & Grove Sts, the private **Lewis Hayden House 12** is among Boston's most important abolitionist sites, having served as refuge to hundreds of runaway slaves. An underground tunnel ran from Hayden's house, allowing slaves a secret means of entry or escape. Legend has it that Hayden – himself a former slave of Senator Henry Clay – never allowed his house to be searched. He apparently kept a stash of gunpowder in the basement and threatened to blow up the house if its threshold was crossed. When slavecatchers came to his doorway, the militant Hayden proclaimed 'leave in peace or leave in pieces.'

Turn south on Grove St, then take a right onto Revere St to Charles St. These are the 'flats,' which Otis and Bulfinch filled in after leveling peaks on the Hill. Asher Benjamin designed the classically Federal **Charles St Meeting House 13** at No 70. The meeting house provided a pulpit for abolitionist leaders William Lloyd Garrison, Frederick Douglass, Harriet Tubman and Sojourner Truth during the 19th century. Charles St is Beacon Hill's main commercial street – an excellent opportunity to stop to refuel (see p136).

End your Beacon Hill hike at the **Public Garden 14** (p76), or head across the Boston Common to return to Park St.

CHARLES RIVER BIKE LOOP

The Charles River, once lined with sawmills and leather manufacturers, was a smelly, marshy tidal estuary until the early 1900s, when the Charles River Dam was built. Today, both sides of the curvaceous Charles River are graced with grassy banks and weaving byways. The paved paths are perfect for bicycling, in-line skating, jogging and walking; the waterway suits sailing and sculling. Storrow Dr snakes along the Boston side of the river, Memorial Dr along the Cambridge side.

If you intend to bicycle the entire loop, you can actually start at any spot along either side of the river. But for the purposes of this tour, we'll start at the **Harvard Bridge 1**, sometimes also called the Mass Ave Bridge, which leads from Back Bay to Massachusetts Institute of Technology (MIT). And why does the bridge that leads directly into the heart of MIT bear the name of its neighboring university up the river? The fact is that the Harvard Bridge was first constructed in 1891, and MIT moved to its current location only in 1916.

Descend to the **Charles River Esplanade** (p199), another green masterpiece designed by Frederick Law Olmsted. On warm days, Bostonians migrate to this most popular and picturesque portion of the park to sunbathe, picnic and feed waterfowl gliding by the tranquil riverbank; children romp on the playscape; and a nonstop flow of joggers, skaters, bikers and walkers travels these paths. Cross the little stone bridge to the sunny strip of land that lies between the Charles River Basin and the Sturrow Lagoon. Just west of the Arthur Fiedler Footbridge is the aluminum **Arthur Fiedler bust 3**, a 1984 sculpture of the maestro who led the Boston Pops for 50 years.

Back on the mainland, the path winds around the **Hatch Memorial Shell 4** (p190), a 1940 art-deco semicovered stage where free outdoor movies and concerts are held throughout the summer. Most of the sailboats tacking back and forth on the Charles originate from **Community Boating 5** (p200), a public boathouse that rents sailboats, kayaks and windsurfers.

Follow the path under the **Longfellow Bridge 6**, nicknamed the Salt & Pepper Bridge because its towers resemble shakers. The Longfellow Bridge offers one of the best views of the Boston skyline.

The last stretch of bike path on the Boston side traverses the Charlesbank Park, which has recently been revamped. Tennis courts, baseball field and swimming pool attract active types. The path ends at the busy intersection around Science Park T station. You'll have to share the sidewalk with pedestrians, as you maneuver your way across the old **metal drawbridge 7**, which crosses the river at its narrowest point. On your left, the **Museum of Science 8** is impossible to miss if you look for the Tyrannosaurus rex standing out front.

Turn left onto Edwin Land Blvd and again onto Cambridge Parkway, where the bike path picks up and continues southwest along the Charles. Pass in front of some swanky highrise apartments with a private marina out front. Continue underneath the Longfellow Bridge. You are now entering the vicinity of MIT (p118), which is easily recognizable from the classical architecture. If you wish to get a closer look at some of the public art that dots the campus, cross busy Memorial Dr at the Wadsworth St crosswalk.

Between the **Walker Memorial 9** and the **Hayden Memorial Library 10**, you can catch a

LOOP FACTS

Start Harvard Bridge (🚇 Hynes or Kenmore)
Finish Harvard Sq (🚇 Harvard)
Distance 8.6 miles
Duration 3 hours
Fuel Stops Shays (p171), Café Pamplona (p170)

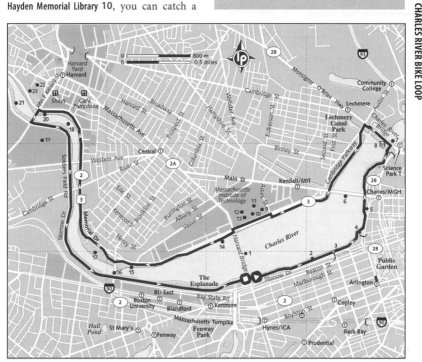

glimpse of Alexander Calder's impressive sculpture **La Grande Voile 11**. Sculptures also dot the lawn of the library. Further along, the wings of the domed **Maclaurin Buildings 12** enclose **Killian Court 13**, which contains sculptures by Henry Moore and Michael Heizer.

The next intersection is Massachusetts Ave, which heads north into the heart of the campus. Cross back to the south side of Memorial Dr and continue along the river. You'll pass the **MIT boathouse 14** and the **Boston University boathouse 15** along this stretch. The MIT boathouse contains one of the nation's best rowing simulators, complete with honest-to-goodness water currents of 10mph. The **BU Bridge 16** is painted with graffiti supporting the BU Terriers. Apparently, this bridge is the only place in the world where a boat can sail under a train driving under a car driving under an airplane. It's a popular spot for photographs, as a gaggle of geese tends to congregate beneath the railroad bridge on the riverbank.

West of the BU Bridge is **Magazine Beach 17**. Despite the progress of clean-up efforts, Magazine Beach is not expected to open for swimming at any time in the near future. It is, however, a popular spot for kite-flying and dog-running. From here, Memorial Dr turns north, passing the River St Bridge and the Western Ave Bridge, both of which head into Central Sq.

As you continue north of Western Ave, you are entering the neighborhood of Harvard University (p117). The red brick buildings and shady courtyards are dormitories and classrooms, and no less than five lofty spires and cupolas grace this skyline. The **Weeks Memorial Bridge 18** is a charming footbridge that offers an excellent vantage point for watching the sculls on the water. It leads across the river to the campus of the prestigious **Harvard Business School 19**.

The most picturesque boathouse is **Weld Boathouse 20**, just east of the Larz Anderson Bridge. Harvard's other boathouse is **Newell Boathouse 21**, on the opposite shore. On the northwest side of JFK St, Harvard's school for public policy – the **Kennedy School of Government 22** – overlooks serene **JFK Park 23**, a pleasant place to recuperate.

Turn right on JFK St to ride into the heart of Harvard Sq. This is an excellent opportunity to refuel (see p156). From here, you can hop on the T (bikes are allowed on the T after 7pm) and catch a ride back into the city. Alternatively, cross the Anderson Bridge and pedal back on the Boston side for a new perspective. More ambitious riders can follow the Charles River route all the way to Watertown, which adds about nine miles to the distance.

LITERARY CAMBRIDGE

Home of the country's first university and its first printing press, Cambridge has made its mark on historical and literary history. Over the centuries, countless writers and thinkers have passed through Johnson Gates, walked the shady lanes of Harvard Yard and lived in the clapboard houses surrounding Harvard Sq. Poet Emily Dickinson went so far as to claim Cambridge 'as hallowed or as unbelieved' as Westminster Abbey. These days, Harvard Sq is still a sort of a pilgrimage place for all types of readers and writers – not only to visit the hallowed halls of its namesake university, but also to peruse the aisles of the countless bookstores that crowd these streets.

Start your tour in the center of Harvard Sq, where **Out of Town News 1** (p220) has been selling newspapers and magazines from around the world since 1928. This prominent spot – directly opposite Harvard Yard – is where Anne Bradstreet had her home in 1631. A poet and autobiographer, she is considered America's first published author. Across the street, the **Coop 2** (p221) is the country's oldest college cooperative, founded in 1882 in response to students' perception that local merchants were price fixing and gouging. Now it is the largest bookstore in the square and managed by Barnes & Noble.

Turn right on Dunster St and look for the **plaque honoring Stephen Day 3**, who ran America's first printing press, founded in 1638. While not many books from this ancient press survive, Day's legacy lives on in Harvard Sq.

Cut down to Mount Auburn St, where you'll find a strip of specialty bookstores offering something for everyone: the **Globe Corner Bookstore 4** (p221) specializes in guidebooks, maps and travel literature (come here for the latest by your favorite Lonely Planet author); **Schoenhof's 5** (p222) is a long-standing and much-loved foreign-language bookstore; inside Holyoke Center, the **Harvard University Press Bookstore 6** (p221) is filled with the latest academic offerings.

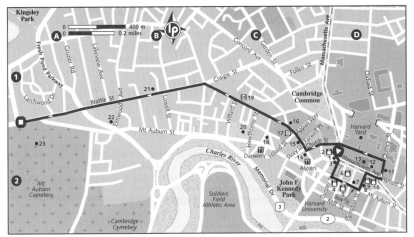

At the corner of Mt Auburn and Plympton Sts, the oddly shaped building at 44 Bow St houses the offices for the long-running humor magazine, **Harvard Lampoon 7**. The university newspaper, **Harvard Crimson 8** is up the street at 14 Plympton. Both publications have nurtured many writers that have gone on to become journalists, novelists and screenwriters, including John Updike and George Plympton. Turn left on Plympton St and return to Mass Ave.

WALK FACTS

Start Harvard Sq (🚇 Harvard)
Finish Mount Auburn Cemetery
Distance 2.3 miles
Duration 3 hours
Fuel Stops Darwin's (p156), Algiers (p170)

At the corner stand two Harvard Sq institutions. **Grolier Poetry Shop 9** (p221) is a famous poetry bookstore that has been hosting poetry readings and discussions since 1927. The independent **Harvard Bookstore 10** (p221) has a basement full of bargains, including second-hand books and remnants.

Cross the street and continue up Quincy St. The site of the Harvard Faculty Club, at No 20, was once the **residence of the James family 11**. Henry James, author of *The Bostonians* and *Daisy Miller*, did most of his writing when he lived in England. His troubled sister Alice, a prolific journal-writer, also lived here, and her journals were published posthumously.

From Quincy St, walk through the iron gates and enter Harvard Yard (p117), the geographic and historic heart of the university. The list of well-known writers who have attended Harvard is too long to mention; among those who have taught here are William James, Henry Wadsworth Longfellow, TS Eliot and Robert Frost. **Houghton Library 12** is the university's repository focusing on European and American literature and history. It contains many rare books, manuscripts and personal papers of writers ranging throughout history. **Widener Library 13** (p118) is the imposing granite building behind it.

Walk straight across Harvard Yard and emerge through Johnson Gates onto Mass Ave. Cross the street and stroll up Church St to Brattle St. Across the street, the 1727 clapboard colonial known as Brattle House now houses the **Cambridge Center for Adult Education 14** (p272). In the 19th century, it was the home of Margaret Fuller, a prominent feminist and editor of the transcendentalist publication *The Dial*. Down the street at No 54, the **Blacksmith House 15** was the home of Dexter Pratt, the namesake character in Longfellow's poem, *The Village Blacksmith*. The sculpted steel chestnut tree memorial is complete with an anvil and a set of blacksmith tools.

Past Hillard St, Brattle St cuts through the middle of the former Radcliffe campus. Radcliffe University has also spawned countless literary luminaries, including Gertrude Stein, Margaret Atwood and Anne Sexton. Lovely **Radcliffe Yard 16** is on the right-hand side; on the left, the **American Repertory Theater 17** (p185) is renowned for its productions of Chekhov's works and other dire plays. Turn left down Ash St and stroll down this shady lane to **No 14 18**, where TS Eliot lived when he was a lecturer at Harvard in 1913.

Return to Brattle St and continue west. Brattle Street's most prominent resident, the esteemed poet Henry Wadsworth Longfellow lived for 45 years in the yellow house at No 105, now known as the **Longfellow National Historic Site 19** (p116). Here, he wrote his most famous works, including *Hiawatha, Paul Revere's Ride* and *The Village Blacksmith,* and hosted all the literati of the day, including Emerson, Thoreau and Hawthorne. Between Brattle and Mount Auburn Sts, the lovely **Longfellow Park 20** ensures an unimpeded river view from the mansion.

Continuing west on Brattle St, you'll pass the distinguished **home of John Bartlett 21** of quotation fame at No 165.

Turn left on Elmwood Ave and walk down to the **urban estate at No 33 22**. This gracious property was once the home of Elbridge Gerry, signer of the Declaration of Independence and namesake of the term 'gerrymandering.' But its more erudite resident was James Russell Lowell – poet, political essayist and first editor of the *Atlantic Monthly*. Elmwood is now the residence of the president of Harvard University.

Return to Brattle St and continue west until the road ends at the intersection with Mount Auburn St. Cross this busy road and enter through the Egyptian revival gates to **Mount Auburn Cemetery 23** (p116), final resting place of Boston's most distinguished writers and thinkers. You can walk back into Harvard Sq or take bus 71 or 73, both of which pass the cemetery gates.

NORTH END NOSH

This warren of streets and alleys retains the old-world flavor brought by southern European immigrants. And when we say 'flavor', we're not being metaphorical. We mean garlic, basil and oregano, sautéed in extra virgin olive oil; rich tomato sauces that have simmered for hours; amaretto and anise, Barolo, Bardolino and Chianti; dark, rich coffee; smooth, sweet cheese; and cold, creamy gelato. The North End is famous for its Italian restaurants, wine bars and pizza parlors (see p139 for some suggestions). But even North Enders must cook at home occasionally. And when they do, they pick up their ingredients in the specialty shops that carry products imported from Italy, so they can re-create their grandmother's pasta sauce.

As you explore the North End, you can shop for authentic ingredients for an Italian extravaganza. But don't resist sampling the meats, cheeses and pastries as you go, which will undoubtedly add to your appreciation of the neighborhood's Italian 'flavor'.

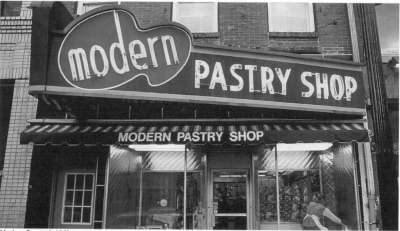

Modern Pastry (p139)

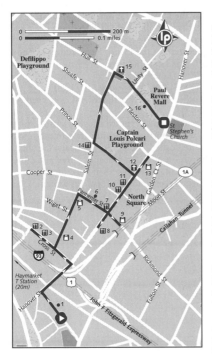

Start at **Haymarket 1** (p134), Boston's vibrant, open-air market. On Friday and Saturday, Hanover St and Blackstone St are jam-packed with shoppers, haggling over the city's freshest, cheapest and most delicious produce. You're unlikely to hear shoppers and vendors conversing in Italian (though you will hear Cantonese, Vietnamese and plenty of Bostonese), but the volume and energy level are just as high as you might expect in a Roman marketplace.

Head up Hanover St into the North End and turn left on Cross St. For years, this corner was a forbidding construction site, but now it is an enticing park-side outdoor seating area. **J Pace & Son 2** (p139) is a neighborhood Italian grocer with fresh cheese, olives, pasta and meats. A daily changing menu offers made-to-order sandwiches and pasta dishes.

Next door, **Maria's Pastry 3** (p139) is considered the neighborhood's most authentic pastry shop. Take your pick from cookies, cakes and confections made with love by the women of the Merola family.

Now duck back up Salem St, which is chock-a-block with specialty markets and restaurants at the southern end. Stop at **Dairy Fresh Candies 4** (p211), for an unsurpassed selection of nuts, chocolates, candies and dried fruit; and at the aromatic **Polcari's Coffee 5** (p211) for coffee, tea and spices. Turn right and head east on Parmenter St. Pop into the **North End Branch Library 6** (closed Sun) at No 25 to check out the impressive plaster model of Doge's Palace in Venice.

NOSH FACTS

Start Haymarket (Haymarket)
Finish Paul Revere Park
Distance 1 mile
Duration 1-2 hours
Fuel Stops J Pace & Son (p139), Caffé Vittoria (p163)

On a hot day, nothing is more refreshing than an icy treat from the **Gelateria 7** (p139) at the corner of Hanover St. Or, if you prefer your desserts baked, turn right on Hanover St and make a beeline to **Modern Pastry 8** (p139), another sweet dream-come-true.

Then retrace your steps and head down Richmond St to the **Salumeria Italiana 9** (p211), an old-fashioned deli and grocery shop. Here you'll find fixings for an Italian-style picnic: salami, prosciutto di Parma, cheese, classic white bean spread and olives. (Refrain from buying bread here, because the best bakery is yet to come.)

Head back to Hanover St and turn right. This is the North End's main commercial thoroughfare, lined with shops, cafés, restaurants and double-parked cars. It is the epicenter of all things Italian in Boston, from pizza and pasta to Saints' celebrations (see p82) in the streets and soccer matches on TV. This is where – in early evening – you'll start to see lines forming in front of favorite restaurants that don't take reservations. At No 300, you'll find yet another institution of Italian desserts: **Mike's Pastry 10**. Next door, **Caffé Vittoria 11** (p163) serves a mean cappuccino.

Fortified with caffeine and sugar, head up to the Roman Catholic **St Leonard Church 12**, at the corner of Prince St. Founded in 1873, St Leonard is the first church in New England built by Italian immigrants. If the church is open, peek inside to see the city's oldest shrine to St Anthony, most beloved of Italian saints. The attached Peace Garden is always open for a sacred moment of serenity.

Oenophiles should take a quick detour across the street to the **Wine Bottega 13** (p212), a boutique wine shop that's crammed with interesting and unusual varieties from Italy and around the world. If you're lucky, you'll happen upon one of the weekly tastings.

From here, head up Prince St, the founding location of the Prince Pasta company (now one of the largest pasta producers in the US). It was here that local boy Anthony Martignetti taught America that 'Wednesday is Prince spaghetti day.' At the corner of Prince and Salem Sts, stop at the **Bova Italian Bakery 14** (p139) for Italian loaves straight from the oven, any time of day or night. By now you should have all the ingredients you need for an Italian feast of a picnic.

Continue north on Salem St to the **Old North Church 15** (p82), the North End's most noteworthy historic site. Stroll through the lovely brick courtyards behind the church, cross Unity St and descend to the **Paul Revere Park 16**. Often called 'the prado' by locals, the shady brick mall perfectly frames the Old North Church. In addition to being a lively meeting place for North-Enders of all generations, it's also one of the few places in the cramped quarter where you can rest as long as you want (which makes it an ideal spot for a picnic).

Eating

Eating

Nowadays, you'll have to look hard to find the old standards of New England cuisine: boiled dinner (corned beef, potatoes and cabbage); seafood Newburg (fish, shrimp and scallops in heavy cream sauce); and – of course – Boston baked beans (navy beans and salt pork in molasses). Some chef might prepare these dishes on a cold winter's day under the trendy label of 'comfort food,' but they no longer define dining in Boston.

Seafood still reigns supreme (and foodies are well advised to take advantage of every opportunity to eat it). It is frequently fried, but also grilled, pan-seared or prepared in any number of creative ways.

Boston presents some fine opportunities to feast on Italian and Chinese fare, but other ethnic cuisines are also well represented (see the boxed text, p146). In recent years, Mediterranean influences have become more pronounced. Whether they're called tapas or meze, 'small plates' are gaining popularity, as diners recognize the benefit of sampling lots of different menu items.

Opening Hours

Most restaurants are open every day from 11am or 11:30am to 9:30pm or 10pm, with longer hours on Friday and Saturday nights. For the purposes of this book, opening hours are listed only where they differ from this standard.

Some restaurants close in the afternoon from about 3pm to 5:30pm, while others may be open only for dinner. Restaurants and cafés that serve breakfast during the week usually open at 7am, and many places offer a special brunch menu on Sunday.

If you get the late-night munchies, your choices are unfortunately limited, as Boston has few 24-hour establishments. Your best bet is to head to Chinatown (p145), where several places serve until 4am. For other ideas, see the boxed text on p145.

How Much

Eating in Boston can be expensive, but there are ways to save. The city boasts plenty of pizza parlors, seafood shacks, burger joints and gourmet delis where you can eat cheap. At upscale restaurants, lunch menus offer smaller portions and lower prices. Many fancy restaurants offer once-a-week tasting menus, usually a three-course meal (often with wine pairings) for a fixed price. Though not exactly inexpensive, it can be an adventurous – and relatively affordable – way to sample some fine dining. The last two weeks in August are Restaurant

---

FARMERS MARKETS

Touch the produce at **Haymarket** (Map pp300–1; Blackstone St; 8am-5pm Fri & Sat; Haymarket) and you risk the wrath of the vendors ('They're a friggin' dollar – quit looking at the strawberries and just buy 'em!'). But no one else in the city matches these prices on ripe-and-ready fruits and vegetables.

Most neighborhoods have a seasonal farmers market from mid-May to late November. In addition to just-picked fruit and local vegetables, you might find Vermont farmstead and other artisanal cheese, crusty loaves and tempting fruit tarts, all fresh, fresh, fresh. Locations (617-626-1700) include:

Central Sq (Map p311; 617-727-3180; cnr Norfolk St & Bishop Allen Dr; noon-6pm Mon; Central)

Charles Hotel (Map p310; 1 Bennett St, Cambridge; 10am-3pm Sun; Harvard)

City Hall Plaza (Map pp300–1; 11am-6pm Mon & Wed; Government Center)

Copley Sq (Map pp306–7; 11am-6pm Tue & Fri May-Oct; Copley)

Week. Participating restaurants offer excellent-value prix-fixe menus (lunch/dinner $20/30). See p15 for details.

Expect to pay less than $15 per person for a meal at a budget eatery, and from $15 to $30 per person at a midrange establishment (not including drinks). Top-end restaurants will set you back at least $30 per person.

PRICE GUIDE	
$	under $15
$$	$15 to $30
$$$	more than $30

Booking Tables

Reservations are recommended for most top-end restaurants, especially on Friday and Saturday evenings. You can make reservations for most Boston restaurants at www.open table.com, a free online service that provides immediate confirmation. During the week it is usually possible to get a table without a reservation, especially if you don't mind waiting for a short while.

Take Out

Boston has plenty of excellent options 'to go.' Your traditional carry-out items – Chinese food and pizza – are areas where Boston restaurants excel (for starters, see Chinatown on p145 and the North End on p139). But these days, almost all budget and midrange restaurants will pack your food so you can take it with you. There is no shortage of gourmet food shops and specialty delis that sell pre-made soups, salads and dishes, as well as made-to-order sandwiches, for your carry-out convenience.

Tipping

Norms for tipping in the United States are different from those in many other parts of the world. In restaurants with sit-down service (where somebody brings your food to your table), customers should leave a 15% tip for acceptable service and a 20% tip for good service: tipping at a lower level reflects dissatisfaction with the service. Waiters normally are paid significantly below minimum wage and they depend on tips for their earnings; the same is true of bartenders.

Don't be confused, however, by the 'tip jars' that grace the counters at other service establishments, such as delis, ice-cream parlors and coffeehouses. The barista who makes your caffe latte and the teenager who scoops your ice cream are not so dependent on your generosity. While you may be moved to drop your change into their bucket (especially if your scoop is extra big), you are not obliged.

Haymarket (opposite)

Eating

BOOKING TABLES

BEACON HILL & BOSTON COMMON

For an afternoon of people-watching and coffee-drinking or a night of starry eyes and sweet nothings, Beacon Hill's old-world ambience lends romance, and there are some gems hidden away amid these cobblestone streets. Climbing up Charles St, you'll find a mix of cute cafés, quick bites and gourmet delicatessens, plus no shortage of swanky spots. On the back side of Beacon Hill, Cambridge St is a bit more businesslike, catering mainly to workers from nearby Massachusetts General Hospital.

UPPER CRUST

Map pp302–3   Pizzeria $

☎ 617-723-9600; 20 Charles St; meals $8-12; 🚇 Charles/MGH

Place your order, pick your seat, sit back and enjoy the aromas of the Upper Crust. Although outlets are sprouting up around Boston, the simple Beacon Hill storefront is the original. The décor is minimalist, at best, so keep your eyes on the open kitchen, where the magic happens. Neapolitan-style pizza features crispy thin crust and fresh, straightforward toppings. Order your pie as you like it or sample the 'slice of the day.'

PARIS CREPERIE

Map pp302-3   French $

☎ 617-589-0909; 326 Cambridge St; meals $8-12; 🕑 7am-10pm Mon-Fri, 8am-10pm Sat & Sun; 🚇 Charles/MGH

The 'Paris' part is a misnomer, as the crêpes at this little café are more inventive than authentic. Savory mains include tuna melts, Asian stir-fry, chicken burritos and many vegetarian options, all disguised as a French pastry. Your sweet tooth will also be sated. Dessert options range from traditionally French (with butter and sugar) to modern American ('smores' with marshmallow and Nutella). The place feels comfortable, with mismatched furniture and well-read magazines scattered about. You won't be fooled into thinking you are on the shores of the Seine… but what's the Seine got over the Charles?

PANIFICIO Map pp302-3   Café $$

☎ 617-227-4340; 144 Charles St; lunch $8-12, dinner $15-25; 🕑 8am-9:30pm Mon-Fri, 10am-9:30pm Sat & Sun; 🚇 Charles/MGH

It's not easy to snag a spot in this cozy, sun-filled bistro. By day, regulars stop in for fresh soup and sandwiches, buttery pastries and piping hot coffee. In the evenings, the menu expands to include homemade pastas and hot mains. Don't miss the weekend Italian brunch, featuring toasted bread with decadent toppings.

PARAMOUNT

Map pp302-3   Cafeteria $$

☎ 617-720-1152; 44 Charles St; breakfast & lunch $8-12, dinner $15-30; 🕑 7am-10pm Mon-Thu, 7am-11pm Fri, 8am-11pm Sat, 8am-10pm Sun; 🚇 Charles/MGH

Not what you'd expect on tony Charles St, this old-fashioned cafeteria is a favorite neighborhood hangout. Basic diner fare includes pancakes, steak and eggs, burgers and sandwiches, and big, hearty salads. For dinner, add table service and candlelight,

FIVE FOR FOODIES

If you're all about the food, here are five places that are all about you:

- **Figs** (opposite or p141) When is a pizza more than just a pizza? When it's invented by Todd English, Boston's more celebrated celebrity chef.
- **Butcher Shop** (p149) You never knew there were so many delicious ways to eat meat. Try it cured, smoked or sausaged; or select a premium cut for the grill.
- **Clio** (p153) Clio never ceases to surprise, whether it's the sassy-yet-classy interior design or Ken Oringer's innovative and unexpected fusion of French and Asian flavors.
- **Neptune Oyster** (p140) Sample the best of Boston seafood, spiced up with enticing, international influences.
- **Ten Tables** (p156) Do you appreciate the simple things in life? Ten Tables' clean preparations show off the freshness of the food and the fullness of the flavors.

and the place goes upscale without losing its down-home charm. The menu is enhanced by homemade pastas, a selection of meat and fish dishes and an impressive roster of daily specials.

KING & I Map pp302-3 — Thai $

☎ 617-227-3320; 145 Charles St; lunch $10, dinner $12-20; ☷ 11:30am-9:30pm Mon-Sat, 5-9:30pm Sun; ☷ Charles/MGH

This Thai standby is simple (Spartan, even) but service is efficient and the meals are satisfying. Noodle and rice dishes are served straight up, without much flare but with plenty of flavor. The specialty of the house is the 'famous' Pad Thai, but more adventurous diners should sample the recommended spicy curries. The menu offers many 'no oil' mains for the health-conscious, and almost unlimited vegetarian options for the animal-conscious.

ZEN Map pp302-3 — Sushi $$

☎ 617-371-1230; 21A Beacon St; lunch $10-15, dinner $20-30; ☷ 11:30am-10pm Mon-Thu, 11:30am-11pm Fri & Sat, 2:30-10pm Sun; ☷ Park St

Affordable lunch specials make this a popular lunchtime spot for State House staffers and other professional types. The minimalist décor and extensive menu are typical sushi-bar stuff, but the menu also features mains such as rack of lamb and soft-shell crab, as well as items cooked on the authentic Japanese stone grill.

ANTONIO'S CUCINA ITALIANA

Map pp302-3 — Italian $$

☎ 617-367-3310; 288 Cambridge St; meals $15-30; ☷ 11am-3pm & 5-10pm Mon-Fri, 5-10pm Sat & Sun; ☷ Charles/MGH

Antonio offers all the charms of your favorite North End eatery: the cramped quarters and scrumptious southern Italian fare are straight from Hanover St, without the crowds. Huge portions and friendly service are reminiscent of eating in the kitchen of your beloved Italian aunt. This neighborhood favorite is little known off of Beacon Hill.

FIGS Map pp302-3 — Pizzeria $$

☎ 617-742-3447; 42 Charles St; meals $15-30; ☷ Charles/MGH

This creative pizzeria – which also has an outlet in Charlestown – is the brainchild

of celebrity chef Todd English, who tops whisper-thin crusts with interesting, exotic toppings. Case in point: the namesake fig and prosciutto with gorgonzola cheese, which receives rave reviews. The menu also includes sandwiches and fresh pasta. While the food tastes gourmet, the dining room is dark, comfy and casual. And it's usually packed, so be prepared to wait.

SCOLLAY SQUARE

Map pp302-3 — American $$

☎ 617-742-4900; 21 Beacon St; meals $15-30; ☷ 11:30am-10pm Mon-Thu, to 11pm Fri, 5:30-11:00pm Sat, 11am-2pm & 5:30-11pm Sun; ☷ Park St

Down the road from the former Scollay Sq (see the boxed text, p79), the retro restaurant hearkens back to the glory days of its namesake. Old photos and memorabilia adorn the walls, including a series of burlesque beauties peering out from behind the bar; suits sip martinis to big-band music. The classic American fare is reliably good, while service – formally dressed in black and white – is excellent. If you're not into the nostalgia, dine on the pleasant sidewalk patio and watch what's happening today.

LALA ROKH Map pp302-3 — Persian $$$

☎ 617-720-5511; 97 Mt Vernon St; meals $30-40; ☷ noon-3pm Mon-Fri, 5:30-10pm daily; ☷ Charles/MGH

Lala Rokh is a beautiful Persian princess, the protagonist of an epic romance by poet Thomas Moore. The tale epitomizes the exotic East, as does the aromatic, flavorful food served at this Beacon Hill gem. While the ingredients will be familiar to fans of Middle Eastern cuisine, but the subtle innovations – an aromatic spice here or savory herb there – set this cooking apart. Don't be afraid to ask for advice from the knowledgeable waitstaff. Reservations recommended.

GROTTO Map pp302-3 — Italian $$$

☎ 617-227-3434; 37 Bowdoin St; meals $30-40; ☷ 11:30am-3pm & 5-10pm Mon-Fri, 5-10pm Sat & Sun; ☷ Bowdoin

Tucked into a basement on the back side of Beacon Hill, this cozy, cave-like place lives up to its name. The funky décor – exposed brick walls decked with rotating art exhibits – is emblematic of the innovative menu (which also changes frequently). Pastas, seafood

BOSTON RUNS ON DUNKIN'

Across America and around the world, mouths water at the sight of the pink and orange box, instantly recognizable as a dozen doughnuts. Pastry-lovers know that box contains an assortment of jelly-filled, honey-dipped and chocolate-glazed doughnuts – sweet, chewy and delicious.

Although Dunkin' Donuts exists worldwide, in Boston this chain is ubiquitous. Indeed, we don't need to list any outlets here, since you can find a Dunkin' Donuts by going out to any street corner and looking around. Of the 6000 franchises worldwide, almost 200 of them are right here in Boston.

So there is no doubt that Bostonians love doughnuts. Dunkin' Donuts was founded in Massachusetts: the first store opened in Quincy (a south-shore suburb) in 1950, and still operates there today.

In 2003, Dunkin's southern rival, Krispy Kreme, recognized the potential of the New England market and opened eight stores in Massachusetts. Bostonians were exuberant, lining up hours in advance on opening day to sample the highly touted super-sweet doughnuts. But Krispy Kreme couldn't hack this market. Three years later, most of the New England stores have closed, including the only Boston outlet. Analysts blamed the Atkins diet, yet Dunkin' Donuts continues to thrive.

Although doughnuts are the *pièce de résistance* of the chain, the dunkin' is also crucial. We're talking about coffee. Dunkin' Donuts franchises use only certified, fairly traded coffee beans, and they now serve all the fancy espresso drinks. But you have to know how to order. Here's your guide to getting a cup o' joe the way the locals do:

- Regular: Cream and sugar, and lots of it
- Light: Cream only
- Sweet: Sugar only
- Black: No sugar, no cream, as usual

But no matter how you take your coffee, don't forget the honey-dipped doughnut.

and steaks are served with an unexpected twist. Spaghetti and meatballs is a tried and true favorite thanks to an 'insanely fabulous tomato sauce.'

NO 9 PARK Map pp302-3 European $$$

☎ 617-742-9991; 9 Park St; lunch $40, dinner $60; ☺ 11am-3pm & 6-10pm Mon-Fri, 6-10pm Sat; 🚇 Park St

Set in a 19th-century mansion opposite the State House, this swanky place tops many fine-dining lists. Chef-owner Barbara Lynch has been lauded by food and wine magazines for her delectable French and Italian culinary masterpieces (featured in a daily changing tasting menu, $135 with wine) and her first-rate wine list. Reservations usually required.

GOVERNMENT CENTER & WEST END

After the massive redevelopment of the 1950s and more recent construction related to the Big Dig, this neighborhood is suffering from a shortage of eating options. If you are looking for someplace to chow down before an event at the Banknorth Garden,

head to the Bullfinch Triangle, southeast of the arena.

OSTERIA RUSTICO Map pp300-1 Italian $

☎ 617-742-8770; 85 Canal St; meals $10-15; ☺ 9am-3pm Mon-Sat; 🚇 North Station

Open only for breakfast and lunch, this family-run Italian joint is one of Boston's best-kept secrets. But those in the know keep coming back for more – staff seem to know everyone by name, or at least by favorite sandwich. Seating is in short supply, but everything is available for take-out. Pastas, salads and subs are all highly recommended: you can't go wrong with a simple antipasto or a panini 'Rustico' (prosciutto, mozzarella and tomato).

ANTHEM

Map pp300-1 American $$

☎ 617-523-8383; 138 Portland St; lunch $15-20, dinner $15-40; ☺ 11:30am-3:30pm Mon-Fri, 5-10pm Mon-Sat; 🚇 North Station

This sophisticated restaurant exudes a cool, quirky Goth ambience. Velvet drapes, heavy furniture and rich colors seem dark, but the windows stretch from shiny wood floors to super-high ceilings, allowing in plenty of light. The menu is equally mod, offering upscale comfort food, like mighty meatloaf, tasso mac and four cheeses, and baked tuna and noodle casserole. Reservations recommended on event nights.

NORTH END

The streets of the North End are lined with *salumerias* and *pasticcerias* and more *ristoranti* per block than anywhere else in Boston. Hanover St is the main drag, but the southern end of Salem St is loaded too. Many do not take reservations, so arrive early or be prepared to wait. To make your own Italian feast, visit one of the North End's authentic *salumerias* (see p210) or take the North End Nosh tour (see p130).

BOVA ITALIAN BAKERY

Map pp300-1   Bakery $

☎ 617-523-5601; 134 Salem St; ☽ 24hr; 🚇 Haymarket

At any time of day or night, head to this little corner store with the window overlooking Salem St. Besides the sublime Italian loaves, pulled straight from the oven, you'll find an amazing selection of cookies, cannolis and other pastries. Bonus: Bova also makes mean sandwiches on homemade bread.

MARIA'S PASTRY

Map pp300-1   Bakery $

☎ 617-523-1196; 46 Cross St; ☽ 7am-7pm; 🚇 Haymarket

Maria Merola believes she is one of the few people who know how to make a *sfogliatelle* (layered, shell-shaped pastry filled with ricotta). Presumably she has passed this secret on to her successors, as three generations of Merola women are now working to bring you Boston's most authentic Italian pastries. Maria's has survived the Big Dig and now has a prime location on the Cross St plaza.

MODERN PASTRY

Map pp300-1   Bakery $

☎ 617-523-3783; 257 Hanover St; ☽ 8am-10pm Sun-Thu, 8am-11pm Fri & Sat; 🚇 Haymarket

While crowds of tourists and suburbanites are queuing out the door at Mike's Pastry across the street, pop into the Modern Pastry, where the local folk come for dessert.

The place has recently expanded to accommodate a seating area, which detracts from the feeling that you have stumbled upon a hidden treasure; but the Italian cookies and cannolis are still divine.

GELATERIA

Map pp300-1   Dessert $

☎ 617-720-4243; 272 Hanover St; ☽ 10am-midnight; gelatos $3.75; 🚇 Haymarket

Gelato, ice-cream's Italian cousin, is a denser, softer version of America's frozen treat. Plus it's made with milk instead of cream, which means it has a lower fat content. But it is no less satisfying on a hot day, as happy customers at this *gelateria* can attest. Some 50 flavors range from traditional *cioccolato* to fanciful fruits.

GALERIA UMBERTO

Map pp300-1   Pizzeria $

☎ 617-227-5709; 289 Hanover St; meals $2-5; ☽ 11am-2:30pm Mon-Sat; 🚇 Haymarket

This lunchtime legend closes as soon as the slices are gone. And considering their thick and chewy goodness, that's often before the official 2:30pm closing time. Loyal patrons line up early so they are sure to get theirs.

J PACE & SON Map pp300-1   Italian $

☎ 617-227-9673; 42 Cross St; meals $8-10; ☽ 7am-7pm; 🚇 Haymarket

J Pace used to be a little neighborhood grocery, so crammed with jars of olive oil that it was difficult to navigate. The new spacious quarters on Cross St have room for a fully stocked kitchen, so the place now offers freshly prepared sandwiches, salads, soups, calzones and pasta. Order at the counter and take your lunch to the pleasant plaza.

PIZZERIA REGINA

Map pp300-1   Pizzeria $

☎ 617-227-0765; 11½ Thatcher St; meals $8-15; ☽ 11am-11pm; 🚇 Haymarket

Pizza rivalries are intense in this 'hood, where tomato sauce is as thick as blood. But the grandmother of North End pizzerias is the legendary Pizzeria Regina, famous for brusque but endearing waitresses and crispy, thin-crust pizza. Reservations are not accepted, so be prepared to wait.

GIACOMO'S RISTORANTE

Map pp300-1   Italian $$

☎ 617-523-9026; 355 Hanover St; meals $20-30;
🕑 5-10pm; 🚇 Haymarket

Customers usually line up before the doors open so they are guaranteed a spot in the first round of seating at this North End favorite. Enthusiastic and entertaining waiters, plus cramped quarters, ensure that you get to know your neighbors. The cuisine is no-frills southern Italian fare, served in unbelievable portions. The specialty of the house is Zuppa di Pesce ($50 for two), chock full of shrimp, scallops, calamari, mussels and lobster.

POMODORO Map pp300-1   Italian $$

☎ 617-367-4348; 319 Hanover St; mains $25-40;
🕑 5-11pm Tue-Sun; 🚇 Haymarket

This hole-in-the-wall on Hanover is one of the North End's most romantic settings for delectable Italian. This place is basic but cozy. The food is simply but perfectly prepared: fresh pasta, spicy tomato sauce, grilled fish and meats, and wine by the glass. Credit cards are not accepted and there's no restroom, but that's all part of the charm.

L'OSTERIA Map pp300-1   Italian $$

☎ 617-723-7847; 104 Salem St; meals $25-40;
🚇 Haymarket

This family-run ristoranti typifies the mouthwatering magic and old-world charm of the North End. It's nothing fancy, but the service is friendly and the southern Italian fare is always delicious. Generous portions guarantee that you will have leftovers for lunch. The basement is sort of drab, so it's worth waiting for a table upstairs.

DAILY CATCH

Map pp300-1   Italian/Seafood $$

☎ 617-523-8567; 323 Hanover St; meals $25-40;
🚇 Haymarket

Although owner Paul Freddura long ago added a few tables and an open kitchen, this shoebox fish joint still retains the atmosphere of a retail fish market; fortunately, it also retains the freshness of the fish. There's not much room to maneuver but you can certainly keep an eye on how your monkfish Marsala or lobster *fra diavolo* is being prepared. The specialty is calamari, fried to tender perfection.

TRATTORIA IL PANINO

Map pp300-1   Italian $$

☎ 617-720-5720; 11 Parmenter St; meals $25-40;
🕑 11am-midnight; 🚇 Haymarket

A rare opportunity for al fresco dining, this charming trattoria offers seating in the ever-pleasant *giardino* during summer months. When weather is foul, settle into a cozy corner of the dimly lit dining room. Either way, it's a romantic rendezvous, only enhanced by your sweet-talking, Italian-accented waiter. The wide-ranging menu features a risotto and lasagna *del giorno*, which are uniformly divine. Budget-minded travelers can head across the street, where Il Panino's express outlet sells some of the same exquisite pasta dishes.

NEPTUNE OYSTER

Map pp300-1   Seafood $$

☎ 617-742-3474; 63 Salem St; meals $25-40;
🕑 11:30am-11pm Sun-Wed, 11:30am-midnight
Thu-Sat; 🚇 Haymarket

Neptune's menu hints at Italian, but you'll also find elements of Mexican, French Cajun and old-fashioned New England. The daily seafood specials and impressive raw bar (featuring three kinds of oysters, plus littlenecks, crabs and mussels) confirm that this newcomer is not your traditional North End eatery. The retro interior offers a convivial – if crowded – setting. The marble bar is an excellent option for solo diners.

RISTORANTE FIORE

Map pp300-1   Italian $$$

☎ 617-371-1176; 250 Hanover St; meals $30-
40; 🕑 4-11pm Mon-Fri, noon-11pm Sat & Sun;
🚇 Haymarket

Come to Fiore – not for anything so special out of the kitchen, but for the fabulous roof deck (the only one in the North End). It's a wonderful place for a cocktail on a warm summer evening. The menu offers all of your favorite Italian standards, most served with Fiore's signature homemade pasta: you'll certainly be sated if you decide to stay for dinner.

CARMEN Map pp300-1   Italian $$$

☎ 617-742-6421; 33 North Sq; meals $30-40;
🚇 Haymarket

Exposed brick and candlelit tables make this tiny wine bar cozy yet chic. The innovative menu offers a selection of small plates providing a fresh take on seasonal vegetables; mains like roast cornish hen and seared tuna sit alongside classic pasta dishes. Reservations recommended.

MARE Map pp300-1 Italian/Seafood $$$
☎ 617-723-6273; 135 Richmond St; meals $40-50; 🕐 5-11pm; 🚇 Haymarket

Mare, meaning 'ocean,' is where all of your favorite creatures of the sea are prepared in creative, contemporary ways, like pan-seared scallops served over lemon angel-hair pasta, or rock shrimp tossed with zucchini over spinach gnocchi. The kicker is that almost all of the ingredients are organic, from the first-press olive oils to the unpasteurized cheeses to the impressive wine list. The progressive menu is complemented by an over-the-top, trendy dining room.

CHARLESTOWN

Traditionally, Charlestown has not been a major stop for Boston foodies. In recent years, however, the neighborhood's gentrification has attracted the attention of some top chefs. Now Charlestown's best restaurants draw patrons from all over the city. Stroll along Main St or check out the options on City Sq.

SORELLE BAKERY CAFÉ Map p304 Café $
☎ 617-242-5980; 100 City Sq; meals $8-12; 🕐 7:30am-9pm; 🚇 North Station

Sorelle's has earned a loyal following of regulars who take coffee at the counter, devour fresh sandwiches and scones, and bus their own tables. The original location (open only for breakfast and lunch) retains some charm in its cramped quarters and central location on Main St. But the new, more spacious location on City Sq trumps with its contemporary interior, outdoor seating area and free wi-fi access.

WARREN TAVERN Map p304 Pub $$
☎ 617-241-8142; 2 Pleasant St; lunch $10, dinner $15-20; 🚇 North Station

Dating to circa 1780, this neighborhood pub is named for General Warren, a revolutionary hero who died in the Battle of Bunker Hill (see the boxed text, p84). The snug, dark quarters still retain a historic air,

with boisterous local crowds contributing to the congeniality. Typical pub fare is on the menu, the highlight being the namesake Warren burger.

TAVERN ON THE WATER
Map p304 Pub $$
☎ 617-242-8040; 18th St, Pier 6; meals $10-20; 🚇 North Station

Set at the end of the pier behind the Navy Yard, this understated tavern offers one of the finest views of the Boston harbor and city skyline. The menu combines typical pub grub with a few passable seafood specialties. The food is not so memorable, but it's a fine place to go to catch some rays on your face, the breeze off the water, and an ice cold one from behind the bar.

FIGS Map p304 Pizzeria $$
☎ 617-242-2229; 67 Main St; meals $15-20; 🚇 North Station

The original branch of this gourmet pizzeria is now Charlestown's favorite lunch spot. The convivial crowd and the open kitchen create a bustling atmosphere into the evening. See p137 for the full review.

COPIA Map p304 Mediterranean $$
☎ 617-242-6742; 100 City Sq; lunch $10-20, dinner $25-40; 🚇 North Station

This Mediterranean steakhouse is named for the Roman goddess of abundance, an apt metaphor for the rich flavors featured on the menu. A vast array of small plates and a more modest selection of mains showcase the flavors of Greece, Italy, Portugal and North Africa. The large, airy dining room also offers incredible views of the Zakim Bridge.

TANGIERINO Map p304 Moroccan $$$
☎ 617-242-6009; 83 Main St; mains $20-28; 🕐 5:30-11:30pm; 🚇 North Station

This unexpected gem transports guests from a colonial town house in historic Charlestown to a sultan's palace in the Moroccan desert. The menu features North African specialties like *harira,* couscous and *tajine,* all with a modern flare. But the highlight is the exotic interior, complete with thick Oriental carpets, plush pillows and rich, jewel-toned tapestries. Hookah pipes are available in the adjoining casbah lounge.

DOWNTOWN

The streets east of the Boston Common (also known as the Ladder District) boast some of Boston's finest fine dining. The nearby Financial District is the workaday world for thousands of bankers, lawyers and office managers, so there is no shortage of sandwich shops and lunch spots. The cheapest eats in Boston are hawked at Downtown Crossing, on Summer between Washington and Chauncy Sts, where lunch-cart vendors offer tasty, inexpensive fast food like burritos, sandwiches and hot dogs.

CHACARERO

Map pp302-3   Chilean $

☎ 617-367-1267; 26 Province St; breakfast $5-7, lunch $6-10; ⊙ Downtown Crossing

A Chacarero is a traditional Chilean sandwich made with grilled chicken or beef, muenster cheese, fresh tomatoes, guacamole and the surprise ingredient – steamed green beans. Stuffed into homemade bread, the sandwiches are the handsdown favorite for lunch around Downtown Crossing. The location in the old Filene's building has long attracted hungry patrons who queue up outside and sit at tables on the plaza. With the closing of Filene's, the future of this original outlet is unknown, so Chacarero has opened a new, more spacious restaurant with indoor seating.

MILK ST CAFÉ

Map pp302-3   Sandwiches $

☎ 617-350-7275; Post Office Sq; meals $6-10; ⊙ 7am-5pm Mon-Fri; ⊙ Downtown Crossing

This is a favorite lunchtime spot of the suit crowd. Pastas, salads, soups and sandwiches include lots of vegetarian options. The park location is pleasant in summer, when café tables are set out and diners spill onto the greenery. There is a second location (minus the garden seating) on Milk St near the Old South Meeting House.

PRESSED Map pp302-3   Sandwiches $

☎ 617-482-9700; 2 Oliver St; lunch $8-12; ⊙ 7am-3pm Mon-Fri; ⊙ Downtown Crossing

The simple, straightforward menu features almost 20 different sandwiches, all made on fresh bread and pressed in a heated grill. Our favorite is the Cuban (pork, ham, cheddar and pickles on ciabatta) but there are many authentic Italian options and

loads of ideas for vegetarians. Look for the new outlet opening in the Seaport District.

SAM LA GRASSA'S

Map pp302-3   Deli $

☎ 617-357-6861; 44 Province St; meals $10-15; ⊙ 11am-5pm; ⊙ Downtown Crossing

Step up to the counter and place your order for one of Sam La Grassa's signature sandwiches, then find a spot at the crowded communal table. You won't be disappointed by the famous Romanian pastrami or the 'fresh from the pot' corned beef. All of the sandwiches are so well stuffed that they can be tricky to eat, which is part of the fun.

SAKURABANA Map pp302-3   Sushi $$

☎ 617-542-4311; 57 Broad St; lunch $12-20, dinner $20-30; ⊙ 11am-2:30pm & 5-9pm Mon-Fri, 5-9:30pm Sat; ⊙ Downtown Crossing

The surroundings aren't too snazzy, but the fish is fresh and tasty at this hole-in-the-wall sushi bar. The place gets packed at lunchtime as white collars descend from the surrounding office buildings to fill up on sashimi, teriyaki and tempura. If you come in the evening, you are less likely to wait for a table and you can take advantage of good-value dinner specials.

SILVERTONE Map pp302-3   Pub $$

☎ 617-338-7887; 69 Bromfield St; meals $15-30; ⊙ 11:30am-11pm Mon-Thu, 11:30-midnight Fri & Sat; ⊙ Park St

Black-and-white photos and retro advertising posters create a nostalgic atmosphere

Milk St Café (left)

KIDS' MENU

If you've got children in tow, you want a place with recognizable food, room for them to move around and no waits for tables. Here are our suggestions for your kiddies:

Bertucci's (p144) You can't go wrong with pizza, and Bertucci's serves it fast.

Jasper White's Summer Shack (p151) Any place you can get 'lobster hats' is bound to be a hit with kids.

Milk St Café (opposite) The parkside setting offers room to run around.

Mr Bartley's Burger Cottage (p156) A menu full of kid favorites: giant burgers, Boston's best onion rings, raspberry-lime rickeys and more.

Quincy Market (right) There's something for everyone at this giant market, and plenty of room to spread out in the central eating area.

Rosebud Diner (p160) Counter seating – need we say more?

at this still-trendy pub and grill. The old-fashioned comfort food is always satisfying (mac and cheese comes highly recommended), as is the cold beer drawn from the tap. The only downside is that the service suffers when the place gets crowded – and it does get crowded.

IVY Map pp302-3 Italian $$
☎ 617-451-1416; 49 Temple Pl; meals $20-30; ⏰ 11:30am-3pm & 5-11pm Mon-Fri, 5pm-midnight Sat & Sun; 🚇 Park St
Ivy is the rare place that manages to combine all the elements: chic, urban décor; cool but unpretentious vibe; and excellent, innovative food and drink. All this, and it won't break the bank. The menu is mostly small plates – pastas, salads and seafood – meaning more *piatti* to sample and share. Afterwards, all guests receive a complementary scoop of organic gelato – a fine finish to your meal.

LOCKE-OBER Map pp302-3 American $$$
☎ 617-542-1340; 3 Winter Pl; meals $40-60; ⏰ 11:30am-2:30pm & 5:30-10pm Mon-Fri, 5:30-11pm Sat; 🚇 Park St
According to an 1883 guide to Boston: 'The leading French restaurant of the city is Ober's, on Winter Place… This has more than a local fame. It is most patronized by

the possessors of long purses.' The description still rings true. Many 19th-century artworks and architectural details have survived in the sumptuous dining rooms. Happily, the exclusive men-only policy has not. Chef-owner Lydia Shire has brought Locke-Ober into the 21st century while maintaining a traditional menu and elegant atmosphere. Reservations required.

WATERFRONT

Faneuil Hall and its environs are packed with touristy places touting baked beans, live lobsters and other Boston specialties. It's hard to get off the beaten track, but that doesn't mean you won't find some fun, funky and delicious places to eat.

QUINCY MARKET

Map pp302-3 Food Court $
☎ 617-338-2323; ⏰ 10am-9pm Mon-Sat, noon-6pm Sun; 🚇 Haymarket
Northeast of Congress and State Sts, this food hall offers a variety of places under one roof: the place is packed with about 20 restaurants and 40 food stalls. Choose from chowder, bagels, Indian, Greek, baked goods and ice cream, and take a seat at one of the tables in the central rotunda.

SULTAN'S KITCHEN Map pp302-3 Turkish $
☎ 617-570-9009; 116 State St; lunch $8-12; ⏰ 11:30am-8:30pm Mon-Fri, 11am-4pm Sat; 🚇 State
Seasonal vegetables, whole grains, legumes and olive oil are among the ingredients that go into the healthful and delicious dishes at this Turkish deli. The kebabs are the house specialty, especially *kofta*, made from lean ground lamb. Other options include homemade soups, gigantic pita sandwiches and endless meze. Counter service and scattered tables don't make for the most atmospheric setting, but the photos of Istanbul help.

DURGIN PARK

Map pp302-3 American $$
☎ 617-227-2038; North Market, Faneuil Hall; lunch $8-12, dinner $15-30; 🚇 Haymarket
Known for its no-nonsense service and sawdust on the floorboards, Durgin Park hasn't changed much since the restaurant opened in 1827. Nor has the menu,

which features New England standards like prime rib, fish chowder, chicken pot pie and Boston baked beans, with strawberry shortcake and Indian pudding for dessert. Be prepared to make friends with the other parties seated at your table.

BERTUCCI'S Map pp302-3   Plzzeria $

☎ 617-227-7889; 22 Merchants Row; meals $10-20; 🚇 Aquarium or State

Despite its nationwide expansion, Bertucci's remains a Boston favorite for brick-oven pizza. The location near Faneuil Hall Marketplace is one of several in the Boston area; others are in the Back Bay and in Harvard Sq. Lunch is a real bargain: all mains ($8 to $10) come with unlimited salad and fresh, hot rolls.

KINGFISH HALL

Map pp302-3   Seafood $$

☎ 617-523-8862; South Market, Faneuil Hall; lunch $10-20, dinner $20-30; 🚇 Haymarket or Government Center

Chef-entrepreneur Todd English, of Olives and Figs fame, has struck again. The imaginative menu offers seafood specialties like catch of the day roasted on the spit, and crispy lobster served 'Cantonese style' (with ginger and scallions). Whimsical, under-the-sea décor includes tile tables inlaid with crustacean mosaics and fish mobiles suspended from high ceilings. Watch the Faneuil Hall activity from the outdoor terrace or sit inside and observe the goings-on in the open kitchen.

Legal Seafood (right)

LEGAL SEAFOOD

Map pp302-3   Seafood $$

☎ 617-227-3115; 255 State St; lunch $10-20, dinner $25-40; 🚇 Aquarium

With a reputation and now-national empire built on the motto 'If it's not fresh, it's not Legal,' Legal Seafood has few rivals. The menu is simple: every kind of seafood, broiled, steamed, sautéd, grilled or fried. Some think Legal's clam chowder is New England's best. This outlet on the waterfront is one of many around town.

SEL DE LA TERRE

Map pp302-3   French $$$

☎ 617-720-1300; 255 State St; lunch $10-20, dinner $30-40; 🚇 Aquarium

Local produce and seafood – as well as fresh-baked bread from the attached *boulangerie* – are the focus of the country French menu at this gem of a bistro on the waterfront. The atmosphere is rustic and relaxed, but service is always attentive. If you are hungry during off-hours, the *boulangerie* is open early for breakfast, while the bar offers a late-night menu (until 12:30am) from Wednesday to Saturday.

UNION OYSTER HOUSE

Map pp302-3   Seafood $$

☎ 617-227-2750; 41 Union St; meals $25-40; 🚇 Haymarket

The oldest restaurant in Boston, ye olde Union Oyster House has been serving seafood in this historic red-brick building since 1826. Countless history-makers have propped themselves up at this bar, including Daniel Webster and John F Kennedy. Apparently JFK used to order the lobster bisque, but the raw bar is the real draw. Order a dozen on the half-shell and watch the shucker work his magic.

SEAPORT DISTRICT

There was a time when hanging around the Seaport District meant you were eating seafood, because there was no other reason to be here. With the opening of the convention center and the ICA, this district is quickly developing as a hotspot for new restaurants. It's still mostly seafood, but check out the hotel restaurants for a change of pace.

LATE-NIGHT GRUB

Boston might be called 'the city that goes to bed early' for all its late-night eating options. If you have a case of the midnight munchies, you have to know where to look for your cure:

- Bova Italian Bakery (p139) may be out of the way, but it's open around the clock for fresh-baked bread, pastries and sandwiches.
- Brasserie Jo (p151) is popular with the post-symphony crowd for its French bistro fare.
- Charlie's (p171) provides grilled cheese, burgers and omelets, hot off the grill.
- Franklin Café (p149) is the South End's most beloved place for meeting and eating; it's even more beloved after midnight.
- Intermission Tavern (p148) feeds the post-theater crowd until 2am.
- Peach Farm (p146) is one of several Chinatown haunts that cater to post-clubbing crowds, until 3am or 4am.
- South Street Diner (p147) serves breakfast around the clock. Amen.

BARKING CRAB

Map pp302-3   Seafood $$

☎ 617-426-2722; 88 Sleeper St; meals $15-25; 🚇 South Station

Big buckets of crabs (Jonah, blue, snow, Alaskan, etc, depending what's in season), steamers dripping in lemon and butter, paper plates piled high with all things fried…the Barking Crab is everything a clam shack should be. The food is plentiful and cheap, and you eat it at communal picnic tables overlooking the water. Beer flows freely, so it's no wonder the atmosphere is so jovial. Be prepared to wait for a table.

NO NAME

Map pp298-9   Seafood $$

☎ 617-338-7539; 151/2 Fish Pier; meals $15-25; 🚇 South Station

Another no-frills fish restaurant, this one on the fish pier. The location lends credence to the motto 'Where the fresh are so fresh, they jump out of the water and onto your plate.' This place has lost some of its charm since being discovered by outsiders, but that doesn't stop dock workers from showing up for fried clams and fish chowder.

LTK BAR & KITCHEN

Map pp298-9   Seafood $$

☎ 617-330-7430; 255 Northern Ave; meals $20-30; 🚇 South Station

LTK stands for Legal Test Kitchen: this is where Legal Seafood is exploring 'dining in the 21st century.' The idea is to incorporate technology into the dining room, offering computerized menus, wireless internet access and iPod docks. Foodwise, LTK has incorporated multicultural cuisine into the menu, like sushi, *pho* and tempura. This all takes place in a sleek, pared-down setting, a contrast to Legal's traditional dining room. LTK is not actually all that cutting-edge, but the vibe is contemporary and creative – appropriate for the up-and-coming Seaport District.

DAILY CATCH

Map pp302-3   Italian/Seafood $$

☎ 617-772-4400; 2 Northern Ave, Moakley Federal Courthouse; meals $25-40; 🚇 South Station

This North End favorite has opened a more spacious branch on Fan Pier. Despite the waterfront location, it lacks the charm of the original (see p140). But you are here to eat, right? You'll find the same fresh seafood (including the famous calamari), garlicky sauces and squid-ink pasta, so grab a table – you probably won't have to wait – and enjoy.

CHINATOWN, LEATHER DISTRICT & THEATER DISTRICT

The most colorful part of Chinatown is overflowing with authentic restaurants (many open until 4am), bakeries and markets. This is some of Boston's best budget eating. The Leather District has a trendy scene unfolding in the streets between Chinatown and South Station, and the Theater District has no shortage of restaurants catering to hungry, show-going crowds.

KEEPING IT REAL

Even the most devout fans of seafood are bound to eventually tire of boiled lobster and fried clams. Fortunately, many restaurants allow your palate to take a mini-vacation. Authentic ethnic restaurants offer some of Boston's best-value eating and the opportunity to sample a little local subculture. The obvious options – Italian and Chinese – are well covered in these listings. This box offers some suggestions for lesser-known international cuisines:

Brazilian Famous for its *churrascaria*, or steakhouse. To feast on grilled meat, try the Midwest Grill (p159) in Inman Sq.

Indian Excellent options are Punjabi Dhaba (p158) in Inman Sq and Tanjore (p157) in Harvard Sq.

Korean Experiment with *kal-gook-su* (steaming noodles with onions) or *bi-bim bab* (rice mixed with vegetables). The most typical Korean dish is a spicy cabbage salad called *kimchi*. To try it, head to Koreana (p158) near Inman Sq or Suishaya (opposite) in Chinatown.

Portuguese For seafood stews and other delicacies made with *bacalhau* (salted cod), head to Atasca (p159) in Kendall Sq.

Russian Start with a hearty peasant soup and follow up with chicken cutlet or sturgeon in cream sauce. Save room for several vodka shots along the way. Do this at Café Samovar (p155) in Brookline Village.

Thai Lighter and spicier than Chinese, Thai cuisine also features lots of saucy dishes served over rice. Thai restaurants are sprouting up all over Boston; the best are Brown Sugar Café (p153), Rod Dee (p154), House of Siam (p148) and Montien (p148).

Vietnamese Who can resist a steaming bowl of *pho?* These spicy Vietnamese noodles are a meal by themselves. Try them at Pho Pasteur (below), at locations in Chinatown or Back Bay.

CHINATOWN

PHO PASTEUR

Map p305   Vietnamese $
☎ 617-482-7467; 682 Washington St; meals $8-15;
🕑 9am-11pm; 🚇 Chinatown

Serves hearty, hot and cheap meals in big bowls. Most people come for *pho* (pronounced 'fuh'), the sometimes exotic, always fragrant and flavorful noodle soup. Another location on Newbury St serves the same great food in more elegant digs.

PEACH FARM Map p305   Chinese/Seafood $
☎ 617-482-3332; 4 Tyler St; meals $10-20;
🕑 11am-3am; 🚇 Chinatown

Popular wisdom says that if you don't know where to eat in Chinatown, you should ask some locals where *they* like to eat. Chances are they will direct you to the Peach Farm, a Chinatown haunt where the focus is on the food. It's not much to look at, but fried noodles and rice, *moo shi* and Szechuan dishes are plentiful and cheap.

CHINA PEARL

Map p305   Chinese/Dim Sum $
☎ 617-426-4338; 9 Tyler St; meals $10-20;
🕑 8:30am-11pm; 🚇 Chinatown

The dull roar at China Pearl (the sound of a restaurant packed with patrons) is a good indication that this place is the best of the bunch for dim sum. Choose your treats as the carts cruise past your table or – if you don't know what's what – copy the Chinese people at the next table.

BUDDHA'S DELIGHT

Map p305   Asian/Vegetarian $
☎ 617-451-2395; 2nd fl, 3 Beach St; meals $10-20;
🚇 Chinatown

Non-meat eaters will be thrilled with the low-as-they-go prices and the stagger-ing number of vegetarian options at this hole-in-the-wall. The many imitation meat dishes – from roast pork to meatballs – are made exclusively from soy. While the taste and texture get mixed reviews, it's safe to say that no animals were harmed in the making of this food.

JUMBO SEAFOOD

Map p305   Chinese/Seafood $$
☎ 617-542-2823; 5-7-9 Hudson St; lunch $6-10,
dinner $20-30; 🕑 11am-1am Sun-Thu, 11am-4am
Fri & Sat; 🚇 Chinatown

You know the seafood is fresh when you see the huge tanks of lobster, crabs and fish that constitute the décor at this China-town classic. But it's not only seafood on the menu, which represents the best of Hong Kong cuisine. Other specialties include braised duck with mushrooms and Szechuan-style shrimp. Lunch specials ($4.75 to $6.25 including soup and fried rice) are a bargain.

SUISHAYA Map p305 Korean/Japanese $$
☎ 617-423-3848; 2 Tyler St; ☻ 11:30am-2am; meals $15-25; ☒ Chinatown
Serving the best Korean food this side of the river, Suishaya is also recommended for sushi and sashimi. Late-night hours make it popular with the clubbing crowd. As with many Chinatown joints, it's not the prettiest place to look at, but at 2am, who notices the décor?

PENANG Map p305 Malaysian $$
☎ 617-451-6373; 685 Washington St; meals $15-30; ☻ 11:30am-11:30pm Sun-Thu, to midnight Fri & Sat; ☒ Chinatown
Serves Malaysian fare in a festive, tiki-bar atmosphere. Some items are listed with the admonition 'Ask your server for advice before you order!!!' Fortunately, most of Penang's menu items are delightfully different, but not too intimidating. Regulars rave about the *roti canai,* crispy pancakes with a curry dipping sauce.

APOLLO GRILL
Map p305 Japanese/Korean $$
☎ 617-423-3888; 84-86 Harrison Ave; meals $20-30; ☻ 11:30am-2:30pm Mon-Fri, 5pm-4am nightly
This Japanese-Korean late-night hot spot features tables with built-in hibachi grills for Korean BBQ doused in a secret sauce. Hot soups, tempura and sushi are also on the menu. Nobody will argue that it's authentic or outstanding, but that doesn't stop the post-club crowd from showing up at all hours of the night.

GINZA Map p305 Japanese $$
☎ 617-338-2261; 16 Hudson St; lunch $20, dinner $30; ☻ 11:30am-2:30pm & 5-11pm Mon-Thu, 11:30am-2:30pm & 5pm-4am Fri, 11am-4am Sat, 11am-11pm Sun; ☒ Chinatown
Named after Tokyo's upscale center of culture and finance, this traditional Japanese restaurant (complete with waitstaff in kimonos) rates among Boston's best sushi places. The freshest pieces of *nigiri,* sashimi and *maki* are artfully presented, offering a feast for the eyes as well as the palate. There is a second outlet near Kenmore Sq.

SHABU-ZEN
Map p305 Japanese $$
☎ 617-292-8828; 16 Tyler St; lunch $20, dinner $30; ☻ 11:30am-11pm Mon-Wed, to midnight Thu-Sun; ☒ Chinatown
For something different, try 'Shabu-Shabu', also known as hot pot cuisine. Choose from a variety of thinly sliced seafood and meats, a plate of fresh vegetables and an array of homemade broths, then cook it up the way you like it. Very hands-on. It's a divine sensory experience, if only for the enticing aromas of the food cooking all around.

LEATHER DISTRICT
SOUTH STREET DINER
Map p305 Diner $
☎ 617-350-0028; 178 Kneeland St; meals $10-15; ☻ 24hr; ☒ South Station
A divey diner that does what a diner is supposed to do – that is, serve bacon and eggs and burgers and fries, at any time of the day or night. So plunk yourself into a vinyl upholstered booth and let the sass-talking waitstaff satisfy your midnight munchies. Considering the location, this place is bound to attract some sketchy characters. But again, that's what a diner is supposed to do.

LES ZYGOMATES Map p305 French $$
☎ 617-542-5108; 129 South St; lunch $15, dinner $30-40; ☻ 11:30am-1am Mon-Fri, 6pm-1am Sat; ☒ South Station
This late-night Parisian bistro serves up live jazz music alongside classic but contemporary French cuisine. Daily prix-fixe menus and Tuesday-night wine tastings ($30; 6pm and 8pm) attract a clientele that is sophisticated but not stuffy. Dinner is definitely pricey; but the tempting selection of starters and cocktails make it a perfect pre- or post-theater spot.

THEATER DISTRICT
FINALE DESSERTERIE
Map p305 Café $$
☎ 617-423-3184; 1 Columbus Ave; desserts $9-14; ☻ 11:30am-11pm Mon-Wed, 11:30am-midnight Thu-Fri, 6pm-midnight Sat, 4-11pm Sun; ☒ Arlington
Choose from a long list of tempting treats, from crème brulée to chocolate soufflé, and

enjoy them with coffee, wine or port. Mirrors over the pastry chefs' workstation allow patrons to watch their magic. There are also light soups, salads and sandwiches at lunchtime and appetizer-size dinner dishes so you don't eat sweets on an empty stomach.

MONTIEN Map p305 Thai $$

☎ 617-338-5600; 63 Stuart St; lunch $12-15, dinner $20-30; Ⓜ Boylston

Popular with neighborhood residents and theater patrons, this quiet Thai restaurant is perfect for grabbing a bite before the show. Regulars ask for the authentic Thai menu, as opposed to the Americanized version that most visitors see. Otherwise, you can't go wrong with the red curry or tried and true *pad thai*. Montien has another newer outlet in Inman Sq.

JACOB WIRTH Map p305 German $$

☎ 617-338-8586; 31-37 Stuart St; meals $20-30; Ⓨ 11:30am-8pm Mon, to 10pm Tue-Thu, to midnight Fri, to 11pm; Ⓜ Boylston

Boston's second-oldest eatery is this atmospheric Bavarian beer hall. The menu features Wiener schnitzel, sauerbraten, potato pancakes and pork chops, but the highlight is the beer – almost 30 different drafts, including Jake's House Lager and Jake's Special Dark. On Friday night, Jake hosts a sing-along that rouses the *haus*.

INTERMISSION TAVERN

Map p305 Pub $$

☎ 617-451-5997; 228 Tremont St; meals $15-20; Ⓨ 10:30am-2am; Ⓜ Boylston

Enter beneath the masks of Comedy and Tragedy into the cozy interior, where show posters adorn the brick walls. Sandwiches, burgers and old-fashioned American dinners are on the menu at this tiny theatrically themed tavern. The place is a relative newcomer, but reasonable prices and late-night dining are bound to attract clubbers, theater-goers and other night owls.

VIA MATTA

Map p305 Italian $$

☎ 617-422-0008; 79 Park Plaza; enoteca $20-30, lunch $20-30, dinner $30-40; Ⓨ 11:30am-1am; Ⓜ Arlington

Via Matta tries to recreate your finest memories of Italy – the ambience, the romance and of course the flavors. Sample the chef's

whims in the tastefully trendy dining room or better yet in the dark, sexy enoteca. The latter serves pizzas, bruschettas and other small plates late into the night – a perfect place to stop for a bite after the theater.

SOUTH END

Much like the neighborhood itself – where the up-and-coming live next door to the down-and-out – the South End boasts an eclectic mix of trendy, high-end eateries and old-school neighborhood cafés. Tremont St is the main drag, but you'll find plenty of places along Columbus Ave and Washington St too.

SOUTH END BUTTERY

Map p305 Bakery/Café $

☎ 617-482-1015; 314 Shawmut Ave; meals $6-10; Ⓨ 7am-3pm Mon-Fri, 8am-4pm Sat & Sun; Ⓜ Back Bay or South End

Flour (see below) has some competition with the recent opening of the South End Buttery. Breakfast is egg sandwiches or homemade granola. For lunch choose from a selection of old-fashioned sandwiches like BLTs and chicken salad, all served on fresh-baked bread, as well as fresh salads and homemade soups. For your sweet tooth, cookies and cupcakes round out the menu.

FLOUR Map p305 Bakery/Café $

☎ 617-267-4300; 1595 Washington St; meals $6-12; Ⓨ 7am-9pm Mon-Fri, 8am-6pm Sat, 9am-5pm Sun; Ⓜ Back Bay or South End

Flour implores patrons to 'make life sweeter…eat dessert first!' It's hard to resist at this pastry-lover's paradise. But dessert is not all: sandwiches, soups, salads and pizzas are also available. And just to prove there is something for everybody, Flour sells homemade dog biscuits for your canine friend. He can't come inside, of course, so if your pooch is in tow, snag a seat on the sunny patio.

HOUSE OF SIAM

Map p305 Thai $

☎ 617-267-1755; 542 Columbus Ave; lunch $7-8, dinner $10-15; Ⓜ Massachusetts Ave

In a traditional dining room done up in red and gold and decked with souvenirs from Siam, this is the South End's favorite Thai restaurant. The extensive menu includes no shortage of perfectly spiced curries and fried rice. It's not the trendiest place on Columbus Ave, but the gracious service and reliably good food attract a constant stream of regulars.

MIKE'S CITY DINER
Map pp298-9   Diner $

☎ 617-267-9393; 1714 Washington St; meals $10-15; 🕒 7am-3pm; 🚇 Massachusetts Ave
Start the day with a big breakfast of eggs, bacon, toast and other old-fashioned goodness, topped with a bottomless cup of coffee. Or if you need to refuel at lunchtime, go for classics like meatloaf and mashed potatoes or fried chicken and biscuits. Service is friendly and fast, part of the appeal of this South End institution.

PICCO
Map p305   Pizzeria $$

☎ 617-927-0066; 513 Tremont St; meals $10-20; 🚇 Back Bay or South End
The crust of a Picco pizza undergoes a two-day process of cold fermentation before it goes into the oven and then into your mouth. The result is a thin crust with substantial texture and rich flavor. Add toppings to create your own pie, or try one of the house specialties, like spinach and goats cheese or littleneck clam pizza. The menu also features sandwiches, salads and delectable homemade ice cream. The breezy décor and free wi-fi access lure those who might like to linger.

JAE'S CAFÉ & GRILL
Map p305   Korean/Sushi $$

☎ 617-421-9405; 520 Columbus Ave; lunch $10-15, dinner $20-30; 🚇 Massachusetts Ave
'Eat at Jae's…Live forever!' is the inviting motto of this popular pan-Asian restaurant. Enjoy the terrace in fine weather; otherwise, head down to the cozy bar, surrounded by exposed brick walls and colorful fish tanks. The menu of sushi is extensive, but Korean dishes like *bi-bim bab* are the specialty.

BOB'S SOUTHERN BISTRO
Map pp298-9   Southern $$

☎ 617-536-6204; 604 Columbus Ave; meals $12-20; 🕒 5-10pm Mon-Thu, 11:30am-midnight Fri & Sat, 10am-10pm Sun; 🚇 Massachusetts Ave
This is Boston's best down-home soul food: barbecue ribs with a hunk of cornbread or fried chicken with black-eyed peas. Thursday through Saturday, dinner is served with live jazz. Sit at the long counter or in a booth in the recently redone dining room.

FRANKLIN CAFÉ
Map p305   New American $$

☎ 617-350-0010; 278 Shawmut Ave; meals $20-30; 🕒 5:30pm-1:30am; 🚇 Back Bay or South End
Once a favorite neighborhood restaurant (and that's saying something in this restaurant-rich neighborhood), the Franklin has been discovered by outsiders. It's still friendly and hip – a fantastic spot for people-watching (especially the beautiful boys in the 'hood). The menu is New American comfort food prepared by a gourmet chef: pan-seared Atlantic cod with oyster mushrooms, scallions and ginger, or roasted turkey meatloaf with spiced fig gravy and chive mashed potatoes.

TORO
Map pp298-9   Spanish $$

☎ 617-536-4300; 1704 Washington St; meals $20-30; 🕒 4:30-9:45pm Sun-Wed, to 10:45pm Thu-Sat; 🚇 Massachusetts Ave
Much anticipated and highly lauded, this cool tapas bar is the latest effort by celebrity chef Ken Oringer. True to its Spanish spirit, this place is bursting with energy, from the open kitchen to the lively bar to the communal butcher-block tables. The menu features simple but sublime tapas – grilled chilis with sea salt, corn on the cob dripping with lemon and butter, delectable, garlicky shrimp. For accompaniment, take your pick from rioja or sangria or any number of spiced-up mojitos and margaritas.

BUTCHER SHOP
Map p305   European $$

☎ 617-423-4800; 552 Tremont St; meals $25-40; 🚇 Back Bay or South End
Only in the South End does the neighborhood butcher shop double as an elegant eatery and wine bar. The cases filled with tantalizing cuts of meat, fresh foie gras and homemade sausages give you a glimpse of the ingredients and provide the decoration at this bistro. The menu is short and sweet, offering charcuterie and antipasti that highlight the butcher shop's products (not a good place for vegetarians). A nice selection of artisanal wines accompanies the food.

B&G OYSTERS LTD Map p305 Seafood $$$

☎ 617-423-0550; 550 Tremont St; oysters $2 each, meals $30-40; 🚇 Back Bay or South End

Patrons flock to this casually cool oyster bar to get in on another endeavor by chef Barbara Lynch. Sit inside at the tiled raw bar or outside on the peaceful terrace, and indulge in a wide selection of the freshest oysters from local waters. An extensive list of wines and a modest menu of mains and appetizers (mostly seafood) are ample accompaniment for the oysters.

AQUITAINE Map p305 French $$$

☎ 617-424-8577; 569 Tremont St; meals $30-40; 🕒 5-10pm daily, 10am-3pm Sat & Sun; 🚇 Back Bay or South End

Let this chic French bistro whisk you away to Paris. Sip fine wines at the super-cool wine bar up front; then settle into the lively dining room for classics like onion soup, steak frite and *filet au poivre*. Sunday brunch is a highlight, featuring omelets and eggs Benedict from different regions, not to mention an excellent prix fixe for $10.

HAMERSLEY'S BISTRO

Map p305 French $$$

☎ 617-423-2700; 553 Tremont St; dinner $40-60; 🕒 5-10pm Mon-Fri; 🚇 Back Bay or South End

Consistently at the top of every 'best restaurants' list, Hamersley's serves perfectly prepared French and country American cuisine. The seasonal menu is diverse, but the house specialty is a simple, delicious roast chicken with garlic, parsley and lemon ($25). The ambience is warm and inviting – not at all pretentious for such a classy place. Reservations highly recommended. For more on chef Gordon Hamersley, see p55.

BACK BAY

Boston's swankiest neighborhood is also one of its finest dining spots. Newbury St is lined with trendy bars, classy grills and cozy cafés. The abundance of students ensures that some of them are actually affordable.

PHO PASTEUR Map pp306-7 Vietnamese $

☎ 617-262-8200; 119 Newbury St; meals $8-15; 🚇 Copley

One of three branches in the area, this Vietnamese restaurant is almost always

BEST FOR BRUNCH

Sunday brunch is becoming an urban tradition in America, and Boston is no exception. Here are our picks for the hottest spots on Sunday at noontime:

Bob's Southern Bistro (p149) Down-home Southern cookin' and spirited gospel music. Do I hear 'Alleluia'?

Centre Street Café (p155) A little hip, a little hippy.

China Pearl (p146) Chinatown's top spot for dim sum.

East Coast Grill (p159) Let the Bloody Mary bar beat your hangover blues.

Sel de la Terre (p144) Divine French pastries straight from the *boulangerie*, plus omelets, crêpes and quiche, like in Provence.

Zaftigs Delicatessen (p154) Be prepared to wait for the classic Jewish deli fare.

crowded. Regulars keep returning for big bowls of spicy stir-fry and delicious vermicelli at prices you can't beat. For a full review, see p146.

CAFÉ JAFFA

Map pp306-7 Turkish $

☎ 617-536-0230; 48 Gloucester St; meals $10-20; 🚇 Hynes/ICA

A surprising bargain in the middle of blue-blood Back Bay. Fill up on delicious *shwarma* and falafel, and wash it down with palatable Israeli beer or rich dark Turkish coffee. With polished wood floors and painted murals, it's more stylish than your typical Turkish deli.

PARISH CAFÉ & BAR

Map pp306-7 Sandwiches $

☎ 617-247-4777; 361 Boylston St; meals $10-20; 🕒 noon-2am; 🚇 Arlington

Sample the creations of Boston's most famous chefs without exhausting your expense account. The menu at Parish features an impressive roster of sandwiches, each designed by a local celebrity chef, including Lydia Shire, Ken Oringer, Barbara Lynch and Jasper White. Despite the creative fare, this place feels more 'bar' than 'café.' The long bar – backed by big TVs and rich red walls – attracts a lively after-work crowd.

BANGKOK BLUE

Map pp306-7   Thai $
☎ 617-266-1010; 651 Boylston St; meals $10-20;
🕒 11:30am-3pm & 5-10pm Mon-Fri, noon-10pm
Sat & Sun; 🚇 Copley

Cash-strapped travelers with the Back Bay blues will find the cure at Bangkok Blue, where the spicy Thai staples will sate your appetite without busting the bank. This understated eatery does a brisk lunchtime business, as hearty portions draw a regular clientele and efficient service ensures quick turnover. Patio seating is a pleasant alternative in warm weather.

TRIDENT BOOKSELLERS & CAFE

Map pp306-7   International $$
☎ 617-267-8688; 338 Newbury St; lunch $10-15,
dinner $20-30; 🕒 9am-midnight; 🚇 Hynes/ICA

Is Trident a bookstore with an amazingly eclectic menu or a café with a super selection of reading material? The collection of books is wide, but leans toward political and New Age themes. The food menu is equally varied, ranging from the comforting (muffins, soups, smoothies) to the daring (spinach arancini, Tibetan dumplings). Vegetarians rejoice over vegan cashew chili.

BRASSERIE JO

Map pp306-7   French $$
☎ 617-425-3240; 120 Huntington Ave; lunch
$15-20, dinner $20-30; 🕒 7am-1am Sun-Thu, to
1:30am Fri & Sat; 🚇 Prudential

Both classy and convivial, this French brasserie is a prime place to catch a bite before the symphony. The kitchen stays open late, so you can also stop by afterwards, when you might see the Maestro himself feasting on classic French fare like steak frite, mussels *marinière* and *croques monsieur*. Regulars crow about the *coq au vin*.

BAR LOLA
Map pp306-7   Spanish $$
☎ 617-266-1122; 160 Commonwealth Ave; meals
$20; 🕒 4pm-1am Mon-Fri, 10am-1am Sat & Sun;
🚇 Copley

This authentic Spanish eatery is tucked into a subterranean space on residential Commonwealth Ave. The menu is exclusively tapas, prepared by a team of chefs trained in España, plus an impressive list of Spanish wines, including *cava* and sangria. Mural-painted walls and flamenco music create an inviting old-world ambience, and a lively, Spanish-speaking crowd (and staff) adds to it.

PIATTINI
Map pp306-7   Italian $$
☎ 617-536-2020; 226 Newbury St; meals $20-30;
🚇 Copley

If you have trouble deciding what to order, Piattini can help. The name means 'small plates,' so you don't have to choose just one. The list of wines by the glass is extensive, each accompanied by tasting notes and fun facts. This intimate enoteca is a delightful setting to sample the flavors of Italy, and you might just learn something while you are there.

JASPER WHITE'S SUMMER SHACK

Map pp306-7   Seafood $$
☎ 617-867-9955; 50 Dalton St; meals $20-30;
🕒 11am-11pm Sun-Thu, to 1am Fri & Sat;
🚇 Hynes/ICA

This Back Bay outlet of Jasper White's famous restaurant is as big and noisy as the lobster is delectable. Portions are large and preparations are straightforward: specialties include traditional lobster rolls, steamed clams and a magnificently huge raw bar. This is a great spot for kids, but solo diners aren't shafted either. The original location is bit out of the way – in North Cambridge near Alewife T station.

CROMA

Map pp306-7   Pizzeria $$

☎ 617-247-3200; 269 Newbury St; meals $20-30; ☺ 11:30am-11pm Sun-Thu, to midnight Fri & Sat; 🚇 Copley or Hynes/ICA

Newly revamped, this stylish pizzeria has a hip European feel. The sleek interior – with exposed brick walls and floor-to-ceiling windows – is a hot spot to see and be seen, as is the outdoor patio. Enjoy a crispy-crust, Neopolitan-style pizza or a selection from the extensive wine-by-the-glass menu.

CASA ROMERO

Map pp306-7   Mexican $$$

☎ 617-536-4341; 30 Gloucester St; meals $30-40; ☺ 5-10pm; 🚇 Hynes/ICA

The entrance to this hidden treasure is in the public alley off Gloucester St. Step inside and find yourself in a cozy *casa* – filled with folk art and Talavera tiles – which is wonderful and warm during winter months. In pleasant weather, dine under the stars on the delightful patio. This is not your average *taqueria* – be prepared to pay for the experience.

SONSIE Map pp306-7   International $$$

☎ 617-351-2500; 327 Newbury St; meals $30-40; ☺ 7am-midnight; 🚇 Hynes/ICA

Where Boston's beautiful people go to see and be seen, this trendy spot continues to attract devotees with its interesting, eclectic menu, not to mention the eye candy that patronizes the place. Tiny, café-style tables are crammed into the front of the restaurant, offering a fabulous view through French windows onto Newbury St. The menu is pricey, but creative pastas and brick-oven pizzas provide a reasonable alternative for the cost-conscious.

L'ESPALIER

Map pp306-7   French $$$

☎ 617-262-3023; 30 Gloucester St; prix fixe $70-88 without wine; ☺ 5:30-10:30pm Mon-Sat; 🚇 Hynes/ICA

The *crème de la crème* of Boston's culinary scene is this very elegant French affair. A variety of prix-fixe and tasting menus

(with or without wine) offer an exceptional dining experience that tops many short lists. The menus change daily, but usually include a degustation of caviar, a degustation of seasonal vegetables and recommended wine pairings. The 1880 Back Bay town house is the perfect setting for such luxury.

KENMORE SQUARE & FENWAY

Most places in Kenmore Sq target the large local student population, meaning cheap ethnic eats and divey sandwich shops. The square's recent revitalization means that upscale restaurants are finding their way here too. The quiet streets between the Back Bay Fens and Fenway Park are home to a few neighborhood favorites: indeed, Peterborough St is one of the best streets in Boston for cheap eats.

KENMORE SQUARE

CAMPO DE' FIORI

Map pp308-9   Pizza/Italian $

☎ 617-236-2066; 580 Commonwealth Ave; breakfast $3-6, lunch & dinner $6-12; ☺ 8am-8pm Mon-Fri, 11am-6pm Sat; 🚇 Kenmore

It looks like a fast food place but it tastes like *la dolce vita*. Scrumptious sandwiches – including many veggie options – are served on fresh-baked Roman flat bread. Crispy thin pizzas are topped with interesting toppings (perhaps not authentically Italian, but still delicious). If this is how they do fast food in Rome, then absolutely, do as the Romans!

OTHER SIDE COSMIC CAFÉ

Map pp308-9   Café $

☎ 617-536-9477; 407 Newbury St; meals $10-12; ☺ 11am-1am daily; 🚇 Hynes/ICA

The 'other side' refers to the other side of Massachusetts Ave, which few strollers crossed before this place opened. 'Cosmic' alludes to its funky, Seattle-inspired style and 20-something crowd. The 1st floor is done in cast iron, while the 2nd floor is softened by velvet drapes, mismatched couches and low ceilings. Vegetarian chili, sandwiches, fruit and veggie drinks and strong coffee are the order of the day.

INDIA QUALITY Map pp308-9 Indian $$

☎ 617-267-4499; 484 Commonwealth Ave; lunch $10, dinner $15-20; ⏱ 11:30am-3pm & 5-11pm Mon-Fri, 3-11pm Sat & Sun; Ⓚ Kenmore

India Quality has been serving chicken curry and shrimp *saag* to hungry students, daytime professionals and baseball fans since 1983. The place is rather nondescript, but the food is anything but, especially considering the reasonable prices. Service is reliably fast and friendly.

PETIT ROBERT BISTRO

Map pp308-9 French $$

☎ 617-375-0699; 468 Commonwealth Ave; lunch $10-15, dinner $20-30; ⏱ 11am-11pm; Ⓚ Kenmore

Once upon a time the legendary Maison Robert represented the finest dining in Boston. The ultrachic institution has now closed, but chef Jacky Robert has reapplied his talents to this welcoming, working-class bistro. The French fare is straightforward and hearty, with daily specials posted on the blackboard. The surroundings are casual chic, including a tiny patio. Happily, prices are not prohibitive; the trade-off is that service is not always particularly professional.

EASTERN STANDARD

Map pp308-9 American/French $$

☎ 617-532-9100; 528 Commonwealth Ave; meals $20-30; Ⓚ Kenmore

Whether you choose to sit in the sophisticated, brassy interior or on the heated patio (open year-round), you're sure to enjoy the upscale atmosphere at this Kenmore Sq newcomer. French bistro fare, with a hint of New American panache, caters to a pre-game crowd that prefers wine and cheese to peanuts and crackerjacks. Great people-watching on game nights.

GREAT BAY Map pp308-9 Seafood $$$

☎ 617-532-5300; 500 Commonwealth Ave; lunch $20-25, dinner $30-40; ⏱ 6-10am & 11:30am-2:30pm Mon-Fri, 7am-noon Sat & Sun, plus 5-10pm or 11pm daily; Ⓚ Kenmore

A newish fancy seafood restaurant. Grey-orange hues and loungey leather chairs surround a circular bar in the center of the eating area, while a side dining room is bathed in silkscreen flowers, jewel tones

and subdued light. The food is no less delightful – seafood standards like salmon and scallops come alive with fresh herbs, seasonal veggies and spicy island influences.

CLIO Map pp308-9 French $$$

☎ 617-536-7200; Eliot Hotel, 370 Commonwealth Ave; meals $40-60, sushi $12-20; ⏱ 5:30-10pm or 10:30pm Tue-Sun; Ⓚ Hynes/ICA

Art deco posters and leopard-print rugs lend a funky feel to this ultrachic boutique restaurant. It is an appropriate setting for one of Boston's most innovative chefs: Ken Oringer is masterful when it comes to creative cuisine and pleasing presentation. Look for a French- and Asian-influenced menu that changes frequently according to what's fresh and in season. The on-site sashimi bar, Uni, also gets rave reviews.

FENWAY
EL PELON TAQUERIA

Map pp308-9 Mexican $

☎ 617-262-9090; 92 Peterborough St; meals $6-8; Ⓚ Museum

If your budget is tight, don't miss this chance to fill up on Boston's best burritos, tacos and *tortas*, made with the freshest ingredients. The *tacos de la casa* are highly recommended, especially the *pescado*, made with Icelandic cod and topped with chili mayo. Plates are paper and cutlery is plastic.

BROWN SUGAR CAFÉ

Map pp308-9 Thai $$

☎ 617-266-2928; 129 Jersey St; lunch $10-15, dinner $15-20; ⏱ 11am-10pm Mon-Fri, noon-10pm Sat & Sun; Ⓚ Museum

This crowded, unassuming neighborhood joint is often lauded for the best Thai food in the city. The delectable dishes are beautifully presented – try the mango curry, with tender chicken simmered in a yellow curry with chunks of ripe mango, tomato, red and green pepper, onion and summer squash.

SORENTO'S Map pp308-9 Pizza/Italian $$

☎ 617-424-7070; 86 Peterborough St; lunch $10-15, dinner $20-30; ⏱ 11am-11pm Mon-Fri, to midnight Sat & Sun; Ⓚ Museum

Little known outside of Fenway, Sorento's is a fabulous find for its romantic ambience and tasty pizzas and pastas. The umbrella-shaded patio is the perfect spot to linger over lunch after spending the morning at the MFA. The interior has an open kitchen and candlelit tables. It's not exactly upscale, but it's definitely the classiest option along this stretch of Peterborough St.

AUDUBON CIRCLE Map pp308-9   Pub $$

☎ 617-421-1910; 838 Beacon St; meals $15-25; ◷ 11:30am-1am; ⓡ St Mary's

The long black bar, wood floors and high ceilings lend an industrial feel to this lively pub and restaurant. It exudes a good vibe for catching a bite, watching the game or both. Burgers are highly recommended, or try the unique appetizers, like spicy beef *quesadilla* or pork-filled wontons.

UMI Map pp308–9   Asian $$

☎ 617-536-6688; 90 Peterborough St; meals $15-25; ⓡ Museum

This sushi bar is a delightful addition to this strip of ethnic eateries. The sushi and sashimi are always fresh and fantastic, but the menu does not stop there. Mains span Asia, including tempura, teriyaki, *pad thai* and even *bib-im bab*. There is not much to this simply decorated storefront, but it's an excellent and still undiscovered option.

ELEPHANT WALK
Map pp308-9   French/Cambodian $$

☎ 617-247-1500; 900 Beacon St; lunch $15-20, dinner $20-40; ◷ 11:30am-2:30pm Mon-Fri, 5-10pm daily; ⓡ St Mary's

Highly regarded for its dual menus of classic French and traditional Cambodian cuisine, the Elephant Walk offers a unique – but delectable – dining experience. The large dining room has an understated and exotic décor to match the menu. For the adventurous eater, the team of chefs offers tasting menus (three/four courses for $30/40) and cooking classes.

BROOKLINE

Brookline is worth the trip for an eclectic assortment of dining options, including kosher delis, Russian restaurants and many other ethnic eats. Coolidge Corner, which is around the intersection of Harvard and Beacon Sts, is the hub for the Brookline dining scene. Brookline Village – about 1km south – also hosts a cluster of restaurants and pubs.

COOLIDGE CORNER
BOTTEGA FIORENTINA

Map pp308-9   Italian $

☎ 617-232-2661; 313B Harvard St; meals $10-15; ◷ 11am-8pm Mon-Sat; ⓡ Coolidge Corner

A tiny, self-service storefront, this place boasts 'the best sandwiches outside of Florence.' But this tiny *bottega* offers much more. Daily specials – ranging from lasagna bolognese to pumpkin tortellini to baked stuffed zucchini – are a surprising bargain ($6 to $8). If you can't stand the cramped quarters, head around the corner for fine dining at the sister restaurant Firenze.

ROD DEE Map pp298-9   Thai $

☎ 617-738-4977; 1430 Beacon St; meals $10-20; ◷ 11:30am-11:30pm; ⓡ Coolidge Corner

Rod Dee is recommended for take-out, as the tiny storefront has hardly any seating and it's often steamy inside. Thai noodles and curry plates will only make you hotter, as they are loaded with spice. Specialties include drunken chicken (chicken and vegetables stir-fried in chili sauce) and *pad* paradise (shrimp and chicken with vegetables and cashews in a secret 'delicious sauce'). Great value for penny pinchers. Another outlet is on Peterborough St in Fenway.

ZAFTIGS DELICATESSEN

Map pp308-9   Diner $$

☎ 617-975-0075; 335 Harvard St; meals $15-20; ◷ 8am-10pm; ⓡ Coolidge Corner

'Let us be your Jewish mother,' Zaftigs implores. And on Saturday and Sunday mornings, patrons craving potato pancakes with smoked salmon, challah French toast and cheese blintzes line up out the door to oblige. Fortunately, breakfast is served all day, so no one has to miss it. Otherwise, the deli turns out a huge selection of sandwiches, including classics like *reubens*, egg salad and pastrami. The funky interior has interesting art adorning the walls.

FUGAKYU Map pp308-9   Japanese $$

☎ 617-734-1268; 1280 Beacon St; meals $15-30; ◷ 11:30am-3pm & 5pm-1:30am; ⓡ Coolidge Corner

The name aptly translates as 'house of elegance.' Upscale and over-the-top, Fugakyu offers a gorgeous array of sushi and sashimi, as well as traditional cooked meals, served by staff dressed in kimonos. The sushi bar features a water canal; watch for your order to arrive by boat.

BROOKLINE VILLAGE

KOOKOO Map pp308-9   Café $
☎ 617-730-5525; 7 Station St; meals $8-12; ☽ 7am-6pm Mon-Fri, 8am-5pm Sat; ⓡ Brookline Village

Across from the T stop, Kookoo is a sooper-cute café serving delicious soups and salads – most with some hint of the magic of the Middle East. The seven sandwich rollups all are fresh, healthy and vegetarian, including the signature kookoo rollup (parsley, spinach, coriander and minty yogurt). Pastries and coffee drinks also get whipped up behind the counter. The tiny space is crowded with an eclectic display of knickknacks and only three tables.

CAFÉ SAMOVAR Map pp308-9   Russian $$
☎ 617-232 0055; 236 Washington St; lunch $10-15, dinner $20-30; ⓡ Brookline Village

Floral babushka scarves serve as tablecloths and the bar is bedecked with a silver samovar, creating an old-world atmosphere in this aptly named restaurant. The menu is alarmingly authentic – handmade *pelmeni* (dumplings), both sweet and savory; a good selection of rich and hearty soups (the salty, sour *solyanka* is recommended); salads with non-descriptive names. A pianist serenades guests Friday and Saturday nights.

POMODORO Map pp308-9   Italian $$
☎ 617-556-4455; 24 Harvard St; meals $20-30; ⓡ Brookline Village

If you love the North End's cuisine but not its crowds, check out this spacious branch of the Hanover St favorite. For a full review, see p140.

LA MORRA Map pp308-9   Italian $$$
☎ 617-739-0007; 48 Boylston St; meals $30-40; ⓡ Brookline Village

This sleek interior at La Morra is the setting for equally sophisticated dining, featuring small plates of antipasti and homemade pastas. A daily changing prix-fixe menu ($35) offers wine pairings ($15) to complement the three-course meal. The staff is pleasant and professional, though service can be harried when the place gets hopping.

JAMAICA PLAIN

Funky, progressive Jamaica Plain hosts an ever-growing restaurant scene. The neighborhood's diverse population enjoys a variety of spunky cafés and international eateries, most of which are lined up along Centre St. The atmosphere is informal, so fine dining is limited.

BON SAVOR   French $$
☎ 617-971-0000; 605 Centre St; breakfast & lunch $8-12, dinner $20-30; ☽ 7:30am-3pm Mon-Fri, 8:30am-4pm Sat & Sun, plus 5:30-10pm Tue-Sat; ⓡ Green St

The crêpes at Bon Savor are made from 'a Russian grandmother's recipe,' which guarantees they are thin and buttery and melt-in-your-mouth divine. Savory options include beef stroganoff and chicken with mushrooms, but the overwhelming favorite is the sweet banana crêpe with whipped cream. New to Centre St, this place was still getting some kinks out at the time of research.

JUNE BUG CAFE   Sandwiches $
☎ 617-522-2393; 403A Centre St; meals $10; ☽ 8am-11pm Mon-Fri, 9am-11pm Sat & Sun; ⓡ Stony Brook

Dressed up like a June bug, this bohemian café's green and purple walls show off the work of local artists. Big, comfy couches (not to mention wi-fi access) invite surfers to settle in for an afternoon, sipping bubble tea or noshing on well-stuffed sandwiches. Vegetarians are well catered for, especially if they indulge in nutritious imitation meat.

CENTRE STREET CAFE   International $$
☎ 617-524-9217; 669 Centre St; meals $15-30; ☽ 11:30am-10pm Mon-Sat, 10am-3pm Sun; ⓡ Green St

This artistic, eclectic restaurant embodies the essence of Jamaica Plain. Smart but idiosyncratic staff serve dishes that range from 'Shrimp Nirvana' to 'Danno's Szechwan Shaboom.' It's not particularly fancy fare, but ingredients are organic and locally grown, and the outcome is – as the menu promises – 'outrageously good!' A highlight is Sunday brunch, when patient would-be patrons wait in lines that stretch down the block.

CAFÉ D
International $$

☎ 617-522-9500; 711 Centre St; meals $20-30;
⏰ 5-10pm; 🚇 Green St

This fun and funky 'global kitchen' borrows from all corners, including Asia (ginger and soy marinated chicken breast), Africa (Moroccan spiced lamb), Europe (risotto with asparagus and mushrooms) and the Americas (Baja fish tacos). What these items have in common is that they are perfectly prepared and easy on the palate. Set in a playful space – wallpapered in newsprint with colorful splashes – this JP newcomer is artful and adventurous.

TEN TABLES
International $$

☎ 617-524-8810; 597 Centre St; meals $20-30;
⏰ 5:30-9pm Mon-Thu, 5:30-10pm Fri & Sat, 5-9pm Sun; 🚇 Green St

True to its name, this gem has only 10 tables. Brick walls are hung with black-and-white photos, and the galley kitchen is framed by pots and pans, a motif that recurs around the restaurant. The emphasis is on simplicity – appropriate for a restaurant that specializes in traditional cooking techniques. The menu is short but changes frequently to highlight local, organic produce, handmade pastas, fresh seafood and homemade sausages. For a sampler plate, try Tuesday night wine dinners (first Tuesday of the month, $35), a joint effort with South End Formaggio (see p215).

CAMBRIDGE

Head across the Charles for more bustling neighborhoods. The most famous, Harvard Sq, has coffeehouses, sandwich shops, ethnic eateries and upscale restaurants to suit every budget and taste. Some regulars complain that rising rents have caused Harvard Sq to lose its edge, but you won't hear that about neighboring Central and Inman. Even post-industrial Kendall Sq boasts Boston's best pizza.

HARVARD SQUARE
GARAGE
Map p310
Food Court $

Cnr Mount Auburn & Dunster Sts; 🚇 Harvard

You're bound to find something fast, filling and cheap at the Garage, where a dozen places to eat are under one roof. Your op-

tions include pizza, tacos, sandwiches and ice cream.

SABRA GRILL Map p310
Lebanese $

☎ 617-868-5777; 20 Eliot St; meals $8-12;
⏰ 10am-10pm; 🚇 Harvard

Sabra served fresh and delicious Middle Eastern takeout long before it was trendy. Vegetarians can't do better than the daily special that never seems to change, a garlicky and delicious roasted veggie sandwich. Others swear by *shwarma* of any kind. Seating is limited, so pick a sandwich and head over to JFK Park for a picnic.

DARWIN'S
Map p310
Sandwiches $

☎ 617-354-5233; 148 Mt Auburn St; meals $8-12;
⏰ 8am-5pm; 🚇 Harvard

Punky staff serve fat sandwiches – made to order and stuffed with meats, cheeses and veggies – fresh soup and salads, and delicious coffee and pastries, all with a generous helping of attitude. The limited seating is often occupied by students who are in for the long haul (thanks to wireless access). So unless you intend to surf, take your lunch to enjoy at JFK Park or Radcliffe Yard. A new location is on Cambridge St near Irving House.

MR BARTLEY'S BURGER COTTAGE
Map p310
Burgers $

☎ 617-354-6559; 1246 Massachusetts Ave; meals $10-12; 🚇 Harvard

Packed with small tables and hungry college students, this burger joint has been a Harvard Sq institution for more than 40 years. Bartley's offers at least 40 different burgers; if none of those suits your fancy, create your own 7oz juicy masterpiece with the toppings of your choice. Sweet potato fries, onion rings, thick frappes and raspberry-lime rickeys complete the classic American meal.

HI-RISE BREAD CO
Map p310
Sandwiches $

☎ 617-492-3003; 56 Brattle St; meals $10-15;
⏰ 8:30am-5pm Mon-Fri, 9am-5pm Sat, 10am-4pm Sun; 🚇 Harvard

Eating at Hi-Rise feels like somebody invited you over for lunch. The cozy dining room upstairs is crowded with mismatched tables; when weather is fine, find a seat on the terrace. You'll be joined by academic types, who frequent this place for steaming soups and well-stuffed sandwiches, as well as crusty loaves and fresh-baked sweets. Everybody agrees it's overpriced, but somehow they can't resist.

VEGGIE PLANET

Map p310   Vegetarian Pizzeria $
☎ 617-661-1513; 47 Palmer St; meals $10-15;
🚇 Harvard
Vegetarians and vegans can go nuts on creative interpretations of pizza (literally nuts: try the peanut curry pizza with tofu and broccoli). Oddly shaped pies call on all the ethnic cuisines – but none of the animals – for their tantalizing tastes. The menu also offers plenty of soups and salads, fresh juices and fairly traded coffee, but no alcohol. This place is for the pure of body and spirit (2% of profits are donated to feed the hungry, so order away!) By night, these basement digs double as the famous folk music venue, Club Passim (see p180).

TANJORE

Map p310   Indian $$
☎ 617-868-1900; 18 Eliot St; lunch $10, dinner $15-25; 🕐 11:30am-11pm; 🚇 Harvard
Tanjore's lunchtime buffet has been a favorite of Harvard Sq locals for years. The buffet changes daily, but it always features perfectly fluffy basmati rice, fresh, hot *naan* bread and subtly delicious *kheer* (rice pudding). This place is good enough to come for dinner, but the buffet offers superior value.

CAMBRIDGE, 1

Map p310   Pizzas $$
☎ 617-576-1111; 27 Church St; meals $20-30;
🕐 noon-midnight; 🚇 Harvard
Set in the old fire station, this pizzeria's name comes from the sign chiseled into the stonework out front. The interior is sleek, sparse and industrial, with a slate bar, an open kitchen and big windows overlooking the Old Burying Ground in the back. The menu is equally simple: nine pizzas, five salads and one dessert. These pizzas are delectable, with oddly shaped, crispy crust and creative topping combos. You cannot create your own pie here, but you don't need to. Try the Sopresetta and fontina, wash it down with a Maretti.

RED HOUSE

Map p310   International $$
☎ 617-576-0605; 98 Winthrop St; meals $20-30;
🕐 noon-midnight Sun & Tue-Thu, noon-1am Fri & Sat; 🚇 Harvard
Formerly known as the Cox-Hicks House, this quaint clapboard house dates to 1802. Reminiscent of an old-fashioned inn, it retains its historic charm with its wide-plank wood floors, cozy (sometimes crowded) layout and functioning fireplace. In summer, the draw is the patio overlooking a quiet corner of Harvard Sq. The menu is varied, but always includes a good selection of seafood and pasta. Almost all mains come in half portions – a boon for your budget.

CASABLANCA

Map p310   Mediterranean $$
☎ 617-876-0999; 40 Brattle St; meals $20-30;
🕐 bar until 1am or 2am Mon-Sat; 🚇 Harvard
Below the Brattle Theater, this Harvard Sq classic has long been the hangout of film fans, local literati and other arty types. Regulars skip the formal dining room and slip in the back door to the boisterous bar. A colorful mural depicting Rick's Café sets the stage for innovative Mediterranean delights, including a great selection of meze.

HARVEST

Map p310   American $$$
☎ 617-868-2255; 44 Brattle St; lunch $20-30, dinner $40-50; 🚇 Harvard
A Harvard Sq classic. This place is simple but sophisticated, a description that applies to the menu as well as the space. The modern American fare allows for some regional influences, such as the seductive raw bar. Local luminaries, especially Harvard faculty, are often spotted here. Foodies will enjoy Harvest Review ($39), a monthly event that features a four-course dinner, wine pairings and a speaker – usually somebody who caught, killed, produced or prepared some part of the meal.

CHEZ HENRI

Map pp298-9   French/Cuban $$
☎ 617-354-8980; 1 Shepard St; meals $30-40, bar menu $7-15; 🕐 6-10pm Mon-Thu, 5:30-10pm Fri & Sat, 5:30-9:30pm Sun; 🚇 Harvard
This French-Cuban blend is a dark, romantic bistro offering saffron-soaked mussels, smoked salmon frisée and *blanquette de*

veau (veal stew). It may sound all French, but the undeniable favorite is the Cubano, a pressed sandwich with succulent, slow-roasted pork. The dining room has a fancy feel, but the lively bar serves up lime daiquiris, mojitos and other rum cocktails to a casual crowd.

UPSTAIRS ON THE SQUARE

Map p310   International $$$
☎ 617-864-1933; 91 Winthrop St; meals $40-60;
⏰ 11am-1am; 🚇 Harvard

Pink-and-gold hues, zebra- and leopard-skin rugs, and lots of glamor and glitz: such is the décor that defines this restaurant, the successor to once-renowned Upstairs at the Pudding. The creative menu and carefully chosen wine list have earned high praise. The downstairs Monday Club Bar is open for lunch, offering a more casual atmosphere, a slightly cheaper menu and a wall of windows overlooking Winthrop Park.

CENTRAL SQUARE

BARAKA CAFÉ

Map p311   North African $$
☎ 617-868-3951; 801/2 Pearl St; meals $15-25;
⏰ 11:30am-3pm & 5:30-10pm Tue-Sat; 🚇 Central

This tiny storefront offers an opportunity for the adventurous eater to sample exotic flavors in a setting reminiscent of a Mediterranean kitchen. The enticing menu offers hot and cold *kemiette* (small plates), as well as classic North African dishes like couscous and *bastilla*. Vegetarians have no shortage of options, while meat-eaters might indulge in the M'Katef (lamb chops with an almond pastry). There's no alcohol, but lemonade – spiced with orange essence and rose water – quenches any thirst.

KOREANA

Map p311   Korean $$
☎ 617-576-8661; 154 Prospect St; lunch $10-15, dinner $20-30; 🚇 Central

Consistently rated as one of Boston's best Korean restaurants. It's worth the short walk up from Central Sq to sample the specialties from the BBQ grill, especially the prime beef ribs. Sushi, hot pots and plenty of vegetarian items guarantee something for everyone. And never fear...the service-oriented staff is sure to oblige newbies who may not know what to order.

CUCHI CUCHI Map p311   International $$
☎ 617-864-2929; 795 Main St; meals $20-30;
⏰ 5:30-11pm; 🚇 Central

Features an international menu of small plates, encouraging you to sample your way around the globe. The lavishly baroque décor bucks the minimalist design trends omnipresent in Boston's hip eateries. Stained-glass windows, gold-veined mirrors and ornate tiles make the sophisticated clientele feel right at home. And yes, the place is named in honor of Charo.

CENTRAL KITCHEN Map p311   French $$
☎ 617-491-5599; 567 Massachusetts Ave; meals $20-30; ⏰ 5:30-11pm; 🚇 Central

Serving rustic Mediterranean fare in a gritty urban setting. Look for bistro classics like mussels *marinière*, pan-seared foie gras and cassoulet. If you think this place is cool, head upstairs to the lounge, the Enormous Room. Through the unmarked door, you'll find a dark room filled with beautiful people, reclining on couches and sipping fancy, fruity cocktails.

INMAN SQUARE

PUNJABI DHABA Map p311   Indian $
☎ 617-547-8272; 225 Hampshire St; meals $8-12;
⏰ 11am-midnight; 🚇 Central

A 'dhaba' is a roadside diner, often found in India's northern Punjab region, known for fast service, minimal décor and super-tasty food. This 'dhaba' fits that description, serving up huge platters of chicken tikka masala, *saag paneer* and other Indian specialties. The tiny, counter-service place is usually crammed with Indian patrons, who appreciate the authentic food and cheap prices.

ALL-STAR SANDWICH BAR

Map p311   Sandwich Bar $
☎ 617-868-3065; 1245 Cambridge St; meals $10-15; ⏰ 11am-9pm Mon-Thu, 11am-10pm Sat; 🚇 Central

Sandwich-lovers will have a hard time choosing at this Inman Sq newcomer (which has declared itself a `wrap-free zone'). Fortunately, you can't really go wrong. The dozens of sandwiches on offer are all prepared with fresh tasty ingredients and just a touch of innovation. Additional perks: fresh-squeezed lemonade, heaping plates of French fries and beers on draught. Cash only.

S&S DELI Map p311 Diner $

☎ 617-354-0620; 1334 Cambridge St; meals $10-20; ⏱ 7am-11pm Mon-Wed, 7am-midnight Thu-Fri, 8am-midnight Sat, 8am-11pm Sun; ⓣ Central

This Jewish deli is an Inman Sq institution, great for homemade soups, hearty sandwiches and breakfast served all day. Enjoy old black-and-white photos of the neighborhood while you wait for a table, especially if you come for weekend brunch. Skeptics complain about the lackadaisical service and nondescript décor, but they keep coming back for more.

MIDWEST GRILL Map p311 Brazilian $$

☎ 617-354-7536; 1122 Cambridge St; meals $20-30; ⏱ 11:30am-11:30pm; ⓣ Central

Carnivores will be in seventh heaven at this authentic Brazilian *churrascaria*. Skewer after skewer of beef, pork, lamb and sausage are served *rodizio*-style, which means they just keep coming until you can eat no more. A buffet of roasted vegetables is also included, but this is not a vegetarian-friendly place. Connoisseurs recommend the roasted chicken hearts. Live Brazilian music adds to the atmosphere.

EAST COAST GRILL

Map p311 Seafood $$$

☎ 617-491-6568; 1271 Cambridge St; meals $30-40; ⏱ 5:30-10pm daily, plus 11am-2:30pm Sun; ⓣ Central or Harvard

Seafood with southern spice. Sample appetizers like a chili-crusted tuna taco or buttermilk fried oysters, before diving into a fine, fresh seafood main. If fish is not your thing, there is also a selection of ribs from the oak-smoked pit barbecue. The do-it-yourself Bloody Mary bar makes the East Coast Grill one of the city's top spots for Sunday brunch.

OLEANA Map p311 Mediterranean $$$

☎ 617-661-0505; 134 Hampshire St; meals $30-40; ⏱ 5:30-10pm Sun-Thu, to 11pm Fri & Sat; ⓣ Central

Foodies sing the praises of this Mediterranean masterpiece in Inman Sq. Ana Sortun's exotic yet still accessible cuisine evokes Greece, Morocco and Turkey. Grilled lamb with fava-bean moussaka is a perennial favorite, while the meat-free will appreciate the vegetarian tasting menu ($40). Like the menu, the setting changes seasonally, with a roaring fire in winter and a delightfully fragrant patio in summer.

KENDALL SQUARE

EMMA'S

Map p311 Pizzeria $$

☎ 617-864-8534; 40 Hampshire St; meals $10-20; ⏱ 11:30am-10pm Mon-Fri, 4-10pm Sat; ⓣ Kendall

Before or after a flick at the Kendall Sq Cinema, make a point of stopping here. The friendly neighborhood pizzeria instills a maniacal devotion in its customers. Crispy thin crust and creative topping combinations cause Emma's to be consistently rated among the city's best pizza. Slices and salads are sold from the front window.

ATASCA

Map p311 Portuguese $$

☎ 617-621-6991; 50 Hampshire St; meals $20-30; ⏱ 11:30am-11pm Mon-Sat, noon-10pm Sun; ⓣ Kendall

This is home-cooking like they do in the Azores (which is where your hostess is from). The specialty of the Cerqueira family is the *bacalhau de cebolada*, salted cod with caramelized onions, roasted red peppers and fried potatoes; but if you like seafood, you'll find something to sate your appetite. The menu also features a wide range of small plates, or *petiscos*, and a nice selection of Portuguese wines. Sit out on the spacious patio and spend a spectacular summer evening.

BLUE ROOM Map p311 International $$$

☎ 617-494-9034; 1 Kendall Sq; brunch $23, dinner $30-40; ⏱ 5:30-10:30pm daily, plus 11am-2:30pm Sun; ⓣ Kendall

Staff at the Blue Room takes pride in the restaurant's reliance on organic farms and 'mom-and-pop purveyors' as the source of produce and meats. They use them to create a menu that is constantly changing according to what's in season and fresh, but is always innovative and delicious. One of Cambridge's top-rated restaurants, the Blue Room still manages to maintain a casual, comfortable atmosphere.

EAST CAMBRIDGE

HELMAND
Map pp298-9   Afghan $$

☎ 617-492-4646; 143 First St; meals $20-30; ☯ 5-10pm Sun-Thu, to 11pm Fri & Sat; ⓡ Lechmere

Fusing flavors and techniques from India and the Middle East, the Helmand shows off the rich, diverse and little-known cuisine of Afghanistan. The active, open kitchen – complete with an oven that turns out melt-in-your-mouth flatbread – is entertainment enough in this simple dining room. And the dishes it produces are exotic and enticing. Not to mention that the place is owned by the brother of Afghan President Hamid Karzai. It's across the street from Cambridge-side Galleria Mall.

OUTLYING AREAS

SOMERVILLE

Filled with students, artists and musicians, this up-and-coming 'hood has no shortage of excellent eating options. Some are so good that they are attracting diners from nearby Cambridge and even from Boston. Ever-hip Davis Sq is busting with bars and cafés, with the occasional upscale restaurant thrown in for special occasions. There is a small but growing cluster of bars and restaurants at the corner of Beacon and Washington Sts (known as Kirkland Corner). Up the road, Union Sq is like an outdoor food court, with a huge selection of pizza places, coffeehouses, bakeries, sub shops and *taquerias* (and more than a few Irish pubs; see p173).

ROSEBUD DINER
Map pp298-9   Diner $

☎ 617-666-6015; 381 Summer St; meals $10-15; ☯ 8am-midnight; ⓡ Davis

A classic American diner, housed in a railroad dining car, complete with plastic booths and counter service. Snappy waitresses serve burgers and sandwiches with sass, as well as the obligatory all-day breakfast.

REDBONES Map pp298-9   BBQ $$
☎ 617-628-2200; 55 Chester St; meals $20-30; ⓡ Davis

Redbones is usually packed with locals craving barbecue ribs, collard greens and corn bread. Portions are huge, but if you can save room for sweet potato pie you won't regret it. The bar is always bustling, as ice-cold beers stave off the hunger for waiting patrons. There is additional seating downstairs, where quarters are dark, but enlivened by the creepy, colorful wall murals.

DALÍ Map pp298-9   Spanish $$$
☎ 617-661-3254; 415 Washington St; meals $30-40; ☯ 5:30-10:30pm; ⓡ Harvard

Crowded with kitsch and craziness, this bustling bar sets the standard for imaginative and appetizing tapas. Don Juan waiters deliver an endless array of goodies, all of which will make you think you've died and gone to Andalusia. The place is usually packed (reservations are not accepted), so order a pitcher of sangria to sip while you wait. From Harvard, walk across the yard and up Kirkland St.

Drinking

Drinking

Taken as a whole, Boston's drinking scene is dominated by four categories: dive bars, authentic Irish bars, irritating Irish knock-offs and sports bars. Truly hip places can be counted on one sober hand or two drunken fists. These and the cooler spots will be found in Cambridge, Somerville, Jamaica Plains and Allston. If you're stuck on the Boston peninsula, get your ass away from the Freedom Trail – a desolate wasteland if you're looking to imbibe in style – and head elsewhere to the South End (gay-friendly), Back Bay (yuppies and students) or Chinatown (the diviest of dives). A notable exception to the Freedom Trail rule is the North End, where a handful of cafés serve coffee and Campari along Hanover St. While open at night, they are primarily daytime venues.

When lubricating your mind away from the center, remember that the T stops running around 12:20am, an hour and a half before last call. Budget an extra $15 to $20 for a cab ride if you don't feel like taking a long walk.

BEACON HILL & BOSTON COMMON

Thanks to the staid Brahmin culture that retains a tight grip on the character of Beacon Hill (and on what businesses are allowed to operate within it), there are very few bars in the city's venerable neighborhood.

21ST AMENDMENT Map pp302-3
☎ 617-227-7100; 150 Bowdoin St; ⏲ 11:30-2am; ⓡ Park St
A quintessential tavern, this basement-level spot has been an ever-popular haunt for overeducated and underpaid statehouse workers to bitch about the wheels of government. The place feels especially cozy in the winter, when you'll feel pretty good about yourself as you drink a stout near the copper-hooded fireplace.

CHEERS Map pp302-3
☎ 617-227-9605; 84 Beacon St; ⏲ 11-2am; ⓡ Arlington
This place not only doesn't look like its famous TV alter ego, it's also ugly. Tables are usually unavailable for the drinks-only crowd until after midnight, and staff banter with bar patrons is restricted to drink orders only. If you're after the mediocre grub, be prepared to pay over $20 for an 'eNORMous burger' ($16.95) and a beer ($5.25).

SEVENS ALE HOUSE Map pp302-3
☎ 617-523-9074; 77 Charles St; ⏲ noon-1am; ⓡ Charles/MGH

Beach Hill's long-standing favorite looks old school, with its wooden bar placed under hanging glasses, and a few comfortable booths. A sedate crowd plays chess and either stares at a mural of a dying Minuteman or admires a jersey signed by Doug Flutie. A single dartboard is in good shape.

GOVERNMENT CENTER & WEST END

In a word: ouch. When the city fathers bulldozed and rebuilt this area in the 1950s and 1960s, one casualty that never recovered was nightlife. Most of deadsville is either a wasteland of residential towers or the empty City Hall complex itself. However, several of the city's most popular rowdy sports bars are clustered near the Boston Garden, home of the Bruins and Celtics. Canal St and gritty Friend St are the best bets.

BOSTON BEER WORKS Map pp300-1
☎ 617-896-2337; 112 Canal St; ⏲ 11:30-1am; ⓡ North Station
Boston's famed beer hall/sports bar features a revolving list of seasonal microbrews (try the pumpkin pie). There's plenty of room to drink and nosh (the French fries are almost as popular as the brews), watch sporting events and shoot pool.

FOURS Map pp300-1
☎ 617-720-4455; 166 Canal St; ⏲ 11-1am; ⓡ North Station
Boasting all sports, all the time, this makes a great place to appreciate Bostonians'

WHEN IN BOSTON, DRINK LIKE THE BOSTONIANS

There is no beverage that truly typifies the Boston drinking experience. Imbibing like a Bostonian is largely a question of which neighborhood you happen to be in. Should you brave your way to Chinatown, expect to see a lot of Bud and shots of rail liquor. Along the cluster of bars on Union St near Faneuil Hall, expect more of the same and maybe someone choking back their puke (that counts as drinking, no?). The Back Bay, South End and spots near the Common are more likely to vend cocktails, some of them very fine, as well as stock decent wine selections.

Perhaps because of the huge numbers of students and sports fans, the booze you're most likely to see is beer. While you might find popular Sam Adams, the city's most famous brew, in the hands of many, bear in mind that the stuff is a bit more bitter than you'd usually choose. Many Bostonians don't have sophisticated enough palettes to tell the difference, which is why they are pleased to drink almost anything in a pint glass that is colored a shade of brown.

near fanatical obsession with sporting events. The large two-level bar was established in 1976 and retains a dash of character from that period. In addition to the game of your choice, admire a Jersey collection and loads of pictures depicting legendary events in Boston's sporting past.

NORTH END

Despite the vibrancy of Hanover St, the colorful North End is devoid of proper bars. If you weave your way through all the late-night bakeries and restaurants, you'll find a handful of cafés where you can drink in Italian American style.

CAFE PARADISO Map pp300-1

☎ 617-742-1768; 255 Hanover St; ⏰ 7am-11pm; 🚇 Haymarket

The Saturday morning regulars are so dedicated that some painstakingly organize their business calendars so they don't miss their spot at the counter. As he has for years, Luigi masterfully attends to the espresso machine and pours neat cognacs with efficient and understated flourish. It's a good spot to watch overseas soccer matches. Excellent desserts are also on offer.

CAFFE DELLO SPORT Map pp300-1

☎ 617-523-5063; 308 Hanover St; ⏰ 6am-midnight; 🚇 Haymarket

An informal shorts-and-T-shirt crowd of tourists and thick accented guys from the 'hood sit at glass-topped tables and drink coffee and Campari. The relic of a sign out front portrays a '70s-looking soccer player about to strike in faded glory.

CAFFÉ VITTORIA Map pp300-1

☎ 617-227-7606; 290-96 Hanover St; ⏰ 8-1am; 🚇 Haymarket

For absolutely superb cappuccino in a frilly parlor displaying antique espresso machines, grab a marble-topped table and live it up in Victorian pleasure. Also on offer are ports and dessert.

CHARLESTOWN

Pretty as historic Charlestown is, the bar scene is miniscule. You can find a drink in one of several restaurants (see eating) or make your way to Sullivan's, the only real bar in the center. Nearby is our favorite vending machine.

SULLIVAN'S PUB Map p304

☎ 617-242-9515; 85 Main St; ⏰ 11:30am-midnight Tue-Sun; 🚇 Community College

Lady behind bar, 'You just sit there and look pretty.' Drunk old-timer, 'I've never looked pretty in my whole life.' Head to this archetypal local (everyone calls it Sully's) for more of such dialogue in a generic bar, beloved by its patrons because of its perfect ordinariness and lack of a trendy crowd.

VENDING MACHINE Map p304

34 Winthrop St; 🚇 Community College

The kind firefighters at Engine Company 50 work in a sweet 19th-century firehouse with the Freedom Trail (p106) passing close by. On most summer days, they open up one of the bays so that hot walkers have access to a vending machine embedded in some old wooden lockers covered in departmental patches. Sit on the bench out front and admire the charming streetscape.

DOWNTOWN

After the department store at Downtown Crossing locks up for the night, the street life quiets considerably. Embedded nearby are some perennial favorites, some of them quite crowded on weekends.

JJ FOLEY'S Map pp302-3
☎ 17-695-1556; 21 Kingston St; ⊗ 11-2am; 🚇 Downtown Crossing

Dating to 1909, this lovely Irish gem is well positioned in the middle of the peninsula, and exudes the authenticity of a well-aged bar. Expect tall ceilings, wooden booths, 8ft-high wainscoting and sweet cabinetry behind the bar.

LAST HURRAH Map pp302-3
☎ 617-227-8600; 60 School St; ⊗ 11:30-12:30am Sun-Fri, 4:30-11:30pm Sat; 🚇 Park St

Having been a haunt for Boston's 19th-century intelligentsia and politicians, the beautiful lobby bar of the Omni Parker Hotel is a throwback to Old Boston. Enjoy a dish of hot nuts, drink a bourbon and don't wear shorts – you'll look woefully out of place.

MR DOOLEY'S BOSTON TAVERN
Map pp302-3
☎ 617-338-5656; 77 Broad St; ⊗ 11:30-2am; 🚇 State

With Irish bands playing traditional tunes several nights a week, and a decent list of appropriate beers, this cozy bar is one of the best bets in the area. Sit in a booth and linger over a copy of the *Irish Immigrant* or *Boston Irish Reporter* to learn about current events on the other side of the Atlantic.

FANEUIL HALL

While it's easy enough to find a bar around Faneuil Hall, most of them actively cater to the tourist crowd and have an underwhelming, generic vibe. Just to the north of Quincy Market, you'll find Union St with an assortment of popular bars that look very 1770 on the outside and very 1989 once you pass the threshold.

BELL IN HAND Map pp300-1
☎ 617-227-2098; 45-55 Union St; ⊗ 11:30-2am; 🚇 Haymarket

Sample the local brew, Samuel Adams beer

With a tourist-trail location and plaque proclaiming its status as 'the oldest tavern in the US,' this spot no longer recalls the days of Jimmy Wilson. At night, expect to see a meat-market, bridge-and-tunnel crowd.

GREEN DRAGON Map pp300-1
☎ 617-367-0055; 11 Marshal St; ⊗ 11-2am; 🚇 Haymarket

Also purporting itself to be a historic watering hole, the Green Dragon is almost indistinguishable from the Bell in Hand. The place is full of overdeveloped biceps kept in perfect tone by constant high-fiving.

SEAPORT DISTRICT

The Seaport District isn't oozing with hot spots, but it does contain a few salty treats. One of these is the harborside Barking Crab (p145) and the other, following, is mentioned with love.

LUCKY'S Map pp302-3
☎ 617-357-5825; www.luckyslounge.com; 355 Congress St S; ⊗ 11-2am Sun-Fri, 6pm-2am Sat; 🚇 South Station

One of Boston's top-notch bars, Lucky's earns street-cred by having no sign. Step inside, and you'll return to a delightfully gritty lounge that looks straight from 1959. Enjoy well-priced drinks, excellent martinis and, frequently, Motown-inspired bands playing tunes to which people actually dance. Sinatra Sundays remain a perpetual favorite, and the after-work scene is one of the liveliest around.

CHINATOWN, LEATHER DISTRICT & THEATER DISTRICT

While the streets in Chinatown and the Leather District can be a touch desolate and seedy at night, they do contain a few old-school dive bars where you'll encounter bohemians and some people that are tougher than you. If you find a Chinese restaurant open past last call, chances are that you can order some 'cold tea' which is code for beer in a teapot.

If you want a beer hall that looks like it hasn't changed a thing since 1868, check out Jacob Wirth (p148) in the nearby Theater District. Readers interested in some swanky drinks should wander to Boylston St.

EXCELSIOR Map p305
☎ 617-426-5684; 272 Boylston St; ⏰ 4:30pm-1am Sun-Thu, 4:30pm-2am Fri & Sat; 🚇 Arlington
A trendy(ish), tame crowd of 30-something urbanites drink in style under a ceiling

covered with sophisticated geometric tapestries. The room swims pleasantly in warm tones of dark teak and amber, the whole thing set around a glass-and-steel cube that contains the wine collection. Efficient, professional staff will hurry oysters to your table as you admire the Public Garden across the street. We lament the ridiculously out-of-character flatscreen.

FOUR SEASONS BOSTON Map p305
☎ 617-338-4400; 200 Boylston St; ⏰ 11-1am Mon-Thu, 11-2am Fri & Sat, 11am-midnight Sun; 🚇 Arlington
Enjoy a dish of complimentary hot nuts while drinking from a menu of seasonal drinks. In summer, this might mean a specialty sangria (rioja, riesling, Cointreau, syrup, cranberry-and-orange juice, fruit and soda), while on a brisk autumn day you might drink a concoction of cider, brandy and pumpkin. The expansive and modern hotel bar has lots of private spaces and soft leather couches.

WEGGIE'S PUB Map pp302-3
☎ 617-542-7080; 162 Lincoln St; ⏰ to 2am; 🚇 South Station
Stuffed with massive trophies from various competitions (such as the 38th Annual

SUPERIOR COCKTAILS

While the following are primarily restaurants, they've all got attached bars staffed by either super-scientists or actual wizards. Expect to pay between $7 and $12 for your libation.

No 9 Park (p138) Carefully handpicked, these bartenders are not performing the job as a stopover to something else. Several have degrees in chemistry, can talk about drinks with authority, and are knowledgeable about the social, commercial and chemical history of cocktails. They use rare mixers that you won't find elsewhere – many people end up consuming drinks they thought they didn't have a taste for and finding out they actually love it. Elegant, dressy room.

29 Newbury (☎ 617-536-0290; 29 Newbury St; ⏰ 4pm-2am; 🚇 Arlington) While proportions of traditional cocktails are strictly adhered to, the volume is not. Meaning the pours can be pleasantly oversized without being either too strong or watered down. The place is gay friendly, and at least one bartender will excitedly tell you about his cruise with the boys, if correctly prompted. There's good outdoor seating in summer.

Beacon Hill Bistro (p228) Because there are only 10 seats, satff will labor over your drink to make it to your precise specifications. The bar is attached to a bistro and looks like a little chapel, backlit with stained glass. It's almost as though you are standing before an altar with the bartender handing out communion bourbon. Also, enjoy the fireplace.

Eastern Standard (p153) Around 10pm, the dinner scene dies down and an industry crowd takes over to guzzle from a menu that features seven kinds of bitters, 14 rums (only two of them shitty) and innovative concoctions. Try the Metamorphosis (Becherovka, honey, lemon) or the Old Cuban (rum, lime, mint and sparkling white wine) – yes, it's girly, but it's so delicious you won't care.

Chinese North American Invitational Volleyball Tournament, held in Toronto in 1982), Weggie's has been a neighborhood fixture for decades. Supposedly, the place was originally 'Reggie's,' but the Chinese line cooks who come here couldn't pronounce the name. This loungie dive is characterized by cheap red vinyl, colorful lampshades and Formica.

BACK BAY

While there are a few places to imbibe on bustling Newbury St, most of the drinking action lies parallel on Boylston. The closer you get to Mass Ave, the more likely you are to find a grimy student haunt. Work your way toward the Public Garden, and you'll find a collection of places catering to people with money. A few of these are elegant, many more of them tacky. In addition to the following, Other Side Cosmic

Café (p152) makes for a delightful late-night spot.

BUKOWSKI TAVERN Map pp306-7
☎ 617-437-9999; 50 Dalton St; ⏰ 11-2am ⓣ Hynes/ICA
This sweet-ass bar lies inside a parking garage next to the canyon of the Mass Pike. Expect sticky wooden tables, loud rock, lots of black hoodies and more than 100 kinds of beer.

COTTONWOOD CAFÉ Map pp306-7
☎ 617-247-2225; 222 Berkeley St; ⏰ 11:30-2am ⓣ Copley
Dressed in warm 'southwestern' tones, come to this bar and restaurant for well-prepared margaritas made from a decent list of tequilas. Big windows overlook sidewalk action, and a pleasant patio is open most of the year. Beware the food; the quality varies greatly.

GET YOUR GAME ON

When every other bar in town has a pool table, sometimes it's hard to know when the felt will be clean and the surface level. Use this crib sheet to figure out good places to shoot stick and chuck darts.

Billiards

Flat Top Johnny's (Map p311; ☎ 617-494-9565; 1 Kendall Sq; ⏰ noon-1am Sat & Sun, 3pm-1am Mon-Fri; ⓣ Kendall Sq) Twelve tournament tables are set in a tall-ceilinged space surrounded by brick walls and comic-book murals. Weekly 9-Ball tournaments.

Diesel Cafe (p173) The back room of this lesbian-friendly café has multiple tables and some of the most skilled ladies in town.

Kings (p191) Play 8-Ball on reconditioned vintage Brunswick Gold Crowns in a plush air-conditioned room to the tune of $14 per hour.

Jillian's Billiard Club (Map pp308-9; ☎ 617-437-0300; 145 Ipswich St; ⏰ 11-2am Mon-Sat, noon-2am Sun; ⓣ Kenmore Sq) With over 50 tables in pristine condition, this enormous three-story place has seven bars and a full-service menu. People also come here to play darts and table tennis.

Sacco's Bowl Haven (p191) Step back into the '50s in this relic of a room attached to the famous bowling alley. Incredibly cheap rates, but no booze.

Darts

Cornwall's (p169) It's got two boards, both in great repair, as well as a side room with multiple pool tables.

Crossroads (opposite) Head upstairs to find a room with six boards and a lot of fellows from nearby MIT fraternities using them.

Field (Map p311; ☎ 617-354-7345; 20 Prospect St; ⓣ Central Square) This pretentious neighborhood pub offers two boards, though you might be tossing the darts over people exiting a nearby bathroom.

Super Chexx Hockey

Milky Way (p192) If you've got a buck, you know you want to play 1983's hottest game, a foosball-like, bubble-topped table pitting the USSR and USA in a hockey match.

CROSSROADS Map pp306-7
☎ 617-262-7371; 495 Beacon St; ⏰ noon-2am; 🚇 Hynes/ICA
Being a low-budget, cheap drinks kind of place, it attracts lots of students, sports fans and folks looking for a good game of darts. It's heavy duty Irish and isn't the kind of place where you want to order Bushmills.

POUR HOUSE Map pp306-7
☎ 617-236-1767; 907 Boylston St; ⏰ 8-2am; 🚇 Hynes/ICA
For years, young college students have introduced themselves to urban nightlife by enjoying cheap drinks and cheaper burgers in this pleasantly ratty bar. At least one of the TVs is playing Kino, not the Sox game.

SOUTH END

This neighborhood contains some of Boston's hippest bars, many of them inside the pleasantly converted brownstones which typify the area. As the South End serves as home base for much of Boston's gay community, you'll find plenty of spots catering to the fellas. The lesbian presence is also felt, but is more prevalent in Jamaica Plain.

BERKELEY PERK CAFE Map p305
☎ 617-426-7375; 69 Berkeley St; ⏰ 6:30am-5pm Mon-Fri, 7:30am-5pm Sat; 🚇 Arlington
A big bay window overlooks a bustling South End street. Look inside to find small café tables, tile inlaid high tops and a few dark wood art deco booths in this airy neighborhood coffeehouse.

CLERY'S Map p305
☎ 617-262-9874; 113 Dartmouth St; ⏰ 11:30-2am; 🚇 Back Bay
Big, popular and very sanitized, Clery's attracts droves of heads accustomed to wearing baseball hats to its weekly trivia night. Some criticize it for fake Irishness, and poor acoustics turn collective conversation into cacophony. Emblematic song played during visit: U2's 'She Moves in Mysterious Ways.'

DELUX CAFÉ & LOUNGE Map p305
☎ 617-338-5258; 100 Chandler St; ⏰ 5pm-1am Mon-Sat; 🚇 Back Bay
If Boston has a laid-back hipster bar, this is it. The small room on the 1st floor of a

brownstone comes covered in knotty pine paneling, artwork from old LPs and Christmas lights. A small TV in the corner plays silent cartoons (not sports), and a noteworthy kitchen serves incredible grilled-cheese sandwiches and inspired comfort food, including coleslaw that you actually want to eat.

DISH Map p305
☎ 617-426-7866; 253 Shawmut Ave; ⏰ 5-11pm Mon-Thu, 5pm-midnight Fri & Sat; 🚇 Arlington
For a romantic date spot in an old brick room redone with intentional graffiti and Mondrian-esque bathroom doors, this trendy bistro serves a dozen wines by the glass and has a small terrace if you feel like lounging outside. It's used more as a restaurant and less as a bar until around 10pm. The bartender likes to play The Sea and Cake.

FLASH'S Map p305
☎ 617-574-8888; 310 Stuart; ⏰ 11-3am Mon-Sat, 5pm-2am Sun; 🚇 Arlington
While mostly full of fellows, this not-quite industrial bar shoots for a modern vibe with its flashy neon sign. Inside, find hardwood floors, a lot of TVs broadcasting Sox games and a few ladies. Strong, bargain martinis.

FRITZ Map p305
☎ 617-482-3450; 26 Chandler St; ⏰ noon-2am; 🚇 Arlington
Inside the Chandler Inn Hotel, enjoy a long bar full of chatty men and lots of bottles of booze, all dimly lit by pink Christmas lights that enhance Fritz's atmosphere without it feeling kitschy. The place swerves toward romantic with several breakaway spots, though you'll be obliged to pay homage to Boston sports on one of several TVs.

JACQUES CABARET Map p305
☎ 617-426-8902; www.jacquescabaret.com; 76 Broadway; ⏰ 11am-midnight Mon-Sat, noon-midnight Sun; 🚇 Arlington
Head to this dive on a dark side street to experience the gay culture of the South End before gentrification took over. A shaded-lamp and pool-table kind of place, Jacques hosts outstanding low-budget

TRIVIA NIGHTS

The great preponderance of Boston's dozens of trivia nights is organized by one company: **Stump! Pub Trivia** (www.trailsideentertainment.com). One of our recommendations hails from this collection, the rest are charming independent operations.

Matt Murphy' Pub (p170) The laid-back contest occurs every Wednesday, where losing teams are often chastised for their failure.

TC's Lounge (below) In the South End, this dive's Thursday night trivia regularly attracts Boston College professors who know a lot about cooking duck.

PJ Ryan's Pub (Map pp298–9; ☎ 617-625-8200; 239 Holland St, Somerville; 🚇 Davis Sq) Expect incredibly challenging questions and stiff competition at this Irish Pub in Teele Sq. The Tuesday contest is popular and reliable enough to charge each team $5.

Thirsty Scholar (Map pp298–9; ☎ 617-497-2294; 70 Beacon St, Somerville; 🚇 Central Sq) A great bar for competitive Sunday evening trivia (organized by Stump!), the dark-wood Thirsty Scholar gets overly packed on weekends with a yuppie crowd. Contents of several bookcases reveal the bar's gloomy secret: it isn't really for scholars.

drag shows every night. We think Mizery is the cat's pajamas.

SISTER SOREL Map p305

☎ 617-266-4600; 647 Tremont St; 🕐 5:30-11pm; 🚇 Back Bay

A pleasantly cracked concrete slab forms the floor of this small bar. Sister Sorel's brick walls and bay window compete against images of roosters in various stages of abstraction in a historic-versus-artistic battle. A few patio tables provide sidewalk seating in front of the charming building. No TV!

TC'S LOUNGE Map pp306-7

☎ 617-247-8109; 1 Haviland St; 🚇 Hynes/ICA

This extraordinarily awesome dive features a collection of faded posters of near-naked celebrities (Farrah Fawcett), old beer ads, pinball and ugly bathrooms. A truly mixed crowd ranges from rising-class Brazilian laborers to Berklee students to hard-core Sox fans. Expect cheap drinks and only two beers on tap, both shitty.

LAUREL GRILL AND BAR Map p305

☎ 617-424-6711; 142 Berkeley St; 🕐 5:30-10pm Mon-Sat; 🚇 Back Bay or Arlington

After the dinner rush, gay boys and a small mixed crowd cluster around the heavy bar at Laurel Grill and Bar. Good-looking lamps from the early 20th century hang amid tall windows and hardwood floors. Pity about that incongruously ugly drop ceiling.

KENMORE SQUARE & FENWAY

Unless you're sipping cognac at Petit Robert Bistro (p153), you'll find that most bars in the vicinity of mecca (otherwise known as Fenway Park) cater to sports fans. While many are forgettable, a few complement and enhance the hysteria.

BOSTON BEER WORKS Map pp308-9

☎ 617-536-2337; 61 Brookline Ave; 🕐 11:30am-1am; 🚇 Kenmore

With 16 microbrews on tap, this somewhat slick, modern room uses blond-wood tones and simple trim stools to create a design effect better than most sports bars. Decked out with scads of televisions that form a ring around the bar, this place is also in a prime location – directly across the street from all the action at Fenway Park.

CASK'N FLAGON Map pp308-9

☎ 617-536-4840; 62 Brookline Ave; 🕐 11:30am-2am; 🚇 Kenmore

Boston's iconic sports bar has long served the Fenway faithful and it occupies a conspicuous site opposite the Green Monster. What this means, particularly for those who are lucky and early enough to score a pre-game sidewalk seat at the Cask'n Flagon, is that you'll have a prime spot from which to watch Lansdowne St reach its frenzied best. It is also a popular destination for Red Sox fans watching away games.

CORNWALL'S Map pp308-9
☎ 617-262-3749; 654 Beacon St; ☻ noon-2am Mon-Sat; ☷ Kenmore

For an extensive list of English and Scottish beers plus a few interesting local brews (Tuckerman's Pale Ale), stop by this family-owned pub where the bartenders (Billy and JR) commonly pour samples should you be curious about an unknown ale. Though close to Fenway Park, the crowd doesn't get too ridiculous during Sox events, and there are board games, darts and pool tables in good repair. The lamb steak is a bargain.

LINWOOD GRILL & BAR Map pp308-9
☎ 617-247-8099; 81 Kilmarnock St; ☻ 11:30am-1am; ☷ Kenmore

You'll be glad to grab a beer or sangria in this converted industrial building, if only because it's one of the few acceptable bars in its vicinity. The place is a hangout for Simmons students, and if you're lucky you'll overhear a heated debate about the Dewey Decimal System from future library scientists. Linwood has some sidewalk seating.

SQUEALING PIG Map pp308-9
☎ 617-566-6651; 134 Smith St; ☻ 11:30-1am; ☷ Longwood Medical Area

This pub is a fries-and-gravy kind (on the menu) of place that attracts dweeby guys in long-sleeved dress shirts and aspiring engineers being trained at nearby Wentworth. The place looks ye olde English, although the wainscoting is fakey. Tunes you can expect to hear are best characterized by 'Desperado,' the Eagle's masterful ballad.

BROOKLINE

Sleepy Brookline is short on drinking spots. You'll find a single pub in the Village (listed in this section) and not much more in Coolidge Corner. Bear in mind that Coolidge Corner is a short 15-minute walk to bustling Allston, however Brookline Village is more remote.

COOLIDGE CORNER CLUBHOUSE
Map pp308-9
☎ 617-566-4948; 307 Harvard St; ☻ noon-1:30am Mon-Sat, 10-1am Sun; ☷ Coolidge Corner

A tiny closet of a sports bar, the 'three Cs' somehow manages to fit several dozen TVs onto its limited wall space, and you can reli-

---

FIVE JOINTS FOR BEER LOVERS

If you're looking for something other than a Sam Adams, Boston has a handful of microbreweries where you can drink the sauce. For those who have concluded that 'local' does not always mean 'good tasting,' there are several bars where the selection is designed to impress.

Bukowski Tavern (p166) Dark, narrow and loud, Boston's favorite bar in a parking garage comes with plenty of street cred and offers an enormous menu of beer (more than 100, organized by province). This menu provides lots of explanatory text to help you make selections. For those that find the task overwhelming, there is a giant wheel behind the bar that can choose for you (though most patrons will scoff at its use).

Boston Beer Works (opposite) This place has two locations: one near Fenway Park and the other near the building that replaced the Boston Garden. The happy consequence is that you'll have plenty of sports fanatics to bump elbows with as you drink seasonal concoctions such as Boston Red and Blueberry Ale. Expect brick walls and exposed tanks and pipes.

Cornwall's (above) This pleasant pub near Kenmore Sq is a family-run spot with a nice balance of English, Scottish and Irish beers plus some fine picks from a few small New England breweries.

Cambridge Brewing Co (Map p311; ☎ 617-494-1994; 1 Kendall Sq; ☻ 11:30am-11pm Mon, 11:30am-midnight Tue-Thu, 11:30-12:45am Fri, noon-12:45am Sat, 5-11pm Sun; ☷ Kendall Sq) For a packed weekend experience, this Kendall Sq brewery keeps MIT grads happy with strong porter and reputable seasonal ales, bitters and black beer. We prefer to stick to the bar and avoid the food.

John Harvard's Brew House (Map p310; ☎ 617-868-3585; 33 Dunster St; ☻ 11:30-12:30am Mon-Thu, 11:30-2am, Fri & Sat, 11:30am-midnight Sun; ☷ Harvard Sq) The beer they brew has a pleasant taste, but you'll be obliged to knock it back in a subterranean bar that is trying so hard to look like ye olde England or colonial Boston (it's hard to make sense of the source of inspiration) that the place ends up mocking itself.

ably watch almost every major college and professional football match. Though the vibe is great for fanatics, the crowd is often uncomfortably large for the small space.

MATT MURPHY'S PUB Map pp308-9
☎ 616-232-0188; 14 Harvard St; ⏲ noon-2am; 🚇 Brookline Village

For a friendly crowd and lots of bartenders from the Emerald Isle, this laid-back pub pours a fine stout and sometimes hosts folk bands. At dinnertime, tables are jammed together and are full more with diners than drinkers. Enjoy hearty Irish fare including fish and chips and a fine rabbit stew.

JAMAICA PLAIN

While the thriving Jamaica Plain (JP) scene is more attributable to its fine restaurants, there are a handful of pubs and bars where you'll hang out with neighborhood locals far from central Boston's tourist traps. In them you'll find a number of lesbians, recent college graduates and creative types, as well as an increasing number of new professionals who have begun infiltrating the area. Be sure to check out the Milky Way (p192) for an additional place to damage your liver.

BRENDAN BEHAN PUB Map pp298-9
☎ 617-552-5386; 378 Centre St; ⏲ noon-1am Mon-Sat; 🚇 Stony Brook

A top-notch Irish pub, candle lit tables, stained glass and old liquor cabinets combine to make a cozy den full of regulars of all ages and sexual orientations. On Tuesday, watch underground movies rented from an independent video store across the street.

DOYLE'S CAFE Map pp298-9
☎ 617-524-2345; 3484 Washington St; ⏲ 9-1am; 🚇 Green St

This Irish bar dates to 1882 and provides an unadulterated glimpse into some vanishing bits of Irish American culture. Distant pressed-tin ceilings hang far above a completely worn-out floor that was long ago covered in linoleum, itself almost entirely worn away. No tourists come here, just locals and off-duty cops drinking from a huge selection of ryes. Also see an enormous (and ghastly) mural of Paul Revere high-fiving a Minuteman.

ST JAMES GATE Map pp298-9
☎ 617-983-2000; 5 McBride St; ⏲ 11:30-1am Tue-Sat, noon-1am Sun, 4pm-1am Mon; 🚇 Forest Hills

A newcomer to JP, this gastropub and its small wooden interior has a prissy, faux-Irish feel. But its enormous fireplaces are still fine things to sit by in the winter. A big outdoor seating area is a popular place to drink during warmer months.

CAMBRIDGE

The watering holes across the river easily beat Boston's in terms of hipness, diversity and quality. Central Sq, convenient to MIT's and Harvard's campuses, provides the greatest density of bars. Elsewhere, Harvard Sq has several cool spots, Kendall Sq is quieter and Inman Sq is off the beaten track.

HARVARD SQUARE

Since Harvard Sq has long been a destination for both out-of-towners and Bostonians to shop and gawk, you'll find plenty of folks to rub elbows with who aren't affiliated with the H-Bomb across the street. Even so, the smart aura lingers, so it might be a good idea to read some literary theory before attempting to make conversation.

ALGIERS COFFEE HOUSE Map p310
☎ 617-492-1557; 40 Brattle St; ⏲ 8am-midnight; 🚇 Harvard

Proceed to the 2nd story of this charming café to find a pleasant wood-paneled room with a mirror-lined octagon cut into the floor, allowing voyeurs to peak into the goings-on below. On offer are Turkish coffee, mint chocolate frappes, beer and port. If not busy, it's a fantastic place to read.

CAFÉ PAMPLONA Map p310
☎ 617-547-2763; 12 Bow St; ⏲ 11-1am; 🚇 Harvard

The lack of background music and simple black-and-white interior at this spare and unassuming coffee shop will either quieten your mind or leave you edgy. The coffee is cheap and the reading material trends esoteric. Waitstaff at Café Pamplona match the décor.

CHARLIE'S Map p310

☎ 617-492-9646; 10 Eliot St; 11-2am; 🚇 Harvard
Charlie's has two floors: downstairs is tamer and upstairs is where the scene thrives. Packed by 9:30pm on a Saturday night, come inside to hear the Cars, Descendants and Pixies played at inordinate volumes from a rock-oriented jukebox. Otherwise drink Pabst and eat patty burgers and lobster rolls while bumping the tattooed elbows of your screaming neighbors.

GRENDEL'S DEN Map p310

☎ 617-491-1160; 89 Winthrop St; 🕙 11-1am; 🚇 Harvard
Though a sign out front falsely claims that this subterranean tavern was established in 1271, Grendel's Den has only been a Harvard mainstay since the '70s. A big draw is the bargain pub food (beef stroganoff, burgers, token vegetarian stuff). When you buy a drink from 5pm to 7pm (on weekdays, 9:30pm to 11pm), all menu items are half price.

LA BURDICK CHOCOLATES Map p310

☎ 617-491-4340; 52-D Brattle St; 🕙 8am-9pm Sun-Thu, 8am-10pm Fri & Sat; 🚇 Harvard
This boutique chocolate store doubles as a café full of patrons drinking cocoa and wine. Though it offers some of the best chocolate you're likely to drink for hundreds of miles, snotty Harvard scholars from Berlin sniff the inferior brew with unmitigated horror.

NOIR Map p310

☎ 617-661-8010; 1 Bennet St; 🕙 4pm-2am; 🚇 Harvard
Nearly elegant with artful red lights and summer terrace seating, Boston's ubiquitous flatscreen emerges to sabotage the atmosphere, analogous to the reasonably well-dressed ladies being attended to by men failing to hold up their end of the style bargain. It's located in the Charles Hotel.

OM Map p310

☎ 617-576-2800; 57 John F Kennedy St; 🕙 5pm-1am Sun-Wed, 5pm-2am Thu-Sat; 🚇 Harvard
A well-dressed crowd heads to Om's fashionable lounge where big windows fold away for views over a small city square. Chic

décor includes a rough brick wall behind the bar, illuminated with eerie green light. Elsewhere, a sheet of water slides over another textured wall, this time illuminated purple. Come for frilly drinks and avoid the food.

SHAY'S PUB & WINE BAR Map p310

☎ 617-864-9161; 58 John F Kennedy St; 🕙 noon-1am; 🚇 Harvard
A pleasant basement level bar, Shay's is a long-standing favorite among Harvard graduate students. It's a small wooden pub where you'll sit on a stool and pretend to look thoughtful. Out front is a small brick patio full of smokers jockeying for one of the few tables. Shay's stocks a decent list of English beers and a limited selection of wine.

KENDALL SQUARE

The square itself is pretty dead, though you'll be able to find some cool spots by penetrating the MIT campus itself. Note that two of these bars, the R&D and Muddy Charles, have abnormal hours. A third spot, the fantastic B-Side, is hidden a few blocks away.

B-SIDE LOUNGE Map p311

☎ 617-354-0766; 92 Hampshire St; 🕙 11:30-2am Mon-Sat, 11-2am Sun; 🚇 Kendall/MIT
Sliding into a booth at the B-Side feels like sitting in the back of a 1962 Cadillac – a really nice one that someone took great care of. The place makes good mint juleps, plays rockabilly and is casually stylish.

MUDDY CHARLES Map p311

☎ 617-253-2086; 142 Memorial Dr (MIT's Bldg 50); 🕙 4pm-midnight Mon-Thu, noon-midnight Fri; 🚇 Kendall/MIT
Opposite the MIT sailing pavilion and run by an MIT student association, come for a sweet riverside locale and signed photographs of astronauts on the wall. Feel like pizza? Order at the bar and some guy from a local joint will deliver it. He's here so often he has a private parking spot.

R&D Map p311

☎ 617-253-0192; 32 Vassar St; 🕙 4-10pm Thu & Fri; 🚇 Kendall/MIT
Take an odyssey through Frank Gehry's Stata Center (MIT's building 32 – the giant angular thing that looks like a pile of windsails) to enjoy style cred in this quiet bar

and restaurant, which has a cool skylight. Clue: it's on the 4th floor. Other clue: some elevators only go down.

INMAN SQUARE

Central Sq's little brother, Inman serves as a haunt for SCUL (a squadron of misfits riding absurd bicycles) as well as graduate students looking to escape the crowds in the Harvard vortex.

1369 COFFEE HOUSE Map p311

☎ 617-576-1369; 1369 Cambridge St; ☿ 7am-10pm Mon-Thu, 7am-11pm Fri, 8am-11pm Sat, 8am-10pm Sun; 🚇 Central

If you're looking for a coffee shop where people linger for hours, you might be unnerved by the 1369, where it seems some folks stay for years. Countless term papers and novels have been written at the small tables, though some come for board games. Also a sister café at 757 Massachusetts Ave.

ABBEY LOUNGE Map p311

☎ 617-441-9631; Beacon St; ☿ 11-2am; 🚇 Central

Drink your long neck and don't sniff the base of the bottle – it might smell like something incredibly foul that is better not described in print. Inman's favorite dive also serves as a small rock venue, and is a holdout against the recent gentrification of the square.

DRUID Map p311

☎ 617-497-0965; 1357 Cambridge St; ☿ 11:30-2am; 🚇 Central

Inman's main bar is a small Irish place serving pub food that costs a few dollars more than it should. It's a comfortable spot, though locals grumble about the loss of its cool edge when the place changed ownership a few years back. Bartenders suffer the indignity of lame, logo-bearing polo shirts.

CENTRAL SQUARE

While impossible to escape student crowds when drinking in Cambridge, historically seedy Central Sq has avoided complete gentrification. The resulting concentration of nightlife is among Boston's best. Here there are divey holdouts, neighborhood pubs and flashy haunts for Biotech workers getting bored in Kendall Sq.

CELLAR Map pp298-9

☎ 617-876-2580; 991 Massachusetts Ave; ☿ 4:30pm-1:30am; 🚇 Central Sq

It doesn't look like much from the outside, but descend the stairs to find a rockabilly bartender trying to avoid a conversation about the merits of 7-card stud and a room where the acoustics are decent enough that you won't have to shout. The space really is a cellar – a wall of crumbling brick and enormous stone blocks provides an interesting cross section of old foundation techniques.

ENORMOUS ROOM Map p311

☎ 617-491-5550; 569 Massachusetts Ave; ☿ from 5:30pm; 🚇 Central

Enter through the door marked with an elephant to find a harem-like room with people draped on cushions. The New York–inspired lounge was almost obnoxiously cool when it opened, though modish waitstaff seems oblivious to the fact that it has now jumped the shark (and thus nicely mellowed the crowd). Good olives.

GREEN STREET Map p311

☎ 617-876-1655; 280 Green St; ☿ 4pm-1am Sun-Wed, Thu-Sat 4pm-2am; 🚇 Central

At first glance, the place looks like a classic Irish dive on a hidden side street. Hipsters like that they can drink inside without needing to be ironic. A phenomenal kitchen turns out jerked chicken and spicy Caribbean-inspired fare.

MIRACLE OF SCIENCE BAR & GRILL
Map p311

☎ 617-868-2866; 321 Massachusetts Ave; ☿ 11-1am; 🚇 Central

With good beer on tap, this triangular shaped bar caters to MIT brainiacs with its periodic table-inspired blackboard menu (eat a burger). Large windows open garage-style on summer nights and there's some weird sciencey crap near the bar.

PEOPLE'S REPUBLIK Map p311

☎ 617-492-8632; 876 Massachusetts Ave; ☿ noon-1am Sun-Wed, noon-2am Thu-Sat; 🚇 Central

Outside, older drunk expats discuss with bravado the merits of deer hunting (neither had done it) while sitting under the Soviet-inspired signage of this watering-hole for townies, bike messengers and

Miracle of Science Bar and Grill (opposite)

students. Inside, find darkness, a few darts boards in good repair and seats arranged around a U-shaped bar allowing for awkward stares or new friendships depending on your approach.

PLOUGH & STARS Map p311
☎ 617-576-0032; www.ploughandstars.com; 912 Massachusetts Ave; ⊗ 11:30-2am Mon-Fri, noon-2am Sat & Sun; ⊛ Central

Stringed bands play Irish tunes in this charming neighborhood pub. While many Boston bars fraudulently and irritatingly exaggerate their 'Irishness,' the Plough & Stars is the real deal. It serves up bangers, eggs and gastro-pub fare in a cozy wooden room with stout on tap and bottles of Fin du Monde and Narragansett (Rhode Island's best worst beer). Weekend soccer matches.

RIVER GODS Map p311
☎ 617-576-1881; 125 River St; ⊗ 3pm-1am; ⊛ Central

The décor of this small cramped room (max 45 people) leans toward kitsch with a cluttered assortment of sparkly leather stools and red velvet chairs that look too much like Gothic thrones. Art-house movies and documentary footage project silently on the wall while DJs spin from a second-story alcove. Monday features a themed showdown, where you might see DJ Curtis attempt to one-up Captain Tipsy with country tunes.

OUTLYING AREAS

Those willing to ride the T to the end (or near the end) of the line will be rewarded if they head to Somerville and Allston. In Somerville, Davis Sq is a bustling and pretty center of urban nightlight with a village feel.

Union Sq has less to offer, but is gritty and more low-key. Those making their way to Allston will find some of Boston's liveliest bars, which seem to attract either hipsters or loud undergrads.

SOMERVILLE

Since Somerville is populated by lots of 20-somethings and bohemians, it's no surprise that places to drink the hooch have arisen to serve them.

Davis Square

Just a few stops past Harvard Sq, compact Davis offers a neighborhood vibe with ample street life. Sometimes it's overrun by Tufts students, whose campus is a short walk away.

DIESEL CAFE Map pp298-9
☎ 671-629-8717; 257 Elm St; pool per hr $8 after 7pm; ⊗ 7am-midnight Mon-Fri, 8am-midnight Sat & Sun; ⊛ Davis

One of Boston's best late-night coffee-houses attracts a regular patronage of lesbians. It has a large industrial room decorated with oversized street signs and boldly painted walls of blue, green and orange. In the back, desperate Tufts students compete for space at worktables with old mechanical pencil sharpeners. Meanwhile sharp-shooting ladies run the pool tables.

DIVA LOUNGE Map pp298-9
☎ 617-629-4963; 248 Elm St; ⊗ 5pm-1am Sun-Thu, 5pm-2am Fri & Sat; ⊛ Davis

For cocktails made from ginger-infused rum or allspice vodka, check out this trendy bar with a décor crossing the ship from *Space Odyssey* and a Lego set. The walls and ceiling are entirely covered with large panels of white plastic bubbles against which pastel lights reflect. Decent DJs spin on weekends.

BURREN Map pp298-9
☎ 617-776-6896; 247 Elm St; ⊗ noon-1am; ⊛ Davis

This cavernous and good-looking Irish pub seems to stretch back forever. Along the way, find plenty of booths, wainscoting and wooden floorboards well seasoned with spilt beer. In the rear room, there's a stage where midweek open-mic sessions attract both the skilled and a lame J-Crew wearing

BA IRISH PUBS

Boston's stuffed full of Irish bars, some extraordinary and some extraordinarily bad. The following pubs transcend the rest and pour their stouts with style.

Brendan Behan Pub (p170) Enjoy the dark wooden womb of this friendly neighborhood favorite.

Burren (p173) Join a rowdy crowd in this cavernous bar with multiple rooms.

Doyle's Café (p170) Sit with the townies in this tall-ceilinged relic, little changed since 1882.

Plough & Stars (p173) Small and cozy, listen to traditional bands in a pub reminiscent of grandma's dining room.

Tir Na Nóg (below) Thank the god of your choosing if you score an evening table in this tiny charmer.

mock-mohawks, trying to get punk sounds from acoustic guitars and making feeble attempts at jokes.

Union Square

Since distant Central Sq is the closest T stop (a 25-minute walk), getting to Union can be a challenge. If you make it here, you'll discover a racially mixed neighborhood on the brink of gentrification with a subdued bar scene.

INDEPENDENT Map p311

☎ 617-440-6022; 75 Union Sq; ⏰ 5pm-1am Mon-Fri, 2pm-1am Sat & Sun; 🚇 Central

A favorite haunt of local playwrights such as Tim Blevins (author of *Love's First Thing*), the tall-ceilinged space occupies a former bank and the bar serves the members of area kickball teams. An attached bistro space is dominated by yuppies and dark-brown furniture that currently has that overly-stained-and-new feel.

TIR NA NÓG Map pp298-9

☎ 617-628-4300; www.thenog.com; 366a Somerville Ave; ⏰ to 1am; 🚇 Central

This tiny Irish bar has cheerful brick walls with glass cabinets displaying old booze, broken-spined encyclopedias and a couple of backgammon sets. There's a minuscule stage wedged in the corner that sometimes hosts folk bands.

ALLSTON

If you're a boy with really tight black pants and deliberated, mussed hair or a girl who looks like a boy of said description, then you'll fit very well into the Allston scene. If you aren't so cool and happen to look like a frat boy (or enjoy dating fellows of said description), you're also in luck.

MODEL Map pp298-9

☎ 617-254-9365; 7 Beacon St N; ⏰ noon-2am Mon-Sat, 5pm-2am Sun; 🚇 Harvard Ave

This two-room joint and its loud jukebox attract droves of precisely dressed hipsters and rockers who enjoy drinking cheap beer and crappy liquor while complaining about how either (1) the place is too much of a cool-kid haunt or (2) the place used to be cool. Either way, it's a scene near closing time and the pool table is too close to the wall.

REEL BAR Map pp298-9

☎ 617-783-3222; 477 Cambridge St; ⏰ 7pm-1am Wed-Sun; 🚇 Harvard Ave

Among the trendy spots in Allston, this bar ranks among the cleanest and most laid-back. Nuzzle up to the bar, nurse a reasonably priced beer from a good selection and ask someone to pass you the joystick for a remote-controlled Galaga arcade experience. Odd movies often play on a screen.

SILHOUETTE Map pp298-9

☎ 617-254-9306; 200 Brighton Ave; ⏰ noon-1am; 🚇 Harvard Ave

Yes, it's an overlit dive full of sticky tables, $6.75 pitchers of Pabst, overturned baskets of popcorn and several Keno monitors, but it still feels good on rowdy weekends. Inside find bike messengers and philosophical college dropouts.

WHITE HORSE TAVERN Map pp298-9

☎ 617-254-6633; 116 Brighton Ave; ⏰ 11:30-2am; 🚇 Harvard Ave

For some, this is a fun bar with 'great' music like Dave Matthews. For others, it's a meat market with a no-tank-top dress code. Either way, it has a stupid rope outside to imply nonexistent exclusivity. The best time to visit is when it's really crowded, as the masses provide a vibe of excitement in an otherwise humdrum mega bar.

Ententainment

Entertainment

Despite the grave of Cotton Mather, Boston has long been a hotbed in terms of its entertainment offerings. The venerable symphony is consistently first-rate and the city's theater district enjoys international accolades, with many troupes performing in staggering gilded palaces from the turn of the 20th century. Live rock is particularly plentiful, with dozens of stages in Cambridge, Allston and Somerville. Jazz venues are more limited in number, but those that exist are reliably stellar. Nightclubs abound, and though they take some flak for not being as cool as those in New York, they still get packed on weekends.

For listings and notices of special events, check out the *Weekly Dig* and *Phoenix*, which thoroughly cover everything from comedy to ballet.

Tickets & Reservations

Depending on the event, buying a ticket can sometimes be a hassle. At most rock, indie and jazz clubs, you can buy tickets at the door at the time of a performance. For bigger or popular shows in danger of selling out, many venues allow advance purchase through Ticketmaster (www.ticketmaster.com) or sometimes by calling the club directly.

Theatrical events, particularly weekend performances, sell out early. Most theaters have a box office, which is usually open during the day from 10am to 5pm. The Boston Ballet and many classical music and theater companies use Telecharge (www.telecharge.com) to handle their online sales.

If you buy from a box office, you'll avoid service charges incurred through Ticketmaster and other such operations.

Festivals

Following are some of the major entertainment festivals and events that occur in the Hub. Also check out the web pages of Mass Art, Harvard and other colleges, as they regularly book special events open to the public.

Independent Film Festival of Boston (www.iffboston.org; late April or early May) Enjoy scores of independent features, documentaries and shorts with special appearances by visiting filmmakers such as Robert Vaughn and John Waters. See the goods at the Brattle, Coolidge Corner and Somerville Theatres.

NEMO Music Festival (www.nemoboston.com; September) This annual three-day-long frenzy takes over nearly every venue in Boston, and stages over 300 bands.

Boston Pride Festival (www.bostonpride.org; June) The week-long celebration of gay culture attracts over 400,000 to its capstone – a famously flamboyant parade followed by a day of block parties.

First Thursdays On the first Thursday of every month, the cafés, restaurants and shops of Jamaica Plain become impromptu galleries and display the work of local artists. The main drag for this event is Centre St.

The New England Film and Video Festival (www.befva.org; early October) A properly independent festival, the NEFVF often works with Coolidge Corner Theatre. Watch fare like *Checkout* about 'a highly trained ninja assassin settling for a job as a supermarket stockboy amid a very tight job market.'

Boston Folk Festival (www.bostonfolkfestival.org; September) For banjoes, fiddles and a few socialist labor songs, this outdoor festival attracts scads of aficionados and lawn chairs. Listen to Richie Haven and Jud Caswell.

Boston Underground Film Festival (www.bostonundergroundfilmfestival.com; March) This festival purports to seek the insane, the bizarre and the controversial, and sometimes even succeeds in the difficult task of finding it.

Boston Film Festival (www.bostonfilmfestival.org; September) It does a lot with AMC Loews Boston Common Theatre. It's essentially a festival for good major releases.

SUBVERSIVE CHOPPER URBAN LEGION

Anyone who's lived in Cambridge or Somerville for long has likely seen a pack of oddly dressed bohemians whiz by on oddly constructed bikes. Actually, whiz isn't the right word, as many of these rides have been altered so radically that they are tremendous pains to move whatsoever, even at slow speeds. The 'ships' and the 'pilots' attached to them comprise SCUL (Subversive Chopper Urban Legion), a collection of improbables who assemble each Friday to ride lengthy late-night missions across vast swathes of the Boston area.

The chopper gang began in 1995 under the leadership of Skunk, the fleet's admiral. Over the years, hundreds of science geeks, set designers, doctors, grad students, burnouts and business types have formed a bizarre group linked by a singular interest in riding impossible bikes. Most (but not all) also enjoy wearing freakish costumes accented with lots of tubes and fake fur. Anyone that joins the ride is encouraged to take a SCUL name (WalTor, DangerMouse, Moose, Moneyshot) and it is generally bad form to ask another pilot about whatever tag they happen to file their taxes under.

The SCUL riders are a welcoming bunch, so if you have some wheels (conventional bikes OK), five bucks to chip in for fleet maintenance, and are able to abide by SCUL's stated philosophy ('to defend the bicycle and pedestrian population in a leisurely manner') contact the group through www.scul.org and they'll tip you off about the time and location of the next flight.

LIVE MUSIC

While rock and indie are king in Boston, jazz spots offer strong competition even if they are fewer in number. Nearly all venues are located away from the peninsula in Cambridge, Somerville, Jamaica Plain or Allston.

ROCK, HIP-HOP & INDIE

Boston has a ton of venues that dispense loud music, in part because of all those students and in part because it's the biggest city for hundreds of miles. To figure out who's playing where, check out the websites of the following clubs or take a look at the listings in the *Phoenix* or *Weekly Dig*, Boston's two alternative newspapers. Most shows are for those aged 21 and over. Be sure to check out the Lizard Lounge (p180), which sometimes books rock.

GREAT SCOTT Map pp298-9
☎ 617-566-9014; www.greatscottboston.com; 1222 Commonwealth Ave; cover $5-12; Ⓣ Harvard Ave
The current 'it' place for rock and indie, Great Scott recently transformed itself from a crappy bar to music palace, thanks to the efforts of booker Ben Sistoe, a cool guy dedicated to Boston music. The place rarely gets uncomfortably crowded, and the stage is well raised.

MIDWAY CAFÉ Map pp298-9
☎ 617-524-9038; www.midwaycafe.com; 3496 Washington St; cover $5; Ⓣ Green St

In addition to hosting a kick-ass dyke night (p191), this queer-friendly rock and punk bar books some of Boston's finest independent music, ranging from rockabilly to dub. Inside, find Pabst beer signs of antique vintage, some long horn skulls, pinball and a genuinely friendly atmosphere.

TT & THE BEARS Map p311
☎ 617-492-2327; www.ttthebears.com; 10 Brookline St; cover $7-10; Ⓣ Central
A dirty dive with two bars in two rooms, one of which provides partial refuge for those who discovered that, though the opening act might have an interesting name, not all local bands are actually worth listening to. So grab a beer and stuff some earplugs while waiting for Northern State, Wayne Hancock or the Queers.

TOAD Map pp298-9
☎ 617-497-4950; www.toadcambridge.com; 1912 Massachusetts Ave; Ⓣ Porter
This laidback place never charges a cover and it's OK to bring in food from next door. It looks like a woody Irish pub. The remaining members of Morphine play here regularly. Otherwise, you might see the Danny Adler Band (of Roogalator fame).

ORPHEUM THEATER Map pp302-3
☎ 617-679-0810; www.orpheumtheatertickets.com; 1 Hamilton Pl; Ⓣ Park St
A lovely worn out old theater dating to the mid-1850s, the Orpheum hosts the likes of the Decemberists, Brian Wilson, the Scissor Sisters and Alice Cooper. Since the hall has

TOP 5 LIVE MUSIC VENUES

Among Boston's plethora of music joints, the following are at the top of the heap.

- **Great Scott** (p177) King of the indie and rock scene, Great Scott not only books good shows but it also looks nice on the inside.
- **Boston Symphony Orchestra** (p186) With talented musicians and a breathtaking hall, the Symphony and Pops transcend beauty.
- **Wally's** (opposite) For many, this divey jazz club is the city's best attribute.
- **Club Passim** (p180) A legendary club, Passim's schedule is a who's-who list of folk musicians.
- **Paradise Lounge** (below) Expect great rock in a small club.

great acoustics, it comes as no surprise that the New England Conservatory began here and the Boston Symphony Orchestra first played here in 1881. One theory has it that the term 'Brahmin' originated here, too: many proper Bostonians stormed out during a Brahms premiere and those who stayed to hear the wild new symphony were dubbed 'Brahmins.'

MUSEUM OF FINE ARTS Map pp308-9

☎ 617-369-3306; www.mfa.org; 365 Huntington Ave; tickets $20-30; ☒ Museum of Fine Arts
For a tame, seated show, try the MFA where you'll often see iconic rockers perform solo gigs for slightly inflated prices. Recent artists include Isabelle from Belle and Sebastian, Cat Power, and psychedelic folkster Vashti Bunyan.

PA'S LOUNGE Map p310

☎ 617-776-1557; www.paslounge.com; 345 Somerville Ave; cover $5-15; ☒ Porter
Oh PA's Lounge! We love you and you book cool shows, but couldn't you maybe buy some Christmas lights or something and at least pretend to decorate? Come see Final Fantasy, Christina Carter and lots of indie acts. There's no stage so shorter patrons might need to push to the front.

PARADISE LOUNGE Map pp308-9

☎ 617-562-8800; www.thedise.com; 967-969 Commonwealth Ave; tickets $10-30; ☒ Pleasant St
A small club known for eclectic musical tastes and for booking big acts, it hosts live rock bands nightly such as Lambchop,

Apollo Sunshine, and Badly Drawn Boy. Most shows are for those aged 18 and up.

MIDDLE EAST Map p311

☎ 617-354-8238; www.mideastclub.com; 472 Massachusetts Ave, cover $10-15; ☒ Central
While the Middle East sometimes gets itself together to book top rock acts (Frank Black, Zui Zui, the Wrens), the two stages (meaning there are two shows at once) of this club spend most of their time under the feet of lousy acts in a protracted battle of the bands event called Emmergenza. The club is emphatically not recommended at such times, which annoyingly last for months in a row.

O'BRIENS Map pp298-9

☎ 617-782-6245; www.obrienspubboston.com; 3 Harvard Ave; cover $6-8 ☒ Harvard Ave
For serious punk and loud amps, head for this shithole where the stage is shoved oddly into a corner, making for weird sight lines. It looks like a wood-paneled basement from the '70s with a sound system.

HARPERS FERRY Map pp298-9

☎ 617-254-9743; www.harpersferryboston.com; ticket $10-15; 158 Brighton Ave; ☒ Harvard Ave
On some nights, this cavernous room gets decent acts like Farside, Lisa Light and Nashville Pussy. On others, you'll hear bands covering U2. Either way, there's a pool table and large bar to sit at if you want to get away from the stage. Sometimes the crowd isn't big enough to properly fill the huge space and it feels weirdly dead.

ABBEY LOUNGE Map p311

☎ 617-441-9631; www.abbeylounge.com; Beacon St; cover $5-10; ☒ Central
Inman Sq's nastiest lovable dive doubles as a venue where a lot of local bands get their first gigs. Expect zero frills, cheap beer and some regulars who either should be in recovery or are cheating in their recovery efforts.

JOHNNY D'S Map pp298-9

☎ 617-776-2004; www.johnnyds.com; 17 Holland St; cover $5-15; ☒ Davis
While you may or may not be impressed by easy-listening adult contemporary bands, whoever books at Johnny D's mixes up the sound with klezmer fiddlers, funk covers

and notable blue grass acts like King Wilkie. Don't feel like paying the cover? Head to the pink Formica bar where the farsighted can still see the stage.

AVALON Map pp308-9
☎ 617-262-2424; www.avalonboston.com; 15 Lansdowne St; tickets $20-25; ⚇ Kenmore
Doubling as Boston's biggest dance club, the Avalon also books serious national and international bands such as Sonic Youth, Asia and Clap Your Hands Say Yeah. It's a standing-room, general-admission kind of place with some elevated spots. Shows usually start early (between 7pm and 8pm) so that the venue can be cleared for the clubbing that will happen later in the night.

AXIS Map pp308-9
☎ 617-0262-2437; 13 Lansdowne St; tickets $10-15; ⚇ Kenmore
Much like the Avalon, Axis transforms itself into a dance club around 10pm, clearing the way for some early live shows. Axis is a mid-sized venue and tends to book a loud, aggressive sound with bands like Clap Your Hands Say Yeah

BANK OF AMERICA PAVILION
Map pp302-3
☎ 617-728-1600; www.livenation.com; 290 Northern Ave
This white sail-like summertime tent with sweeping harbor views hosts nationally known pop, rock (Megadeth) and jazz performers . Shuttle buses run from South Station before and after shows.

JAZZ & BLUES
While the blues scene is kind of weak in Boston, you can sometimes find the goods either in some of the following venues or at Harpers Ferry (opposite) which occasionally books major talent like Bo Diddley. Jazz aficionados will have way more luck. The New England Conservatory (p186) sometimes stages jazz and blues acts, as does the Zeitgeist Gallery (p183).

WALLY'S Map pp306-7
☎ 617-424-1408; www.wallyscafecom; 427 Massachusetts Ave; ⚇ Massachusetts Ave
Old-school, gritty and small, Wally's is the kind of place where someone on stage

will recognize a high-caliber out-of-town musician in the crowd and convince them to play. It's been an institution since the '60s and is one of the most successfully racially mixed bars you'll find in Boston. A lot of Berklee students stop in and there are half-priced drinks before the bands start playing.

CANTAB Map p311
☎ 617-354-2685; www.cantab-lounge.com; 738 Massachusetts Ave; ⚇ Central
While some nights feature bluegrass or low-budget open mics, the perennial draw is Little Joe Cook & the Thrillers, a soul-inspired band with a Top 40 hit from 1957 (called 'Peanuts') to their legendary credit. So come eat a greasy patty burger, grab a Miller and watch Little Joe rock the house and leer at the younger ladies in attendance (which they seem to enjoy).

SCULLERS JAZZ CLUB Map pp298-9
☎ 617-642-4111; www.scullersjazz.com; 400 Soldiers Field Rd; tickets $15-35; ⚇ Central
This club books huge names (Dave Brubeck, Keely Smith, Herb Reed) in a relatively intimate room serving stiff drinks. Many prefer to buy a package where you get a three-course dinner plus seats practically in the laps of the performers. Though it enjoys impressive views over the Charles, the room itself lacks the grit you might hanker for in a jazz club and definitely feels like it sits inside a Doubletree Hotel (which it does).

REGATTABAR Map p310
☎ 617-661-5000; www.regattabarjazz.com; 1 Bennett St; tickets $15-35; ⚇ Harvard
Why does Boston have such clean jazz clubs? Like Scullers, Regattabar looks just like a conference room in a hotel – in this case the Charles Hotel. They get big enough names (Irma Thomas, Slaid Cleaves) to transcend the mediocre space. As it only has 225 seats, you'll at least have a good view and the sound system is quality.

RYLES JAZZ CLUB Map p311
☎ 617-876-9330; www.rylesjazz.com; 212 Hampshire St; cover $10-15; ⚇ Central
Upstairs you'll find a largish dance hall where there are often early evening instructors on hand to get you primed to swing or merengue. On the 1st level you'll find a

Performers at the Berklee Performance Center (below)

dining room. Both are done up with a natty jazz-inspired décor, and each has its own stage on which both local talent and national names play (Arturo Sandoval, Maynard Ferguson). A popular Sunday brunch makes a great time to visit, though you might need a reservation.

LIZARD LOUNGE Map pp298-9

☎ 617-547-0759; www.lizardloungeclub.com; 1667 Massachusetts Ave; 🚇 Harvard
Surprisingly big acts get booked in a room that can't fit more than a hundred. It doubles as both a jazz and rock venue, and the lounge's interior is done up with red lights and upholstery along with good-looking people. The bar stocks an excellent list of New England beers.

BERKLEE PERFORMANCE CENTER

☎ 617-747-2261; www.berkleebpc.com; 136 Massachusetts Ave; tickets $5-25; 🚇 Hynes/ICA
For high energy jazz recitals, smoky-throated vocalists and oddball sets by keyboard playing guys that look like they dabble at being dungeon masters, the performance hall at this notable music college marks an eclectic spot on Boston's musical landscape. Depending on the night, you'll hear student recitals (ranging from awful to excellent), the Ultra Sonic Rock Orchestra, invited musicians or instructors from the college.

FOLK & WORLD

In addition to perusing our drinking chapter to find Irish pubs with traditional music. In particular, see Matt Murphy's Pub (p170), Plough & Stars (p173), Tir La Nóg (p174) and the Burren (p173).

CLUB PASSIM Map p310

☎ 617-492-7679; www.clubpassim.org; 47 Palmer St; tickets $10-15; 🚇 Harvard
This club is a legendary Boston institution. Though Boston folk music seems to be endangered outside of Irish Bars, Club Passim does such a great job booking top-notch acts that it practically fills in the vacuum by itself. The colorful and intimate room is hidden off a side street in Harvard Sq, and those attending shows are welcome to order filling dinners from Veggie Planet (p157), an incredibly good restaurant that shares the space.

CLUBBING

Boston has two main centers for big dancing action. One is the nucleated bunch of thematically over-the-top mega clubs that arise with hype and glory around the Theater District (and often fade into oblivion when they pass from fashion a few years later). The other major center is Lansdowne St near Fenway Park, where the clubs are a bit out-of-date but consistently packed. Both the Theater District and Lansdowne St tend to be urban and upscale, though many students also infiltrate. Major student hangouts can be found in Cambridge and Allston.

Many of Boston's trendiest bars book experimental DJs who sometimes put a few patrons in the mood to move instead of fashionably lounging. Mostly, though, they'll observe the action with blasé expressions and thumping hearts. Among the best of these are the **Reel Bar** (p174), the **Enormous Room (p172)**, the **Independent** (p174) and **River Gods (p173)**. The **Midway Cafe (p177)** transcends the rest and gets a lively dancing crowd on the nights it hosts DJs. Additionally, **Milky Way (p192)** has a salsa night on Sunday.

THEATER DISTRICT, CHINATOWN & SOUTH END

Boylston St is the main clubbing drag in this area. Unless on an off night or otherwise specified, expect to pay a cover of $10 to $15. Most of these clubs attract a well-dressed set in fancy duds, and a no athletic-wear, hats, tank-tops or sneakers policy is enforced. The idea is to give the illusion of class, but since many venues occasionally host tacky events (pantie modeling) you can at least roll your eyes with appropriate dignity if you are turned away at the door.

LIQUOR STORE Map p305

☎ 617-357-6800; 25 Boylston Pl; cover $5; ☽ 9pm-2am Fri & Sat; 🚇 Boylston
Even too cool for school hipsters secretly like this over-the-top club. To start, it's got a mechanical bull. And you can ride it, though cheeseball management generally prefers that you be a girl wearing a bikini top when you get in line. Better: they serve 40s in brown paper bags. Also on offer are packed dance floors and elevated stages with poles.

MOJITOS Map pp302-3

☎ 617-988-8123; www.mojitoslounge.com; 48 Winter St; ☽ 9pm-2am Thu-Sun; 🚇 Downtown Crossing
Come inside this large, Latin-inspired club to experience two spaces. On one level, find a lounge where house bands play salsa and timba tunes (free salsa lessons

at 9:15pm most nights). In the basement, a club caters to the scantily clad with hip-hop, Brazilian, reggaeton and sounds related to the Tropic of Capricorn.

BIG EASY Map p305

☎ 617-351-7000; www.bigeasyboston.com; 1 Boylston Pl; ☽ 9pm-2am Fri & Sat; 🚇 Boylston
This club splices together iconic emblems from the great southern city in a superficial pastiche that has caused it to be ridiculously successful. It's hard to tell whether the place is mocking New Orleans, but come inside anyway to experience knock-off wrought-iron balconies that overlook the dancefloor, huge open spaces and oversized cocktails (hurricanes, of course). While most people will be perspiring to pop DJs, sometimes you'll be forced to deal with a cover band. Lots of bachelorettes.

ALLEY CAT LOUNGE Map p305

☎ 617-351-7000; 1 Boylston Pl; ☽ 8pm-2am Tue-Sat; 🚇 Boylston
Part owned by Boston Celtic Paul Pierce, the Alley Cat might be faux-sophisticated in the ways you'd expect a populist nightclub to be, but they've got a pretty sweet karaoke setup complete with music videos and a captive audience who won't run away from you since the line outside is probably too long to bother renavigating.

CLUB CAFE Map p305

☎ 617-536-0966; www.clubcafe.com; 209 Columbus Ave; 🚇 Arlington
For a glossy gay dance club, stop in this Boston mainstay where you can admire the fellas as you all listen to the Madonna dance remix of the moment. They must import their bartenders from a place that animates Greek statuary.

WEST STREET GRILL Map pp302-3

☎ 617-423-0300; 15 West St; 🚇 Downtown Crossing
On weekends, the after-work crowd at this smallish bar gives way to dancing set to pop music and hip-hop. The place can get pretty packed and serves as a pick-up place for college graduates disenfranchised with the large clubs in the area. It's a good spot to make out with someone you never want to see again.

KENMORE SQ & FENWAY

Boston's biggest clubs can be found in Kenmore Sq, which attracts droves of students plus a lot of 'Euro' Americans as well as actual Europeans. If you're after guys wearing cologne and trim black pants, head to Lansdowne St, where you'll find a maze-like complex containing several clubs operated by the same management (Avalon, Modern, Axis, Embassy). On many nights, when there are no celebrity DJs, you can move freely from one club to the next to best suit your fancy (the cover in all is usually $15).

AVALON Map pp308-9

☎ 617-262-2424; www.avalonboston.com; 15 Lansdowne St; Ⓡ Kenmore
Here it is: Boston's largest and most popular mega club. Though it often books bands, weekend nights (Thursday to Saturday) are reserved for DJs and dancing. Fridays see the best international DJs (Tiesto, Paul van Dyk) and thousands of people working themselves into a frenzy. It plays a lot of techno and there's a popular gay night on Sunday.

MODERN Map pp308-9

☎ 617-351-2581; 36 Lansdowne St; Ⓥ 10pm-2am Tue & Thu-Sat; Ⓡ Kenmore
With clean lines and a sleek chrome and glass bar, this narrow lounge is the most elegant space in the Lansdowne complex. Though there's little in the way of a dance-floor, high heel depressions in a long leather couch running along a wall reveal how some girls improvise when the hip-hop gets loud. Dress to impress or be denied entry.

EMBASSY Map pp308-9

☎ 617-536-2100; 36 Lansdowne St; Ⓥ 10pm-2am Tue & Thu-Sat; Ⓡ Kenmore
With a small dancefloor and plenty of breakaway space, this two level club attracts lots of internationals into its dark womb. A voyeuristic window in the hallway allows a tinted (but relatively clear) view of a pair of urinals in the men's bathroom.

AXIS Map pp308-9

☎ 617-262-2437; 13 Lansdowne St; Ⓥ 10pm-2am; Ⓡ Kenmore
The black, white, grey and red color palette and painting scheme feels very dated

(think 1994), but they've got stripper poles and sometimes hire professional dancers (clothed ones) to use them. Thanks to the smoking ban, the lack of cigarette odor reveals that the place smells like feet, even when empty. There's a large floor and complicated light arrangements to make you feel glamorous.

ALLSTON & BRIGHTON

Most Allston clubs cater to students at nearby Boston University (BU) and Boston College. If you're looking for the jeans-and-baseball-cap crowd, you've found it – though some places do have a no-athletic-wear policy at night. Cover runs between $5 and $15.

SOHO Map pp298-9

☎ 617-562-6000; www.sohoboston.com; 386 Market St; Ⓡ Warren St
The warm wood tones of this two-level club evoke a kind of Scandinavian modern design. Since this is Boston, there are also TVs everywhere, including the bathrooms. The result is a confusing mix – yeah, there are a hundred young professionals dancing, but the West Coast feed of that Bruins game might also demand your attention. Despite all those TVs, watch out for the enforced dress code.

KELLS Map pp298-9

☎ 617-782-9082; 161 Brighton Ave; Ⓥ 4pm-2am Mon-Fri, 10-2am Sat & Sun; Ⓡ Boston College
If you'd like to gaze at the midriffs of hundreds of gussied-up BU students (or perhaps expose your own), head to the Kells where you can find a lot of dance partners with itchy crotches. It's the kind of place where Bacardi sponsors special events, management comes up with lots of gimmicks to attract the ladies and there's beer pong on Monday.

HARPERS FERRY Map pp298-9

☎ 617-254-9743; www.harpersferryboston.com; 158 Brighton Ave; Ⓡ Harvard Ave
Though normally a joint to hear live music, Thursday at Harpers Ferry is given to an event called Paper, essentially a dance night where the club soundtrack is mixed more to the taste of indie scenesters.

CAMBRIDGE & SOMERVILLE

For some of Boston's coolest clubs, cross the Charles. Though they tend to be smaller, the places tend to be more sophisticated (Middlesex) or more delightfully skuzzy (Hong Kong).

MIDDLESEX Map p311

☎ 617-686-6739; www.middlesexlounge.com; 315 Massachusetts Ave; cover $5 (Fri & Sat only); 🚇 Central

The sophisticated minimalist design of this beautiful modern room uses a well-done sequence of wood paneling reminiscent of Japanese tatami mats. Black modular furniture sits on heavy casters, allowing the cubes to be easily rolled aside when the place transforms from lounge to club on nights when the fashionable crowd becomes entranced with DJs experimenting with French pop and electronica.

HONG KONG Map p310

☎ 617-864-5311; www.hongkongharvard.com; 1238 Massachusetts Ave; 🚇 Harvard

Climb straight past the 1st floor's greasy low-mein dispenser to the low-budget disco above. One level is a bar full of people drinking giant Scorpion Bowls (use a long straw to suck a future hangover out of communal mixing crockery). Above it is a dark room illuminated by a single disco ball packed with a racially diverse mix of townies, Harvard kids and slumming BU students. Slightly seedy.

TOAST Map p311

☎ 617-623-9211; www.toastlounge.com; 70 Union Sq; 🕙 Wed-Sun; 🚇 Central

Descend through deep sidewalk cuts to a designy bar in the lower levels of a former police building from the 1920s. An assortment of DJs spin tunes for various theme nights. Wednesday and Saturday attract heaps of Goths and misfits, while Friday has become one of Boston's most popular dyke nights thanks to DJ Susan Esthera.

CANTAB Map p311

☎ 617-354-2685; www.cantab-lounge.com; 738 Massachusetts Ave; 🚇 Central

Go to the basement of this kick-ass dive, where the rec-room feel and Top 40 hits go well with a crowd where everyone dances, everyone sings along and few look cool.

ART GALLERIES

Boston's 'gallery row' lies on Newbury St, particularly those blocks closest to the Public Garden. We recommend a few galleries from this street below, but there are about a dozen of them in a small crush of space that are worth checking out. Elsewhere, you'll find a thriving artist community in Fort Point near the Waterfront and a few alternative places scattered around the outlying neighborhoods (eg Zeitgeist and Green Street Gallery).

FORT POINT ARTS COMMUNITY
Map pp302-3

☎ 617-423-4299; www.fortpointarts.org; 300 Summer St; 🚇 South Station

Since 1978, dozens and dozens of artists have lived and worked in a refurbished big-windowed warehouse from the turn of the 20th century. This artists building is the hub of the Fort Point Arts Community, which contains a gallery featuring work from the talented collective. See huge psychedelic oils, prints inspired by 14th-century Venetian Laces, lampshades made from birch and mixed media films. Every October, a hugely popular open-studios event allows you to see the artists' live-work spaces as they display and sell their creations. Other such events occur near Christmas and in spring.

ZEITGEIST Map p311

☎ 617-876-6060; www.zeitgeist-gallery.org; 186 Hampshire St; 🚇 Central

A gallery and minimalist performance space, Zeitgeist attracts a hodgepodge of the bizarre and good, both in terms of the art that it displays (such as robots or a videography of a girl achieving the uncanny through a freakish yet appealing dance ritual in unusual places) and in terms of the crowd. The gallery is independent, small and reliably interesting. There are frequently musical performances, including jazz and shakuhachi.

GREEN STREET GALLERY Map pp298-9

☎ 617-522-0000; www.greenstreetgallery.com; 141 Green St; 🚇 Green St

To see thoughtful shows by talented young artists, stop by this contemporary glass and steel gallery attached to the Green Street T station. The director, James Hull, is well connected with Mass Art and is really open minded, ensuring a selection of art that is often odd and always worth checking out. Once a year they display 150 pieces, each one on sale for 150 bucks. A shitload of people line up outside and almost everything is claimed within 90 seconds.

ALPHA GALLERY Map pp306-7
☎ 617-536-4465; www.alphagallery.com; 38 Newbury St; ⓡ Arlington
Presenting the work of some headline-grabbing artists (sometimes local, sometimes international), this starkly minimalist gallery mostly shows oils (some figurative, some abstract), though occasionally you'll see sculpture, mixed media and prints. They have an annual new talent exhibition and intermittently have special shows of masters such as Max Beckman and Milton Avery.

BARBARA KRAKOW GALLERY
Map pp306-7
☎ 617-262-4490; www.barbarakrakowgallery.com; 10 Newbury St; ⓡ Arlington
The catalogue of artists represented by this older gallery (established 1964) reads like something you'd expect from a major museum. Among the famous are Josef Albers, Ellsworth Kelly, Sol LeWitt and Jasper Johns. Though it's very much a house of the modernists, the gallery sometimes displays the work of an emerging artist.

GALLERY NAGA Map pp306-7
☎ 617-267-9060; www.gallerynaga.com; 67 Newbury St; ⓡ Arlington
Inside the Gothic digs of the Church of the Covenant, Gallery Naga exhibits contemporary painters (eg Bryan McFarlane) and has a warm place in many hearts for their specialization in unique and limited-edition furniture.

GASP Map pp308–9
☎ 617-731-2500; 362 Boylston St; www.g-a-s-p.net; ⏰ 11am-5pm Thu-Sat; ⓡ Brookline Hills
Created by the wife-and-husband team of MM Campos-Pons and Neil Leonard, ambitious and independent GASP serves as a gallery, studio and performance space for cutting-edge contemporary art. Don't be fooled by the somewhat remote Brookline location: while plenty of Boston artists and performers use the space as a second home, this is an international house of ex-

perimentation, inviting curators and artists from Norway, Montreal and Egypt.

ALLSTON SKIRT GALLERY Map p305
☎ 617-482-3652; www.allstonskirt.com; 65 Thayer St; ⏰ 11am-5pm Wed-Sat; ⓡ Back Bay
For stunning exhibits by rising-star artists, visit the Allston Skirt Gallery. The work displayed often combines material beauty with rich interpretations of art theory. Works by Tina Feingold, David Robbins (if you haven't seen his snowmen, you should), Heather Holber-Keene and more.

THEATER
Though it lives in the shadow of New York, Boston's theatrical culture is impressively strong for a city of its size. Multiple big-ticket venues consistently book top shows, produce premieres and serve as testing grounds for many plays that eventually become hits on Broadway.

Tickets
Tickets for all venues are available online or at the individual theater box offices. Availability varies greatly, but most shows do not sell out far in advance. BosTix (www.bostix.com) offers discounted tickets to productions citywide. Discounts up to 25% are available for advanced purchases online. Discounts up to 50% are available for same-day purchase: check the website to see what's available, but purchases must be made in person, in cash, at outlets on Copley Sq or at Quincy Market.

THEATER DISTRICT
Home to the major companies, the stages in the theater district tend to be located in gilded palaces of monumental architecture.

HUNTINGTON THEATRE COMPANY
Map pp306-7
☎ 617-266-0800; www.huntingtontheatre.org; 264 Huntington Ave (Boston University Theatre); ⓡ Symphony or Massachusetts Ave
For award-winning theater, it's tough to outdo the Huntington, whose trophy cabinet has long been full. It stages many shows before its production is transferred to Broadway (at least three of these have won Tonys)

and seven major works by August Wilson were performed by the Huntington before going on to fame in New York. The company's credentials also include over 50 world premieres of works by playwrights such as Tom Stoppard and Christopher Durang.

Plays occur in two venues, the fine Boston University Theatre (built in 1925) and the Calderwood Pavilion at the Boston Center for the Arts (built in 2004), which contains state-of-the art gizmos and is more intimately scaled.

WANG THEATRE Map p305
☎ 617-482-9393; www.wangcenter.org; 270 Tremont St; tickets $45-95; ⓧ Boylston
Restored in 1989, this opulent 3600-seat theater with mural-covered vault and chandelier-festooned lobby are the definition of early-20th-century grandeur. A variety of shows are presented, usually of the kind with a sizable budget for set design. See Broadway, theater, music, dance and live performances by celebrities like John Stewart. The Boston Ballet uses it as home base.

SHUBERT THEATRE Map p305
☎ 617-482-9393; www.wangcenter.org; 270 Tremont St; tickets $45-95; ⓧ Boylston
Administered by the Wang Center, the Shubert Theatre hosts dance and popular theater (eg Boston Lyric Opera's Madama Butterfly, James Kirkwood's Legends! starring Joan Collins and Linda Evans). Like the Wang Theatre, this is an old architectural beauty, though smaller (1600 seats) and less lavish.

CHARLES PLAYHOUSE & BLUEMAN GROUP Map p305
☎ 617-931-2787; www.blueman.com; 74 Warrenton St; ⓧ Boylston
If you're in the dark tank that is the Charles Playhouse, it likely means that you're about to watch the Blueman Group embarrass someone seated near you. Why? Because the troupe has been playing here for years (in fact, the Charles Playhouse is their original home), and it is a rare occasion when another act uses the stage.

OPERA HOUSE Map pp302-3
☎ 617-880-2442; 539 Washington St; ⓧ Downtown Crossing
After more than a decade of neglect, the Opera House reopened its doors in 2004

for a highly acclaimed production of Disney's Lion King. The lavish theater has been restored to its 1928 glory, complete with mural-painted ceiling, gold-gilded molding and plush velvet curtains. The glitzy theater regularly hosts productions from the Broadway Across America series, as well as the Christmas-time performance of The Nutcracker by the Boston Ballet.

ALT/INDIE & UNIVERSITY TROUPES

Alternative theater in Boston is sometimes more impressive than the main stages in the Theater District. You can thank the huge numbers of academics and students who live in the city for this culturally impressive phenomenon.

AMERICAN REPERTORY THEATER Map p310
☎ 617-547-8300; www.amrep.org; 64 Brattle St; tickets $40-75; ⓧ Harvard
For Tony-award winning experimental theater, this company packs their small house at Harvard's contemporary Loeb Drama Center. Set designs are generally creative, and even if you do see something of traditional appeal, such as Romeo & Juliet or Carmen, it will be staged and performed with care and intelligence.

COMPANY ONE
☎ 617-277-7032; www.companyone.org
For inspired, independent performances, Company One has broken ground and hearts with fare like Den of Thieves, The Last Days of Judas Iscariot, and A More Perfect Union. While often esoteric, works that are staged are dynamic and engaging and they simultaneously appeal to youth culture, hipster and academic audiences. Most shows are performed in the Boston Center for the Arts (BCA) theaters.

BOSTON CENTER FOR THE ARTS Map p305
☎ 617-933-8600; www.bcaonline.org; 539 Tremont St; ⓧ Copley
The BCA serves as a nexus for excellent small theater productions. The playwrights represented reflect the edgy, contemporary minds and times of the diverse cultural and socioeconomic backgrounds

found throughout the region. Each year over 20 companies present more than 45 separate productions ranging from comedies to drama and modern dance to musicals. The BCA occupies a complex comprised of several buildings, including a cyclorama from 1884 built to display panoramic paintings, a former organ factory, and the Mills Gallery.

HASTY PUDDING THEATRICALS
Map p310

☎ 617-495-5205; 12 Holyoke St; 🚇 Harvard
The oldest theater company in the States, Harvard's undergraduate dramatic society was founded in 1795. While you can see several kinds of events, including the annual Hasty Pudding Awards, mostly it's all about musical comedy with guys in drag.

CLASSICAL MUSIC, OPERA & DANCE

As a legacy of Brahmin culture, Boston contains excellent options in big budget performances set to orchestral music.

CLASSICAL MUSIC

Home to the Boston Symphony Orchestra and the New England Conservatory of Music, Boston boasts some of the country's oldest and most prestigious houses for symphonic experiences.

BOSTON SYMPHONY ORCHESTRA
Map p305

☎ 617-266-1200; www.bso.org; 301 Massachusetts Ave; tickets $30-111; 🚇 Symphony
Conductor James Levine leads a masterful orchestra through Schoenberg, Beethoven, Vaughan Williams and Shostakovich with great finesse. Though occasionally playing outdoors at the Hatch Schell on the Esplanade, their usual home, the breathtaking Symphony Hall, is a beauty with an ornamental high relief ceiling where most in the crowd will be dressed in their finest. It was designed in 1861 with the help of a Harvard physicist who pledged (and succeeded) to make the building acoustically perfect.

Occasionally, you can get tickets to rehearsals which are cheaper than full-fledged shows.

BOSTON POPS Map p305

☎ 617-266-1200; www.bostonpops.org; 301 Massachusetts Ave; tickets $30-111; 🚇 Symphony
Also playing out of the audibly and visually delightful Symphony Hall, the Boston Pops arranges crowd-pleasers for the orchestra to tackle. Usually this means seasonal fare such as Christmas carols, movie scores and thematic mischief. The business is conducted by the dashing Keith Lockhart, making Boston hearts swoon since 1995. Tickets are booked out far in advance, especially for shows during the winter holidays.

CHAMBER MUSIC TEAS Map p305

☎ 617-266-1200; www.bso.org; 301 Massachusetts Ave; tickets $15; 🚇 Symphony
On some Fridays, members of the Boston Symphony Orchestra get together to perform during afternoon teas in the Cabot-Cahners room of Symphony Hall (doors open at 1:30pm, concert at 2:30pm). Consume coffee, tea and baked goods in the finest style.

NEW ENGLAND CONSERVATORY OF MUSIC Map p305

☎ 617-585-1260 box office; Jordan Hall, 30 Gainsborough St; admission free (usually); 🚇 Symphony
Founded in 1867, the NEC is the country's oldest music school and hosts professional and student chamber and orchestral concerts in the acoustically superlative hall that dates from 1904. Perhaps for better sight lines, the floor pitches slightly forward, and while perfectly safe, it gives some on the balcony an odd sensory experience. The Boston Philharmonic, Boston Modern Orchestra Project and From the Top (of National Public Radio fame) all make use of the hall.

OPERA & DANCE

Though options are limited, these three options will blow you away with melodrama or pointy-toed shoes.

OPERA BOSTON Map p305

☎ 617-451-3388; www.operaboston.org; 219 Tremont St (Cutler Majestic Box Office); tickets $24-99; 🚇 Boylston
Playing out of the gilded Cutler Majestic Theater, this acclaimed opera company

Live music at Regattabar (p179)

has been impressing Boston for almost three decades. Expect innovative set design and intelligently selected shows that bring to life the rarely heard works of masters, plus innovative repertoires of more recent vintage. Recent performances include Mozart's *La Clemenza di Tito* and Weill's *The Rise and Fall of the City of Mahagonny*.

BOSTON LYRIC OPERA Map p305
☎ 617-542-6772; 265 Tremont St (Shubert Theatre Box Office); tickets $33-112; 🚇 Boylston
Another longstanding company, the BLO is often featured on NPR and stages classic performances, such as a popular outdoor production of *Carmen* in the Boston Common. Their usual house is the Shubert Theatre, where you'll see *Madama Butterfly*, *The Little Prince* or *The Barber of Seville*.

BOSTON BALLET
☎ 617-695-6950; www.bostonballet.org; tickets $15-100
Boston's skilful ballet performs classical and modern works. During the Christmas season, they stage wildly popular performances of the *Nutcracker* at the Wang

Theatre (p185). Students can often get rush tickets for $15 on the day of a show.

CINEMA
Boston is home to several old-school theaters that show cult flicks and classics in art deco or gilded style. It also boasts several brand new, high-tech movie houses where your seat will be soft, your screen huge and your film a warm blanket of Hollywood special effects.

FIRST-RUN THEATERS
Want to see a first-run film? You'll likely be giving your $10 to one of several theaters affiliated with the Landmark or AMC chains. For other options, take in some IMAX at a museum or check the independent theater listings below, as these also show first-run fare.

LANDMARK KENDALL SQUARE CINEMA Map p311
☎ 617-499-1996; 1 Kendall Sq; adult/child $9.25/7; 🚇 Kendall/MIT
Part of the Landmark chain, this modern theater screens popular foreign films and

the usual collection of hits from the Sundance Festival (eg *Half Nelson, Little Miss Sunshine*). Seats are steeply sloped and the concession stand actually serves snacks that taste good.

AMC LOEWS BOSTON COMMON 19
Map pp302-3

☎ 617-423-3499; 175 Tremont St; adult/student/child/matinee $10/9/7/8; ☒ Park St

For first-run blockbusters, this generic megaplex offers big screens, plush seats and a central location opposite the Common. Though it has large theaters and 19 screens, popular weekend shows can sell out hours early. Should you need a stiff one to help you through *Step Up,* there's a bar on site.

AMC FENWAY 13 Map pp308-9

☎ 617-424-6266; 401 Park Dr; adult/student/child $9.50/6.50/6.50; ☒ Fenway

This Loews is one of the only multiplexes that has a decent student discount – which is great, unless you don't want to be surrounded by students, who sometimes interrupt viewings with lame witticisms. The place has all the bells and whistles, including superior sound and reclining stadium seats.

AMC LOEWS HARVARD SQUARE
Map p310

☎ 617-864-4580; 10 Church St; adult/student/child/matinee $9.25/8.25/6.25/7.25; ☒ Harvard

After eating at the nearby Veggie Planet, don't miss out on an opportunity to wait in line in the rain to buy tickets. This plus other historical anomalies lend character to this chain-operated venue, which screens a blend of somewhat mainstream independent movies and major-studio releases. All shows before noon Friday to Sunday cost $5.

SIMONS IMAX THEATRE
Map pp302-3

☎ 617-973-5200; www.neaq.org; Central Wharf; adult/child $10/8; ☒ Aquarium

At the New England Aquarium, this IMAX bad-boy plays lots of educational films on a six-storey screen, in 3D. That way when you have a gander at *Sharks,* you'll actually feel like you're about to be eaten. Try not to poop your pants. They occasionally play

IMAX versions of popular fare (eg *Superman Returns*).

MUGAR OMNI THEATRE Map pp300-1

☎ 617-723-2500; www.mos.org; Science Park; adult/child $6.50/4.50; ☒ Science Park

For more IMAX immersion, check out the space- and natural science–oriented flicks at the Museum of Science's theater. A sweet sound system will help you believe that you're actually searching for endangered animals in a distant rainforest.

COMCAST IMAX 3D THEATER AT JORDAN'S FURNITURE Map pp298-9

☎ 508-424-0088; www.jordansimax.com; 1 Underprice Way (Rte 9), Natick; tickets $11

For a bizarre and hellish experience, rent a car and allow yourself 45 minutes to an hour to drive to this suburban nospace. It's in a fucking furniture store on a fake street (Underprice Way!?).

INDEPENDENT, ARTS & REVIVAL THEATERS

Boston's independent theaters are some of the best you'll find anywhere, and screen amazing calendars of hard-to-find or just plain excellent films.

BRATTLE THEATRE Map p310

☎ 617-876-6837; www.brattlefilm.org; 40 Brattle St; adult/child $9/6, student & matinee $7.50; ☒ Harvard

From thriller double features of *Psycho* and *Death Trance* to screenings of film noir, movies for children that don't suck (eg *Dark Crystal* or the *5000 Fingers of Dr T*) to the work of the Italian masters, the legendary old Brattle has been satisfying Harvard Sq for decades.

COOLIDGE CORNER THEATRE
Map pp308-9

☎ 617-734-2501; www.coolidge.org; 290 Harvard St; adult/child/matinee $9.50/6.50/7.50; ☒ Coolidge Corner

An art deco neighborhood palace, this old theater blazes with exterior neon. Inside, view select Hollywood hits, cult flicks, popular independent fare and special events such as 'open mic for movies' where you bring self-made masterpieces less than

10 minutes in length (all formats including 35mm, Super8, VHS and DVD) for a pastiche of amateur weirdness. Fifty cents of every ticket goes to upkeep of the building.

SOMMERVILLE THEATRE Map pp298-9
☎ 617-625-5700; www.somervilletheatreonline .com; 55 Davis Sq; adult/child/matinee 6.50/4.75/4; 🚇 Davis

This classic neighborhood movie house dates from 1914 and features plenty of gilding and pastel murals of muses in excellent condition. On offer are first- and second-run Hollywood hits, live chamber music, the Chuck Norris Film Festival and the Independent Film Festival of Boston screenings. The main theater is the biggest, best and oldest and has the added treat of a balcony.

HARVARD FILM ARCHIVE
Map p310
☎ 617-495-4700; http://hcl.harvard.edu/hfa; 24 Quincy St; adult/student $8/6; 🚇 Harvard

For retrospectives of distinguished actors, screenings of rare films, thematic groupings (eg Chinatown: *Broken Blossoms, The Lady from Shanghai, Chan is Missing*) and special events where filmmakers (William Klein, Bibi Anderson) appear to discuss their work, head to Le Corbusier's Carpenter Center (p42). Tickets for most screenings are sold at the Cinematheque 45 minutes ahead of show times, which often sell out.

MUSEUM OF FINE ARTS Map pp308-9
☎ 617-369-3306; 365 Huntington Ave; tickets $10.50; 🚇 Museum of Fine Arts

If you packed your thinking cap, the MFA screens highbrow film events (ie retrospectives of Syrian cinema focusing on surrealist narratives, documentaries and social commentary) where visiting artists frequently attend screenings to discuss their work. Recent shows include *Wondrous Oblivion, Return of the Idiot* and a collection of British advertising shorts from the previous year.

COMEDY

People with weird accents from Boston make good comedians. It's a fact you can't ignore. We've selected the following spots from the dozen that exist in town.

SHEAR MADNESS Map p305
☎ 617-426-6912; www.shearmadness.com; 1 Shear Madness Alley; admission $38; 🚇 Boylston

America's longest running comedy operates out of the Charles Playhouse, situated on a sleazy street (don't worry, it adds to the mood) in a former church. An odd mix of half-play and half-improvision, the show features an outrageous gay hair stylist and various freak-show characters in a whodunit-style performance where actors ad-lib the plot based on cues from the audience.

COMEDY STUDIO AT HONG KONG
Map p310
☎ 617-661-6507; www.thecomedystudio.com; 1236 Massachusetts Ave; admission $7-10; 8pm Tue-Sun; 🚇 Harvard

The 3rd floor of this noodle house contains a low-budget comedy house with a reputation for hosting cutting-edge acts and where talented future stars (eg Brian Kiley, now a writer for Conan O'Brien) refine their racy material. They usually sponsor a comedian of the month and on Tuesday host a weird magician show.

DICK'S BEANTOWN COMEDY VAULT
Map p305
☎ 617-482-0110; 124 Boylston St; ⏰ 9pm Thu-Sun; admission $10-15; 🚇 Boylston

In the basement of Remington's (a restaurant), local comedian Dick Doherty and a collection of regular helpers work the room into painful howls with surgical precision. Note that Sunday nights are open mic, and the pain you feel on such occasions might feel very different than at other times during the week.

COMEDY CONNECTION Map pp302-3
☎ 617-248-9700; Quincy Market, Faneuil Hall Marketplace; tickets $15-25; 🚇 Government Center

Of Boston's comedy clubs, you can most reliably find big-name acts here. The room lies on the 2nd floor of Quincy Market, above the food court, and charges an obligatory two item admission fee (meaning drink or forgettable food) in addition to the cost of your ticket. Thursday features an R-rated hypnotist who despite being corny is also pretty funny. Seats are really close together and the earlier you buy your ticket, the closer you will be to the stage.

READINGS & LECTURES

Most universities offer various special events which are open to the public, and you can learn about the goings-on by poking through their websites. Some universities are more active than others in this field, and Harvard in particular seems to have some kind of public and esoteric lecture almost every day of the week. For a regular poetry slam, visit the Cantab Lounge (p179) on Wednesdays.

HARVARD UNIVERSITY Map p310

www.community.harvard.edu/happeningharvard
Harvard hosts a staggering number of lectures, symposia, meetings and tours, many of which are open to the public and many of which are free. Topics are as diverse as the university itself and are impossible to encapsulate in a review such as this. Representative events are gallery talks on botanical motifs in East Asian art, urbanism in Carthage or post-communist politics. Or go see a lecture by a NASA astronaut.

BROOKLINE BOOKSMITH Map pp308-9

☎ 617-566-6660; www.brooklinebooksmith.com; 279 Harvard St; 🚇 Brookline Village
Head to this top-notch mom-an-pop bookstore for readings in a homey brick room where patrons sit on a collection of bridge chairs and listen to Elinor Lipman (*The Pursuit of Alice Thrift*) or Jon Katz (*A Good Dog*) while others chat.

LIZARD LOUNGE Map pp298-9

☎ 617-547-0759; www.lizardloungeclub.com; 1667 Massachusetts Ave; cover $5; 🚇 Harvard
On Sundays at 7:30pm, head to the Lizard Lounge to sit in a room that recalls a red-light district done up with Persian rugs to hear poetry recited in slam fashion. You'll usually find a featured poet accompanied by the improvisational Jeff Robinson Trio.

HARVARD BOOKSTORE Map p310

☎ 800-542-7323; www.harvard.com; 1256 Massachusetts Ave; usually free, sometimes $3; 🚇 Harvard
Established in 1932, this famous and independent bookstore has long been a center of intellectual activity in Harvard Sq. A regular series of readers and speakers range from novelists (such as Nell Freudenberger and William Boyd) to academics. Many readings are held in the store itself, others in the Brattle Theatre. There's a Friday forum at 3pm.

BOSTON PUBLIC LIBRARY

Map pp306-7
☎ 617-536-5400; 700 Boylston St; 🚇 Copley
For a schedule of free events, check out the BPL, where you might hear an author talk

---

FREE FUN

For those short on bread, several entertainment options don't charge admission. Be aware that many Irish pubs host traditional folk bands and jam sessions and rarely require patrons to pony up for the listening experience.

Toad (p177) Live Indie and local bands play every night in this low-key bar.

New England Conservatory (p186) Top-notch student performers and national acts give orchestral performances in a weird concert hall.

Esplanade Performances (☎ 617-626-4970) May through September, the Boston Symphony Orchestra, the Boston Pops and the city itself provide free outdoor performances at the Hatch Shell. Hear Cool & the Gang, classical music and on Friday evenings, watch movies.

Shakespeare on the Common (☎ 617-532-1212; www.freeshakespeare.org) Each summer, the Commonwealth Shakespeare Company stages a major production often with a populist twist. Thus *Taming of the Shrew,* set in a North End restaurant.

Wally's (p179) Stellar musicians perform in the city's smallest, oldest and grittiest jazz club.

Hong Kong (p183) Crowds of students drink awesomely large scorpion bowls in this cover free low-budget nightclub.

GAY & LESBIAN BOSTON

If you wander through the South End, you'll discover that Boston's queer population has cornered some of the prettiest real estate in town. In it you'll find the highest concentration of bars that are either gay or gay friendly. Elsewhere, special events and dance nights occur with regularity. Consult www.edgeboston.com for more information.

ID (p179) In the same complex as the Avalon, ID hosts Pink, a lesbian dance party, every Saturday night in a souped up mainstream club.

Toast (p183) For one of the most popular dyke nights in town, this stylish neighborhood bar features a top-notch local DJ on Friday.

Diesel Cafe (p173) Shoot stick, drink coffee and swill beer in this industrial café popular with Tufts University students and queers.

Avalon (p179) Since the late '70s, Boston's biggest dance club has been reserved for the lads on Sunday nights.

Midway (p177) For hip-hop and classic pop, this Thursday night lesbian party is intermittently interrupted throughout the evening when a phenomenon known as 'queeraoke' takes over with dubious singing and gayer-than-gay costumes.

by a well-known novelist (eg Janet Fitch or James R Benn) or a discussion about how to buy a home in Boston. Most events are held in the Rabb Lecture Hall, which lies inside a painfully ugly addition attached to the celebrated main library building. Others occur in more beautiful and stimulating environs.

BOSTON HISTORICAL SOCIETY

Map pp302-3

☎ 617-720-1713; 206 Washington St; Ⓜ Downtown Crossing

For lectures, special events and children's activities on a wide range of Boston topics, stop by the historical society for evenings devoted to the Boston Strangler, abolitionism in Boston and a reading by Nancy Seasholes, author of *Gaining Ground: A History of Landmaking in Boston*.

FORD HALL FORUM

☎ 617-373-5800; www.fordhallforum.org

The oldest continuing public lecture series in the country (begun in 1908), it sponsors lively and spirited dialogues on topical world events from stem-cells to terrorism via attitudes toward ageing. Venerable past speakers have included Martin Luther King Jr, Maya Angelou, Winston Churchill, Cokie Roberts, Al Gore and MacArthur Genius Award recipient John Bonifaz. Lectures are held in the fall, winter and spring at Faneuil Hall, Old South Meeting House and Northeastern University.

BOWLING

Though Boston's alleys are few in number, many of them offer distinctive evening entertainment. Sacco's is probably the oldest bowling interior you'll experience in life, while Kings provides so many visual goodies that you might feel like you are bowling in an action movie, with large video screens spewing flashy graphics, and an impressive sound system.

SACCO'S BOWL HAVEN Map pp298-9

☎ 617-776-0552; 45 Day St; game/shoe rental $2.75/1.50; Ⓨ 10am-midnight Mon-Sat, noon-midnight Sun; Ⓜ Davis

For an incredible time warp, head to Sacco's – an unchanged and slightly beaten-up treasure last renovated in 1950. Inside you'll find lots of worn wood lanes, faux-marble benches, a giant stuffed swordfish and old metal lockers. The game de jour is candlepin. If you ever bowl here you'll never want to go anywhere else.

KINGS Map pp306-7

☎ 617-266-2695; www.kingsbackbay.com; 10 Scotia St; game/shoe rental $6.50/$4; Ⓨ 5pm-2am Mon, 11:30-2am Tue-Sun; Ⓜ Hynes/ICA

For an over-the-top tenpin experience, roll a few at Kings where high-tech lanes in pristine condition are lined with neon lights and surrounded by walls painted with trippy graphics. Behind deck is an enormous cocktail lounge done up in a retro style

WHAT'S WRONG WITH THOSE PINS?

If you go bowling in Boston, chances are very good that you'll encounter candlepin, a frustrating variant with skinny pins that hate to fall down. The game was developed in Massachusetts in the 1880s and is only found in New Brunswick and in some New England states.

The setup looks similar to conventional tenpin, only the pins are about 12in high and 2in thick, with a taper at each end. Bowling balls are palm-sized and weigh less than 4lbs. Though the balls' diminutive proportions allow you to chuck them pretty hard, it also means that they don't exactly bulldoze the targets at the other end of the lane. And when you do hit a target, its limited girth doesn't help much in taking down its neighbors. Factor these two circumstances together, and you'll see why a novice getting a strike is about as common as a cow milking itself.

Luckily for players, they get three balls, not two. Further, deadwood (pins that have been knocked over) doesn't get cleared away. The positive here is that if you hit some deadwood it can spin into standing pins to help you topple your remaining wooden adversaries. The small balls also allow children to play more easily.

Want to play? Both Sacco's Bowl Haven and the Milky Way are specialists in candlepin action.

reminiscent of the *Jetsons*, a *Howard Johnson's* or the house from the *Brady Bunch*.

MILKY WAY Map pp298-9

☎ 617-524-3740; www.milkywayjp.com; 405 Centre St; lane per hr $25; ⏱ 6pm-midnight Mon-Thu, 6pm-12:45am Fri & Sat, 6-11pm Sun; 🚇 Stony Brook

Though this subterranean bar acts more as a retro lounge and nightclub, it was originally a bowling alley back in the 1960s and six of the old lanes have been retained for your candlepin pleasure. The hourly charge covers shoe rentals and everyone in your party (up to six people). If there's an event (band, karaoke) you'll also have to pay a cover. While individual kids are cool, bringing a group of them is a no-no.

LUCKY STRIKE LANES Map pp308-9

☎ 617-437-0300; 145 Ipswich St; game/shoe rental $6/3.50; ⏱ 11-2am; 🚇 Kenmore

Run by a national chain, this high-tec bowling alley is embedded inside Jillian's, a large entertainment complex containing a dance club, arcade and pool hall. As the place fills with the Lansdowne St crowd, sometimes the wait for a lane can take a long time. The alley is exclusive to patrons 21-years and over after 8pm on weekends.

Activities ■

Activities

Considering Boston's large student population and extensive green spaces, it's no surprise to see urban outdoorsmen and women running along the Esplanade, cycling the Emerald Necklace and skating the Minuteman Trail. For seafaring types, the Charles River and the Boston Harbor offer myriad opportunities for kayaking and canoeing, sailing and sculling, and even swimming in their brisk waters.

On any given sunny weekend, you're bound to see fierce Frisbee competitions, league softball games and rigorous tennis matches. And that's just on the Boston Common; the same scene is played out in parks around the city.

All this goes on, and the keenest of sports fans are planted in front of their TVs watching the Red Sox. When it comes to spectator sports, Boston is a baseball town. Other sports have their fans, especially during a strong season. The Patriots' recent string of Super Bowl championships guaranteed a loyal following of football fans. And Boston natives still remember the not-so-distant past, when Larry Bird won successive championships for the Celtics and Bobby Orr played for the Bruins. But baseball is like a religion in Boston. (That's a warning to Yankee fans, who should remember what happens to religious heretics here.)

WATCHING SPORTS

Boston loves its sports teams. And why not, with the three-time world champion New England Patriots and the long-overdue World Series–winning Red Sox? Emotions run high around every sports season, especially baseball (see the boxed text, opposite). There is no better way to strike up a spirited conversation than to inquire about the Sox. For sports talk radio all the time, tune into 850AM.

Tickets

The easiest way to get tickets is to order them online in advance. Tickets can also be purchased at the box office in the days leading up to the games. Red Sox and Patriots games usually sell out, which means it is difficult to get tickets through the regular channels. If you have your heart set on seeing the hometown team, many online ticket agents will be pleased to sell you tickets, often with a hefty mark-up:

Ace Tickets (☎ 800-697-3287; www.aceticket.com)

Beantown Tickets (www.beantowntickets.com)

Buy Baseball Tickets (www.buy-baseball-tickets.com)

Buy Sell Tix (☎ 800-451-8499; www.buyselltix.com)

Tickets Now (☎ 800-927-2770; www.ticketsnow.com)

Alternatively, check **Craig's List** (www.boston.craigslist.org), where there is always a lot of buying and selling.

BASEBALL

No other Boston team is loved and hated as much as the Red Sox. From April to September, watch the Red Sox play at **Fenway Park** (Map pp308–9; ☎ 617-267-1700; www .redsox.com; 4 Yawkey Way; ⓡ Kenmore), the nation's oldest and most storied ballpark. It is also the most expensive. Tickets in the bleachers are $23 to $27, while more comfortable grandstand seats are $45. Even at these prices, tickets are hard to come by, but single seats and obstructed-view tickets are sometimes available on the website during the week leading up to a game. First-come, first-serve standing-room-only tickets are sold on game day; head to the ticket windows at Gate C on Landsdowne

CURSE? WHAT CURSE?

'And there is pandemonium on the field!' With the final out of baseball's 2004 World Series, the Boston Red Sox had overcome more than just the brawny St Louis Cardinals, but the heavy weight of 86 years of futility and fatalism. Woe is the Fenway Faithful, it was long said, for their team is cursed.

It had all started so well for the Olde Towne team. Then known as the Pilgrims of the upstart American League, Boston captured the first ever World Series in 1903 against the Pittsburgh Pirates of the senior circuit National League. By 1918, Boston, now renamed the Red Sox, had won four more championships. But fortunes soon changed.

On the day after Christmas in 1919, Boston owner Harry Frazee, unwilling to meet the demands of his star player, sold his contract to New York owner Colonel Jacob Ruppert. Ruppert acquiesced to the player's demand to receive a $20,000 contract and to be moved from the pitching mound to the outfield. Now bedecked in Yankee pinstripes, Babe Ruth became baseball's foremost power hitter and, arguably, the greatest player who ever played the game. Led by the Sultan of Swat, the Yankees became perennial contenders, as the Red Sox faded into perpetual also-rans.

Thus the legend was born of the Curse of the Bambino. Over the years, success eluded the Red Sox, while the Yankees piled up championship upon championship. Whenever it appeared that a Red Sox season might end in triumph, inexplicable and unnatural forces intervened against them. Bad breaks, botched balls and hanging sliders would suddenly steal defeat from the jaws of victory. The Red Sox–Yankee rivalry was the most intense in all sports, and the most one-sided. As the disappointments accumulated, only one conclusion prevailed – the team was hexed. Sizing up the problem and seizing the initiative, concerned fans even hired a well-known Salem witch to exorcise the angry ghost, to no avail.

The Red Sox were indeed a cursed team for much of the 20th century – cursed by bad management, that is. In 1933 Tom Yawkey turned 30 years old and gained access to a $40 million trust fund. With his birthday allowance, he purchased the Red Sox and Fenway Park. Yawkey was an avid sportsman and a passionate fan, who loved hanging out with and indulging his players. In an era of stinginess, he spent lavishly on his team. The Boston franchise was seen as a country club, where Yawkey employed his drinking buddies in management and his favorite players called the shots.

The Yawkey-led Red Sox were further burdened by the legacy of racism. As society changed, the city and the team did not. Red Sox management passed on the chance to sign Jackie Robinson and Willie Mays. The Red Sox was the last all-white team in the major leagues. The racist reputation of the organization, as well as the city, plagued the franchise well after Yawkey's death in 1976. Not until the 1990s did the team shed this ugly image.

For Red Sox Nation, the past is finally past. On a cold October night in 2004, in the same House that Ruth Built, the unkempt and unfazed Red Sox thrashed the clean-cut and choked-up Yankees in the final game of the American League championship. Desperate and disbelieving, Yankee fans tried in vain to conjure up the spirit of the Babe, which likely had gone out for hot dogs and beer. Next up, the Red Sox throttled its old National League nemesis, the St Louis Cardinals, who fell to the hose in four straight. Hell had frozen over. The curse was reversed. The Boston Red Sox were World Series champs.

St. Otherwise, you can always get tickets from scalpers around Kenmore Sq. If the Sox are doing well, expect to pay two times face value.

FOOTBALL

Three-time Super Bowl champs New England Patriots play football in the state-of-the-art **Gillette Stadium** (☎ 508-543-8200, 800-543-1776; www.patriots.com; Gillette Stadium, Foxborough), 32 miles south of Boston in Foxborough. The season runs from late August to late December. Again, it's hard to get tickets, as most seats are sold to season ticket holders. Seats run from $60 to $125 and standing-room tickets are sometimes available for $49. From I-93, take I-95 south to Rte 1. Otherwise, direct trains go to Foxborough from South Station.

Now part of the competitive Atlantic Coast Conference (ACC), the BC Eagles play football in the new **Alumni Stadium** (☎ 617-552-3000; www.bceagles.com; 140 Commonwealth Ave; $27-42; ⓑ Boston College) every second Saturday from September to November. Staunch Ivy League rivalries bring out alumni and fans to see the Harvard Crimson play at **Harvard Stadium** (Map pp298–9; ☎ 617-495-2211; www.gocrimson .com; N Harvard St & Soldiers Field Rd), across the river from Harvard Square.

BASKETBALL

The Boston Celtics have not attracted much attention lately, but they have won more basketball championships than any other NBA team. From October to April, they play at the **Banknorth Garden** (Map pp300–1;

Baseball practice, Fenway Park (p101)

☎ information 617-523-3030, tickets 931-2000; www.celtics.com; 150 Causeway St; tickets upper deck $15-55, middle deck $55-135; Ⓡ North Station). Formerly called the Fleet Center, the arena sits on top of North Station. Tickets start at $15, but you won't be able to see anything from there. Expect to pay $35 for a decent seat in the upper deck and anywhere from $55 to $135 for something closer.

The Boston College Eagles basketball team is competitive in the ACC and is usually still standing for March Madness. The Eagles play at **Conte Forum** (☎ 617-552-3000; www.bceagles.com; 140 Commonwealth Ave; ⊙ Nov-Mar; Ⓡ Boston College).

HOCKEY

From mid-October to mid-April, the Boston Bruins play ice hockey at the **Banknorth Garden** (Map pp300–1; ☎ information 617-624-1900, tickets 931-2000; www.bostonbruins .com; 150 Causeway St; Ⓡ North Station). College hockey is also huge in Boston, as Harvard, Boston College and Boston University teams earn the devotion of spirited fans. The competition culminates in April, when local college teams play the annual Bean Pot Tournament, college hockey's premier event:

Agganis Arena (Map pp308–9; ☎ 617-353-4628; www .agganisarena.com; Commonwealth Ave; Ⓡ St Paul St) BU opened this brand new fancy arena to host its basketball and hockey teams.

Bright Hockey Center (Map pp298–9; ☎ 617-495-2211; www.gocrimson.com; N Harvard St & Soldiers Field Rd; Ⓡ Harvard) Harvard's hockey team sits at the top of the Ivy League.

Conte Forum (☎ 617-552-3000; www.bceagles.com; 140 Commonwealth Ave; Ⓡ Boston College)

SOCCER

Boston's soccer team, the New England Revolution, plays at **Gillette Stadium** (☎ 877-438-7387; www.revolutionsoccer.net; Rte 1, Foxborough) from mid-April to early October. The cheapest tickets are $18, but for $34 you can sit right behind the team benches.

HORSERACING

From May to October, horseracing takes place at **Suffolk Downs** (☎ 617-567-3900; www.suffolkdowns.com; Rte 1a, East Boston; admission $2; ⊙ 12:45pm Mon-Wed & Sat; Ⓡ Suffolk Downs) in East Boston. Live racing takes place four days a week, but the track is open for simulcasting daily (free admission).

OUTDOOR ACTIVITIES

Boston's young, active population is always moving. Whether sailing on the River Charles or cycling along its banks, whether inline skating on a summer day or ice skating in the cold of winter, this energetic city does not miss the chance to get outside and get going. Miles of off-road trails and acres of parkland provide an excellent opportunity to escape the city traffic, as do the chilly waters of the Charles River and the Boston Harbor.

Equipment Rental

Ata Cycle (Map pp298–9; ☎ 617-354-0907; www .atabike.com; 1773 Massachusetts Ave, Cambridge; bike hire per day $25; ⏰ 10am-7pm Mon-Fri, 9am-6pm Sat, noon-5pm Sun; 🚇 Porter) Located between Harvard and Porter Sqs; convenient to the Minuteman Trail.

Beacon Hill Skate (Map p305; ☎ 617-482-7400; 135 Charles St S; per hr/day $10/25; ⏰ 11am-5:30pm Mon & Wed-Sat, noon-4pm Sun; 🚇 New England Medical Center) Sells and services skateboards, inline skates and ice skates. Convenient for skating along Southwest Corridor Park.

Bicycle Exchange (Map pp298–9; ☎ 617-864-1300; www .cambridgebicycleexchange.com; 2067 Massachusetts Ave, Cambridge; per day/week $20/75; ⏰ 9am-6pm Tue-Wed & Fri-Sat, to 8pm Thu, noon-5pm Sun; 🚇 Porter) Just north of Porter Sq. Convenient to the Minuteman Trail.

Boston Bicycle (Map pp308–9; ☎ 617-236-0752; 842 Beacon St; per day/week $25/$125; ⏰ 10am-7pm Mon-Sat, noon-6pm Sun; 🚇 St Mary's) Rents bikes and equipment; also offers customized bike tours through the affiliate Urban Adventours (see p72). This is a convenient place to pick up a bike for riding along the Emerald Necklace. You cannot bring your bike on the green line.

Cambridge Bicycle (Map p311; ☎ 617-876-6555; www .cambridgebicycle.com; 259 Massachusetts Ave; per day/week $25/$125; ⏰ 10am-7pm Mon-Sat, noon-6pm Sun; 🚇 Central) The Cambridge affiliate of Boston Bicycle. Convenient for cycling along the Charles River.

RUNNING & WALKING

Boston is a compact city, which makes it easy to get around on foot. Walking the city streets is in fact one of the best ways to get to know Boston (see the Walking Tours chapter, p124, for some suggested routes). If you prefer to stay off the streets, miles of trails through Boston's parks offer an easy escape from the traffic. The Boston Harbor Islands (p91) also contain many miles of unpaved trails to explore.

BACK BAY FENS Map pp308-9
☎ 617-635-7275; ⏰ dawn to dusk; 🚇 Museum
This narrow winding park is a long link in the Emerald Necklace (see the boxed text, p104). The Back Bay Fens, also called the

---

BOSTON MARATHON

Patriot's Day – officially celebrated on the third Monday in April – means more than Paul Revere's ride and 'the shot heard around the world.' Since 1897, Patriot's Day means the **Boston Marathon** (☎ 617-236-1652; www.boston marathon.org). Fifteen people ran that first race (only 10 finished); these days, the Boston Marathon annually attracts over 20,000 participants.

The 26-mile race starts in rural Hopkinton, MA and winds its way through the western suburbs of Ashland, Natick, Wellesley, Newton and Brookline to Boston. Some of the marathon's most dramatic moments occur between mile 20 and 21, on Commonwealth Ave near Boston College. The course runs through the notorious Newton Hills, which culminate at the aptly named Heartbreak Hill, rising a steep 80ft. It's all downhill from there.

Runners cruise up Beacon St, through Kenmore Sq, down Commonwealth Ave, turning right on Hereford St and left on Boylston St, and into a triumphant finish at Copley Sq (p99). This final mile is among the most exciting places to be a spectator.

Women began running in the Boston Marathon only in the 1960s. Roberta Gibb was the first woman to run in 1966, but she ran without properly registering, hiding in the bushes until the race start. The following year, Katherine Switzer entered as 'KV Switzer.' When race officials realized a female was running the Boston Marathon, they tried to physically remove her from the course. The official rules were changed in 1971, and the following year eight women ran the Boston Marathon.

The most infamous participant (loosely defined) is probably Rosie Ruiz, who in 1980 seemingly emerged from nowhere to win the women's division. In fact, it was determined that she did emerge from nowhere and had skipped most of the race. She was disqualified, but remains a marathon legend.

Other marathon celebrities include Rick and Dick Hoyt, a famous father-son team. Rick suffers from cerebral palsy, due to severe brain damage at birth. Dick is his father, who was determined to give his son the chance to pursue his passions, including sports. With Dick pushing his son in a wheelchair and using other special equipment, they have competed in 64 marathons and over 200 triathlons. The Hoyts have completed the Boston Marathon 25 times. Are you inspired yet?

BOSTON'S BEST REGATTAS & ROAD RACES

Boston's fastest fun:

Best Buddies Challenge (www.bestbuddiesmassachusetts.org) Cycle 20 or 90 miles, from the JFK Library in Dorchester to the Kennedy compound on Cape Cod, where everybody 'parties like the Kennedys.' Occurs annually in May.

Boston Marathon (www.bostonmarathon.org) The world's oldest marathon, attracting tens of thousands of ambitious runners to pound the pavement for 26.2 miles (see the boxed text, p197). Patriot's Day (third Monday in April).

Boston Triathlon (www.bostontriathlon.org) It's a sprint triathlon: short and sweet. Swim half a mile in the Boston Harbor, cycle 11 miles along Memorial Dr and run 3.1 miles through the Seaport District. Sunday before Labor Day (first Monday in September).

Head of the Charles (www.hocr.org) This famous rowing regatta is open to a limited number of singles, doubles and quads, though applications must be filed well in advance. The 3-mile course, from the BU boathouse to Artesani Park (just past the Eliot Bridge) features five bridge crossings and many twists and turns. Third weekend in October.

Tufts 10K for Women (www.tufts-healthplan.com/tufts10k) The largest 10K road race specifically for the ladies. Join more than 6000 women running through Cambridge and Back Bay, ending on the Boston Common. Columbus Day (second Monday in October).

Fenway, follows the Muddy River, an aptly named creek that is choked with tall reeds. Following the shoreline of this slow-moving waterway, the Fenway stretches south from the Charles River Esplanade (at Park Dr or Charlesgate East) and winds through the neighborhood of the same name, forming its border with Brookline. The Fens features well-cared-for community gardens, the elegant Kelleher Rose Garden, and plenty of space to toss a Frisbee, play pick-up basketball or lie in the sun. It's not advisable, however, to linger after dark.

CHARLES RIVER ESPLANADE
Map pp302-3

www.esplanadeassociation.org; ⓔ Charles/MGH
The southern bank of the Charles River Basin is an enticing urban escape, with grassy knolls and cooling waterways, all designed by Frederick Law Olmsted. The park is dotted with public art, including an oversized bust of Arthur Fiedler, long-time conductor of the Boston Pops. Paths along the river are ideal for bicycling, jogging or walking. The Esplanade stretches almost 3 miles along the Boston shore of the Charles River, from the Museum of Science to BU Bridge.

HARBORWALK Map pp302-3
www.harborwalk.org; ⓔ Aquarium
In theory, HarborWalk extends for almost 47 miles, following the perimeter of Boston Harbor north through Charlestown and south through South Boston and Dorchester, as well as across the harbor in East

Boston. In reality, the most accessible and best-marked portion of HarborWalk is along the Waterfront between Lewes Wharf and Fort Point Channel. The paved or boardwalk path weaves around the wharves and marinas, affording many magnificent harbor views. Christopher Columbus Park often hosts live musical performances on summer weekends, as does the Boston Harbor Hotel. Ponder David von Schlegell's *Untitled Landscape*, an odd piece of public art on India Wharf. Or admire the mega-yachts moored at the Commercial Wharf marina. This portion of the walk is very busy. To get off the beaten path, continue north around the edges of the North End or head across the Northern Ave Bridge to the less touristy corners of the Seaport District.

BIKING

More than 50 miles of bicycle trails originate in the Boston area. While riding through the downtown streets can be tricky, these mostly off-road trails offer a great opportunity for bikers to avoid traffic and explore the city on two wheels. You can take your bike on any of the MBTA subway lines except the green and silver lines, but you must avoid rush hours (7am to 10am and 4pm to 7pm weekdays) and always ride on the last train car.

Mass Bike (☎ 617-542-2453; www.mass bikc.org) is an excellent nonprofit organization with loads of information about bike trails, tours and other events, as well as details about biking laws in Massachusetts and other tips for riding in the city.

Rubel BikeMaps (☎ 617-776-6567; www
.bikemaps.com) produces laminated 'Pocket
Rides,' 50 different loop rides in greater
Boston or from area commuter rail stations.
For the metro Boston area, look for the 'BU
Bridge Bike Pack,' in which all tours start
from the bridge. See Bike Tours on p72.

CHARLES RIVER ROUTE
One of the most popular circuits runs along
both sides of the Charles River between the
Museum of Science and the Mt Auburn St
Bridge in Watertown Center (5 miles west of
Cambridge). The round trip is 17 miles, but
10 bridges in between offer ample opportunity to turn around and shorten the trip.
This trail is not particularly well maintained
(watch for roots and narrow passes) and is
often crowded with pedestrians. On Sundays
(mid-April to mid-November), Memorial Dr is
closed to cars between the Eliot Bridge and
River Rd, which helps to relieve some of the
traffic. See also p126.

EMERALD NECKLACE
This chain of parks runs through the middle of the city, from the Fenway to Jamaica
Way to Arnold Arboretum (see the boxed
text, p104). The packed dirt is fine for
mountain bikes and hybrids, but not really
suitable for road bikes. This shady path is
not as crowded as the Charles River route,
but beware of a few dangerous intersec-
tions and road crossings.

MINUTEMAN TRAIL
The best of Boston's bicycle trails starts in
Arlington (near Alewife station) and leads
10 miles to historic Lexington center (see
p246), then traverses an additional 4 miles
of idyllic scenery and terminates in the rural
suburb of Bedford. The wide, straight, paved
path is in excellent condition, though it gets
crowded on weekends. The Minuteman Trail
is also accessible from Davis Sq in Somerville
(Davis station) via the 2-mile Community
Path to Arlington.

SOUTHWEST CORRIDOR PARK
Almost 5 miles long, the Southwest Cor-
ridor is a beautiful paved and landscaped
walkway, running between and parallel to
Columbus and Huntington Aves. The path
leads from Back Bay, through the South
End and Roxbury, to Forest Hills in Jamaica
Plain. Take the orange line to any stop

between Back Bay/South End and Forest
Hills. Forest Hills Cemetery is also a pleasant place to pedal.

INLINE SKATING
All of the routes listed under Biking are also
suitable for inline skating (with the exception of some sections of the Emerald Necklace that are not paved). The most popular
spots are the Charles River Esplanade and –
on Sundays – Memorial Dr in Cambridge.

Inline Club of Boston (ICB; www.sk8net.com)
is a local group that hosts organized group
skates for different skill levels. Participants
must sign a waiver before participating in
the free events. Sunday morning city skates
depart at 10:30am from JFK Park in Cambridge (beginners and intermediate), while
Midweek on the Minuteman (MOM) departs from Arlington center at 6:30pm every
Wednesday. Departures are prompt so arrive early. Helmets required.

CHARLES RIVER SKATEPARK
Map pp300-1
☎ 617-619-2850; www.charlesriverskatepark.org;
East Cambridge; 🚇 Lechmere
This fantastic new facility is currently being
built in East Cambridge, underneath ramps
leading to the Zakim Bridge. The idea was to
create a state-of-the-art park that would lure
skateboarders away from the public plazas
and city streets. The 40,000-acre facility will
feature paved paths, ramps and jumps to
cater to skateboarders and inline skaters.
Parklands will eventually be connected by
a paved path to the Paul Revere Park in
Charlestown (see p84) and the HarborWalk
(opposite). Construction has started, but
fundraising is ongoing, so it's not clear when
the park will be open for skating business.

GOLF
While there is only one public course in
Boston proper, there are a few other options
in nearby Brookline and Cambridge.

BROOKLINE GOLF CLUB AT
PUTTERHAM
☎ 617-730-2078; www.brooklinegolf.com; Newton
St, Brookline; 18 holes weekday/weekend $30/45
The Brookline Country Club is famous for
hosting the 1999 Ryder Cup. You probably

can't get on that private course, but you can play next door at Putterham, a less famed but perfectly pleasant public course. Wide fairways and a lack of water hazards make this a suitable course for all levels. Take Huntington Ave west out of the city. Continue on Boylston St (Rte 9) when it enters Brookline. Turn left on Hammond St, then turn on Newton St at the rotary.

FRANKLIN PARK GOLF COURSE

☎ 617-265-4084; 22 Circuit Dr, Dorchester; 9 holes weekday/weekend $16/18
In the midst of Franklin Park, this 18-hole course is America's second-oldest public golf course. Apparently Grand Slam winner Bobby Jones honed his skills here when he was a student at Harvard. Take Columbia Rd south to Blue Hills Ave.

FRESH POND GOLF COURSE

☎ 617-349-6282; www.freshpondgolf; 691 Huron Ave, Cambridge; 9 holes weekday/weekend $21/25
About 2 miles west of Harvard Sq, the Fresh Pond is a nine-hole public course that wraps around the city's reservoir. It's easily accessible but the setting is suburban. Drive west on Mount Auburn St and turn right on the Fresh Pond Parkway and left on Huron Ave.

TENNIS

Besides these public courts, tennis courts at the local universities are also open to the public at various times.

Boston Common (Map pp302–3; ☉ 24hr; ⓡ Boylston or Park) The lights stay on at the Common all night, so you can come play tennis on these two courts after your night on the town. (Indeed, you have a better chance getting on the courts.) First come, first served.

Cambridge Ringe & Latin School (Map p310; ☎ 617-349-6279; 1640 Cambridge St, Cambridge; ☉ dawn to dusk; ⓡ Harvard) The two courts behind the Cambridge high school cannot be reserved; players are requested to limit their playing time to one hour when others are waiting.

Charlesbank Park (Map pp300–1; Charles St; ☉ dawn to 10pm; ⓡ Science Park) This newly revamped park along the Charles River Esplanade has four courts with lights. They are right next to the highway, so don't let the honking horns distract you from your serve.

North End Park (Map pp300–1; Commercial St; ☉ dawn to dusk; ⓡ North Station) A sweet neighborhood park looking across the Boston Harbor. Two tennis courts are not lit.

BOATING & KAYAKING

Between the Boston Harbor and the River Charles, boaters have plenty of opportunities to get out on the water. If you are not intent on doing the work yourself, see Boat Tours on p72.

CHARLES RIVER CANOE & KAYAK CENTER – BOSTON Map pp298-9

☎ 617-462-2513; www.ski-paddle.com; Soldiers Field Rd; rates per hr canoe $15-20, kayak $14-20, kids' kayak $7; ☉ 4-8pm Thu, 1-8pm Fri, 10am-8pm Sat & Sun early May–mid-Oct; ⓡ Harvard
Besides canoe and kayak rental, Charles River Canoe & Kayak offers classes and organized outings, including a Friday-night Barbecue Tour (per person $63, 6:30pm Friday, May to August), including an introductory lesson, a paddle along the Charles and a barbecue on the shores of the river. From Harvard Sq, cross the Charles and walk west along the river bank for about 20 minutes.

CHARLES RIVER CANOE & KAYAK CENTER – NEWTON

☎ 617-965-5110; www.ski-paddle.com; 2401 Commonwealth Ave; ☉ 10am-8pm Mon-Fri, 9am-8pm Sat & Sun Apr-Oct; ⓡ Riverside
The Newton branch of this outfit offers the same services as its Boston counterpart. The difference is the setting: this is a tranquil stretch of the Charles without the urban atmosphere. Known as the 'lakes district,' it encompasses 6 miles of flat water between Newton and Waltham. Rates are the same as the Boston branch, but there are also rowing shells available for $18 per hour if you can demonstrate your competence. A Moonlight Canoe Cruise (per person $39) is offered throughout the summer.

COMMUNITY BOATING Map pp302-3

☎ 617-523-1038; www.community-boating.org; Charles River Esplanade; per 2 days kayak $50, sailboat $100; ☉ 1pm-sunset Mon-Fri, 9am-sunset Sat & Sun Apr-Oct; ⓡ Charles/MGH
Offers experienced sailors unlimited use of sailboats and kayaks on the Charles River, but you'll have to take a test to demonstrate your ability. A 30-day 'Learn to Sail'

The cleanup efforts in the Boston Harbor have yielded more visible results. Several races take place in the harbor, including the Boston Triathlon (see the boxed text, p198). And there are a handful of decent, clean urban beaches that are great places to experience summer in the city. Besides the beaches listed below, see also Spectacle Island (p92) and Lovells Island (p92).

CARSON BEACH
Day Blvd, South Boston; 🕑 dawn-dusk;
🚇 Broadway
West of Castle Island, 3 miles of beaches offer opportunities for swimming in an urban setting. L and M St beaches are adjacent to each other along Day Blvd. Further west, Carson Beach has recently been revamped with a new bathhouse, a new fishing pier and – get this – new sand. All the beaches have nice harbor views, but it's not the most pristine setting to soak. The HarborWalk (p198) connects Castle Island to Carson Beach and continues all the way to the John F Kennedy Memorial Library in Dorchester (p121).

REVERE BEACH RESERVATION
☎ 616-626-4972; www.reverebeach.com; Ocean Blvd, Revere; 🕑 dawn to dusk; 🚇 Wonderland
Little remains from Revere Beach's heyday, when families would flock to this vacation wonderland. It was Boston's version of Coney Island, complete with dance halls, roller coasters and carousels. Now backed by high-rise condominiums, the crescent-shaped beach is not nearly so atmospheric. But you can still get Boston's best roast-beef sandwich at the famous beachfront sandwich shop, Kelly's Roast Beef. Look for the blue flag, which means the water is safe for swimming.

Swimming Pools
The state Department of Conservation & Recreation (☎ 617-626-4972; www.mass.gov/dcr) oversees outdoor public swimming pools throughout Massachusetts.

BOSTON COMMON FROG POND
Map pp302-3
☎ 617-635-2120; Boston Common; admission free;
🕑 11am-6pm daily Jun-Aug; 🚇 Park St
In summer, the Frog Pond on the Boston Common becomes a spray pool. OK, it's not

Community Boating (opposite) on the Charles River

package is $80, while a 60-day boating pass is $135.

COURAGEOUS SAILING Map p304
☎ 617-242-3821; www.courageoussailing.org; 1 First Ave, Charlestown; half-day $95; 🕑 2pm-dusk Tue-Fri, from noon Wed, 10am-dusk Sat & Sun;
🚇 North Station
The half-day fee allows you to take a Rhodes 19 out for a four-hour sail around the harbor. Otherwise, an unlimited month-long membership is $250. A variety of lesson packages, member clinics and organized outings are also available.

SWIMMING
Beaches
In the last decade, the Charles River has undergone a massive cleanup effort, which has been lauded as successful. Indeed, in 2006 the Charles River Swimming Club (www .charlesriverswimmingclub.org) hosted the first annual Charles River One-Mile Swim, the first open-water swim in Boston's beloved 'dirty water' (see p24). But that does not mean that just anybody can swim in the Charles. The swimming club conducted countless tests, monitored the weather and water flows and made special arrangements for a safe swimming dock along the Esplanade. The club estimates that the river will not actually be open for public swimming for another 10 years.

exactly swimming, but it's loads of fun for the little ones.

LEE MEMORIAL POOL
Map pp300-1

☎ 617-727-1058; 280 Charles St; ☽ 9:30am-5pm late Jun–mid-Aug; ⓢ Science Park

Located at Charlesbank Park, this facility has a larger pool with lanes for lap swimming, as well as a smaller wading pool for children. At the time of research, the larger pool was closed due to ongoing renovations at the park, but the wading pool was open.

VETERANS MEMORIAL POOL
Map pp298-9

☎ 617-727-1058; 719 Memorial Dr, Cambridge; ☽ 10am-6pm late Jun–mid-Aug; ⓢ Central

You can't swim at Magazine Beach, except for this swimming pool in the park. It's often overrun with local kids, but who can blame them for seeking refuge from the hot city streets at the cool city pool?

WHALE-WATCHING

Whale sightings are practically guaranteed at Stellwagen Bank, a fertile feeding ground 25 miles out to sea. The big humpback whales are most impressive while breaching and frolicking; in the spring and fall, huge pods of dolphins making their way to and from summers in the Arctic are also impressive. Trips are three to four hours with onboard commentary provided by naturalists. Dress warmly even on summer days.

BOSTON HARBOR CRUISES
Map pp302-3

☎ 617-227-4320; www.bostonharborcruises .com; 1 Long Wharf; adult/senior/child $35/32/29; ☽ 10am & noon Mon-Fri, 10:30am, 12:30pm, 2:30pm & 5:30pm Sat & Sun Jul-Aug; ⓢ Aquarium

Boston Harbor uses a high-speed catamaran, which (they claim) means less travel time and more whale-watching time on this three-hour tour. Outside of peak months, weekend cruises are also offered throughout September (10am Monday to Friday, 10:30am, 12:30pm and 2:30pm Saturday and Sunday) and October (10am Monday to Friday, 10:30am Saturday and Sunday).

NEW ENGLAND AQUARIUM WHALE WATCH
Map pp302-3

☎ 617-973-5277; www.neaq.org/visit/wwatch; Central Wharf; adult/child $32/26; ☽ 10am daily Apr-Oct, additional cruises May-Sep; ⓢ Aquarium

Naturalist guides explain how they monitor the marine life and collect data. Whale sightings are guaranteed (otherwise, you receive a coupon for a free trip at a later date). No children under 30in tall are permitted.

WINTER SPORTS

In Boston there is plenty of winter to go around. The snow usually arrives in December and it sticks around until March, if not April. While Bostonians maintain a long tradition of whingeing about the weather, they also know how to endure winter: that's right, put on your big boots and your warm, woolly hat and go out and play in the snow.

BOSTON COMMON FROG POND
Map pp302-3

☎ 617-635-2120; www.bostoncommonfrogpond .org; Boston Common; admission adults/children $4/free; ☽ 10am-9pm Sun-Thu, 10am-10pm Fri & Sat mid-Nov to mid-Mar; ⓢ Park St

In winter, the Frog Pond gets flooded for ice-skating. It's a fun, festive way to celebrate winter in Boston. Skate rentals (adults/children $8/5), lockers and restrooms are available. Weekends are often crowded, as are weekdays around noon, as local skate fiends spend their lunch break on the ice.

DANEHY PARK
Map pp298-9

☎ 617-349-4895; 99 Sherman St, Cambridge; ⓢ Alewife

This park sits on the site of a former city landfill. You wouldn't know it, though, for its lovely landscaping, running paths and fields. But it does explain that big hill in the middle of the park. And *that* is what draws thrill-seekers in blizzard (or post-blizzard conditions); it's the Boston area's best sledding. From Alewife T stop, walk a half-mile east on Rindge Ave and turn south on Sherman St.

FLAGSTAFF HILL
Map pp302-3

Boston Common; ⓢ Park St

Flagstaff Hill, topped by the Soldiers & Sailors Monument (see p78), is a popular spot

Activities

OUTDOOR ACTIVITIES

⚓RBAN ADVENTURE

It is a rare opportunity to camp in a major metropolitan area, but you can do it on the Boston Harbor Islands. Of the 34 islands contained within Boston Harbor's State Park, four of them allow camping: Peddock, Lovell, Grape and Bumpkin. To make reservations, contact the **Department of Environmental Management** (DEM; ☎ 877-422-6762; www .mass.gov/dem/parks/bhis.htm).

Each island has 10 to 12 individual sites and one large group site. Camping is allowed on Saturday from early May to mid-October and nightly between Memorial Day and Labor Day. For more information on the individual islands (and how to get there), see p91.

Keep in mind the following dos and don'ts:
- Do bring your own water and supplies.
- Do carry everything (including trash) in and out.
- Do hang your food high in the trees out of reach of animals.
- Don't bring pets or alcohol.
- Don't make open fires.
- Don't expect anything more than primitive sites and decomposing toilets.

for sledding when the wintry white stuff covers the ground. It's pretty tame, but central. Daredevil sledders will have more fun at Danehy Park (see opposite page).

RINK AT THE CHARLES Map p310

☎ 617-661-5096; adult/child $5/3, skate rental $5; ☾ 2-8pm Mon-Fri, 10am-8pm Sat & Sun Dec-Mar; ⊠ Harvard

The plaza in front of the Charles Hotel is a fine place for some pirouettes (or some plunges, as the case may be). The setting – in the shadow of the giant Christmas tree – is festive. The skating rink at the Charles is a relatively new phenomenon, so it does not get as crowded as the Frog Pond.

HEALTH & FITNESS

When in Boston, there is no need to forego your regular routine of downward-facing dogs or holistic aromatherapy. The city has plenty of health spas and fitness centers to meet your workout and chill-out needs.

GYMS & FITNESS CENTERS

In the dead cold of winter and in the humid heat of summer, Boston gyms are packed with type-As. The good news is that you can join them. Most hotels have some small fitness center on site (see the boxed text, p231) or they offer guests a discounted day rate at a nearby fitness center. Otherwise, join the Village People at the local YMCA.

CAMBRIDGE FAMILY YMCA
Map p311

☎ 617-661-9622; www.cambymca.org; 820 Massachusetts Ave, Cambridge; 1-week membership $40; ☾ 5:30am-10pm Mon-Thu, 5:30am-9pm Fri, 6am-7pm Sat, 9am-5pm Sun; ⊠ Central

Facilities include two gyms (with basketball courts etc), a full schedule of yoga and aerobics classes and a three-lane, 20-yard swimming pool.

CENTRAL YMCA Map pp308-9

☎ 617-927-8060; www.ymcaboston.org; 316 Huntington Ave; day rate $10; ☾ 5am-11pm Mon-Thu, 5am-9pm Fri, 7am-7pm Sat & Sun; ⊠ Northeastern

The admission fee allows access to a slew of classes, from yoga to Latin dance to virtual cycling. Other facilities include weights, circuit training, basketball courts and swimming pool. All facilities are well used, so be prepared to reminisce about high-school gym class. Check the online schedule for details.

WANG YMCA OF CHINATOWN Map p305

☎ 617-426-2237; www.ymcaboston.org; 8 Oak St W; day rate $10; ☾ 5am-10pm Mon-Fri, 6am-7pm Sat, 9am-10pm Sun; ⊠ New England Medical Center

This YMCA was recently renovated, making this one of the nicer Y facilities around. It offers cardiovascular equipment, free weights and various fitness classes. The 25-yard lap pool is open for lap swimming, or you can soak in the whirlpool. Childcare is also available.

Activities

HEALTH & FITNESS

MARTIAL ARTS

Since the 1960s, Taekwondo has become the most practiced form of martial arts worldwide, and Boston is no exception. Other popular practices are karate and tai chi, and you won't have any problem finding classes and clubs.

Besides these better-known forms of martial arts originating in Asia, *capoeira* is also an increasingly popular phenomenon in Boston. Capoeira is a form of martial arts with roots in Africa, but slaves brought this practice to the New World, where it was popularized in Brazil. Classes are held at various times and places around the city. Get more information from the **Grupo Capoeira Brazil Boston** (☎ 617-513-5858; www.capoeira brasilboston.com) or **Capoeira with Mestre Chuvisco** (☎ 617-259-5628; www.mestrechuvisco .com).

BOSTON KUNG FU TAI CHI INSTITUTE Map pp306-7
☎ 617-262-0600; www.taichi.com; 883 Boylston St; ☒ Copley
Offering a wide range of classes in Chinese martial arts and general fitness, including tai chi, kung fu and san shou. Classes include strengthening and conditioning and line drills, as well as practicing the forms themselves.

CW TAEKWONDO@BOSTON Map p311
☎ 617-876-4853; www.cwtkd.com; 600 Massachusetts Ave; ☒ 6:30-10:30pm Mon-Thu, 6-7pm Fri, 10:30am-1pm Sat; ☒ Central
This nonprofit Taekwondo club was founded by seven black-belt instructors who were all trained under Master Han Don Cho in Ithaca, NY. The friendly club offers evening classes in cardio kickboxing, self-defense and competitive Olympic-style Taekwondo.

JAE HUN KIM TAEKWON-DO INSTITUTE – BOSTON Map pp308-9
☎ 617-266-5050; www.tkd-boston.com; 102 Brookline Ave; ☒ 10am-9pm Mon-Fri, 10am-6pm Sat, 10am-4pm Sun; ☒ Kenmore
Grandmaster Kim founded this respected institute in 1974, and he still teaches some of the classes, alongside other certified instructors. Some classes are suitable for all levels, while others are designed specifically

for beginners or the more advanced. Other classes focus on sparring and stretching.

JAE HUN KIM TAEKWON-DO INSTITUTE – CAMBRIDGE Map pp298-9
☎ 617-492-5070; www.tkd-boston.com; 2000 Massachusetts Ave; ☒ 10am-9pm Mon-Fri, 10am-6pm Sat, 11am-4pm Sun; ☒ Porter
See left for review.

JKA BOSTON Map pp308-9
☎ 617-566-2966; www.jkaboston.com; 310 Harvard St; per class $10, 1-month intro $75; ☒ 6-8:30pm Mon, Wed & Fri, 4:30-8:30pm Tue & Thu, 9:15-11:45am Sat; ☒ Coolidge Corner
The Japan Karate Association of Boston operates this studio in Coolidge Corner. Classes include meditation and warm-up before proceeding to basic punches, kicks and blocks and Shotokan *kata*, or forms. More advanced classes also incorporate sparring. Classes end with calisthenics and warm-down. Beginners are encouraged to take a month-long introductory class (6pm Tuesday and Thursday), which begins the first Tuesday of every month.

DAY SPAS

When you are in need of some self-indulgence, Boston has no shortage of decadent day spas. Just wander down Newbury St for a virtually unlimited choice of places to get foot reflexology or hot rocks treatment.

CARRIAGE HOUSE SALON Map p310
☎ 617-868-7800; www.carriagehousesalon.com; 33 Church St, Cambridge; ☒ Harvard
The Carriage House is primarily a hair salon (and if you have curly hair, this is the place to have it done). But this welcoming spot also offers a full range of facial, massage and body treatments. Half-day ($105 to $140) and full-day ($175 to $205) packages are a relatively affordable way to treat yourself to the works.

DEBÚ SALON Map p305
☎ 617-292-3328; www.debuboston.com; 184 South St; ☒ 9am-8pm Tue-Fri, 9am-5pm Sat; ☒ South Station
Body treatments range from sea salt exfoliation to Monticelli mud wraps, while

EXTREME BOSTON

Boston does not pretend to compete with its West Coast counterparts when it comes to inventing and engaging in adventure sports. But that doesn't mean that Bostonians are not willing to give it a go. Here are a few options for the extreme-ly adventurous.

Boxing

'Old school boxing meets extreme fitness.' So goes the motto at the Ring, an old-time boxing club appealing to a newfound interest. Boxing clubs around Boston make a point of differentiating themselves from kickboxing and other aerobic workouts you might do at your local gym. This is the real deal: complete with boxing gloves and dummy bags. It's not pretty, but boxing is one of the best ways to burn calories and build muscle. Sparring in the ring is optional, but many boxers agree it is the most fun part of the workout.

Boston Boxing & Fitness (☎ 617-926-0362; www.bostonboxing.com; 125 Walnut St, Watertown; ✆ 4-11pm Mon-Thu, 4-9pm Fri, noon-5pm Sat) Offers special classes for women and kids.

Ring (Map pp308–9; ☎ 617-782-6946; www.ringboxingclub; 971 Commonwealth Ave; ✆ noon-10pm Mon-Fri, noon-6pm Sat; ⓡ BU Central) Take a free trial lesson and see what it's all about.

Kite Surfing

With a colorful kite overhead harnessing the wind, and a surfboard underfoot riding the waves, kite surfing combines the thrills of sailing and waterskiing. Kite surfing originated in the late 1990s on the West Coast, but it didn't take long for adventure-seekers in the east to follow suit. Now it's popular in beach areas. You'll find kite surfing operations on Cape Cod and the islands, and others along the New Hampshire coast, but only one outfit in Boston proper.

Leading Edge Kite School (☎ 617-650-5483; www.kiteboston.com; intro/full $80/150) Gives lessons in Pleasure Bay near Castle Island, as well as Nahant Beach in Lynn and other locations on Cape Cod. Introductory lessons demonstrate setting up the gear and choosing a launch site, as well as kite flying on land. The full lesson also includes body dragging (in the water) and water starts.

Rock Climbing

Combining physical challenge with high altitudes will give anyone a rush. Add a spectacular setting and that goes a long way toward explaining the appeal of rock climbing. The natural setting for this popular sport is the mountains – and the White Mountains are no exception – but a mountain face is not always so accessible, and weather can be prohibitive.

The Boston area has several impressive, state-of-the-art indoor climbing facilities with thousands of square feet of climbing walls, catering to climbers of all skill levels. All facilities offer instruction for beginners and clinics for more advanced climbers.

Boston Rock Gym (☎ 781-935-7325; www.bostonrockgym.com; 78 Olympia Ave, Woburn; admission $14; ✆ 10am-10pm Mon-Fri, 10am-6pm Sat & Sun) One of the first dedicated rock climbing facilities in the country. Take the Washington St exit off of I-95/Rte 128 and turn right on Olympia Ave.

MetroRock (☎ 617-387-7625; www.metrorock.com; 69 Norman St, Everett; adult/senior/student $16/12/12; ✆ noon-10pm Mon, Wed & Thu, 10am-10pm Tue & Fri, 10am-6pm Sat & Sun; ⓡ Wellington) The 17,000 sq ft of climbing walls includes some space dedicated to bouldering. MetroRock also organizes trips to the White Mountains for outdoor climbing. Take the free shuttle bus that runs from the T stop at Wellington.

facials hydrate, stimulate and invigorate. Also on the menu: waxing, tweezing, trimming, coloring, straightening, filling and painting. Receives rave reviews for the 'Bostonian bikini wax' – like the Brazilian, but not quite.

EMERGE BY GIULIANO Map pp306-7

☎ 617-437-0006; www.emergespasalon.com; 275 Newbury St; ⓡ Hynes

Occupying a gorgeous 19th-century town house on tony Newbury St, this day spa tempts both men and women. The mahogany Men's Club offers not only a shave and a haircut, but also manicures, pedicures, waxing and sport massage – everything the metrosexual in you might desire. Women are not neglected, of course, and there's a whole host of treatments (mostly massage) for couples. After being pampered, relax in the fireside lounge or the rooftop garden.

ÉTANT Map p305
☎ 617-423-5040; www.etant.com; 524 Tremont St; ⏰ 11am-9pm Mon-Fri, 9am-6pm Sat; ⓡ Back Bay/South End

The focus at Étant is not just on painting your nails or cutting your hair, but on 'well-being,' meaning acupuncture, aromatherapy and ear candling (a fancy way of cleaning out ear wax). Align your personal energy with an hour of polarity therapy ($80).

EXHALE SALON Map pp306-7
☎ 617-532-7000; www.exhalesalon.com; 28 Arlington St; ⓡ Arlington

If you are waiting to exhale, now you can do it. This subterranean spa specializes in very expensive facials, utilizing all kinds of light and laser treatments. A menu of acupuncture treatments – combined with massage, facials and detox programs – address health and wellness issues. A full schedule of Vinyasa and restorative yoga classes ($18 for 75 minutes) is also on offer.

G SPA Map pp306-7
☎ 617-267-4772; www.gspa.biz; 35 Newbury St; ⓡ Arlington

Lauded for its menu of 'Quickie' treatments, facials, massage, manicures and pedicures that provide a quick pick-me-up in 25 minutes or less. These speedy treaties save you time and money, as they are priced $45 and under. If you've got the time (and money), splurge on the 'Menage-a-Spa.'

YOGA

For detailed listings of yoga studios around the city, see www.bostonyoga.com.

BACK BAY YOGA STUDIO Map pp308-9
☎ 617-375-0785; www.backbayyoga.com; 1112 Boylston St; per class $15; ⏰ 6am-9pm Mon-Thu, 6am-7pm Fri, 10am-2pm Sat, 8am-8pm Sun; ⓡ Hynes

Services from massage to meditation, as well as all forms of yoga. Three to seven classes are offered daily, with a particularly full schedule on Sunday.

BAPTISTE POWER VINYASA YOGA – BOSTON Map pp306-7
☎ 617-423-9642; www.baronbaptiste.com; 139 Columbus Ave; per class $12; ⏰ 6:30am-7:30pm Mon-Thu, 6:30am-5:45pm Fri, 7:15am-4:15 Sat, 7:15am-6:45 Sun; ⓡ Arlington

Courses take place in a room where temperatures reach 90°F, allowing for great flexibility and lots of sweating. Four to six classes offered daily. Mats available to rent; bring a towel and drink plenty of water.

BAPTISTE POWER VINYASA YOGA – CAMBRIDGE Map pp298-9
☎ 617-661-9642; www.baronbaptiste.com; 2000 Massachusetts Ave, Cambridge; ⓡ Porter

See above for a full review. Walk two blocks north from Porter Sq.

BIKRAM YOGA – BOSTON Map p305
☎ 617-555-9926; www.bikramyogaboston.com; 108 Lincoln St; adult/senior/student $20/15/15; ⏰ 6am-7:30pm Mon-Thu, 9am-5:30pm Fri-Sun; ⓡ South Station

Baron Baptiste's number-one competition is Bikram Choudhury. Classes are 90 minutes long and go through a series of 20 poses in a heated room (arrive hydrated). The price includes two towels: you'll need them both.

BIKRAM YOGA – CAMBRIDGE Map p310
☎ 617-556-9926; www.bikramyogaboston.com; 30 JFK St, Cambridge; ⏰ noon & 6pm Mon, Wed & Fri, 6am & 6pm Tue & Thu, 9am & 4pm Sat & Sun; ⓡ Harvard

See above for a full review.

SOUTH END YOGA Map p305
☎ 617-247-2716; www.southendyoga.com; 11 W Concord St; $12; ⓡ Back Bay/South End

Offering courses in a variety of yoga forms, including Ashtanga, Mysore and Vinyasa. The number of classes is limited and the schedule of classes varies, so check the website to see what fits your schedule.

Activities

HEALTH & FITNESS

Shopping

Shopping

Boston is not famous for its fashion sense. But this town is getting more chic with each passing year, encouraged by the constant influx of students, internationals and other trendsetters. Boston, Brookline and Cambridge are good for bookstores and music shops; but they also boast plenty of bohemian boutiques, offbeat shops and distinctive galleries.

While these unique and fashionable shops will not thrill bargain-hunters, Filene's Basement will (see p212). Thrifty shoppers will find more than enough factory outlets and second-hand shops to test their pay-off-the-credit-card resolve.

The challenge for the souvenir hunter is to find something uniquely Boston. The city loves its sports teams, so you may go home with a Patriots jersey or a Red Sox cap. College gear is another obvious option: a Boston College sweatshirt, a Harvard insignia necktie, an MIT slide rule.

Many specialty food and wine stores whet the appetite of shoppers. For the ultimate edible souvenir, purchase a complete lobster dinner, packed in dry ice to ship or take home, from Legal Seafood (p144). See below for other suggestions for souvenirs made in Boston.

Shopping Areas

If you like to shop for the sake of shopping, go directly to the Back Bay. Between the swanky Shops at Prudential Center and Copley Place and the boutiques and galleries that line Newbury St, no other place in Boston offers such an enticing mix of high fashion, high art and high prices. Others may prefer the hustle and bustle of Downtown Crossing, where large department stores and smaller practical retail outlets cater to everyday Bostonians.

Beacon Hill is the traditional spot for antiquing, although Charles St is also home to cutesy boutiques, fancy galleries and neighborhood shops. In Cambridge, Harvard Sq has always been famous for its used bookstores and second-hand record shops. While critics complain about its undeniable 'mall-ification,' the student population guarantees that these vestiges of old-time Harvard Sq will never disappear completely.

Opening Hours

Stores are generally open Monday through Saturday from 9am or 10am until 6pm or 7pm, unless otherwise noted. Most are also open on Sunday from noon to 5pm.

Sales & Taxes

The state of Massachusetts charges a 5% sales tax on all items that are not considered necessities. Foodies and fashionistas will be happy to hear that food (purchased from a store, not a restaurant) and clothing (up to $175) are indeed considered necessities!

MADE IN BOSTON

Looking for a souvenir that is uniquely Boston? Check out the merchandise at these local retailers.

- **Aunt Sadie's Candles** (p214) Scented candles for any season. 'Greetings from Boston' candles available, but also fresh cut grass, pumpkin pie or the famous pine scent.
- **Cibeline** (p224) A designer-owned boutique for ladies in search of fun, flirty and (relatively) affordable fashions.
- **Hempest** (p216) Stylish clothing and soothing body products, all made from controversial cannabis.
- **Life is Good** (p216) Brothers Bert and John Johnson – and their lovable stick-figure friend Jake – tout their upbeat message on T-shirts and other gear.
- **New Balance** (p224) Avid runners swear that once you wear New Balance sneakers, you'll never run in anything else.
- **Temper Chocolates** (p218) To die for. Candies, cakes and even perfume, from the finest artisial chocolate.

BEACON HILL

There was a time when Charles St was lined with antique shops and nothing else: some historians claim that the country's antique trade began right here on Beacon Hill. There are still enough antique shops to thrill the Antique Rd Show lover in you; but you'll also find plenty of contemporary galleries, preppy boutiques and practical shops to go along with all that old stuff.

BOSTON ANTIQUE CO-OP

Map pp302-3   Antiques & Collectibles
☎ 617-227-9810; www.bostonantiqueco-op.com; 119 Charles St; 🚇 Charles/MGH
This cooperative antique market is a collection of 40 dealers under one roof. Most of the merchandise comes from area estates, so there is a good collection of furniture and household accessories, especially fine porcelain and textiles.

BOSTON RUNNING CO

Map pp302-3   Sportswear
☎ 617-723-2786; 121 Charles St; 🕐 11am-7pm Mon & Wed-Fri, 11am-3pm Tue, 11am-5pm Sat & Sun; 🚇 Charles/MGH
Note that this is a 'running company' not a sports shop. Here, former Olympic athlete and marathon record-holder Mike Roche brings his expertise to average-joe-runner. Using Video Gait Analysis (basically, he films you on the treadmill then replays in slow-mo), Roche will evaluate your stride and determine the best sneaker for you. All footwear and apparel meet his rigorous requirements.

EUGENE GALLERIES

Map pp302-3   Antiques & Collectibles
☎ 617-227-3062; 76 Charles St; 🚇 Charles/MGH
This tiny shop has a remarkable selection of antique prints and maps, especially focusing on old Boston. Follow the history of the city's development by examining 18th- and 19th-century maps; witness the filling-in of Back Bay and the greening of the city. Historic prints highlight Boston landmarks.

FLAT OF THE HILL

Map pp302-3   Women's Clothing & Accessories
☎ 617-619-9977; 60 Charles St; 🚇 Charles/MGH
This girly-girl boutique is filled with 'cute' things: look for bright colors and bold prints, jewel-studded accessories and smelly soaps and lotions. Technically, it's a gift shop – but any she-shopper with a hint of prepster in her will be tempted to treat herself too.

FRENCH DRESSING

Map pp302-3   Lingerie
☎ 617-723-4968; 49 River St; 🕐 11am-7pm Mon-Sat; 🚇 Charles/MGH
Crystal chandeliers, paisley prints and soft pink and blue hues make shopping for underwear the romantic affair that it should be. Putting the French accent in 'lingerie,' this sweet spot features light and lacy under-things, as well as luxurious loungewear. Great gift idea: membership in the thong-of-the-month club (now that's the gift that keeps on giving).

HELEN'S LEATHER

Map pp302-3   Shoes & Accessories
☎ 617-742-2077; 110 Charles St; 🕐 10am-6pm Mon-Sat, to 8pm Thu, noon-6pm Sun; 🚇 Charles/MGH
You probably didn't realize that you would need your cowboy boots in Boston. Never fear, you can pick up a slick pair right here on Beacon Hill. (Somebody is buying them, because this place has been in business for over 30 years.) Helen also carries stylish dress boots and work boots, as well as Birkenstock sandals, gorgeous jackets, classy handbags and sharp wallets and belts, all crafted from soft, supple leather.

KOO DE KIR Map pp302-3   Housewares
☎ 617-723-8111; 65 Chestnut St; 🕐 10am-7pm Mon-Fri, 10am-5pm Sat; 🚇 Charles/MGH
That's coup de coeur for you French-speakers. This innovative design shop aims to give patrons a 'strike to the heart' with its sexy, stylish home furnishings and accessories. The style is urban and sophisticated, but not cold or off-putting. Besides the interesting light fixtures, pillows and dishes, there is a small selection of gift-type items.

MARIKA'S ANTIQUE SHOP

Map pp302-3   Antiques & Collectibles
☎ 617-523-4520; 130 Charles St; 🚇 Charles/MGH
Over 50 years ago, a Hungarian immigrant opened this treasure trove in Boston's

antique central. Today, it's run by her grandson, but it still holds an excellent selection of fine collectibles – most notably jewelry, beads and pocket watches.

MOXIE

Map pp302-3   Shoes & Accessories

☎ 617-557-9991; 51 Charles St; Ⓡ Charles/MGH
'No outfit is complete without that perfect pair of shoes.' And 'Why have one bag when you can have a collection?' These bits of wisdom are what inspired avid shopper Karen Fadden Fabbri to open a store dedicated to shoes, handbags and other accessories. She pulls it off with much aplomb, enticing shoppers with unique styles, designer labels and top-notch service.

PIXIE STIX

Map pp302-3   Children's Clothing

☎ 617-523-3211; 131 Charles St;
Ⓡ Charles/MGH
This sweet boutique caters to 'tweens' – that awkward age between kid and teenager – and does so with cuteness *and* coolness, if that's possible. The fun fashions at Pixie Stix will appeal to mother and daughter with bright colors, bold patterns and preppy styles. Down the street, the Red Wagon carries equally adorable outfits for smaller tykes.

SAVENOR'S

Map pp302-3   Food & Drink

☎ 617-723-6328; 160 Charles St; Ⓡ Charles/MGH
Famous for catering to the likes of the legendary 'French Chef' Julia Child when she lived in Cambridge (technically, she shopped at the store's other location in Somerville). This gourmet shop is small, but packed to the brim with fancy selections of cheese, deli meats, freshly baked bread and pastries, fruit and vegetables.

WISH

Map pp302-3   Women's Clothing

☎ 617-227-0170; 49 Charles St; Ⓡ Charles/MGH
Some skeptics complain about the more-fashionable-than-thou attitude, but others argue that does not detract from the way-cool women's wear at Wish. Snazzy suits and sweaters by top-end designers have price tags to match; the dress selection is superb so it's a nice place to splurge on a special occasion gown.

Hilton's Tent City (below), outdoor adventure specialists

GOVERNMENT CENTER & WEST END

This institutional section of town is not much for shopping. But the warehouse-type buildings house a few gems for the serious bargain-hunter.

HILTON'S TENT CITY

Map pp300-1   Outdoor Gear

☎ 617-227-9242; 272 Friend St; ⏱ 9am-9pm
Mon-Fri, 9am-6pm Sat, noon-6pm Sun; Ⓡ North
Station
It's dusty and musty, but it boasts four floors of tents (set up to test out), as well as outdoor apparel, camping gear, backpacks and just about any other outdoor accessory you might need. From water shoes to snow shoes, from sleeping bags to duffle bags, Hilton's has it. Prices are competitive and staff members are helpful (they have to be because it's nearly impossible to find anything on your own).

NORTH END

Every visitor to Boston goes to the North End to savor the flavors of Italian cooking. But as a local community directory points out: 'Where do you think the chefs get their food from?' These old streets are filled with specialty markets selling imported food products, wine, spices, fresh produce, meats and seafood (see the North End Nosh walking tour on p130). The constant flow of foot traffic has started to attract funky boutiques and galleries, too.

DAIRY FRESH CANDIES

Map pp300-1   Food & Drink

☎ 617-742-2639; www.dairyfreshcandies.com; 57 Salem St; ☯ 9am-7pm Mon-Fri, 8am-7pm Sat, 11am-6pm Sun; ☯ Haymarket
Walking through the doors of this tiny storefront is like entering Charlie's Chocolate Factory, with its unsurpassed selection of nuts, chocolates, candies and dried fruit. To some, it's baking supplies; but to others, it's an irresistible array of sweets.

IN-JEAN-IUS Map pp300-1   Jeans

☎ 617-523-5326; 441 Hanover St; ☯ 11am-8pm Mon-Fri, 10am-7pm Sat, noon-6pm Sun; ☯ Haymarket
You know what you're getting when you waltz into this denim haven. Offerings from over 30 designers include tried-and-true favorites and little-known gems, and staff are on-hand to help you find the pair that fits you perfectly.

KARMA Map pp300-1   Used Clothing

☎ 617-723-8338; 26 Prince St; ☯ Haymarket
Designer consignments: that's what you'll find that this newish – and very upscale – second-hand shop. Look for the fanciest names in fashion, and not only the Italian ones. Also look for prices that are about half-off the original.

MODO GATTO Map pp300-1   Men's Clothing

☎ 617-523-4286; 424 Hanover St; ☯ Haymarket
Gentlemen, if your lady friend has vanished into the dressing room at In-jean-ius, you may wish to pop across the street to Modo Gatto to find your own pair of designer jeans. If the fashion doesn't do it for you, perhaps the baseball game on the big screen will.

NORTH BENNET ST SCHOOL

Map pp300-1   Arts & Crafts

☎ 617-227-1055; 39 North Bennet St; ☯ Haymarket
The North Bennet St School has been training craftspeople and artisans for over 100 years. Established in 1885, the school offers programs in traditional skills like bookbinding, woodworking and locksmithing. The school's onsite gallery sells incredible hand-crafted pieces made by students and alumni. Look for unique jewelry, handmade journals and exquisite wood furniture and musical instruments.

POLCARI'S COFFEE Map pp300-1 Food & Drink

☎ 617-227-0786; 105 Salem St; ☯ 10am-6pm Mon-Sat; ☯ Haymarket
Since 1932, this corner shop is where North Enders stock up on their beans. Look for 27 kinds of imported coffee, over 150 spices and an impressive selection of legumes, grains, flours and loose teas. Don't bypass the chance to indulge in a fresh Italian ice.

SALUMERIA ITALIANA

Map pp300-1   Food & Drink

☎ 617-523-8743; www.salumeriaitaliana.com; 151 Richmond St; ☯ Haymarket
Shelves stocked with extra virgin olive oil and aged balsamic vinegar; cases crammed with cured meats, hard cheeses and olives of all shapes and sizes; boxes of pasta, jars of sauce: this little store is the archetype of North End specialty shops. Shopping tip: inquire about the Rubio aged balsamic vinegar made exclusively for the Salumeria Italiana by an artisan in Modena, Italy. Made from Trebbiano grapes and aged in oak barrels, this is the secret ingredient of many North End chefs.

TUTTO ITALIANO Map pp300-1   Food & Drink

☎ 617-557-4002; 20 Fleet St; ☯ Haymarket
When they say 'tutto' they mean 'tutto.' All the products at this little grocery store are imported from Italy, including meats, cheeses, sauces and pastas. This little shop also carries a selection of salads and pasta dishes. Delectable frozen tortellini, ravioli and gnocchi tastes homemade.

V CIRACE & SON, INC

Map pp300-1   Food & Drink

☎ 617-227-3193; 127 North St; ☯ Haymarket
It's the third generation of the Cirace family that runs this North End institution. Established in 1906, V Cirace & Son carries an impressive selection of Italian wines and spirits. Other specialties include gift baskets and cigars – a veritable cornucopia of indulgences.

WINE BOTTEGA Map pp300-1 Food & Drink
☎ 617-227-6607; 341 Hanover St; 🚇 Haymarket
A relative newcomer, the Wine Bottega has a large choice of wines packed into a small space. It's a delightful place to browse, though you'll face a challenge if you're looking for something specific. Ownership is enthusiastic about little-known wineries, so the selection is eclectic – perfect for the adventurous oenophile.

DOWNTOWN

Downtown Crossing is an outdoor pedestrian mall with practical shops geared to everyday needs. Washington St, Winter St and Summer St are lined with stores selling music, books, shoes, clothing, electronics, jewelry, gifts and everything else your consumer heart desires.

With the recent closing of the Boston institution Filene's, the big department store that anchors the shopping district is Macy's. Never fear: Filene's Basement is under separate ownership and remains open in its original location (see below).

BRATTLE BOOK SHOP

Map pp302-3 Bookstore
☎ 617-542-0210, 9 West St; ⏰ 9am-5:30pm Mon-Sat; 🚇 Park St
Since 1825, the Brattle Book Shop has been catering to Boston's literati: it is a treasure trove crammed with out-of-print, rare and first-edition books. Ken Gloss – whose family has owned this gem since 1949 – is an expert on antiquarian books, moonlighting as a consultant and appraiser (see him on the Antiques Roadshow!).

CITY SPORTS Map pp302-3 Sportswear

☎ 617-423-2015; 11 Bromfield St; 🚇 Downtown Crossing
City Sports is second only to the Red Sox when it comes to T-shirts spotted around Boston. This local chain was founded in 1983 by 'a couple of local joes' who didn't have anywhere to buy sporting goods. Now City Sports is up and down the East Coast (including five in Boston and Cambridge), selling sports apparel and footwear, with a limited selection of equipment. And with that ubiquitous City Sports T-shirt, they don't even need to advertise.

LONDON HARNESS COMPANY

Map pp302-3 Leather Goods
☎ 617-542-9234; 60 Franklin St; ⏰ 9:30am-6pm Mon-Fri, 10am-4pm Sat; 🚇 Downtown Crossing
The history of the London Harness Company goes back to 1776, when local saddle maker Zachariah Hicks joined forces with WW Winship, a well-established trunk maker. This historic partnership claimed Ben Franklin as a customer, and today the London Harness Company is the country's

BARGAIN BASEMENT

The granddaddy of bargain stores is **Filene's Basement** (Map pp302–3; ☎ 617-542-2011; 426 Washington St). Originally, Filene's sold its overstocked and irregular items in the basement of the flagship store. Shoppers would flock from miles around for a chance to browse the merchandise at deeply discounted rates. The store became so popular that Filene's Basement started opening outlets in malls around metropolitan Boston and up and down the East Coast. But this is the original, right here on Washington St, in the basement of the original Filene's building (even if Filene's is no longer here).

It's not just the everyday low prices that make this concept so appealing. Items are automatically marked down the longer they remain in the store. With a little bit of luck you could find a $300 designer jacket for $30. In reality, the chances of finding something perfect are pretty slim, but that shouldn't keep you from trying!

The maddest day at Filene's Basement is the famous Running of the Brides, the annual wedding gown sale, typically held in August. Anxious brides-to-be in bodysuits and bikinis line up before dawn and stampede in when the doors open. They grab dresses at random, regardless of size or style. Participants estimate the racks are cleared in one minute or less. As mothers and friends guard the stashes, hundreds of women try on dresses in the aisles and negotiate trades for appropriate size. Those left standing after the melee usually depart with a designer gown at a fraction of retail price.

Even on a normal day, patience is a prerequisite for shopping at Filene's Basement. But it's a shopping experience unique to Boston; and you never know what bargain might be uncovered. For the time being, Filene's Basement remains open in its original location on Washington St. The future of the building is unsure, however. So Filene's Basement has also opened a huge new outlet in the Back Bay (see p216).

oldest luggage retailer (you can't buy saddles here anymore). Look for high-quality leather and classic styles in handbags, briefcases and suitcases.

WINDSOR BUTTON

Map pp302-3   Sewing Supplies

☎ 617-482-4969; 35 Temple Place; ☷ 10am-6pm Mon-Sat, to 7pm Thu; ☒ Park St

Windsor Button has Boston's most extensive collection of buttons and yarn, as well as sewing and craft products. Designer buttons, hand-painted buttons, leather buttons, seashell button... not to mention a whole line of New England themed buttons (lighthouses, lobsters, swan boats, etc) – the perfect souvenir for sewers.

WATERFRONT

The Faneuil Hall & Quincy Market area is possibly Boston's most popular tourist shopping spot: upwards of 15 million people visit annually. The five buildings are filled with 100-plus tourist-oriented shops, pushcart vendors and national chain stores.

BOSTON PEWTER COMPANY

Map pp302-3   Souvenirs

☎ 617-523-1776; 1 Faneuil Hall Marketplace; ☒ State

In the basement of Faneuil Hall, this specialty shop is pretty much what the name implies. Think tableware, picture frames and light fixtures, all crafted from the elegant metal. The collection is supplemented with other New England collectibles like scrimshaw, copper weather vanes and handblown glass.

BOSTONIAN SOCIETY MUSEUM SHOP

Map pp302-3   Souvenirs

☎ 617-720-3284; Quincy Market; ☷ 10am-9pm Mon-Sat, noon-6pm Sun; ☒ State

Run by the Boston Historical Society, the museum shop carries a good selection of souvenirs with the Americana theme: woven throws featuring flags, eagles and other all-American goodness; presidential prints; reproductions of Paul Revere's depiction of the Boston Massacre; patriotic themed coffee mugs, etc. The most clever souvenirs are in the food aisle: Boston Harbor Tea, Stars & Stripes pasta and other treats to enliven your next July 4th cookout.

BUILD-A-BEAR WORKSHOP

Map pp302-3   Toys

☎ 617-227-2478; 6 North Market; ☷ 10am-9pm Mon-Sat, noon-6pm Sun; ☒ State

Here's a cure for cranky kids. This fun store is 'where best friends are made.' Literally. Children pick out the cuddly creature they like, stuff it, give it a heart, dress it and create a personalized birth certificate. All furry friends come with a Cub Condo carrying case.

CELTIC WEAVERS Map pp302-3   Clothing

☎ 617-720-0750; 6 North Market; ☒ State

If you really wanted to vacation in the isles (the British Isles, that is), you may wish to bring home a souvenir from Celtic Weavers. Beautiful handmade sweaters, hats and blankets will keep the chill away on a rainy afternoon. Other items include expensive jewelry and fine china from Ireland, Scotland and Wales.

GEOCLASSICS Map pp302-3   Jewelry

☎ 617-523-6112; 7 North Market; ☷ 10am-9pm Mon-Sat, noon-6pm Sun; ☒ State

Geoclassics showcases minerals, fossils and gemstones in jewelry and other decorative settings. The natural beauty of the stones is enhanced by their artistic presentation. The collection of fossils – from dinosaur eggs to dragonflies – is incredible.

CHINATOWN, LEATHER DISTRICT & THEATER DISTRICT

This district is more for eating than shopping, but Chinatown is a great place to come looking for specialty Asian ingredients. Nearby in the Leather District, artists (and developers) are converting these former warehouses for studio and gallery space, so something is bound to catch your eye if you stroll down South St or Lincoln St.

BOSTON COSTUME

Map p305   Vintage Clothing

☎ 617-482-1632; 69 Kneeland St; ☷ 9:30am-6pm Mon-Sat; ☒ New England Medical Center or Chinatown

Perfectly placed to cater to the actors in the Theater District and the drag queens in the South End. In addition to costume rental, this vintage clothing store has fishnet stockings and feather boas. Why? You might consider picking something up before heading to Crypt night, Wednesdays at Toast (see p183).

CALAMUS BOOKSTORE

Map p305   Bookstore

☎ 617-338-1931; 92 South St; 🚇 South Station

Calamus – son of the Greek river god – was transformed with grief into a reed when his lover drowned. The character (and the namesake plant) inspired Walt Whitman's *Calamus Poems*, which celebrates gay love. And now, he has inspired Boston's biggest and best GLBT bookstore. With a full calendar of author talks and art exhibitions, as well as a regular electronic newsletter, Calamus is not only a bookstore but also a community center.

CENTRAL CHINA BOOK CO

Map p305   Bookstore

☎ 617-426-0888; 44 Kneeland St; 🚇 Chinatown

Tucked into a basement in the heart of Chinatown, this little bookstore carries fiction, reference and children's books, as well as CDs and DVDs. The impressive inventory (over 100,000 titles) is almost exclusively Chinese language products.

JACK'S JOKE SHOP Map p305   Novelty Shop

☎ 617-426-9640; 226 Tremont St; 🕐 9:30am-5:30pm Mon-Sat; 🚇 Boylston

Jack Goldberg founded his joke shop in 1922, which means this fun house has been cracking people up for over 80 years. Still run by the same funny family, Jack's carries over 3000 items: masks, wigs, magic, tricks, disguises, hats, noise makers, moustaches, exploding stuff, squirty stuff, stinky stuff, wacky stuff… wait, isn't this all wacky stuff?

SUPER 88 Map p305   Food & Drinks

☎ 617-423-3749; 73-79 Essex St; 🕐 8:30am-7pm; 🚇 Chinatown

The leading Asian supermarket chain in Boston specializes in exotic vegetables, tropical fruits and live seafood. Founded by a Vietnamese immigrant, Super 88 stores are successful because they appeal not only to Asian customers, but also to Boston's diverse, food-loving population.

SOUTH END

Deep in the throes of gentrification, the South End boasts ever-changing speciality stores along Tremont St, as well as an increasing number of galleries and quirky shops along lower Washington St, Shawmut Ave and Columbus Ave.

AUNT SADIE'S CANDLESTIX

Map p305   Gift Shop

☎ 617-357-7117; 18 Union Park St; 🚇 Back Bay or South End

Aunt Sadie's is famous for her namesake candles, it's true. But there is more to this little gift shop than wicks and wax. Besides the never-ending array of candles (summertime bestseller: Beach in a Can), look for bubble bath, smelly soaps, scented sachets and other sweet-smelling products.

FRESH EGGS Map p305   Housewares

☎ 617-247-8150; 58 Clarendon St; 🚇 Back Bay or South End

No, it's not an artisinal dairy in the heart of the South End, though you might see a baker's dozen for sale here. Its appeal, however, would be purely aesthetic, to complement some quaintly crafted basket or a carved wooden bowl. This sweet spot features 'everything for your nest,' and the eclectic selection includes clever kitchen gadgets, functional tableware and stylish furnishings.

PARLOR Map p305   Women's Clothing

☎ 617-521-9005; 1248 Washington St; 🚇 New England Medical Center

The selection of super-cool duds and hot name brands receives rave reviews all around, but it's the friendly fashion advice that makes Parlor so popular. Regulars agree that these girls know their stuff, and they want you to know it too. Parlor's alluring outfits often feature local designers.

SOOKI Map p305   Boutique

☎ 617-536-0809; 505 Tremont St; 🕐 10am-7pm Mon-Wed, 10am-9pm Thu-Sat, noon-5pm Sun; 🚇 Back Bay or South End

Sooki's wide-ranging product line is hard to categorize. Distinctive fashions in bold colors. Chunky, funky jewelry and sleek Italian leather goods. Luxurious throws and pillows; interesting, exotic glassware. And this sleek boutique does not forget your four-legged friend: the all-encompassing store has decked out Boston's most fashionable dogs with its cool selection of sweaters and collars.

SOUTH END FORMAGGIO

Map p305   Food & Drink

☎ 617-350-6996; 268 Shawmut Ave; ☽ 9am-8pm Mon-Fri, 9am-7pm Sat, 11am-5pm Sun; ☒ Back Bay or South End

Weave your way through this tiny store – past the shelves piled high with dry goods, past the eclectic selection of wines. Way in the back, you'll find what you're looking for: the cheese. The smallish case is virtually overflowing with artisinal cheeses: hard cheeses, soft cheeses, pungent cheeses, mild cheeses, spreadable cheeses, shredded cheeses. To really get to know your cheeses, join the cheesemongers for a Sunday-night wine and cheese pairing (per person $35).

SOUTH END OPEN MARKET

Map p305   Market

☎ 617-481-2257; www.southendopenmarket .com; 540 Harrison Ave; ☽ 10am-4pm Sun May-Oct; ☒ New England Medical Center

Part flea market and part artists' market, this weekly outdoor event is a fabulous opportunity for strolling, shopping and people-watching. Over 100 vendors set up shop under white tents. It's never the same two weeks in a row, but there's always plenty of arts and crafts, as well as edgier art, vintage clothing, jewelry, antiques, local farm produce and homemade sweets.

UNIFORM Map p305   Men's Clothing

☎ 617-247-2360; 511 Tremont St; ☒ Back Bay or South End

Modish men no longer need to feel neglected. With its cool collection of men's casual wear, Uniform is catering to you and only you. Hot men looking good in hot fashions: it's very South End.

BACK BAY

Boston's premier shopping street, Newbury St (www.newbury-st.com) is lined with chic boutiques, cafés and art galleries running the gamut from stodgy to funky. Second only to New York's Fifth Ave in price-per-sq ft, these eight high-rent blocks have some seriously tempting places to lighten your wallet. In addition to Newbury St, two luxurious indoor malls on Boylston St might entice you to part with your cash.

If you're not among the 'old money' elite, or you don't happen to have your father's gold card handy, do not distress. Even Back Bay has a few second-hand shops for those of us who don't mind gently used clothing, as long as the label is still legible. And if you are not buying, Newbury St is entertaining enough for its window-shopping and people-watching.

BEADWORKS

Map pp306-7   Beads

☎ 617-247-7227; 167 Newbury St; ☒ Hynes/ICA

For the creatively inclined, Beadworks has all the components for making your own jewelry. Come here for the impressive selection of shiny gemstones, hand-painted beads and other delightful charms. Avid beaders agree that much of this stuff is overpriced; so treat yourself to a rare stone or a funky bead but look elsewhere to stock up on supplies. There's another shop in Harvard Sq.

CLOSET, INC

Map pp306-7   Used Clothing

☎ 617-536-1919; 175 Newbury St; ☒ Copley

For shoppers with an eye for fashion but without a pocketbook to match. The Closet (and it does feel like some fashion maven's overstuffed closet) is a second-hand clothing store that carries high-quality suits, sweaters, jackets, jeans, gowns and other garb by acclaimed designers. Most items are in excellent condition.

CONDOM WORLD

Map pp306-7   Sex Shop

☎ 617-267-7233; 332 Newbury St; ☒ Hynes/ICA

Boston's best selection of condoms, in all sizes, colors and textures. Cinnamon-flavored condoms are not the only way to spice up your sex life, however. Friendly staff can also help you pick out lubricants, adult toys and other sex paraphernalia. And for the easily amused: provocatively-shaped ice-cube trays, pasta, and straws; X-rated fortune cookies; etc etc.

Shopping

BACK BAY

COPLEY PLACE

Map pp306-7   Shopping Mall
☎ 617-369-5000; www.simon.com; 100 Huntington Ave; ☽ 10am-9pm Mon-Sat, 11am-6pm Sun; ⓡ Back Bay or South End

This upscale site is much more than a shopping mall: glass walkways connect two luxury hotels, a first-run cineplex, a slew of restaurants and 100 elegant shops. Besides housing the only Neiman Marcus department store in New England, Copley Place contains other distinctive names like Tiffany & Co, Barneys New York and A/X Armani Exchange.

EASTERN MOUNTAIN SPORTS

Map pp306-7   Outdoor Gear
☎ 617-236-1518; 855 Boylston St; ☽ 10am-8pm Mon-Sat, noon-6pm Sun; ⓡ Copley

EMS is all over the East Coast, but it started right here in Boston, when a couple of rock climbers started selling the equipment they couldn't buy elsewhere. Now this tree-hugger retailer sells not only rock climbing equipment, but also camping gear, kayaks, snowboards, and all the special apparel you need to engage in the aforementioned activities. Additional stores are in Harvard Sq and on Commonwealth Ave near Boston University (BU).

FILENE'S BASEMENT

Map pp306-7   Department Store
☎ 617-424-5520; 497 Boylston St; ⓡ Copley

The new Back Bay location of this Boston institution is upscale compared with the original. You may appreciate the doorman at the entrance and the actual doors on the dressing room stalls; but you won't find the same Basement bargains.

GARGOYLES, GROTESQUES & CHIMERA

Map pp306-7   Art
☎ 617-536-2362; 262 Newbury St; ⓡ Copley or Hynes/ICA

'Goth boutique' seems like an oxymoron, but that's the most apt description of this dimly lit showroom of gloom and doom. Like the crypt of a medieval cathedral, the store carries a scary selection of gargoyles, sculpture and stained glass, much of which was salvaged from now-demolished churches.

HEMPEST

Map pp306-7   Clothing & Home Accessories
☎ 617-421-9944; 207 Newbury St; ☽ 11am-8pm Mon-Sat, noon-6pm Sun; ⓡ Copley

All of the products at the Hempest are made from cannabis hemp, the botanical cousin of marijuana. The idea behind this store is to bring hemp products into the marketplace and 'counter the misinformation and ignorance that has surrounded this plant.' It's all on the up and up: men's and women's clothing; organic soaps and lotions; and fun home furnishing items. These folks argue that hemp is a rapidly renewable and versatile resource that is economically and environmentally beneficial… if only it were legal to grow. A second store is in Harvard Sq.

LIFE IS GOOD

Map pp306-7   Clothing & Accessories
☎ 617-262-5068; 285 Newbury St; ⓡ Copley

Life *is* good for this locally designed brand of T-shirts, backpacks and other gear. Styles depict the fun-loving stick figure Jake engaged in guitar-playing, dog-walking, coffee-drinking, mountain climbing and just about every other good-vibe diversion you might enjoy. Jake's activity and message vary, but his 'life-is-good' theme is constant. Check out the sister store, Everything's Jake, in the Garage (p221) in Harvard Square.

LOUIS BOSTON Map pp306-7 Department Store
☎ 617-262-6100; 234 Berkeley St; ☽ 11am-6pm Mon, 10am-6pm Tue-Wed, 10am-7pm Thu-Sat; ⓡ Arlington

This beautiful four-story town house occupies the entire block between Newbury and Boylston Sts. As such, there is plenty of room inside for ultra-trendy (and pricey) clothing and cool, contemporary housewares. The 1st floor is filled with gift ideas like gourmet foods, fancy bath accessories, nostalgic books and sweet pet gear. Upstairs, you'll find the fashion: Louis caters disproportionately to the males of the species, but somebody's got to. If you have not reached your credit limit, when you're done shopping have a bite to eat at Restaurant L.

LUNA BOSTON Map pp306-7 Accessories
☎ 617-262-3900; 286 Newbury St; ☽ 11am-7pm; ⓡ Hynes/ICA

If you have a thing for handbags, then Luna has a thing for you. With a mile-long list of designers, Luna will have no problem finding you the perfect tote, clutch or satchel. Luna caters to the working girl with its great selection of stylish laptop carriers. Also beach bags, backpacks and baby bags.

MATSU Map pp306-7   Clothing
☎ 617-266-9707; 259 Newbury St; ☽ 11am-6pm Mon-Sat, 1-5pm Sun; ⊠ Copley or Hynes/ICA
This internationally inspired boutique sells exquisite clothing and gifts influenced by a Japanese Zen aesthetic. Matsu encourages shoppers to indulge their senses, with sweet-smelling fragrances, enticing, exotic music and clothing in a rich palette of colors and fabrics.

NEWBURY COMICS

Map pp306-7   Music
☎ 617-236-4930; 332 Newbury St; ⊠ Hynes/ICA
Any outlet of this local chain is usually jam-packed with teenagers clad in black and sporting multiple piercings. Apparently these kids know where to find cheap CDs and DVDs. The newest alt-rock and the latest movies are on sale here, plus comic books, rock posters and other silly gags. No wonder everyone is having such a wicked good time. Another outlet is in the Garage (p221) in Harvard Sq.

NIKETOWN Map pp306-7   Sportswear
☎ 617-267-3400; 200 Newbury St; ⊠ Copley
Covering some 9000 sq ft, this palatial footwear emporium is more of a destination than a store. Gone are the days when the shoe salesperson disappears into the back-room to look for your size. Here, they plug the numbers into the computer, and your shoe arrives via shoe-tube. While Niketown is a sight to see, you'll pay top dollar for your sneakers here, so there is no point in buying unless you have your heart set on Nike's newest styles. It's worth stopping by around Patriot's Day to check out the tribute to the Boston Marathon.

RICCARDI Map pp306-7   Clothing
☎ 617-266-3158; 116 Newbury St; ⊠ Copley
Fresh from Florence in 1978, Riccardo Dallai showed up on Newbury St and introduced Boston to European fashion. Ever since, his store has attracted Boston's hippest and hottest, who appreciate the ultra-cool-but-casual designs. Dallai's latest brainchild

is Relic, featuring more affordable, more denim-focused modes.

SECOND TIME AROUND

Map pp306-7   Used Clothing
☎ 617-247-3504; 219 Newbury St; ☽ 11am-7pm Mon-Fri, 10am-7pm Sat, 10am-6pm Sun; ⊠ Copley
This contemporary used-clothing shop is a gold mine of barely worn designer clothing (including lots of denim). Merchandise is all in perfect condition and no more than two years old. Come early and come often, because you never know what you're going to find; but you can be sure it will have a designer label. If you are interested in gently used designer furniture for your home, Second Time Around Furniture is down the street at 176 Newbury St. Additional clothing outlets are in Harvard Sq and on Beacon Hill.

SHOPS AT PRUDENTIAL CENTER

Map pp306-7   Shopping Mall
☎ 617-236-3100; www.prudentialcenter; 800 Boylston St; ⊠ Prudential
Back Bay's urban shopping center is home to many stores that you will recognize from your favorite mall back home. It also has two major department stores – Lord & Taylor and Saks Fifth Ave – and the requisite food court. Lest you forget you are not in Kansas anymore, let the elevator whisk you to the Skywalk Observatory on the 52nd floor (see p100).

SOCIETY OF ARTS & CRAFTS

Map pp306-7   Arts & Crafts
☎ 617-266-1810; 175 Newbury St; ⊠ Copley
This prestigious nonprofit gallery was founded in 1897. With retail space downstairs and exhibit space upstairs, the society promotes emerging and established artists and encourages innovative handicrafts. The collection changes constantly, but you'll find high-quality weaving, leather, ceramics, glassware, furniture and other hand-crafted items.

TANNERY Map pp306-7   Shoes & Accessories
☎ 617-267-0899; 402 Boylston St; ⊠ Arlington
It's not really a place to come for bargains, but the Tannery carries hundreds of top brands in fashionable yet functional footwear. These are shoes that you can wear

every day, and your feet will thank you for it. A second outlet is in Harvard Sq.

TRIDENT BOOKSELLERS & CAFÉ

Map pp306-7   Used Bookstore

☎ 617-267-8688; 338 Newbury St; ☺ 9am-midnight; 🚇 Hynes/ICA

Pick up a pile of books and retreat to a quiet corner of the café (see p151) to decide which ones you really want to buy. You'll come away enriched, as Trident's stock tends toward New Age titles. But there's a little bit of everything here, as the 'hippie turned back-to-the-lander, turned Buddhist, turned entrepreneur' owners know how to keep their customers happy.

KENMORE SQUARE & FENWAY

Because of its proximity to the Berklee School of Music, there are loads of stores selling new and used records and CDs, musical instruments and other noisemakers. Also, in the streets surrounding Fenway Park, there is no shortage of souvenir stalls, just in case you have not yet found that pretty pink Red Sox cap.

COMMONWEALTH BOOKS

Map pp308-9   Bookstore

☎ 617-236-0182; 526 Commonwealth Ave; ☺ 10am-7pm Mon-Wed, 10am-8pm Thu-Sat, 11am-7pm Sun; 🚇 Kenmore

Floor-to-ceiling bookcases provide the ambience at this little bookstore in the heart of Kenmore Sq. Specializing in arts, architecture, history, literature, philosophy, and religion, Commonwealth Books also has outlets on Boylston St and in the basement of the Old South Meeting House.

LOONEY TUNES Map pp308-9   Used Music

☎ 617-247-2238; 1106 Boylston St; ☺ 10am-9:30pm, noon-8pm; 🚇 Hynes/ICA

Vinyl junkies should not miss Looney Tunes, which claims a rotating collection of hundreds of thousands of records. They are not all packed into this tiny store near Berklee School of Music (though it feels like it) – there is another store in Harvard Sq and a huge stock of items in storage. All records are graded so you know the

condition of the product. Also carries CDs and DVDs.

TEMPER CHOCOLATES

Map pp308-9   Food & Drink

☎ 617-375-2255; 500 Commonwealth Ave; 🚇 Kenmore

Get a taste of the divine inside the Hotel Commonwealth. Indulge in this boutique selection of artisinal chocolates, each infused with an element of the exotic – hazelnut, espresso, or maybe mango. And chocolate is not just for eating anymore: sample Temporare, the line of custom perfumes.

BROOKLINE

Coolidge Corner is the commercial center of Brookline. While it's not a shopping destination in and of itself, there are shops and galleries to keep your credit card occupied.

BEST CELLARS Map pp308-9   Wine

☎ 617-232-4100; 1329 Beacon St; 🚇 Coolidge Corner

The team at Best Cellars believes that everybody should drink and enjoy wine as much as they do. They are dedicated to teaching their customers, encouraging them to discover what they like and then giving it to them at affordable prices. Enjoy nightly wine tastings (5pm to 8pm Monday to Friday and 2pm to 4pm Saturday) and prices mostly under $15. Cheers to that. Another store is located on Boylston St in Back Bay.

BROOKLINE BOOKSMITH

Map pp308-9   Bookstore

☎ 617-566-6660; 279 Harvard St; ☺ 8:30am-11pm Mon-Sat, 10am-8pm Sun; 🚇 Coolidge Corner

Year after year, this independent bookstore wins 'Best Bookstore in Boston.' Customers love the line-up of author talks, the emphasis on local writers and the Used Book Cellar in the basement. Extra long hours are also a perk.

CLAYROOM Map pp308-9   Arts & Crafts

☎ 617-566-7575; 1408 Beacon St; ☺ 10am-10pm Tue-Sat, 10am-8pm Sun & Mon; 🚇 Coolidge Corner

Clayroom will sell you the pottery piece you've been dreaming of, but first you have to make it. The concept is simple: pick out a piece (platter, trivet or coffee mug), summon up your inner Picasso and paint! The Clayroom takes care of glazing and firing, and your masterpiece is ready in four days. Great creative fun for anyone with an artistic eye.

GOOD VIBRATIONS Map pp308-9 Sex Shop
☎ 617-264-4400; 308 Harvard St; 🚇 Coolidge Corner

Now you can get good vibrations on the East Coast, too. This San Francisco-based, woman-focused sex shop offers 'sex-positive products,' not to mention newsletters, workshops and pleasure parties. Thinking of experimenting in your sex life? Here is your chance to get some ideas. No question is too probing for the ladies at Good Vibes. And it would seem that no product is either.

POD Map pp308-9 Gift Shop
☎ 617-739-3802; 313 Washington St; 🚇 Brookline Village

Befitting of its tiny space, Pod celebrates the art of minimalism. Organic lotions and body oils. Cotton towels and sheets in soft textures and soothing hues. Candles and incense giving off enticing aromas. There is a wide variety of goods – including women's and children's clothing – but the common theme is its simplicity and purity.

SIMONS SHOES
Map pp308-9 Shoes
☎ 617-277-8980; 282 Harvard St; 🚇 Coolidge Corner

Simons carries only a few designers, but the styles are unique, eye-catching and – above all – easy on the feet. Specializes in Dansko (famous for their ultra-comfy clogs straight from Denmark) and Naot (an Israeli brand known for flexibility and flair).

STUDIO Map pp308-9 Women's Clothing
☎ 617-738-5091; 233 Harvard St; 🕑 10am-5:30pm Mon-Sat, to 8pm Wed; 🚇 Coolidge Corner

The Studio has developed a devoted following for its always interesting but not-too-trendy fashions and its practical, down-to-earth advice. Women of all ages, shapes and sizes rave that the Studio helps them put together outfits that make them look and feel beautiful. What more do we want from our clothes?

WILD GOOSE CHASE
Map pp308-9 Gift Shop
☎ 617-738-8020; 1431 Beacon St; 🕑 10am-6:30pm Mon-Sat, to 8pm Thu, noon-6pm Sun; 🚇 Coolidge Corner

The 'Wild Goose Chase' refers to the search for the perfect gift. If you can't find it here, it's certainly not for lack of options. The store specializes in American-made crafts and so-called Judaica (mezuzahs, menorahs and more). If all else fails, go for the luxuriously colorful slippers by Goody Goody – in silk, velvet and suede, whose feet wouldn't appreciate the indulgence?

CAMBRIDGE

Harvard Sq (www.harvardsquare.com) is home to upwards of 150 shops, all within a few blocks of the university campus. The area used to boast an avant-garde sensibility and dozens of independent stores, and vestiges of this free spirit, remain. Certainly, there are still more bookstores in Harvard Sq than anywhere else in the Boston area. However, many of the funkier shops have been replaced by chains, leading critics to complain that the square has become an outdoor shopping mall.

Meanwhile, Massachusetts Ave – north of Harvard Sq – is still lined with quirky boutiques. And east of here, Central and Inman Sqs are welcoming the small-shop owners driven out of Harvard by rising rents.

HARVARD SQUARE

BERK'S Map p310 Shoes
☎ 617-492-9511; 50 John F Kennedy St; 🕑 10am-9pm Mon-Sat, 11am-7pm Sun; 🚇 Harvard

Berk's is a little store with a great selection of shoes – half for your sensible feet and half for your fancy feet. Prices can be prohibitively high, unless you hold out for the awesome end-of-season sales. You know they're going on when you see tables on the sidewalks piled high with shoes.

BOB SLATE STATIONER
Map p310 Stationery
☎ 617-547-1230; 1288 Massachusetts Ave; 🚇 Harvard

This old-fashioned, family-owned stationery shop is packed with pens, pencils and paper, plus gift wrap, greeting cards and

GET OUT OF TOWN

Harvard Sq's favorite landmark is **Out of Town News** (Map p310; ☎ 617-354-7777; Harvard Sq; 🚇 Harvard). Indeed, dating to 1927, it is a national historic landmark. This quintessential newsstand sells newspapers from every major US city, as well as dozens of cities around the world. Even if you're not looking for reading material, you need to know this place, as it's the top spot to hook up with friends coming off the T.

art supplies. It's been around since the 1930s, catering to Harvard students and other Cambridge writers and artists. Two additional, smaller stores are located on Church St and on Massachusetts Ave near Porter Sq.

CAMBRIDGE ARTISTS COOPERATIVE

Map p310   Arts & Crafts

☎ 617-868-4434; 59A Church St; 🚇 Harvard
Owned and operated by Cambridge artists, this three-floor gallery displays an ever-changing exhibit of their work. The pieces are crafty – handmade jewelry, woven scarves, leather products and pottery. The craftspeople double as sales staff, so you may get to meet the creative force behind your souvenir.

CARDULLO'S GOURMET SHOP

Map p310   Food & Drink

☎ 617-491-8888; 6 Brattle St; 🚇 Harvard
We've never seen so many goodies packed into such a small space. You'll find every sort of imported edible your heart desires,

from caviar to chocolate. The excellent selection of New England products is a good source for souvenirs. Cardullo's newest gourmet 'treat' is flavored edible bugs – that's right, crickets, scorpions and ants, organically grown and charmingly packaged. That's got to be a good source of protein.

CLOTHWARE Map p310   Women's Clothing

☎ 617-661-6441; 52 Brattle St; 🚇 Harvard
When Clothware started way back when, it produced its own original line of clothing. These days, the boutique carries a variety of designers, but it remains true to the fashion ideals that won over its loyal customers: vibrant colors, clean lines and durable fabrics. This is fashion for notoriously unfashionable Cantabrigians, who value comfort over cool.

COLONIAL DRUG Map p310   Pharmacy

☎ 617-864-2222; 49 Brattle St; ⏱ 8am-7pm Mon-Fri, 8am-6pm Sat; 🚇 Harvard
This old-time apothecary carries hundreds of scents, including many hard-to-find

fragrances which are their specialty. Besides cosmetics, colognes and soaps they also stock old-fashioned shaving kits – complete with razor, bowl and brush – like your grandfather used to use.

COOP Map p310 Bookstore

☎ 617-499-2000; 1400 Mass Ave; ☾ 9am-10pm Mon-Sat, 10am-9pm Sun; ◉ Harvard

Harvard students started this cooperative bookstore back in 1882, when they needed a place to buy books, school supplies and wood to stoke their stove. They don't sell wood here anymore, but you will find three floors of books and other 'essentials.' At the branch on Palmer St, anyone can buy just about anything emblazoned with the Harvard logo. Alas, the place is now owned by Barnes & Noble.

CURIOUS GEORGE GOES TO WORDSWORTH

Map p310 Children's Bookstore

☎ 617-498-0062; 1 John F Kennedy St; ◉ Harvard

In the olden days, there was Wordsworth, a great independent bookstore, and there was Curious George goes to Wordsworth, the separate shop for children's books. Wordsworth has since gone the way of the independent bookstore, but Curious George Store continues to thrive. Of course you can find your favorite story about that mischievous monkey, but there are also thousands of other books and toys to choose from.

DICKSON BROS Map p310 Hardware Store

☎ 617-876-6760; 26 Brattle St; ☾ 8:30am-6pm Mon-Sat, 10am-4pm Sun; ◉ Harvard

Locals know that you can find just about anything you need for your home at this old-timer hardware store. From house paint to cleaning supplies, from kitchen accessories to storage bins, it's all crammed into this three-story space in the heart of Harvard Sq.

GARAGE Map p310 Shopping Mall

36 John F Kennedy St; ◉ Harvard

This mini mall in the midst of Harvard Sq houses an eclectic collection of shops and a good food court. Highlights include Newbury Comics (see p217) and Everything's Jake (see Life is Good on p216), as well as the crazy costume store Hootenanny.

GLOBE CORNER BOOKSTORE

Map p310 Bookstore

☎ 617-497-6277; www.globecorner.com; 90 Mount Auburn St; ☾ 9:30am-9pm Mon-Sat, 11am-6pm Sun; ◉ Harvard

In new digs, the Globe Corner Bookstore specializes in travel literature, guide books and maps. There is no better selection of books about Boston and New England. Also, a great source of topographical maps. Look here for the latest Lonely Planet guide.

GROLIER POETRY BOOKSHOP

Map p310 Bookstore

☎ 617-547-4648; 6 Plympton St; ◉ Harvard

Founded in 1927, Grolier is the oldest – and perhaps the most famous – poetry bookstore in the USA. Through the years, TS Eliot, ee cummings, Marianne Moore and Allen Ginsberg all passed through these doors. Today, Grolier continues to foster young poets and poetry-readers. Besides selling written and spoken poetry, the store hosts readings and festivals.

HARVARD BOOKSTORE

Map p310 Bookstore

☎ 617-661-1515; 1256 Massachusetts Ave; ☾ 9am-11pm Mon-Sat, 10am-10pm Sun; ◉ Harvard

Family-owned and operated since 1932, the Harvard Bookstore is not officially affiliated with the university, but it is the university community's favorite place to come to browse. While the shop maintains an academic focus, there is plenty of fiction for the less lofty, as well as used books and bargain books in the basement.

HARVARD UNIVERSITY PRESS DISPLAY ROOM Map p310 Bookstore

☎ 617-495-2625; 1350 Massachusetts Ave, Holyoke Center; ☾ 9am-7pm Mon-Sat, noon-6pm Sun; ◉ Harvard

For all the latest releases from Harvard University Press, stop by its little showroom in Holyoke Center. The Bargain Alcove sells slightly damaged books for half-price or less.

IN YOUR EAR Map p310 Used Music

☎ 617-491-5035; 72 Mount Auburn St; ◉ Harvard

In an out-of-the-way spot on the edge of the square, this underground (literally) record shop is everything it should be.

Crammed with LPs and 45s, there's also a huge selection of CDs, DVDs and even eight-tracks. The albums on the wall will catch your eye, but they are expensive; look down below for unbelievable bargains.

JASMINE SOLA & SOLA MEN

Map p310   Clothing & Shoes

☎ 617-354-6043; 37 Brattle St; 🚇 Harvard

With multiple stores in the Prudential Center and on Newbury St, Jasmine Sola has a devoted following of fashion fans, who are effusive about its great selection of sexy dresses, cool jeans and funky jewelry. This outlet is the largest and it keeps expanding, now offering shoes, denim and men's fashions. If you are put off by the high prices, visit the warehouse store on Commonwealth Ave in Brighton.

MUDO Map p310   Women's Clothing

☎ 617-876-8846; 9 John F Kennedy St; 🕑 10am-7pm Mon-Thu, 10am-8pm Fri & Sat, noon-7pm Sun; 🚇 Harvard

Tiny tops and slinky jeans. Shimmering dresses and strappy sandals. Short skirts and tall boots. Come here to clothe yourself for a night on the town. It's not exactly practical (or cheap), but such fun never is. Another branch is on Newbury St.

OONA'S EXPERIENCED CLOTHING

Map p310   Used Clothing

☎ 617-491-2654; 1210 Massachusetts Ave; 🚇 Harvard

Oona's sells kitschy clothes from all eras. Dress-up dandies come here for Halloween costumes, drag wear, retro attire from any decade and outfits for every theme. Not that you need an excuse to go vintage: Oona's merchandise is cheap enough that you can buy it just for fun.

RAVEN USED BOOKS Map p310   Used Books

☎ 617-441-6999; 52 John F Kennedy St; 🕑 10am-9pm Mon-Thu, 10am-10pm Fri & Sat, 10am-8pm Sun; 🚇 Harvard

It's refreshing to see a used bookstore open in Harvard Sq, where the trend is that rising rents and increasing competition are driving independent shops out. Tucked into a tiny basement, Raven knows its audience: its 14,000 titles focus on scholarly titles, especially in the liberal arts. Bibliophiles

Shopping

CAMBRIDGE

CLOTHING SIZES

Measurements approximate only, try before you buy

Women's Clothing

Aus/UK	8	10	12	14	16	18
Europe	36	38	40	42	44	46
Japan	5	7	9	11	13	15
USA	6	8	10	12	14	16

Women's Shoes

Aus/USA	5	6	7	8	9	10
Europe	35	36	37	38	39	40
France only	35	36	38	39	40	42
Japan	22	23	24	25	26	27
UK	3½	4½	5½	6½	7½	8½

Men's Clothing

Aus	92	96	100	104	108	112
Europe	46	48	50	52	54	56
Japan	S		M	M		L
UK/USA	35	36	37	38	39	40

Men's Shirts (Collar Sizes)

Aus/Japan	38	39	40	41	42	43
Europe	38	39	40	41	42	43
UK/USA	15	15½	16	16½	17	17½

Men's Shoes

Aus/UK	7	8	9	10	11	12
Europe	41	42	43	44½	46	47
Japan	26	27	27½	28	29	30
USA	7½	8½	9½	10½	11½	12½

agree that the quality and condition of books is top-notch.

SCHOENHOF'S FOREIGN BOOKS

Map p310   Bookstore

☎ 617-547-8855; 76A Mt Auburn St; 🚇 Harvard

Since 1856, Schoenhof's has been providing Boston's foreign-language-speaking literati with reading material. Special booklists keep regulars abreast of new arrivals in their language of choice, whether it's scholarly or literary works, language instruction materials or children's books. If you are wondering which languages and dialects are available, the official count is over 700, so Schoenhof's probably has you covered.

CENTRAL SQUARE

CHEAPO RECORDS Map p311   Used Music

☎ 617-354-4455; 538 Massachusetts Ave; 🕑 10am-6pm Mon-Wed, 10am-9pm Thu-Sat, 11am-5pm Sun; 🚇 Central

With tunes blasting out from its new digs, Cheapo Records lures music-lovers to browse through its huge selection of vinyl and decent selection of CDs. And yes, they really are cheap-o. Don't come here looking for a new release, though. These are oldies but goodies: classic rock, R&B, jazz and blues.

HARVEST CO-OP Map p311 — Food & Drink

☎ 617-661-1580; 581 Massachusetts Ave; ⏰ 8am-10pm; 🚇 Central

Socially conscious shoppers will appreciate this cooperative market. Besides being community owned, Harvest also supports sustainable agriculture, certified organic, fair trade, and local and small family farms. In front of the store, the Café @ Harvest is a pleasant place to stop for lunch (and there is free wi-fi access).

SANDY'S MUSIC

Map p311 — Musical Instruments

☎ 617-491-2812; 896A Massachusetts Ave; 🚇 Central

Bills itself as 'Cambridge's funkiest music shop.' Sandy is quite a character: a DJ on the local folk radio program, self-proclaimed 'banjo maniac,' and purveyor of all things stringed, including acoustic and electric guitars, mandolins, fiddles, basses, ukuleles and more. If you're into folk, stop by for the weekly Old Timey Jam (8pm Monday).

TEN THOUSAND VILLAGES

Map p311 — Imported Goods

☎ 617-876-2414; 694 Massachusetts Ave; 🚇 Central

A unique nonprofit store, Ten Thousand Villages imports handicrafts from developing countries for a fair price, so you won't find any incredible bargains here. On the other hand, the craftsmanship on baskets, pottery and textiles is excellent, and you can rest easy knowing your purchase helps to pay for food, education, health care or housing for somebody who needs it.

INMAN SQUARE

LOREM IPSUM Map p311 — Used Bookstore

☎ 617-497-7669; 157 Hampshire St; 🚇 Central

Thanks to fancy inventory-tracing software developed inhouse, you can browse Lorem Ipsum's extensive catalogue online. But why would you want to, if you can go to the brick and mortar bookstore and browse the old-fashioned way. Floor-to-ceiling shelves, hardwood floors and lots and lots of books. Anyone with voyeuristic tendencies should visit the restroom to peruse the collection of personal notes, things-to-do and shopping lists, garnered from the used books.

STELLA BELLA Map p311 — Toys

☎ 617-491-6290; 1360 Cambridge St; 🚇 Central

If you would let them, kids could play all day at Stella Bella. Toys are strewn across the floor in the designated play area, and kids are busy building blocks, making music and reading books. Even parents can't keep from playing (the challenge is keeping them in the designated play area). Stella Bella is especially strong for creative and educational toys and games.

KENDALL SQUARE

GARMENT DISTRICT

Map p311 — Vintage Clothing

☎ 617-876-5230; 200 Broadway; ⏰ 11am-9pm Sun-Fri, 9am-9pm Sat; 🚇 Kendall

If your memories of the fashion-conscious '60s and '70s have faded like an old pair of jeans, this store will bring it all back. Downstairs, Dollar-a-Pound has different merchandise and pricing methods. Like a flea market gone berserk, piles of clothing are dumped on the warehouse floor and folks wade through it looking for their needle in the haystack. Upon checkout, your pile is weighed and you pay 'by the pound.' The price per pound is usually $1.50, but on Friday it's lowered in order to move the merchandise faster.

EAST CAMBRIDGE

CAMBRIDGE ANTIQUE MARKET

Map pp298-9 — Antiques

☎ 617-868-9655; 201 McGrath-O'Brien Hwy; ⏰ 11am-6pm Tue-Sun; 🚇 Lechmere

This old brick warehouse looks foreboding from the outside, but inside is an antiquer's paradise. With over 150 dealers on five floors, this antique market is a trove of trash and treasures. The constant turnover of dealers lends a flea market feel, guaranteeing that you never know what you will find.

CAMBRIDGESIDE GALLERIA

Map p311   Shopping Mall

☎ 617-621-8666; 100 Cambridgeside Place;

🕙 10am-9:30pm Mon-Sat, 11am-7pm Sun;

🚇 Lechmere

A shopping mall in the old-fashioned sense of the word. Three floors of Anywhere, USA stores include a gigantic Best Buy and a Borders bookstore. Sears and Filene's are the department stores that anchor the place down.

OUTSKIRTS

BRIGHTON

NEW BALANCE FACTORY STORE

Map pp298-9   Sportswear

☎ 877-623-7867; 40 Life St, Brighton

Factory seconds and overruns of running shoes, fleece jackets and synthetic clothing made by New Balance. You may have to search for your size, but you can easily save 25% to 50% off any given item. Look for the automatic 20% reduction when you trade in an old pair of shoes of any brand. This place is not so easy to find: take bus 64 from Central Sq.

SOMERVILLE

CHINOOK OUTDOOR ADVENTURE

Map pp298-9   Sportswear

☎ 617-776-8616; 93 Holland St; 🚇 Davis

Chinook knows its market – selling warm, fuzzy fleeces to the Cambridge-Somerville area's young, active types. This adventure boutique features durable, comfortable and fashionable brands like Horny Toad, Icebreaker and Prana; sports sandals and boots are by Teva, Keen, Dansko and Ugg. Even your little guys (kids, that is) will stay warm in Polartec blankets, hats and jackets.

CIBELINE

Map pp298-9   Women's Clothing & Accessories

☎ 617-625-2229; 85 Holland St; 🚇 Davis

Showcasing the fashions of local designer Cibeline Sariano, whom you'll probably see working in her sewing room attached to the boutique. Her Hepburn-inspired styles include gorgeous gowns, classic jackets, fun and fresh skirts and slacks. An annual 'swap and shop' lets you clean out your closet and trade those clothes you no longer wear for somebody else's gently worn outfit.

MCINTYRE & MOORE BOOKSELLERS

Map pp298-9   Used Bookstore

☎ 617-629-4840; 255 Elm St; 🕙 10am-11pm Mon-Sat, noon-11pm Sun; 🚇 Davis

McIntyre & Moore is one of Boston's best and biggest used bookstores, with over 85,000 titles in 200 subject areas. Subject matter ranges from scholarly to New Age to fiction, with an excellent selection of children's books and even cookbooks. This well-organized place is great for browsing. Also home of the Davis Sq Philosophy Cafe, which meets here monthly (from 7:30pm to 9:30pm, every third Tuesday).

Sleeping

Sleeping

From poor student backpackers to high-class business travelers, Boston's tourist industry caters to all types of visitors. That means the city offers a complete range of accommodations, from dorms and hostels, to inviting guesthouses in historic quarters, to swanky hotels with all the amenities.

Most hotels, particularly upscale chains, have no set rates. Instead, rates fluctuate seasonally, if not daily. The high season for hotel rates is roughly defined as April through October, although it's more accurately driven by occupancy and high-profile events. So holidays, university graduations, baseball games and pride parades all affect hotel rates. Rates quoted do not include the 12.45% room tax (not applicable to B&Bs).

Keep in mind that calling a hotel will rarely yield the cheapest rates. Hotels often offer their rack rate, which is a base rate with no discount or special criteria applied. No smart traveler should ever pay rack rates, however. Better rates are almost always available via hotel websites, booking services (p270) and bidding and discount websites (see the boxed text, opposite).

Rates quoted in this book are based on published rack rates. You can count on finding rooms for less than $125 at any of the budget accommodation options. Midrange rates run between $125 and $250, while top-end hotels charge $250 and up.

PRICE GUIDE	
$	under $100
$$	$100 to $200
$$$	more than $200

B&Bs

Boston B&Bs haven't exactly sprouted like weeds in city sidewalks, but visitors will find a range from budget to fancy. With the exceptions noted in the text, your best bet is to contact an agency that will try to match your neighborhood desires with the thickness of your wallet. Another benefit is there's no room tax on B&Bs with fewer than three rooms.

Bed & Breakfast Agency of Boston (☎ 617-720-3540, 800-248-9262, 0800-89-5128 free from the UK; fax 617-523-5761; www.boston-bnbagency.com) Lists over 100 different properties, including B&Bs (single $70 to $90, double $100 to $160) and furnished apartments (studios $90 to $140, one-bedroom apartments $120 to $180). Properties are located in Beacon Hill, Back Bay, North End and South End. Many are pet-friendly and all offer weekly and monthly rates, as well as the occasional low-season deal.

Bed & Breakfast Associates Bay Colony (☎ 781-449-5302, 888-486-6018, from UK 08-234-7113; www.bnbboston.com) A huge database of furnished rooms and apartments in Boston, Brookline, Cambridge and the suburbs. Most are unhosted. Prices vary but weekly and monthly rates are usually available.

Private Homes

The internet is a mine of information about apartment rentals, home swaps and other person-to-person methods of finding a place to stay. Check out the following websites for more:

Craig's List (www.boston.craigslist.org) The mother of all informal exchanges. You can find anything on Craig's List, including vacation rentals, house swaps, roommates, summer sublets and more. See 'housing'.

CouchSurfing.com (www.couchsurfing.com) This innovative site allows individuals to take advantage of the hospitality of fellow travelers, crashing on couches or staying in guest rooms. Couchsurfing does not – obviously – allow for too much privacy, but it's a great way to make

BOOK ACCOMMODATIONS ONLINE

For more accommodation reviews and recommendations by Lonely Planet authors, check out the online booking service at www.lonelyplanet.com. You'll get the true, insider lowdown on the best places to stay. Reviews are thorough and independent. Best of all, you can book online.

BIDDING FOR TRAVEL

The internet has revolutionized many aspects of travel, not the least of which is finding and booking hotel rooms. Savvy surfers utilize bid-for-booking sites, which offer great rates and an element of adventure. Generally, you can choose a general location and a level of service, but you never know exactly what you're going to get until the deal is done. Here are a few sites and how they work:

www.biddingfortravel.com The goal of this website is to promote informed bidding when using the services of priceline.com (see below). Visitors are invited to post their successful bidding history on specific hotels so that others learn the lowest acceptable prices. The site is monitored by an administrator, who answers questions and gives advice to subscribers who want to bid.

www.hotwire.com Choose your dates and your preferred neighborhood (up to four), and hotwire.com will provide a general location, list of amenities, price and star-rating for several options. You learn the hotel name and exact location only after you buy your reservation.

www.priceline.com Choose your desired neighborhood, desired star-rating and desired price; enter dates and credit-card info. If priceline.com finds something that meets your criteria your reservation is automatically booked, and you learn the hotel specifics afterwards. There's nothing to stop you from starting very low and gradually increasing your bid so you get the best price possible. Use this site in conjunction with biddingfortravel.com for a great hotel deal.

---

friends while you travel, assuming you are a good guest. The idea is that you will return the favor when one of your fellow surfers wants to sleep on your couch.

Vacation Rentals By Owner (www.vrbo.com) Plenty of apartments available by the day or week in all parts of Boston, as well as Cape Cod and surrounding areas.

Long-Term Accommodations

With hordes of students and other transients moving around town, Boston, Brookline and Cambridge are full of summer sublets and longer-term apartments available to rent. Signs are often posted at coffee shops, bookstores and other student hangouts. University housing offices are also good sources of information.

Boston Apartments (www.bostonapartments.com)

Boston Realty Hub (www.bostonrealtyhub.com)

Grand Central Apartments (www.grandcentralapartments.com)

Just Rentals (www.justrentals.com)

Sabbatical Homes (www.sabbaticalhomes.com) Advertises houses and apartments to rent or swap, mostly available for six months to a year. Caters to academics but open to all.

BEACON HILL

Site of the State House and steps from the Boston Common and the Public Garden, Beacon Hill combines history and greenery. A short stroll across the Common lands you on the Freedom Trail and the city's major tourist attractions; but Beacon Hill is also a lived-in (if luxuriously so) residential neighborhood, with some of the city's best restaurants, galleries and antique shops. Charles St and Beacon St are the main commercial avenues.

JOHN JEFFRIES HOUSE

Map pp302-3   Hotel $

☎ 617-367-1866; www.johnjeffrieshouse.com; 14 David Mugar Way; s/d $99/129, ste $155-165; 🚇 Charles/MGH; 🅿 🔀

Reproduction furnishings, original molding, hardwood floors and mahogany accents warmly recall the era when Dr John Jeffries founded what is now the world-renowned Massachusetts Eye & Ear Infirmary. Many patients reside here when they come to town for treatment, as do travelers like you. While the parlor is a lovely spot to enjoy your complimentary breakfast, you can also whip up your own meal in your in-room kitchenette (available in most rooms).

BEACON HILL BED & BREAKFAST

Map pp302-3   B&B $$

☎ 617-523-7376; www.lanierbb.com/inns/bb1384 .html; 27 Brimmer St; r $200-250; Ⓖ Charles/MGH; ✖ ▯

This private home is the only place to stay on the quiet back streets of Beacon Hill, allowing travelers to sample residential life in this historic neighborhood. The two rooms are sumptuous and stylish, filled with antiques, ornamental fireplaces and oriental rugs (as befits this Victorian brownstone). Breakfast is served in the posh parlor downstairs. The owner manages the place herself, so you can't expect all the amenities of a full-service hotel. But you can expect the warmest of welcomes, especially from the two delightful resident dogs.

CHARLES STREET INN

Map pp302-3   B&B $$$

☎ 617-314-8900, 877-772-8900; 94 Charles St; r $225-375; Ⓥ 9am-9pm; Ⓖ Charles/MGH; ✖ ▯

Built in 1860 as a showcase home, this Second Empire Victorian inn is now a model for how to meld the best of the 19th and 21st centuries. Each room is a veritable museum with an emphatic 'please snuggle right on in' policy. Ornate plaster cornices, ceiling medallions and window styles grace the nine rooms and common areas, where you're never vying for space or staff attention. Rooms are fitted with Victorian fabrics, handmade Turkish rugs, whirlpool tubs and working fireplaces. For added romance, a complimentary continental breakfast is served in your room.

BEACON HILL HOTEL & BISTRO

Map pp302-3   Boutique Hotel $$$

☎ 617-723-7575; www.beaconhillhotel.com; 25 Charles St; r $245-305, ste $365; Ⓖ Charles/MGH; Ⓟ ✖ ▯

This upscale European-style inn blends without flash or fanfare into its namesake neighborhood. Carved out of former residential buildings typical of Beacon Hill, the hotel's guest rooms are small, but they certainly make up for that in low-key style and comfort. You can expect individually decorated rooms, complete with

black-and-white photographs, a designer's soothing palette of paint choices, select accessories, plush duvets, pedestal sinks and louvered shutters. Added perks include the exclusive roof deck and complimentary breakfast at the urbane, on-site bistro.

XV BEACON Map pp302-3   Boutique Hotel $$$

☎ 616-670-1500; www.xvbeacon.com; 15 Beacon St; r from $375; Ⓖ Park St; Ⓟ ✖ ▯

Housed in a turn-of-the-20th-century Beaux Arts building, XV Beacon sets the standard for Boston's boutique hotels. Guest-room décor is utterly soothing, taking advantage of color schemes rich with taupe, espresso and cream. You'll find custom-made gas fireplaces and built-in mahogany entertainment units; heated towel racks and rainforest shower heads in the bathrooms; canopy beds dressed in Frette linens; and a healthy selection of CDs in your room. Free in-town taxi service, along with 24-hour room service and complimentary health-club privileges, are a few of the first-class trappings that guests can expect.

GOVERNMENT CENTER & WEST END

Sometimes called Bulfinch Triangle, the streets that are tucked in between North Station and Government Center have long housed Boston's least expensive lodging options. While the immediate vicinity did not have very much to offer, it was just a cobblestone's throw from Faneuil Hall and the North End. With the completion of the Big Dig, however, this low-rent district is changing fast, as restaurants and hotels race to develop the prime real estate. Fortunately, there are still a few cheapie options around.

BOSTON BACKPACKERS' YOUTH HOSTEL Map pp300-1   Hostel $

☎ 617-723-0800, 774-287-9602; www.boston backpackers.com; 234 Friend St; dm $25; Ⓖ North Station; ▯

Rising rents drove out two other hostels that were housed on this block. Enter the new Boston Backpackers' Youth Hostel. At the time of research, new owners were still gearing up, struggling to accommodate the travelers who were trickling through. But they were off to a good start. The space is architecturally appealing, with wide plank floors, exposed brick walls and sky-high ceilings. Six rooms on two levels are furnished with sturdy bunk beds. Tiled showers and bathrooms are spotless, although they may not be enough to accommodate the 48 beds. Laundry facilities are available, plus discounts at the pub downstairs.

SHAWMUT INN Map pp300-1   Hotel $

☎ 617-720-5544, 800-350-7784; www.shawmut inn.com; 280 Friend St; r/ ste $99/$189; 🚇 North Station; 🅿 ❌ 🖳

This small hotel offers just the basic goods in each room: cable/satellite TV and dial-up internet access. Kitchenettes have a refrigerator, microwave and coffee/tea maker. Smallish, darkish rooms are not overly appealing, but they are ideal for travelers who don't spend much time holed up in their hotel. Weekly rates also available.

ONYX HOTEL Map pp300-1   Boutique Hotel $$

☎ 617-557-9955; www.onyxhotel.com; 155 Portland St; d $229-289, d specials from $143; 🚇 North Station; 🅿 ❌ 🖳

The Onyx has received publicity for its Britney Spears room, designed by the pop star's mother to resemble her bedroom ($349 per night, 10% of revenue goes to the singer's foundation). But this boutique hotel has much more to offer than this over-the-top tribute. Done up in jewel tones and contemporary furniture, the Onyx exudes warmth and style – two elements that do not always go hand in hand. Other attractive features include morning car service, passes to a local gym and an evening wine reception. 'Pet-friendly' goes to a whole new level with gourmet doggy biscuits and dog-sitting service.

BULFINCH HOTEL

Map pp300-1   Boutique Hotel $$

☎ 617-624-0202; www.bulfinchhotel.com; 107 Merrimac St; d $199-249; 🚇 North Station; 🅿 ❌ 🖳

Exemplifying the up-and-coming character of this once-downtrodden district, the namesake hotel occupies a fully restored 19th-century flatiron building on the western edge of the Bulfinch Triangle. This place oozes with understated sophistication. Inside, creamy coffee colors complement the modern walnut furniture in the guest rooms, all of which are fully equipped

with flat-screen TVs and other amenities. By contrast, the hotel's on-site restaurant is the Angus Beef Steakhouse, which is gaining respect for its good old-fashioned food.

NORTH END

This close-knit Italian community is not known for welcoming visitors – for dinner, yes, but not to spend the night. But times are changing, and now you can stay in the heart of this historic residential neighborhood. Besides the incredible array of Italian restaurants, the North End offers easy access to the Freedom Trail, Faneuil Hall and the Boston Harbor waterfront.

LA CAPPELLA SUITES

Map pp300-1   B&B $$

☎ 617-523-9020; www.lacappellasuites.com; 290 North St; ste $150-210; 🚇 Haymarket; ❌ 🖳

'La Cappella' refers to the small chapel of La Societá di San Calogero di Sciacca that previously occupied this red-brick building. Now it is a private home with three spacious guest suites on the upper floors, topped off by a shared roof deck. Look for Italian marble flooring, panoramic views of the skyline and the harbor, and access to kitchen and common areas.

CHARLESTOWN

Charlestown is a short, scenic boat ride from downtown Boston (take the ferry from Long Wharf), as well as the end of the Freedom Trail. But Charlestown is a destination in its own right, as the Navy Yard and the sights around this 18th-century neighborhood will keep you entertained.

CONSTITUTION INN Map p304   Hotel $$

☎ 617-241-8400, 800-495-9622; www.constitution inn.org; 150 Second Ave; d $170-180; 🚇 Aquarium; 🅿 ❌ 🖳 🛇

Housed in a granite building in the historic Charlestown Navy Yard, this excellent budget hostel accommodates active and retired military personnel. But civilian guests are welcome too. Strident antiwar types needn't be put off sleeping here, nor will you see a preponderance of crew cuts. What you'll find, among other things, is crisp, modern rooms with all the basics (some with kitchenettes), plus an Olympic-class fitness center. It's no surprise that service is excellent: this place is run like a tight ship. Discounts for military, veterans and government employees.

DOWNTOWN

Some of Boston's classiest places to stay are lined up along Tremont St. And no wonder. The Freedom Trail goes right past your front door, and the city's major sights and best restaurants are a few steps away. The Financial District is also nearby, so these hotels are also the haunts of business travelers, especially during the week (when prices are often higher).

NINE ZERO

Map pp302-3   Boutique Hotel $$$
☎ 617-772-5810; www.ninezero.com; 90 Tremont St; r from $249, d specials from $159; 🚇 Park St; 🅿 ❌ 🖳
Chic. Boutique. With its striking juxtaposition of colors and textures, this Ladder District landmark knows how to maximize its impact. The Kimpton Group's latest

acquisition also caters to diverse audiences. Deluxe rooms have high-speed internet access and all sorts of business-friendly high-tech gadgets. Bold splashes of color and mod bathrooms appeal to urbanites, while Egyptian cotton bedding tempts upper-crust doyennes. Foodies appreciate the Mediterranean flavors churned out of the acclaimed on-site restaurant, Spire. All of the above enjoy the marvelous views of the State House and the Granary (if they are willing to pay for them).

HILTON BOSTON FINANCIAL DISTRICT

Map pp302-3   Hotel $$$
☎ 617-556-0006; www.hilton.com; 89 Broad St; d from $259 Mon-Fri, from $219 Sat & Sun; 🚇 Downtown Crossing; 🅿 ❌ 🖳
Multimedia Art Deco melds with 21st-century comforts in this gorgeously renovated 1928-era skyscraper. From exquisite lobby décor to period room appointments and boutique service, at the Hilton, the delight is in the details. Ride the brass elevator to your room where you'll find 12ft ceilings, rich woods and lots of space, glorious space. Designer ergonomic chairs are a pleasure, whether you've just landed or had a day of exploring. Amenities cater to every imagined need of savvy business travelers, globetrotters and families looking for top-notch accommodations. Great discounts are available, that is if you are willing to make an advance, nonrefundable booking.

OMNI PARKER HOUSE

Map pp302-3   Hotel $$$
☎ 617-227-8600, 800-843-6664; www.omnihotels.com; 60 School St; r $289-389; 🚇 Park St; 🅿 ❌ 🖳
Even though cold facts won't keep you warm at night, history and Parker House go hand in hand like JFK and Jackie O (who got engaged here). To wit: Malcolm X was a busboy here; Ho Chi Minh was a pastry chef here; and Boston Cream Pie, the official state dessert, was created here. As for the rooms, they're handsome and elegant, furnished with cherry furniture and antique heirlooms. But they do not lack for modern amenities either. History buffs might choose one of the individually decorated suites paying tribute to a historic

Omni Parker House (right)

LET'S GET PHYSICAL

Do you think a high heart rate is more important than a high thread count? Check out these hotel fitness centers for a good workout.

Charles Hotel (p240) Guests have access to the on-site Wellbridge Health & Fitness Center, a state-of-the-art facility with yoga, pilates, kickboxing, countless cardiovascular machines and an 'aquatic atrium'.

Constitution Inn (p229) The two-storey fitness center includes basketball courts, free weights, Olympic-size pool, plus all the classes and machines your little body desires.

Four Seasons (p232) This 24-hour facility will push you *and* pamper you. Treadmills, stairmasters and stationary bikes are fitted with televisions and headsets to entertain you while you run or ride; the swimming pool is equipped with whirlpool and sauna; and guests are treated to fresh fruit after their workout.

Colonnade (p236) Pump those biceps as you lift your fruity cocktail to your parched lips, while lounging poolside at the RTP. But seriously, there is also a brand new fitness center with all the standard cardio and weight machines. Flat-screen TVs and reading material also provided.

YMCA of Greater Boston (p238) This is Boston's biggest YMCA, complete with free weights and weight machines, indoor track, basketball and squash courts and swimming pool. A full schedule of exercise classes is open to Y residents.

Boston figure. Fitness buffs can request a room with a portable treadmill and healthy snack pack.

MARRIOTT CUSTOM HOUSE

Map pp302-3   Hotel $$$

☎ 617-310-6300, 800-845-5279; www.marriott .com; 3 McKinley Sq; ste $299-389; 🚇 Aquarium; P ☒ 🖳

With its grand clock towering above the harbor, the old Custom House is one of the most distinctive buildings on the Boston city skyline. So you can imagine the views from the inside of this magnificent landmark. Even if you are not staying here, you might check it out from the open-air observation deck that wraps around the 26th floor (see p86). If you are staying here, you may enjoy the same view from your spacious suite (each with kitchenette and dining area), or from the fully-equipped fitness center on the 25th floor, with a wonderful panorama to distract you from your workout.

WATERFRONT

It's a rare opportunity to camp in a major metropolitan area, but you can do it in Boston (see p203). If that's not your (sleeping) bag, take in sunrise *and* room service from a prime waterfront location. With the completion of the Big Dig, this neighborhood has been reconnected to the rest of the city and is very foot-friendly.

HARBORSIDE INN

Map pp302-3   Boutique Hotel $$

☎ 617-723-7500; www.harborsideinnboston .com; 185 State St; d from $189; 🚇 Aquarium; P ☒ 🖳

Ensconced in a respectfully renovated 19th-century warehouse, this tasteful hostelry strikes just the right balance between historic digs and modern conveniences. In its former life as a mercantile building, the massive structure played an integral role in the bustling waterfront port. Fortunately, the architects who renovated it in the late 1990s cared about preserving historic details. Guest rooms have original exposed brick and granite walls and hardwood floors. They're offset perfectly by Oriental area carpets, sleigh beds and reproduction Federal-era furnishings. Add $20 for a city view.

MILLENNIUM BOSTONIAN HOTEL

Map pp302-3   Hotel $$$

☎ 617-523-3600; www.millenniumhotels.com; Faneuil Hall Marketplace; d $249-299; 🚇 Haymarket; P ☒ 🖳

The Bostonian proudly touts its roots as part of the Blackstone Block, the city's oldest block – dating to the late 1600s. From the moment you enter the discreet, sit-down check-in area, to the time you step out on your balcony overlooking the colorful bustle of Haymarket, you'll appreciate the singular position this hotel has carved out. It incorporates two historic buildings: traditional rooms are located in the

Harkness Wing, modern ones in the Bostonian Wing. Glass walkways between the two buildings allow guests to peer down onto a narrow cobblestone passageway.

BOSTON MARRIOTT LONG WHARF
Map pp302-3   Hotel $$$

☎ 617-227-0800, 800-627-7468; www.marriott .com; 296 State St; r $279-319 Sat & Sun, $399-419 Mon-Fri; 🚇 Aquarium; 🅿 🗙 🖵 🐾

The best aspect of this hotel? You're minutes from historic landmarks like Faneuil Hall and the Freedom Trail. You're moments from the North End – the next best thing to Italy itself. You're within haggling distance of the city's most colorful market. All that's at your doorstep, which doesn't begin to address what goes on inside this classy place. Restaurants, a health club, an outdoor terrace with Boston's finest harbor views, high-speed internet and Web TV in every room... Services galore keep business travelers and touring guests well cared for.

SEAPORT DISTRICT

With the opening of the convention center, this district has become a hotbed of hotel development. It's a bit removed from the action, unless you are actually attending an event at the convention center. But it's nirvana for seafood eaters and art connoisseurs. And with the new Silver Line up and running, it's an easy trip from the airport.

SEAPORT HOTEL
Map pp298-9   Hotel $$

☎ 617-385-4000; 1 Seaport Lane; www.seaport boston.com; r $219-309; 🚇 South Station; 🅿 🗙 🖵 🐾

With glorious views of the Boston Harbor, this business hotel is up-to-snuff when it comes to high-tech amenities. All rooms come equipped with automatic motion-sensitive lights so you never have to enter a dark room and privacy/service lights instead of the old-fashioned 'Do not disturb' signs (in addition to standards like wireless access). Soothing tones, plush linens and robes, and a unique no-tipping policy guarantee a relaxing retreat. Now the Seaport is reaching out to families, offering Nintendo, baby gear and treats for your pet.

CHINATOWN, LEATHER DISTRICT & THEATER DISTRICT

For the purposes of sleeping, the only neighborhood in this group that really matters is the Theater District (although isn't it nice to have Chinatown nearby when you get the munchies at 2am?).

MILNER HOTEL Map p305   Hotel $$

☎ 617-426-6220, 800-453-1731; www.milner -hotels.com; 78 Charles St S; d $140-175; 🚇 Boylston; 🅿 🖵

Some folks find the golden filigrees, faux marble and chandeliers at the Milner to be on the gaudy side. Get over that and you'll enjoy the spirit that infuses the youthful yet professional staff with a sense of fun and irony. Since this is a roost for performers as well, you might come home to see performers and stage crew in their civvies. As for the rooms, they are small and darkish, with plain but passable décor. As Mr Milner said back in 1918, 'A bed and a bath for a buck and a half.' (Prices have gone up a little since 1918.)

COURTYARD BOSTON TREMONT
Map p305   Hotel $$

☎ 617-426-1400, 800-331-9998; www.courtyard bostontremont.com; 275 Tremont St; d $219-299; 🚇 Boylston; 🅿 🗙 🖵

Built in 1925 as the national Elks headquarters, this hotel retains an ornate and elegant lobby, while its rooms are smallish but contemporary. After recently becoming part of a national hotel chain, the Tremont's rough edges got smoothed out a bit and its character dulled in the process. Still, it's a comfortable and fun hotel, as befits any place that is sprinkled with elk heads. And it still houses the historic Roxy nightclub in its ballroom. Discounts available on weekends.

FOUR SEASONS BOSTON
Map p305   Hotel $$$

☎ 617-338-4400; www.fourseasons.com; 200 Boylston St; r $325 Sat & Sun, $475 Mon-Fri; 🚇 Arlington; 🅿 🗙 🖵 🐾

Utter the two words 'Four Seasons' and you might as well be uttering a whole paragraph of superlative adjectives to describe one of the finest hotel chains on the planet. And this link in the chain is no exception. Coolly contemporary and never stuffy (despite the crystal chandelier in the porte-cochere and the grand staircase), the Four Seasons excels because of its seamless attention to details and service. Luxurious rooms packed with amenities don't hurt either. Aujourd'hui, the on-site dining room, is one of the best splurges in Boston.

SOUTH END

Boston's gay-friendliest neighborhood is edgy in more ways than one. It is home to avant-garde art galleries and daring new restaurants, making it edgy in the metaphorical sense of the word. And geographically, it sits on the edge of the city center, sandwiched between upscale Back Bay and downtrodden Roxbury. While the places listed here are in safe areas, travelers should take care walking around south of Washington St and west of Massachusetts Ave, especially at night.

BERKELEY RESIDENCE YWCA

Map p305   Hostel $

☎ 617-375-2524; www.ywcaboston.org/berkeley; 40 Berkeley St; s/d/tr $60/90/105, weekly $280/430/495; 🚇 Back Bay or South End
Straddling the South End and Back Bay, this Y rents over 200 small rooms (some overlooking the garden) to guests on a nightly and long-term basis. Most are open to women only, although one floor is open

for men. Bathrooms are shared, as are other useful facilities such as the telephone, library, TV room and laundry. It's a safe, friendly and affordable place for travelers. All rates include breakfast, while dinner is also included in long-term rates.

ENCORE Map p305   B&B $$

☎ 617-247-3425; www.encorebandb.com; 116 W Newton St; r $145-190; 🚇 Back Bay, South End or Massachusetts Ave; P 🚗 🖥
If you love the theater, or if you love innovative contemporary design, or if you just love creature comforts and warm hospitality, you will love Encore. Co-owned by an architect and a set designer, this 19th-century town house sets a stage for both of their passions. Exposed brick walls are adorned with exotic masks, interesting art and theatrical posters; bold colors and contemporary furniture pieces furnish the spacious guestrooms. All three rooms have a sitting area or private deck that offers a spectacular skyline view.

CHANDLER INN

Map p305   Hotel $$

☎ 617-482-3450; www.chandlerinn.com; 26 Chandler St; r $151; 🚇 Back Bay or South End
This building's original use as a dormitory for the Coast Guard shows through in the spare design and furnishings of the rooms. In a neighborhood of brownstones and cobbled sidewalks, the Chandler Inn may offer spartan quarters, but the location posits you within roll-me-home range of some of Boston's best restaurants and tourist hot spots. Gay travelers will feel right at home,

HIP HOTEL BARS

If you like to tipple with your fellow travelers, check out these hip hotel bars.

Charlesmark Lounge, Charlesmark at Copley (p235) Understated but urbane. The newish lounge spills out onto a sweet patio fronting Boylston St.

Cuffs, Jury's Boston Hotel (p236) An upscale Irish pub that attracts a lively mixed crowd, especially to the outdoor terrace. Great menu of fancy martinis ($11) and classy pub grub.

Fritz, Chandler Inn (above) Boston's favorite neighborhood sports bar. It just happens to be in a gay neighborhood, making it a gay sports bar. It seems incongruous, but in the South End, it works.

Spire Lounge, Nine Zero (p230) A sophisticated, after-hours hotspot. Bonus: all of the scrumptious items from the restaurant menu are available in the lounge.

Tia's, Marriott Long Wharf (opposite) Sip drinks under the stars and get a taste of Boston's singles scene on the waterfront. But don't stay for dinner!

as most of the patrons at the hopping bar downstairs – and residents and neighborhood business owners, for that matter – are gay as well.

CLARENDON SQUARE INN

Map p305   B&B $$

☎ 617-536-2229; www.clarendonsquare.com; 198 W Brookline St; r $165-445; 🚇 Prudential; P ♿ 💻

Located on a quiet residential street, the completely renovated brownstone is a designer's dream. A dramatic open entry sets the tone and is continued with a curved staircase leading up to the 2nd floor. Guestroom details might include Italian marble wainscoting, French limestone floors, a silver leaf barrel-vaulted ceiling or a hand-forged iron and porcelain washbasin. Common areas are decadent (case in point: roof-deck hot tub); continental breakfast is served in the paneled dining room and butler's pantry. Staying here will certainly give you a great sense of gay, chichi South End living.

BACK BAY

Expense-account travelers can take their pick from the many fancy four- and five-star hotels that are clustered around Copley Sq and the Hynes Convention Center. Fortunately, the residential parts of the Back Bay are also home to some friendly, affordable guesthouses, which allow travelers to experience all the charm and convenience of this neighborhood without spending a fortune. Particularly good deals are hidden among the streets between Huntington Ave and the Southwest Corridor Park – on the edge of the South End.

463 BEACON ST GUEST HOUSE

Map pp306-7   Guesthouse $

☎ 617-536-1302; www.463beacon.com; 463 Beacon St; d with shared bathroom $79, with private bathroom $149-64; 🚇 Hynes/ICA; P

What's more 'Boston' than a handsome, historic brownstone in the Back Bay? This gorgeous guesthouse lets you live the blue-blood fantasy – and save your cash for the chichi boutiques and martini bars of Newbury St. This c 1880 building retains plenty of highfalutin' architectural frolics, like a gorgeous spiral staircase, painted wrought-

iron filigrees and impossibly high ceilings and windows in each room. Rooms vary in size, but they all have the basics like TV and telephone. Bathrooms are cramped, but hopefully you won't be spending too much time in there. Also available: furnished apartments for longer-term rental.

COPLEY HOUSE

Map pp306-7   Apartments $

☎ 617-236-8300, 800-331-1318; www.copley house.com; 239 W Newton St; studio $85-135, 1-bedroom $135-65; 🚇 Prudential; 💻

Wrought-iron fences, ivy-covered brownstones, trees whispering in the breeze – it only takes a couple of quiet neighborhood blocks to reach this oasis and escape the blur of the city. With a full kitchen in each room, Copley House offers a comfortable spot to hole up for some well-deserved peace and quiet. The simple, just-shy-of-beautiful apartment-style rooms are located in four different buildings, straddling the Back Bay and the South End. A judicious use of antique wood and big windows beaming with light make this Queen Anne–style inn a place of respite and a handy base of operations for exploring Boston. Weekly rates available.

COMMONWEALTH COURT GUEST HOUSE Map pp306-7   Guesthouse $

☎ 617-424-1230, 888-424-1230; www.common wealthcourt.com; 284 Commonwealth Ave; r $99-140; 🚇 Hynes /ICA

These 20 rooms with kitchenettes are not super spiffy, but the price is right for this great location. The Euro-style guesthouse is housed in a turn-of-the-century brownstone in the heart of Back Bay. Once a private residence, it retains a homey feel and lots of lavish architectural details. Service is pleasant but not overly attentive (maid service occurs only twice a week). Inquire about long-term rates and weekly in-season deals.

COLLEGE CLUB

Map pp306-7   Guesthouse $

☎ 617-536-9510; www.thecollegeclubofboston .com; 44 Commonwealth Ave; s with shared bathroom $99-105, d with private bathroom $170-90; 🚇 Arlington; 💻

Despite the name, you don't need a college degree or any sort of club membership to

College Club (opposite)

stay here. But you do need to have the smarts to recognize a great deal when you see one. Originally a private club for female college graduates, the College Club has 11 enormous rooms with high ceilings, now open to both sexes. Period details, typical of the area's Victorian brownstones, include claw-tooth tubs, ornamental fireplaces and bay windows. Local designers are lending their skills to decorate the various rooms, as a part of the ongoing 'Dream Room Makeover Challenge,' with delightful results. Prices include a continental breakfast.

NEWBURY GUEST HOUSE

Map pp306-7   Guesthouse $$
☎ 617-437-7666, 800-437-7668; www.hagopian hotels.com; 261 Newbury St; s/d from $120/135; ⛳ Hynes/ICA or Copley; ⓟ ⛟ ▣
Dating to 1882, these three interconnected brick and brownstone buildings offer big bang for the buck. Repeat guests are drawn by the historic neighborhood and its proximity to Boston's best attractions. Although guest rooms aren't as ornate as they once were, 19th-century details like molded ceilings, carved mantles and bay windows are still visible. A complimentary continental breakfast is laid out next to the marble fireplace in the salon.

COPLEY INN Map pp306-7   Guesthouse $$
☎ 617-236-0300, 800-232-0306; www.copleyinn .com; 19 Garrison St; r $145; ⛳ Prudential
Although much of the old brownstone's character has been rehabbed right out of it, the Copley Inn is still a very nice vanilla-flavored establishment. And you can't argue with the location: it's about as close as you can get to the shops, galleries and cafés and restaurants of Newbury St, while preserving the sense that you're nesting in a slightly quieter neighborhood. Equipped with kitchens, rooms in this four-storey walk-up are relatively roomy – there's plenty of pay-off in sacrificing atmosphere for elbow room.

CHARLESMARK AT COPLEY

Map pp306-7   Boutique Hotel $$
☎ 617-247-1212; www.thecharlesmark.com; 655 Boylston; r $159-89; ⛳ Copley; ⓟ ⛟ ▣
At the crossroads of Euro-style luxury and ingenious functionality, this place doesn't leave you gazing longingly at expense-account suites down the street. The design is classic modernism. And the effect is upscale, urbane and surprisingly affordable. This hip hostel is backed by a small group of warmly efficient staff that sees to details you didn't even know you wanted. The downstairs lounge spills out onto the sidewalk where the people-watching is tops.

Sleeping

BACK BAY

MIDTOWN HOTEL

Map pp306-7   Hotel $$

☎ 617-262-1000, 800-343-1177; www.mid
townhotel.com; 220 Huntington Ave; r $159-239;
🚇 Symphony; Ⓟ ✖ 🖥 🔉

This low-rise motel looks like it belongs
by the side of the highway, instead of in
the shadow of the Prudential Center. But
its spacious rooms fill up with families,
businesspeople and tour groups. That's
because the price is right and the location
is unbeatable. Service is friendly and ef-
ficient; rooms are plain but clean. Perks for
families: kids under 18 stay for free, and
they'll enjoy splashing around in the pri-
vate outdoor swimming pool.

COLONNADE

Map pp306-7   Hotel $$

☎ 617-424-7000; www.colonnadehotel.com;
120 Huntington Ave; r $179-249; 🚇 Prudential;
Ⓟ ✖ 🖥 🔉

The reason to stay at the Colonnade is not
its handsome guest rooms, which are well
equipped with both high-tech gadgetry and
simple pleasures (like a rubber duck in your
bathtub). It's not the vibrant Parisian bistro,
Brasserie Jo, a hotspot for symphony-goers
(see p151). It's not even the prime location,
straddling the Back Bay and the South End.
The real reason to stay at the Colonnade is
the rooftop pool, or RTP, as it's known. A
glamorous place to see and be seen in your
bikini, it's also optimal for alfresco dining,
sunbathing and yes, even swimming. Open
to nonguests weekdays only.

COPLEY SQUARE HOTEL

Map pp306-7   Hotel $$

☎ 617-536-9000, 800-225-7062; www.cop
leysquarehotel.com; 47 Huntington Ave; s/d
$189/219; 🚇 Copley or Back Bay; Ⓟ ✖ 🖥

It's downright heroic when a fine hotel
wins awards for its environmental vision.
Everything from how the hotel does its
laundry (no chlorine) to the fuel used in
hotel vans (compressed natural gas) dimin-
ishes its environmental footprint without
diminishing the elegance that pervades
the Copley. This superlative attention to
environmental impact goes hand-in-green-
hand with superior attention to its guests.
Personal service is a hallmark here, with
impeccable concierge service, bike rentals,

baby-sitting and access to a nearby fitness
centre. Traditionally decorated rooms vary
in size (some are quite small) but all include
conveniences you'd expect.

LENOX HOTEL

Map pp306-7   Hotel $$$

☎ 617-536-5300, 800-225-7676; www.lenox
hotel.com; 61 Exeter St; r $229-329; 🚇 Copley;
Ⓟ ✖ 🖥

The Lenox bundles together good service,
great location and nice rooms at not-quite-
exorbitant prices. What more can you hope
for? Although 'value' is a word you don't
often hear associated with Boston hotels,
it's an apt watchword here. And while the
atmosphere is a tad old-world, you don't
have to forego modern conveniences
to live with that ethos. Guest rooms are
comfortably elegant (with chandeliers and
crown molding), without being stuffy. If
your pockets are deep enough, it's worth
splurging for a junior suite; they boast the
best views.

JURY'S BOSTON HOTEL

Map pp306-7   Hotel $$$

☎ 617-266-7200; www.jurysdoyle.com; 350 Stuart
St; r $235-265; 🚇 Back Bay; Ⓟ ✖ 🖥

Perched on the border of the Back Bay and
the South End, this fashionable newcomer
is housed in the former Boston Police
Headquarters. The Irish brand brings a
modern Euro flare to this historic edifice,
with funky floor lights, intriguing artwork
and flowing waterfall. Rooms are luxuri-
ous, draped in rich ivory, green and copper
tones, and well stocked with amenities. The
on-site bar, Cuffs, is a popular hangout for
the local gay community.

KENMORE SQUARE & FENWAY

Home to myriad students and sacred haunt
of Red Sox fans, this area has a bunch of
inexpensive places to stay, including a few
hostels. (For late-night clubbers, this may
be your best bet for stumbling home with-
out the aid of a taxi.) With the revamping
of Kenmore Sq also comes new high-class
hotels for free-spenders, while a few smaller
hotels and guesthouses offer a friendly and
affordable alternative.

KENMORE SQUARE
FENWAY SUMMER HOSTEL

Map pp308-9   Hostel $

☎ 617-267-8599, reservations 617-536-1027; www.bostonhostel.org; 575 Commonwealth Ave; dm/r $35/89 + $3 for nonmembers; 🚇 Kenmore; 🔀 🖳

This former Howard Johnson hotel turned HI youth hostel doubles as a Boston University dorm, so it's open for travelers only from June to August. Rooms have three beds each: rent the bed or rent the room. Each room has its own bathroom, which allows plenty of privacy in hostel-hopping terms. The top floor, once a lively nightclub, is now a kick-ass common area surrounded by windows, offering breathtaking views over the Charles River and Beantown.

HOTEL BUCKMINSTER

Map pp308-9   Hotel $$

☎ 617-236-7050, 800-727-2825; www.boston hotelbuckminster.com; 645 Beacon St; r from $120; 🚇 Kenmore; 🅿 🔀

Designed by the same architect who designed the Boston Public Library and many gracious Back Bay town houses, the Buckminster is an elegant convergence of Old Boston charm and up-to-date amenities. It offers nearly 100 affordable rooms, including 24 spacious apartment suites, that are filled with authentic touches of another era. European-style rooms and suites are quite roomy, with all the tools and toys of comfort and convenience. As well, each floor has its own laundry and kitchen facilities.

GRYPHON HOUSE

Map pp308-9   B&B $$

☎ 617-375-9003; www.innboston.com; 9 Bay State Rd; r $149-265; 🚇 Kenmore; 🅿 🔀 🖳

A premier example of Richardson Romanesque, this beautiful five-storey brownstone is a paradigm of artistry and luxury overlooking the picturesque Charles River. Eight spacious suites have different styles, including Victorian, Gothic, Arts and Crafts, but they all have 19th-century period details. And they all have home-away-from-home perks like big TVs with VCRs, CD players, wet bars and gas fireplaces. Inquire about discounts for Red Sox fans (seriously!).

Hotel Buckminster (left) on Kenmore Sq

HOTEL COMMONWEALTH

Map pp308-9   Hotel $$$

☎ 617-933-5000, 866-784-4000; www.hotel commonwealth.com; 500 Commonwealth Ave; r $229-329; 🚇 Kenmore; 🅿 🔀 🖳

Set amid Commonwealth Ave's brownstones and just steps away from Fenway Park, this independent, luxury hotel enjoys prime real estate. Step off the busy street and into an oasis of contemporary calm. The rooms feature dark wood and rich fabrics, lending an Old World feel to the otherwise modern décor. If you came to New England for seafood, don't miss Michael Schlow's latest endeavor, Great Bay (see p153).

ELIOT HOTEL

Map pp308-9   Hotel $$$

☎ 617-267-1607, 800-443-5468; www.eliothotel .com; 370 Commonwealth Ave; r $245-285, ste $285-345; 🚇 Hynes/ICA; 🅿 🔀 🖳

Akin to a small London hotel, the Eliot offers two-room suites, each with a bedroom and a sitting room separated by French doors. The posh quarters are furnished in English chintz and Queen Anne mahogany and adorned with botanical prints. Bathroom walls are dressed with Italian marble. Other upscale amenities include two televisions, plush terry robes, complimentary shoeshine service and more. The acclaimed restaurant Clio (see p153) is on the 1st floor.

FENWAY

HOSTELLING INTERNATIONAL
BOSTON Map pp308-9   Hostel $
☎ 617-536-1027; www.bostonhostel.org; 12 Hemenway St; dm $28-45, d $70-100; Ⓣ Hynes/ICA; ✂ 🖳

This international travel hub offers some of Boston's cheapest beds, in a prime location. Same-sex and coed dorm-style bunk rooms hold four to six people each, plus there are some private rooms for couples. The price includes sheets, towels, soap and shampoo, as well as breakfast. The 200 beds are almost always full, so be sure to reserve as far in advance as possible; book online for the cheapest rate. On-site laundry and kitchen facilities are decent, but the best feature of this hostel is the daily activities arranged by the events coordinator: walking tours, museum visits and comedy clubs, all at discounted (if not free) rates.

YMCA OF GREATER BOSTON
Map pp308-9   Hostel $
☎ 617-536-7800; www.ymcaboston.org; 316 Huntington Ave; s/d/tr/q $46/66/81/96; Ⓣ Northeastern; 🖳

The Village People were right: It *is* fun to stay at the YMCA. You get to use the gyms, indoor track, basketball and squash courts and swimming pool; and you get a hearty breakfast and free passes to various programs. Rooms (rented to both genders May to August but only to men the rest of the year) are small, with miniscule closets, tiny desks and why-bother bureaus. Stark, battered furnishings are on par with local hostels. But the place is pretty clean, in a locker-room sort of way. The staff is brusquely friendly and enthusiastically encourages use of everything the Y has to offer. Discounted rates available for members.

OASIS GUEST HOUSE
Map pp308-9   Guesthouse $
☎ 617-267-2262, 800-230-0105; www.oasisgh.com; 22 Edgerly Rd; s with shared bath $89-99, with private bath $149; Ⓣ Hynes/ICA or Symphony; Ⓟ ✂ 🖳 ⸍

True to its name, this homey guesthouse is a peaceful, pleasant oasis in the midst of Boston's chaotic city streets. Thirty-odd guest rooms occupy four attractive, brick, bow-front town houses on this tree-lined lane. The modest, light-filled rooms are tastefully and traditionally decorated, most with queen beds, floral quilts and nondescript prints. The common living room does not exactly encourage lingering, but outdoor decks and kitchen facilities are nice touches.

BROOKLINE

Brookline is a sweet retreat if the city makes you feel claustrophobic. Grand elm trees shade the wide green lawns and gracious mansions in this 'streetcar suburb.' As this moniker implies, a short ride on the green line brings you into Kenmore Sq, the Back Bay and Downtown.

ANTHONY'S TOWN HOUSE
Map pp308-9   Guesthouse $
☎ 617-566-3972; www.anthonystownhouse.com; 1085 Beacon St; r $90-120; Ⓣ Hawes St (C-line); ✂ 🖳

Halfway between Coolidge Corner and Kenmore Sq, this family-operated guesthouse puts the rolled 'r' in rococo. With more frills and flourishes than should be allowed in one place at one time, the Victorian-era brownstone is downright girly. While over the top by some standards, the 10 rooms are spacious and comfortable and filled with antiques and lacy linens. Each of the four floors has its own bathroom. Affable owners and cheap rates attract plenty of repeat visitors and some long-term guests.

BEECH TREE INN Map pp308-9   B&B $
☎ 617-227-1620; www.thebeechtreeinn.com; 83 Longwood Ave; r $109-79; Ⓣ Longwood (D-line); Ⓟ ✂ 🖳

This turn-of-the-century Victorian home now contains 10 guest rooms, each individually decorated with period furnishings and wallpaper, ornamental fireplaces with hand-painted screens, floral quilts and lacy curtains. Common areas include a cozy parlor and a pleasant patio. It's a romantic return to yesteryear, located on a quiet residential street not far from Coolidge Corner and the Back Bay Fens.

BEACON INN

Map pp308-9   Guesthouse $$

☎ 617-566-0088, 888-575-0088; www.beaconinn .com; 1087 Beacon St; r $129-229; ⓧ Hawes St (C-line); P ⊠ ⌨

This gorgeous guesthouse occupies another beautiful brownstone on Beacon St, midway between Coolidge Corner and Kenmore Sq. Fourteen rooms – each named for a Boston landmark personality or neighborhood – vary in size: some have king-size beds and sitting areas, while other cozier quarters are designed for solo travelers. Architectural flourishes – like ornamental fireplaces in some rooms – as well as elegant antique furnishings and original woodwork enhance the Old World atmosphere. A second location is west of Coolidge Corner at 1750 Beacon St.

BERTRAM INN Map pp308-9   B&B $$

☎ 617-566-2234, 800-295-3822; www.bertraminn .com; 92 Sewall Ave; r $149-189; ⓧ St Paul (C-line); P ⊠ ⌨

Brookline's tree-lined streets shelter this dreamy, Arts and Crafts–style inn, located a quick jaunt from downtown Boston. A quiet elegance is accented with beautifully carved oak panels, leaded windows and, if you play your cards right, a working fireplace in your room. Amenities and services match those of high-end hotels, including a full gourmet breakfast buffet. The same owners run the Sewall Inn across the street, an exquisitely restored Victorian with even more rooms. Both places boast tree-shaded decks, a warm welcome to pets and a location that's a heartbeat from the Hub of the Universe.

JAMAICA PLAIN

Slightly isolated from the main sights of the city, Jamaica Plain is a vibrant, artsy neighborhood filled with restaurants, galleries and a lively gay and lesbian population. The Franklin Park Zoo, Jamaica Pond and the rest of the Emerald Necklace are in the immediate vicinity, while Boston proper is a 30-minute T-ride away.

TAYLOR HOUSE   B&B $$

☎ 617-983-9334; www.taylorhouse.com; 50 Burroughs St; s $125-159, d $145-220; ⓧ Green St; P ⊠ ⌨

Sitting pretty pond-side, this gracious Italianate Victorian mansion has undergone a loving restoration – apparent from the ornamental details throughout the house and the gorgeous gardens outside. (If you have any doubt, check out the 'before' and 'after' photos on hand.) The three spacious guest rooms have dark polished wood floors, sleigh beds and plenty of sunshine. Dave and Daryl are your designers, decorators and amazing hosts. PS: Must love dogs (two friendly golden retrievers live here too).

CAMBRIDGE

Cambridge has its own collection of quaint B&Bs and upscale hotels, which are particularly inviting for travelers attending events at the local universities. The red line guarantees a short and convenient commute into the city for serious sightseeing, but Cambridge also boasts a vibrant cultural scene of its own. Harvard Sq is a hub for such things. Several upscale hotels are also located along the Charles River between MIT and the Museum of Science – a location that's convenient to Boston and Cambridge alike.

HARVARD SQUARE
A FRIENDLY INN

Map pp298-9   Guesthouse $

☎ 617-547-7851; www.afinow.com/afi; 1673 Cambridge St; r $97-137; ⓧ Harvard; P ⊠

While this Victorian-era inn gets mixed reviews, nobody disputes that it is indeed 'a friendly inn.' Service is accommodating and efficient, offering a clean and quiet respite for budget travelers. The old maxim holds true, however: you get what you pay for. Be prepared to sleep in cramped quarters and to forego the fancy-pants amenities you may find at an upscale hotel. A continental breakfast is included, but you are better off heading down the street to Darwin's (p156) for your morning meal.

IRVING HOUSE

Map pp298-9   B&B $

☎ 617-547-4600, 877-547-4600; www.irving house.com; 24 Irving St; r with shared bathroom $100-160, with private bathroom $125-225; 🚇 Harvard; 🅿 🔀 💻

Call it a big B&B or a homey hotel, this property welcomes even the most world-weary traveler. The 44 rooms range in size, but every bed is covered with a quilt and big windows let in plenty of light. There is a bistro-style atmosphere in the brick-lined basement, where you can work on your novel, plan your travels or munch on the free continental breakfast. Perks include museum passes and laundry facilities. Steps from Harvard Yard, the Irving House attracts lots of parents and visiting scholars, so prices increase dramatically during commencement and other university events.

HARVARD SQUARE HOTEL

Map p310   Hotel $$

☎ 617-864-5200; www.harvardsquarehotel.com; 110 Mount Auburn St; d $149-249; 🚇 Harvard; 🅿 🔀 💻

After a recent revamp, the square's namesake hotel offers a suitable (if unremarkable) place to sleep smack dab in the middle of lively Harvard Sq. The downside: rooms are small and not particularly stylish; service is not particularly attentive; and you'll pay extra for amenities like parking and internet access. The upside: location, location, location.

INN AT HARVARD

Map p310   Inn $$

☎ 617-491-2222; www.theinnatharvard.com; 1201 Massachusetts Ave; d $169-269; 🚇 Harvard; 🅿 🔀 💻

The inn's collegiate atmosphere is appropriate for its setting, just outside the gates of Harvard Yard. But these accommodations are not outmoded. A recent renovation means that all guest rooms are decorated with contemporary colors, cherry wood furniture and original artwork, not to mention flat-screen TVs and ergonomic chairs. On-site services are limited – this is not a full-service hotel after all – but guests are allowed to use the university gym and all the resources of Harvard Sq are at your doorstep.

MARY PRENTISS INN

Map pp298-9   B&B $$

☎ 617-661-2929; www.maryprentissinn.com; 6 Prentiss St; r $194-264; 🚇 Harvard or Porter; 🅿 🔀 💻

A perfect blend of urban living and gracious New England hospitality. This upscale inn is housed in a neoclassical Greek revival gem, complete with front porch, fluted columns and Ionic capitals. The stylish guest rooms are decorated with soothing fabrics and colorful chintzes. All have a smattering of 19th-century antiques – perhaps a sleigh bed, a cannonball post bed, Windsor chairs or armoires. The walled deck – filled with fragrant potted herbs, container-grown vines and colorful annuals – is an ideal place to enjoy the bountiful breakfast.

CHARLES HOTEL

Map p310   Hotel $$$

☎ 617-864-1200; www.charleshotel.com; 1 Bennett St; r from $269; 🚇 Harvard; 🅿 🔀 💻

'Simple, Stylish, Smart.' Harvard Sq's most illustrious hotel lives up to its motto. Overlooking the Charles River, this institution has hosted the university's most esteemed guests, ranging from Bob Barker to the Dalai Lama. Design at the Charles – including rooms and restaurants – is surprisingly clean, but the facilities do not lack the luxuries and amenities one would expect from a highly rated hotel.

CENTRAL SQUARE
HARDING HOUSE

Map p311   Hotel $

☎ 617-876-2888, 877-489-2888; www.irving house.com; 288 Harvard St; r with shared bathroom $100-125, with private bathroom $155-240; 🚇 Central; 🅿 🔀 💻

This delightful treasure brilliantly blends refinement and comfort, artistry and efficiency. Rooms are spacious and bright. Old, wooden floors toss back a warm glow and sport gorgeous throw rugs. Lovely antique furnishings complete the inviting atmosphere. The complimentary Thursday-night wine-and-cheese hour is a chance to meet your fellow inn-mates, or sip and nosh in thoughtful solitude, gazing at the garden. Other perks include all-day munchies, a thoughtfully designed continental breakfast and complimentary museum passes.

HOTEL @ MIT

Map p311   Hotel $$

☎ 617-577-0200, 800-222-8733; www.hotelat mit.com; 20 Sidney St; r $179-259; Ⓡ Central; Ⓟ ✖ ▣

The Hotel @ MIT fuses art, design and science. Rooms and suites are awash with wood, chrome and ergonomically designed furniture. Computer boards equipped with high-speed internet connections are built into wood armoires. Guests may be world-famous geneticists or Nobel Prize–winning technologists, so this hip Hilton hotel doesn't skimp on providing them all the high-tech and luxury amenities they expect.

KENDALL SQUARE
KENDALL HOTEL

Map p311   Hotel $$

☎ 617-577-1300; www.kendallhotel.com; 350 Main St; r $194-264; Ⓡ Kendall/MIT; Ⓟ ✖ ▣

Once the Engine 7 Firehouse, this city landmark is now a cool and classy all-American hotel. The 65 guest rooms retain a fire-fighter riff, without a whiff of 'cutesy.' Bold color choices include mustard yellow, burnt orange and deep-sea blue. An artful mix of bedsteads, lamps, wall hangings and window treatments makes each room sing. There's no scrimping at the breakfast table, either, with a full buffet included. The on-site Black Sheep restaurant, filled with memorabilia from old days of fightin' fires, features organic, locally grown produce pleasing to omnivores and vegetarians alike.

EAST CAMBRIDGE
HOTEL MARLOWE

Map pp298-9   Hotel $$

☎ 800-825-7140; www.hotelmarlowe.com; 25 Edwin Land Blvd; d $229-289, specials d $129; Ⓡ Lechmere; Ⓟ ✖ ▣

The Kimpton Group's first property in the Boston area, just steps from Cambridgeside Galleria Mall and the Charles River, embodies chic and unique as this organization

always tries to do. The rooms are defined by rich colors, playful styles and (some) fantastic river views. Perks include down comforters, Sony Playstations and the *New York Times* delivered to your doorstep – enough to please everyone from creature of comfort to free spirit to intellectual snob.

NORTH CAMBRIDGE
A CAMBRIDGE HOUSE

Map pp298-9   B&B $$

☎ 617-491-6300; www.acambridgehouse.com; 2218 Massachusetts Ave; r $129-229; Ⓡ Davis; Ⓟ ✖ ▣

This gracious Victorian throwback overlooks Massachusetts Ave about a mile north of Harvard Sq. An endless array of frills – from plush oriental rugs and floral wallpaper to piles of lacy pillows – evoke the romance of the era. A continental breakfast is included, but there are also plenty of cafés and restaurants within walking distance.

BEST WESTERN HOTEL TRIA

Map pp298-9   Hotel $$

☎ 617-491-8000, 800-528-1234; www.hoteltria .com; 220 Alewife Brook Parkway; r $159-219; Ⓡ Alewife; Ⓟ ✖ ▣ Ⓡ

It's hard to stand out as part of a big chain, but the three Greek sisters who own Hotel Tria have pulled it off. At check-in, guests can choose their own scents from a selection of locally handmade soaps, rather than endure the ennui of yet another industrial white cake. Head up to your room, pop in the complimentary 'calming' CD and wrap yourself in a thick, leopard-patterned robe for a restful evening. Better still, call for the free Harvard Sq shuttle for a night on the town. The neighborhood is not so charming but it has its advantages: notably, its proximity to the Minuteman Trail (see p199) that runs from Davis Sq in Somerville to Lexington Center.

OUTLYING AREAS

One option for budget-conscious travelers is to stay on the outskirts of the city and commute in for sightseeing and other fun. The T offers easy access into town, while the local neighborhoods have their own selection of eateries and entertainment.

SOMERVILLE

MORRISON HOUSE Map pp298-9   B&B $

☎ 617-627-9670; www.morrisonhousebnb.com;
221 Morrison Ave; s $75-120, d $105-135; 🚊 Davis;
🅿 ✂ 💻

Ron and Linde Dynneson are musicians,
cyclists and – now – innkeepers, as they
have opened their home in the heart of
the Davis Sq to guests. Their beautiful turn-
of-the-century Italianate has three cheerful
guestrooms, as well as a sunny patio and a
comfortable common room. Best of all, it's
a short walk to the restaurants, cafés and
bookstores of Davis Sq, not to mention a
quick ride on the red line into the city.

BRIGHTON

BEST WESTERN TERRACE INN

Map pp298-9   Motel $$

☎ 617-566-6260, 800-242-8377; www.bestwestern
.com/terraceinn; 1650 Commonwealth Ave; d $159-
209; 🚊 Washington St (B-line); 🅿

About 2 miles west of Kenmore Sq and
a mile east of Boston College, this Best

Western has 72 rooms, some with kitch-
enettes. They are exactly what you would
expect from a Best Western: clean and
spacious, but lacking any special style. This
hotel is located in the heart of the 'student
ghetto,' which means lots of pizza places
and beer pubs.

DORCHESTER

RAMADA INN   Motel $$

☎ 617-287-9100; www.bostonhotel.com; 800
Morrissey Blvd; d $129-149; 🚊 JFK/UMass;
🅿 ✂ 🚲

Simple and straightforward, this midrange option is about 5 miles south of
the center, right off the I-93. This excellent choice for families offers an outdoor
pool, a recreation center and three on-site
restaurants. While the nondescript neighborhood lacks the charm of other outlying
areas, it is only a mile from the JFK library,
and a van shuttles guests between the
hotel and the nearby T-station. The nearby
Comfort Inn offers a slightly more upscale
alternative.

Excursions

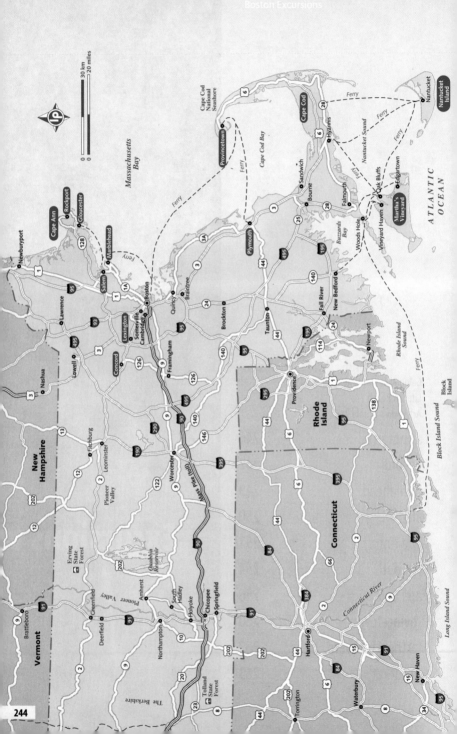

Excursions

Famous village greens, national parks and historic harbors, rich in the evocation of New England's past, lie within an hour's excursion from Boston. History buffs can relive the travails of the earliest European settlers in the New World from the 17th century, witness the events leading up to the American War for Independence in the 18th century, experience the heyday of maritime New England and remember the cultural greats of the 19th century.

But history is not the only draw. Generations of artists have been inspired by the soft light at sunset and the surf crashing on the sand along the coast. Hiking, wildlife-watching, canoeing, kayaking, biking and beaching tempt the wild at heart. Fried clams, grilled striper and boiled lobster will delight seafood lovers. And miles of secluded sandy beaches lure sunbathers and picnickers.

So get on the bus, catch a train, rent a car or saddle up your bike. But by all means, get out of town.

COLONIAL & MARITIME HISTORY

To trace the events leading to the outbreak of the American Revolution in 1775, travelers can follow patriot Paul Revere's famous ride to **Lexington** (p246), 18 miles northwest of Boston, where the revolution's first battle broke out on **Battle Green** (p246). Then continue another six miles along the **Battle Road** (p246) to **Concord** (p247), where the feisty colonists were able to beat back the Redcoats.

To go back even further in time, head to the South Shore. See where the Pilgrims first landed at **Provincetown** (p260), and where they had their first skirmish with Native Americans in **Brewster** (p257) on Cape Cod. The hearty crew finally settled in **Plymouth** (p254), and you can experience the challenges they faced on board the **Mayflower II** (p254) and at **Plimoth Plantation** (p254).

The entire coast of Massachusetts claims a rich history, but no part offers more seafaring lore than the North Shore. **Salem** (p250) was among America's wealthiest ports in the 19th century; **Gloucester** (p252) is the nation's most famous fishing port; and **Marblehead** (p249) remains one of the premier yachting ports in the USA. Further north, at the mouth of the mighty Merrimac River, **Newburyport** also prospered as a shipping port. Trade and fishing brought wealthy residents, sumptuous houses and great collections of art and artifacts to this area. Explore the region's rich maritime history and spectacular coastal scenery and don't miss the opportunity for a seafood feast.

LIFE'S A BEACH

Nothing relieves the hellish heat and humidity of summer in the city like a trip to the beach; and Massachusetts has several appealing options. On the North Shore, the craggy coast of Cape Ann conceals several sandy stretches, including **Good Harbor Beach** (p252) between East Gloucester and Rockport, **Back Beach** (p252) on Sandy Bay near Rockport, and **Wingaersheek Beach** (p252) on Ipswich Bay. Just north of Cape Ann, in the midst of the Crane Wildlife Refuge, **Crane Beach** is four miles of fine-sand barrier beach on Ipswich Bay. Further north, near Newburyport, **Plum Island** has nine miles of wide, sandy beaches surrounded by acres of wildlife sanctuary.

Alternatively, head south to Cape Cod, an arm that reaches more than 60 miles into the Atlantic. On the northern and western shore, the gentle waters of Cape Cod Bay lap up onto sweet sanctuaries like **First Encounter Beach** (p258). On the eastern shore, the **Cape Cod National Seashore** (p258) protects 42 sq miles of sand dunes, coastal forest and utter tranquillity.

If only an island will do, hop on a ferry to Martha's Vineyard or Nantucket, just south of Cape Cod. Nantucket's bicycle trails lead to the island's most popular surfing and swimming destinations, including **Dionis**, **Surfside** and **Sconset Beaches** (p263). On the Vineyard, catch some rays at **Lighthouse Beach** (p262), pedal south to **Katama** (p262) or retreat to the deserted shores of **Chappaquiddick Island** (p262).

ART-LOVER'S AMBLE

Artsy-fartsy travelers to Boston could spend days – if not weeks – exploring galleries, haggling with antique dealers and finding treasures to bring home as souvenirs. If your pocketbook is thin, don't miss the world-class **Peabody Essex Museum** (p250) in Salem or the **DeCordova Sculpture Park & Museum** (p248) near Concord, where you can marvel at the masterpieces but you won't be tempted to buy.

Otherwise, go north to Cape Ann, where you can see the impressive collection of Fitz Hugh Lane at the **Cape Ann Historical Museum** (p252) in Gloucester and compare it to the work of his contemporary counterparts at the **Rocky Neck Artists' Colony** (p252). For a seemingly endless collection of art galleries and antique shops, drive out Cape Cod along Rte 6A, especially in **Dennis, Brewster** and **Wellfleet** (p256). Keep going as far as Provincetown, and you'll have a field day at the **Provincetown Art Association & Museum** (p260) and in the countless galleries at the east end of Commercial St.

LEXINGTON

This upscale suburb has a bustling village of white churches, historic taverns and tour buses surrounding the historic **Battle Green**. Here, the skirmish between patriots and British troops jumpstarted the War for Independence. This history is celebrated and preserved, but it is a stark contrast to the peaceful, even staid, community of Lexington today. Each year on April 19, however, historians and patriots don 18th-century costumes and grab their rifles for an elaborate reenactment of the events of 1775.

At the southeast end of Battle Green, the **Minuteman statue** (crafted by Henry Hudson Kitson in 1900) stands guard, honoring the bravery of the 77 Minutemen who met the British here and the eight who died. The **Parker Boulder**, named for the commander of the Minutemen, marks the spot where they faced a force almost 10 times their strength. It is inscribed with his instructions to his troops: 'Stand your ground. Don't fire unless fired upon. But if they mean to have a war, let it begin here.' Cross the street to see how history buffs have preserved the **Old Belfry** that sounded the alarm signaling the start of the revolution.

> ## TRANSPORTATION
>
> **Distance from Boston** 12 miles
>
> **Direction** West
>
> **Bicycle** The Minuteman Commuter Bikeway runs six miles from Alewife in Cambridge to Lexington. From here you can follow the Bikeway another four miles west to its terminus in Bedford, or ride the Battle Rd Trail to Concord. See p199 for details.
>
> **Bus** MBTA bus 62 (Bedford VA Hospital) and 76 (Hanscom Field) run from the red-line T terminus at Alewife through Lexington center hourly on weekdays, less frequently on Saturday, with no Sunday service.
>
> **Car** Take MA 2 west from Boston or Cambridge to exit 54 (Waltham St) or exit 53 (Spring St). From I-95 (MA 128), take exit 30 or 31.

Southeast of the green in **Isaac Harris Cary Memorial Hall**, Henry Sandham's painting *The Dawn of Liberty* is the most famous depiction of the battle.

Facing the green, **Buckman Tavern**, built in 1709, was the headquarters of the Minutemen. Here, they spent the tense hours between the midnight call to arms and the dawn arrival of the Redcoats. Today, it is a museum of colonial life. The **Lexington Historical Society** maintains two other historic houses that are open sporadically.

Two miles west of Lexington center, the route that British troops followed to Concord has been designated The **Minute Man National Historic Park**. The visitors center at the eastern end of the park shows an informative multimedia presentation depicting Paul Revere's ride and the ensuing battles. Within the park, **Battle Rd** is a wooded trail that connects the historic sites related to the battles – from Meriam's Corner, where gunfire erupted while British soldiers were retreating, to the Paul Revere capture site.

Information

Lexington Historical Society (☎ 781-862-1703; www.lexingtonhistory.org; 1332 Mass Ave)

Lexington Visitor Center (Lexington Chamber of Commerce; ☎ 781-862-1450; www.lexingtonchamber.org; 1875 Mass Ave, Lexington; 🕙 9am-5pm Apr-Oct, 10am-4pm Nov-Mar) Opposite Battle Green next to Buckman Tavern.

MBTA (☎ 617-222-5215; www.mbta.com)

Sights

Buckman Tavern (☎ 781-862-5598; 1 Bedford Rd; adult/senior/child $5/5/3; 🕙 10am-5pm Mon-Sat, 1-5pm Sun Apr-Oct)

Isaac Harris Cary Memorial Hall (☎ 781-862-0500; 1625 Mass Ave; admission free; 🕙 8:30am-4:30pm Mon-Fri)

Liberty Ride (☎ 781-862-0500; www.libertyride.us; adult/child $20/10; 🕙 10am-5pm) For those who prefer to follow in Paul Revere's footsteps in the comfort of an air-conditioned bus.

Minute Man National Historic Park Visitors Center (☎ 978-862-7753; www.nps.gov/mima; 🕙 9am-5pm Apr-Oct)

Eating

Rancatore's (☎ 781-862-5090; 1752 Mass Ave; ice cream $3-5; 🕙 10am-11pm) Cool off with a scoop of homemade ice cream or sorbet from this family-run parlor.

Upper Crust (☎ 781-274-0089; 41 Waltham St; meals $8-12; 🕙 11:30am-10pm Sun-Thu, 11:30am-11pm Fri & Sat) Crispy, Neopolitan pizza with tangy garlic, fresh tomatoes and spicy pepperoni, served up in a clean, no-frills setting.

Vila Lago Gourmet Foods (☎ 781-861-6174; 1845 Mass Ave; meals $8-12; 🕙 7am-7pm Mon, 7am-8pm Tue-Wed, 7am-9pm Thu-Sat) High ceilings, intimate tables, a scent of fresh-roasted coffee and a great deli case.

Sleeping

Battle Green Inn & Suites (☎ 781-862-6100, 800-343-0235; www.battlegreeninn.com; 1720 Mass Ave; d/tw weeknights $79/99, d/tw weekends $99/109) A motel-style lodging right in the center of Lexington's historic district.

Mary Van's My Old House (☎ 781-861-7057; www.maryvansmyoldhousebandb.com; 12 Plainfield St; r $75-85, breakfast $10) Featured on the PBS series *This Old House*, Mary Van's place is nestled on the corner of a shady residential street, about a mile south of the center.

Morgan's Rest (☎ 781-652-8018; www.morgansrestbandb.com; 205 Follen Rd; r Nov-Mar $95-115, r Apr-Oct $105-125) A friendly B&B about two miles from Lexington center. Guests enjoy gourmet breakfast served in the elegant library, complete with gorgeous grand piano and working fireplace.

CONCORD

White church steeples rise above ancient oaks and elms in colonial Concord, giving the town a stateliness that belies the Revolutionary War drama that occurred centuries ago. Indeed, it is easy to see how writers such as Ralph Waldo Emerson, Nathaniel Hawthorne, Henry David Thoreau and Louisa May Alcott found their inspiration here.

The grassy center of **Monument Square** is a favorite resting and picnicking spot for cyclists touring Concord's scenic roads. A half-mile north of here, the wooden span of **Old North Bridge**, now part of Minute Man National Historic Park, is the site of the 'shot heard around the world' (as Ralph Waldo Emerson wrote in his poem *Concord Hymn*). Daniel Chester French's first statue, the **Minuteman**, presides over the park from the opposite side of the bridge. On your way up here, look for the yellow **Bullet Hole House**, where British troops fired at the owner of the house as they retreated from North Bridge.

Next to Old North Bridge, the **Old Manse** was built in 1769 by the Reverend William Emerson, Ralph Waldo's grandfather, and was owned by successive generations of the Emerson family. Today it's filled with mementos, including those of Nathaniel and Sophia Hawthorne, who lived here for a few years. The highlight of Old Manse is the gorgeously

---

TRANSPORTATION

Distance from Boston 18 miles

Direction West

Car Take Rte 2 west from Cambridge.

Train MBTA commuter rail trains ($5, 40 min, eight daily) run between Boston's North Station and Concord Depot on the Fitchburg/South Acton line.

maintained grounds: the fabulous organic garden was planted by Henry David Thoreau as a wedding gift to the Hawthornes.

Southeast of Monument Square, the **Concord Museum** brings together the town's diverse history under one roof. The museum's prized possession is one of the 'two if by sea' lanterns that hung in the steeple of the Old North Church in Boston as a signal to Paul Revere and his cohorts. This place also has the world's largest collection of Henry David Thoreau artifacts, including his writing desk from Walden Pond.

Across the street is the **Emerson House Museum**, where Ralph Waldo Emerson (1803–82) lived for almost 50 years. He was the paterfamilias of literary Concord, one of the great literary figures of his age and the founding thinker of the Transcendentalist movement.

Louisa May Alcott was a junior member of Concord's august literary crowd, but her work proved to be durable: *Little Women* (1868–69) is among the most popular young-adult books ever written. Her childhood home, **Orchard House** is just east of Emerson's house.

These famous figures rest in **Sleepy Hollow Cemetery**. Walk east along Bedford St to **Authors' Ridge**. Henry David Thoreau and his family are buried here, as are the Alcotts and the Hawthornes. Emerson's tombstone is the large uncarved rock of New England marble, an appropriate Transcendentalist symbol.

Henry David Thoreau took the naturalist beliefs of Transcendentalism out of the realm of theory and into practice when he left the comforts of town and built a rustic cabin at **Walden Pond**. The glacial pond is now a state park, surrounded by acres of forest preserved by the nonprofit Walden Woods project. The **site of Thoreau's cabin** is on the northeast side, marked by a cairn and signs. To escape the crowded summertime beach, follow the path along to the other side of the pond.

Located near Walden Pond, the magical **DeCordova Sculpture Park** encompasses 35 acres of green hills, providing a spectacular natural environment for a constantly changing exhibit of outdoor artwork. As many as 75 pieces are on display at any given time. Inside the complex, a **museum** hosts rotating exhibits of sculpture, painting, photography and mixed media.

Information

Concord Chamber of Commerce Visitor Center (☎ 978-369-3120; www.concordchamberofcommerce.org; 58 Main St; guided walking tours adult/senior & student/child $18/12/7, 11am Fri-Mon; ☽ 9:30am-4:30pm daily Apr-Oct, 9am-2pm Mon-Fri Nov-Mar) Tours of revolutionary and literary Concord.

MBTA (☎ 617-222-5215; www.mbta.com)

North Bridge Visitor Center (☎ 978-369-6993; Liberty St; ☽ 9am-4pm, to 5pm Apr-Oct)

Sights

Concord Museum (☎ 978-369-9609; www.concord museum.org; 200 Lexington Rd; adult/senior/student/child $8/7/7/5; ☽ 9am-5pm Mon-Sat & noon-5pm Sun Apr-Dec,11am-4pm Mon-Sat & 1-4pm Sun Jan-Mar)

DeCordova Sculpture Park & Museum (☎ 781-259-8355; www.decordova.org; 51 Sandy Pond Rd, Lincoln; museum adult/senior/student/child $9/6/6/6; ☽ museum 10am-5pm Tue-Sun, park dawn-dusk daily)

Emerson House Museum (☎ 978-369-2236; 28 Cambridge Turnpike; adult/senior & child/child under 7 yrs $7/5/free; ☽ 10am-4:30pm Thu-Sat, 1-4:30pm Sun mid-Apr–mid-Oct)

Old Manse (☎ 978-369-3909; www.thetrustees.org; 269 Monument St; adult/senior/child $8/7/5; ☽ 10am-5pm Mon-Sat, noon-5pm Sun mid-Apr–Oct)

Orchard House (☎ 978-369-4118; www.louisamayalcott .org; 399 Lexington Rd; adult/senior & student/child $8/7/5; ☽ 10am-4:30pm Mon-Sat & 1-4:30pm Sun Apr-Oct, 11am-3pm Mon-Fri, 10am-4:30pm Sat & 1-4:30pm Sun Nov-Mar)

Sleepy Hollow Cemetery (☎ 978-371-6299; Bedford St)

Walden Pond (☎ 978-369-3254; www.mass.gov/dem/parks/wldn.htm; 915 Walden St; admission free; ☽ dawn-dusk; P $5)

Eating

Cheese Shop (☎ 978-369-5778; 29 Walden St; lunch $4-8; ☽ closed Mon) Stop here for a huge luncheon sandwich like the mixed grilled veggie pocket ($6) or for picnic supplies. Wine tasting starts at noon on Saturday.

Helen's Café (☎ 978-369-9885; 17 Main St; meals $8-12; ☽ 7am-9pm) This popular breakfast and lunch spot hums with the sound of silver and plates hitting the Formica table tops. Hungry patrons come looking for homemade soups and grinders, or a thick frappe from the ice cream counter.

Walden Grille (☎ 978-371-2233; 24 Walden St; lunch $10-15, dinner $20-30) A tavern-restaurant with soft lighting, exposed brick walls and lyrical landscape paintings. The New American menu gets mixed reviews, but the former fire station setting is welcoming and cool.

Sleeping

Best Western at Historic Concord (☎ 978-369-6100, 800-528-1234; www.bestwestern.com; 740 Elm St; r with breakfast $99-124; P ⚡) Freshly appointed, well-scrubbed units typical of this chain. The motel is at MA 2 near the Concord rotary; several restaurants are nearby.

Colonial Inn (☎ 978-369-9200, 800-370-9200; www .concordscolonialinn.com; 48 Monument Square; r $149-229; P) The oldest part of this 1716 inn houses 12 of the more expensive guest rooms, a lobby, dining rooms and tavern (featuring afternoon tea). The other less expensive 48 guest rooms are in a modern brick annex.

North Bridge Inn (☎ 978-371-0014; www.northbridge inn.com; 21 Monument St; r $165-250; P) Six rooms are decked out with down comforters, plush pillows, tile bathrooms and kitchenettes; a gourmet breakfast is served in the flower-filled dining room; and the friendly dog Posey greets every guest who walks through the door.

MARBLEHEAD

First settled in 1629, Marblehead's Old Town is a maritime village with winding streets, brightly painted colonial and Federal houses, and 1000 sailing yachts bobbing at moorings in the harbor. This is the Boston area's premier yachting port and one of New England's most prestigious addresses.

Pick up a map from the Marblehead Chamber of Commerce information booth on Pleasant St near its intersection with Essex and Spring Sts. Many restaurants and historic buildings are clustered

---

TRANSPORTATION

Distance from Boston 16 miles

Direction Northeast

Bus Take MBTA bus 441 or 442 from Haymarket Sq (near North Station), or bus 448 or 449 from Downtown Crossing or South Station.

Car From Salem, follow MA 114 southeast for 4 miles to Marblehead, where it becomes Pleasant St.

---

around the intersection of Pleasant and Washington Sts. The red-brick building with a lofty clock tower is the **Old Town House** and contains artifacts of Marblehead's history, including the original title deed to Marblehead from the Nanapashemet Indians, dated 1684. The famous patriotic painting *The Spirit of '76* (c 1876) by Archibald M Willard, hangs in the Selectmen's Meeting Room in **Abbott Hall**, home of the Marblehead Historical Commission. The **Marblehead Museum & Historical Society** organizes exhibits and maintains historic sites, including the Georgian **Jeremiah Lee Mansion**.

From Pleasant St (MA 114) south of the Marblehead center, Ocean Ave leads east over a causeway onto Marblehead Neck, a 2-sq-mile swathe of land that juts into the ocean. On the southeastern side, a short walk takes you to **Castle Rock**, with views of the Boston Ship Channel and Boston's Harbor Islands. At the northern tip of Marblehead Neck, **Chandler Hovey Park**, by Marblehead Light, offers views of Cape Ann and the islands of Salem Bay.

Information

Marblehead Chamber of Commerce (☎ 781-639-8469; www.marbleheadchamber.org; 62 Pleasant St; ☉ noon-5pm Mon-Fri, 10am-6pm Sat & Sun)

MBTA (☎ 617-222-5215; www.mbta.com)

Sights

Abbott Hall (☎ 781-631-0000; 188 Washington St; admission free; ☉ 9am-4pm, longer hours in summer)

Jeremiah Lee Mansion (☎ 781-631-1768; 161 Washington St; admission $5; ☉ 10am-4pm Tue-Sat Jun-Oct, gardens open year-round)

Marblehead Museum & Historical Society (☎ 781-631-1768; 170 Washington St; admission free; ☉ 10am-4pm Tue-Sat Nov-May, 10am-4pm Tue-Fri Jun-Oct)

Eating

The Barnacle (☎ 781-631-4236; 141 Front St; meals $10-20) Perched on a rocky outcrop at the harbor's edge, this is what waterside dining is meant to be. Specialties include steaming hot clam chowder and lobsters straight off the boat. Excellent outdoor seating.

Jack Tar (☎ 781-631-2323; 126 Washington St; meals $15-20) This pleasant place boasts 'creative takes on

traditional dishes,' including reliably tasty brick-oven pizzas, homemade pastas and seafood entrées.

Crosby's Market (☎ 781-631-1741; 118 Washington St;
deli $2-7; ☺ 9am-9pm) Visit this place in Old Town for all
of your picnic needs.

Maddie's Sail Loft (☎ 781-631-9824; 15 State St; meals
$15-30) The place to come for local color. Set in a historic
house, oldtimers pack into this little pub to wolf down
fried seafood and swill some beers. One block inland from
State St Landing.

Sleeping

Marblehead's dozens of B&Bs cater mostly
to weekend visitors (expect higher prices

on Friday and Saturday nights). Most of
them have only a few rooms, so reservations
are essential. You will find a complete list of
B&Bs at the Marblehead Chamber of Commerce (see p249), which will also help with
reservations.

Harbor Light Inn (☎ 781-631-2186; www.harborlight
inn.com; 58 Washington St; r $145-345; P 💻 🐾) A
larger but no less romantic spot, with canopy beds, working fireplaces and in-room hot tubs.

Marblehead Inn (☎ 781-639-9999; www.marblehead
inn.com; 264 Pleasant St; r $184-195; P) Ten cozy suites
in a gracious Victorian.

SALEM

This town's very name conjures up images
of diabolical witchcraft and women being
burned at the stake. The famous Salem
witch trials of 1692 are engrained in the national memory. Indeed, Salem goes all out
at Halloween, when the whole town dresses
up for parades and parties and shops sell all
manner of Wiccan accessories.

Of more than a score of witchy sites,
the most authentic is the **Witch House**. This
was the home of Jonathan Corwin, a local
magistrate who investigated witchcraft
claims. Corwin examined several accused
witches, possibly in the first-floor rooms
of this house. The **Salem Witch Museum** holds
dioramas, exhibits, audiovisual shows and
costumed staff who explain the witchcraft
scare.

The witch phenomena obscure Salem's
true claim to fame: its glory days as a center
for clipper-ship trade with China, started
by Elias Hasket Derby. The **Salem Maritime
National Historic Site** comprises the custom
house, the wharves and the other build-

TRANSPORTATION

Distance from Boston 20 miles

Direction Northeast

Bus MBTA bus 450 and 455 from Boston's Haymarket Sq (near North Station) take longer than the
train and cost no less.

Car A 35-minute drive (non-rush hour). Follow US
1 north across the Mystic River (Tobin) Bridge and
bear right onto MA 16 toward Revere Beach, then
follow MA 1A (Shore Rd) to Salem. MA 1A becomes
Lafayette St in Salem and takes you right to Essex St
Mall and the common.

Train Both the Newburyport and Rockport lines of
the MBTA commuter rail ($3.75, 30 minutes) run
from Boston's North Station to Salem Depot. Trains
run every 30 minutes during the morning and
evening rush hours, hourly during the rest of the
day, and less on weekends.

ings along Derby St that are remnants of the shipping industry that once thrived along
this stretch of Salem. In all, the site comprises ten different historic locations within a
two-block area.

Many Salem vessels followed Derby's ship *Grand Turk* around the Cape of Good Hope,
and soon the owners founded the East India Marine Society to provide warehousing
services. The new company's charter required the establishment of a museum 'to house
the natural and artificial curiosities' brought back by member ships. The collection was
the basis for what is now the world-class **Peabody Essex Museum**. Predictably, it is particularly
strong on Asian art and includes a Chinese house that was shipped from Huizhou province.
The museum also has extensive collections focusing on New England decorative arts and
maritime history.

The **House of the Seven Gables** was made famous in Nathaniel Hawthorne's 1851 novel of the
same name. The novel brings to life the gloomy Puritan atmosphere of early New England
and its effects on the people's psyches; the house does the same.

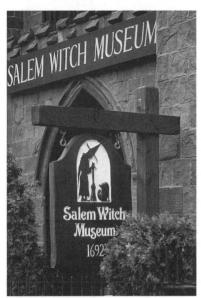

Salem Witch Museum (right)

Information

Central Wharf Visitor Center (☎ 978-740-1650; www
.nps.gov/sama; 193 Derby St; admission free; ⏱ 9am-5pm)

Destination Salem (☎ 978-744-3663; www.salem.org;
54 Turner St) The office of tourism and cultural affairs.

Haunted Happenings (☎ 877-744-3663; www.haunted
happenings.org) Everyone in Salem celebrates Halloween,
not just the witches. For most of October, there are special
exhibits, parades, concerts, pumpkin carvings, costume
parties and trick-or-treating. It all culminates on October
31, with the crowning of the king and queen of Halloween.

MBTA (☎ 617-222-5215; www.mbta.com)

National Park Service (NPS) Regional Visitor Center
(☎ 978-740-1650; 2 Liberty St; ⏱ 9am-5pm)

Sights

Cry Innocent (☎ 978-867-4747; www.cryinnocent.com;
Old Town Hall; adult/senior & student $8/7; ⏱ 11:30am,
1:30pm & 3pm daily Jun-Aug, Sat only in Sep, 11am & 1pm
daily in Oct) A historical reenactment of the witch trial of
Bridget Bishop, in which the audience plays the jury.

House of the Seven Gables (☎ 978-744-0991; www
.7gables.org; 115 Derby St; adult/senior & student/child
$12/11/7.25; ⏱ 10am-5pm Nov-Jun, 10am-7pm July-Oct)

Peabody Essex Museum (☎ 866-745-1876, 978-745-
9500; www.pem.org; Essex St Mall, New Liberty St;
adult/senior/student/child $13/11/9/free; ⏱ 10am-5pm)

Salem Maritime National Historic Site (☎ 978-740-
1650; www.nps.gov/sama; 174 Derby St; adult/child $5/3)

Salem Witch Museum (☎ 978-744-1692; www
.salemwitchmuseum.com; Washington Square North;
adult/senior/child $7.50/6.50/4.50; ⏱ 10am-5pm Sep-
Jun; 10am-7pm July & Aug)

Witch Dungeon (☎ 978-741-3570; www.witchdungeon
.com; 16 Lynde St; adult/senior/child $6/5/4; ⏱ 10am-
5pm Apr-Nov) Stages re-creations of a witch trial based on
historical transcripts.

Witch House (☎ 978-744-8815; www.salemweb
.com/witchhouse; 310 Essex St; adult/senior/child $8/6/4;
⏱ 10am-5pm May-Nov, extended hours in Oct)

Eating

Finz (☎ 978-774-8485; 76 Wharf St; meals $15-30) Three
walls of windows overlooking Salem Harbor. The seductive
raw bar and carefully chosen wine list are added perks.

Front Street Coffeehouse (☎ 978-740-6697; 20 Front St;
meals $5-8) A cool place to sip a caffe latte or munch on a
giant sandwich. Also offers free wi-fi access.

Rockafellas (☎ 978-745-2411; www.rockafellasofsalem
.com; 231 Essex St; sandwiches $7-11, mains $18-20;
⏱ 11:30am-midnight Sun-Wed, 11:30am-1am Thu-Sat)
With live entertainment Wednesday through Sunday, this
lively restaurant and lounge draws an upscale crowd to
kick back and enjoy the semi-swanky setting.

Rockmore Floating Restaurant (☎ 978-740-1001;
Pickering Wharf; meals $10-15; ⏱ 11am-9pm Jun &
Aug) That's right: floating. Set on a barge in the middle
of Salem Harbor, this clam shack is the ultimate place to
refuel on a hot summer day. Catch the free shuttle boat
from the Congress St Bridge, but don't forget to tip the
captain.

Sleeping

Hawthorne Hotel (☎ 978-744-4080, 800-729-7829;
www.hawthornehotel.com; 18 Washington Square West;
r $104-309) This historic Federalist-style hotel is in the
heart of Salem center. Also operates the Suzanna Flint
House, a small B&B in an 1808 Federal house.

Salem Inn (☎ 978-741-0680, 800-446-2995; www
.saleminnma.com; 7 Summer St; d $129-189) Thirty-three
rooms are located in three different historic houses, including the Captain West House, a large brick sea captain's
home from 1834.

Salem Waterfront Hotel (☎ 978-740-8788; www
.salemwaterfronthotel.com; 225 Derby St; r $159-189)
Prime location overlooking Pickering Wharf and Salem
Harbor. Eighty-six spacious rooms have graceful decor and
all the expected amenities.

CAPE ANN

Cape Ann offers a combination of natural beauty, maritime history and New England charm that is hard to resist.

Founded in 1623 by English fisherfolk, Gloucester is among New England's oldest towns. This port on Cape Ann has made its living out of fishing for 400 years, and inspired books and films like Rudyard Kipling's *Captains Courageous* and Sebastian Junger's *The Perfect Storm*. Despite recent economic diversification, this town still smells of fish. Fishing boats, festooned with nets, dredges and winches, are tied to the wharves or motor into the harbor with clouds of hungry seagulls hovering above. Visit the **Gloucester Maritime Center** and see the ongoing restoration of wooden boats, watch the operation of a marine railway that hauls ships out of the water, and compare the different fishing boats that were used over the years. This working waterfront is also a good place to pick up a **whale-watching cruise**.

TRANSPORTATION

Distance from Boston Gloucester 35 miles, Rockport 40 miles

Direction Northeast

Car You can reach Cape Ann quickly from Boston or North Shore towns via four-lane Rte 128, but the scenic route on MA 127 follows the coastline through prim New England villages. MA 127/127A loops around Cape Ann, connecting these towns to Rockport. Driving the entire loop is worth it for seaside scenery in East Gloucester, Laneville, and Annisquam.

Local Bus The Cape Ann Transportation Authority operates bus routes between the towns on Cape Ann.

Train The Rockport line of the MBTA commuter rail ($5.50, one hour) goes from Boston's North Station to both Rockport and Gloucester.

The **Cape Ann Historical Museum** has an impressive collection of paintings by Gloucester native Fitz Hugh Lane. This artistic legacy endures, as Gloucester still boasts a vibrant artists community at **Rocky Neck Artists' Colony.** Check out the galleries operated by the **North Shore Arts Association.**

Don't leave Gloucester without paying your respects at **St Peter's Square,** where Leonard Craske's famous statue, *Gloucester Fisherman* is dedicated to 'They That Go Down to the Sea in Ships, 1623–1923.'

Meanwhile, at the northern tip of Cape Ann, Rockport is a quaint contrast to gritty Gloucester. **Dock Square** is the hub of Rockport. Visible from here, the red fishing shack decorated with colorful buoys is known as **Motif No 1** because so many artists painted and photographed it over the years. **Bearskin Neck** is the peninsula that juts into the harbor, lined with galleries, lobster shacks, and souvenir shops.

Cape Ann has several excellent beaches that draw Boston-area sun-and-sea worshippers on any hot day in July or August. Just north of Dock Square is **Back Beach**, on Sandy Bay. Perhaps biggest and best, however, is **Wingaersheek Beach**, a wide swath of sand surrounded by Ipswich Bay and guarded by **Annisquam Lighthouse.** East of East Gloucester on the way to Rockport, **Good Harbor Beach** is a spacious, sandy beach. Parking is very limited here, so arrive early.

A few miles north of Rockport is **Halibut Point State Park.** A 10-minute walk through the forest brings you to yawning, abandoned granite quarries, huge hills of broken granite rubble and a granite foreshore of tumbled, smoothed rock perfect for picnicking, sunbathing, reading or painting. The surf can be strong here, making swimming unwise.

Information

Cape Ann Chamber of Commerce (☎ 978-283-1601, 800-321-0133; www.capeannvacations.com; 33 Commercial St, Gloucester; ☒ 8am-5:30pm Mon-Fri, 10am-6pm Sat, 10am-4pm Sun) South of St Peter's Square.

Cape Ann Transportation Authority (CATA; ☎ 978-283-7916; www.canntran.com) Operates buses between Cape Ann towns.

MBTA (☎ 617-222-5215; www.mbta.com)

Rockport Chamber of Commerce (☎ 978-546-6575, 888-726-3922; www.rockportusa.com; 3 Whistlestop Mall, Rockport; ☒ 9am-5pm Mon-Fri) Near the train station.

See Cape Ann (www.seecapeann.com) Cape Ann's online information booth.

Sights & Activities

Cape Ann Historical Museum (☎ 978-283-0455; www.capeannhistoricalmuseum.org; 27 Pleasant St, Gloucester; adult/senior/student $6.50/6/4.50; ☒ 10am-5pm Tue-Sat & 1-4pm Sun Mar-Jan)

Capt Bill & Sons Whale Watch (☎ 978-283-6995, 800-339-4253; www.captbillandsons.com; 33 Harbor Loop; adult/senior/child $39/33/24) The boat leaves from behind Captain Carlo's Seafood Market & Restaurant.

Gloucester Maritime Center (☎ 978-281-0470; www.gloucestermaritimecenter.org; 23 Harbor Loop, Gloucester; admission by donation, Sea Pocket Lab adult/senior/child $5/4/2; ☒ 10am-5:30pm daily Jun & Aug, Sat-Sun only Sep-May)

Good Harbor Beach (Thatcher Rd, Rte 127A; P $20 Mon-Fri, $25 Sat-Sun)

Halibut Point State Park (☎ 978-546-2997; www.halibutpointstatepark.com; admission $2; ☒ 8am-9pm; P $2)

North Shore Arts Association (☎ 978-283-1857; www.northshoreartsassoc.org; 197 East Main St, Gloucester; ☒ 10am-5pm Mon-Sat, noon-5pm Sun)

Wingaersheek Beach (Atlantic Rd, Gloucester; P $20 Mon-Fri, $25 Sat-Sun)

Eating

Rockport is a dry town, meaning that alcohol is not sold in stores or restaurants and there are no bars.

Brackett's (☎ 978-546-2797; 25 Main St, Rockport; lunch $10-15, dinner $20-30; ☒ closed Nov-Mar) The casual pub atmosphere, ocean views and daily specials draw a consistent crowd.

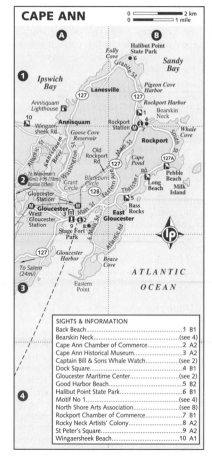

Crow's Nest (☎ 978-281-2965; 334 Main St, Gloucester) The down-and-dirty fisherfolk bar made famous in *The Perfect Storm*.

Franklin Cape Ann (☎ 978-283-7888; 118 Main S, Gloucester; meals $20-30; ☒ 5pm-10:30pm Sun-Thu, 5pm-midnight Fri & Sat) The North Shore branch of a South End favorite (see p149).

Maria's Pizza (☎ 978-283-7373; 35 Pearl St, Gloucester; pizza $10-15) Gloucester's favorite pizzeria is across from the train station. Bring your own beer from the 'packie' across the street.

Roy Moore Lobster Company (☎ 978-546-6696; 29 Bearskin Neck, Rockport; meals $10-20) This takeout kitchen has the cheapest lobster-in-the-rough (around $11) on the Neck. You can sit in the back with the fishing boats on a few tables fashioned from lobster traps; or go next door to the restaurant if you prefer a little more refinement.

Excursions

CAPE ANN

Sleeping

Every year, new B&Bs are opening around Cape Ann. Search out this emerging market at www.capeannvacations.com or www .innsofrockport.com.

Bear Skin Neck Motor Lodge (☎ 978-546-6677; 64 Bear Skin Neck, Rockport; r $99-149; P) The only lodging on Bear Skin Neck is this motel-style lodge near the end of the strip. Needless to say, every room has a great view – and a balcony from which to enjoy it.

Cape Ann Motor Inn (☎ 978-281-2900; www.capeann motorinn.com; 33 Rockport Rd, Gloucester; r $75-145; P) Halfway between Rockport and Gloucester and right on Long Beach. All rooms feature glass sliding doors that open onto private balconies with ocean views.

Captain's Bounty Motor Inn (☎ 978-546-9557; www .captainsbountymotorinn.com; 1 Beach St; r $150-180; P) The draw here is the prime location, right on Front Beach and only a few minutes' stroll from Dock Sq. The 24 rooms are simple, but they have lovely views of the sunrise over the beach and the local lobstermen checking their traps.

PLYMOUTH

Historic Plymouth, 'America's Home Town,' is synonymous with Plymouth Rock. Thousands of visitors come here each year to look at this weathered granite ball and to consider what it was like for the Pilgrims, who stepped ashore this strange land in the autumn of 1620. You can see **Plymouth Rock** in a mere minute, but the rock is just a symbol of the Pilgrims' struggle, sacrifice and triumph, which are elucidated in many museums and exhibits.

If Plymouth Rock tells us little about the Pilgrims, **Mayflower II** speaks volumes. Climb aboard this replica of the small ship in which they made the fateful voyage, where 102 people lived together for 66 days as the ship passed through the stormy North Atlantic waters.

During the winter of 1620–21, half of the Pilgrims died of disease, privation and exposure to the elements. But new arrivals joined the survivors in 1621; and by 1627, Plymouth colony was on the road to prosperity. The **Plimoth Plantation**, a mile or so south of Plymouth Rock, authentically re-creates the Pilgrims' 1627 settlement. Everything in the village – costumes, implements, vocabulary, artistry, recipes and crops – has been painstakingly researched and remade. **Hobbamock's (Wampanoag) Homesite** replicates the life of a Native American community in the area at the same time.

Claiming to be the oldest continually operating public museum in the country, **Pilgrim Hall Museum** was founded in 1824. At the opposite end of town, the **Jenney Grist Mill** is located on the site of the first grist mill established in 1636.

As New England's oldest European community, Plymouth also has its share of fine old houses. The oldest is the **Richard Sparrow House**, built in 1640, which now houses a gallery. The 1667 **Howland House** is the only house in Plymouth that was home to a known *Mayflower* passenger. The **Mayflower Society Museum** is housed in the magnificent 1754 Winslow House. The Plymouth Antiquarian Society maintains three additional historic houses, but only the 1749 **Spooner House** was open for tours at the time of research.

TRANSPORTATION

Distance from Boston 40 miles

Direction South

Boat The Plymouth-to-Provincetown Express Ferry (adult/senior/child/one-way $35/30/25/20, 90 minutes, once daily) departs Plymouth at 10am and leaves Provincetown at 4:30pm.

Bus Plymouth & Brockton (P&B) buses travel to South Station or Logan Airport in Boston (adult/child $12/6, hourly). Heading south, these buses continue as far as Hyannis.

Car Take I-93 South to MA3.

Train MBTA commuter trains ($6, one hour, four daily) to Plymouth leave from South Station. GATRA buses connect the P&B terminal and the train station at Cordage Park to the town center.

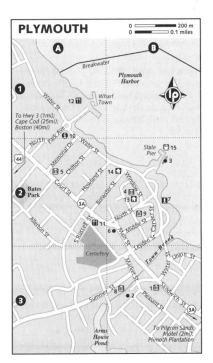

PLYMOUTH

0 |———| 200 m
0 |———| 0.1 miles

Plymouth & Brockton (P&B) Bus (☎ 508-746-0378, 778-9767; www.p-b.com)

Plymouth Guide Online (www.plymouthguide.com) Lots of information about tourist attractions, dining and accommodation in the area.

Plymouth-to-Provincetown Express Ferry (☎ 508-747-2400, 800-242-2469; provincetownferry.com; State Pier)

Sights

Howland House (☎ 508-746-9590; 33 Sandwich St) adult/senior & student/child $4/3/2; ☻ 10am-4:30pm late May to mid-Oct)

Jenney Grist Mill (☎ 508-747-4544; www.jenneygrist mill.org; 6 Spring Lane; adult/child $6/3; ☻ 9:30am-5pm Mon-Sat, noon-5pm Sun Apr-Nov)

Mayflower II (☎ 508-746-1622; www.plimoth.org; State Pier; adult/senior/child $8/7/6, combined ticket to Plimoth Plantation adult/senior & student/child $24/21/14; ☻ 9am-5pm Apr-Nov)

Mayflower Society Museum (☎ 508-746-2590; www .mayflower.org; 4 Winslow St; admission $4; ☻ 10am-4pm Jul & Aug, 10am-4pm Sat-Sun only Jun, Sep & Oct)

Pilgrim Hall Museum (☎ 508-746-1620; www .pilgrimhall.org; 75 Court St; adult/senior/child $6/5/3; ☻ 9:30am-4:30pm Feb-Dec)

Plimoth Plantation (☎ 508-746-1622; www.plimoth .org; MA 3A; adult/senior/child $21/19/12, combined ticket to *Mayflower II* adult/senior & student/child $24/21/14; ☻ 9:30am-5pm Apr-Nov)

Richard Sparrow House (☎ 508-747-1240; www.sparrow house.com; 42 Summer St; adult/child $2/1; ☻ 10am-5pm Thu-Tue Apr-Dec)

Spooner House (☎ 508-746-0012; www.plymouthanti quariansociety.org; 27 North St; adult/child $4.50/2; ☻ 2-6pm Thu & Fri, 9am-noon Sat)

Information

Destination Plymouth (☎ 508-747-7533; www.visit-ply mouth.com; 170 Water St; ☻ 9am-5pm Apr-Nov, to 8pm Jun-Aug) Located at the rotary across from Plymouth Harbor.

GATRA (☎ 508-747-1819; www.gatra.org)

MBTA (☎ 617-222-5215; www.mbta.com)

Eating

Fast-food shops line Water St opposite the *Mayflower II*. For more options, walk a block inland to Main St, where restaurants are open year-round.

Jubilee (☎ 508-747-3700; 22 Court St; meals $10-15) Soups, salads, pastas and entrées with international panache. Look for weekly specials and signature sandwiches.

Lobster Hut (☎ 508-746-2270; Town Wharf; meals $10-20) A seafood shack with big plates of fried clams, fish and chips, and – of course – lobster in every form. Outdoor seating available.

Sleeping

1782 Whitfield House (☎ 508-747-6735; www
.whitfieldhouse.com; 26 North St; r $120, ste $170-220;
P) A gracious Federal house in the heart of
historic Plymouth. It has only four rooms – each
uniquely decorated with the utmost attention to detail.

Governor Bradford Inn (☎ 508-746-6200, 800-332-
1620; www.governorbradford.com; 98 Water St;
r $125-165; P) Named for William Bradford,
the second governor of Plymouth Colony and author
of the historical reference *Of Plimouth Plantation*.
Conveniently located smack dab in the middle of
town.

Pilgrim Sands Motel (☎ 508-747-0900, 800-729-7263;
www.pilgrimsands.com; 150 Warren Ave; d beach view
$185-195, plantation view $155-165; P ⊠) This typical
beach motel is another good option for families, as it's
right on a private beach and directly opposite Plimouth
Plantation.

CAPE COD

The Cape is New England's favorite summertime destination. Vacationers come in search of fresh seafood and sandy beaches that cover most of 400 miles of shoreline. They come for sleepy sand dunes, studded with scrub oak and pine, for salt marshes teeming with birdlife, and for quaint beach towns with historic roots. Although you can see parts of Cape Cod in a day trip, if you have three or four days it's all the better.

The Sagamore and Bourne Bridges span the Cape Cod Canal, linking the Cape to the mainland. Stop by the **Cape Cod Canal Visitor Center** to view interactive exhibits or inquire about guided tours. Each side of the Cape Cod Canal has a well-maintained **bike trail** that follows its banks. (Rent a bicycle at **Sandwich Cycles**.)

The first town of note that you encounter across the Sagamore Bridge is Sandwich (founded in 1637). The town was a center for glassmaking in the 19th century, and this heyday is celebrated at the **Sandwich Glass Museum**. The highlight of sylvan Sandwich, however, is the 76-acre **Heritage Museum and Garden**, with an amazing collection of Americana.

MA 6A continues through **Barnstable** as a tranquil, winding route dotted with antique stores and art galleries. Barnstable's best attraction is **Sandy Neck Beach**, a 6-mile stretch of barrier beach with a trail through dunes and salt marshes.

The Cape's commercial and transportation hub is **Hyannis**, with a rejuvenated waterfront and Main St. Hyannis was the summer home of JFK and remains the family compound; Kennedy fans can visit the **JFK Hyannis Museum & Memorial**.

Yarmouth is green and genteel with shady trees and historic buildings. The historic **Hallet's Store** (an apothecary still sporting its original soda fountain) dates to 1889. Grety's Beach stretches out into the marsh on the bay side, while **Seagull Beach** is the town's best south-side beach.

Continuing east along MA6A, **Dennis** has rolling hills, cranberry bogs, salt marshes and artsy boutiques. The **Cape Museum of Fine Arts** holds modern, airy galleries that exhibit local artists. Dennis is also the beginning of the 22-mile **Cape Cod Rail Trail**, which follows the Old Colony Railroad bed all the way to Wellfleet. Rent a bike at **Barbara's Bike & Sports**.

TRANSPORTATION

Distance from Boston Sandwich 64 miles, Barnstable 70 miles, Hyannis 79 miles, Brewster 84 miles, Chatham 90 miles, Orleans 88 miles, Wellfleet 101 miles, Truro 105 miles

Direction Southeast

Bus Services of the Plymouth & Brockton Bus Co run the length of the Cape from Boston at least four times daily, with more frequent services from Boston to Hyannis ($16, 1½ hours). The Flex ($1, every 30 minutes) is a bus service that runs the length of the Lower Cape, from Harwich to Truro, with stops in each of the towns along the way. The Cape Cod Regional Transit Authority operates a shuttle which runs between Provincetown and North Truro ($1, every 30-60 minutes). These regional shuttle run from Memorial Day to Labor Day only.

Car MA28, which heads south from the Bourne Bridge to Falmouth, runs along the southern shore of the Cape, past Hyannis and into Chatham, heading north to Orleans. US 6, also called the Mid-Cape Hwy is an inland highway from the canal to Orleans and on to Provincetown. The alternative is MA 6A, a scenic two-lane road between Sandwich and Orleans.

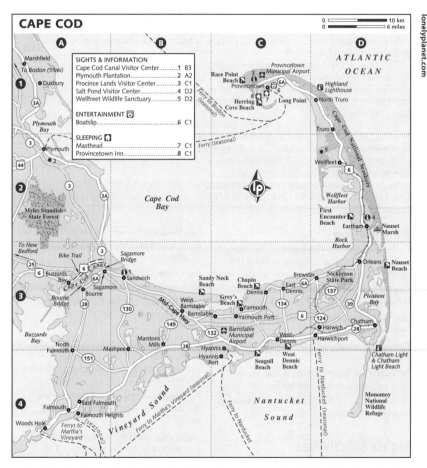

0 ————— 10 km
0 ————— 6 miles

lonelyplanet.com

SIGHTS & INFORMATION
Cape Cod Canal Visitor Center..........1 B3
Plymouth Plantation.........................2 A2
Procine Lands Visitor Center............3 C1
Salt Pond Visitor Center...................4 D2
Wellfreet Wildlife Sanctuary.............5 D2

ENTERTAINMENT
Boatslip...6 C1

SLEEPING
Masthead...7 C1
Provincetown Inn..............................8 C1

Dennis has beaches on both sides, including the long, dune-backed **Chapin Beach** on the bay side and the narrow **West Dennis Beach** on Nantucket Sound.

Brewster is also known for antique shops and art galleries set amid old captains' homes. It is home to the **Cape Cod Museum of Natural History**, with excellent naturalist-led programs, and the 2000-acre **Nickerson State Park**, which boasts a network of trails for walking and cycling. When the tide goes out on Cape Cod Bay, the **tidal flats** extend a mile into the bay, offering opportunities to commune with crabs, clams and gulls. The best access to the tidal flats is via the Point of Rocks or Ellis Landing beach.

The patriarch of Cape Cod towns, **Chatham** has a genteel refinement that is evident along its shady Main St. For expansive vistas of sand and sea, head to **Chatham Light**; Chatham Light Beach is the long, wide sandy beach just below. Off the elbow of the Cape, the 2700-acre **Monomoy Island Wildlife Refuge** – accessible only by boat – is a haven for birds and seals. Swimmers and sunbathers make the journey to the remote **South Beach**. The water taxi/tour service **Beachcomber** can take you to either destination.

To some, **Orleans** is the place where MA28 and US6 converge and continue north to Provincetown. But those in the know go no further. The nine-mile **Nauset Beach** offers the Cape's loveliest walking, surfing and sunning. The protected waters of **Nauset Marsh** entice explorers in canoes and kayaks. Stop in at **Goose Hummock Outdoor Center** to rent kayaks or arrange tours in this tranquil bay.

Excursions

CAPE COD

Eastham is Cape Cod's quietest, most compact town, home to its **oldest windmill**, which dates to 1680. It was here that the Pilgrims first came across Native Americans at the site now called **First Encounter Beach**. Another lovely beach is **Nauset Light Beach**, guarded by its namesake red-and-white striped tower.

Eastham is the southern terminus for the **Cape Cod National Seashore**, which includes the whole eastern shoreline of the Outer Cape, comprising more than 42 square miles of pristine beaches, dunes, marshes and forests. The **Salt Pond Visitor Center** shows excellent exhibits and films about the Cape's geology and geography. Two short walking trails lead from the center.

Wellfleet is famous for its oysters, but it also boasts interesting art galleries, pristine beaches, scenic roads and the old-fashioned **Wellfleet Drive-In**. The Audubon Society's 1000-acre **Wellfleet Bay Wildlife Sanctuary** has walking trails that crisscross tidal creeks, salt marshes and a bay beach. The **Cape Cod Rail Trail** terminates at LeCount Hollow Rd; rent bikes at the **Black Duck Sport Shop** at the end of the trail.

In North Truro, **Highland Light** – also known as Cape Cod Light – replaced the Cape's first lighthouse, which was built here in 1798. The beach to beat is **Head of the Meadow**, with limited facilities.

Information

Each town on the Cape has a chamber of commerce that can assist with hotel reservations and other tourist information.

Cape Cod Canal Visitor Center (☎ 508-833-9678; Ed Moffitt Dr, Sandwich; ☸ 9am-5pm May-Oct)

Cape Cod Regional Transit Authority (☎ 800-352-7155; www.capecodtransit.org)

Plymouth & Brockton (P&B) Bus (☎ 508-746-0378, 778-9767; www.p-b.com)

Salt Pond Visitor Center (☎ 508-255-3421; Eastham; ☸ 9am-4:30pm year-round, until 5pm Mar-Oct)

The Flex (☎ 800-352-7155; www.theflex.org) Bus service between Cape Cod towns.

Sights & Activities

UPPER CAPE

Heritage Museums & Gardens (☎ 508-888-3300; Grove St, Sandwich; adult/senior/child $12/10/6; ☸ 9am-6pm Thu-Tue & 9am-8pm Wed May-Oct, 10am-4pm Wed-Sun Nov-Apr)

John F Kennedy Hyannis Museum & Memorial (☎ 508-790-30077; 397 Main St, Hyannis; adult/child $5/2.50; ☸ 9am-5pm Mon-Sat & noon-5pm Sun mid-Apr–mid-Oct, 10am-4pm Thu-Sat & noon-4pm Sun mid-Oct–Dec & mid-Feb–mid-Apr)

Sandwich Cycles (☎ 508-833-2453; 40 MA 6A)

Sandwich Glass Museum (☎ 508-888-0251; 129 Main St, Sandwich; adult/child $4.50/1; ☸ 9:30am-5pm Apr-Dec, 9:30am-4pm Wed-Sun Feb-Mar)

MID CAPE

Barbara's Bike & Sports (☎ 508-760-4723; 450 MA 134, Dennis; per 2hr/day $10/20)

Cape Museum of Fine Arts (☎ 508-385-4477; MA 6A, Dennis; adult/child $7/free; ☸ 11am-5pm Tue-Sat & noon-5pm Sun)

Hallet's Store (☎ 508-362-3362; 139 MA 6A, Yarmouth; ☸ 11am-3pm Apr-Dec)

Sandy Neck Beach (☎ 508-362-8300; Barnstable; Ⓟ weekdays/weekends $10/12)

LOWER CAPE

Beachcomber (☎ 508-945-5265; Chatham; adult/senior/child $20/18/14) Ferry to Monomoy Island Wildlife Refuge.

Black Duck Sport Shop (☎ 508-349-9801; 1446 US6, Wellfleet; bikes per day/week adult $20/65, child $10/40)

Cape Cod Museum of Natural History (☎ 508-896-3867; 896 Main St, Brewster; adult/child $7/3.50; ☸ 10am-4pm Wed-Sun Apr-May, 10am-4pm daily Jun-Sep, 10am-4pm Sat & Sun Oct-Dec)

Eastham Windmill (cnr US6 & Samoset Rd; admission free; ☸ 10am-5pm Jun-Aug)

Goose Hummock Outdoor Center (☎ 508-255-2620; www.goose.com; Town Cove, Orleans; canoes & kayaks per 4hr $25-35)

Highland House Museum (☎ 508-487-3397; Light House Rd, North Truro; adult/child $3/free; ☸ 10am-4:30pm Jun-Sep)

Little Capistrano Bike Shop (☎ 508-255-6515; Salt Pond Rd, Eastham; per 2/8 hours $10/16)

Wellfleet Bay Wildlife Sanctuary (☎ 508-349-2615; 291 State Hwy/US6; adult/child/senior $5/3/3; ☸ 8:30am-5pm daily late May–mid-Oct, 8:30am-5pm Tue-Sun mid-Oct–late May)

Wellfleet Drive-In (☎ 508-349-7176, 800-696-3532; US 6; adult/child $7/4)

Eating
UPPER & MID CAPE

Contrast Bistro and Espresso Bar (☎ 508-385-9100; 605 MA 6A, Dennis; lunch $7-9, dinner $10-22) A modern bistro with a varied menu. Serves such disparate dishes as frittatas, lasagna, meat loaf and moussaka.

Dunbar Tea Shop (☎ 508-833-2485; 1 Water St, Sandwich) Often crowded. Specializes in ploughman's lunch, quiche, Scottish shortbread and authentic English tea.

RooBar City Bistro (☎ 508-778-6515; 586 Main St, Hyannis; meals $20-30; ☻ 4pm-1am) The New American fusion cuisine rocks, as does the late-night bar scene.

LOWER CAPE

All of these local spots have reduced hours (or close completely) in the off-season.

Brewster Fish House (☎ 508-896-7867; 2208 MA 6A, Brewster; lunch $15-20, dinner $20-30) Highly regarded for fresh, creatively prepared seafood, eg spicy lobster bisque and scallops with sundried tomatoes. Expect to wait if you arrive after 6:30pm.

Finely JP's (☎ 508-349-7500; 665 MA6, Wellfleet; meals $20-30) One of the premier places to sample Wellfleet's famous oysters ($10 per half-dozen).

Jo Mama's New York Bagels (☎ 508-255-0255; 125 MA6A, Orleans; meals $5-8; ☻ 7am-2pm) Bagels direct from New York, smoked whitefish, kosher pastrami, yadda, yadda.

Marion's Pie Shop (☎ 508-432-9439; 2022 MA28, Chatham; small $6-10, large $12-20; ☻ 8am-6pm Tue-Sat, 8am-4pm Sun) Get your pies for the big pie fight. Choose sweet or savory and enjoy.

Moby Dick's (☎ 508-349-9795; US 6, Wellfleet; meals $15-30) This self-service place with indoor picnic tables and great clam chowder is the best fried-fish joint on the Outer Cape. Bring your own beer or wine.

Terra Luna (☎ 508-487-1019; 104 Shore Rd, North Truro; meals $30-40; ☻ 5pm-10pm) A surprisingly hip bistro with local art on barnboard walls and creative cooking on the menu.

Sleeping

All of the area's chambers of commerce can assist with reservations at local motels and B&Bs. Most places are open from April or May to September or October, so you're better off making advanced arrangements outside this season.

UPPER & MID CAPE

MA 6A is lined with places that were once sea captains' houses and have now been converted into romantic B&Bs.

All Seasons Moor Inn (☎ 508-394-7600; www.all seasons.com; 1199 MA28, South Yarmouth; d $129-160; ☐ ☻) Yarmouth's best motel deal, with 114 rooms and plenty of facilities catering to families.

Captain Gosnold Village (☎ 508-775-9111; www .captaingosnold.com; 230 Gosnold St, Hyannis; d/studio/cottage $105/90/170; ☻) Named for a locally significant explorer. A small, informal and value-priced complex.

Lighthouse Inn (☎ 508-398-2244; www.lighthouseinn .com; Lighthouse Rd, West Dennis; s/d $122/218; ☐ ☻) A former lighthouse, dating to 1856. Nine acres of grassy grounds offer plenty of outdoor activities.

Scargo Manor (☎ 508-395-5534; www.scargomanor .com; 909 Main St, Dennis; d $135-235) Abutting lovely Scargo Lake. Besides the elegant accommodations, offers free use of boats and bikes.

LOWER CAPE

Bow Roof House (☎ 508-945-0848; 59 Queen Anne Rd, Chatham; d $85-95) Within walking distance of town and beach, this 18th-century house has six homey rooms that are delightfully old-fashioned in price and style.

HI Mid Cape (☎ 508-255-2785, 800-909-4776; www .capecodhostels.org; 75 Goody Hallet Dr, Eastham; dm member/nonmember $20/24) Offers 48 dorm beds and three private rooms in quaint, clean, clapboard cabins. Reservations are essential in summer. From US 6 and the Orleans traffic circle/rotary, follow Harbor Rd to Bridge Rd to Goody Hallet Dr.

HI Truro (☎ 508-349-3889, 888-901-2086; www .capecodhostels.org; N Pamet Rd, Truro; d $24-30) A former Coast Guard station just five minutes from the beach with 42 beds and two private rooms.

Holden Inn (☎ 508-349-3450; www.theholdeninn.com; 140 Commercial St, Wellfleet; s/d from $55/75) Dating to 1840, this old captain's house has not changed much since it became an inn in the 1920s. Nonetheless, its 26 rooms and surrounding gardens are well-maintained.

Nauset House Inn (☎ 508-255-2195; www.nauset houseinn.com; 143 Beach Rd, Orleans; d $75-170) Fourteen comfortable rooms (some with shared bath) within walking distance to Nauset Beach.

Nickerson State Park (☎ 508-896-3491, 877-422-6762; 3488 MA 6A, Brewster; camp sites $12-15; ☻ May-Oct) The Cape's best campsites. Period. There are 420 wooded sites, some with pond views.

PROVINCETOWN

This is it: as far as you can go on Cape Cod (and not just geographically). 'P-town' is the region's most lively resort town and New England's gay mecca. On any given day on Commercial St, you'll see dressed-up drag queens, dressed-down beach-goers, leather-clad motorcyclists, barely-clad in-line skaters, same-sex couples strolling hand-in-hand and heterosexual couples, perhaps wondering what they've stumbled into on their way to whale-watching.

Commercial St – a one-way street that functions as a boardwalk – is lined with restaurants and bars, kitschy souvenir shops, classy art galleries and everything in between. The east end is the hub of the art scene, with dozens of galleries packed into a few blocks. The **Provincetown Art Association & Museum** is one of the country's foremost small museums, showcasing work by Lower Cape artists.

The **Expedition Whydah** is one of more than 3000 shipwrecks that occurred off the coast of the Cape, but it is the only authentic pirate ship ever raised. Visit the museum on MacMillan Wharf to see the booty, as well as the crew's weapons, supplies and clothing. Though pirate ships no longer ply these waters, **whale-watching cruises** leave from MacMillan Wharf.

The Pilgrims first set foot on American soil in 1620 at Provincetown, at the western end of Commercial St. The **bas-relief** at the corner of Freeman and Gosnold Sts commemorates the Mayflower Compact. Up the street, the **Pilgrim Monument & Provincetown Museum** remembers their struggle with a 252ft tower, offering fantastic views, and an old-fashioned museum of Provincetown history.

Even with all this art and history, the main draw to Provincetown is the **Cape Cod National Seashore**, which includes seven miles of bike trails leading through sand dunes and coastal forest. Two spurs lead to the pounding surf at **Race Point Beach** and the calmer waters of **Herring Cove**. Pick up information at **Province Lands Visitor Center**; rent bicycles at **Ptown Bikes**.

TRANSPORTATION

Distance from Boston 128 miles

Direction Southeast

Air Cape Air operates daily flights from Boston Logan to Provincetown Municipal Airport, about 4 miles from town.

Boat Both Bay State Cruise Co (adult/senior/child/bike $44/40/28/5, 90 minutes, three daily) and Boston Harbor Cruises (adult/senior/child/bike $45/40/35/5, 90 minutes, twice daily, three times daily on weekends) operate ferries between Boston and Provincetown. The Plymouth-to-Provincetown Express Ferry (adult/senior/child/one-way $35/30/25/20, 90 minutes, once daily) departs Plymouth at 10am and leaves Provincetown at 4:30pm.

Bus The Plymouth & Brockton bus travels from Boston to Provincetown ($24, 3½ hours, four daily) between Provincetown and Boston and stops at the chamber of commerce. The Cape Cod Regional Transit Authority operates a shuttle which runs between Provincetown's main points of interest and North Truro ($1, every 30-60 minutes).

Car Estimate 2½ hours to make the drive from Boston; but weekend traffic can be brutal and will surely slow you down.

Information

Bay State Cruise Co (☎ 617-748-1428; www.baystate cruisecompany.com; 200 Seaport Blvd, Boston)

Boston Harbor Cruises (☎ 617-227-4321; www.boston harborcruises.com; One Long Wharf, Boston)

Cape Air (☎ 508-487-0241, 800-352-0714; www.fly capeair.com)

Provincetown Chamber of Commerce (☎ 508-487-3424; www.ptownchamber.com; 307 Commercial St, MacMillan Wharf; ⊙ 9:30am-4:30pm May-Oct, 10am-4pm Nov-Apr)

Plymouth-to-Provincetown Express Ferry (☎ 508-747-2400, 800-242-2469; provincetownferry.com; State Pier, Plymouth)

Police station (☎ 508-487-1212; 26 Shank Painter Rd)

Post office (☎ 800-275-8777; 211 Commercial St)

Sights

Expedition Whydah (☎ 508-487-8899; 16 MacMillan Wharf; adult/senior/child $8/6/6)

Pilgrim Monument & Provincetown Museum (☎ 508-487-1310, 800-247-1620; High Pole Hill Rd; adult/senior/student/child $7/5/5/3; ⊙ 9am-5pm Apr-Nov, to 7pm Jul & Aug)

Province Lands Visitor Center (☎ 508-487-1256; Race Point Rd; ⊙ 9am-5pm early May–late Oct) Beach parking $10.

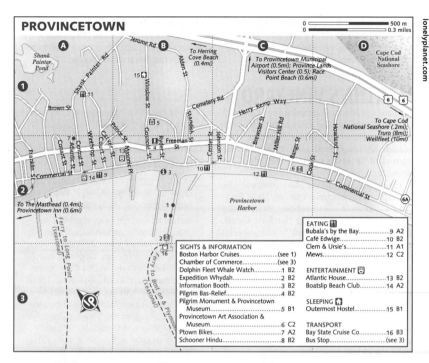

PROVINCETOWN

0 _____ 500 m
0 _____ 0.3 miles

To Herring Cove Beach (0.4mi)

To Provincetown Municipal Airport (0.5mi); Province Lands Visitors Center (0.5); Race Point Beach (0.6mi)

Cape Cod National Seashore

To Cape Cod National Seashore (.2mi); Truro (8mi); Wellfleet (10mi)

Provincetown Harbor

To The Masthead (0.4mi); Provincetown Inn (0.6mi)

Ferry to Long Point (seasonal)

Ferry to Boston & Plymouth (seasonal)

EATING 🍴
Bubala's by the Bay.................9 A2
Café Edwige..........................10 B2
Clem & Ursie's......................11 A1
Mews...................................12 C2

ENTERTAINMENT 🎭
Atlantic House.......................13 B2
Boatslip Beach Club...............14 A2

SLEEPING 🛏
Outermost Hostel...................15 B1

TRANSPORT
Bay State Cruise Co...............16 B3
Bus Stop............................(see 3)

SIGHTS & INFORMATION
Boston Harbor Cruises......................(see 1)
Chamber of Commerce.....................(see 3)
Dolphin Fleet Whale Watch............1 B2
Expedition Whydah.......................2 B2
Information Booth.........................3 B2
Pilgrim Bas-Relief.........................4 B2
Pilgrim Monument & Provincetown
  Museum...................................5 B1
Provincetown Art Association &
  Museum...................................6 C2
Ptown Bikes................................7 A2
Schooner Hindu...........................8 B2

Provincetown Art Association & Museum (☎ 508-487-1750; www.paam.org; 460 Commercial St; admission free; ☼ 11am-8pm Mon-Thu, 11am-10pm Fri, 11am-5pm Sat & Sun Jun-Aug, noon-5pm Thu-Sun Sep-May)

Activities

Boston Harbor Cruises (☎ 617-227-4321; MacMillan Wharf; adult/senior/child $18/15/10)

Dolphin Fleet Whale Watch (☎ 508-349-1900; MacMillan Wharf; adult/senior/child $24/22/20)

Ptown Bikes (☎ 508-487-8735; 42 Bradford st; per 2hrs $8-10, per 24hrs $18-20)

Eating

Bubala's by the Bay (☎ 508-487-0773; 183 Commercial St; lunch mains $10-15, dinner mains $20-30) Good food, great people-watching. It's hard to resist the shaded patio seating on a sunny afternoon.

Cafe Edwige (☎ 508-487-4020; 33 Commercial St; breakfast $5-12, dinner mains $30-40) P-town's most popular breakfast spot doubles as a romantic bistro at night.

Clem & Ursie's (☎ 508-487-2333; 85 Shank Painter Rd; meals $15-30) A colorful counter-service roadhouse with tables decorated by local artists.

The Mews (☎ 508-487-1500; 429 Commercial St; meals $20-30) Dine right on the beach, or retreat to the dimly-lit dining room upstairs. Exceptional food and martinis.

Entertainment

Atlantic House (☎ 508-487-3821; 4 Masonic Pl) P-town's gay scene got its start here and it's still the leading bar in town. Includes an intimate 1st-floor pub with fireplace, as well as a dance club and cabaret through a separate entrance.

Boatslip (☎ 508-487-1669; 161 Commercial St; $5; ☼ 4-7pm) Hosts wildly popular afternoon tea dances, often packed with gorgeous guys.

Sleeping

Provincetown has a hundred delightful small inns and guesthouses lining Commercial St and the side roads. Most require reservations in summer, but inquire at the chamber of commerce if you arrive unannounced.

Outermost Hostel (☎ 508-487-4378; 26-28 Winslow St; beds $22) The cheapest place to sleep in P-town, though the facilities do not match its counterpart in nearby Truro (see p259).

Provincetown Inn (☎ 508-487-9500; www.province towninn.com; 1 Commercial St; d from $140; ⊗) Valuing function over form, this motel boasts a quiet location in the west end, surrounded by water on three sides.

The Masthead (☎ 508-487-0523; www.themasthead .com; 31-41 Commercial St; d from $70) One mile west of the center, this conglomeration of cottages, apartments and simple rooms sits at the water's edge.

MARTHA'S VINEYARD

In 1602, mariner Bartholomew Gosnold cruised the New England coast. The story goes that when Gosnold stopped on this island, he discovered wild grapes, so he named it 'Martha's Vineyard' after his daughter.

From these quaint beginnings, the Vineyard has become one of New England's premier destinations, attracting vacationers from all over the East Coast. **Vineyard Haven** is the island's commercial center, and may be your port of entry. As the ferry approaches the dock, you'll see traditional wooden schooners and sloops bobbing around, while stately homes line the shore.

Other ferries arrive at **Oak Bluffs**, famous for its colorful Victorian gingerbread houses. You can't miss the **Flying Horses Carousel**, a national historic landmark that claims to be the oldest operating merry-go-round. Two public beaches are nearby.

Edgartown is classic New England. Its Greek Revival houses, formerly owned by whaling captains, are perfectly maintained, complete with clipped lawns, blooming gardens and white picket fences. Here you'll find the **Martha's Vineyard Historical Society**, which displays whaling and maritime relics, as well as the huge Fresnel lens from Gay Head Lighthouse. **Lighthouse Beach** is easily accessible from the end of N Water St.

Besides running the museum, the historical society offers sunset tours of **East Chop Lighthouse** in Oak Bluff and **Gay Head Lighthouse** at the western tip.

The Trustees of Reservations administers two wildlife refuges on **Chappaquiddick Island**, off the eastern end of the Vineyard. The 516-acre Cape Poge is more interesting topographically, while the 200-acre Wasque is famous for fishing, beaches and currents. The Trustees offers natural history tours, lighthouse tours and canoeing trips. To reach the island, catch the **Chappy Ferry** from Edgartown.

The most convenient way to get around Martha's Vineyard is by bike. Bike trails run from Edgartown to Oak Bluffs, Vineyard Haven and **Katama Beach**. Chappaquiddick is also perfect for pedaling. Rent bikes at **Strictly Bikes**, near the ferry terminal in Vineyard Haven, or **Edgartown Bicycles**.

TRANSPORTATION

Distance from Boston 88 miles

Direction Southeast

Air Cape Air operates shuttles to/from Boston ($126, 35 minutes, hourly), Hyannis ($49, 20 minutes, 2-3 daily) and Nantucket ($49, 15 minutes, 2-3 daily).

Boat Car and passenger ferries, operated by the Steamship Authority, run from Woods Hole on Cape Cod to Vineyard Haven (adult/child/car/bike $13/7/62/6, 45 minutes, nine daily) or Oak Bluffs (4-5 daily). Between Hyannis and Oak Bluffs, Hy-Line Cruises runs a seasonal traditional ferry (adult/child/bike $16.50/8.25/5, 90 minutes, daily) and a year-round high-speed ferry (adult/child/bike in-season $29/22/5, off-season $10/5/5, one hour, five daily). Two services run from Falmouth on Cape Cod: the Island Queen to Oak Bluffs (adult/child/bike $7/6/6, 35 minutes, seven daily) and the Falmouth Ferry Service to Edgartown (adult/child/bike $15/12/8, 35 minutes, five daily). All services have a reduced schedule outside the summer months.

Information

Cape Air (☎ 508-771-6944; www.flycapeair.com)

Chappy Ferry (☎ 508-627-9427; cnr Daggett & Dock Sts, Edgartown; car/bike/person $8/5/2; ⊗ 7am-midnight Jun–mid-Oct, reduced service off-season)

Falmouth Ferry Service (☎ 508-548-9400; www .falmouthferry.com)

Hy-Line Cruises (☎ 508-693-0112; www.hy-linecruise.com)

Island Queen (☎ 508-548-4800; www.islandqueen.com)

Martha's Vineyard Chamber of Commerce (☎ 508-693-0085; Beach Rd, Vineyard Haven; ⊗ 9am-5pm Mon-Fri & 10am-2pm Sat)

Steamship Authority (☎ 508-693-0367; www.island ferry.com)

Sights & Activities

Chappaquiddick Island (☎ 508-627-3599; www.thetrust ees.org; ⏱ dawn to dusk late May to mid-Oct)

Edgartown Bicycles (☎ 508-627-9008; www.edgar townbicycles.com; 212 Upper Main St, Edgartown; bike rental daily/weekly adult $20/80, child $15/60)

Flying Horses Carousel (☎ 508-693-9481; cnr Lake & Circuit Aves; $1.50; ⏱ 10am-10pm daily late May to early Sep, weekends only in Apr, May & Oct)

Lighthouse tours (☎ 508-627-4441; www.marthasvine yardhistory.org; $3; ⏱ 1½ hour before dusk, Fri-Sun Gay Head, Sun only Eastern Chop mid-Jun–mid-Sep)

Martha's Vineyard Historical Society (☎ 508-627-4441; www.marthasvineyardhistory.org; 59 School St; adult/ off-season/child $7/6/4; ⏱ 10am-5pm Tue-Sat mid-Jun–mid-Oct, reduced hours off-season)

Strictly Bikes (☎ 508-693-0782; 24 Union St, Vineyard Haven; per day $20)

Eating

Black Dog (☎ 508-693-9223; 20 Beach St Extension, Vine-yard Haven; breakfast & lunch $10-20, dinner $25-40) Once-humble harborfront tavern made famous by T-shirt sales.

Giordano's (☎ 508-693-0184; 107 Circuit Ave, Oak Bluffs; meals $20-30) Since 1930, Giordano's must be doing some-thing right. Pizza is the family favorite, but pasta and fried seafood are also excellent. Next to the carousel.

Jimmy Seas Pan Pasta (☎ 508-696-9922; 20 Kennebec Ave, Oak Bluffs; meals $25-40; ⏱ 5pm-10pm) A great se-lection of pasta dishes, tossed with fresh seafood, veggies and homemade sauces, and served in a cast-iron skillet.

Main Street Diner (☎ 508-627-9337; 65 Main St, Edgartown; breakfast & lunch mains $10-12, dinner mains $20-30; ⏱ 8am-10pm) A kitschy 1950s-style diner featuring classics like grilled cheese and PB&J.

Sweet Life Cafe (☎ 508-696-0200; 63 Circuit Ave, Oak Bluffs; meals $30-50; ⏱ 5pm-10pm) Sweet life, indeed. A frequently changing New American menu, enjoyed in the Victorian dining room or in the lovely gardens. The same owner-chef runs A Slice of Life down the street.

Sleeping

Many stately captains' homes have been turned into elegant B&Bs. It's useful to make reservations before arriving, espe-cially since accommodation options are spread out over the island. Otherwise, in-quire at the chamber of commerce.

Clark House (☎ 866-493-6550; www.clarkhouseinn.com; 20 Edgartown Rd, Vineyard Haven; d $135-225) A rustic house, furnished with antiques and graced with a sunny porch. Cheaper rooms share bathrooms.

Edgartown Inn (☎ 508-627-4794; www.edgartowninn .com; 56 N Water St, Edgartown; d $125-275) This old inn (1798) is friendly and tidy: Edgartown's best bargain.

Narragansett House (☎ 508-693-3627; www.narragan setthouse.com; 46 Narragansett Ave, Oak Bluffs; d $100-165) This Victorian has 13 simple, old-fashioned rooms; across the street, the spiffy Iroquois Cottage is renovated and romantic ($200-275).

NANTUCKET

One need not be a millionaire to visit Nan-tucket, but it doesn't hurt. This compact island, 30 miles south of Cape Cod, grew rich from whaling in the 19th century and recent decades have seen its rebirth as a summer playground for CEOs and society types.

It's easy to see why. Nantucket is New England at its most rose-covered, cobble-stoned, cedar-shake, picture-postcard per-fect. Even in the peak of summer, there's always a stretch of sandy beach to be found; and outdoor activities abound on the water-ways, grassy moors, salt marshes and bike paths.

Nantucket Town is the island's only real population center. You can catch up on its history at the **Nantucket Historical Asso-ciation**, which operates nine different muse-ums covering everything from Nantucket's

TRANSPORTATION

Distance from Boston 100 miles
Direction Southeast
Air Cape Air & Nantucket Airlines operates daily shut-tles to/from Boston ($132, 45 minutes, hourly), Hyan-nis ($49, 20 minutes, hourly), and Martha's Vineyard ($125, 35 minutes).
Boat The Steamship Authority has a high-speed service (adult/child/bike $29/22/6, one hour, five daily), in addition to its regular ferry (adult/child/bike $14/7/6, two hours, six daily) to/from Hyannis. Hy-Line Cruises also goes to/from Hyannis via high-speed catamaran (adult/child/bike $36/27/5, one hour, five daily) and traditional ferry (adult/child/bike $16.50/8.25/5, two hours, three daily). Hy-Line also operates a high-speed inter-island passenger ferry to Martha's Vineyard (adult/child/bike $25/12.50/5), departing Oak Bluff at 1:25pm and Nantucket at 2:50pm daily.

agricultural roots to its whaling heyday. The **Maria Mitchell Association** is devoted to America's first female astronomer, who hales from Nantucket. The complex includes her birthplace house and two observatories where she worked.

Small **Children's Beach** is closest to town, but it's worth hopping on a bicycle to travel to the island's prime swim and surf spots. Call **Easy Riders** to rent a bike. Five different cycling routes are marked with color-coded signs. Cliff Bike path is the shortest, leading to **Cliff Beach** and on to **Dionis Beach**. To reach **Surfside Beach**, pedal three miles along the path of the same name. Two alternate routes lead to **Sconset Beach**. Sconset Trail (also called Milestone Path) is a seven-mile trail beginning east of the historic district; Polpis Rd Bike Path is a more lush route that passes the **Lifesaving Museum** along the way.

Information

Cape Air & Nantucket Airlines (☎ 800-352-0714; www
.flycapeair.com)

Hy-Line Cruises (☎ 508-778-2600; www.hy-linecruises
.com)

Post office (5 Federal St; ⏱ 5:30am-5pm Mon-Fri,
8:30am-noon Sat)

Steamship Authority (☎ 508-477-8600; www
.steamshipauthority.com)

Visitor Services & Information Bureau (☎ 508-
228-0925; www.nantucketchamber.org; 25 Federal St;
⏱ 9am-5:30pm May-Nov, Mon-Sat Dec-Apr)

Sights & Activities

Easy Riders Bike Rental (☎ 508-325-2722; www.easy
ridersbikerentals.com; bike rentals adult/child daily
$20/15, weekly $90/65) Includes delivery and helmets.

Lifesaving Museum (☎ 508-228-1885; 158 Polpis Rd;
adult/child $5/2; ⏱ 9:30am-4:30pm mid-Jun to mid-Oct,
reduced hours off-season)

Maria Mitchell Association (☎ 508-228-9198; www
.mmo.org; 2 Vestal St; combo ticket adult/senior/child
$10/7/7; ⏱ variable)

Nantucket Historical Association (☎ 508-228-1894;
www.nha.org; 15 Broad St; adult/child whaling museum
$15/8, historic sites $6/3, combo $18/9; ⏱ 10am-5pm
Mon-Sat & noon-5pm Sun, reduced hours off-season)

Eating

Black-Eyed Susan's (☎ 508-325-0308; 10 India St;
breakfast $10-15, dinner $20-30) Young and old, hip and
square, everyone adores eating at this casual gourmet

gem. Choose between the welcoming patio or the comfy
hardwood dining room.

Cambridge Street Victuals (☎ 508-228-7109; 12
Cambridge St; meals $20-30) Dim and boisterous C-Street
is a hot spot for youngish foodies who don't want to spend
a fortune.

Fog Island Cafe (☎ 508-228-1818; 7 S Water St;
breakfast & lunch mains $10-20, dinner mains $20-30)
Suitably noisy and good for those in search of upscale
diner fare.

Nantucket Lobster Trap (☎ 508-228-4200; 23 Washington St; meals $20-30) Don your bib and get cracking. The
early bird special (⏱ 5-7pm) is a bargain.

Sleeping

The Nantucket Visitor Services & Information Bureau can provide assistance if you show up without reservations. Check out www.nantucketchamber.org for a complete list of lodging options. Otherwise, take a stroll along N Water St, which is known as guesthouse row.

Barnacle Inn (☎ 508-228-1332; www.thebarnacleinn
.com; 11 Fair St; s/d/tr $85/145/205) A quaint, quiet inn
surrounded by green space. Substantial discounts for rooms
with shared baths.

Nesbitt Inn (☎ 508-228-0156; 21 Broad St; r $55-125) A
centrally-located 1872 house with 12 rooms (shared bath),
Victorian furniture and a breezy deck.

Point Breeze Hotel (☎ 508-228-0313, 800-365-4371;
www.pointbreeze.com; 71 Easton St; d $99-300, cottages
from $275; 🐾) This rambling turn-of-the-century hotel
has 23 simple but clean rooms and 14 cottages that are
well-suited to families. Walk 10 minutes north from
Main St.

Directory

Directory

TRANSPORTATION

Flights, tours and rail tickets can be booked online at www.lonelyplanet.com/travel_services.

AIR

In the aftermath of September 11, security has become more stringent at US airports, as it has all over the world. Count on arriving at the airport at least one hour before your flight (airlines recommend two hours for international flights) to allow time for security checks. Remember that carry-on baggage is severely restricted: for the latest information on what not to carry and what not to check, reference the **Department of Homeland Security** (www.tsa.gov).

Flying to Boston is like flying anywhere in the US. For the cheapest tickets, be sure to book early; avoid weekends and holidays; and always keep your eyes open for airline sales. **STA Travel** (☎ 800-777-0112; www.statravel.com), which offers discounts for student travel, has offices in major cities nationwide.

Otherwise, the cheapest fares are often available online. Search these online services for good fares:

Cheap Tickets (www.cheaptickets.com) Search engine covers airline tickets, hotels, rental cars and cruises.

Expedia (www.expedia.com) A flexible search engine allows for one-way fares and multiple-leg journeys.

Orbitz (www.orbitz.com) 'Flex Search' allows you to compare fares on different dates – an excellent tool if you have a flexible travel schedule.

Smarter Travel (www.smartertravel.com) Offers tips for finding the lowest fare, as well as a list of current published fares and last-minute deals.

Travel Zoo (www.travelzoo.com) Highlights sales and specials; also includes discount airlines that are often overlooked by other search engines.

Airlines

All of the airlines have offices at Logan International Airport.

Air Canada (☎ 888-247-2262; www.aircanada.com)

American Airlines (☎ 800-433-7300; www.aa.com)

British Airways (☎ 800-247-9297; www.british-airways.com)

CLIMATE CHANGE & TRAVEL

Climate change is a serious threat to the ecosystems that humans rely upon, and air travel is the fastest-growing contributor to the problem. Lonely Planet regards travel, overall, as a global benefit, but believes we all have a responsibility to limit our personal impact on global warming.

Flying & Climate Change

Pretty much every form of motorized travel generates CO_2 (the main cause of human-induced climate change) but planes are far and away the worst offenders, not just because of the sheer distances they allow us to travel, but because they release greenhouse gases high into the atmosphere. The statistics are frightening: two people taking a return flight between Europe and the US will contribute as much to climate change as an average household's gas and electricity consumption over a whole year.

Carbon Offset Schemes

Climatecare.org and other websites use 'carbon calculators' that allow travelers to offset the level of greenhouse gases they are responsible for with financial contributions to sustainable travel schemes that reduce global warming – including projects in India, Honduras, Kazakhstan and Uganda.

Lonely Planet, together with Rough Guides and other concerned partners in the travel industry, support the carbon offset scheme run by climatecare.org. Lonely Planet offsets all of its staff and author travel. For more information, check out our website at www.lonelyplanet.com.

GETTING INTO TOWN

Downtown Boston is just a few miles from Logan International Airport and is accessible by subway (the T), water shuttle, van shuttle, limo, taxi and rental car.

The T, or the **MBTA subway** (☎ 617-222-3200, 800-392-6100; www.mbta.com; per ride $1.70; ✆ 5:30am-12:30am), is normally the fastest and cheapest way to reach the city from the airport. From any terminal, take a free, well-marked shuttle bus (22 or 33) to the blue-line T station called Airport and you'll be downtown within 30 minutes.

The Silver Line is the MBTA's new 'bus rapid transit service.' It travels between Logan International Airport and South Station (which is the railway station as well as a red-line T station), with stops in the Seaport District. Silver Line buses pick up directly at the airport terminals. This is the most convenient way to get into the city if you are staying in the Seaport District, Theater District or South End.

Taxis are plentiful but pricey; traffic snarls can translate into a $25 fare to downtown. The regional bus lines (Concord Trailways, Peter Pan and Plymouth & Brocktonp268) operate **Logan Direct** (☎ 800-235-6426, $8), which provides direct bus service between Logan airport and the South Station Transportation Center.

Several water shuttles operate between Logan and the Waterfront district in Boston:

City Water Taxi (☎ 617-422-0392; www.citywatertaxi.com; one-way/round-trip $10/17; ✆ 7am-10pm Mon-Sat, 7am-8pm Sun) Serves 15 destinations in Boston Harbor, including Long Wharf, the Seaport District and the North End. Use the checkerboard call box at Logan dock to summon the water taxi.

Rowes Wharf Water Taxi (☎ 617-406-8584; www.roweswharfwatertaxi.com; one-way/round-trip $10/17; ✆ 7am-7pm) Serves Rowes Wharf near the Boston Harbor Hotel, the Moakley Federal Courthouse on the Fort Point Channel and the World Trade Center in the Seaport District.

Delta (☎ 800-221-1212; www.delta.com)

Jet Blue (☎ 800-538-2583; www.jetblue.com)

KLM (☎ 800-374-7747; www.klm.com)

Lufthansa (☎ 800-645-3880; www.lufthansa.com)

Northwest (☎ 800-225-2525; www.northwest.com)

Spirit Air (☎ 617-772-7117; www.spiritair.com)

United (☎ 800-241-6522; www.ual.com)

US Airways (☎ 800-428-4322; www.usairways.com)

Airports

On MA 1A in East Boston, **Logan International Airport** (Map pp298–9; ☎ 800-235-6426; www.massport.com) has five separate terminals that are connected by a frequent shuttle bus (bus 11). Public information booths are located in the baggage claim areas of Terminals A, B, C and E.

A quiet alternative to Logan, **Manchester Airport** (☎ 603-624-6556; www.flymanchester.com) is just 55 miles north of Boston in New Hampshire.

Just outside the city of Providence (Rhode Island), **TF Green Airport** (☎ 401-737-4000; www.pvdairport.com) is also serviced by major carriers. Southwest Airlines, in particular, offers very competitively priced tickets. The airport is one hour south of Boston.

BICYCLE

Boston has been rated 'Worst City for Cycling' by Bicycle magazine. That is because Boston's streets are old and narrow and they are often overcrowded with cars. Many roads in Cambridge have marked bicycle lanes but in Boston they do not.

That said, plenty of students, commuters and messenger services get around by bike. Boston drivers are used to sharing the roads with their two-wheeled friends (and they are used to arriving *after* their two-wheeled friends, who are less impeded by traffic snarls). Bikers should always obey traffic rules and ride defensively.

You can bring bikes on the T for no additional fare. Bikes are not allowed on green-line trains or Silver Line buses, nor are they allowed on any trains during rush hour (7am to 10am and 4pm to 7pm, Monday to Friday). Bikes are not permitted inside the buses, but many MBTA buses have bicycle racks on the outside. For information about off-road bicycle trails see p198, and for information about bike rental, see p197.

BOAT

For information on the airport water shuttle, see above. For information on cruises, see p72.

Bay State Cruise Company (Map pp298–9; ☎ 617-748-1428; www.boston-ptown.com; Commonwealth Pier; adult/senior/child/bike $44/40/20/5; ⏱ depart Boston 8am, 1:30pm & 5:30pm, depart Provincetown 10am, 3pm & 7:30pm mid-May–Sep; ⓡ South Station) Operates boats from the World Trade Center in the Seaport District to Provincetown at the tip of Cape Cod.

Boston Harbor Cruises (Map pp302–3; ☎ 617-227-4321; www.bostonharborcruises; Long Wharf; ⓡ Aquarium) Operates a ferry to Provincetown (adult/senior/child/bike $45/40/35/5; ⏱ depart Boston 9am & 2pm, depart Provincetown 11am & 4pm mid-June–mid-October, reduced schedule Sep-Oct) and a commuter service to Charlestown Navy Yard (adult/child $1.50/0.75; ⏱ 6:30am-8pm Mon-Fri, 10am-6pm Sat & Sun).

City Water Taxi (Map pp302–3; ☎ 617-422-0392; www.citywatertaxi.com; $10; ⏱ 7am-10pm Mon-Sat, 7am-8pm Sun) Makes on-demand taxi stops at about 15 waterfront points, including the airport, the Barking Crab, the Seaport District, Long Wharf, Sargents Wharf in the North End and the Charlestown Navy Yard. Call to order a pick-up.

Harbor Express (Map pp302–3; ☎ 617-222-6999; www.harborexpress.com; adult/senior & child $6/3; ⏱ 5:45am-11:45pm Mon-Fri, 8am-11:45pm Sat & Sun; ⓡ Aquarium) Operates commuter boats from Long Wharf to Quincy and Hull on the South Shore. Also operates boats from Long Wharf to George's Island and Spectacle Island. See p91 for details.

Salem Ferry (Map pp302–3; ☎ 978-741-0220; www.salemferry.com; Central Wharf; round-trip adult/senior/child $22/18/14; ⏱ 9am-9pm mid-Jun–Aug, 9am-7pm Mon-Fri & 11am-7pm Sat & Sun Sep-Oct; ⓡ Aquarium) A new service between Boston Central Wharf (at the New England Aquarium) and Salem. From Boston, the boat docks in Salem, leaving early enough so commuters can be in Boston before 8am on weekdays. The last return to Boston is at 8pm Sunday to Thursday and at 10pm Friday to Saturday (June to August), 6pm Sunday to Thursday and 8pm Friday and Saturday (September and October).

BUS

The **MBTA** (☎ 617-222-5215; www.mbta.com) operates bus routes within the city. These can be difficult to figure out for the short-term visitor, but schedules are posted on its website and at some bus stops along the routes. Bus fare is $1.25; exact change is required. Bus fare is free with a transfer from the T.

The new Silver Line, a so-called 'rapid' bus, starts at Downtown Crossing and runs along Washington St in the South End to Roxbury's Dudley Sq. Another route goes from South Station to the Seaport District, then under the harbor to Logan International Airport. This waterfront route costs $1.70 instead of the normal $1.25 fare.

For inter-city travel, Boston has a modern, indoor, user-friendly **bus station** (Map pp302–3; 700 Atlantic Ave; ⓡ South Station), at Summer St, conveniently adjacent to the South Station train station and above the red-line T stop.

The nationwide bus company is **Greyhound** (☎ 617-526-1800, 800-231-2222; www.greyhound.com). Buses depart for New York City throughout the day. Express buses take only 4½ hours, but others take up to two hours longer. One-way adult fares are $30 for a non-refundable ticket, $35 for a more flexible ticket. Greyhound buses travel across the country. A seven-day advance purchase on one-way tickets often beats all other quoted fares.

All of these regional lines operate out of South Station:

Concord Trailways (☎ 617-426-8080; 800-639-3317; www.concordtrailways.com) Plies routes from Boston to NH (Concord, Manchester, and as far up as Conway and Berlin) and ME (Portland and Bangor). Its partner Dartmouth Coach goes to Hanover, NH.

C&J Trailways (☎ 603-430-1100, 800-258-7111; www.cjtrailways.com) Provides daily service to Newburyport, MA, as well as Portsmouth and Dover, NH. Kids travel for free when accompanied by a full-paying adult.

Peter Pan Bus Lines (☎ 800-343-9999; www.peterpanbus.com) Serves 52 destinations in the northeast, as far north as Concord NH and as far south as Washington, DC, as well as western Massachusetts. Fares are comparable to Greyhound.

Plymouth & Brockton Street Railway Co (☎ 508-746-0378; www.p-b.com) Provides frequent service to the South Shore and to most towns on Cape Cod, including Hyannis and Provincetown.

Vermont Transit (☎ 800-552-8737; www.vermonttransit.com) The route from Boston goes via Manchester and Concord, NH to White River Junction, Montpelier and Burlington, VT, then all the way to Montréal, Québec in Canada. Another route runs up the coast to Newburyport, MA; Portsmouth, NH; and Portland, Augusta, Bangor and Bar Harbor, ME.

The cheapest way to get to New York city is on one of the **Chinatown Buses** (www.chinatown-bus.com). These are bus companies that run between the major cities on the East Coast, from Chinatown to Chinatown. It's crowded, it's confusing, but it sure is cheap ($15). This rock-bottom price is already more expensive than it used to be, but the buses actually leave from South Station, which makes life easier for the non-Chinese traveler. Buses depart at the top of every hour:

Fung Wah Bus Company (☎ 212-925-8889; www .fungwahbus.com; ⊙ 7am-10pm & 11:30pm) Fung Wah started the Chinatown service eight years ago.

Lucky Star Bus (☎ 800-881-0887; www.luckystarbus .com; ⊙ 7am-8pm & 11:30pm) Arrive 30 minutes before your scheduled departure to assure that your seat is not given away.

CAR & MOTORCYCLE

With any luck you won't have to drive in or around Boston. Not only are the streets a maze of confusion, choked with construction (see p25) and legendary traffic jams, but Boston drivers use their own set of rules. Driving is often considered a sport – in a town that takes its sports very seriously.

Driving

From western Massachusetts, the Massachusetts Turnpike ('Mass Pike,' or I-90, a toll road) takes you right into Downtown. After paying a toll in Newton, drive east 10 more minutes on the pike and pay another toll; then the fun begins.

There are three exits for the Boston area: Cambridge, Copley Sq (Prudential Center) and Kneeland St (Chinatown). Then the turnpike ends abruptly. At that point, you can head north or south of the city on the I-93 Expressway or directly past South Station, into Downtown.

Two highways skirt the Charles River: Storrow Dr runs along the Boston side and the more scenic Memorial Dr parallels it on the Cambridge side. There are exits off Storrow Dr for Kenmore Sq, Back Bay and Government Center. Both Storrow Dr and Memorial Dr are accessible from the Mass Pike and the I-93 Expressway.

If you're driving from the airport into Boston or to points north of the city, the Sumner Tunnel ($3 toll) will lead you to Sturrow Dr or over the Zakim Bridge to I-93 North. To points south of Boston, use the Ted Williams Tunnel ($3) to I-93 South. To or from points west, the Mass Pike should connect directly with the Ted Williams Tunnel. When you're heading to the airport from downtown Boston, take the Callahan Tunnel. All three tunnels are off I-93 and free when heading inbound.

At the time of research, the I-90 connector tunnel was closed for repairs, so it's useful to double-check your route before you set out. See www.massport.com for details on alternative routes.

Rental

All major rental car agencies are represented at the airport; free shuttle vans will take you to their nearby pick-up counters. When returning rental cars, you'll find gas stations on US 1, north of the airport. Rental car companies with offices downtown include:

Avis (Map pp300–1; ☎ 617-534-1400, 800-331-1212; www.avis.com; 3 Center Plaza; Ⓣ Government Center) Another outlet is in the Charles Hotel in Harvard Sq (p240).

Budget (Map p305; ☎ 617-497-1800, 800-527-0700; www.budget.com; 24 Park Plaza; Ⓣ Arlington)

Enterprise (Map pp306–7; ☎ 617-262-8222, 800-736-8222; Prudential Center, 800 Boylston St; ⊙ 7am-6pm Mon-Fri, 9am-3pm Sat, 9am-1pm Sun; Ⓣ Prudential)

Hertz (Map p305; ☎ 617-338-1500, 800-654-3131; www.hertz.com; 30 Park Plaza; ⊙ 7am-7pm Sun-Thu, 7am-8pm Fri, 7am-6pm Sat; Ⓣ Arlington)

National (Map pp298–9; ☎ 617-661-8747, 800-227-7368;www.nationalcar.com; 1663 Massachusetts Ave, Cambridge; ⊙ 8am-5:30pm, to 7pm Fri; Ⓣ Porter) Between Harvard Sq & Porter Sq.

Thrifty (Map p310; ☎ 617-876-2758; www.thrifty .com; 110 Mt Auburn St, Harvard Square Hotel, Cambridge; Ⓣ Harvard)

Parking

Folks on Beacon Hill pony up $150,000 to own a space at the Brimmer Street Garage. The explanation is simple economics: supply and demand. Since on-street parking is limited, you could end up paying $25 to $35 daily to park in a lot. Some cheaper lots include:

Boston Common Garage (Map pp302–3; ☎ 617-954-2096; $10; ⊙ after 4pm Mon-Fri, all day Sat & Sun; Ⓣ Park St) Enter from Charles St.

Boston University Lot (Map pp308–9; 286 Babcock St; $6)

Center Plaza Garage (Map pp300–1; ☎ 617-742-7807; 1 Center Plaza; $8; ⊙ after 4pm Mon-Fri, all day Sat & Sun; Ⓣ Government Center) Great option for Garden events.

Clarendon Garage (Map pp306–7; 100 Clarendon St; $9; ⊙ after 5pm; Ⓣ Kenmore) Walk to Fenway Park in about 15 minutes. Price for game days only; game ticket required.

Farnsworth Street Garage (Map pp302–3; Farnsworth St; $8 Mon-Fri, $5 Sat & Sun; 🚇 South Station) Requires validation from the Children's Museum.

Parcel 7 Garage (Map pp300–1; cnr New Sudbury & Congress Sts; with validation 2/3 hr $1/3; 🚇 Haymarket) Convenient for dining in the North End. Be sure to get your ticket validated at the restaurant where you eat.

Prudential Center (Map pp306–7; ☎ 617-236-3100; 800 Boylston St; 4hr $10, daily $20; 🚇 Prudential) Requires a $10 purchase from the Shops at Prudential Center (save your receipts). Discounted rates available for Red Sox games ($15) and other special events ($13).

Rowes Wharf Parking (Map pp302–3; ☎ 617-439-0328; 30 Rowes Wharf; Mon-Fri $18, Sat-Sun $13; 🚇 Aquarium) Requires validation from New England Aquarium.

Sargent's Wharf Parking (Map pp300–1; 269 Commercial St; $12 all day; 🚇 Aquarium)

South Boston Fan Pier (Map pp302–3; $7 all day; 🚇 South Station or Aquarium)

State Street Parking (Map pp302–3; ☎ 617-742-7275; 75 State St; $12; ☾ after 5pm Mon-Fri, all day Sat & Sun; 🚇 State)

SUBWAY (THE T)

The **MBTA** (Map p312; ☎ 617-222-3200, 800-392-6100; www.mbta.com) operates the USA's oldest subway, built in 1897, known locally as the 'T.' There are four lines – red, blue, green and orange – that radiate from the principal downtown stations: Park St, Downtown Crossing, Government Center and State. When traveling away from any of these stations, you are heading outbound.

LinkPasses with unlimited travel (on subway, bus, water shuttle and some commuter rail trains) are available for seven days ($15) and one day ($9). Kids ages five to 11 pay half-fare. Passes may be purchased at the visitor information center on Tremont St (p278) and at most T stations. For longer stays, buy a monthly LinkPass allowing unlimited use of the subway and bus ($59).

Otherwise, buy Charlie Cards (adult/senior/child $1.70/60¢/80¢) at the T stations. Children under 11 ride for free. The price of the subway includes a free transfer to the bus. Green-line stations west of Symphony (E branch) and Kenmore (B, C and D branches) are above ground.

The T operates from about 5:30am to 12:30am. The last red-line trains pass through Park St at about 12:30am (depend-ing on the direction), but all T stations and lines are different: check the posting at the station.

TAXI

Cabs are plentiful (although you may have to walk to a major hotel to find one) but expensive. Rates are determined by the meter, which calculates miles. Expect to pay about $10 to $15 between most tourist points within the city limits, without much traffic. You'll have lots of trouble hailing a cab during bad weather and between 3:30pm and 6:30pm weekdays. Again, head to major hotels or Faneuil Hall. Recommended taxi companies include **Independent** (☎ 617-426-8700) and **Metro Cab** (☎ 617-242-8000).

TRAIN

The national railway line is **Amtrak** (☎ 800-872-7245; www.amtrak.com; South Station; 🚇 South Station). Trains leave from South Station (Map pp302–3), located at Atlantic Ave and Summer St; the trains also stop at Back Bay Station (Map pp306–7) at Dartmouth St. Service to New York City's Penn Station costs $54 to $73 one-way and takes four to 4½ hours. Service to Manhattan on the high-speed Acela train (three to 3½ hours) is a lot more expensive ($99 to $116 one-way); reservations are required. Amtrak's online 'Rail Sale' program offers substantial discounts on many reserved tickets.

The **MBTA commuter rail** (☎ 617-222-3200, 800-392-6100; www.mbta.com) services destinations in the metropolitan Boston area. Trains heading west and north of the city, including to Concord, leave from bustling North Station (Map pp302–3) on Causeway St. Catch the 'beach trains' to Salem, Gloucester and Rockport here. Trains heading south, including to Plymouth, leave from South Station (Map pp302–3).

PRACTICALITIES

ACCOMMODATIONS

Boston offers an array of accommodation options, from small B&Bs (some with only a handful of rooms) to large, luxury chain hotels. Many B&Bs and inns are housed in historic or architecturally significant buildings. In recent years, Boston has also become a hot-spot for boutique hotels – small, stylish hotels, usually with personalized service and contemporary flair. The classiest boutique hotels are not cheap, but most offer competitive rates to attract tourists and business people.

Inexpensive accommodations are rare, but the savvy traveler should have no problem locating an acceptable option. Boston has only a few hostels catering to traditional backpacking budget travelers. Other budget options include guesthouses, offering simple accommodation and personal service and usually catering to international types, students and long-term guests. Posted rates at independent hotels and B&Bs are generally more affordable than at the high-end hotels in the city. But even the latter post promotions and off-season sales on their websites.

While rack rates are quoted in this book, cheaper rates are often available, especially using online booking sites. See 'Bidding for Travel' (p227) for cost-saving accommodation options. Other hotel booking sites include:

www.hoteldiscounts.com Enter your destination and dates and the website will provide information and prices for hotels with rooms available. You can book through the website at the discounted rate offered.

www.hotels.com This website uses the same system as hoteldiscounts.com and seems to come up with the same results.

www.lastminutetravel.com The address says it all. Offers deals for last-minute bookings.

www.lonelyplanet.com Includes booking service and expanded author reviews.

www.placestostay.com This site is not as user-friendly as the others, but it's worth checking for good deals.

Reviews indicate rates for single occupancy (s), double occupancy (d) or simply a room (r) if there is no appreciable difference in the rate for one or two people. Unless otherwise noted, breakfast is not included, bathrooms are private and lodging is open year-round. Rates do not include a 5.2% lodging tax (not applicable to B&Bs).

A room in our budget category ($) costs $125 or less; midrange rooms ($$) cost $125 to $250; and top-end rooms ($$$) start at $250. This book quotes high-season rates throughout, which generally means April to October. Often the most expensive period is from mid-September to mid-October. You also expect rates to spike for special events in the city or in the specific neighborhood (eg university graduations, festivals, etc).

BUSINESS HOURS

For the purposes of this book, hours are included in the reviews only where they do not conform to the norm, which follows:

Banks 8:30am to 4pm Monday through Friday; some banks open until 6pm Friday and 9am to noon Saturday.

Bars & Clubs Until midnight daily, often until 1am or 2am Friday and Saturday.

Businesses 9am to 5pm Monday through Friday

Restaurants 11:30am to 9pm or 10pm daily; some restaurants close from 2:30pm to 5:30pm; others open for breakfast from 6am to 10am.

Shops 9am or 10am to 6pm or 7pm Monday to Saturday; some also open noon to 5pm Sunday; major shopping areas and malls keep extended hours.

CHILDREN

When in Boston with children, don't forget to think outside the box; many adult-oriented museums and historic sites have special programs geared toward kids. See 'Boston for Children' on p81 for details. A handy reference book is *Kidding Around Boston*, by Helen Byers.

Keep in mind that many services exist to make it easier to travel with children. Most sites and activities offer discounted rates for children, while the youngest tots often enjoy free admission. Many hotels also invite kids to stay free in the same room as their paying parents; car rentals offer child-safety seats; restaurants offer half-portions and kids' menus. Families are a prime target market for the tourist industry in Boston, so most hotels, restaurants and tour services will do their best to accommodate the needs of you and your children.

We're not sure if America's first public park is home to its first playground, but rest assured, the **Boston Common** (Map pp302–3; Park St) has a huge playscape with swings, jungle gyms and all the rest. Other parks with playgrounds include:

Back Bay Fens (Map pp308–9; Museum)

Cambridge Common (Map p310; Harvard)

Charles River Esplanade (Map pp302–3; Hynes/ICA)

Charlesbank Park (Map pp300–1; Science Park)

Magazine Beach (Map p311; Central)

Child Care

If you're leaving them behind, a few agencies offer temporary babysitting services. Most upscale hotels also offer babysitting services or referrals.

Boston Best Babysitter (☎ 617-268-7148; www.bbbaby sitters.com; per hour$10-15, plus $35 registration fee)

In Search of Nanny, Inc (☎ 978-921-1735; www .insearchofnanny.com; per hour $11-18, plus $40 referral fee, four-hour minimum)

Nanny Poppins (☎ 617-227-5437; www.nannypoppins .com; per hour $10-18, plus $30-50 placement fee)

CLIMATE

For more information see p23.

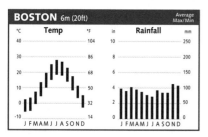

COURSES

The local adult education centers in Boston are incredible sources for courses, from walking historical city tours, to writing workshops hosted by local authors, to massage courses for couples. Most of the classes take place once a week over the course of a semester or season. But the centers also offer many short courses and one-day workshops on just about any subject.

Boston Center for Adult Education (Map pp306-7; ☎ 617-267-4430; www.bcae.org; 5 Commonwealth Ave, Boston; ☼ 9am-7pm Mon-Thu, 9am-5pm Fri; ⓡ Harvard)

Cambridge Center for Adult Education (Map p310; ☎ 617-547-6789; www.ccae.org; 42 Brattle St, Cambridge; ☼ 9am-9pm Mon-Thu, 9am-7pm Fri, 9am-2pm Sat; ⓡ Harvard)

Studio 122 (Map p305; 122 Arlington St; ⓡ Arlington) A branch of BCAE that houses art, woodworking, photography and dance studios.

Boating

Charles River Canoe and Kayak Center (☎ 617-965-5110; www.ski-paddle.com; 2401 Commonwealth Ave,

Newton) Introductory kayaking classes are two or three sessions, for a total of six hours ($139). Also offers day-long introductory kayaking trips for $129.

Community Boating (Map pp302-3; ☎ 617-523-1038; www.community-boating.org; Charles River Esplanade; ⓡ Charles/MGH) Offers a wide variety of courses for paddlers, windsurfers and sailors (for beginners to racers).

Courageous Sailing (Map p304; ☎ 617-242-3821; www.courageoussailing.com; 1 First Ave, Charlestown) Small-group lessons are $250 for four three-hour sessions; also includes one-month unlimited membership. Private lessons are $75 per hour.

Cooking

Cambridge School of Culinary Arts (☎ 617-354-2020; www.cambridgeculinary.com; 2020 Massachusetts Ave, Cambridge; $60-75; ⓡ Porter) The recreation division of this professional school offers one-time courses focusing on seasonal meals such as 'An American Gathering' or 'A Tuscan Christmas,' or on other crucial cooking skills such as 'All you Knead' (basic breads). The most popular course, offered monthly, is based around cooking for couples.

Music

New School of Music (☎ 617-492-8105; 25 Lowell St; ☼ 9am-4:45pm Mon-Fri) Classes range from string ensembles to scat singing to Australian didgeridoo. Most classes meet once a week for 10 to 14 weeks, but one-time workshops are also available. Also offers yoga classes with live musical accompaniment on the sitar.

Writing

Grub Street (Map pp306-7; ☎ 617-695-0075; www .grubstreet.org; 160 Boylston St; 3-hour seminar $45, weekend seminar $165-185; ☼ 9am-5pm Mon-Fri; ⓡ Boylston) Designed to offer a supportive environment for would-be writers, Grub Street sponsors long-term writing workshops, evening and weekend seminars and countless readings and other events. Programs tend to focus on a genre (fiction, poetry, screenplays, etc) and involve a lot of writing and rewriting.

CULTURAL CENTERS

Boston Irish Visitors Center (Map pp302-3 ; ☎ 617-723-5252; www.bostonirishvisitorcenter.com; 25 Union St; ☼ 9am-8pm; ⓡ Haymarket) Offers walking tours of Irish pubs and Irish history.

French Library (Map pp306-7; ☎ 617-912-0400; www .frenchlib.org; 53 Marlborough St; ☼ 10am-6pm Mon, Tue & Thu, 10am-8pm Wed, 10am-5pm Fri; ⓡ Arlington) Sponsors regular lectures, films and language classes. The library hosts an annual Bastille Day celebration (July 14) during which Marlborough St is closed off.

Goethe Institute (Map pp306–7; ☎ 617-262-6050; www.goethe.de/boston; 170 Beacon St; ☒ 9am-1pm & 2pm-5:30pm Mon-Thu, 9:30am-1pm & 2pm-4:30pm Fri; ☒ Arlington) Sponsors a cultural program of German events and classes; its reference library is also well-stocked with books, tapes and periodicals.

CUSTOMS

Each visitor is allowed to bring 1L of liquor and 200 cigarettes duty-free into the US, but you must be at least 21 and 18 years of age, respectively. In addition, each traveler is permitted to bring up to $100 worth of gift merchandise into the US without incurring any duty. For up-to-date information, see www.customs.gov.

DANGERS & ANNOYANCES

As with most big US cities, there are run-down sections of Boston in which crime is a problem. These are primarily in Roxbury, Mattapan and Dorchester (where tourist attractions are limited). Parts of the South End border Roxbury, as does Jamaica Plain. In the South End, avoid areas southeast of Washington St and southwest of Massachusetts Ave after dark. In Jamaica Plain, stay on the west side of Hyde Park Ave and Columbus Ave at night. You may find a few vestiges of 'skankiness' along Washington and Essex Sts in Chinatown, where one or two X-rated shops hang on by the thread of a G-string.

Avoid parks such as Franklin Park and the Back Bay Fens after dark. The same goes for streets and subway stations that are otherwise empty of people.

DISABLED TRAVELERS

Boston attempts to cater to disabled residents and visitors with cut curbs, accessible restrooms and ramps on public buildings; but old streets, sidewalks and buildings mean that facilities are not always up to snuff. These organizations specialize in the needs of disabled travelers:

Access-Able Travel Source (☎ 303-232-2979; www .access-able.com; PO Box 1796, Wheat Ridge, CO 80034) Specializes in services for elderly travelers.

MBTA Office for Transportation Access Services (☎ 617-222-5438; ☒ 8:30am-5pm Mon-Fri; ☒ Downtown Crossing, Back Bay and South End) The office in

charge of making sure Boston's public transportation is accessible to all.

Society for Accessible Travel and Hospitality (SATH; ☎ 212-447-7284; www.sath.org; Suite 610, 347 Fifth Ave, New York, NY 10016)

Twin Peaks Press (☎ 360-694-2462; PO Box 129, Vancouver, WA 98666) Publishes directories and access guides.

DISCOUNT CARDS

Thanks to its student-heavy population, Boston is one of the few US cities that usually offers students discounted admission; so bring your student ID and always inquire.

Other programs that offer discounted admission to area museums and attractions:

Boston City Pass (www.citypass.com; adult/child $39/21) Includes admission to six popular spots: the John F Kennedy Memorial Library, Museum of Fine Arts, Harvard Museum of Natural History, Museum of Science, New England Aquarium and Skywalk Observatory. You have nine days to use your tickets. It makes for a busy week, but if you use them all, you'll save $40.

Go Boston Card (www.gobostoncard.com; adult/child one-day $49/29, three-day $109/49, seven-day $159/69) This card allows unlimited admission to over 60 Boston area attractions, including most museums, tours and historic sites. Also offers 15% to 20% discounts at local restaurants and shops. The card is good for any number of days (from one to seven, depending on what you pay for), so squeeze in as much as you can to get your money's worth. In reality, you have to have a pretty ambitious itinerary to make this worthwhile.

ELECTRICITY

Electric current in the USA is 110V-115V, 60Hz AC. Outlets may accept flat two-prong or three-prong grounded plugs. If your appliance is made for another electrical system, you will need a transformer or adapter – readily available at drugstores and anywhere that sells hardware.

EMBASSIES & CONSULATES

For a complete list of US embassies and consulates overseas, see http://usembassy. state.gov. Most foreign embassies in the US are in Washington, DC, but many countries have consular offices in Boston, including the following:

Canada (Map pp306–7; ☎ 617-262-3760; www.dfait -maeci.gc.ca; Suite 400, 3 Copley Pl; ☒ Back Bay or South End)

France (Map pp306–7; ☎ 617-542-7374; www
.consulfrance-boston.org; Suite 750, 31 St James Ave;
🚇 Arlington)

Germany (Map pp306–7; ☎ 617-369-4900; www
.germany.info/boston; Suite 500, 3 Copley Pl; 🚇 Back Bay
or South End)

Ireland (Map pp306–7; ☎ 617-267-9330; www.ireland
emb.org/boston; 535 Boylston St; 🚇 Copley)

Japan (Map pp302–3; ☎ 617-973-9772; www.boston.us
.emb-japan.go.jp; 14th fl, 600 Atlantic Ave; 🚇 South
Station)

Netherlands (Map p305; ☎ 617-542-8452; www
.netherlands-embassy.org; 20 Park Plaza; 🚇 Arlington)

UK (Map p311; ☎ 617-245-4500; www.britainusa
.com/boston; 1 Memorial Dr, Cambridge; 🚇 Kendall/MIT)

EMERGENCY

Ambulance/police/fire ☎ 911

Bay Cove Substance Abuse Treatment Center ☎ 617-
371-3000; www.baycove.org

Boston Area Rape Crisis Center ☎ 617-492-7273; www
.barcc.org

Suicide Prevention Resource Center ☎ 1-800-273-TALK
(8255); www.sprc.org

GAY & LESBIAN TRAVELERS

Out and active gay communities are visible all around Boston, especially the South
End and Jamaica Plain. Pick up the weekly
Bay Windows (www.baywindows.com) and
monthly *Sojourner* at Calamus Bookstore
(see p214), which is also an excellent source
of information about community events
and organizations. Other resources include:

BGL Advertising Co (www.bgladco.com) Lists many gay and
lesbian social and community groups, as well as entertainment venues and other general information.

Bisexual Resource Center (Map p305; ☎ 617-424-9595;
www.biresource.org; 29 Stanhope St; 🚇 Back Bay or
South End)

Edge (www.edgeboston.com) An informative e-zine with
lots of news, entertainment and commentary, targeting
gay audiences.

The biggest event of the Boston gay and lesbian community is Boston Pride, a week of
parades, parties, festivals and flag-raisings.
See p14 for details.

There is no shortage of entertainment options catering to GBLT travelers. From drag
shows to dyke nights, this sexually diverse

community has something for everybody.
Gay and lesbian venues are listed throughout the chapters on Drinking (p162) and
Entertainment (p180). See the boxed text
on p191 for our favorites.

HOLIDAYS

See also p13.

New Year's Day January 1

Martin Luther King Jr's Birthday January – third Monday

Presidents' Day February – third Monday

Evacuation Day March 17

Patriot's Day April – third Monday

Memorial Day May – last Monday

Independence Day July 4

Labor Day September – first Monday

Columbus Day October – second Monday

Veterans Day November 11

Thanksgiving Day November – fourth Thursday

Christmas Day December 25

INTERNET ACCESS

Boston Public Library (Map pp306–7; ☎ 617-536-5400;
www.bpl.org; 700 Boylston St; access free; ⌚ 9am-9pm
Mon-Thu, 9am-5pm Fri-Sat, 1-5pm Sun Oct-May only;
🚇 Copley) Internet access free for 15-minute intervals. Or
get a visitor courtesy card at the circulation desk and sign
up for one hour of free terminal time. Arrive first thing in
the morning to avoid long waits.

FedEx Kinko's (www.fedexkinkos.com) Copley Sq (Map
pp306–7; ☎ 617-262-6188; 187 Dartmouth St; ⌚ 24hr;
🚇 Back Bay or South End); Government Center (Map
pp300–1; ☎ 617-973-9000; 2 Center Plaza; ⌚ 24hr
Mon-Thu, noon-10pm Fri, 7am-10pm Sat, 7am-midnight
Sun; 🚇 Government Center); Harvard Sq (Map p310;
☎ 617-497-0125; 1 Mifflin Pl; ⌚ 24hr; 🚇 Harvard)

WI-FI BOSTON

Wireless access is free at most hotels and many cafés,
including Darwin's (p156), Harvest Co-op (p223), June
Bug Cafe (p155), Sonsie (see p152) and Trident Booksellers and Cafe (p218). For a long list of wi-fi locations
around the city, see http://boston.wifimug.org/.

In 2006, Boston Mayor Thomas Menino proposed a
plan called Wireless Boston, which would use wireless
technology to bridge the digital divide by installing a
citywide wireless network. For more on this effort, see
www.bostonwag.org.

NewburyOpen.net (Map pp306–7; ☎ 617-267-9716; www.newburyopen.net; 252 Newbury St; per hr $5, per 15 min $3; ✆ 9am-8pm Mon-Fri, noon-7pm Sat-Sun; ⓡ Hynes/ICA)

LEGAL MATTERS

If you are arrested for a serious offence, you are allowed to remain silent, entitled to have an attorney present during any interrogation and presumed innocent until proven guilty. You have the right to an attorney from the very first moment you are arrested. If you can't afford one, the state must provide one for free. All persons who are arrested have the right to make one phone call. If you don't have a lawyer or family member to help you, call your embassy or consulate.

The minimum age for drinking alcoholic beverages is 21. You'll need a government-issued photo ID (such as a passport or a US driver's license). Stiff fines and jail time can be incurred if you are caught driving under the influence of alcohol.

MAPS

Excellent street atlases and maps of Boston are published by Arrow and Streetwise. **Professor Pathfinder** (☎ 800-933-6277; www.hed bergmaps.com) produces detailed maps of Harvard Sq and Harvard University, Massachusetts Institute of Technology and other parts of Cambridge, as well as a laminated folding map of Back Bay.

If you plan on bicycling beyond the banks of the Charles River, get hold of the fantastic *Boston's Bike Map*, produced by **Rubel BikeMaps** (☎ 617-776-6567; www .bikemaps.com). Rubel also produces 50 little laminated 'Pocket Rides' (usually sold in packs of five for $9) for trips within Greater Boston and from commuter train stations in the area.

All of these maps are available at the Globe Corner Bookstore (see p221).

MEDICAL SERVICES

In case of a medical emergency, the failsafe response is to go to the emergency room at any local hospital, where staff are required to treat everyone that shows up. Unfortunately, if your life is not threatened, ER waits can be excruciatingly long and the cost is exorbitant. Therefore, the ER should be reserved for true emergencies.

Massachusetts General Hospital (MGH; Map pp300–1; ☎ 617-726-2000; ⓡ Charles/MGH) Arguably the city's biggest and best. It can often refer you to smaller clinics and crisis hotlines.

MGH International Patient Center (Map pp300–1; ☎ 617-726-2787; 55 Fruit St, Blake 180; ⓡ Charles/ MGH) Provides assistance with interpreting services, housing arrangements and financial arrangements.

MONEY

The US dollar is divided into 100 cents. Coins come in denominations of 1¢ (penny), 5¢ (nickel), 10¢ (dime), 25¢ (quarter) and the rare 50¢ piece (half dollar). Bank notes come in $1, $2, $5, $10, $20, $50 and $100 dollar denominations. See the Quick Reference section inside this book's front cover for exchange rates.

ATMs

Automatic teller machines (ATMs) are great for quick cash influxes and can negate the need for traveler's checks entirely, but watch out for ATM surcharges. Most banks in Boston charge at least $1.50 per withdrawal.

The Cirrus and Plus systems both have extensive ATM networks that will give cash advances on major credit cards and allow cash withdrawals with affiliated ATM cards. Look for ATMs outside banks and in large grocery stores, shopping centers and gas stations.

If you are carrying foreign currency, it can be exchanged for US dollars at Logan International Airport. Bank outlets around the city are not so reliable about offering currency exchange services.

Credit & Debit Cards

Major credit cards are accepted at hotels, restaurants, gas stations, shops and car-rental agencies. In fact, you'll find it hard to perform certain transactions, such as renting cars or purchasing concert tickets, without one. Some small B&Bs and family-owned shops and restaurants may not accept credit cards (noted in reviews where relevant).

Visa and MasterCard are the most widely accepted. Places that accept Visa and MasterCard are likely to accept debit cards, which deduct payments directly from the user's checking account and charge a minimal transaction fee.

If your credit card gets stolen, use the following toll-free numbers:

American Express (☎ 800-528-4800)

Diners Club (☎ 800-234-6377)

Discover (☎ 800-347-2683)

MasterCard (☎ 800-826-2181)

Visa (☎ 800-336-8472)

Changing Money & Traveler's Checks

Traveler's checks provide protection from theft and loss. For refunds on lost or stolen traveler's checks, call **American Express** (☎ 800-992-3404) or **Thomas Cook** (☎ 800-287-7362). Keeping a record of check numbers and those you have used is vital for replacing lost checks, so keep your records separate from the checks themselves. Traveler's checks are as good as cash in the US, but only if they are in US dollars.

Not all banks exchange foreign currency, but this service is provided at any full-service branch of the **Bank of America** (☎ 800-841-4000) Copley Sq (Map pp306–7; 557 Boylston St; Ⓣ Copley); Downtown (Map pp302–3; 100 Federal St; Ⓣ Downtown Crossing); Government Center (Map pp300–1; 6 Tremont St; Ⓣ Government Center); Harvard Sq (Map p310; ☎ 877-353-3939; 1414 Massachusetts Ave, Cambridge; Ⓣ Harvard); Kenmore Sq (Map pp308–9; 540 Commonwealth Ave; Ⓣ Kenmore).

NEWSPAPERS & MAGAZINES

Bay Windows (www.baywindows.com) Serves the gay and lesbian community.

Boston Globe (www.boston.com) One of two major daily newspapers; publishes an extensive Calendar section every Thursday and the daily Sidekick, both of which include entertainment options.

Boston Herald (www.bostonherald.com) The more right-wing daily, competing with the *Globe*; has its own Scene section published every Friday.

Boston Magazine (www.bostonmagazine.com) The city's monthly glossy magazine.

Boston Phoenix (www.boston phoenix.com) The 'alternative' paper that focuses on arts and entertainment; published weekly.

WHAT'S GOING ONLINE?

Blogs, chats and other internet randomness for your entertainment and edification:

- **www.boston.indymedia.org** The Boston Independent Media Center, an alternative voice for local news and events
- **www.boston-online.com** Source of such valuable info as public restroom reviews and English-Bostonese glossary
- **www.dogboston.com** Everything man's best friend needs to know about Boston
- **www.sonsofsamhorn.com** Dedicated to discussion of all things Red Sox
- **www.universalhub.com** Bostonians talk to each other about whatever is on their mind (sometimes nothing)
- **www.worstofboston.com** Why don't you tell us how your really feel?

Improper Bostonian (www.improper.com) A sassy biweekly distributed free from sidewalk dispenser boxes.

Stuff@Night (www.stuffatnight.com) A free offbeat bi-weekly publication focusing on entertainment events.

PHARMACIES

CVS Cambridge (☎ 617-354-4420; 1446 Massachusetts Ave; ☾ 24hr; Ⓣ Harvard); Government Center (☎ 617-523-3653; 2 Center Plaza; ☾ 6am-7pm Mon-Fri, 9am-6pm Sat & Sun; Ⓣ Government Center); Back Bay (☎ 617-236-4007; 240 Newbury St; ☾ 7am-midnight daily; Ⓣ Hynes/ICA)

Skenderian Apothecary (☎ 617-354-5600; 1613 Cambridge St; ☾ 8am-8pm Mon-Sat; Ⓣ Harvard) For a more personal touch, visit this old-time family-run pharmacy.

PHOTOGRAPHY & VIDEO

For a complete short course on photographic ins and outs, dos and don'ts, consult Lonely Planet's *Travel Photography*.

Most local camera shops service both 35mm cameras and digital cameras (for photo developing and prints from CDs, see also Pharmacies, above). Whether you are a traditional photographer with slide and print film or an up-to-date techie with digital gadgetry, you'll find all the supplies and services you need at the following:

Bromfield Camera (Map pp302–3; ☎ 617-426-5230; 10 Bromfield St; ☾ 8:30am-6pm Mon-Fri, 9am-5pm Sat; Ⓣ Downtown Crossing) Buys and sells new and used equipment.

Color Tek (Map p305; ☎ 617-451-2714; 727 Atlantic Ave; ⓧ South Station) This full-service photo service center offers a digital lab, scanning, restoration and all the traditional print services.

Hunt's Photo & Video (Map p310; ☎ 617-576-0969; 99 Mt Auburn St, Cambridge; ⓧ Harvard) For purchasing and repairing equipment.

Video systems use the NTSC color TV standard, not compatible with the PAL system.

POST

Boston's **main post office** (Map pp302–3; ☎ 800-275-8777; 25 Dorchester Ave; ⓨ 24hr; ⓧ South Station) is just a block southeast of South Station. Mail can be sent to you here marked c/o General Delivery, Boston, MA 02205, USA. Post offices are generally open from 8am to 5pm weekdays and 9am to 3pm on Saturday, but it depends on the branch. Other convenient branches include:

Back Bay (Map pp306–7; ☎ 617-267-8162, 800 Boylston St, Prudential Center; ⓨ 8am-7pm Mon-Fri, 8am-2pm Sat; ⓧ Prudential)

Beacon Hill (Map pp302–3; ☎ 617-723-1951, 136 Charles St; ⓨ 8am-5:30pm Mon-Fri, 8am-noon Sat; ⓧ Charles/MGH)

Central Sq (Map p311; 770 Massachusetts Ave; ⓨ 7:30am-7pm Mon-Fri, 7:30am-2pm Sat; ⓧ Central)

Harvard Sq (Map p310; 125 Mt Auburn St; ⓨ 7:30am-6:30pm Mon-Fri, 7:30am-3:30pm Sat; ⓧ Harvard)

North End (Map pp300–1; 217 Hanover St; ⓨ 8am-6pm Mon-Fri, 8am-2pm Sat; ⓧ Haymarket)

RADIO

Boston is blessed with two public radio stations – WGBH (89.7 FM) and WBUR (90.9 FM) – broadcasting news, classical music and radio shows. For sports talk radio all the time, tune into 850AM. See also 'Shtick Shift' on p116.

TAXES

Although there is no national sales tax (such as VAT), there are state and local taxes to consider. Hotel rooms are subject to 8.45% sales tax in Boston and Cambridge. B&Bs with three rooms or less are exempt from this tax.

All sales are subject to a 5% sales tax, except food (purchased in a store, not in a restaurant) and clothing up to $175. Prices in this book don't include taxes.

TELEPHONE & FAX

The separate Boston Area Yellow Pages and White Pages, which include Brookline, Cambridge and Somerville, are comprehensive directories.

All USA phone numbers consist of a three-digit area code followed by a seven-digit local number. Boston's area code is ☎ 617, while surrounding areas may have codes of ☎ 508, ☎ 781 or ☎ 978. Even if you are calling locally in Boston, you must dial ☎ 617 + the local seven-digit number. If you are calling long distance, dial ☎ 1 + area code + seven-digit number.

Local calls from pay phones are usually 50¢; hotels' access charges are often astronomical. Toll-free phone numbers begin with ☎ 800, ☎ 888, ☎ 866 or ☎ 877. Numbers beginning with ☎ 900 usually incur high fees.

For local directory assistance, dial ☎ 411. When dialing outside your area code, dial ☎ 1 + three-digit area code of the place you want to call + 555-1212. For directory assistance regarding toll-free numbers, dial ☎ 1-800-555-1212. Dial ☎ 0 for the operator.

Calling from abroad, the international country code for the USA is ☎ 1. For direct international calls from Boston, dial ☎ 011 + country code + area code + number.

Cellular Phones

The US uses a variety of cell-phone systems, most of which are incompatible with the GSM 900/1800 standard used throughout Europe and Asia. The main cell phone companies that have extensive coverage in Boston and around New England are **Cingular** (www.cingular.com), **Sprint** (www.sprint.com) and **Verizon** (www.verizon.com). Cingular and Sprint outlets are located around Boston (see websites for details).

TELEVISION

Local networks include:

New England Cable News (www.necn.com)

New England Sports Network (www.nesn.com)

Univision New England (www.wunitv.com) Spanish language programming, channel 27.

WBZ-TV (http://cbs4boston.com) CBS, channel 4.

WCBV-TV (www.thebostonchannel.com) ABC, channel 5.

WGBH (www.wgbh.org) PBS, channel 2.

WHDH-TV (www.whdh.com) NBC, channel 7.

WLVI-TV (http://bostonscw.trb.com) WB, channel 56.

WSBC (http://tv38.com) UPN, channel 38.

TIME

Boston is on Eastern Standard Time, five hours behind Greenwich Mean Time. This region observes daylight saving time, which involves setting clocks ahead one hour on the first Sunday in April and back one hour on the last Sunday in October.

TIPPING

Many members of the service culture depend on tips to earn a living. Tip taxi drivers (10% to 15%), baggage carriers ($1 per bag), and housekeepers ($3 to $5, more for longer stays). Waiters and bartenders get paid less than minimum wage in the US, so tips constitute their wages. Tip 20% for good service and 15% for adequate service; any less than 15% indicates dissatisfaction with the service.

TOILETS

For an online guide to public restrooms (including cleanliness ratings) in Boston, have a look at www.boston-online.com/restrooms. Restrooms that receive a four-roll rating include:

Borders Bookstore, Cambridgeside Galleria Mall (p224)

Charles Hotel, Harvard Square (p240)

Lenox Hotel, Back Bay (p236)

Marriott Long Wharf, Waterfront (p232)

Mary Baker Eddy Library, Back Bay (p100)

TOURIST INFORMATION

Appalachian Mountain Club Headquarters (AMC; Map pp302–3; ☎ 617-523-0636; www.outdoors.org; 5 Joy St; ☻ 8:30am-5pm Mon-Fri; ☒ Park St) The resource for outdoor activities in Boston and throughout New England.

Boston Harbor Islands Information Center (Map pp302–3; Moakley Federal Courthouse; ☒ South Station)

Cambridge Visitor Information Kiosk (Map p310; ☎ 617-441-2884, 800-862-5678; www.cambridge-usa .org; Harvard Sq; ☻ 9am-5pm Mon-Sat & 1-5pm Sun;

☒ Harvard) Detailed information on current Cambridge happenings and self-guided walking tours.

Charlestown Navy Yard Visitor Center (Map p304; ☎ 617-241-7575; www.nps.gov/bost; Monument Sq; admission free; ☻ 9am-5pm Apr-Nov, 9am-6pm Jun-Aug; ☒ North Station)

GBCVB Information Center (Map pp302–3; ☎ 617-426-3115; Tremont & West Sts; ☻ 8:30am-5pm daily; ☒ Park St)

Greater Boston Convention and Visitors Bureau (GBCVB; Map pp306–7; ☎ 617-536-4100, 800-888-5515; www .bostonusa.com, Suite 105, 2 Copley Pl, Boston, MA 02116; ☒ Back Bay or South End) Write in advance for an information packet, or stop in for a subway or bus route map or other information.

Harvard University Information Center (Map p310; ☎ 617-495-1573; www.harvard.edu; Holyoke Center, 1350 Massachusetts Ave, Cambridge; ☒ Harvard)

MIT Information Center (Map p311; ☎ 617-253-4795; Lobby 7, 77 Massachusetts Ave, Cambridge; ☻ 9am-5pm Mon-Fri; ☒ Central)

Massachusetts Office of Travel & Tourism (Map p305; ☎ 617-973-8500, 800-227-6277; www.massvaca tion.com; State Transportation Building, Suite 4510, 10 Park Plaza; ☻ 9am-5pm Mon-Fri)

National Park Service Visitor Center (NPS; Map pp302–3; ☎ 617-242-5642; 15 State St; ☻ 9am-5pm) Plenty of historical literature, a short slide show and free walking tours of the Freedom Trail (see p106).

Prudential Center Visitor Center (Map pp306–7; 800 Boylston St; ☻ 9am-6pm; ☒ Prudential)

VISAS

Since the establishment of the Department of Homeland Security following the events of September 11, 2001, immigration now falls under the purview of US Citizenship and Immigration Service (www.uscis.gov).

Getting into the United States can be a bureaucratic nightmare, depending on your country of origin. To make matters worse, the rules are rapidly changing. For up-to-date information about visas and immigration, check with the US State Department (www .unitedstatesvisas.gov).

Most foreign visitors to the US need a visa. However, there is a visa waiver program through which citizens of certain countries may enter the US for stays of 90 days for less without first obtaining a US visa. This list is subject to continual re-examination and bureaucratic rejiggering. Currently, these countries include: Andorra, Australia, Austria, Belgium, Brunei, Denmark, Finland, France, Germany, Iceland, Ireland, Italy, Japan, Liechtenstein, Luxembourg, Monaco, the Netherlands, New Zealand, Norway, Portugal, San Marino, Singapore, Slovenia, Spain, Sweden, Switzerland and UK. Under this program, you must have a round-trip ticket or ticket to any onward foreign destination and you will not be allowed to extend your stay beyond 90 days.

Because the Department of Homeland Security is continually modifying its entry requirements, even those with visa waivers may be subject to enrollment in the US-visit program. This program may require that visa recipients have a machine-readable passport and/or a digital scan of their fingerprints. See http://travel.state.gov/visa for details.

In any case, your passport should be valid for at least six months longer than your intended stay and you'll need to submit a recent passport-size photo with the visa application. Documents of financial stability and/or guarantees from a US resident are sometimes required, particularly for those from developing countries. Visa applicants may be required to 'demonstrate binding obligations' that will ensure their return home. Because of this requirement, those planning to travel through other countries before arriving in the US are generally better off applying for their US visa while they are still in their home country.

The validity period for a US visitor visa depends on your home country. The actual length of time you'll be allowed to stay in the US is determined by the citizen and immigration services at your port of entry.

WOMEN TRAVELERS

Contemporary women in Boston take comfort in knowing that generations of women have won respect and equality for females in business, arts, science, politics, education, religion and community service. Nonetheless, women travelers everywhere do face challenges particular to their gender. Avoiding vulnerable situations and conducting yourself in a common-sense manner will allow you to avoid most problems. Be aware that drinking, using drugs and going out alone increases your vulnerability. If you don't want company, most men will respect a firm but polite 'no, thank you.'

If you are assaulted, call the **police** (☎ 911) or the **rape crisis hotline** (☎ 617-492-7273). Other resources:

National Organization for Women (NOW; ☎ 617-232-4764; www.bostonnow.org; 214 Harvard Ave, Brighton)

Planned Parenthood (☎ 617-616-1600, ☎ hotline 617-616-1616 hotline; www.plannedparenthood.org; 1055 Commonwealth Ave)

WORK

Foreigners entering the US to work must have a visa that permits it. Apply for a work visa from the US embassy in your home country before you leave. The type of visa varies, depending on how long you are staying and the kind of work you plan to do. Generally, you need either a J-1 visa, which you can obtain by joining a visitor-exchange program, or an H-2B visa, when you are sponsored by a US employer. The latter can be difficult to procure unless you can show that you already have a job offer from an employer who considers your qualifications to be unique and not readily available in the US.

Behind the Scenes

THE LONELY PLANET STORY

The story begins with a classic travel adventure: Tony and Maureen Wheeler's 1972 journey across Europe and Asia to Australia. There was no useful information about the overland trail then, so Tony and Maureen published the first Lonely Planet guidebook to meet a growing need.

From a kitchen table, Lonely Planet has grown to become the largest independent travel publisher in the world, with offices in Melbourne (Australia), Oakland (USA) and London (UK). Today Lonely Planet guidebooks cover the globe. There is an ever-growing list of books and information in a variety of media. Some things haven't changed. The main aim is still to make it possible for adventurous travelers to get out there – to explore and better understand the world.

At Lonely Planet we believe travelers can make a positive contribution to the countries they visit – if they respect their host communities and spend their money wisely. Every year 5% of company profit is donated to charities around the world.

THIS BOOK

This third edition of Boston was written by Mara Vorhees and John Spelman. Earlier editions were written by Kim Grant. This guidebook was commissioned in Lonely Planet's Oakland office, and produced by the following:

Commissioning Editor Jay Cooke

Coordinating Editor Elisa Arduca

Coordinating Cartographer Kusnandar

Coordinating Layout Designer Carol Jackson

Managing Editor Melanie Dankel

Managing Cartographers Alison Lyall, Julie Sheridan

Assisting Editors David Andrew, Simone Egger, Melissa Faulkner, Kate James

Assisting Cartographer Andy Rojas

Assisting Layout Designer Wibowo Rusli

Cover Designer Marika Kozak

Project Manager Craig Kilburn

Thanks to Sin Choo, Sally Darmody, Ryan Evans, Mark Germanchis, Laura Jane, Chris Love, Raphael Richards, Suzannah Shwer, Cara Smith, Phillip Tang, Kate Whitfield, Celia Wood, David Wood

Cover photographs Autumn Ivy Red, Back Bay, Boston, Steve Dunwell/Getty Images (top), Rowers ready to embark on the Charles River, Kim Grant/Lonely Planet Images (bottom), Zakim Bridge at Night, Lou Jones/Lonely Planet Images, (back).

Internal photographs p24, p 111, Eoin Clarke/Lonely Planet Images; p7 (#3), p112, Richard Cummins/Lonely Planet Images; p109, Juliet Coombe/Lonely Planet Images; p 252, Jon Davison/Lonely Planet Images; p5 (#3), p49, p83, p105, Lee Foster/Lonely Planet Images; p2, p4 (#1, #2), p5 (#1, #2), p6 (#2), p7 (#1), p21, p31, 35, p45, p63, p67, p71, p78, p90, p97, p106, p107, p108, p110, p126, p142, p144, p164, p180, p187, p201, p220, Kim Grant/Lonely Planet Images; p7 (#2), p8, p15, p54, p135, p196, Lou Jones/Lonely Planet Images; p3, p6 (#1, #3), p102, p130, p151, p173, p210, Angus Oborn/Lonely Planet Images; p4 (#3), Neil Setchfield/Lonely Planet Images.

All images are copyright of the photographer unless otherwise indicated. Many of the images in this guide are available for licensing from Lonely Planet Images: www.lonelyplanet images.com.

THANKS

MARA VORHEES
Thanks to my team at LP – Jay Cooke, our fearless leader, and John Spelman, who so willingly sacrificed himself to Boston's bars and entertainment venues – for turning out a great book. To ScottyB, for your endless supply of wisdom and enthusiasm for your hometown. Thanks especially to Jerzy for teaching me about baseball, making me lobster rolls and sharing the best of Boston with me. Couldn't (or wouldn't) do it without you.

JOHN SPELMAN
At LP, my deepest gratitude goes to Jay Cooke for his generosity, grace and patience. Thanks also to Alison, Elisa, Kusnandar and Kate, the doughnuts to my hole. In Boston, Mara, my excellent co-author, provided duck and useful advice. Thanks to Michael and Amie for extensive research assistance; to George, Sandra for generous hospitality; to Joe and John at Cahill Swift; to Mark, Raime, K-Tron and Skunk; to Eric for dive bars; to the future librarians at Simmons College, particularly Heather, Darin and Amy; and to Sarah Stroud. Everything cool about the architecture chapter, including the organization framework, was stolen from Matt Lasner. Jason Fox provided helpful criticism.

OUR READERS

Many thanks to the travelers who used the last edition and wrote to us with helpful hints, useful advice and interesting anecdotes:

Nuria Batet Barcelo, Earl Bautista, Cindy Burke, Briar Campbell, Chungwah Chow, Robert Cook, Natalie Dixon, David Fong, Alicia Glover, Steven Greenberg, Paul Guzyk, Margarite Howe, Amy Johnson, Heather Mackay, Erica Misfeldt, Christina Pappas, Jason Poole, Yana Rykova, Jörn Schmidt, Elisa Valentin

ACKNOWLEDGEMENTS

Many thanks to the following for the use of their content: Massachusetts Bay Transportation Authority: MBTA Transit Map (c) 2006

SEND US YOUR FEEDBACK

We love to hear from travelers — your comments keep us on our toes and help make our books better. Our well-traveled team reads every word on what you loved or loathed about this book. Although we cannot reply individually to postal submissions, we always guarantee that your feedback goes straight to the appropriate authors, in time for the next edition. Each person who sends us information is thanked in the next edition — and the most useful submissions are rewarded with a free book.

To send us your updates — and find out about Lonely Planet events, newsletters and travel news — visit our award-winning website: www.lonelyplanet.com /contact.

Note: We may edit, reproduce and incorporate your comments in Lonely Planet products such as guidebooks, websites and digital products, so let us know if you don't want your comments reproduced or your name acknowledged. For a copy of our privacy policy visit www.lonelyplanet.com/privacy.

Notes

Notes

Notes

Index

See also separate indexes for Drinking (p292), Eating (p292), Entertainment (p293), Shopping (p294) and Sleeping (p294).

000 map pages
000 photographs

Index

Index

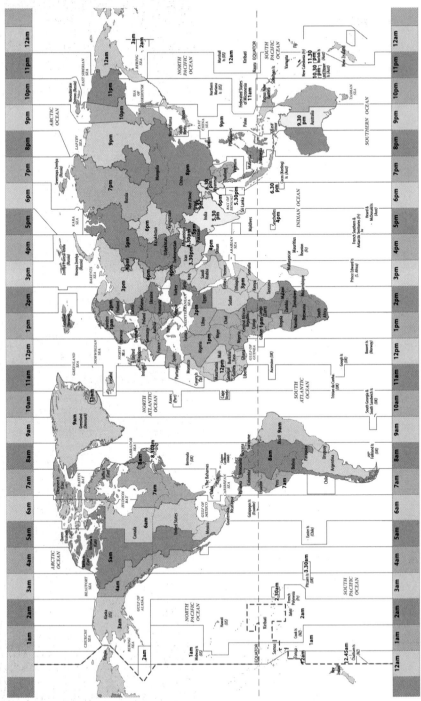

MAP LEGEND

ROUTES

Tollway	One-Way Street
Freeway	Mall/Steps
Primary Road	Tunnel
Secondary Road	Walking Tour
Tertiary Road	Walking Tour Detour
Lane	Walking Trail
Under Construction	Walking Path
Track	Pedestrian Overpass

TRANSPORT

Ferry	Rail
Metro	Bus Route

HYDROGRAPHY

River, Creek	Canal
Intermittent River	Water

BOUNDARIES

International	Regional, Suburb
State, Provincial	Ancient Wall

AREA FEATURES

Airport	Forest
Area of Interest	Land
Beach, Desert	Mall
Building, Featured	Park
Building, Information	Reservation
Building, Other	Rocks
Building, Transport	Sports
Cemetery, Christian	Urban

POPULATION

✪ **CAPITAL (NATIONAL)**	◉ **CAPITAL (STATE)**
● **Large City**	○ **Medium City**
● Small City	○ Town, Village

SYMBOLS

Sights/Activities
- ▶ Beach
- ♜ Castle, Fortress
- ✝ Christian
- ▮ Monument
- ▥ Museum, Gallery
- ● Other Site
- ⚑ Ruin
- ▣ Swimming Pool
- ▣ Zoo, Bird Sanctuary

Eating
- ▯ Eating

Drinking
- ▯ Drinking

Entertainment
- ▣ Entertainment

Shopping
- ▣ Shopping

Sleeping
- ▣ Sleeping

Transport
- ✈ Airport, Airfield
- ▣ Bus Station
- Ⓟ Parking Area

Information
- ⑤ Bank, ATM
- ❷ Embassy/Consulate
- ✚ Hospital, Medical
- ❶ Information
- @ Internet Facilities
- ❸ Police Station
- ✉ Post Office, GPO
- ☎ Telephone

Geographic
- ▮ Lighthouse
- ⚑ Lookout

Maps

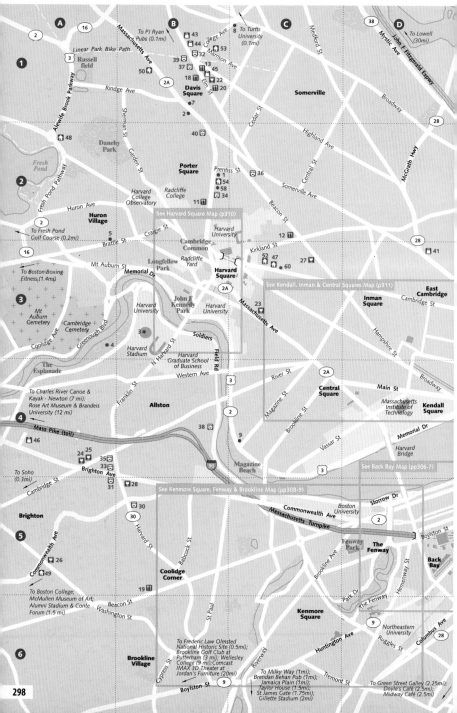

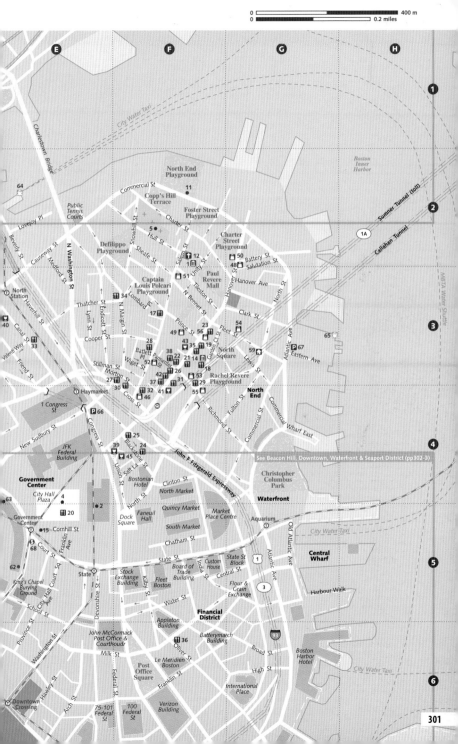

BEACON HILL, DOWNTOWN, WATERFRONT & SEAPORT DISTRICT

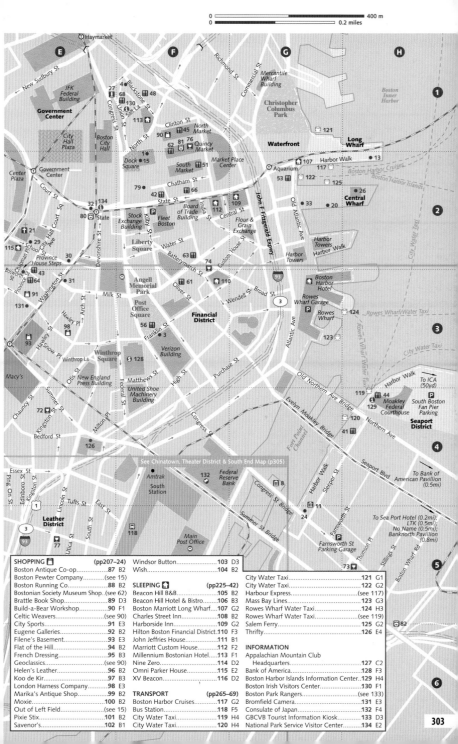

CHARLESTOWN

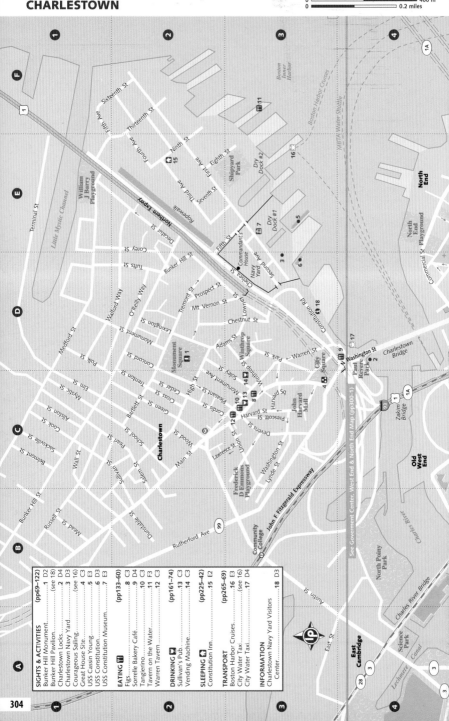

0   400 m
0   0.2 miles

SIGHTS & ACTIVITIES	(pp69–122)
Bunker Hill Monument	1 D2
Bunker Hill Pavilion	(see 18)
Charlestown Locks	2 D4
Charlestown Navy Yard	3 D3
Courageous Sailing	(see 16)
Great House Site	4 C3
USS Cassin Young	5 D3
USS Constitution	6 D3
USS Constitution Museum	7 E3

EATING	(pp133–60)
Figs	8 C3
Sorrelle Bakery Café	9 D4
Tangierino	10 C3
Tavern on the Water	11 F3
Warren Tavern	12 C3

DRINKING	(pp161–74)
Sullivan's Pub	13 C3
Vending Machine	14 C3

SLEEPING	(pp225–42)
Constitution Inn	15 E2

TRANSPORT	(pp265–69)
Boston Harbor Cruises	16 E3
City Water Taxi	(see 16)
City Water Taxi	17 D4

INFORMATION	
Charlestown Navy Yard Visitors	
Center	18 D3

0 _____ 200 m
0 _____ 0.1 miles

ENTERTAINMENT 🎭 (pp175–92)
Alley Cat Lounge	.45	D1
Big Easy	.45	D1
Boston Center for the Arts & Cyclorama	.46	C3
Club Café	.47	B2
Dick's Beantown Comedy Vault	.48	D1
Hub Ticket Agency	.49	D1
Liquor Store	.50	D1
Matrix	(see 69)	
Opera Boston	.51	D1
Shear Madness	.52	D1

SHOPPING 🛍 (pp207–24)
Aunt Sadie's Candlestix	.53	C3
Boston Costume	.54	D1
Brix Wine Shop	.55	C3
Calamus Bookstore	.56	E1
Central China Book Co	.57	D1
Fresh Eggs	.58	B2
Jack's Joke Shop	.59	D1
Parlor	.60	C3
Sooki	.61	C2
South End Formaggio	.62	C3
South End Open Market	.63	C1
Super 88	.64	E1
Uniform	.65	C2

SLEEPING 🛏 (pp225–42)
Berkeley Residence YWCA	.66	C2
Chandler Inn	.67	C2
Clarendon Square Inn	.68	A3
Courtyard Boston Tremont	.69	D2
Encore	.70	A3
Four Seasons Boston	.71	C1
Milner Hotel	.72	C1

TRANSPORT (pp265–69)
Budget	.73	C1
Hertz	.74	C1

INFORMATION
Bisexual Resource Center	.75	B2
Colotek	.76	E1
Consulate of the Netherlands	.77	C1
Grub Street	.78	C1
Massachusetts Office of Travel & Tourism	.79	C1
Studio 122	.80	C1

SIGHTS & ACTIVITIES (pp69–122)
Beacon Hill Skate	.1	A3
Bikram Yoga	.2	E1
Cathedral of the Holy Cross	.3	C4
Chinatown Gate & Park	.4	D2
Community Bicycle Supply	.5	C3
Debu Salon	.6	E1
First Corps of Cadets Armory	.7	B4
South End Yoga	.8	B4
Wang YMCA of Chinatown	.9	D2
Étant	.10	C3

EATING 🍴 (pp133–60)
Aquitaine	.11	B3
B&G Oysters	.12	B3
Buddha's Delight	.13	D1
Butcher Shop	.14	B3
China Pearl	.15	D1
Finale Desserterie	.16	C1
Flour	.17	B3
Franklin Café	.18	C3
Ginza	.19	E1
Hamersley's Bistro	.20	B3
House of Siam	.21	A3
Intermission Tavern	.22	D1
Jacob Wirth	.23	D1
Jae's Café & Grill	.24	A3
Jumbo Seafood	.25	D1
Les Zygomates	.26	E1
Montien	.27	D1
Peach Farm	(see 34)	
Penang	.28	D1
Pho Pasteur	.29	D1
Picco	.30	C2
Shabu-Zen	.31	D1
South End Buttery	.32	C3
South Street Diner	.33	E1
Suishaya	.34	D1
Via Matta	.35	C1

DRINKING 🍷 (pp161–74)
Berkeley Perk Café	.36	C2
Clery's	.37	B2
Delux Café & Lounge	.38	B3
Dish	.39	C2
Excelsior	.40	C1
Flash's	.41	C2
Four Seasons Boston	(see 71)	
Fritz	.42	C2
Jacques Cabaret	.43	B2
Laurel Grill & Bar	.43	B2
Sister Sorel	.44	B3

See Beacon Hill, Downtown, Waterfront & Seaport District Map (pp302–3)

See Back Bay Map (pp306–7)

To Symphony Hall (0.2mi);
Boston Symphony Orchestra (0.2mi);
Boston Pops (0.2mi); New England
Conservatory of Music (0.2mi)

To Alston
Skirt Gallery
(109yd)

To Mike's City
Diner (0.1mi);
Toro (0.1mi)

To Bob's Southern
Bistro (17yd)

Ⓐ　　Ⓑ　　Ⓒ　　Ⓓ

SIGHTS & ACTIVITIES	(pp69–122)	
Arlington St Church	1	H2
Baptiste Power Yoga - Boston	2	H3
Boston Kung Fu Tai Chi Institute	3	D3
Boston Public Library	4	F3
Christian Science Church	5	D5
Duck Tours	6	E4
Emerge by Guiliano	7	D3
Exhale Salon	8	H2
French Library	9	G1
G Spa	10	G2
Gibson House Museum	11	G1
John Hancock Tower	12	F3
Mary Baker Eddy Library & Mapparium	13	D5
New Old South Church	14	F3
Prudential Center Skywalk	15	E3
Trinity Church	16	F3

EATING 🍴	(pp133–60)	
Bangkok Blue	17	F3
Bar Lola	18	F2
Brasserie Jo	(see 66)	
Café Jaffa	19	D3
Casa Romero	20	D3
Croma	21	D3
Emack & Bolio's	22	D3
Farmers Market	23	E3
Herrell's	24	E3
Jasper White's Summer Shack	25	D4
JP Licks	26	C3
L'Espalier	27	D3
Parish Café & Bar	28	G2
Pho Pasteur	29	F2
Piattini	30	E3
Sonsie	31	C3
Trident Booksellers & Café	32	C3

DRINKING 🍷	(pp161–74)	
29 Newbury	33	G2
Bukowski Tavern	34	D4
Cottonwood Café	35	G2
Crossroads	36	C2
Pour House	37	D3
TC's Lounge	38	C4
Tealuxe	39	F2

ENTERTAINMENT 🎭	(pp175–92)	
Alpha Gallery	40	G2
Barbara Krakow Gallery	41	G2
BosTix	42	F3
Boston Public Library	(see 4)	
Gallery Naga	43	G2
Huntington Theatre Company	44	D6
Kings	45	D4
Symphony Hall	46	D5
Wally's Café	47	E6

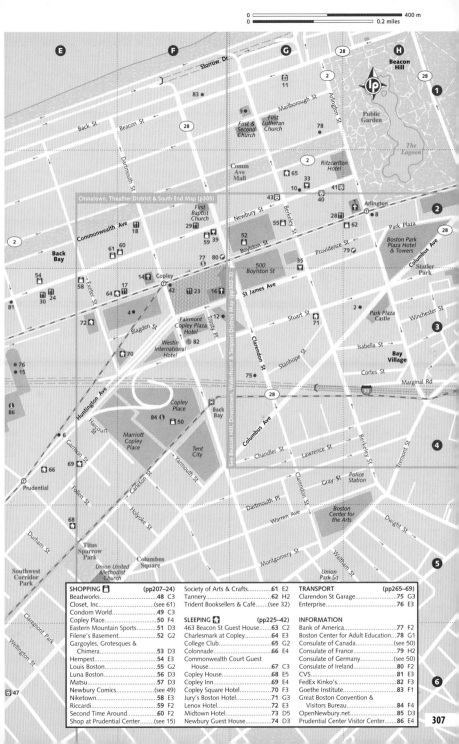

KENMORE SQUARE, FENWAY & BROOKLINE

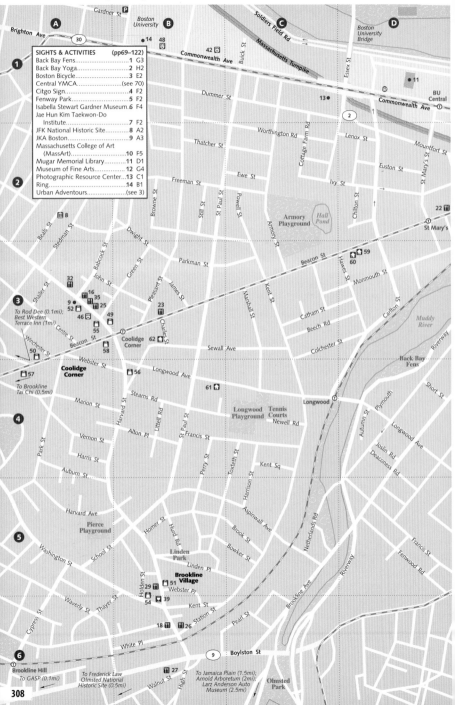

SIGHTS & ACTIVITIES (pp69–122)

Back Bay Fens	1 G3
Back Bay Yoga	2 H2
Boston Bicycle	3 E2
Central YMCA	(see 70)
Citgo Sign	4 F2
Fenway Park	5 F2
Isabella Stewart Gardner Museum	6 F4
Jae Hun Kim Taekwon-Do	
Institute	7 F2
JFK National Historic Site	8 A2
JKA Boston	9 A3
Massachusetts College of Art	
(MassArt)	10 F5
Mugar Memorial Library	11 D1
Museum of Fine Arts	12 G4
Photographic Resource Center	13 C1
Ring	14 B1
Urban Adventours	(see 3)

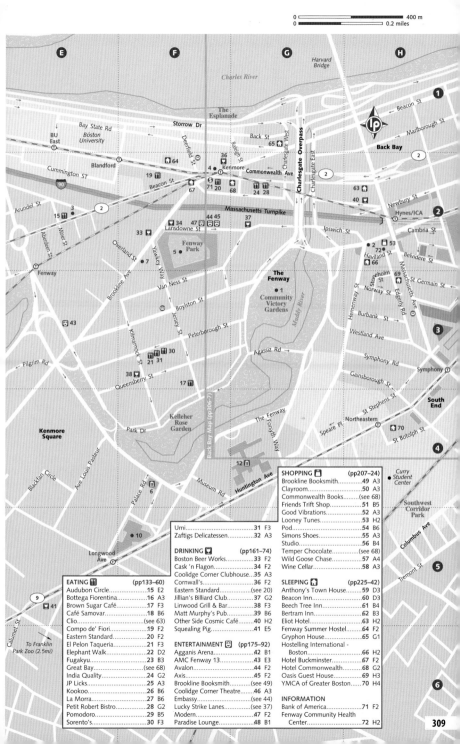

0 — 400 m
0 — 0.2 miles

SHOPPING (pp207–24)
Brookline Booksmith........49 A3
Clayroom........50 A3
Commonwealth Books........(see 68)
Friends Trift Shop........51 B5
Good Vibrations........52 A3
Looney Tunes........53 H2
Pod........54 B6
Simons Shoes........55 A3
Studio........56 B4
Temper Chocolate........(see 68)
Wild Goose Chase........57 A4
Wine Cellar........58 A3

SLEEPING (pp225–42)
Anthony's Town House........59 D3
Beacon Inn........60 D3
Beech Tree Inn........61 B4
Bertram Inn........62 B3
Eliot Hotel........63 H2
Fenway Summer Hostel........64 F2
Gryphon House........65 G1
Hostelling International -
  Boston........66 H2
Hotel Buckminster........67 F2
Hotel Commonwealth........68 G2
Oasis Guest House........69 H3
YMCA of Greater Boston........70 H4

INFORMATION
Bank of America........71 F2
Fenway Community Health
  Center........72 H2

Umi........31 F3
Zaftigs Delicatessen........32 A3

DRINKING (pp161–74)
Boston Beer Works........33 F2
Cask 'n Flagon........34 F2
Coolidge Corner Clubhouse........35 A3
Cornwall's........36 F2
Eastern Standard........(see 20)
Jillian's Billiard Club........37 G2
Linwood Grill & Bar........38 F3
Matt Murphy's Pub........39 B6
Other Side Cosmic Café........40 H2
Squealing Pig........41 F3

ENTERTAINMENT (pp175–92)
Agganis Arena........42 B1
AMC Fenway 13........43 E3
Avalon........44 F2
Axis........45 F2
Brookline Booksmith........(see 49)
Coolidge Corner Theatre........46 A3
Embassy........(see 44)
Lucky Strike Lanes........(see 37)
Modern........47 F2
Paradise Lounge........48 B1

EATING (pp133–60)
Audubon Circle........15 E2
Bottega Fiorentina........16 A3
Brown Sugar Café........17 F3
Café Samovar........18 B6
Clio........(see 63)
Compo de' Fiori........19 F2
Eastern Standard........20 F2
El Pelon Taqueria........21 F3
Elephant Walk........22 D2
Fugakyu........23 B3
Great Bay........(see 68)
India Quality........24 G2
JP Licks........25 A3
Kookoo........26 B6
La Morra........27 B6
Petit Robert Bistro........28 G2
Pomodoro........29 B5
Sorento's........30 F3

309

0 — 200 m
0 — 0.1 miles

SIGHTS & ACTIVITIES	(pp69–122)
Birkram Yoga	1 C4
Carriage House Salon	2 C3
Christ Church	3 C3
Gund Hall	4 D3
Harvard Art Museums (Fogg Art Museum & Busch-Reisenger Museum)	5 D3
Harvard Art Museums (Arthur M Sackler Museum)	6 D3
Harvard Hall	7 C3
Harvard Museum of Natural History	8 D2
Harvard Yard	9 C3
Longfellow National Historic Site	10 A2
Massachusetts Hall	11 C3
Peabody Museum of Archaeology & Ethnology	(see 8)
Science Center	12 C2
Sever Hall	13 D3
Stonghton House	14 A3
Widener Library	15 D4

EATING 🍴	(pp133–60)
Cambridge, 1	16 C3
Casablanca	17 B4
Darwin's	18 A3
Farmers Market	19 B4
Garage	(see 52)
Harvest	20 B4
Herrell's	21 C4
Hi-Rise Bread Co	22 B3
Mr Bartley's Burger Cottage	23 D4
Red House	24 B4
Sabra Grill	25 B4
Tanjore	26 B4
Toscanini's	27 C4
Upstairs on the Square	28 B4
Veggie Planet	(see 38)

DRINKING 🍷	(pp161–74)
Algiers Coffee House	(see 17)
Cafe Pamplona	29 D4
Charlie's	30 B4
Grendel's Den	31 B4
John Harvard's Brew House	32 C4
LA Burdick Chocolates	33 B3
Noir	(see 61)
Om	34 B4
Shay's Pub & Wine Bar	35 B4

ENTERTAINMENT 🎭	(pp175–92)
AMC Loews Harvard Square	36 C3
American Repertory Theater	(see 43)
Arrow St Theater	37 D4
Brattle St Theatre	(see 17)
Club Passim	38 C3
Harvard Bookstore	(see 55)
Harvard Box Office	39 C4
Harvard Film Archive & Film Study Library	40 D4
Hasty Pudding Theatricals	41 D4
Hong Kong	42 D4
Loeb Drama Center	43 B3
Regattabar	(see 64)

SHOPPING 🛍	(pp207–24)
Berk's	44 B4
Bob Slate Stationer	45 C4
Cambridge Artists' Cooperative	46 B3
Cardullo's Gourmet Shop	47 C4
Clothware	48 B3
Colonial Drug	49 B3
Coop	50 C4
Curious George Goes to Wordsworth	51 C4
Garage	52 C4

Globe Corner Bookstore	53 C4
Grolier Poetry Bookshop	54 D4
Harvard Bookstore	55 D4
Harvard University Press Display Room	56 C4
In Your Ear	57 C4
Jasmine Sola & Sola Men	58 C4
Mudo	59 C4
Oona's Experienced Clothing	60 D4
Out of Town News	61 C4
Raven Used Books	62 B4
Schoenhof's Foreign Books	63 C4

SLEEPING 🛏	(pp225–42)
Charles Hotel	64 B4
Harvard Square Hotel	65 B4
Inn at Harvard Square	66 D4

TRANSPORT	(pp265–69)
Thrifty Rental Car	(see 65)

INFORMATION	
Bank of America	67 C4
Cambridge Center for Adult Education	68 B3
Cambridge Visitor Information Kiosk	69 C4
CVS	70 C3
FedEx Kinko's	71 B4
Harvard University Information Office	(see 39)
Hunt's Photo & Video	72 C4

KENDALL, INMAN & CENTRAL SQUARES

0 _____ 200 m
0 _____ 0.1 miles

BOSTON TRANSPORT MAP

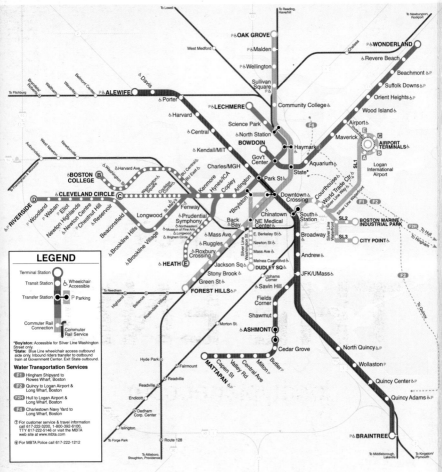

LEGEND

Terminal Station

Transit Station   &⚲ Wheelchair Accessible

Transfer Station   P Parking

Commuter Rail Connection   Commuter Rail Service

*Boylston: Accessible for Silver Line Washington Street only.
*State: Blue Line wheelchair access outbound side only. Inbound riders transfer to outbound train at Government Center. Exit State outbound.

Water Transportation Services

F1   Hingham Shipyard to Rowes Wharf, Boston
F2   Quincy to Logan Airport & Long Wharf, Boston
F2H   Hull to Logan Airport & Long Wharf, Boston
F4   Charlestown Navy Yard to Long Wharf, Boston

For customer service & travel information call 617-222-3200, 1-800-392-6100, TTY 617-222-5146 or visit the MBTA web site at www.mbta.com

For MBTA Police call 617-222-1212